Insurance Marketing

Thomas Köhne

Insurance Marketing

Marketing and Sales in Insurance Companies: Theory and Practice

Springer

Thomas Köhne
Berlin School of Economics and Law
Berlin, Germany

ISBN 978-3-658-47344-0 ISBN 978-3-658-47345-7 (eBook)
https://doi.org/10.1007/978-3-658-47345-7

This book is a translation of the original German edition "Versicherungsmarketing," 2nd edition, by Thomas Köhne, published by Springer Fachmedien Wiesbaden GmbH in 2024. The translation was done with the help of an artificial intelligence machine translation tool. A subsequent human revision was done primarily in terms of content, so that the book will read stylistically differently from a conventional translation. Springer Nature works continuously to further the development of tools for the production of books and on the related technologies to support the authors.

This Springer imprint is published by the registered company Springer Fachmedien Wiesbaden GmbH, part of Springer Nature.
The registered company address is: Abraham-Lincoln-Str. 46, 65189 Wiesbaden, Germany

Preface

The aim of this textbook is to provide the reader with a comprehensive and up-to-date overview of the issues and content of insurance marketing. For this purpose, it combines—in relation to insurance marketing this is still unique—a broad theoretical foundation with an application-oriented presentation. The reference to theory is served by a theoretical basic part and research windows in the individual chapters with references to relevant research findings and in-depth literature. The necessary application and practical reference is made through appropriate content presentations and concretizations, by considering current legal framework conditions and market developments, and by incorporating various examples and current practice cases (best-in-class) from insurance companies. The textbook is therefore aimed at bachelor and master students, scientists as well as practitioners who want to deepen and supplement their knowledge.

The present textbook is a fundamentally revised new edition of the identically titled textbook from 2016. This involves numerous content revisions, which include, in particular, the updating of the extensive regulatory provisions, market and company data, as well as the addition of research windows. These content revisions also include restructurings and the insertion of the new research window on digitalization in insurance distribution. Moreover, many new topics have been incorporated that have gained increasing importance in recent years, including Customer Dominant Logic (including Customer Centricity, Customer Experience Management and Customer Journey), Multi Cumulative Prospect Theory, ecosystems, Embedded Insurance, InsurTechs, digitalization, Big Data, AI, EU retail investment strategy, Mystery Shopping, customer typologies, income and consumption sample (EVS), ecological and health framework conditions and developments (including climate change, sustainability, anchoring of ESG sustainability criteria in the regulation of insurance companies, pandemics), Business Model Canvas and Mobile Marketing.

The book is structured as follows: The introductory chapter serves to justify insurance marketing. In Part II, fundamentals are addressed: The status quo of insurance marketing in research and practice, the derivation of a comprehensive insurance marketing conception, the insurance market as the target of marketing, theoretical explanatory approaches for a deeper understanding of customer behavior, and marketing research as a tool. In the following Parts III to VI, the insurance marketing conception of the insurance company is then comprehensively dealt with and discussed in terms of implementation. Specifically, this involves the analysis of the marketing situation (Part III), strategic marketing with its goals, strategies, and tasks (Part IV), operational marketing with the various marketing tools (product, price and premium, service, claims settlement, sales and communication policy) (Part V), and as a procedural bracket, marketing management with the planning, implementation, and control of activities (Part VI). New compared to other insurance marketing textbooks is also the consideration of marketing tasks and claims settlement as a marketing tool.

The textbook is the result of 30 years of teaching and research activity at universities and the Berlin School of Economics and Law (HWR Berlin). The latter supported its creation by granting a research semester, during which the author was able to produce part of the book. For this, my thanks go to HWR Berlin.

Likewise, explicit thanks are given to some individuals who have made a valuable contribution to the practical relevance of the present textbook with their inputs:

Dr. Oliver Gaedeke, Managing Director of Sirius Campus, has on the one hand updated and supplemented his guest contribution on marketing research from the first edition, and on the other hand, he has provided me with various studies from his company with current market research findings and approved the use of selected illustrations. Dr. Anja Theis has supplied me with extensive sources (and references) on economic and market economic aspects as well as political and regulatory aspects on the part of the GDV and beyond. Both of the aforementioned individuals have supported me in a goal-oriented manner and have thus significantly contributed to the fact that the presented market data is comprehensive, high-quality, and current. This is essential for a marketing textbook, and I would like to thank both of them for it.

My thanks also go to various individuals who have contributed to the five comprehensive and current practice cases (so-called marketing highlights) that have all been developed in close coordination with the marketing managers of the respective insurance companies, thus originating from the companies themselves and therefore ensuring the representation of the actual circumstances. The marketing highlights refer—listed in alphabetical order—to Allianz, HanseMerkur, HUK-Coburg, Versicherungskammer and VHV. I would like to express my special thanks in this regard to Thomas Lukowsky (Head of Marketing and Communication, Allianz Kunde Markt GmbH) and Dr. Olaf Tidelski (Chief Customer Officer, member of the management, Allianz Kunde und Markt GmbH), Eric Bussert (member of the board (sales and marketing), HanseMerkur Holding AG), the marketing department of HUK-Coburg, Christina Koch (Marketing Manager, Konzern Versicherungskammer) and Stefan Weller (Head of Corporate Marketing, Konzern Versicherungskammer) as well as Elke Frerichmann (Brand Management/Brand Communication, VHV Allgemeine Versicherung AG) and Christian Seidel (Head of Brand Management/Brand Communication, VHV Allgemeine Versicherung AG).

While theoretical, definitional, and systematizing statements on insurance marketing generally have a rather long validity, market and company data as well as legal framework conditions are subject to a comparatively high dynamic of change. Therefore, it is important to note that the status of the literature and data is as of December 2023/January 2024.

May the textbook benefit the readers!

Berlin, Germany
Spring 2024

Thomas Köhne

Contents

List of Figures

List of Tables

Directory of Marketing Highlights

Directory of Research Windows

Part I

Introduction

1 Justification of Insurance Marketing and Concept of this Textbook

This introductory chapter aims to briefly discuss why insurance companies should engage in strategic (Sect. 1.1) and industry-specific (Sect. 1.2) marketing, what reference points it has (Sect. 1.3), and what concept this textbook follows (Sect. 1.4).

1.1 Why must Actors in the Insurance Market have a Strategic Understanding of Marketing?

Insurance companies must understand and operate marketing from strategic and increasingly existential perspectives—at least three different, all significant aspects are responsible for this:

- Firstly, there are the always existing peculiarities of insurance products compared to products from other industries (Sect. 1.1.1).
- In addition, there are the existing conditions and current environmental and market developments to which the actors in the insurance market must respond (Sect. 1.1.2).
- Finally, consumer policy developments can even have an existential impact if they increasingly question the benefit of individual insurance solutions in general (e.g., endowment insurance, Riester pension, private health and accident insurance) and thus endanger entire business areas or even business models (Sect. 1.1.3).

1.1.1 Characteristics of Insurance Services

From a business perspective, **insurance** is the "coverage of an individually uncertain, overall estimated need for funds based on risk equalization in the collective and over time" (Farny 2011, p. 8 f.). It is extremely difficult to explain to the general private

T. Köhne, *Insurance Marketing*, https://doi.org/10.1007/978-3-658-47345-7_1

customer what this means, how insurance works, and what the specific economic benefit of taking out insurance is. The insurer or intermediary would therefore have to first make clear to his customer what this means. This rarely happens in reality, and often due to a lack of customer interest and time constraints, the customer's risks and abstract possible solutions through insurance products are discussed directly. Thus, (later emerging) misunderstandings between customers and insurers and/or intermediaries are preprogrammed.

The background to the often lacking customer understanding and lack of interest are the **peculiarities of insurance products**. These are composed of typical characteristics of services in general, financial services, and finally the insurance services themselves (see Sect. 2.2.1).

The characteristics of the insurance product resulting from its service nature and its essential features, in combination, lead to the following **circumstances on the part of private customers**. Taken individually, these already have high relevance for marketing; in their interaction, they represent a peculiarity compared to all other industries, which constantly challenges insurance marketing:

1. **Lack of product understanding**: The abstract, insubstantial, and legally defined insurance product is usually only partially understood and comprehended by private customers and therefore requires explanation (Farny 2011, pp. 429–431).
2. **Difficult to recognize benefit**: The insurance protection concept, according to which every customer receives the benefit from the promised long-term protection upon conclusion of an insurance policy, is factually correct, but requires a rational and abstracting penetration that few customers fully carry out. The same applies to the capture of the insurance product over the entire service process.
3. **Lack of customer interest**: Private customers show a low propensity to consume and low involvement in almost all types of insurance; market research repeatedly shows that the majority of private households do not want to deal with insurance issues (Krüger-Barvels 1971, p. 121; Farny 2011, pp. 429–431; Sirius Campus 2019a).
4. **Dual function of the customer**: The insurance customer is both a demander and thus premium payer, as well as a factor of production and thus cost factor. As a factor of production, he provides the insurer with information about his risk, which serves to calculate the expected loss value resp. the expected loss costs. The customer thus influences the insurer's revenues and expenses (Harbrücker 1992, pp. 47 f.).
5. **Situational customer behavior**: The first four aspects apply more or less generally; behavior-related aspects additionally lead to the fact that the behavior of insurance customers is very situation-specific: These include the cultural circle, societal developments of lifestyles, personal factors, and especially psychological factors such as individual risk perception, emotions, needs, and attitudes (Köhne 1997, pp. 58–103; Görgen 2007, pp. 23–36). Situational customer behavior is very relevant to marketing. It can be observed in many industries (Kotler et al. 2022, pp. 292 f.), but also shows insurance-relevant patterns.

These circumstances have **consequences for the demand behavior** towards insurance: From the outset, most private customers are only vaguely aware of their insurance needs—if at all—and at the same time have little interest in dealing with them in more depth. Awareness and interest must therefore be aroused first. Once this hurdle is overcome, further product characteristics make it difficult to bring about purchase decisions: The lack of tangibility, the widespread lack of product understanding, and the abstract benefit of insurance mean that private customers can neither adequately assess the advisory service of an insurer or intermediary, nor the long-term protection promise, thus taking on a **high purchase risk**. These characteristics require a high level of trust from the customer at the time of purchasing the insurance product.

The task of insurance marketing is therefore to

- awaken the latent customer need,
- interest customers in managing their risk situation, and
- finally build the necessary trust to reduce the customer's purchase risk.

1.1.2 Framework Conditions of the Insurance Market and Current Challenges for Insurance Companies

1.1.2.1 Basic Conditions of the Insurance Market

Apart from the fundamental characteristics of insurance services, various long-standing conditions of the insurance market require insurers to conduct marketing from a strategic perspective.

The insurance market in the private customer business has always been a **buyer's market**, where the supply, due to almost arbitrary reproducibility, exceeds the demand per se and where customers must be courted. This alone would necessitate strategic marketing—for decades now (Delisle 1981, p. 97; Köhne 1997, pp. 19 f.; Köhne and Lange 2020, p. 30).

The insurance market is a functioning market economy system in which—increasingly international—**competition** takes place. Since deregulation in 1994, this also applies to product and tariff or pricing policy, and thus to all marketing tools, after previously only distribution and communication policy could be freely designed. Although this market economy system is comparatively heavily regulated, especially for consumer protection reasons, by numerous legal provisions, particularly of supervisory and insurance contract law, compared to other sectors and their markets, it is still a market with essentially free supply and demand, free market access and competition. The degree of concentration is low compared to other sectors (see Sect. 3.4.1), and 198 property & casualty/accident insurers, 80 life insurers and 46 health insurers in 2022 (GDV 2023a, p. 2) suggest a tendency towards polypolistic market structures. There is therefore a need to assert oneself in this market or submarkets against the competition

(Delisle 1981, pp. 98 f., 5; Görgen 2007, pp. 19–21; Lohse and Will 2019, p. 10; Werth et al. 2020, p. 171).

In addition to competition, the **persistently negative industry image** is a constant challenge to overcome, which refers to the insurance companies as well as—increasingly articulated by politicians and consumer advocates—to the insurance intermediaries (see Sect. 1.1.3). Although customers' close-up view of their own insurance company and intermediary is significantly better than the distant view of the industry and its actors, the image is an obstacle, especially in the context of new customer acquisition and the recruitment of junior staff.

Finally, the—also long-observed—**demographic development** does not play into the hands of insurance companies; it complicates the calculation of attractive life and health insurance products, the recruitment of qualified and motivated employees, and—as a result of exhausted demand—not least growth. However, it does bring with it an increasing senior segment with partially high purchasing power, which, however, still needs to be tapped (Kotler et al. 2022, pp. 155 f., 257 f.).

1.1.2.2 Current Challenges for Insurance Companies

In recent years and decades, various developments—some of which also offer considerable opportunities—have presented new challenges to the management of insurance and intermediary companies. Without claiming to be exhaustive, the following are worth mentioning in this regard (among others, Görgen 2007, pp. 16–22; Farny 2011, pp. 98–104; Lohse and Will 2019; GDV 2021b, 2023a, pp. 31, 64):

- a certain **market saturation**, particularly in life insurance branches, whose premium volume has been stagnating for almost 20 years now;
- market saturation in various property insurance branches such as buildings, home contents and legal expense insurance, as well as accident insurance, whose contract numbers have been stagnating for several years;
- since deregulation in 1994, a tendency towards **shortening product life cycles**;
- the **entry of new competitors** from other industries, e.g., car manufacturers, automobile clubs, internet portals in motor vehicle insurance, and initial attempts by Big Tech's like Amazon;
- the **increasing regulation**, e.g., with regard to Solvency II or the anchoring of sustainability goals, through numerous EU regulations and adjustments in German insurance supervision and insurance contract law with comprehensive information obligations;
- new rules of the game through **jurisprudence**, e.g., the Unisex ruling of the CJEU or the BGH ruling on the participation of policyholders in life insurance in the hidden reserves;
- **technological developments** that come with novel risks, such as cyber risks, eavesdropping techniques with potential danger to personality and data protection rights, and negative reporting or word-of-mouth propaganda in social networks;

- the **progressing digitalization**, which fundamentally changes processes within companies, as well as the customer interface and communication with customers, and has significant transformation potential;
- **societal developments** such as rural exodus in Eastern Germany resulting in a loss of customers, increasingly individual life paths of citizens, the decreasing importance of professional careers and wealth accumulation in large parts of the population, and the beginning of a new phase of demographic change due to the retirement of the baby boomers;
- the increasing prevalence of mobile and **home-office work**;
- potentially and **partially** actually **better informed customers** in conjunction with higher price transparency through internet portals and the consequence of sometimes increasing switching frequency, as well as a changed information behavior induced by the internet, when customers inform themselves online but buy offline, i.e., exhibit so-called RoPo behavior (Research online, purchase offline) (see Sect. 6.1.4);
- **negative reporting**, which is multiplied by new media and is increasingly used by consumer protectors as a "marketing platform";
- **current events** such as the global Corona pandemic in the years 2020–2022, the ongoing war in Ukraine and as a result sharply increased energy costs, **inflation** and **sharply rising prime rates** after a decade-long low-interest phase, which has been challenging for all companies from industries with capital accumulation character.

The developments outlined require an even more market-oriented approach than in the past, which aims at designing and generating customer benefits from a profitability perspective and shapes the company-wide culture, in short, strategic insurance marketing.

1.1.3 Negative Image Spiral due to Consumer Advocates, Media, and Politics

The **image problems of the insurance industry are not new**. They date back to the replacement of the principle of charity with the market economy principle of profit-seeking at the end of the 19th century. This was accompanied by the introduction of the acquisition commission, a remuneration dependent on the mediated new business, which brought about the intended sales increases and a nationwide growth of the insurance industry. But at the same time, the image of the industry deteriorated (keywords: "door-to-door salesmen", "pushy sales teams", etc.). For decades, the insurance agent has consistently ranked last (out of 32 surveyed professions) in a professional ranking of the reputation of individual professional groups, including in 2023 (forsa 2023, p. 14). And claims settlement has also—rightly or wrongly—often been a bone of contention. At the same time, the already mentioned lack of understanding of insurance benefits in the private customer segment is not conducive to the image; the understanding problem arises from complex and often opaque functional and calculation mechanisms, legally formulated conditions, and not least from a lack of customer interest (Arps 1965, pp. 81 f.; Krüger-Barvels 1971, pp. 121–125; Nickel-Waninger 1987, pp. 166 f.; Surminski 1987, pp. 3 f.). This has not changed significantly to this day (Görgen 2007, p. 22; Farny 2011, p. 104). In addition, products and processes in the industry comparison are less digitized, appear rather backward, and thus do not ignite a positive image effect (Oster 2019, p. 172; Werth et al. 2020, p. 172).

In addition to these self-inflicted image problems, there are external factors of image formation. These have always included the media. About twenty years ago, the tendency in journalism was identified to significantly overweight negative news in relation to positive, to accuse industries that are already struggling with image problems, and to dramatize specific individual cases "with a face" (experience reporting), e.g., to illustrate a claim denial or poor claims settlement using a specific example (Görgen 2007, p. 22).

Although it is true: The industry has been **economically successful despite these image problems** in recent decades and was able to achieve high growth rates for a long time. At least two circumstances may have been helpful for this originally: First, the "cycle" of news was low overall, and citizens, as mentioned, were little interested in the topic of insurance and retirement provision. Therefore, the impact of isolated negative news was also low. Second, market research then and now shows that the image of the industry and its insurance agents in general (distant image) is very negative, but that of their own insurers and agents (close image) is predominantly good (Farny 2011, p. 104).

But in recent years, the **environment has changed**: The issue of consumer protection has gained significantly in relevance, particularly on the political agenda. The European Commission and national governments are assigning ever greater importance to consumer protection. Accordingly, consumer policy issues are increasingly and rigorously anchored in directives, laws, and regulations, and the **influence of consumer protection institutions** on legislation has increased. To position themselves and be noticed by politicians and consumers, they also engage in marketing. In doing so, they have to uncover grievances to legitimize themselves. The best arena for this is the media.

The **media logic** in turn is more and more consistently oriented towards ratings than in previous years. Individual media (TV stations and broadcasting companies, print and online media) and journalists themselves are subject to a competition that has intensified greatly over the last 10–15 years. Journalists and media can distinguish themselves in this competition by uncovering a scandal. Emotionally negative topics are also stirred up more strongly and more often in the media than positively charged topics. The basic pattern of the "David-Goliath comparison" dominates as a mechanism of scandalization in the insurance industry: The insurers as Goliath are anonymous, large and powerful, the individual insurance customer is powerless and defenseless in comparison. Individual cases or case examples are easier and more understandable to present than complicated facts. And due to the high number of insured persons in Germany, there is a large arsenal of experiences in which insured persons feel unfairly treated. Finally, people tend to solidarize against the actually or supposedly stronger one (Stefanidis 2013). Therefore, media logic demands "sensational" statements, concrete and negative experience reports.

Consumer protection organizations as advocates of consumers (and thus Davids) against the anonymous insurers (or Goliaths) offer exactly that. And most citizens feel much more addressed by this than by factual, but often abstract arguments and highly aggregated (rather economic) performance indicators of insurers, or as *Kepplinger* puts it: "They [the insurers] confront the reporting with what they know about their own industry. And here there is an extreme difference between their insider knowledge and what is being discussed in public" (quoted in Stefanidis 2013, p. 14).

The **politics** in turn is oriented towards voter voices and topics popularly placed by media and consumer advocates and also picks up on these. Although the insurers have always had a strong representation of interests with their numerous associations, foremost among them the German Insurance Association (GDV). However, what is new is the negative image spiral shown, which results from the interaction of consumer advocates (as representatives of consumer interests), media logic and politics. It leads to the fact that consumer advocates can continuously maintain the media pressure and the negative industry image can be used and confirmed at the same time. As a consequence, even entire business models are now being (prematurely) questioned in terms of their benefits, such as private health insurance and endowment insurance for some time now, and in recent years the Riester pension and the (too expensive) occupational disability insurance. Compared to previous years, the frequency and extent of negative reporting and opinion formation in the population have thus significantly increased, and it is no longer just individual aspects that are criticized, but entire business models are pilloried (Surminski 2015a, p. 140).

It should not be evaluated here whether this development is good or not, who is responsible for it and whether and how it can be overcome. But it should be undisputed that such an **image spiral has a far-reaching and lasting effect on consumers** and thus also on current and potential insurance customers. Since no real alternative offers are presented to them, this inevitably leads to a strong increase in uncertainty among citizens.

For insurers, this has led to the sobering realization in recent years: A negative image spiral influences the demand for insurance, and insurers have to deal with it. A key task of strategic marketing in this context is to communicate the benefits of their business models and products and to restore customer trust. If this does not succeed, certain insurance branches and thus partially entire business models and individual insurers are existentially threatened. It seems that this development of mutual escalation has relaxed somewhat in recent years; it is not foreseeable whether this is sustainable or simply due to more pressing crises such as the Corona pandemic and the war in Ukraine. In any case, the **legitimate function and role of consumer protection institutions and the public interest in consumer protection issues will remain**. Because this represents consumer interests and thus partially compensates for the largely passive customer behavior. What *Delisle* interestingly already stated in 1981 applies more than ever in 2024:

> "The discussion on consumer protection, which has also fully flared up against the insurance industry, could at least be mitigated by systematic customer orientation through marketing. Legal provisions and insurance supervision do not prevent customer-friendly progress, there is and remains enough room for [marketing-] initiatives of the companies, which should be used." (Delisle 1981, p. 96; [...] author's note)

Interim Conclusion: Good Reasons for Strategic Marketing

Insurance services exhibit a number of characteristics that, in combination, make them a unique product: Their need for explanation to mostly uninterested private customers and the necessary trust advance when concluding an insurance policy form a generally unfortunate constellation from a marketing perspective. Moreover, the demand for insurance in reality is characterized by situational customer behavior: It is influenced in individual cases by numerous factors such as socio-economic personal characteristics and various psychological effects, which require individual customer approach and consultation. Other challenging market conditions of the private customer business such as its characteristic as a buyer's market, competitive pressure, the poor industry image, and the demographic development are also stable over time. In conjunction with new, sometimes suddenly emerging challenging developments in the capital markets, in legislation and case law, or in the social sphere, as well as with a public pressure that is greatly increasing due to consumer advocates, media, and politics, insurers (and also intermediaries) are today required to deal much more consistently than in the past with market structures, competitors, distribution channels, and changing customer behavior. Digitalization fuels these developments. In increasingly saturated markets, some of which are completely questioned, growth no longer comes by itself, but must be hard-earned. Customer acquisition reaches its limits, customer retention becomes the (existential) goal for almost all insurers. Strategic marketing is therefore more important than ever.

1.2 Why is Industry-specific Marketing Necessary?

So far, it has been shown why actors in the insurance market must conduct marketing from a strategic perspective. Now it needs to be clarified whether the insights and design guidelines of classical marketing are sufficient for this, or whether—in addition—an industry-related and thus more specific insurance marketing is necessary. Based on the explanations in the previous sub-chapter and also the book title, it should not surprise the reader that an insurance marketing as industry-specific marketing, which cannot be explained solely from classical marketing and service marketing, exists and is also necessary. It makes sense to use the insights of classical and also service marketing, but to supplement these with industry-specific insights, designs, and procedures. This will now be briefly clarified and justified—as should the entire textbook express.

The **general marketing** fulfills a business function and ideally also serves as a management philosophy. Both must and can in principle be carried out and implemented in a similar form in every company. Accordingly, general marketing textbooks claim to make **industry-independent statements**. The marketing thought has historically originated in the consumer goods industry and is influenced by it, which is reflected accordingly in the general marketing doctrine (Meffert et al. 2019, p. 6–9, 12; Becker 2019, p. 2). This raises the question of whether its insights apply without restrictions or at least with very minor restrictions to all industries.

The fact that almost all classic marketing textbooks dedicate special chapters to consumer goods, capital goods, trade, and service marketing can be seen as a first indication that these sectors apparently have specific characteristics relevant to marketing, which also entail special aspects and design recommendations. Corresponding specialist literature underpins this indication. With regard to **service marketing**, the literature accordingly refers to the characteristics of services as well as their production and sales peculiarities (e.g. Meffert et al. 2018, p. 23–30). But even within the service sector, the spectrum of services offered is so broad that their characteristics are very differently pronounced and require an adapted marketing design (e.g. Kotler et al. 2022, p. 426). Therefore, the inclusion of insurance companies in a unified conception of management and marketing of services proves difficult, because production technology, products, and sales differ significantly from other service industries (Farny 1990, p. 4).

A subcategory of services are financial services, which, for example, have in common their indirect benefit (money as a means to an end) resulting from the exchange of purely monetary services and benefits in return. Even this subcategory (between sector and industry) has dedicated textbooks and specialist literature on **financial services marketing** (e.g. Kühlmann et al. 2002; Richter 1996).

Finally, insurance as an economic sector and service product forms a subcategory of financial services. There are also several textbooks and numerous specialist literature on **insurance marketing** (see Sect. 2.1.2). Even with reference to the insurance industry, it can be observed that insurance marketing from a corporate perspective cannot simply be transferred to insurance intermediaries, as both actors play quite different roles and functions in the value chain and therefore perform different tasks. There is also specific literature on this (Eickenberg 2009).

The fact that there are specific textbooks and specialist literature on insurance marketing is an indication, but not a justification for their meaningfulness and necessity. To justify this, industry-specific peculiarities from the areas of law, ethics, customer specifics, and competitive situation are proposed in the literature (Tscheulin and Helmig 2001, p. 22). These can indeed be found in the insurance industry (law, customer specifics), but need to be supplemented by essential, specific peculiarities. The justification therefore primarily arises from the **specific marketing conditions of the insurance industry** (see also Delisle 1981, pp. 61–87; Kühn and Fassnacht 2001, pp. 84–89): These include the already mentioned characteristics of insurance services and the resulting peculiarities with high marketing relevance. These are compiled in Table 1.1.

Table 1.1 Peculiarities of insurance service and implications for marketing

Lack of product understanding on the customer side	Explanation of insurance coverage Creation of transparency Simplification of insurance products
Difficult to recognize benefit	Direct clarification of the benefits of insurance coverage Indirect clarification of the benefits of insurance coverage (e.g., activities made possible by insurance coverage) Marketing of all partial services of the service process Benefit increase through additional services
Need for trust on the customer side	Creation of trust through brand, intermediary, rating, quality seal, customer review, guarantees, etc. Personal advice and sales
Lack of customer interest	Direct activation of customer demand Indirect activation of customer demand (through other topics and products) Stimulating customer interest in the company or intermediary Sensitizing the public
Dual function of the customer as a demander and production factor	Motivating customers to provide information Creating customer interest in his risk progression Acquisition of many, "good" customers

Nickel-Waninger (1987, pp. 175–198) extensively represents and justifies the view that the often mentioned peculiarities of the insurance product do not represent peculiarities and therefore do not provide a justification for industry-specific insurance marketing. However, this argument falls short: While it is generally understandable that most characteristics are not industry-specific in themselves, there are exceptions such as the abstract promise of long-term protection and the design of claims services as a central product component (see Sect. 2.2.1), both of which are very specific to the industry. Secondly, the peculiarity of the insurance service results from the unique interplay of challenging characteristics.

Specific marketing conditions in the insurance industry include not only the peculiarities of insurance services but also the framework conditions of insurance providers, which can be divided into internal and external company factors.

Internally, the extraordinary **importance of sales and sales channels** in the insurance industry must be emphasized. A timeless, pointed saying in the industry is: "Insurances are *sold*, not *bought*." This refers to the previously mentioned disinterest on the customer side and the need for activation by the insurers or the sales department. The sales department is the area with the greatest customer proximity and—in the case of own or tied agents—also the mouthpiece of the insurer. As a result, sales policy and especially the control of intermediaries are more critical to success than in most industries, for some insurers even existential. Many insurers have their own large representative structures, which, however, cannot be restructured overnight in the event of market changes.

Personal sales, accompanying training, and all further sales promotion measures thus gain very high relevance in the insurance industry. The fact that the insurance market is a buyer's market due to almost unlimited production capacities is an additional reason for the high importance of personal sales.

▶ **Note:** Insurances are *sold*, not *bought*.

Externally, insurers and increasingly also intermediaries—unlike many other industries—are heavily regulated. The Insurance Supervision Act (VAG) regulates the **state supervision** by the Federal Financial Supervisory Authority (BaFin) over insurance companies. The numerous regulations that define and sometimes also limit the business model of an insurer will be discussed in detail later. In addition to the numerous, industry-specific laws and regulations, the market conditions in the insurance industry are very strongly and sometimes largely influenced by **jurisprudence**: In disputes, judgments are made on the specific interpretation of insurance contracts and certain regulations in the insurance conditions, which may then possibly apply to all further contracts and thus change the "rules of the game". Prominent examples are the Unisex ruling of the CJEU, which led to the abandonment of the premium calculation taking into account gender, which had always been practiced in several affected insurance branches, or the BGH ruling on the calculation of surrender values in life insurance with the obligation to involve customers in the hidden reserves of the life insurer in the event of early termination of the contract.

Interim conclusion: Necessity of industry-specific insurance marketing

The characteristics of the insurance service and the marketing conditions shown (high importance of sales; strong regulation by supervision, legislation, and jurisprudence) influence all marketing actions and related information as well as marketing management. Therefore, the marketing tools in the insurance industry cannot be used analogously to other industries. This justifies the need for industry-specific insurance marketing.

1.3 Reference Points of Insurance Marketing

1.3.1 Customer, Intermediary, or Company Perspective

Marketing can be conducted from various perspectives, regardless of the industry. Analogous to the main actors in the market, these are the customer, the sales intermediary, and the manufacturer's perspective. The private customer—unlike the commercial customer—is a mere consumer who does not conduct independent procurement marketing. Therefore, the customer perspective is primarily about understanding the view of private customers and their perception of benefits and demand behavior—but ultimately only for the purpose of developing, communicating, and selling one's own services more successfully to the demander. In this respect, in the private customer segment, the customer perspective is a means to an end for both manufacturers and sales intermediaries and thus part of their marketing. However, marketing can be conducted by both the sales intermediary and the provider, each with the intention of marketing and selling their respective services to their customers and clients as best as possible, i.e., supporting sales and profit targets (Meffert et al. 2019, pp. 12–17, 49–52).

The same applies to the insurance market: private policyholders do not conduct their own procurement marketing. As heard, they are usually not interested in insurance topics at all. However, dealing with their demand behavior and a demand theory of policyholders—i.e., the **customer perspective**—helps insurers and intermediaries to better understand their customers. In this respect, customer behavior and insurance demand are natural objects of study for insurance marketing.

From the **company perspective**, insurance marketing, according to the general (marketing) definition (see Sect. 1.2), is a business function and a guiding principle of corporate management with the aim of developing, communicating, and generating customer benefits over the entire period of the service process in order to create value for the insurance company and its stakeholders. The sales policy is a marketing tool, the intermediary a sales intermediary (Kühlmann et al. 2003, pp. 245 f.; Farny 2011, pp. 702 f., 744–747). Insurance marketing is aimed at both the end customer and the intermediaries as sales partners (Lach 1995, pp. 140–149).

From the **intermediary perspective**, insurance marketing essentially means the same thing, but with a different goal and weighting: For the intermediary too, it is a business function and a guiding principle of his activity with the aim of developing, communicating, and generating customer benefits over the entire period of the service process in order to create value for his intermediary business (Kühlmann et al. 2003, pp. 298–300, 305–333; Puschmann 2003, pp. 308–322; Eickenberg 2022, pp. 77–84). The weighting and content of the development, communication, and generation of customer benefits differ from the insurer, but also between the employed intermediary, representative, and broker. For example, market observation (market research) and consulting play a central role in the broker's value creation. Depending on the intermediary status, the marketing is largely predetermined by the provider or largely independently designed by the intermediary (Lach 1995, pp. 121–133, 271–273). Unlike the insurer, insurance marketing for the intermediary is generally only aimed at the end customer.

1.3.2 Insurance Marketing or Insurance Sales

In **theory**, insurance marketing and insurance sales can be clearly distinguished and put into a systematic context: Insurance marketing designs and integrates the entire marketing mix, including sales policy as one of the marketing tools. This makes it theoretically quite possible to coordinate all tools in a goal-oriented manner. In this understanding, **insurance sales is part of insurance marketing**. In **insurance practice**, however, the situation is different: **Marketing** there has a **comparatively subordinate importance** next to sales (see Sect. 2.1.1). While sales always have their own departments, this is still far from being the norm for marketing. Insurance companies in which marketing controls, designs, and coordinates all marketing tools and thus also sales are not known. Direct sales insurers are probably best able to do this, as they have to centrally implement all marketing tools anyway (Köhne 1997, pp. 31–33; Puschmann 2003, p. 290; Homburg 2020, pp. 1250 f.). Theory and practice diverge quite widely in this respect.

1.3.3 Centralized or Decentralized Implementation

Marketing is carried out both **centrally from the head office** and **decentralized at regionally distributed locations by the sales intermediaries** (Kotler et al. 2017a, p. 836; Homburg 2020, p. 1249). In the case of the insurer and its (own or tied) intermediary organization, planning, a large part of the design, and the controlling of marketing activities take place at the company headquarters (Köhne and Lange 2020, p. 172–182); part of the operational implementation is done decentralized by the intermediaries, for example, personal sales with customer communication using sales promotion tools (Eickenberg 2022, p. 74–77). Even large representative agencies have more decision-making leeway and their own marketing budgets for selected regional marketing measures (regional advertising, sponsoring, events), but still have extensive specifications through a more or less centrally designed marketing mix. In the case of independent intermediaries, they naturally carry out their marketing independently in their region or in their business area (Regional marketing). In the case of large, supra-regional intermediary companies, they also centrally design their own marketing mix in the head office—however, tailored to the consulting and brokerage services with certain product design influences as their service product—with equally extensive specifications for the decentralized operating intermediaries as with the insurer and its intermediary organization (Lach 1995, p. 113–137). The two extreme poles of centralized and decentralized insurance marketing management are on the one hand the centrally operated marketing of the (direct sales) insurer and on the other hand the decentralized, individually operated marketing of the legally and economically independent intermediary operation. The former has strategic and operational elements in corporate practice, the latter is predominantly operationally determined.

1.3.4 Uniform or Specific Implementation According to Customer Segment, Insurance Branch, Distribution Channel or Region

The necessity of insurance marketing as industry-specific marketing was justified, among other things, by the fact that it differs from general marketing and service marketing and cannot be explained solely by these. One might be inclined to divide insurance marketing according to further criteria and to develop specific insurance marketing concepts for the resulting case groups. For example, insurers can serve quite different customer segments (private customers, corporate customers), insurance branches (liability, motor vehicle, life insurance), distribution models (direct, representative, bank, broker distribution) and ranges (regional, national, international). These case groups certainly influence the conception of insurance marketing: For example, the content of marketing in industrial insurance looks different than in the private customer segment (Hermann 2009) etc. But the criteria just mentioned can all be captured from the insurance marketing conception. They are **part of the business field determination within the framework of the marketing strategy** (see Sects. 8.2.3.1 and 8.3) and thus a specification for the concrete design of the marketing tasks and marketing tools. In this respect, insurance marketing not only allows a business field-related design and implementation, but even demands it.

1.4 Orientation, Methodology and Content Logic of this Textbook

Against the background of what has been said so far, the aim of this textbook is to **present insurance marketing as industry-specific marketing from the perspective of an insurance company** in a comprehensive **manner**.

In line with this, the consideration is limited as follows (Fig. 1.1): The good to be designed is the insurance product according to the principles of individual insurance. The focus is on the national insurance market and the private customer segment, in which insurances represent a consumer good; nevertheless, the statements largely also apply to the commercial and partly to the industrial customer segment. The actor's perspective is that of the head office and therefore predominantly central, but with points of connection to the decentralized marketing implementation in the branches and agencies.

Target Audience The textbook is intended to meet the demands of academic teaching without losing sight of insurance practice. Therefore, it is designed for undergraduate and graduate students, researchers, as well as interested practitioners and executives with academic aspirations.

Methodologically, both theoretical references and the actual conditions of everyday insurance practice should be taken into account. The scientific claim is ensured by the theoretical references to general marketing, service and insurance marketing (partly also

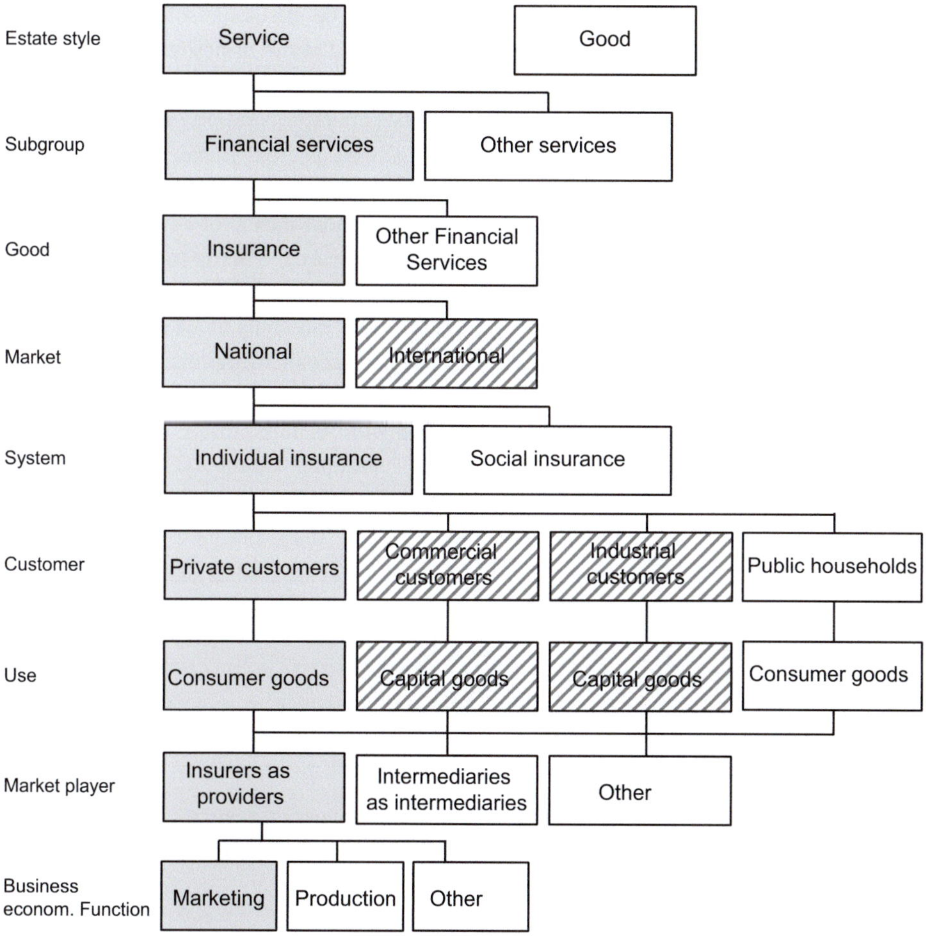

Fig. 1.1 Content delimitation of insurance marketing in this textbook (highlighted in color)

in short excursuses), by the case-by-case integration of research findings in so-called "research windows", and by comprehensive literature references in the individual chapters. Concrete practical examples, current market data and more extensive case studies in so-called "marketing highlights" serve the absolutely necessary practical reference. The marketing highlights were selected according to the best-in-class approach. They were all developed in close coordination with the marketing managers of the respective insurance companies; in terms of content, they originate from the companies and thus correspond to the actual conditions, the author of the present textbook has stylistically adapted them to its terminology and systematics.

The **structure of the textbook** is consistently oriented from Part III onwards to the insurance marketing conception developed in the following basic chapter. This is taken from general marketing and further developed specifically for insurance. Part II initially serves the basics of insurance marketing: In Sect. 2.1 the status quo of insurance marketing in practice and science is illuminated. In Sect. 2.2 some basics of insurance marketing are first discussed and then—as said—transferred into the insurance marketing conception. Chap. 3 serves to present the insurance market as addressees of insurance marketing, i.e., here the financial services market as well as the demanders and providers are described and finally the insurance market for private customers is defined. Chaps. 4 and 5 as further basic chapters deal with the theoretical basics of insurance demand by private customers and the methods of marketing research. This is followed by Parts III to VI, in which the individual components of the insurance marketing conception are successively picked up and explained. Part III refers to the analysis of the initial situation and consists only of Chap. 6, which includes the analysis of the marketing situation of the insurance company and its sub-analyses (macro and micro environment, company analysis, SWOT analysis). Part IV then deals with strategic marketing design: This includes the marketing objectives (Chap. 7), the marketing strategy (Chap. 8) and the marketing tasks (Chap. 9). Part V follows with the presentation and explanation of operational marketing design, which concerns the marketing tools and their interaction. The chapters of this part (Chaps. 10, 11, 12, 13, 14, 15) are dedicated to the individual marketing tools: Chap. 10 to product policy, Chap. 11 to price and premium policy, Chap. 12 to service and claims policy, Chap. 13 to sales policy, Chap. 14 to communication policy and the most important communication tools, and finally Chap. 15 to the integration of the marketing tools. The last Part VI picks up the management perspective of marketing, with Chap. 16 dealing with marketing management and its phases of planning, implementation and controlling.

References

Arps, L. (1965): Auf sicheren Pfeilern – Deutsche Versicherungswirtschaft vor 1914, Göttingen, 1965.

Becker, J. (2019): Marketing-Konzeption: Grundlagen des ziel-strategischen und operativen Marketing-Managements, München, 11. ed., 2019.

Delisle, E. (1981): Marketing in der Versicherungswirtschaft, Beiträge zu wirtschaftswissenschaftlichen Problemen der Versicherung, Band 5, Karlsruhe, 2. ed., 1981.

Eickenberg, V. (2009): Marketing für Versicherungsvermittler, Karlsruhe, 2. ed., 2009.

Eickenberg, V. (2022): Erfolgsfaktor Vertrauen bei der Versicherungsvermittlung. Theorie und Praxis eines effektiven Marketings, Wiesbaden, 2022.

Farny, D. (1990): Versicherungsbetriebslehre: Wirtschaftliche Theorie des Versicherungsunternehmens und seiner Beziehungen zur Umwelt, in: ZVersWiss, Jg. 79, pp. 1–30.

Farny, D. (2011): Versicherungsbetriebslehre, Karlsruhe, 5. ed., 2011.

Forsa (Ed.) (2023): dbb Bürgerbefragung Öffentlicher Dienst 2023, Berlin, 2023.

GDV (Ed.) (2021b): Versicherer – für die Herausforderungen von morgen, in: Makro und Märkte kompakt, Nr. 39, 2021.

GDV (Ed.) (2023a): Statistiken zur deutschen Versicherungswirtschaft 2023, Berlin, 2023.

Görgen, F. (2007): Versicherungsmarketing, Strategien, Instrumente und Controlling, Stuttgart, 2. ed., 2007.

Harbrücker, U. (1992): Wertewandel und Corporate Identity, Perspektiven eines gesellschaftsorientierten Marketing von Versicherungsunternehmen, Wiesbaden, 1992.

Hermann, R. (2009): Überlebenswichtig oder überflüssig? Marketing für Firmensachversicherungen sichert langfristig das Marktpotenzial, in: VW, Jg. 64, 2009, Nr. 19, pp. 1.498–1.504.

Homburg, C. (2020): Marketingmanagement, Strategie – Instrumente – Umsetzung – Unternehmensführung, Wiesbaden, 7. ed., 2020.

Köhne, T. (1997): Die Wirkungsversicherung im Privatkundengeschäft – Implikationen für eine kundenorientierte Marktleistungsgestaltung, St. Gallen, 1997.

Köhne, T./Lange, M. (2020): Marketing und Vertrieb von Versicherungs- und Finanzproduk-ten für Privatkunden, Fach- und Führungskompetenz für die Assekuranz, Karlsruhe, 4. ed., 2020.

Kotler, P./Keller, K.L./Opresnik, M.O. (2017a): Marketing-Management, Konzepte – Instrumente – Unternehmensfallstudien, Halbergmoos, 15. ed., 2017.

Kotler, P./Armstrong, G./Harris, L.C./He, H. (2022): Grundlagen des Marketing, Halbergmoos, 8. ed., 2022.

Krüger-Barvels, R. (1971): Marketing im Versicherungsbetrieb, Freiburg i.B., 1971.

Kühlmann, K./Käßer-Pawelka, G./Wengert, H./Kurtenbach, W. (2002): Marketing für Finanzdienstleistungen, Frankfurt a.M., 2002.

Kühlmann, K./Wolf, H.-P./Wallenwein, C./Swoboda, U. (2003): Marketing und Vertrieb, Funktionsorientierte Qualifikationen, Karlsruhe, 2. ed., 2003.

Kühn, R./Fassnacht, R. (2001): Marketing für Versicherungen, Herausforderungen und Entwicklungstendenzen, gezeigt am Beispiel des schweizerischen Versicherungsmarktes, in: Tscheulin, D.K./Helmig, B. (Eds.), Branchenspezifisches Marketing, Grundlagen – Besonderheiten – Gemeinsamkeiten, Wiesbaden, 2001, pp. 79–98.

Lach, H. (1995): Vertikales Marketing von Versicherungsunternehmen, Berlin, 1995.

Lohse, U./Will, A. (2019): Rahmenbedingungen und strategische Herausforderungen für die Versicherungsbranche, in: Reich, M./Zerres, C. (Eds.), Handbuch Versicherungsmarketing, Berlin, 2. ed., 2019, pp. 3–14.

Meffert, H./Bruhn, M./Hadwich, K. (2018): Dienstleistungsmarketing, Grundlagen – Konzepte – Methoden, Wiesbaden, 9. ed., 2018.

Meffert, H./Burmann, C./Kirchgeorg, M./Eisenbeiß, M. (2019): Marketing, Grundlagen marktorientierter Unternehmensführung, Konzepte – Instrumente – Praxisbeispiele, Wiesbaden, 13. ed., 2019.

Nickel-Waninger, H. (1987): Versicherungsmarketing, auf der Grundlage des Marketing von Informationsprodukten, Karlsruhe, 1987.

Oster, O. (2019): Customer Experience – die Königsdisziplin, in: Reich, M./Zerres, C. (Eds.), Handbuch Versicherungsmarketing, Berlin, 2. ed., 2019, pp. 171–191.

Puschmann, K.-H. (2003): Praxis des Versicherungsmarketing, Karlsruhe, 2. ed., 2003.

Richter, A. (1996): Neuausrichtung des Finanzdienstleistungsmarketings, Wiesbaden, 1996.

Sirius Campus (Ed.) (2019a): Entscheidertypologie im Versicherungsmarkt, Köln, 2019.

Stefanidis, A. (2013): „Das Selbstverständnis der Journalisten hat sich geändert“, Interview mit Prof. Dr. Hans Mathias Kepplinger, in: GDV (Ed.), Positionen zu Politik, Wirtschaft und Gesellschaft, Nr. 87, Berlin, 2013, pp. 12–15.

Surminski, A. (1987): Das Image in der Versicherung, in: ZfV, Jg. 38, 1987, Nr. 1, pp. 2–16.

Surminski, M. (2015a): Lebensversicherung im Fadenkreuz – Wie kann sich die Branche gegen den Medienbeschuss wehren?, in: ZfV, Jg. 66, 2015, Nr. 5, pp. 140.

Tscheulin, D.K./Helmig, B. (2001): Gibt es ein branchenspezifisches Marketing? Zur Bedeutung einer branchenorientierten Sichtweise des Marketing in Wissenschaft, Lehre und Praxis, in: Tscheulin, D.K./Helmig, B. (Eds.), Branchenspezifisches Marketing, Grundlagen – Besonderheiten – Gemeinsamkeiten, Wiesbaden, 2001, pp. 19–33.

Werth, O./Schwarzbach, C./Rodríguez Cardona, D./Breitner, M.H./Schulenburg, J.-M. Graf von der (2020): Influencing factors for the digital transformation in the financial services sector, in: ZVersWiss, Jg. 109, 2020, pp. 155–179.

Part II

Basics of Insurance Marketing

2 Insurance Marketing as a Business Management Function in Insurance Companies

The introductory chapter highlighted the importance of insurers engaging in strategic insurance marketing. This chapter will first examine the current status quo in business practice and science (Sect. 2.1), in order to subsequently develop an industry-specific definition of insurance marketing and a conception for insurance companies based on this foundation (Sect. 2.2).

2.1 Status quo of Insurance Marketing in Practice and Science

2.1.1 Role and Significance of Insurance Marketing in Business Practice

A look into companies makes it clear—still—**there is a need to catch up in terms of establishing strategic insurance marketing**. Marketing has never had it easy in the insurance industry and suffers—in some companies to this day—from a lack of understanding in the management and therefore from too weak, sometimes even completely missing strategic weighting. In the late 60s, it was explicitly and increasingly demanded that insurers should engage in marketing, as was already common in other industries. Although this subsequently happened, insurers' focus was rather on partial aspects, a uniform understanding of marketing was lacking and marketing departments, if they were set up at all, served as an alibi or were limited to advertising measures (Delisle 1981, p. 1 f.). Little changed in the following period: marketing research was very limited, for example in terms of market research, and advertising measures were rather unsystematic and ineffective due to a lack of customer needs and advertising impact analyses (Nickel-Waninger 1987, pp. 206–210; Schmidt 1995, p. 6). Even with deregulation in 1994, this only changed hesitantly. At the turn of the millennium, marketing in

T. Köhne, *Insurance Marketing*, https://doi.org/10.1007/978-3-658-47345-7_2

most insurance companies was still not fully developed and often still led a "wallflower existence" (Köhne 1999, p. 35).

In the first decade after the turn of the millennium, insurance marketing in the insurance market professionalized in many areas (Trumpfheller 2005, p. 11 f.; Görgen 2007, p. 5; Hermann 2009, p. 1498; Müller 2012, pp. 1721 f.):

- Marketing research was established, and some insurers even set up their own department for it;
- Market segments and target groups were increasingly identified and—at least with communication campaigns—addressed;
- Brand policy and with it advertising and advertising success measurement were increasingly consciously and strategically pursued by market leaders, and advertising spending increased across the market;
- Customer Relationship Management programs (CRM) led many companies to consciously collect and evaluate information about their own customers for the first time;
- Product life cycles became shorter, accompanied by the appointment of product managers for certain sectors;
- Insurance products were increasingly enriched with assistance services from marketing considerations and marketed as problem solutions;
- Especially in the motor vehicle insurance market, transparent prices and their comparisons by media led to strong price competition, which is further intensified today by so-called "comparers" (Internet comparison portals) and thus to an increasingly conscious pricing policy;
- Market presence and communication in new media were increasingly professionalized, from initial internet presences to online marketing efforts to the development of online and social media strategies.

Despite this **noticeable development**, insurance marketing in the insurance industry had not yet achieved the same status as, for example, in the consumer goods industry or in retail by 2010. In this regard, the following statement by the then CEO of a large German insurance company was telling: "We have not consistently thought from the customer's perspective for a long time" (o. V. 2010, p. 33). Accordingly, more than ten years ago, it was the goal of two major insurers (AXA, ERGO) to strategically anchor customer orientation and actively differentiate themselves in the market through it (Schwarz 2015; Oletzky et al. 2015).

In the last decade, the possibilities of online, social media, and platform marketing have significantly expanded and improved (Bruhn 2019b, p. 435, 545 f.; Meffert et al. 2018, p. 337; Homburg 2020, p. 882–888), and they are also increasingly being used operationally (Barinka and Wippler 2019; Schumacher 2019). The internet presence of insurers has also become more professional, modern, and often more customer-centric. However, still only a few insurers follow a strategic marketing understanding. In some insurance companies, marketing is still equated—in terms of content and organization—with advertising and sales promotion and is treated accordingly as a stepchild. As advertising and sales promotion, it primarily serves sales and is therefore subordinate to this department, the same applies to online and social media activities. In most companies, sales are still consistently oriented towards selling existing products in the sense of a supply-oriented company management—as a push sales (Hermann 2009, p. 1498). Sometimes different marketing tasks are also performed in different departments, which are assigned to different board departments, e.g. sales promotion and advertising in sales, market research as a staff unit of the board or within the insurance divisions, and product marketing within the divisions (see also Sect. 16.2).

However, there are also some companies with a more comprehensive understanding of marketing, in which at least market research, brand design, advertising, sales support, and product marketing are integrated into a marketing department. This is then assigned to a board department, sometimes (out of embarrassment?) together with other areas to the chairman of the board, or often to the sales department, as this already operates market-oriented. In the latter case, it is often even named at the department level under the designation "Sales & Marketing"—usually in this order. Explicitly, this is the case with 12 of the 30 largest insurers in the German market, only one insurer names the department "Marketing & Sales".

A **separate board department for marketing or customers** (Chief Customer Officer), which is at least equivalent to the division and sales departments in terms of competence, is **rare** (see also Glaser 2021, p. 203 f.). So only one insurer has its own board department under the name "Global Marketing & Customer Experience and Investment Products" and one insurer under the name "Customer Management". Apart from that, however, at least some insurers in the market seem to have newly discovered the customer, the importance of customer orientation, and thus a more consistent market view for themselves and to attach more importance to this in their corporate strategies: positioning as "problem solvers" instead of "check payers", frequent further developments of products, short-term cancellable coverage sections, more differentiated pricing in competitive insurance branches such as motor vehicle insurance, numerous sales cooperations with companies from all sectors, the increasingly widespread use of customer satisfaction scores, and the attempt to participate in so-called ecosystems could be **indications** of this. Also, buzzwords like "customer report", "customer journey", and "customer centricity" are relatively new to the insurance industry and indicate a **more consistent turn towards the customer** (Oster 2019; Laakmann and Rahlf 2019; Allianz Group 2023, p. 3, 108 f.; AXA Insurance AG 2023, p. 6; ERGO Insurance AG 2023, p. 41 f.; HUK-Coburg Insurance Group 2023, p. 49–51; Konzern Versicherungskammer 2023, p. 13 f.).

2.1.2 Role and Importance of Insurance Marketing in Science

Insurance marketing is part of insurance business administration, which in turn is part of the economic examination of insurance and focuses on economic activity within insurance companies. As part of a division of labor, insurance business administration, like general business studies, differentiates various business functions such as research and development, production, marketing (traditionally: sales), financing or human resource management. **Insurance marketing** is therefore primarily a result of functional insurance business administration and takes place as a **business function** within the institutional framework **of the insurance company**. The functional view provides insights into the content design of marketing, i.e., possible design options for strategies, tasks, and tools. In exercising the business function "marketing", the marketing activities are then planned, implemented, and controlled in a marketing management process. Thus, insurance marketing is also accessible to, or even dependent on, insights from decision-oriented or decision-theoretical insurance business administration. The decision-oriented approach views economic activity (here marketing) in the insurance company as a sum of decisions about goals and the means appropriate for achieving these goals, especially about the selection of the corresponding marketing activities (strategies, tasks, tools). Decision theory examines and explains the causal and final relationships between means design and goal achievement, for example, between price design and profit growth or between sales incentive design and premium growth (based on Farny 2011, pp. 1–7).

The demand for a—to date undeveloped—comprehensive and holistic theory of insurance marketing or aspects thereof is the creation of a closed and consistent system of statements that explain facts and relationships (explanatory function) and/or provide recommendations for promising design (design function). However, one should bear in mind how high the complexity of the reality of insurance is and that general marketing science has not yet developed a comprehensive, integrated marketing theory, but rather uses the explanatory contributions of various economic theory approaches in different marketing sub-areas (Meffert et al. 2019, pp. 30–44; Homburg 2020, p. 16). Therefore, it seems **unrealistic to develop a holistic theory of insurance marketing in the foreseeable future**. Much **more promising** is the theory-guided explanation of aspects of insurance marketing and derivation of design recommendations for these aspects while simultaneously integrating them into a **holistic insurance marketing conception**. The associated theoretical contribution can, in relation to individual sub-areas of this marketing conception, make clear statements about the relationship between economic, marketing-related activities and procedures on the one hand and the contributions to achieving marketing goals on the other. This embodies a **practical-normative and application-oriented research**.

Like insurance business administration, insurance marketing is confronted with the fact that insurance as part of its subject of investigation represents a synthesis of many different elements. Therefore, the attempt to explain the reality of insurance marketing often requires, in addition to the **recourse to various economic theory approaches, additional interdisciplinary approaches**. Given this, the precise delimitation of insurance marketing as a science is difficult: Although it is essentially about business processes (microeconomic focus of **insurance business administration**), the policyholders as users (microeconomic focus of the **risk management theory** of the policyholder) as well as the insurance market with its interplay between supply and demand as the addressee of insurance marketing (macroeconomic focus of the **insurance market theory**) must also be examined. For understanding customer behavior and the adequate design of marketing tools, insights from **sociology** and especially **psychology** can be drawn upon; these so-called behavioral sciences are referred to as behavioral economics in the context of explaining customer behavior. As outlined, economic activity in the insurance company is also influenced by numerous legal conditions (**insurance law**), and insurance marketing must take these into account: These include in particular insurance contract law, insurance supervision law, commercial law, competition law, and insurance intermediation law (based on Farny 2011, pp. 16 f.).

The **history of scientific insurance marketing** is relatively young: from the mid to late 1960s, there was an increased demand in specialist media for the insurance industry, like other economic sectors, to pursue a market-oriented, demand-oriented corporate policy, namely marketing. This initially took place in the Anglo-Saxon area and from the end of the 1960s in the German-speaking area (with references Delisle 1981, p. 1; Farny 1990, p. 3).

Accordingly, the first scientific and more systematic treatises on the **entire complex of marketing** in the insurance industry date back to this time (Table 2.1). For the German-speaking area, the first **monographs** on insurance marketing by *Krüger-Barvels* (1971) and *Delisle* (1971) are noteworthy. However, they are almost the only comprehensive scientific works to date that deal with the transfer of a holistic marketing conception to the insurance industry and have insurance marketing as a whole in mind. At the same time and in this direction, there is also the treatise by *Farny* (1971), who, however, avoided the term marketing until 2011 and instead spoke of sales policy (Farny 2011, p. 686 ff.) and defined marketing too narrowly when he described it as "an expression of an attitude in the insurance company, a mindset, according to which all decisions and economic activities are oriented towards the sales market" (p. 689). In contrast to the two aforementioned basic works, his view is very company-oriented, i.e., from inside to outside (inside-out), and thus only partially meets the marketing with its market and customer orientation, i.e., from outside to inside (outside-in). The fourth treatise on a holistic marketing conception in the insurance industry is due to *Köhne* (2006).

While textbooks on insurance marketing naturally also cover the **entire complex of marketing in the insurance industry**, the scientific **monographs** listed in Table 2.1 with a marketing term in the title already refer to sub-aspects such as the demand structure, the information-economic design, the control function, reinsurance, the division of labor between insurer and intermediary, societal developments such as individualization and value change, and marketing in strategic insurance networks.

In addition, various scientific monographs (without a marketing term in the title) have examined **sub-areas of insurance marketing** (e.g., Schütze 1972; Mertens 1992; Müller 1994; Kremer 1994; Rützler 1994; Vielreicher 1995; Lach 1995; Joho 1996; Köhne 1997; Eurich 2001; Reitzler 2001; Krausz 2002; Müller-Reichart 2002; Altenburger 2003; Trumpfheller 2005; Hujber 2005; Hartmann 2006; Friederichs-Schmidt 2006;

Table 2.1 Overview of German-language monographs on insurance marketing

Author	Title (translated into English)	Source	Year
Delisle	Marketing in the Insurance Industry*	Karlsruhe	1971
Krüger-Barvels	Marketing in the Insurance Company*	Freiburg i. B.	1971
Farny	Sales and Sales Policy of the Insurance Company*	Karlsruhe	1971
Perrenoud	Marketing in Reinsurance*	Zurich	1979
Kurtenbach	Insurance Marketing**	Frankfurt a. M.	1981
Duft	Insurance Marketing*	Zurich	1983
Keuper	Basics of a marketing conception in insurance companies with special consideration of the commercial clients demand structure*	Vienna	1986
Puschmann	Practice of Insurance Marketing**	Karlsruhe	1986
Nickel-Waninger	Insurance marketing based on the marketing of information products*	Karlsruhe	1987
Schwake	Considerations for a risk-adequate marketing as a control conception of insurance companies*	Karlsruhe	1987
Harbrücker	Change of values and corporate identity, perspectives of a society-oriented marketing of insurance companies*	Wiesbaden	1992
Schmidt	Marketing in Reinsurance*	Karlsruhe	1994
Lach	Vertical Marketing of Insurance Companies*	Berlin	1995
Kurtenbach et al.	Insurance Marketing (4th ed.)**	Frankfurt a. M.	1995
Kendl	Reengineering in Insurance Marketing*	Wiesbaden	1997
Popp	Individualization and Insurance, Consequences for a Society-Oriented Insurance Marketing*	Wiesbaden	1997
Görgen	Insurance Marketing**	Stuttgart	2002
Puschmann	Practice of Insurance Marketing (2nd ed.)**	Karlsruhe	2003
Kühlmann et al.	Marketing and Sales (2nd ed.)**	Karlsruhe	2003
Köhne	Marketing in the Strategic Corporate Network, Explanatory Model and Practical Application in the Insurance Industry*	Wiesbaden	2006
Görgen	Insurance Marketing (2nd ed.)**	Stuttgart	2007
Köhne and Lange	Marketing and Sales of Insurance and Financial Products for Private Customers**	Karlsruhe	2009
Köhne	Insurance Marketing**	Karlsruhe	2016
Köhne and Lange	Marketing and Sales of Insurance and Financial Products for Private Customers (4th ed.)**	Karlsruhe	2020

* scientific works, not textbooks; ** textbooks
Filter: Marketing or insurance marketing in the title (thus not aspects of marketing in the title)

Schmitz 2007; Schröppel 2017; Sihler 2019; Jost 2022; Thiefes 2022; without treatises on insurance distribution). It is striking that after 2007, apart from textbooks, only a few monographs on insurance marketing or sub-aspects have been created. Pure treatises on insurance distribution are not included here, as this—as mentioned particularly with regard to insurance practice—is usually not seen as part of insurance marketing (see references to this in Chap. 13).

As far as **scientific articles** are concerned, the first papers date back to the late 1960s. Apart from contributions by the aforementioned book authors, there are still **a few fundamental publications** (e.g., Fröhner 1969; Lobscheid 1970; Fädler 1972; Krauth 1979; Koppelmann 1994; Bechmann and Köhne 1997; Kühn and Fassnacht 2001), which, however, like the books, are all of older origin. Nevertheless, there are **on specific aspects** of insurance marketing—these include, for example, the effects of individual measures on customer satisfaction and recommendation readiness or on customer behavior, the development of product innovations, the impact of pricing measures, the design of (digital) communication tools, success factors of cross-selling as well as studies of the effects of customer satisfaction or individual marketing measures on company performance—recently several publications in scientific journals (e.g., Kuzmany 2004; Köhne and Kopp 2007; Burkhardt and Steul-Fischer 2014; Zagel and Steul-Fischer 2014; Heideker and Steul-Fischer 2016; Musiol and Steul-Fischer 2017; Grösch and Steul-Fischer 2018; Trautinger 2018; Pooser and Browne 2018; Klotzki 2018; Köhne and Melashenko 2019; Brutyan et al. 2019; Musiol and Steul-Fischer 2019a, b; Grösch 2020; Klopfer and Steul-Fischer 2020; Leon and Nakayama 2020; Smith and Smith 2021; Klopfer et al. 2022; Eckert et al. 2022; Fritzsche and Bohnert 2022; Staudt and Wagner 2022; Jahnert and Schmeiser 2022; Jahnert et al. 2022; Unger and Steul-Fischer 2023; Dellaert et al. 2024). However, it is noticeable that the recent papers are scientifically demanding, but predominantly process little to no insurance marketing-related literature (and German-language sources). Furthermore, it can be observed that many of these contributions originate at a university location; the same applies in this respect, and it is also noticeable that these publications only refer to general marketing literature and the insurance reference only results from the subject of investigation, as the (empirical) studies relate to insurers, intermediaries or policyholders.

From a **content perspective**, a closer look at the textbooks and scientific publications on insurance marketing reveals that the mentioned **industry specifics are not consistently incorporated into the system of statements**. Instead, the general marketing definition is used as a basis, and there is no industry-specific marketing conception that takes up and considers the characteristics and resulting peculiarities of insurance. These should, however, be reflected in operational marketing. Instead, the existing insurance marketing literature essentially follows general marketing and regularly the classic marketing mix. *Kurtenbach et al.* (1995, p. 31) and *Kühlmann et al.* (2003) at least add the service policy. But in almost no work—with the exception of those by *Köhne* (since 2003)—is the **claims settlement mentioned as a marketing tool** in connection with the marketing mix. Yet it is undoubtedly an important part of the insurance service performance, from the customer's point of view probably even the most important, with which the quality of insurance protection proves itself in the event of a claim (Farny 2011, p. 677).

Interim Conclusion: Insurance Science Does Not Meet the Standards of Insurance Marketing Practice

In the German insurance industry, marketing still does not play the strategic role in most companies that it holds in other sectors and that the market development increasingly requires. In recent years, however, customer orientation has increasingly found its way into strategies, and in particular the operational implementation of marketing has become more professional and modern. In contrast, the importance of insurance marketing in science has only recently seen a certain increase. Individual aspects of insurance marketing are increasingly being examined. Nevertheless, it must be stated that insurance science does not meet the—increased during the same period—developments and requirements of insurance practice. There is further need for research, be it with regard to the still missing application of a comprehensive insurance marketing conception and its insurance-specific characteristics and the examination of their interrelationships, or be it in relation to the integration of new developments affecting the insurance market of an economic, legal, technological and societal nature. Science is therefore called upon to (further) develop theoretical conceptions and models that enable the derivation of solution approaches and recommendations for action for future-oriented, market-oriented corporate policy.

2.2 Insurance Marketing Conception of the Insurance Company

Building on what has been said so far, a specific insurance marketing conception is now being conceptualized. This requires

- consideration of the essential specifics of the insurance service (Sect. 2.2.1),
- and their effects on the role and behavior of insurance customers (Sect. 2.2.2),
- a corresponding insurance marketing definition (Sect. 2.2.3) and
- the derivation of an insurance-related marketing conception based on this (Sect. 2.2.4).

2.2.1 Characteristics and Specifics of the Insurance Service

The insurance service is something special in terms of marketing. This will become clear in this subchapter. The background is the typical characteristics of services, financial services and finally the insurance services themselves.

Insurance products are services. A service is an independent, marketable product that is associated with the provision and/or use of capabilities (**potential orientation**). In the course of its creation process, internal and external factors are combined (**process orientation**). The combination of factors by the service provider is used with the aim of achieving beneficial effects on external factors, on people or their objects (**result orientation**)(Meffert et al. 2018, p. 15).

▶ **Service** is any activity or service offered to another that is essentially immaterial in nature and does not bring about direct changes in possession or ownership.

(Kotler et al. 2017a, p. 498)

The difference between services and goods, despite their close connection in the sales or distribution process, characterizes peculiarities that must be taken into account by (service) marketing. These peculiarities characterize the production and sales (e.g., Meffert et al. 2018, pp. 23–36; Homburg 2020, p. 1055 f.).

Characteristics of Service Production: Industrial products can be manufactured without involving the customer or an object of the customer. Moreover, they remain in the possession of the manufacturer until the product is provided. Both are different for services, as they always aim at a change in people—for example, in insurance, at achieving inner security—or at existing objects, over which the service customer also retains control. The service provider can therefore not provide his service independently of the customer or his object (as an **external factor**). The participation of the demander takes place actively or passively, moreover, different degrees of activity are possible between these poles. It is crucial that the external factor is an indispensable prerequisite for service production. This results in both the necessity and opportunity for **customer integration into service provision** from a marketing perspective.

The production of services usually takes place in two phases: In the pre-combination, the necessary service potentials (capability, willingness to perform) are built up, in the final combination, it is necessary to sell services through the interaction of willingness to perform, marketing and sales impulses, and external factor (customer). The **result quality** measures the final result of services performed on people or objects, the **process quality** measures the process of service provision. In personal services (such as insurance), in addition to the result quality, the process quality (e.g., of advice or claims settlement) plays a major role—however, their measurement presents problems due to subjectivity and situation dependence. Because services with personal involvement are the result of an interpersonal, social interaction process.

Characteristics of Service Sales: The first characteristic of the service is its **immateriality** (lack of materiality). The consequence for marketing is that immaterial services need to be materialized, i.e., made “tangible”. The im materiality of the service is linked to other characteristics that need to be considered: Services cannot be stored and cannot be transported. Not to be confused with the inability to store is the ability to store or save the result of the service. In relation to insurance, for example, the condition guarantee regarding assets (Müller 1981, p. 165) or the resulting mediation of inner security (Haller 1982, pp. 397 f.) are constant. The lack of storage ability as a characteristic of the service results in the requirement for marketing to intensively coordinate between production and demand. The capacity problem addressed in this context affects the insurance business in the private customer sector less due to almost unlimited coverage capacities. However, the coordination between internal (production) and sales force (product demand) is very important for the insurance industry. The inability to transport the service includes the consideration that hardly any service can be consumed at a place other than where it was created (**Uno-actu principle**). However, the spatial distance between provider and customer is not an obstacle for services with low demand frequency. Sales can be made via agencies, telephone, video meeting or correspondence (for active customers), or the service can be provided directly to the customer via sales force (for passive customers). In addition, it should be noted that there is a **high qualitative fluctuation range in the execution** of services, especially when the execution is **done by people**.

Further peculiarities can be the rapid perishability of the benefit, the lack of legal protection and the associated difficulty of innovations, the high importance of customer trust, the important role of personal communication, the significance of the environment of service provision, the necessity of own distribution systems as well as the high emotional attachment of the customer to the service provider, depending on the type of service.

Financial Services are a subgroup of services, for which the described characteristics and peculiarities also apply. However, they distinguish themselves from other services by their exclusive reference to financial or cash flows instead of goods flows.

▶ **Financial Services** are monetary products that are provided in mutual contracts, in which both the service and the service in return are to be fulfilled in cash flows on both sides.

(Tchoumta 2002, p. 21)

Well-known examples of financial services products are financial products (e.g., account, savings book, credit, funds) and insurance products.

The performance of the insurance is thus also a financial service. The insurance product is also found in all three sub-areas of the service concept: The provision of the insurance service (the coverage capacity, the application forms and also the customer service) corresponds to the potential orientation; the external factors (risk and economic situation of the customer, specific damage situation) are taken into account in the "production" of the insurance coverage by internal factors (in the application and claims processing) (process orientation); finally, a benefit-generating effect (internal and/or external security) is achieved for the insurance customer (result orientation).

▶ **Insurance** is the transfer of an uncertain probability distribution of damages from the customer's perspective to the insurer in exchange for a generally fixed premium (**Customer perspective**).

Insurance is the coverage of a need for funds that is uncertain from the insurer's perspective in individual cases, but estimated overall, based on risk equalization in the collective and over time (**Insurer perspective**).

(adapted from Farny 2011, p. 8 f.)

From the service character of insurance and its essential features, some **characteristics of the insurance product** result (e.g., Delisle 1981, p. 66 f.; Kurtenbach et al. 1995, p. 18 f.; Köhne 1997, p. 117 f.; Puschmann 2003, p. 13–16; Farny 2011, p. 584 f.; Köhne and Lange 2020, p. 5): Insurance coverage

- is no object, is not tangible, and not visible;
- is a service that cannot be realized at the moment because it covers a future need that is difficult to grasp;
- therefore offers no concrete equivalent value;
- thus has only an abstract benefit;
- is therefore not a self-promoting good;
- also promises no prestige benefit;
- serves only a latent need that must first be awakened;
- is usually associated with negative associations;
- is time-related and usually leads to a longer-term contract commitment;
- is essentially determined by the general insurance conditions, which are usually formulated in legal terms and are incomprehensible to the general private customer;
- cannot be qualitatively assessed by the customer at the time of purchase and is therefore a classic credence good;
- requires "mass production" and corresponding sales for risk equalization in the collective, but can be increased at will in terms of its supply capacity;
- is produced and sold simultaneously (Uno-actu principle) because the customer provides the insurer with his risk-relevant information in the application and the insurer then presents him with an offer;
- however, is sometimes also first produced and then sold, because the creation of the product documents and the tariff calculation in the private and commercial customer business already take place (long) before the mediation of individual insurance contracts;
- is sometimes also first sold and then produced, because the policy is only created after the sale (application acceptance) and is usually sent to the customer with a time delay;
- can be easily imitated by the competition in terms of the product due to the lack of patent protection.

Excursus on the Credence Good Character of Insurances

The **information economic approach** provides insights for dealing with market-related information and uncertainty problems. It assumes that transaction processes between providers and consumers involve **information asymmetries** that lead to customer uncertainty about the quality and behavior of the provider. The reduction of these information deficits incurs costs. The levels of information deficits and information costs are influenced by the customer's evaluation behavior and the evaluation possibilities of a service offer. Information economics distinguishes between so-called search, experience, and credence goods in terms of the customer's information disadvantage compared to the provider when purchasing a good. A service usually consists of all three types of properties, with the predominance of a certain property having special implications for marketing.

With a **search good**, the customer can inform himself about the quality of the good to be purchased before the purchase by inspecting the good. Typical search properties are, for example, the color, design, or smell of a product, typical search goods are TV magazines, clothing, furniture, or perfume.

With an **experience good**, the customer can assess the quality of the purchased good during or shortly after the purchase by trying out the good, i.e., gaining experience. Compared to the search good, there is a higher information asymmetry between provider and consumer. This can be reduced by suitable marketing measures such as product samples, warranty provision, or exchange rights. Typical experience goods are food, a meal in a restaurant, medications, air or train travel, and further education offers.

With a **credence good**, the customer cannot assess the quality of the purchased good during or shortly after the purchase, but only at the time when he claims the service of the good. Thus, he must trust this service until then. Suitable marketing measures to reduce information asymmetry are information surrogates as a signal for the existence of trust characteristics such as results from test institutes, references from satisfied customers, and certificates. Typical credence goods are, for example, treatment and consulting services from doctors, lawyers, or insurance intermediaries, but also the insurer's promise of protection, combined with actual claims settlement in the event of a claim.

Goods are not per se to be classified into one of these three categories, but sometimes it also depends on the experience of the consumer whether he is dealing with a search or credence good. In the **private customer sector of the insurance market**, it is generally assumed that both the quality of the insurance product and the quality of the insurance advice and the behavior of the intermediary cannot be assessed by the customer and therefore both represent credence goods.

Further reading for in-depth study:

- Bosselmann 1994, pp. 78–111.
- Eckhardt 2007.
- Kaas 1990.
- Kaas 1991.
- Meffert et al. 2018, pp. 51–55.
- Stigler 1961.
- Weiber and Adler 1995.

▶ **Note** In the private customer sector of the insurance market, it is generally assumed that insurance is a credence goods in a double sense, as both the quality of the insurance product and the quality of the insurance advice cannot be assessed by the customer during and shortly after the purchase, and he must trust in them.

Another characteristic of insurance services is the process nature typical of services. In insurance, this has a special manifestation and a particular significance. On the one hand, it is expressed in the insurer's **ongoing protection promise**, which applies not only at the time of sale, but throughout the entire contract period, often lasting decades, and promises the customer insurance coverage. On the other hand, the service is provided in a so-called **service process**, during which partial services are provided to the customer multiple times (Fig. 2.1).

This service process, in the case of insurance, specifically extends over the phases of contact initiation, information and advice, explanation, sale as such, customer care over time (sometimes in the event of a claim, always in the course of contract adjustments or additions) up to contract termination (Lehmann 1989, p. 307 f.; Köhne 1997, p. 317 f.).

The characteristics and peculiarities of insurance services shown must be captured and taken into account by industry-specific insurance marketing. Because the **combination of disinterest, lack of risk awareness, low product understanding, and abstract benefit of insurance** leads to **private customers** being unable to adequately assess either the advisory service of an insurer or intermediary, or the ongoing protection promise, thus taking a **high purchase risk**. The credence good insurance therefore requires a high advance of trust from the customer. Insurance marketing must awaken the latent customer need, interest customers in managing their risk situation, and finally build the necessary trust to reduce the customer's purchase risk. The individual characteristics of the insurance service are not immutable, but can be mitigated or compensated with suitable marketing measures. Industry-related marketing also takes into account the service process and with it the marketing tools of service policy and claims settlement design. Customers must be made aware that the insurance benefit consists not only of possible claims settlement, but of all partial services provided during the service process. And all partial services must be designed with a customer orientation.

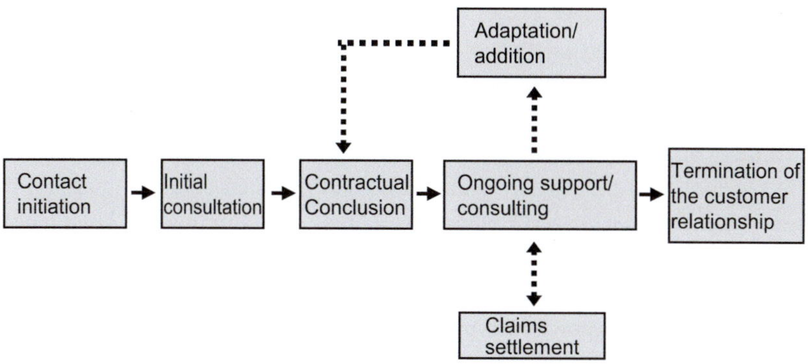

Fig. 2.1 Insurance service process

▶ **Note** Insurance marketing must awaken the latent customer need, interest customers in managing their risk situation, and finally build the necessary trust to reduce the customer's purchase risk.

2.2.2 Impacts on the Functions and Behaviors of Insurance Customers

Due to the presented characteristics of services, the customer, in contrast to classically produced consumer goods, assumes (partly new) functions and roles that go beyond those of the demander. The information and communication technology and societal development lead him to take on further functions. In addition to the classic function of the demander, the industry-typically significant dual role of the revenue and cost factor as well as service-typically the co-producer, the "substitute for leadership" and the marketing and quality assurance resource are added (Lehmann 1998, Chap. 1.3; there in detail for services and with numerous further literature references).

The insurance customer is in a **dual role as a revenue and cost factor**, because he is both a demander and thus premium payer, and a production factor and thus cost causer. As a production factor, he provides the insurer with information about his risk, which serves to calculate the expected loss value or the expected loss costs. The customer thus influences the insurer's revenues and expenses (Harbrücker 1992, p. 47 f.).

As a **co-producer**, the customer is involved in the service creation process, whether this is through the provision of time, information or know-how, or through (partial) assumption of the service creation (Bruhn 2022, p. 57). In the insurance sector, this role is often taken on by the intermediary; commercial and especially private customers usually behave passively and only provide the information requested (in the application). New forms of communication such as social media potentially allow for stronger communication and customer participation (Smith and Smith 2021, p. 110), and the combination of the internet and changed rules of risk compensation constitutes new business models, such as Friendsurance (Zeier Röschmann 2018, p. 286). However, this is countered by a frequently low customer interest in insurance, so it remains to be seen how important the role of the co-producer will really be in the so-called mass business in the future.

The further customer function of the **Substitute for Leadership** means that the customer, in services with particularly pronounced and personal contacts, takes on the role of the supervisor towards the service provider's employees through his direct feedback—usually unconsciously—because he can and does give more direct and personal feedback through his gestures, facial expressions or statements than a supervisor who is not present during the numerous direct customer interactions. In the case of insurance, there is intensive, personal contact with insurance intermediaries and possibly with claims adjusters on site; the contacts with the insurance back office are less intensive, rare and anonymous. Although customer feedback is important for all employees in direct customer contact—including those in the call centers of the back office—the sales force is likely to be more influenced by customer reactions and behavior and align themselves more closely with their (also situational) needs. This feedback function of the customer has always been part of the relationship between the intermediary and the customer.

Finally, customers take on a **marketing and quality assurance function**: Existing customers influence the expectations of other customers through word-of-mouth communication; on the internet and in social media channels, this role takes on enormous importance and influences other users to a large extent (Kotler et al. 2022, p. 262, 821 f.). In these channels, the statements of non-customers are added. In the insurance sector, this customer function is also becoming increasingly important due to technological and societal development, apart from the fact that statements from customers and non-customers are also highly interesting (and cheap) for market research. Customers also contribute to quality assurance before, during or after the service interaction through their competence and experience, when they are involved in service development as lead users, are asked about their satisfaction after interactions or through systematic complaint management. In relation to insurance, the role of the lead user is rather taken on by brokers or large representative agencies. Customer surveys are becoming increasingly important. A holistic and systematic complaint management is increasingly being enforced by corresponding supervisory regulations (see Sect. 12.1).

On the one hand, as shown, customers in the insurance sector are assuming new and additional roles. On the other hand, the mentioned characteristics of the insurance service in their combination simultaneously lead to **circumstances on the part of private customers**, which in their interaction constantly challenge insurance marketing and have already been mentioned (Sect. 1.1.1):

1. Lack of product understanding
2. Benefit difficult to recognize
3. Lack of customer interest
4. Situational customer behavior.

The first two points are interconnected. They lead to customers consciously or unconsciously understanding insurance according to the damage concept and reducing the product benefit to a possible damage payment. The insurance protection concept, according to which every customer receives the benefit from the promised continuous protection promise when concluding an insurance contract, is factually correct, but requires a rational and abstracting penetration that only a few customers carry out. The same applies to the capture of the insurance service over the entire service process.

Excursus on the Perception of Insurance Benefits

Often, customers mentally offset the benefit of insurance with the disadvantage caused by the insured event (Farny 1961, p. 132). The result is that the customer, who does not report any claims during an insurance period, believes that he has not received any benefits in return. In this view, the insurance product is consciously or unconsciously (also by practitioners) equated with the service in the event of a claim (damage concept). Insurance, understood according to the insurance protection concept, primarily provides certainty of being able to achieve certain financial goals despite disruptive events. Despite mere external guarantees, the main content of insurance is the acquisition of knowledge and trust (inner security). This service extends over the entire duration of the service and is not limited to the time of claims settlement. The injured parties, who also receive a cash benefit and thus repair service through the claims settlement, are not preferred, but compensated (Haller 1982, p. 399). This means:

According to the **damage concept**, an insurance policyholder or the injured party only perceives the specific claim payment as the service of the insurance. If the damage and/or the claim payment is absent, no "benefit in return" for the paid premium is perceived.

According to the **protection concept**, the policyholder perceives the financial protection promise as the service of the insurance. Thus, insurance primarily provides certainty of being able to achieve certain (financial) goals despite disruptive events, and the benefit consists in the acquisition of knowledge and trust. The policyholder perceives this "benefit in return" for the paid premium—regardless of whether he experiences a loss and/or a claim payment.

Further literature for deepening:

- Farny 2011, p. 22 f.
- Haller 1982, p. 398–400.
- Krüger-Barvels 1971, p. 60.

The widespread lack of customer interest in insurance is considered empirically proven. In addition, customer behavior is subject to typical perception distortions (see Sect. 4.2.1) and is also situational, i.e., influenced by specific, sometimes situation-dependent factors (see Sect. 4.3).

2.2.3 General Understanding of Marketing and the Term Insurance Marketing

As mentioned, marketing is a significant business function. This was recognized and formulated by *Peter Drucker* as early as 1954:

> "Marketing is so basic that it cannot be considered a separate function. [...] It is about the entire business activity viewed from the perspective of its end result, i.e., from the customer's point of view. Responsibility and accountability for marketing must therefore permeate all areas of the company." (Drucker, 1954, p. 38)

As outlined in the introductory chapter, various—partly timeless and partly current—circumstances are responsible for insurance companies also having to perform this significant function, both from strategic perspectives and industry-specifically as insurance marketing. Since there has been literature on insurance marketing since the 1960s, one would expect to find a definition of insurance marketing there. However, surprisingly, such a definition did not exist until 2016 (Köhne 2016, p. 35). The relevant literature, however, refers to general marketing definitions. Since insurers must practice industry-specific insurance marketing, it seems only consistent to also define it conceptually.

In order to comply with the necessary definition of terms, but not necessarily to open up a separate field of discussion with presumably limited added value, the proposed definition pragmatically follows the most common, often further developed and differentiated marketing definitions, but includes the industry.

The **marketing term** as such was already established around the turn of the last century in the USA, but did not gain acceptance in Western Europe until the end of the 1950s. The shift in corporate perspective from the product to sales and then to the customer was referred to as the marketing revolution at that time. Keith (1960, p. 35) described this rethinking process in research and practice in 1960: "No longer is the company at the center of the business universe. Today the customer is at the center." Thus, even then, the guiding principle of customer orientation was at the heart of marketing.

The classical economic (narrow) understanding of marketing is based on **three perspectives**:

1. **Marketing as a maxim and mindset**: The buyer should be the starting point and goal of the company's management philosophy. An indispensable prerequisite for this is market research.
2. **Marketing as a tool**: Marketing uses sales policy instruments with the aim of systematically influencing and shaping the market.
3. **Marketing as a management task**: As an expression of systematic decision-making and a planned approach, the process of decision-making in marketing is institutionalized.

With *Meffert*, the following classic, economically interpreted Marketing definition can be derived:

> Marketing means [according to the tripartite division] "the planning, coordination and control of all company activities aimed at current and potential markets. Through a lasting satisfaction of customer needs, the company's goals are to be realized." (Meffert 1974, quoted in: Meffert et al. 2019, p. 10)

The most generic and broadest interpretation (from a social perspective) according to *Kotler et al.* applies marketing to any form of exchange between two contracting parties:

> "Marketing is a process in the economic and social fabric, through which individuals and groups satisfy their needs and desires by creating, offering and exchanging products and other things of value." (Kotler et al. 2017a, p. 6)

A modern and expanded understanding of marketing is represented by the definition of the American Marketing Association:

> "Marketing is an organizational function and a set of processes for creating, communicating, and delivering value to customers and for managing customer relationships in ways that benefit the organization and its stakeholders." (AMA 2004, quoted in: Meffert et al. 2019, p. 11)

Weinhold-Stünzi has succinctly defined it as:

> "Marketing is market-oriented and market-appropriate corporate policy." (Weinhold-Stünzi 1988, pp. 33–35)

Here, "market-oriented" means a market-oriented corporate management and "market-appropriate" the development and offering of needs-based and ethically justifiable services.

Even though the last definition appears attractive due to its succinctness, for the definition of insurance marketing, a reference to the AMA definition is preferred, as it has found widespread acceptance and recognition in science and practice (Meffert et al. 2019, p. 11):

▶ **Insurance Marketing** as a business function and guiding principle of corporate management, develops, communicates and generates customer value over the entire service process period, in order to create value for the insurance company and its stakeholders. (Köhne 2016, p. 35)

Insurance marketing is thus a function of insurance business administration. Moreover, it serves as a guiding principle for the insurance company in customer- and market-oriented corporate management. Insurance marketing is responsible for the creation and communication of the insurance company's generated benefit and its distribution or mediation to the insurance customer. This benefit is provided over the entire service process, i.e., during the period between first contact and termination. In doing so, insurance marketing aims to create value for the insurance company and meet the needs of its stakeholders. Or, in short, as expressed by *Weinhold-Stünzi*: Insurance marketing is market-oriented and market-appropriate corporate policy of an insurance company.

2.2.4 Derivation of the Insurance Marketing Conception

A concept or conception in management theory, and thus also in marketing, is to be understood as a basic decision-making grid, with the help of which the most important intentions, connections, structural elements, and processes are presented in a coordinated manner. Concepts influence decisions and thus the central management function. Here and in the following, the term conception is used to avoid conceptual confusion. Because in marketing literature, a **marketing concept** is sometimes understood as a **specific attitude towards the market**, specifically a customer-oriented basic attitude that starts with the customer's wishes in the creation of products and services—in contrast to the product or sales concept (Kotler et al. 2017a, pp. 22–24; Haller 1986a, pp. 1105–1107). In contrast, the **marketing conception** stands for a **basic decision-making grid**. With *Becker*, a marketing conception is "a coherent, holistic action plan ('roadmap') that is oriented towards desired goals ('desired locations'), chooses suitable strategies ('route') for their realization, and on this basis determines the appropriate marketing tools ('means of transport')" (Becker 2019, p. 5).

Marketing as market-oriented corporate management can only be consistently implemented if the entrepreneurial action is based on a secured, company-specific marketing conception. This marketing conception reflects not only the content intentions, connections, and elements of the decision-making process that must be gone through in marketing. The development of a marketing conception makes sense because it creates a **conceptual order**, a **basis for coordination measures** with other basic task areas such as research and development, production, etc., as well as an **action and decision-making framework** for the areas subordinate to marketing. The marketing conception has a high significance within the overall company, as it flows into important company decisions wherever the company management acts according to market conditions. Thus, management decisions and various decisions in other basic task areas are directly linked to marketing decisions. In addition, the marketing conception determines the scope for subordinate decision-making areas such as the sales or advertising conception by defining their essential framework conditions. The marketing conception thus embodies the basic guiding plan of the entire company and thereby exercises a high degree of coordinating function throughout the company (Becker 2019, p. 5). The marketing conception covers all relevant marketing components and their interaction. In this respect, it is the ideal **structuring aid for this textbook**.

The starting point for the substantive concretization of a marketing conception is the realization that marketing is a phenomenon that is as comprehensive as it is multifaceted and complex, which becomes clear not least from the three perspectives already mentioned. Since all three marketing perspectives find their expression in the marketing concept, these will be briefly illuminated in more detail (Meffert 1986, p. 31; Weinhold-Stünzi 1988, pp. 15 f., 33–39; Webster Jr. 2005, pp. 4 f.; Homburg 2020, pp. 7–9):

1. **Marketing as a mindset**: Marketing and directly related to it, an orientation towards the market, customer needs, competition or value-creating partner companies reflects a basic attitude characterized by openness, dynamism, external orientation, opportunity seeking and interaction between individuals or companies. Understanding customer orientation as a corporate philosophy means and brings about more than just the platitude use of the credo of customer orientation in the sense of a me-too strategy or terms such as customer centricity or customer journey as "buzz words". Only when marketing as a mindset is anchored in the minds of employees and corporate management can it be lived and transformed into customer-oriented market services and problem solutions throughout the entire customer relationship with the company (customer journey).

2. **Marketing as a tool**: Marketing can be seen as a tool of a company insofar as it should and can contribute to developing, designing and selling market services and securing the existence of the offering companies. A comprehensive marketing conception includes a careful analysis of the system's internal and external environment, a vision and objective derived from it, a strategy fulfilling these and its implementation in concrete market services and their integrated design. Thus, the marketing conception as a whole is an instrument for successful corporate management. In addition, methods of internal and external environment analysis, goal and strategy formation approaches, and the components of the marketing mix are tools that support the implementation of the marketing conception.
3. **Marketing as a management task and planning process**: The complexity, scope and relevance of marketing require integrated marketing management. This involves both structural aspects (organizational structure and process, technical support and employee potential) and process-oriented aspects (management as a cycle). The implementation of a marketing-friendly mindset through the design of the "marketing" tool requires appropriate management and organizational anchoring in the company, which enables and ensures planning, decision-making, implementation and control in marketing.

Referring to important marketing representatives in the German-speaking and Anglo-Saxon areas, it can be noted that these—partly under the designation conception (Becker 2019, pp. 3–5), marketing management process (Meffert et al. 2019, p. 19) or marketing plan (Kotler et al. 2022, pp. 123 f.; Bruhn 2022, pp. 33 f.)—identify certain components as essential and therefore belonging to a marketing conception:

Components of a Marketing Conception

- **Analysis of the marketing situation**:
  - Analyses and forecasts of the business environment (Marketing as a tool)
  - Analyses and forecasts of the internal business environment (Marketing as a tool)
- **Strategic Marketing**:
  - Long-term objectives (Marketing as a tool)
  - Basic mandate per business field and business field mix (Marketing as a tool)
  - Philosophy, guiding principles and positioning (Marketing as a mindset, Marketing as a tool)
  - Strategy formulation (Marketing as a tool)
- **Operational Marketing**:
  - Determination and derivation of marketing sub-goals (Marketing as a tool)
  - Design of the marketing mix (Marketing as a tool)
  - Program or detailed planning (Marketing as a tool)

- **Accompanying marketing management process**:
  - Planning, decision-making, implementation and control as management tasks (Marketing as a leadership task)

The components 'Analysis of the marketing situation' and 'Marketing management process' do not require further explanation.

In the context of strategic marketing, it should first be noted that **strategic marketing encompasses more** than just the **marketing strategy**; in addition to this, marketing objectives and—as will be shown—marketing tasks are also part of strategic marketing (Meffert et al. 2019, p. 18; Bruhn 2022, Chap. 3).

The **marketing objectives** are a now almost self-evident—component in German-language marketing presentations. In contrast, American marketing literature—otherwise often a model and pattern for modern German-language marketing teaching—does not contain differentiated presentations on corporate and marketing objectives. In German-speaking business administration, the discussion of objectives has come to the fore with decision theory. Initially, the focus was somewhat one-sidedly on the top corporate objectives, the functional area objectives were only considered later with the development of the individual functional area teachings (Becker 2019, p. 13).

The **marketing strategy** refers to both company-wide and business field-related specifications: The former include company-wide positioning and brand policy as well as the selection of strategic business fields to be served, the latter refer to a possible differentiated positioning and brand policy as well as individual market management strategies for each business field (Meffert et al. 2019, p. 298 f.; Tomczak et al. 2023, p. 11 f.).

In the context of operational marketing, the **Marketing Mix** is in focus. The market performance shaped by this mix is the essential output of the marketing conception. The market performance is the result of the combined use of the marketing tools product, price, distribution and communication—i.e., the classic marketing mix according to *McCarthy* (1960). His four-part classification scheme has become known under the name "four P's", which stand for product, price, place (location, distribution) and promotion (sales promotion, communication).

Using these four sub-areas, the market-influencing variables can be classified according to their explanatory contribution to the following questions:

1. What services or problem solutions should be offered in what way in the market? (**Product policy**)
2. Under what conditions should the services be offered in the market? (**Pricing policy**)
3. To whom and by what means should the products be sold or conveyed? (**Distribution policy**)
4. What communicative measures should be taken to sell the services? (**Communication policy**)

The marketing mix has been and continues to be frequently criticized. The main **criticisms** concern the static nature and the need for complementarity of the tools, the product orientation of the approach, and the lack of anchoring at the top corporate level (Tomczak and Reinecke 1999, p. 312). The need for complementarity of the tools was also identified in connection with industry-specific insurance marketing.

The excessive product orientation of the marketing mix is emphasized by Schultz et al. (1993, p. III f.) and they demand a new understanding of marketing in this context: "The days of traditional mass marketing are over. Technology ended them. They will not return […]. Successful marketing in the 1990s and beyond requires real customer orientation. It means communicating with individuals, not shotgunning markets […]. That's what integrated marketing communications is all about. It's the implementation process for the new marketing paradigm." The result of this integrated marketing understanding are *Lauterborn*'s four C's, which he contrasts with *McCarthy*'s four P's (Lauterborn 1990; Schultz et al. 1993, p. 12 f.; Kotler et al. 2011, p. 193):

Customer-oriented Marketing-Mix (according to Schultz et al. 1993)

- **P**roduct ➤ study **C**onsumer wants and needs (**Customer benefit**)
- **P**rice ➤ understanding the consumers **C**osts and Conditions (**Conditions**)
- **P**lace ➤ think **C**onvenience to buy (**Customer contact design**)
- **P**romotion ➤ **C**ommunication (**Communication** in the sense of a dialogue)

Driven by a similar observation of a missing customer perspective, *Sheth and Sisodia* develop their customer-centered marketing system, which addresses the four consumer values of acceptance, affordability, accessibility, and awareness (Sheth and Sisodia 2012, cited in: Kotler et al. 2017a, p. 29). If, according to their understanding, acceptance depends on the extent to which the services meet (or exceed) customer expectations, affordability refers to the price level that customers are able and willing to pay, accessibility means how easily the customer can acquire the product, and finally, awareness stands for the extent to which customers are informed about the product features and are convinced by the product and commit to the brand, then these four comprehensible customer perspectives still strikingly remind of the product, the price, the distribution, and the communication as the four original tools of the marketing mix as well as the more customer-oriented formulation according to *Lauterborn* (1990).

Excursus on the Customer-Dominant Logic and its Approaches

In recent years, various ways of thinking have emerged in service marketing, which take different perspectives when creating services (**marketing logics**).

According to the **Goods-Dominant Logic** (also Product-Dominant Logic), the products and the product-specific customer expectations are at the center, the value creation is done by the providers. Despite customer orientation, the provider's view and "product thinking" are in the foreground.

According to the **Service-Dominant Logic**, the service-centered understanding replaces the product-centered understanding. Service is seen as a process of one person's activity for another person, not as an output unit. The value creation still comes from the provider, but results from the derived service experience of the customer, not from the purchase of a product. Instead, it arises in a mutual process between provider and customer (Value Co-Creation) and from the integration of the customer into the service creation process (Lusch and Vargo 2006). This makes it much more in line with the service approach than the (consumer goods-oriented) product orientation of the Goods-Dominant Logic. The approach also tries to integrate various marketing concepts that have developed partly independently of each other, such as service marketing, quality management, supply chain management, and relationship marketing (Bruhn 2022, p. 57).

According to the **Customer-Dominant Logic**, the customer is not only a buyer of products or user of services and thus an object, but rather involved in value creation. His individual logic, his **Ecosystem** (life world and everyday life) and his value drivers are the basis for the development and provision of service offers, because the value formation is shaped in the life of the customer. The role of the provider changes, in that he becomes a value creation partner in the Ecosystem of the customer and supports the customer's goal achievement through his service offers (Heinonen et al. 2010). Here, in contrast to the customer integration of the Service-Dominant Logic, there is a provider integration into the Ecosystem of the customer (Bruhn 2022, p. 60–62).

Closely connected with a Customer-Dominant Logic are further, current approaches discussed in the marketing literature such as customer centricity, customer experience management, or the customer journey.

Under the **Customer Centricity**, the departure from the classic product-centered company view towards a customer-oriented integration and alignment of all company processes in the sense of an ideal customer-centered company organization is understood. The customer-centered philosophy does not ask how products or services can be sold, but rather how customer benefit and thus company value can be generated through the totality of entrepreneurial activities (Bruhn et al. 2019, p. 819 f.).

Customer Experience Management (CEM) is a customer-oriented concept, at the center of which is the customer and the analysis of the customer experience as the basis for the development and implementation of a customer-centric business strategy. The customer experience arises from a series of interactions of a customer with a product, a company, or parts of the company (interaction), which provoke a reaction in the customer. The customer experience is fundamentally personal (subjective) and is based on the involvement of the customer at various levels (rational, emotional, sensory, physical, mental). Its evaluation depends on the comparison of the expectations of the interaction and its perception at the various contact moments or customer contact points. The goal of CEM is to generate positive customer experiences at all touchpoints ("Customer Touchpoints") that he has with a provider and to generate as holistic an experience as possible in order to create customer enthusiasm and in this way to bind customers sustainably (also emotionally) to the company (Bruhn et al. 2019, p. 354–356).

Closely related to this is the **Customer Journey**, which is essentially the sum of all touchpoints. It represents the sum of the customer's experiences with the company over time and can be divided into the phase(s) before the purchase, phase(s) during the purchase, and phase(s) after the purchase (Lemon and Verhoef 2016). Companies must therefore not only consider the touchpoints during the purchasing process, but also past and future touchpoints of the customer with the company and the product. Due to the advancing digitalization, the number of touchpoints is significantly increasing (Homburg 2020, p. 634 f.).

Individual insurers are now also applying CEM, such as Nürnberger Versicherung, which has been building a cross-company Customer Experience Management for its private customers since 2016 (Klopfer et al. 2022), or Allianz, which has institutionalized the function of the Chief Customer Officer (CCO) in Germany and uses so-called Analytic Driven Marketing (see Sect. 8.2.2, Marketing Highlight on Allianz).

Regarding the **overcoming of the too strong product orientation of the marketing mix**, it can thus be stated: If one follows the marketing idea in connection with its customer orientation as a marketing strategic response to the existence of a buyer's market and thus ultimately the Customer-Dominant Logic (see excursus on marketing logics), the marketing mix should be aligned with customer needs (4 C's) or customer values (acceptance, affordability, accessibility, and awareness) (market view) and the marketing tools should be consistently designed from the customer's perspective. Accordingly, one would have to speak of customer benefit, conditions, customer contact, and communication design or creation of acceptance, affordability, accessibility, and awareness. Pragmatically, however, in order to be able to connect to the actual understanding in business practice, the generally common formulations of product, price, distribution, and communication policy should be retained here. However, this does not exclude that they are each designed oriented towards the generated customer benefit and the serving of customer values.

Interpretation of the Marketing Mix from a Customer Perspective

The market performance across the Marketing-Mix is a bundle of benefits perceived by the customer as a unit, serving various customer values. It is based on the sub-services of product policy (under the premise of benefit generation and acceptance creation), price policy (under the premise of the customer budget), distribution policy (under the premise of the customer benefit of the respective customer contact and the creation of accessibility), and communication policy (under the premise of creating awareness and trust).

Apart from the more customer-oriented interpretation, the **Marketing-Mix** is, as mentioned, to be **further developed in relation to insurance**, because the marketing conditions shown ultimately influence all marketing activities.

Based on the **service-specific characteristics**, for example, process, equipment, and personnel policies could be added as service-typical marketing tools in addition to the classic four P's (Meffert et al. 2018, p. 268; Homburg 2020, pp. 1083–1088). However, in relation to insurance, this seems to be only conditionally purposeful: The equipment policy (e.g., agency equipment) belongs to sales promotion and thus to communication policy, so it can be integrated into the classic marketing mix. Service units (e.g., customer service, claims adjusters) that interact with the customer are also part of this in terms of service provision or internal service. However, not only the equipment in terms of potential quality but also the actual provision in terms of process and result quality is part of the market performance. Therefore, the term equipment policy is not specific enough. Personnel policy as a conceivable additional marketing tool is certainly important for service providers whose staff is in direct contact with customers. But to derive from this that personnel policy should be considered as another marketing tool is not convincing: It is traditionally an independent business function alongside marketing and as such performs a secondary value-adding activity, which provides a service function to the primary value creators such as product creation and design, i.e., it should also recruit and develop personnel with customer contact according to the marketing strategy (Porter 1985, pp. 34–53). For this, personnel policy does not need to become a marketing tool. The situation is different in the case of process design as a third service-typical marketing tool. It results from the time-relatedness typical for many services, which also applies to insurance: The market performance of insurance is provided over the entire service process and thus over a period of time, and it therefore includes various customer contact points over time. The service process thus takes into account the dynamic character of customer relationships. Therefore, service marketing relies on relationship or relationship marketing as a basic concept.

▶ **Relationship Marketing** encompasses all measures of analysis, planning, implementation, and control that serve the initiation, stabilization, intensification, and resumption, and possibly the termination of business relationships with the company's stakeholders—especially with the customers—with the aim of mutual benefit.
(Bruhn 2022, p. 12)

Relationship marketing shifts the focus of marketing conception away from the point-in-time exchange of goods in consumer goods marketing towards longer-term, dynamic customer relationships. Interactions with the customer become as important as the product; the customer lifecycle becomes more important than the product lifecycle. In addition to the classic economic success factors (profit, sales, costs), customer-related key figures such as the customer contribution margin, the customer equity and the value of a customer over the entire expected duration of the business relationship (**Customer Lifetime Value**) gain importance (Meffert et al. 2018, pp. 45–47). With regard to the marketing mix of the insurance company, this requires less a standalone marketing tool, but rather the **dynamic provision of the classic marketing tools along the service process**. This primarily affects the more procedural marketing tools of sales and communication design. This can ultimately overcome the static nature of the traditional marketing mix.

From the **insurance-specific characteristics**, it can now be justified why the generally more or less unreflected transfer of the traditional marketing tools (product, price, communication, and sales policy) to insurance companies is not sufficient and how the Marketing Mix needs to be adapted with regard to the insurance service:

The performance of the insurance is initially determined and shaped by the product and premium policy, communication, and distribution, thus encompassing the classic marketing tools. In addition, however, the insurance service includes services along the entire service process (information, advice, explanation, support) as well as in the specific case of damage (claims settlement), all of which are undoubtedly components of the benefits perceived by the customer and therefore can be designed in a customer-oriented manner (Joho 1996, pp. 127–141; Jara 2000, Chap. 1.1, 1.4; Köhne 2003). Therefore, it seems very obvious to **consider** the **service policy and** the **claims settlement design as insurance-specific marketing tools**. The service policy is to be designed in a potential-, process-, and result-oriented manner and thus picks up the equipment and process policy proposed in the service context. The claims settlement, on the other hand, is industry-specific (see excursus in Sect. 12.1). Thus, the insurer's marketing mix is to be supplemented by the service policy (Kurtenbach et al. 1995, p. 31; Kühlmann et al. 2003, p. 22; Köhne 2006, p. 310) as well as by the claims settlement design or claims policy (Köhne 2003). The now six insurance-typical marketing tools could theoretically be described in a consistently customer-oriented terminology as customer benefit, conditions, contact, communication, comfort design as well as compensation, thus opposing the four P's of consumer goods marketing with the **six C's of the insurance marketing mix** (Fig. 2.2).

As already mentioned above, however, it is more pragmatic in terms of compatibility with the actual understanding in corporate practice to use the more common formulations **product, price, distribution, communication, service and claims settlement policy**. This does not exclude the possibility of designing these six marketing tools in a customer-centric manner, **each oriented towards the generated customer benefit and the servicing of customer values** (Fig. 2.3).

Regarding the weighting of the different elements of a marketing conception, it is important to recall the **special role** of operational marketing: The design **of the marketing mix** gives the insurance service its profile and determines its character, its positioning, and its benefit creation. In addition, the operational product and service design is also the decisive brand-shaping element. Therefore, it should be noted that the marketing mix, despite some justified criticism, plays a decisive role in the context of operational product and service design.

Regarding the criticism that the marketing mix is not sufficiently anchored at the top level of the company, it should be noted that this applies particularly to its integration into the overarching strategic business or corporate planning. *Tomczak and Reinecke* rightly point out in this context that the marketing mix is not particularly well suited to serve as a useful framework for top management, as it aims to create value and pursues the question of which offers can generate sales and profits in which markets. This observation leads them to **supplement** the (operational) **marketing mix with a guiding**

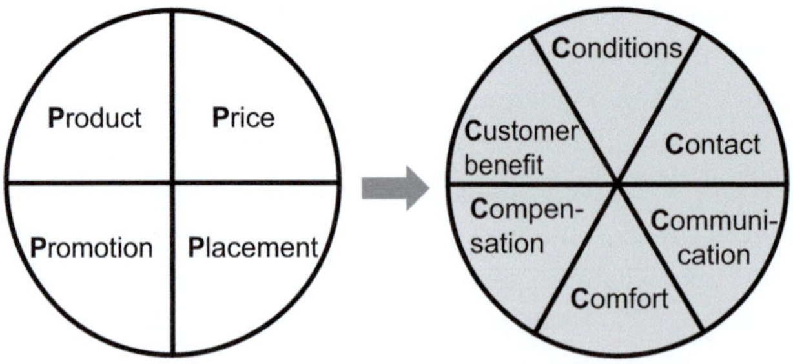

Fig. 2.2 From the 4 P's in consumer goods marketing to the 6 C's in insurance marketing

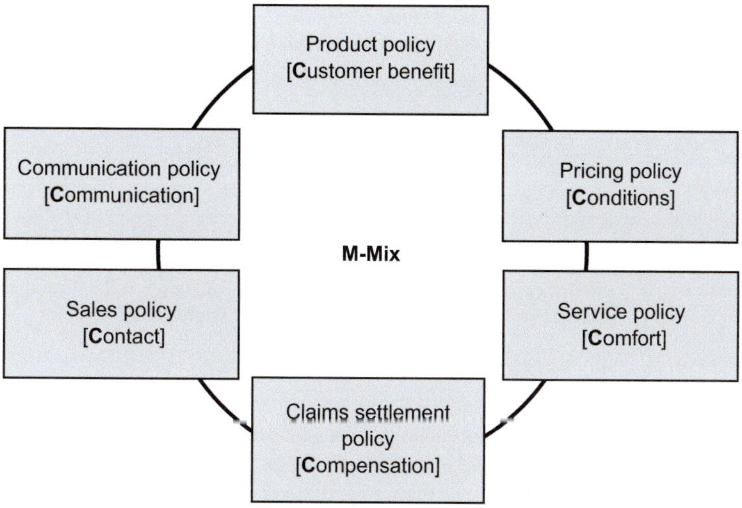

Fig. 2.3 The six marketing tools in the insurance company

plan, so that the marketing tools can be harmonized with the overarching business strategy. The required guiding plan is served by the so-called **core marketing tasks**, which include performance innovation, performance maintenance, customer acquisition, and customer retention. The basic orientation of the four core tasks is the realization of competitive advantages. Accordingly, the task-oriented approach is underpinned by the central theoretical approaches to building, maintaining, and expanding strategic competitive advantages by considering their commonalities with the four basic orientations of customer, resource, innovation, and persistence. These in turn largely coincide with the basic ideas of the four core tasks (Fig. 2.4): Customer potentials are based on a customer orientation, performance potentials on a resource orientation. The development of new customer and performance potentials requires an innovation orientation, while the exploitation of existing customer and performance potentials requires a persistence orientation (Tomczak and Reinecke 1999, pp. 297–308; Reinecke 2004, pp. 185–188; Tomczak et al. 2023, pp. 51–55).

The core task of **customer acquisition** stands for the development of new customer potentials for the respective provider, whether these are the customers of the competition (displacement competition) or previous non-users of the respective service. In the course of the core task of **customer retention**, the aim is to prevent customer migration to the competition and to generate repeat and follow-up purchases in the sense of potential exploitation. **Performance innovations** require the development of new problem solutions using superior resources. They include all measures from the creation of new offers to their enforcement in the market. Finally, the core task of **performance maintenance**

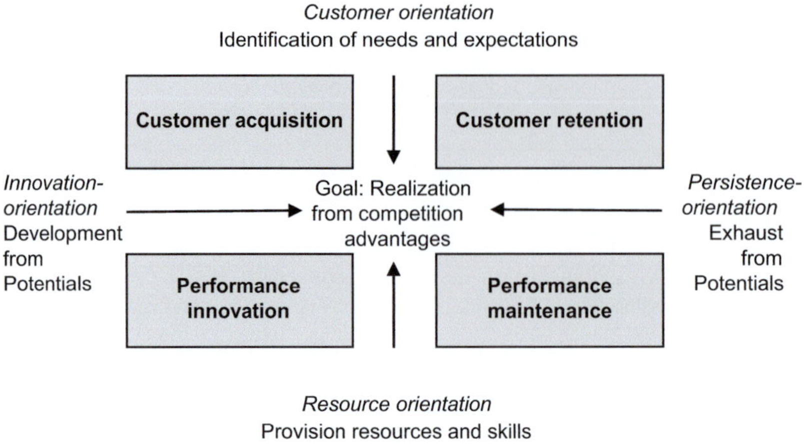

Fig. 2.4 Basic orientations and core tasks in marketing. (Based on Tomczak and Reinecke 1999, p. 308)

aims at the long-term exploitation of performance potential and relies on measures that contribute to extending the life cycle of market services and sustainably exploiting the potential through multiplication. Top management must fundamentally deal with all four core tasks, even if different priorities can be set (Tomczak and Reinecke 1999, pp. 308–315; Reinecke 2004, pp. 189–198; Tomczak et al. 2023, pp. 55–66).

The relationship marketing, which is fundamental for the service sector, and with it the explicit orientation towards long-term business relationships, are becoming increasingly relevant in the financial services sector. Especially in the insurance market, this does not only refer to the customer, but also to the large number of sales partners and intermediaries. Relationship marketing shifts the focus more towards customer retention (Meffert et al. 2018, p. 45 f.). From the importance of sales partners, there is also a need for two additional marketing tasks, **partner acquisition** and **partner retention**. Relationships with current as well as future or potential business and sales partners need to be established, developed or even terminated (Köhne 2006, pp. 159–162).

The core marketing tasks are concretization components of a marketing strategy and are difficult to separate from it (Tomczak and Reinecke 1996, pp. 3–8). Nevertheless, this concretization is necessary and sensible. Therefore, the six marketing tasks are consequently integrated into the "Strategic Marketing" part of the marketing conception (unlike in Meffert et al. 2019, p. 18).

Another important building block for the marketing conception originates from the general marketing mindset, the **thinking in functions**. It essentially anchors the marketing philosophy and customer orientation across all areas in the marketing conception. In the course of developing the marketing strategy, function orientation represents a kind of basic philosophy of strategic marketing (marketing as a mindset). Function-based marketing advocates the thesis that services from a customer's perspective must fulfill certain basic functions in order to create customer benefits. The fulfillment of functions is consistently ensured, while products and their features are transient (Levitt 1960, p. 45). In this respect, thinking in functions also overcomes the product orientation criticized in the marketing mix. Functional thinking ensures the adoption of the customer's perspective and prevents an overly inward-oriented product design. With regard to the theoretical foundation of the marketing conception, it offers a concrete implementation of the **Market-based-View** (MbV). If marketing management is also to play a special role in linking MbV and resource-based theory approaches, it must also take into account its own competencies (resources, abilities, knowledge, and technologies) in order to **connect** the **Resource-based-View** (RbV) with the MbV (Meffert et al. 2019, p. 45 f.). Both strands of theory are thus expressions of marketing as a mindset, but also a formative basis of the (marketing) content design (e.g., in the internal and environmental analysis).

Excursus on Functional Thinking

Thinking in functions consistently adopts the customer's perspective and asks about the **functions that a market service fulfills from the customer's point of view**. Therefore, customer- and function-appropriate product and service design is based on the effects actually achieved with the customer, which are realized on several reference levels (individual, group, society) and in various dimensions (direct/indirect; positive/negative; financial/technical-performance/economic/social). Thus, the focus of consideration is on the effectively realized creation of customer benefits instead of provider-planned benefit creation.

The following questions are at the forefront of functional thinking:

1. What basic function(s) should be fulfilled from the customer's perspective by one or more demanded services?
2. What additional function(s) (positive, but also negative) could also be fulfilled from the customer's perspective?
3. What conceivable products (and product combinations) enable optimal fulfillment of the targeted function(s)?
4. What functions fulfilled by our own company could potentially be fulfilled by potential and current competitors in the future?

Example Smartphone:

The basic function of the smartphone is mobile telephony or communication and goes back to its product predecessors (cordless phone, mobile phone). This function is constant and still needs to be fulfilled, although the associated products (mobile phone) have already been replaced by further developments. The smartphone—unlike its predecessors—fulfills numerous other functions, and the transition between basic functions and additional functions is fluid, partly determined by user needs. Other services—besides telephony—such as SMS, mailing, video telephony, and communication apps round off the **communication function**. Here too, an expansion can be observed: The (originally bilateral) communication function is increasingly becoming a multilateral networking function; this can be demanded privately, but also professionally. This function is particularly served by social networks. In addition, a smartphone serves an **information function**, which can also be interpreted as a basic function: This includes services such as the internet, information apps, or location-based dynamic information such as location-dependent restaurant tips.

Traditional mobile phones have already reached their limits in this respect. Another function is **entertainment**: This includes services such as the internet, radio, TV, but also own pictures, music and videos or game apps. For many users, this is also a basic function, which as a result of technological development in the course of media convergence is nowadays demanded as a **suitable bundle of functions** together with information and communication. In the past (telephony), it would have been a non-mandatory additional function. Apart from these core functions, there are **further additional functions** that a smartphone can fulfill, if they are important to the user: Constant availability, status symbol, belonging to a community ("Apple community"), participation in technological and media progress as positive additional functions, but also negative additional functions such as disruption of personal (face-to-face) communication, disturbance of others by noise, inattention due to distraction etc. On the one hand, the smartphone has supperseded and replaced some traditional products by bundling these diverse, demanded functions (e.g., mobile phone, digital camera, MP3 player, navigation devices), on the other hand, it is currently hardly replaceable due to this unique bundling of functions. This makes it a **marketing masterstroke**, which was made possible by technology, but became successful through creative (function-oriented) bundling.

Further reading for in-depth study:

- Haller 1986a.
- Haller 2006.
- Isaacson 2011.
- Kotler et al. 2022, p. 45, 52–58, 99 f.
- Levitt 1960.

As a coherent, holistic action plan, the **marketing conception** is the **result of a systematic analytical approach** that identifies both the potential of the market of interest and the weaknesses of competitors (according to the MbV) as well as the strengths of one's own company (according to the RbV). The analyses flow into an optimal overall conceptual problem solution, namely the marketing conception. This must satisfy the condition of completeness, i.e., it must include all mentioned levels—namely goals, strategies (incl. tasks), and tools. As practice shows, the determination of objectives does not necessarily follow a systematic analysis of the strategic starting position. However, this would be sensible, as the defined objectives should be realistic.

It is important that the marketing conception, in addition to its content elements, represents a **process** (marketing control) that iteratively goes through the following steps:

- Internal and external analysis, forecasts (marketing research),
- Goal, strategy, and task definition (strategic marketing),
- Market performance determination in relation to the marketing mix (operational marketing),
- Detailed planning, implementation, and control (marketing management process).

Over time, external and internal company factors change, so that individual marketing objectives may need to be adjusted, but not the conceptual guiding plan (Becker 2019, pp. 4 f., 127 f., 822; Tomczak et al. 2023, pp. 10–14).

Figure 2.5 schematically and summarily shows the insurance marketing conception-insurance marketing concept underlying this textbook. Its essential function is to serve as a **basic decision-making grid** to capture the marketing phenomenon as completely as possible and to present the most important intentions, links, structural elements, and processes in a coordinated manner. This provides a systematic basis for developing and presenting the basics of insurance marketing in parts III to VI in the spirit of *Krüger-Barvels* using general marketing theory as well as service and especially industry-specific

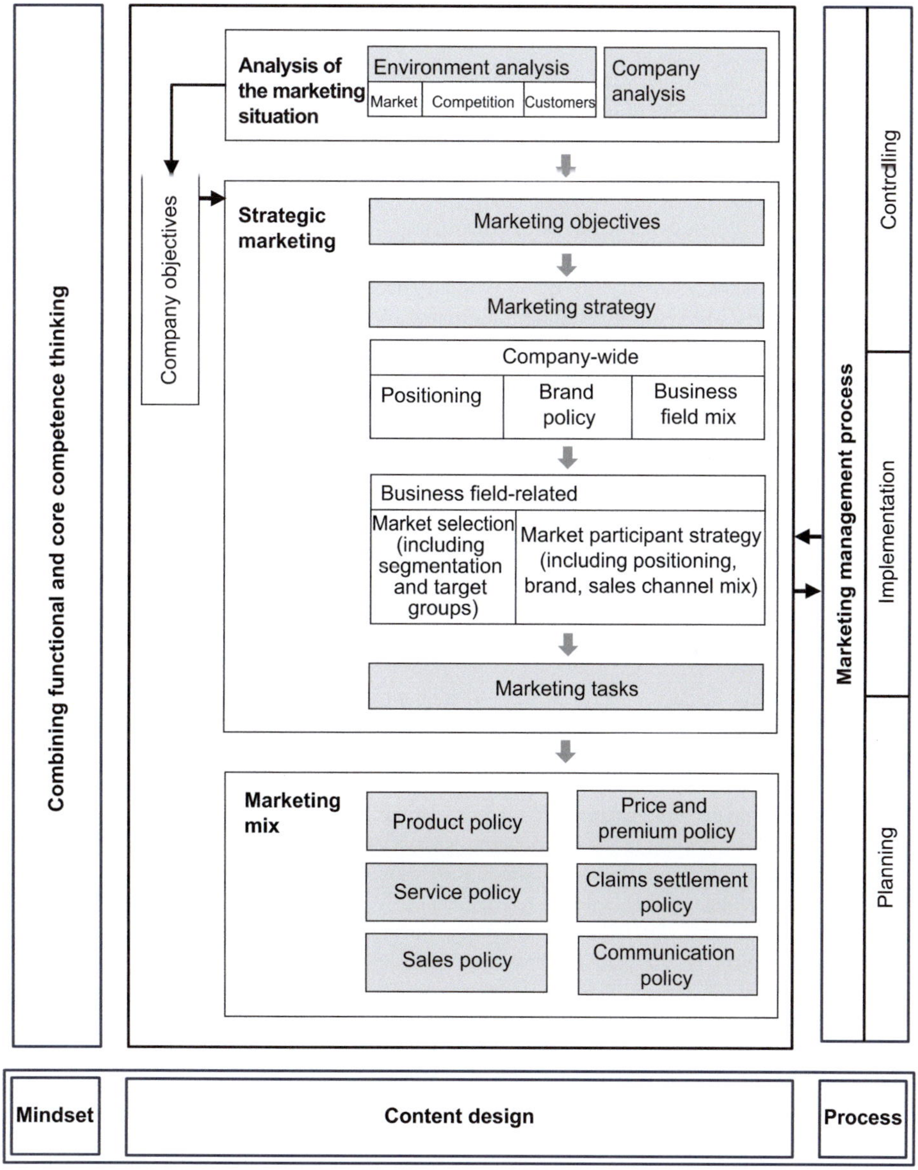

Fig. 2.5 Insurance marketing conception. (Further developed from Köhne 2006, p. 309)

findings (Krüger-Barvels 1971, p. 13). This allows the marketing conception to ensure that insurance marketing can be captured in its **multifaceted complexity**, as well as support the systematic mental **organization of relationships**. The insurance marketing conception can also depict the basic **guiding plan** of the insurance company in implementing a market-oriented corporate management.

References

Allianz Konzern (Ed.) (2023): Allianz Konzern Geschäftsbericht 2022, München, 2023.

Altenburger, R. (2003): Electronic Business im Erstversicherungsunternehmen unter besonderer Berücksichtigung des Marketing, Leipzig, 2003.

AXA Versicherung AG (Ed.) (2023): Geschäftsbericht 2022, Köln, 2023.

Barinka, A./Wippler, P. (2019): Personalisierte Links ersetzen Apps und Portale, in: Reich, M./ Zerres, C. (Eds.), Handbuch Versicherungsmarketing, Berlin, 2. ed., 2019, pp.423–434.

Bechmann, T./Köhne, T. (1997): Integriertes Marketing: Schlüsselfunktion im dynamischen Versicherungsmarkt, Sonderausgabe der IVW Management-Information, Band 1, St. Gallen, 1997.

Becker, J. (2019): Marketing-Konzeption: Grundlagen des ziel-strategischen und operativen Marketing-Managements, München, 11. ed., 2019.

Bosselmann, E.H. (1994): Versicherungsmakler und deregulierte Versicherungsmärkte, Karlsruhe, 1994.

Bruhn, M. (2019b): Kommunikationspolitik, Systematischer Einsatz der Kommunikation für Unternehmen, München, 9. ed., 2019.

Bruhn, M. (2022): Relationship Marketing. Das Management von Kundenbeziehungen, München, 6. ed., 2022.

Bruhn, M./Meffert, H./Hadwich, K. (2019): Handbuch Dienstleistungsmarketing. Planung – Umsetzung – Kontrolle, Wiesbaden, 2. ed., 2019.

Brutyan, A./Guxha, D./Schmeiser, H. (2019): Versicherungen aus Kundensicht: Erkenntnisse aus der Wissenschaft, in: ZVersWiss, Jg. 108, pp. 365–381. (https://doi.org/10.1007/s12297-019-00447-8)

Burkhardt, J./Steul-Fischer, M. (2014): Versicherungsunternehmen in Social Networks – Ein Überblick über aktuelle Forschungsfelder und eine experimentelle Studie zur Kundenansprache, in: ZVersWiss, Vol. 102, 2014, Nr. 5, pp. 473–490.

Delisle, E. (1971): Marketing in der Versicherungswirtschaft, Beiträge zu wirtschaftswissenschaftlichen Problemen der Versicherung, Band 5, Karlsruhe, 1971.

Delisle, E. (1981): Marketing in der Versicherungswirtschaft, Beiträge zu wirtschaftswissenschaftlichen Problemen der Versicherung, Band 5, Karlsruhe, 2. ed., 1981.

Dellaert, B.G.C./Johnson, E.J./Duncan, S./Baker, T. (2024): Choice Architecture for Healthier Insurance Decisions: Ordering and Partitioning Together Can Improve Consumer Choice, in: Journal of Marketing, Vol. 88, 2024, No. 1, pp. 15–30. (https://doi.org/10.1177/00222429221119086)

Drucker, P. (1954): The Practice of Management, New York, 1954.

Duft, C. (1983): Insurance Marketing, Zürich, 1983.

Eckert, C./Neunsinger, C./Osterrieder, K. (2022): Managing customer satisfaction: digital applications for insurance companies, in: GP, Vol. 47, 2022, No. 3, pp. 569–602. (https://doi.org/10.1057/s41288-021-00257-z)

Eckhardt, M. (2007): Insurance Intermediation, An Economic Analysis of the Information Services Market, Heidelberg, 2007.

ERGO Versicherung AG (Ed.) (2023): Geschäftsbericht 2022, Düsseldorf, 2023.
Eurich, A. (2001): Bestandskundenmarketing von Versicherungsunternehmen, Lohmar, 2001.
Fädler, K. (1972): Eine Marketing-Konzeption für den Versicherungsbetrieb?, in: SVZ, Jg. 40, 1972, pp. 66–75.
Farny, D. (1961): Die Versicherungsmärkte, Berlin, 1961.
Farny, D. (1971): Absatz und Absatzpolitik des Versicherungsunternehmens, Karlsruhe, 1971.
Farny, D. (1990): Versicherungsbetriebslehre: Wirtschaftliche Theorie des Versicherungsunternehmens und seiner Beziehungen zur Umwelt, in: ZVersWiss, Jg. 79, pp. 1–30.
Farny, D. (2011): Versicherungsbetriebslehre, Karlsruhe, 5. ed., 2011.
Friederichs-Schmidt, S. (2006): Kundenwert aus Sicht von Versicherungsunternehmen, Wiesbaden, 2006.
Fritzsche, A./Bohnert, A. (2022): Implications of bundled offerings for business development ad competitive strategy in digital insurance, in: GP, Vol. 47, 2022, pp. 817–834. (https://doi.org/10.1057/s41288-021-00244-4)
Fröhner, R. (1969): Lebensversicherung der Assekuranz, Versicherungswirtschaft auf dem Weg zum Marketing, in: die absatzwirtschaft, Jg. 12, 1969, Nr. 5, pp. 17–24.
Glaser, C. (2021): Wettbewerbsfaktor Vertrieb bei Finanzdienstleistern. Ein ganzheitliches Konzept zur Sales Excellence, Wiesbaden, 3. ed., 2021.
Görgen, F. (2002): Versicherungsmarketing, Stuttgart, 2002.
Görgen, F. (2007): Versicherungsmarketing, Strategien, Instrumente und Controlling, Stuttgart, 2. ed., 2007.
Grösch, M. (2020): The impact of product variety on customers' default acceptance and company perception. Experimental studies for the insurance industry, in: ZVersWiss, Jg. 109, 2020, pp. 377–398. (https://doi.org/10.1007/s12297-020-00458-w)
Grösch, M./Steul-Fischer, M. (2018): Less is more: How the number of insurance options influences customers' default acceptance, in: ZVersWiss, Jg. 107, 2018, pp. 517–529. (https://doi.org/10.1007/s12297-018-0415-4)
Haller, M. (1982): Risiko- und Versicherungsprobleme des privaten Haushalts – aus Sicht der Privatversicherung, in: ZVersWiss, Jg. 71, 1982, Nr. 3/4, pp. 383–437.
Haller, M. (1986a): Funktionen-Marketing – zur Bewältigung der „Financial Services (R) Evolution"? in: Belz, C. (Ed.), Realisierung des Marketing, Festschrift zum 60. Geburtstag von Prof. Dr. H. Weinhold-Stünzi, St. Gallen 1986, pp. 1.097–1.124.
Haller, M. (2006): Funktionen-Ansatz, in: Belz, C./Bieger, T. (Eds.), Customer Value, Kundenvorteile schaffen Unternehmensvorteile, Landsberg a. L., 2006, pp. 745–760.
Harbrücker, U. (1992): Wertewandel und Corporate Identity, Perspektiven eines gesellschaftsorientierten Marketing von Versicherungsunternehmen, Wiesbaden, 1992.
Hartmann, C. (2006): Customer Value im Bereich der Automobilität – empirische Analyse und strategische Implikationen für die Kfz-Versicherer als automobile Dienstleistungsanbieter, St. Gallen, 2006.
Heideker, S./Steul-Fischer, M. (2016): Werbeanzeigen von Versicherungsunternehmen zur Aufklärung über Gesundheitsrisiken, in: ZVersWiss, Jg. 105, 2016; pp. 549–561. (https://doi.org/10.1007/s12297-016-0355-9)
Heinonen, K./Strandvik, T./Mickelsson, K.-J./Edvardsson, B./Sundström, E./Andersson, P. (2010): A customer-dominant logic of service, in: Journal of Service Marketing, Vol. 29, 2010, No. 6/7, pp. 531–548.
Hermann, R. (2009): Überlebenswichtig oder überflüssig? Marketing für Firmensachversicherungen sichert langfristig das Marktpotenzial, in: VW, Jg. 64, 2009, Nr. 19, pp. 1.498–1.504.
Homburg, C. (2020): Marketingmanagement, Strategie – Instrumente – Umsetzung – Unternehmensführung, Wiesbaden, 7. ed., 2020.
Hujber, T. (2005): Werbung von Versicherungsunternehmen, Wiesbaden, 2005.

HUK-Coburg Versicherungsgruppe (Ed.) (2023): Bericht über das Geschäftsjahr 2022, Coburg, 2023.

Isaacson, W. (2011): Steve Jobs, Die autorisierte Biografie des Apple-Gründers, München, 2011.

Jahnert, J.R./Schmeiser, H. (2022): The relationship between net promoter score and insurers' profitability: an empirical analysis at the customer level, in: GP, Vol. 47, 2022, pp. 944–972. (https://doi.org/10.1057/s41288-021-00237-3)

Jahnert, J.R./Schmeiser, H./Schreiber, F. (2022): Pricing strategies in the German term life Insurance market: An empirical analysis, in: Risk Management and Insurance Review, Vol. 25, 2022, pp. 19–34. (https://doi.org/10.1111/rmir.12202)

Jara, M. (2000): Zielorientierte Neugestaltung des Schadenmanagements in Versicherungsunternehmen, St. Gallen, 2000.

Joho, C. (1996): Ein Ansatz zum Kundenbindungs-Management für Versicherer, Bern, 1996.

Jost, T. (2022): Kundenbeziehungsmanagement in der Versicherungswirtschaft: Ein Perspektivwechsel vor dem Hintergrund der Digitalisierung und der Entwicklung von Ökosystemen, Karlsruhe, 2022.

Kaas, K.-P. (1990): Marketing als Bewältigung von Informations- und Unsicherheitsproblemen im Markt, in: DBW, Jg. 50, 1990, Nr. 4, pp. 539–548.

Kaas, K.-P. (1991): Marktinformationen: Screening und Signaling unter Partnern und Rivalen,, in: ZfB, Jg. 61, 1991, Nr. 3, pp. 357–370.

Keith, R.J. (1960): The marketing revolution, in: JoM, Vol. 24, 1960, No. 1, pp. 35–38.

Kendl, E. (1997): Reengineering im Versicherungsmarketing, Funktionsverlagerung auf Vermittlerbetriebe, Wiesbaden, 1997.

Keuper, F.W. (1986): Grundlagen einer Marketingkonzeption im Versicherungsunternehmen unter besonderer Berücksichtigung der betrieblichen Nachfragestruktur, Wien, 1986.

Klopfer, L.-M./Steul-Fischer, M. (2020): Weiterempfehlungsprogramme: Die Wirkung des Akquisitionskanals und der Prämienaufteilung auf den Erfolg von Weiterempfehlungen, in: ZVersWiss, Jg. 109, 2020, pp. 361–376. (https://doi.org/10.1007/s12297-020-00466-w)

Klopfer, L.-M./Steul-Fischer, M./Zitzmann, A. (2022): Customer Experience Management – Eine qualitative Studie zur Umsetzung in der Versicherungsbranche, in: ZVersWiss, Jg. 111, 2022, pp. 245–276. (https://doi.org/10.1007/s12297-022-00531-6)

Klotzki, U. (2018): New life insurance products and product complexity in Germany, in: ZVersWiss, Jg. 107, 2018, pp. 143.161. (https://doi.org/10.1007/s12297-018-0404-7)

Köhne, T. (1997): Die Wirkungsversicherung im Privatkundengeschäft – Implikationen für eine kundenorientierte Marktleistungsgestaltung, St. Gallen, 1997.

Köhne, T. (1999): Versicherungsmarketing: Vom „Mauerblümchendasein" zur strategischen Instanz, in: IVW HSG (Ed.): Risk Tomorrow, IVW-Jahresbericht 1998, St. Gallen, 1999, pp. 35–38.

Köhne, T. (2003): Schadenmanagement als Marketinginstrument oder: Kundenorientierung im „Moment of truth", in: El Hage, B./Jara, M. (Eds.), Schadenmanagement, Grundlagen, Methoden und Instrumente, Praktische Erfahrungen, St. Gallen, 2003, pp. 67–90.

Köhne, T. (2006): Marketing im strategischen Unternehmensnetzwerk, Erklärungsmodell und praktische Anwendung in der Versicherungswirtschaft, Wiesbaden, 2006.

Köhne, T. (2016): Versicherungsmarketing. Marketing und Vertrieb im Versicherungsunternehmen in Theorie und Praxis, Karlsruhe, 2016.

Köhne, T./Kopp, F. (2007): Produktinnovationen und Produktmodifikationen in der Versicherungswirtschaft: Rolle und Bedeutung nach der Deregulierung, in: ZVersWiss, Jg. 96, 2007, Nr. 2, pp. 227–259.

Köhne, T./Lange, M. (2009): Marketing und Vertrieb von Versicherungs- und Finanzprodukten für Privatkunden, Fach- und Führungskompetenz für die Assekuranz, Karlsruhe, 2009.

Köhne, T./Lange, M. (2020): Marketing und Vertrieb von Versicherungs- und Finanzprodukten für Privatkunden, Fach- und Führungskompetenz für die Assekuranz, Karlsruhe, 4. ed., 2020.
Köhne, T./Melashenko, I. (2019): Produktinnovationen und Produktmodifikationen in der Versicherungswirtschaft zwischen 2006 und 2017, in: ZVersWiss, Jg. 108, Nr. 3–4, 2019, pp. 275–305.
Konzern Versicherungskammer (Ed.) (2023): Geschäftsbericht Konzern Versicherungskammer 2022, München, 2023.
Koppelmann, U. (1994): Marketingüberlegungen im Versicherungsbereich, in: Schwebler u.a. (Hrsg), Dieter Farny und die Versicherungswissenschaft, Karlsruhe, 1994, pp. 285–306.
Kotler, P./Armstrong, G./Wong, V./Saunders, J. (2011): Grundlagen des Marketing, München, 5. ed., 2011.
Kotler, P./Keller, K.L./Opresnik, M.O. (2017a): Marketing-Management, Konzepte – Instrumente – Unternehmensfallstudien, Halbergmoos, 15. ed., 2017.
Kotler, P./Armstrong, G./Harris, L.C./He, H. (2022): Grundlagen des Marketing, Halbergmoos, 8. ed., 2022.
Krausz, S. (2002): Strategische Unternehmenspolitik von Erstversicherern unter Verbindung von Zielgruppen-Marketing und Kernkompetenz-Management, Karlsruhe, 2002.
Krauth, W. (1979): Absatzstrategien im Versicherungsunternehmen, in: ZVersWiss, Jg. 68, 1979, Nr. 3, pp. 497–548.
Kremer, M. (1994): Das Nachfrageverhalten von Versicherungs- und Bankkunden aus ganzheitlicher Sicht – Konsequenzen für den Finanzdienstleistungsgedanken, St. Gallen, 1994.
Krüger-Barvels, R. (1971): Marketing im Versicherungsbetrieb, Freiburg i.B., 1971.
Kühlmann, K./Wolf, H.-P./Wallenwein, C./Swoboda, U. (2003): Marketing und Vertrieb, Funktionsorientierte Qualifikationen, Karlsruhe, 2. ed., 2003.
Kühn, R./Fassnacht, R. (2001): Marketing für Versicherungen, Herausforderungen und Entwicklungstendenzen, gezeigt am Beispiel des schweizerischen Versicherungsmarktes, in: Tscheulin, D.K./Helmig, B. (Eds.), Branchenspezifisches Marketing, Grundlagen – Besonderheiten – Gemeinsamkeiten, Wiesbaden, 2001, pp. 79–98.
Kurtenbach, W. (1981): Versicherungsmarketing, Frankfurt a.M., 1981.
Kurtenbach, W./Kühlmann, K./Käßer-Pawelka, G. (1995): Versicherungsmarketing, Eine praxisorientierte Einführung in das Marketing für Versicherungen und ergänzende Finanzdienstleistungen, Frankfurt a.M., 4. ed., 1995.
Kuzmany, K. (2004): Werbemitteldesign und Markenpolitik in Versicherungsunternehmen, in: ZVersWiss, Jg. 93, 2004, pp. 739–751.
Laakmann, M. /Rahlf, C. (2019): Customer Journey am Beispiel des Schadenprozesses in der Versicherungswirtschaft, in: Reich, M./Zerres, C. (Eds.), Handbuch Versicherungsmarketing, Berlin, 2. ed., 2019, pp. 401–422.
Lach, H. (1995): Vertikales Marketing von Versicherungsunternehmen, Berlin, 1995.
Lauterborn, B. (1990): New marketing litany – four P's passe; C-words take over, in: Advertising Age, 1990, October, pp. 26.
Lehmann, A. (1989): Dienstleistungsmanagement zwischen industriell-orientierter Produktion und zwischenmenschlicher Interaktion, St. Gallen, 1989.
Lehmann, A.P. (1998): Qualität und Produktivität im Dienstleistungsmanagement. Strategische Handlungsfelder im Versicherungs- und Finanzdienstleistungswettbewerb, Wiesbaden, 1998.
Leon, S./Nakayama, M. (2020): Exploring factors that influence positive WOM in the health insurance industry, in: Health Marketing Quarterly, Vol. 37, 2020, No. 2, pp. 176–192. (https://doi.org/10.1080/07359683.2020.1756124)
Lemon, K.N./Verhoef, P.C. (2016): Understanding customer experience throughout the customer journey, in: Journal of Marketing, Vol. 80, 2016, No. 6, pp. 69–96.

Levitt, T. (1960): Marketing Myopia, in: Harvard Business Review, Vol. 38, No.4, 1960, pp. 45–56.
Lobscheid, H.G. (1970): Grundzüge eines Marketing bei Versicherungsunternehmen, in: DVZ, Jg. 24, 1970, Nr. 5, pp. 111–119.
Lusch, R.F./Vargo, S.L. (2006): Service-Dominant Logic: Reactions, Reflections and Refinements, in: Marketing Theory, Vol. 6, 2006, No. 3, pp. 281–288.
McCarthy, E.J. (1960): Basic Marketing: A Managerial Approach, Homewood, 1960.
Meffert, H. (1986): Grundlagen der Absatzpolitik, Wiesbaden, 1986.
Meffert, H./Bruhn, M./Hadwich, K. (2018): Dienstleistungsmarketing, Grundlagen – Konzepte – Methoden, Wiesbaden, 9. ed., 2018.
Meffert, H./Burmann, C./Kirchgeorg, M./Eisenbeiß, M. (2019): Marketing, Grundlagen marktorientierter Unternehmensführung, Konzepte – Instrumente – Praxisbeispiele, Wiesbaden, 13. ed., 2019.
Mertens, M. (1992): Kundentypologien im Versicherungsgeschäft mit Privatkunden, Bergisch Gladbach, 1992.
Müller, H. (1994): Marktsegmentierung im Privatkundengeschäft von Versicherungsunternehmen, Karlsruhe, 1994.
Müller, R. (2012): Träume, Formeln, Traumata: Das Marketing der Versicherung heute, in: VW, Jg. 67, 2012, Nr. 23, pp. 1.720–1.722.
Müller, W. (1981): Das Produkt Versicherung, in: Jung, M./Ralph, L./Seifert, W. (Eds.), Geld und Versicherung, Festgabe für Wilhelm Seuß, Karlsruhe, 1981, pp. 155–171.
Müller-Reichart, M. (2002): International orientierte Produktinnovationspolitik globalisierter Versicherungsunternehmen, Karlsruhe, 2002.
Musiol, A./Steul-Fischer, M. (2017): The psychological effects on tariff choices for car insurance, in: ZVersWiss, Jg. 106, 2017, pp. 525–538. (https://doi.org/10.1007/s12297-017-0395-9)
Musiol, A./Steul-Fischer, M. (2019a): Price framing and consumers' purchase intention on pay-how-you-drive tariffs, in: ZVersWiss, Jg. 108, 2019, pp. 407–419. (https://doi.org/10.1007/s12297-019-00440-1)
Musiol, A./Steul-Fischer, M. (2019b): Der Einfluss der Produktart und des Weiterempfehlungskanals auf den Erfolg von Weiterempfehlungen bei Versicherungen, in: ZVersWiss, Jg. 108, 2019, pp. 389–406. (https://doi.org/10.1007/s12297-019-00438-9)
Nickel-Waninger, H. (1987): Versicherungsmarketing, auf der Grundlage des Marketing von Informationsprodukten, Karlsruhe, 1987.
Oletzky, T./Staud, N./Boltz, J. (2015): Die Versicherungswirtschaft auf dem Weg zu wirklicher Kundenorientierung, in: Zimmermann, G. (Ed.), Change Management in Versicherungsunternehmen. Die Zukunft der Assekuranz erfolgreich gestalten, Wiesbaden, 2015, pp. 257–272.
Oster, O. (2019): Customer Experience – die Königsdisziplin, in: Reich, M./Zerres, C. (Eds.), Handbuch Versicherungsmarketing, Berlin, 2. ed., 2019, pp. 171–191.
o. V. (2010): Interview mit Dr. Torsten Oletzky, in: Handelsblatt vom 07.12.2010, pp. 33.
Perrenoud, P.-C. (1979): Marketing in der Rückversicherung, Zürich, 1979.
Pooser, D.M./Browne, M.J. (2018): The effects of customer satisfaction on company profitability: Evidence from the property and casualty insurance industry, in: Risk Management and Insurance Review, Vol. 21, 2018, pp. 289–308.
Popp, H. (1997): Individualisierung und Versicherung, Konsequenzen für ein gesellschaftsorientiertes Versicherungsmarketing, Wiesbaden, 1997.
Porter, M.E. (1985): Competitive Advantage, Creating and Sustaining Superior Performance, New York, 1985.
Puschmann, K.-H. (1986): Praxis des Versicherungsmarketing, Karlsruhe, 1986.
Puschmann, K.-H. (2003): Praxis des Versicherungsmarketing, Karlsruhe, 2. ed., 2003.

Reinecke, S. (2004): Marketing Performance Management, Empirisches Fundament und Konzeption für ein integriertes Marketingkennzahlensystem, Wiesbaden, 2004.

Reitzler, R. (2001): Versicherungen für Senioren, Wiesbaden, 2001.

Rützler, P. (1994): Jugendmarketing für Versicherungen, St. Gallen, 1994.

Schmidt, D. (1995): Versicherungsmarketing Heute – Anspruch und Wirklichkeit, in: SCG St. Gallen Consulting Group (Ed.), Handbuch Management Versicherungsvertrieb, Wiesbaden, 1995, pp. 5–18.

Schmidt, M. (1994): Marketing in der Rückversicherung, Karlsruhe, 1994.

Schmitz, M. (2007): Einfluss der Vermittler auf Zufriedenheit und Loyalität von Versicherungskunden, Tönning u.a., 2007.

Schröppel, Lina (2017): Digitalisierung am deutschen Versicherungsmarkt – Einschätzung des moderierenden Effekts der Online-Aktivität auf den Zusammenhang von Convenience instrumentalisierenden Attributen und Kundengewinnung im Neugeschäft der Assekuranz, Univ.-Diss., Neubiberg, 2017.

Schütze, U. (1972). Probleme der Produktgestaltung in der Versicherungswirtschaft unter besonderer Berücksichtigung der Produktinnovation, Karlsruhe, 1972.

Schultz, D.E./Tannenbaum, S.I./Lauterborn, R.F. (1993): The new marketing paradigm. Integrated marketing communications, Lincolnwood/Illinois, 1993.

Schumacher, U. (2019): Versicherung 2.0 – Marketing und Kommunikation im Social Media-Zeitalter, in: Reich, M./Zerres, C. (Eds.), Handbuch Versicherungsmarketing, Berlin, 2. ed., 2019, pp. 457–470.

Schwake, E. (1987): Überlegungen zu einem risikoadäquaten Marketing als Steuerungskonzeption von Versicherungsunternehmen, Karlsruhe, 1987.

Schwarz, S. (2015): Kulturwandel bei AXA: „Kundenzentrierung" als Erfolgsfaktor bei der Strategieumsetzung, in: Zimmermann, G. (Ed.), Change Management in Versicherungsunternehmen. Die Zukunft der Assekuranz erfolgreich gestalten, Wiesbaden, 2015, pp. 153–163.

Sheth, J./Sisodia, R. (2012): The 4A's of Marketing: Creating Value for Customer, Company and Society, New York, 2012.

Sihler, P. (2019): Kundenakzeptanz verhaltensabhängiger Preise, Hamburg, 2019.

Smith, K.T./Smith, L.M. (2021): Analysis of Social Media Usage and Relationship to Profit Margin among Insurance Companies, in: Services Marketing Quarterly, VOL. 42, 2021, No. 1–2, pp. 108–123. (https://doi.org/10.1080/15332969.2021.1948488)

Staudt, Y./Wagner, J. (2022): Factors Driving Duration to Cross-Selling in Non-Life Insurance: New Empirical Evidence from Switzerland, in: Risks, Vol. 10, pp. 187–207. (https://doi.org/10.3390/risks10100187)

Stigler, G. (1961): The Economics of Information, in: Journal of Political Economy, Vol. 63, 1961, No. 3, pp. 213–225.

Tchoumta, J.-M. (2002): Allfinanz aus der Sicht der Assekuranz: eine vergleichende Studie, Frankfurt a.M., 2002.

Thiefes, D. (2022): Influencer Branding in der Versicherungswirtschaft, Wiesbaden, 2022.

Tomczak, T./Reinecke, S. (1996): Der aufgabenorientierte Ansatz, Einen neue Perspektive für das Marketing-Management, Fachbericht für Marketing, Heft 5, St. Gallen, 1996.

Tomczak, T./Reinecke, S. (1999): Der aufgabenorientierte Ansatz als Basis eines marktorientierten Wertmanagements, in: Grünig, R./Pasquier, M. (Eds.), Strategisches Management und Marketing, Festschrift für Richard Kühn, Bern, 1999, pp. 293–327.

Tomczak, T./Reinecke, S./Gollnhofer, J. (2023): Marketingplanung, Einführung in die marktorientierte Unternehmens- und Geschäftsfeldplanung, Wiesbaden, 8. ed., 2023.

Trautinger, M.-J. (2018): Kundenzufriedenheit als Steuerungsinstrument in einem Versicherungsunternehmen – nur Schall und Rauch oder ökonomisch sinnvoll?, in: ZVersWiss, Jg. 107, 2018, pp. 3–39. (https://doi.org/10.1007/s12297-017-0394-x)

Trumpfheller, J. (2005): Kundenbindung in der Versicherungswirtschaft, Eine theoretische und empirische Analyse unter besonderer Berücksichtigung des Versicherungsvertriebs über Versicherungsintermediäre, Karlsruhe, 2005.

Unger, F./Steul-Fischer, M. (2023): Rewards for a Healthy Lifestyle:The Impact of Reward Type and Timing in Pay-As-You-Live Pricing, in: Marketing ZFP, Vol. 45, 2023, No. 1, pp. 66–84.

Vielreicher, P. (1995): Produktinnovationsmanagement in Versicherungsunternehmen, Wiesbaden, 1995.

Webster Jr., F.E. (2005): Back to the Future: Integrating Marketing as Tactics, Strategy, and Organizational Culture. In: JoM, Vol. 69, 2005, pp. 4–6.

Weiber, R./Adler, J. (1995): Informationsökonomische Erkenntnisse für das Marketing bei Qualitätsunsicherheit der Konsumenten, in: ZfBF, Jg. 47, 1995, Nr. 1, pp. 43–65

Weinhold-Stünzi, H. (1988): Marketing in zwanzig Lektionen, St. Gallen, 1988.

Zagel, T./Steul-Fischer, M. (2014): Wahrgenommene Preisfairness bei Preiserhöhungen in der Schadenversicherung, in: ZVersWiss, Jg. 103, 2014, Nr.5, pp. 447–459.

Zeier Röschmann, A. (2018): Digital insurance brokers – old wine in new bottles? How digital brokers create value, in: ZVersWiss, Jg. 107, 2018, pp. 273–291. (https://doi.org/10.1007/s12297-018-0413-6)

3 Insurance Market as the Addressee of Insurance Marketing

This chapter defines the **insurance market for private customers**, as the insurance marketing conception of the insurer, which will be discussed in detail later, is aimed at it. The insurance market is initially a part of the financial services market (Sect. 3.1). Its demand side includes the demand segments of industrial and corporate, commercial, and private customers (Sect. 3.2), its supply side includes financial services and insurance branches (Sect. 3.3). The insurance market for private customers finally has a special structure and operates within certain legal framework conditions (Sect. 3.4).

3.1 Market for Financial Services and Insurance

From an economic perspective, a market stands for the meeting of supply and demand as comprehensive (macroeconomic) quantities: A financial services market is therefore the place of meeting of

- Financial services providers such as banks, insurers, investment companies, building societies, leasing service providers and/or credit card companies,
- Financial services intermediaries, portals and other intermediaries, and
- Demanders of financial services such as companies, public households as customers and private households.

These market participants meet to exchange supply and demand for financial services. Accordingly, the insurance market can be defined as part of the financial services market.

▶ **Insurance market:** It is the place where insurance companies, intermediaries and policyholders meet to exchange supply and demand for insurance coverage.

(Eisen 2017, p. 1010)

T. Köhne, *Insurance Marketing*, https://doi.org/10.1007/978-3-658-47345-7_3

The economic market concept is product-oriented—it bases the naming of the market on the traded good or service, the financial services or the insurance coverage. However, the individual insurance company is in many different exchange relationships with actors of its served market, so that a business market view allows a greater differentiation: From a business perspective, the market concept describes the entire economically relevant environment with which insurers interact externally. This environment certainly includes the overall market, but also sub-markets as well as individual provider-intermediary and provider-customer relationships. In addition to the product view, a customer, intermediary and regional view are therefore added—all describe the economically relevant market from the perspective of the individual provider. This differentiated market description must also be taken into account by the marketing strategy, which will be picked up and discussed in detail later.

3.2 Demand on Financial Services and Insurance Markets

3.2.1 Actors and their Characteristics

The entirety of financial services and insurance customers can be divided into subsets with the same characteristics: External, institution-related characteristics of the customer refer to their position in the overall economic process and their economic activities; internal, person-related characteristics include motives, attitudes, abilities and behaviors of the customer.

The external characteristics often directly indicate the financial and risk situations and the resulting financial services and insurance needs. For example, it can be assumed that an internationally active pharmaceutical corporation, a self-employed master craftsman and a young worker household are exposed to very different financial situations and risk situations and therefore have a correspondingly differentiated financial and insurance need.

The **orientation towards institution-related characteristics** leads to a division into

- Industrial or corporate customers,
- Commercial customers,
- Public households, and
- Private customers.

The separation between **industrial and corporate customers** is not clearly defined, but varies from insurer to insurer. If a separation is made at all, industrial customers are defined as very high-revenue, globally producing or trading companies (international corporations), while corporate customers are defined as less high-revenue or less globally active companies (medium-sized companies). For example, one of the world's largest industrial insurers separates industrial from corporate customers from a turnover size of 500 million €, a direct competitor has, however, set industrial customers from 5 million € for many years (Lohmann et al. 2020, p. 323–326). As a guideline, the thresholds of the Second Property & Casualty Directive could be used, which is still referred to in the new Distribution Directive (IDD) in Art. 2 No. 16: Large risks (and thus industrial customers) would therefore be companies that meet at least two of the following three criteria: net turnover of at least 12.8 million €, balance sheet total of at least 6.2 million €, at least 250 employees on average in the financial year.

Another indication for the distinction between industrial and corporate customers is the presence of a company's own affiliated brokerage company in the case of industrial customers. However, there is no generally accepted and applied demarcation.

In the case of **commercial customers**, commercial and private insurance coverage are often closely intertwined, e.g. in small businesses, in agriculture and forestry, in crafts, in self-employed and freelancers. It is noteworthy that the same insurance product can secure both private consumption and the means of production. In contrast, the industrial and corporate customer always concludes an insurance contract in connection with a productive activity (as a factor of production). Nevertheless, the distinction between corporate and commercial customers is fluid at the border. Whether a supplier with an annual turnover of 5 million €, 20 employees and international sales is a corporate or a commercial customer ultimately depends on the individual classification of financial service providers and insurers.

The **distinction between commercial and private customers**, on the other hand, is generally easier to make: producing companies cover external demand, private households cover their own demand (Kotler et al. 2022, p. 151). It is a characteristic of public and private households to consume insurance coverage, more precisely, to secure their consumption (own demand). This distinguishes them from (commercial) companies that use insurance coverage to secure their production (external demand) and for which insurance coverage thus becomes a factor of production involved in the production of other goods (Farny 2011, p. 425). Although private households also produce goods in a certain sense through the use and combination of factors of production, e.g. the ability to work of household members, insurance coverage nevertheless secures the economic and social existence of the household and thus the ability to consume, but not the ability to work. Thus, the different purchasing motives of insurance demanders speak for a distinction between commercial and private customers. Because it makes a difference whether an insurance policyholder wants to secure his private life or his privacy or whether he wants to secure a company oriented towards economic goals against possible losses. In the latter case, the policyholder will be less emotionally affected by the loss. For the demarcation of the private customer from the commercial policyholder, the respective different goals and expectations play a significant role.

For the **private household**, **goals** can be identified in three spheres (Haller 1982, pp. 392–394):

1. In the social area, there are education-related, societal, and cultural goals or expectations.
2. In the performance economic area, there are generative and regenerative goals: Generative goals are, for example, the establishment, preservation, and expansion of the family, regenerative goals are the procurement and provision of goods and services for preservation and regeneration.
3. In the financial economic area, income, wealth, and liquidity goals can be formulated.

Apart from the goal system, the involvement of the demanders can be used for the demarcation of private customers. In contrast to companies, in private households the demanders are simultaneously the users of the insurance coverage and the carriers of the insured system. They bear the direct responsibility for the safety of their household. Private households always operate for their own needs; companies do not do this, they primarily cover external demand.

▶ **Private customers** primarily seek insurance coverage to secure their private (family) sphere and consumption (personal needs), not to secure a profit goal or production factors to cover external needs.

At least in the case of farmers and foresters, self-employed individuals, or so-called liberal professions such as doctors, architects, lawyers, notaries, and independent consultants, the distinction is difficult. They essentially belong to both target groups, as their business, which is oriented towards economic goals, is based on their person and therefore personal risks (death, accident, illness, occupational disability) affect both the company and the private individual. The securing of a profit goal can hardly be distinguished from the securing of one or more family goals (social, performance-economic, financial-economic). In insurance practice, they are usually attributed to commercial customers due to their also existing business-related risks or served by independent marketing programs, as they have a special insurance need due to specific risks of their professional activities.

Finally, for the sake of completeness, the **public households** (federal, state, local) should be mentioned, which also demand insurance coverage, provided they do not bear risks themselves or finance them through municipal loss compensation. They too are consumers and not producers.

While institution-related characteristics allow for the formation of customer segments, **customer types can be formed based on personal characteristics**. This is because personal characteristics of financial services and insurance customers cause different behaviors in the procurement and use of financial services products and are therefore of great importance to the marketing expert. Although such characteristics ultimately influence the behaviors of all decision-makers, they are particularly relevant in the private customer sector for further subdivision of this demand group. This is due, on the one hand, to the fact that private customers tend to act more emotionally than rationally in their decision-making process. On the other hand, the characteristics in this segment can be more easily collected due to the number of people affected than, for example, with commercial customers (see in detail in Sect. 4.3).

3.2.2 Functions of Financial Services and Insurance from a Customer Perspective

The concept of thinking in functions as a principle of customer orientation has already been presented. It assumes that services from a customer's perspective must fulfill certain basic functions in order to create customer benefits and satisfy needs. The satisfaction of needs on the customer side thus requires the fulfillment of functions by a market service.

To capture the basic needs for financial services and insurance, the so-called **hierarchy of needs by *Maslow*** (1970) is helpful. It ranks human motivation according to its different urgency for behavior into five categories of needs (Fig. 3.1):

1. Physiological (biological) needs such as food, sleep, and preservation of health
2. Security needs, e.g., preservation of employment and retirement provision

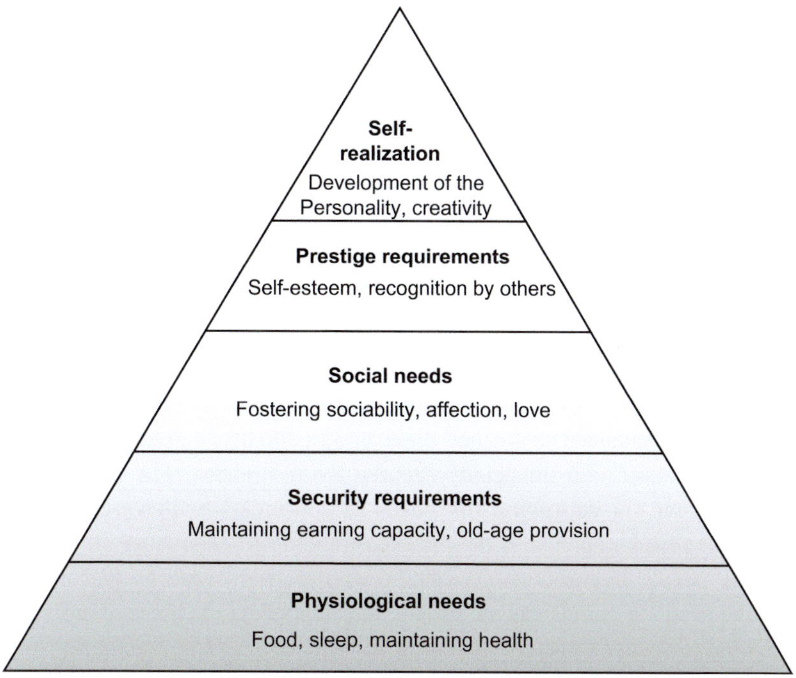

Fig. 3.1 Hierarchy of needs according to *Maslow*. (Meffert et al. 2015, p. 117)

3. Social needs, e.g., needs for affection, love, sociability, belonging to a group (community)
4. Striving for self-esteem and recognition by others (desire for prestige)
5. Striving for self-actualization, i.e., development of personality and creativity in the broadest sense.

The first four layers represent deficit needs: they are the result of a lack of need-reducing stimuli. The fifth, "highest" need represents a growth need, characterized by an individual's active pursuit with the ultimate goal of individual realization. Growth need refers to the phenomenon that the desire for self-realization can never be fully satisfied and therefore the desire for further self-realization is stronger, the more the original need for self-realization is satisfied. The human motivation resulting from these needs becomes effective in a hierarchical order.

Central to *Maslow's* motivation theory is the principle of relative priority in need actualization: All higher motives of the hierarchy are only activated as goals when the respective subordinate goals are fulfilled according to a certain level of demand. The level of demand is dependent on society and the immediate environment of the buyer. Experiences from past purchase decisions also flow into the demands, so that the levels of demand are dynamic sizes. However, this is an ideal-typical view, because firstly, the order of motivation is differently pronounced in many people and secondly, a motivation does not always have to be completely fulfilled before a higher motivation can become effective.

However, if one accepts the hypotheses of this dynamic motivation model despite the objections raised, it makes a helpful contribution to understanding the motivation and underlying needs of consumers. From the general need categories, concrete needs can be derived that influence customer behavior and should therefore be taken into account by marketing measures (Meffert et al. 2019, p. 108; Homburg 2020, p. 31).

Almost all **insurance products** directly serve the **satisfaction of the second need category "security"**, other financial service products such as already created assets or retirement provision products at least partially. In addition, financial services products indirectly serve the satisfaction of the remaining need categories: payment transaction products help with the purchase and sale of existential consumer goods as well as with the purchase of (luxury) goods of the third and fourth need category, asset accumulation products are intended to finance these goods. Finally, activities of the fifth category "self-realization" are financially secured by insurances. The **need pyramid** is particularly suitable for **capturing the needs of** consumers or **private households**. It can in principle also be applied to the other customer segments. After all, decisions are also made by people in corporate customers, who are influenced by personal motives. However, the needs of companies are usually less shaped by the goals of individual people than by the company's goals.

In this respect, the **fundamental needs of companies** towards financial services are **economically determined**: Financial services are means to an end and serve the implementation of financial flows to finance business activities as well as the flow of goods. From a company's perspective, insurance products are essentially intended for the **hedging of conditional risks** to ensure the achievement of objectives (profit, sales, costs) despite occurring disruptions. These conditional risks refer to implicitly assumed (functioning) production conditions such as intact machines, timely arriving, supplied products, capable employees, functioning data exchange, available liquidity, etc. They are to be hedged in order to be able to take on the actual entrepreneurial risks (action risk) (Haller 1986b, p. 13–16). Company-specific demand for insurance coverage thus arises, among other things, from the legal form: Legal entities have insurance needs exclusively due to business activity, while sole proprietors are increasingly forced by tax legislation to strictly separate business and private life. Furthermore, company-specific liability is more complex than that of private individuals according to § 823 BGB; It includes, in addition to classic liability claims, product and environmental liability for manufacturing companies, asset liability for certain companies, and manager liability. Other specific company risks concern production downtime and all kinds of transport risks. The insured objects are company buildings, commercial vehicles, machines, buildings from offices to factories, but also goods and commodities. Finally, the insured persons are company members, whether individuals such as top managers or entire groups of people such as employees (Hermann 2009, p. 1502; Aschoff and Heitmann 2020, p. 89–98). Apart from obtaining (specific) insurance coverage, other motives for the demand for insurance products are of a balance sheet policy nature (balance sheet protection, less need for reserves) or the need for risk management services (Kühlmann et al. 2003, p. 86; Lohmann et al. 2020, p. 335–337).

The fundamental needs outlined above for financial services products can be assigned to **financial services functions**. Financial services then have the following functions to fulfill from the customer's perspective (Bätscher 1989, p. 66–76):

- **Earning**: Only the fulfillment of the function of receiving money (e.g., through wages and salaries, asset income, gifts, inheritances, gambling winnings) leads to its possession and thus financial availability. Financing is also included here.
- **Spending**: The function of spending money is fulfilled when received funds are used for the purpose of livelihood, i.e., used to acquire material and immaterial goods in return.
- **Asset formation and saving**: What is not spent from the income earned serves for saving or asset formation. This complements the time-related income and expenditure with the temporal aspect and the temporal decoupling of income and expenditure.
- **Investing**: The investment function is closely linked to asset formation. Because only the possibility of investing money leads to maintaining and increasing the value of the assets over time.
- **Securing**: Since unexpected factors can positively, but also negatively influence the fulfillment of the mentioned financial functions, another need arises to ensure this fulfillment by securing it. Thus, the function of securing is added as another function.

- **Diversification**: Spreading income across several sources and assets across various investment forms initially complements the function of securing (diversification). In addition, the spread of expenditures across several benefits means a disposition of the available funds.

There are numerous and close economic connections of these functions; at the customer regarding the benefit and at the provider regarding the creation of services and sales. The combination of various financial functions in a total service is referred to as "Allfinanz".

Although the financial services functions have been developed from the perspective of private households, they can also be transferred to corporate customers. These must, as part of their financial activities, take in money, spend it, invest it temporarily, secure it, and diversify it. Wealth accumulation and saving, on the other hand, are of lesser importance (except for the financial services providers themselves).

Excursus on functional thinking in the global financial system

The **functional thinking** can even be **transferred to the global financial system**. In 1995, a group of scientists from Harvard Business School wrote a remarkable book as part of a research project. They show that the global financial system also fulfills (six) basic functions. These are characterized firstly by the fact that they remain constant over time and hardly change. In contrast, the products, institutions, and political framework conditions of these financial systems are constantly changing. Secondly, therefore, the structure or the institutional form must follow the function and not vice versa, so that innovations and competition between the institutions help the financial system to greater efficiency and performance. The scientists explain the logic and functioning of the global financial system based on these functions and not—as often in the literature—from a purely institutional perspective.

They describe the **six functions** as follows:

1. **Clearing and Settlement Payments**: A financial system organizes the processing of payments and invoicing to support the exchange of goods, services, and assets.
2. **Pooling Resources and Subdividing Shares**: A financial system creates a mechanism to simultaneously pool financial resources to carry out large-volume, indivisible undertakings, and to create participations in companies and ventures to enable diversification.
3. **Transferring Resources across Time and Space**: A financial system enables the transfer of economic resources over time, geographical regions, and industries.
4. **Managing Risk**: A financial system creates the conditions to manage uncertainty and control risks.
5. **Providing Information**: A financial system provides price information that supports the coordination of decentralized decisions in different areas of the economy.
6. **Dealing with Incentive Problems**: A financial system regulates the handling of incentive problems that arise when one market party has an information advantage or is a contractor of the other market party.

Further reading for in-depth study:

- Crane et al. 1995, esp. pp. 3–31.

It can therefore be stated that the basic needs of private households as well as the financial management of companies require the fulfillment of classic financial functions. With regard to private households, it is true that the purely monetary needs are already present on the first layer of motivation and require the functions of earning and spending. Security and wealth-building functions only come into play on the second layer—i.e., from a certain level of prosperity. In the upper layers (striving for recognition, self-realization), all financial functions play a significant role—but only indirectly and in different content-related forms.

▶ **Note** The central (basic) **function** that **insurances** fulfill is **financial security against predefined risks.** This applies to typical property, asset, and personal risks as well as to retirement provision, where the risk of "long life" is financially secured.

3.2.3 Current Empirical Data and Facts on Demand in the German Insurance Market

Germany, with its approximately 84.5 million inhabitants (as of June 2023) and a premium volume in primary insurance of about 223 billion € in gross written contributions in 2022, is the **sixth largest insurance market in the world** and the third largest insurance market in Europe. Excluding life insurance, Germany is the third largest insurance market worldwide (GDV 2023a, p. 1, 93, 95[1]).

In the field of indemnity insurance, Germany, together with the United Kingdom, leads Europe in terms of demand and turnover. This is due, among other things, to the comparatively large importance of industry and medium-sized businesses and the correspondingly high demand for property & casualty insurance.

The nearly **41 million private households** in Germany (2022) form the largest customer group. On average, a household comprises 2 people—in 1950 it was still 3 and in 1980 it was 2.5 people. With the continuously increased wealth, their demand for financial services and insurance has also significantly increased in recent decades (Federal Statistical Office 2023a).

In 2022, according to calculations by the Deutsche Bundesbank, the monetary assets of private households amounted to 7.23 trillion €; after deducting existing loans, they had a **net-monetary assets** of 5.14 trillion €. A large part of this (1.09 trillion €) is due

[1] Note: Here and subsequently, premium and loss values from 2022 are always only preliminary values that could still be slightly adjusted.

to claims against life insurers. The **formation of monetary assets** of private households in 2022 amounted to 288 billion €. The newly formed monetary assets of private households with insurance companies (life insurance, property & casualty/accident insurance, and private health insurance) and pension institutions (pension and burial funds, pension funds, and professional pension schemes and supplementary pension institutions) amounted to almost 90 billion €. Of this, 32.7 billion € was attributable to life insurance, 53.7 billion € to pension institutions. The share of life insurance in the total formation of monetary assets was thus 11.3% (2021:13.7%), which was slightly lower compared to the two Corona years 2020 and 2021, but remained almost unchanged compared to the pre-Corona years.

However, the **structure of the formation of monetary assets** of private households in Germany still does not correspond to the goal of long-term accumulation of retirement assets. Looking at the monetary assets by types of investment, it is also evident for 2022 that private households continue to shy away from long-term commitments in the area of investment. Alone 3.11 trillion €, or 42.9% of the total monetary assets of private households, were invested in banks in 2022; this was mainly in the form of sight deposits and savings deposits, but also cash holdings were at 430 billion €, more than double the amount in 2017 (197 billion €). Conversely, this potentially provides considerable funds for funded retirement provision, provided it is possible to overcome the prevailing wait-and-see attitude (Deutsche Bundesbank 2023, pp. 48–51).

In terms of insurance demand, **objective and subjective factors of insurance needs** can be distinguished based on the different risk situations of customers: Objective factors are determinants that are exclusively oriented towards factual circumstances; subjective factors, on the other hand, depend on the customer himself and are expressed in his behavior. They include, for example, his emotional state, his basic attitude and risk propensity, his knowledge related to risk and insurance, and his intelligence (see in detail Sect. 4.3).

Even at the macroeconomic and societal level, the objective and subjective insurance needs of private customers are influenced. An objective factor is the macroeconomic starting situation, i.e., the basic demand potential and its provision with insurance (**degree of market saturation**).

In the insurance industry, private customers represent around 90% of the premium volume—in 2022, their contribution income was therefore around 200 billion € (Hohenstein et al. 2020, p. 19).

The **provision rate**, i.e., the ratio of premium expenditures to the disposable income of private households (in 2022: 2164.47 billion €, Federal Statistical Office 2023b, p. 9), is thus about 9.2%.

In the past, the insurance industry could almost continuously record a significant growth advantage over the overall economy; today, its growth opportunities have obviously become smaller. Accordingly, the ratio of premium income to gross domestic product, the so-called **insurance penetration**, which has been steadily increasing since 1950 to 2010—with a minor dip from 2005 to 2008—has been stagnating since 2010. In

2022, it fell by 0.5% from the previous year to 5.77%; thus, it is only as high as in 1994 (5.72%).

Thus, insurance penetration in Germany is rather below average in international comparison (6.8%). For instance, in 2022, insurance penetration in the USA, UK, Taiwan, South Korea, and South Africa was over 10%, and in France, the Netherlands, Italy, Japan, and Canada between 8 and 9%. The main reason for this in most of these countries is the much greater weight given to life insurance for retirement provision.

The insurance needs of all private households can be roughly gauged by the extent to which they have basic insurance. The **insurance density** referred to here, i.e., the amount of annual premium expenditures per inhabitant, is 2647 € in 2022. Although this is about 30% more than in 2008, Germany does not hold a top position internationally (GDV 2023a, pp. 9, 96).

In trend, insurance penetration and insurance density are likely to increase again or continue to increase in Germany. Private insurance protection is among those products that are disproportionately demanded with increasing levels of prosperity. Those who own more have more to lose or more to insure. This applies—at the latest after a recovery from the globally effective Corona crisis and with the progression of the conversion of energy supply to renewable energies—also and especially to the German insurance market.

The mentioned market data on insurance coverage already allow some conclusions about the provision of private households in Germany with insurance coverage. However, they should be **interpreted with caution** at this level of aggregation. In particular, they are hardly suitable for international comparisons: For example, different insurance densities result not only from different coverage of private households, but also

- from different risks such as country-specific liability systems,
- the distortion caused by the unreported proportion of included insurance premiums from commercial insurance, which also have very different significance in different countries,
- the different proportion of cross-border business in the premiums, and
- the very different social, pension, and tax systems in individual countries.

Thus, market-wide data do not allow any statement about the distribution of existing insurance coverage among different households or about specific insurance gaps in certain types of households. This is made possible by **microdata**, as determined in household surveys. In terms of insurance demand, the Income and Consumption Sample (EVS) collected by the Federal Statistical Office every five years is worth mentioning. From the EVS 2018 survey, high-quality and reliable data on the spread of insurance coverage are available (see excursus).

Excursus on the Income and Consumption Sample (EVS) of the Federal Statistical Office

The Income and Consumption Sample (EVS) is the largest household survey in Europe, with around 60,000 participating households (approximately 0.15% of all households in Germany). In the context of the EVS, private households provide information about their income and expenses, wealth accumulation and assets, the provision of consumer goods, and their living situation.

Interested households voluntarily register for participation in the survey. The Federal Statistical Office then selects the households to be surveyed from these households based on a quota plan, ensuring a very high degree of representativeness. The data collection is carried out through questionnaires that the participating households fill out themselves. Due to the large number of surveyed households and extensive plausibility checks, weaknesses in the selection of participants—voluntariness always also means a certain degree of selection bias ("Selectivity Bias")—are at least partially compensated. With reference to existing insurance coverage, household surveys pose particular challenges due to the often lower willingness of customers to deal with insurance issues compared to other consumer decisions, as well as the frequently low financial literacy.

In the EVS, information is collected on the ownership of various types of insurance, the expenses for insurance coverage, and the monetary assets of households in life insurance contracts. While the information on the spread of insurance coverage shows high response rates and, from the GDV's point of view, also a high plausibility, the data on monetary assets in insurance contracts show a clear under-recording, for example compared to the monetary asset data of the Deutsche Bundesbank (Hohenstein et al. 2020, p. 28).

An analysis by the GDV based on the EVS data from 2018 reveals the following insights into the **degree of insurance coverage in private households**: Most households have extensive insurance coverage, but there are also gaps in coverage. Some of these are indeed due to individual preferences and situations of individual households, but some also result from a lack of understanding and interest in the context of often complex insurance decisions. It can be observed that many households do not have all the insurance products that they consider to be needs-based and desirable from their point of view. The analysis of the empirical data shows groups of households where the risk of insurance gaps is particularly high, even for existential risks. For example, younger households, households with a low monthly net income, and single people and single parents show large gaps in coverage against statutory liability risks.

Across the different types of insurance, it can be seen that households with young main income earners hold fewer insurance contracts. Although the degrees of coverage vary greatly between the types of insurance presented, on average the difference between those under 25 and the group of 35- to 50-year-olds is more than 20 percentage points. This is partly due to a lower risk (e.g., no children or life partners for whom term life protection is required; little home contents) or co-insurance with parents. However, there is also a significantly lower degree of coverage for existential risks, such as the loss of earning capacity. Apart from the increasing age of the main income earner, the spread of insurance coverage increases in multi-person households and couples, as well as linearly with household income: As income increases, both financial risks and the opportunity to conclude insurance contracts increase. The problem is that this correlation apparently also exists for types of insurance where there should regularly be a need for low-income earners and whose premium is also affordable with lower income, such as liability insurance. Based on further data not originating from the EVS, the GDV also identifies disproportionate gaps in insurance coverage among women (Hohenstein et al. 2020, pp. 39 f.).

In addition to the objective need, subjective customer behavior is also influenced by general **(societal) trends**. For example, societal value change and digitalization have led to sustainable changes in consumer behavior. The societal value change has primarily changed the consumption behavior of consumers: Post-materialistic consumption behavior is characterized by an ethical orientation (Consumer Social Responsibility), which may lead to non-consumption or even consumer boycott, by a strong environmental and health consciousness, and by communal consumption (Sharing Economy). Digitalization intensifies this effect even further. At the same time, it is seen as a determinant for central changes in the purchasing behavior of consumers. As mentioned, digitalization leads to customers coming into contact with a multitude of contact points (touchpoints) from companies in the pre-purchase, purchase, and post-purchase phases (see Sect. 2.2.4, Excursus on Customer-Dominant Logic).

An insurer can and must take these developments into account in its marketing policy, i.e., first investigate them as part of its market research (see Chap. 5) and then incorporate them into corresponding product (Chap. 10), service (Chap. 12) and communication concepts (Chap. 14). Equally important, because they are decision-relevant in individual cases, are the **situationally pronounced behavioral characteristics** (Sects. 4.2 and 4.3): They can ultimately only be captured in a situation-specific manner—personal contact, especially through the intermediary, plays a paramount role in this, as will be shown later (Sect. 14.2.3).

3.3 Supply in Financial Services and Insurance Markets

3.3.1 Actors and their Characteristics

In the financials services and insurance markets, essentially two large groups of actors appear: The first group consists of the original providers or producers of the various financial services products: banks, credit card or fund, investment and leasing companies, and insurers. The second group are the financial intermediaries, i.e., companies that act as a link between producers on the one hand and other producers or consumers on the other, whether they mediate financial services products, advise customers, provide market participants with information or perform risk-bearing functions (Fig. 3.2).

Financial services providers in the narrower sense are thus **producers** who are ready to accept payment instruments from the original money providers against the promise of later repayment (investment service) and on the other hand to provide the

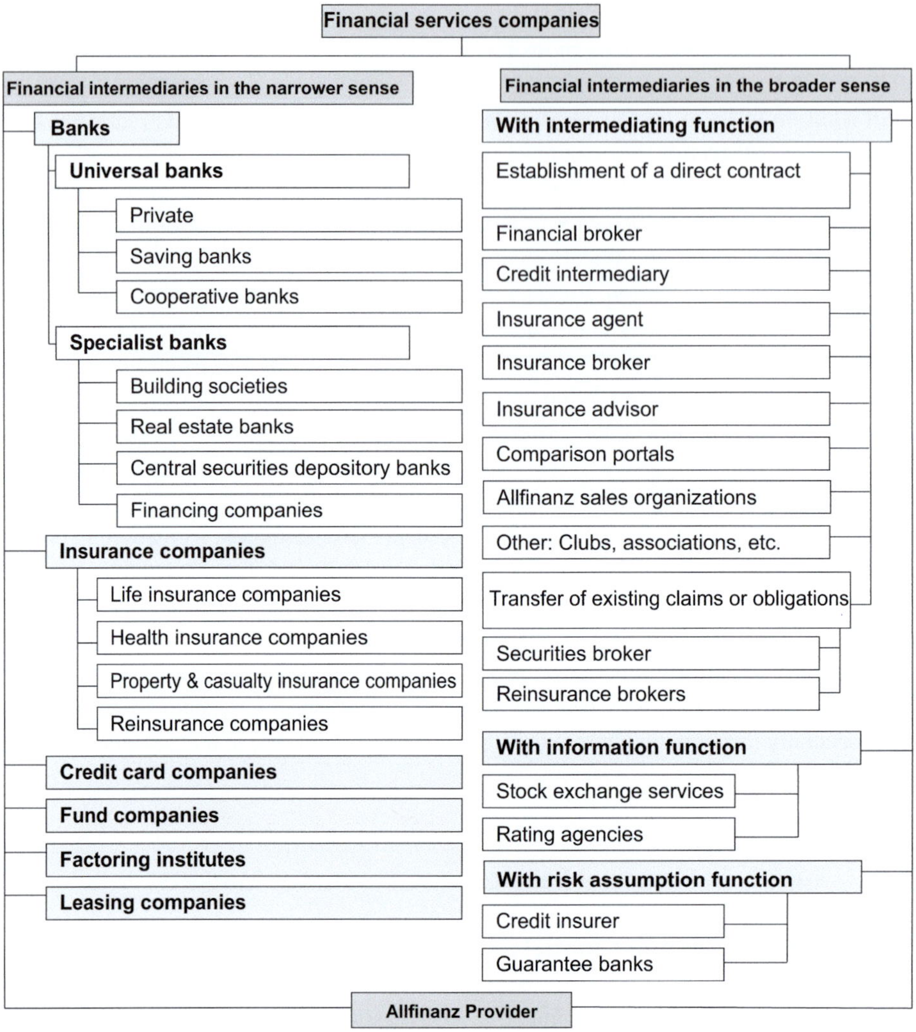

Fig. 3.2 Types of financial services companies. (Further developed from Tchoumta 2002, p. 32)

original money borrowers with the required payment instruments also against the promise of later repayment (financing service).

Financial services providers in the broader sense are then **financial intermediaries**, whose business activity is aimed at facilitating and making more cost-effective the direct conclusion of financial contracts between original and/or intermediary money providers and borrowers, or enabling it in the first place, without, however, themselves acting as a partner in such a contract.

While banks have always been characterized by the investment and financing function—and thus the lot size and term transformation function—insurance companies focus on risk transformation and retirement provision. Banks collect funds in different amounts or sizes from investors than they lend to other customers for financing purposes (**lot size transformation**). In addition, the terms are usually different, i.e., individual accepted investments do not have the same duration as loans issued at the same time (**term transformation**). Insurers transform risks in a similar way through a collective risk equaliziation in their insurance portfolios, so that they can be transferred to the insurer and this is affordable for the customer and acceptable for the insurer (**risk transformation**). Credit card and leasing companies serve the financing function resp. the financial services function of spending, like banks, while investment or fund companies serve investing and wealth creation. Finally, factoring companies support invoice-related payment transactions, especially the collection from the perspective of (commercial) invoice issuers.

Companies that offer insurance coverage must be insurers. They require a license to operate from the Federal Financial Supervisory Authority (BaFin) and are subsequently subject to its supervision. **Insurance companies** are, according to § 1 in combination with § 7 No. 33 Insurance Supervision Act (VAG), those that conduct insurance business and are not carriers of social insurance.[2] Their possible **legal forms** are limited in § 8 para. 2 VAG to the stock corporation (AG) including the European Company (SE), the mutual insurance association (VVaG), and the public-law corporation or institution. In practice, as of 2022, the AG (including the SE) with 272 companies and the VVaG with 235 companies significantly outweigh 14 public-law insurers and 3 branches of foreign insurers based outside the EU (GDV 2023a, p. 3; as of 01.01.2022; as of 01.01.2022). However, a view focused on individual companies does not do justice to the fact that in most cases the acting economic unit is a group in which several legally independent companies are combined under unified management.

The **economic forms of appearance** of insurance companies are, however, very diverse (Farny 2011, pp. 240–248). In addition to primary insurers, who exclusively conclude insurance contracts with policyholders—generally these are the end customers—there are pure reinsurers, who exclusively conduct reinsurance business with other primary or reinsurers, as well as "mixed" insurance companies that offer both types of business. Even more diverse are the company manifestations within the scope of primary insurance, which are oriented towards the operated insurance branch groups (life, health, property & casualty) or the associated individual **insurance branches**. Although numerous, different business designations exist in practice, these can largely be traced back to

---

[2] In addition to insurance companies, insurance holding companies, insurance special purpose entities (for conducting alternative risk transfer), security funds, and pension funds are also subject to the VAG and thus the supervision of BaFin.

the legal list of insurance branches provided by the VAG (Annex A), which according to § 10 II VAG come with a separate license to operate (Table 3.1).

In the insurance market, there are so-called all-lines insurers, which operate (almost) all of the mentioned insurance branches, multi-line insurers, and specialists who focus on one insurance branch, e.g., accident, transport, legal expenses, or credit insurers. Two classic types of multi-line insurers are composite insurers, which cover all or several insurance branches in the area of property & casualty insurance, and SHUK insurers, which offer property, liability, accident, and motor vehicle insurance.

There are also different types of providers regarding the **regional expansion** of business activities. The small mutual insurance associations (VVaG's) and public-law companies usually only operate regionally. Large mutual insurance associations and most large joint-stock companies are nationally oriented, thus focused on Germany, and some large insurance groups are active internationally (e.g., Munich Re, Allianz) or are German subsidiaries of international groups (e.g., AXA, Generali, Zurich).

Furthermore, the providers active in the insurance market can be classified or systematized according to their **size**. For this purpose, one can use both quantity sizes (e.g., contract quantity, number of customers, number of insured risks, number of employees) and value sizes (e.g., premium revenues, volume of capital investments). In practice, orientation towards premium volumes is common. A presentation of the largest property & casualty, life, and health insurers in the German insurance market in terms of sales follows in Sect. 3.3.3.

Table 3.1 Insurance branches in accordance with VAG, Appendix A (in modified order)

Life insurance (incl. term life insurance, endowment insurance, disability insurance, long-term care annuity insurance) (unless listed separately) Unit-linked life insurance Pension funds Health insurance (incl. cost-of-illness insurance, daily sickness allowance insurance, daily hospital allowance insurance, long-term care insurance and long-term care daily benefit insurance) Accident insurance Credit insurance Surety insurance Legal expenses insurance Assistance services (Assistance insurance) General liability insurance Transport insurance	Property insurance (fire, exlosion, storm, land subsidence and natural hazard) Property insurance (hail, frost and other property damage such as theft, water damage) (incl. comprehensive home contents insurance, comprehensive buildings insurance, engineering insurances) Land motor vehicle insurance: • Land vehicle liability • Land vehicle own damage Rail rolling stock insurance • Own damage Aircraft insurance • Aircraft liability • Aircraft own damage Ships insurance • Sea, inland lake and river shipping liability • Sea, inland lake and river shipping own damage

Finally, the actual providers of insurance protection differ in terms of their **company owners**. The ownership can initially be fundamentally with a closed or an open circle of natural and/or legal persons.

Excursus on natural and legal persons

The **BGB** (German Civil Code) distinguishes between natural persons (Book I, Sect. 1, Title 1) and legal persons (Book I, Sect. 1, Title 2). Persons are synonymous with legal subjects. **Legal subjects** are characterized by the fact that they can enter into legal transactions with each other or can generally be connected with each other through legal relationships, in short: legal subjects can be holders of rights and obligations.

Natural persons are individuals who, regardless of their age, gender, nationality, race, intelligence, etc., are holders of rights and obligations (§ 1 BGB). This realizes the idea of the equality of all people and recognizes that legal capacity is not granted to a person by the legislator, but is predetermined on the basis of human dignity.

Legal persons, i.e., persons created by the legal system, are in contrast legally regulated social organizations or institutions that are legally capable as a unit and can participate in legal transactions as independent subjects like natural persons. They have a legal sphere separate from their members, the people acting for them, and third parties, with their own rights and obligations. However, natural persons must act for them as their organs, because legal persons, as conceptual creations of purpose, cannot act independently. In addition, they are liable as a unit, i.e., institutionally, but not their acting organs as persons. Legal persons are thus holders of rights and obligations, have their own (liable) assets, and can sue and be sued in their own name.

(Boemke and Ulrici 2014, pp. 447, 449, 459–461)

The spectrum is broadest in the case of the joint-stock company (AG): In the case of an open shareholder base with many shareholders and shares in free float, a public company is present. There are different degrees regarding the extent of closed shareholder circles—from the minority shareholder (under 50%) to the majority shareholder (over 50%) to the sole shareholder. If the main ownership lies with another insurer, it is a group insurance company—particularly common in Germany as a result of the sector separation requirement. If, on the other hand, the ownership lies with the policyholder, who as an independent company in another industry wants to insure its own risks, this is referred to as a captive insurer. In the case of an association, it is accordingly an association captive insurer. A family business exists when the insurer is in the closed ownership of a person or a family (e.g., ARAG; formerly also Gerling). In the case of the VVaG, the owners are members: Here too, the circle of members can be closed or open to all natural and legal persons. The latter applies to most large VVaGs; smaller VVaGs often have closed member circles, whether the condition for membership is profession-related (e.g., taxi companies, civil servants, pastors, etc.) or environment and thus also need-related (e.g., homeowners, union members, etc.). In the group of public-law insurers, the owners are, according to the idea, public-law corporations and institutions from the public-law banking or savings bank system.

3.3.2 Financial Services and Insurance Products as Market Objects

As mentioned, financial services are characterized compared to other services in that they are purely monetary products, in which both the benefit and the benefit in return must be fulfilled in cash flows on both sides.

Corresponding to the basic functions of financial services from a customer's perspective listed in Sect. 3.2.2, there are a number of **classic and modern financial services products** that each fulfill one or more of these functions (Bätscher 1989, pp. 83–88; Farny 2011, pp. 384–386):

- Earning and spending: payment transactions with account management and EC cards, credit cards, factoring
- Financing: current account, bill discount loans, personal loans (short to medium term); partial payment, consumer, acquisition, mortgage, building society loans (medium to long term); leasing
- Investing with financial service providers i. e. S.: sight and term deposits (short term); savings deposits, issuance of bonds etc. (medium to long term); savings plans, traditional life or pension insurance, building society contracts
- Investing, mediated by financial service providers: securities transactions (issuance, brokerage and management of securities) with shares, fixed-income securities, funds, derivatives (options, futures, swaps etc.); fund savings plans; unit-linked life or pension insurance
- Financial security: all insurance products (see above for insurance branches); derivatives (options, futures, swaps etc.).

The financial services products can be further divided into financial and insurance products, with the former essentially encompassing all financial services products except insurance. In the practice of retail business, this is primarily associated with loans, leasing, building society contracts, funds and credit cards.

The standard insurance products on the market can in turn be further divided by sectors, branches and types (see Table 3.1 for the branches).

▶ **Insurance sector** (insurance branch group) describes a plurality of insurance branches with the same characteristic, e.g. personal, property, financial loss insurance.

▶ **Insurance branch**(= insurance line) stands for the part of an insurance sector that covers a specific type of risk, e.g. life and health insurance as parts of personal insurance; fire and comprehensive motor vehicle insurance as parts of property insurance.

▶ **Type of insurance** is again a part of an insurance branch with a specific form of risk coverage, e.g. pure term life insurance as part of life insurance or daily hospital allowance insurance as part of health insurance.
(Farny 2011, p. 370)

3.3.3 Current Empirical Data and Facts on the Supply in the German Insurance Market

The supply on the German insurance market is determined by the insurance companies as producers of insurance protection. Distributed across the most important product classes, in 2022 in Germany under the supervision of BaFin, there were 80 life insurers, 46 health insurers, 198 property & casualty/accident insurers and 29 reinsurers. These employed around 164,000 internal staff, 10,400 trainees and 29,500 sales force employees. In addition, about 139,000 insurance agents worked for them, who in turn employed another approximately 86,000 employees. In addition, there were another 46,800 independent insurance intermediaries, the majority of them as insurance brokers, as well as about 5100 so-called product accessory intermediaries active in the market. The data underline the strong importance and weighting of sales-oriented activities in the German insurance market (GDV 2023a, pp. 2, 11 f.).

Insurers have continuously increased their premium income in the past and reached the highest value ever in 2022 with a premium volume of about 223 billion € in primary insurance. Since 2003, property & casualty insurance has been growing at plus/minus 3% per year. Life insurance has been stagnating in the area of products against ongoing premium payments since 2005, with larger fluctuations essentially only in the area of single premiums, which rose sharply from 2019 to 2021 due to the low-interest-rate environment, but also fell significantly in 2022 for the same reason (GDV 2023a, p. 31, 59). In 2022, the revenues are distributed among the individual insurance branches according to Table 3.2.

Table 3.2 Premium income 2022 by insurance branches. (GDV 2023a, p. 31, 48, 60)

Insurance branch	Gross written premiums (in million Euro)	Change from previous year (in percent)
Life insurance	97,111	−5.9
Private health insurance	41,991	2.4
Private accident insurance	6,626	−0.9
Motor vehicle insurance	29,129	1.1
Comprehensive buildings insurance	10,169	8.9
Comprehensive home contents insurance	3,403	3.2
Non-private property insurance (incl. engineering insurance and business interruption)	11,425	10.8
General liability insurance	8,255	4.2
Legal expenses insurance	4,728	3.4
Credit, surety, fidelity insurance	2,164	10.8
Transport and aviation insurance	2,159	10.5
Cyber insurance	249	56.3

When considering the largest providers in the three major product categories of life, health, and property& casualty/accident insurance, it is noticeable that there are insurers who are represented in all three areas, as well as those who are only sporadically involved (Tables 3.3, 3.4 and 3.5). Most life insurers made less revenue in 2022 than in 2021; this is primarily due to rising interest rates and the associated falling demand for single premium life insurance. Conversely, some property & casualty insurers in 2022 reported significantly above-average growth of 13.5 to 18%. Affected are the two

Table 3.3 The ten largest life insurers by gross written premiums. (o. V. 2023a, p. 431)

Rank	Company	Gross written premiums in 2022 (in million Euro)	Change from previous year (in percent)
1	Allianz Leben	21,450	−7.8
2	R+V Leben	7,266	−9.6
3	Generali Deutschland Leben	6,002	2.1
4	Debeka Leben	3,863	−1.4
5	Zurich Deutscher Herold	3,017	−6.7
6	Alte Leipziger Leben	2,970	2.2
7	Bayern-Versicherung	2,933	−16.3
8	AXA Leben	2,490	−6.5
9	Nürnberger Leben	2,278	−1.3
10	Proxalto*	2,150	−7.4

*Insurer in run-off

Table 3.4 The ten largest health insurers by gross earned premiums. (Surminski 2023a p. 526)

Rank	Company	Gross Earned Premiums in 2022 (in million Euro)	Change from Previous Year (in percent)
1	Debeka	7,873	5.3
2	DKV	5,144	1.4
3	Allianz	3,991	2.7
4	AXA	3,708	4.2
5	Signal Iduna	3,195	1.9
6	Barmenia	2,229	7.0
7	Generali	2,139	3.5
8	Bayerische Beamten	2,027	3.4
9	Continentale	1,870	2.3
10	HUK-Coburg	1,664	5.5

Table 3.5 The ten largest property & casualty/accident insurers by gross written premiums. (o.V. 2023b, p. 639)

Rank	Company	Gross written premiums in 2022 (in million Euro)	Change from previous year (in percent)
1	Allianz	10,687	3.4
2	AGCS	5,867	18.0
3	HDI Global	5,796	13.5
4	ERGO	5,061	14.5
5	R+V Allgemeine	4,840	4.0
6	AXA	4,221	3.4
7	Provinzial	3,075	6.1
8	LVM	2,916	4.6
9	Generali	2,781	3.8
10	VHV	2,510	3.3

industrial insurers AGCS and HDI Global, and at ERGO the industrial insurance sector may have contributed; the background is premium increases ("Sanierung") in industrial insurance (Surminski 2023b, p. 638).

3.4 Insurance Market for Private Customers

In this textbook, the marketing of an insurer is first considered in general terms and then deepened with a focus on the private customer segment, as this, with a premium share of approximately 90% of the market, is by far the most significant in terms of turnover (Hohenstein et al. 2020, p. 19). It also deals with the insurance market and the insurance services offered there as the core business of insurers, the financial services market is only discussed insofar as it influences the insurance business, and not for its own sake. Therefore, the **insurance market for private customers** needs to be **delineated** as the actual addressee of insurance marketing, and its structural features need to be captured (Sect. 3.4.1). In this market, there are also numerous legal—often industry-specific—regulations that significantly affect insurance marketing and influence its scope of action (Sect. 3.4.2).

3.4.1 Delineation and Structure

The insurance market is part of the market for financial services, for which a whole **series of industry-specific rules** apply in addition to generally valid legal regulations. This starts with the fact that insurances according to § 1 para. 1 in conjunction with § 8 para. 1 VAG can only be "produced" and offered by insurance companies that require a license to operate from BaFin.

Furthermore, the insurance market for private customers is part of the entire insurance market—as mentioned, the largest part in terms of turnover. In addition to this, there are submarkets for industrial and corporate customers, commercial customers, and public households. By definition, **private customers** are characterized by the fact that they primarily demand insurance coverage to secure their private (family) sphere and their consumption. In this context, insurance plays the central role of supporting private households in achieving their goals by providing financial protection against certain risks. Their goals relate to various areas: In the social area, there are education-related, societal, and cultural goals or expectations, in the performance-economic area, it is about building, maintaining, and expanding the family as well as procuring and providing goods and services for preservation and regeneration. In the financial-economic area, income, wealth, and liquidity goals can be formulated. In addition to these rather basic objectives, goals of self-realization are added in the sense of Maslow's growth-oriented needs (1970).

For insurers, the aim is then to serve the approximately **41.5 million private households in Germany** or a desired part of them with insurance coverage in a market-oriented manner, i.e., to support them in a goal-oriented manner with adequate insurance services. At the same time, they have to assert themselves in the lucrative private customer market against numerous competitors from their own industry from home and abroad as well as from other industries such as banks, statutory health insurance funds, associations, or car manufacturers.

The **structure of the insurance market** for private customers can be captured through the power relations between the market parties, the market concentration among the providers associated with this, and the international interlinking.

The power relations determine who dominates in the market, and thus whether a buyer's or a seller's market exists. In a buyer's market, the supply is greater than the demand, i.e., the buyers are in a better position and are therefore courted. In a seller's market, the demand is greater than the supply, so the buyers are happy if they receive a product or service at all. Nowadays, most markets are buyer's markets (Becker 2019, p. 1). And the private customer sector of the insurance market is a **classic buyer's market**. A major reason for this is the fundamentally existing overcapacity on the supply side, which results, among other things, from the fact that insurances are capital collection pools and can "collect" more funds at any time. Therefore, the providers are required to conduct active marketing to win (new customer acquisition) and secure (customer retention) the favor of the customers (Köhne 1997, p. 19).

The **market concentration** among providers can be measured by the degree of concentration. This expresses how much market share the three, five, or ten largest providers combine. In the German insurance industry, concentration has always taken place for two reasons: Firstly, the previously mentioned separation of business lines leads to group formation (as one form of concentration); secondly, the establishment of supra-company statistics as calculation bases for estimating the assumed risks is carried out through cooperation in associations (as another form of concentration). Apart from this, current developments promote the concentration process: An increasing dynamization of the markets, a steadily increasing digitalization and the associated technical requirements, narrower growth opportunities, and a further increasing pressure on profit margins have prompted many insurers to redefine their market positioning.

The degree of concentration in the German insurance industry is nevertheless not particularly high, even though the number of providers has been decreasing for some time. Compared to other European insurance markets or to other goods and service markets in Germany, it does not stand out. The Monopolies Commission also saw no reason in its most recent main report in the summer of 2022 to draw negative conclusions from the concentration in the German insurance industry on competition in this area (Monopolkommission 2022, p. 6).

Given the specific structures in the German insurance industry, the degree of concentration is usually not determined for individual companies, but **for insurance groups** (GDV 2021a, p. 3). The reason for this is that many groups are characterized by a high degree of horizontal integration, e.g., through shared service centers or other forms of group-wide cooperation, such as in the area of capital investment, IT, or product and risk management. If one looks at the market share of the ten largest groups, in 2021 it was 66.7% in life insurance, 76.3% in health insurance, and 62.2% in property & casualty/accident insurance (GDV 2023a, p. 22). The number of providers is still high (see Sect. 3.3.1).

Regarding the **international interconnection** as the third structural feature, it can be said that this has increased somewhat due to the globalization of goods, financial and service markets, the creation of the European Single Market and the introduction of the Euro, as well as the spread of modern information and communication technologies. Some insurance companies have strengthened their European or international orientation, while conversely, the presence of foreign insurers in the German market has also increased. Foreign insurance companies have therefore long been a natural part of the German insurance market. Measured by premium income, their market share has been quite stable at about a quarter for years. Thus, private customers receive offers from Swiss, Dutch, Italian, French, Scandinavian, and Anglo-Saxon providers. This happens on the one hand via the so-called passporting business through German branches of insurers from EEA countries (91 in 2018) and EEA insurers registered in Germany for the free provision of services (828 in 2018!); here, EEA insurers operate in the German market from their home country with their European passport. However, only about 6% of the premium volume of the German insurance market is attributable to this passporting business. On the other hand—and to a greater extent than in the passporting business—the market entry of foreign insurers takes place via their German subsidiaries under the supervision of BaFin (in 2016 about 18% of the premium income of insurers with BaFin license); among the 15 largest insurance groups in Germany, there are three subsidiaries of insurers from other European countries (Theis and Wiener 2018, pp. 8 f.). However, globalization has long since extended beyond the EU. Internationally active primary insurers have significantly expanded their commitment in the so-called emerging markets in Central and Eastern Europe, and the markets in China and India have also been increasingly targeted for some time.

3.4.2 Legal Framework of the Insurance Market

Insurance products as information products are **largely shaped by law**, and their scope of services is legally determined in the insurance documents (policy, general insurance conditions (GIC), special insurance conditions). Against this background alone, it is always possible that individual marketing measures may violate a legal mandate or prohibition, thereby leading to administrative, criminal, or civil consequences. However, the law not only sets a **regulatory framework** for insurance marketing and thus restricts it, but also influences the market under consideration or even defines it, as for example through tax incentives or non-incentives for certain life insurance products, thus becoming a **market maker**. An effective insurance marketing strategy therefore necessarily presupposes that this interaction of law and product is not completely neglected, but is taken into account as far as possible from the outset (Gal 2019, p. 98).

With regard to the regulatory framework, however, this poses quite a challenge: Because first, in many cases the **legal mandate or prohibition is not** so **clearly defined** that the insurance company is inevitably faced with the conscious decision between compliance and violation. Rather, laws often work with general clauses or undefined legal concepts, i.e., norms with a very broad scope of application, which need to be concretized by case law. For example, the Unfair Competition Act (UWG) declares "unfair business practices" to be inadmissible (§ 3 para. 1 UWG). Although the law subsequently declares some practices explicitly unfair, this does not mean in reverse that practices not listed could not also be considered unfair. And secondly, **law is not static, but dynamic**: On the one hand, today's legal violation can be the industry standard of the future. For example, comparative advertising was generally prohibited in Germany until the end of the 1990s. However, as some competitors used this instrument in certain industries despite this, they initiated a differentiating case law, which considered a comparison at least permissible if the products were objectively comparable, there was a sufficient reason for comparison, and the statements were within the limits of necessity and truthful factual discussion. Thus, these actors contributed to a change in the legal situation, so that comparative advertising is now only prohibited under more restricted conditions. On the other hand, an industry standard can become obsolete and suddenly become a legal violation with a stroke of the legislator's pen, as happened with the reform of the Insurance Contract Act (VVG) to the so called "Policen-Modell" previously common for contract conclusion (sending the GIC to the customer along with the policy) (Gal 2019, pp. 100 f.).

In this context, the **legal framework of the insurance market** is already diverse and in some cases very far-reaching (Theis 2015, p. 7; Altemeyer-Bartscher et al. 2019,

p. 28 f.). Increasingly, they are being initiated at EU level by new directives that bring far-reaching consequences and also requirements for national legislation, as well as leading to national laws and regulations. Initially, these were only the various basic directives on life, property & casualty or motor vehicle insurance, but in the last 20 years many more directives have been added (Table 3.6).

The **general legal regulations** that also apply to insurance companies include, at the international level, in particular EU economic and antitrust law, and at the national level, commercial (HGB, BilMoG), tax (income, corporate tax law), corporate (AktG, GWB, UWG), consumer (BDSG, consumer protection) and social law (SGB)—the latter of course with special significance for private insurance, as the regulations on social insurance directly influence the scope for design for private insurance, be it substitutive (= replacing) or complementary (= supplementing). This is followed in the context of needs assessment by the insurance intermediary or the insurance customer by the Act on

Table 3.6 Important EU directives and national laws related to the insurance market

EU Directives	National Laws
• 1.-3. Non-Life Insurance Directive • 1.-3. Life Assurance Directive • 1.-7. Motor Vehicle Insurance Directive • Reinsurance Directive • 1.-2. Markets in Financial Instruments Directive (MiFID 2) • 1.-2. Insurance Mediation Directive (IMD, IDD) • Environmental Liability Directive • Distance Selling Directive • Accounting Directive • Solvency II Directive • Consumer Rights Directive • Corporate Sustainability Reporting Directive (CSRD)	• Insurance Supervision Act (VAG) • Insurance Contract Act (VVG) • Compulsory Insurance Act (PflVG) • Retirement Income Act (AltEinkG) • Retirement Savings Act (AVmG) • Retirement Provision Contracts Certification Act (AltZertG) • Life Insurance Reform Act (LVRG) • Occupational Pensions Act (BetrAVG) • Occupational Pensions Strengthening Act • Act on the Development and Introduction of a Pension Dashboard • Insurance Tax Act (VersStG) • Insurance Mediation Regulation (VersVermG) • Trade, Commerce and Industry Regulation Act (GewO) • Federal Data Protection Act (BDSG) • General Equal Treatment Act (AGG) • Accounting Law Modernization Act (BilMoG) • Supervision of Financial Conglomerates Act (FKAG) • Act to Strengthen Competition in Statutory Health Insurance (GKV-WSG) • Environmental Damage Act (USchadG) • Genetic Diagnosis Act (GenDG) • Act on Corporate Due Diligence Obligations in Supply Chains (LkSG)

the Development and Introduction of a Pension Dashbord of February 11, 2021, which in future is intended to ensure that a realistic overview of the “interim statuses” of pension benefits achieved with various old-age provision measures can be generated, or as the Deutsche Rentenversicherung puts it: “The Digital Pension Overview is an online portal that is intended to help you better understand the status of your individual old-age provision situation. You can use the portal to digitally retrieve your acquired old-age provision entitlements and thus get a complete overview of your statutory, company and private old-age provision entitlements from one source” (Deutsche Rentenversicherung 2023, p. 2).

Industry-specific legal regulations for insurance companies, intermediaries, and insurance customers supplement the general regulations. These include in particular the Insurance Supervision Act (VAG) and the new Insurance Contract Act (VVG), which came into force on 1 January 2008 after a fundamental reform. With it, a law for the reorganization of insurance intermediary law (Insurance Mediation Regulation) was introduced for the first time. In terms of retirement provision, the Retirement Income Act (AltEinkG), the Retirement Savings Act (AVmG), and the Life Insurance Reform Act (LVRG) are also important.[3]

The framework conditions to be observed by insurers result from the interaction of general and industry-specific regulations. The most important regulations in terms of marketing decisions will now be briefly discussed.

In the context of **competition and antitrust law**, it should be noted that according to § 1 of the Competition Act (GWB), market agreements restricting competition are generally prohibited. This includes all agreements between companies (and associations) and coordinated practices that aim at or result in the prevention, restriction, or distortion of competition. With regard to insurance, the peculiarity of the insurance business necessitates the cross-company collection and evaluation of certain data and information—usually via associations—which are permitted under antitrust law, provided they do not result in a restriction of competition. Thus, insurers are allowed to jointly create and evaluate loss statistics, mortality and morbidity tables for risk-appropriate loss calculation, calculate and communicate a net risk premium based on this, and refer to association standard conditions (GDV 2023b). In addition, insurers can jointly cover exposed risks in certain insurance branches through co-insurance and reinsurance communities (pools) or distribute them among various insurers. Co-insurance in individual cases and reinsurance are not subject to the prohibition of cartels.

---

[3] In addition to the laws, there are a whole range of general and industry-specific regulations such as the Regulation on the Principals Underlying the Calculation of the Premium Reserve (DeckRV), Anlage- (AnlV), Finanzrückversicherungs- (FinRVV), Krankenversicherungsaufsichts- (KVAV), Mindeszuführungs- (MindZV), Insurance Mediation (VersVermV) or VVG-Informationspflichten-Regulation (VVG-InfoV). However, these will not be discussed individually here due to their scope. They will be mentioned as needed at the appropriate place.

Since 2006, there has been the **General Equal Treatment Act** (AGG), which is independent of the industry: It prohibits discrimination of the policyholder or the insured person based on race, ethnic origin, gender, religion, age, disability, or sexual identity in mass insurance business in product and premium design. Cases in which personal characteristics justify higher expected loss values and therefore higher premiums according to technical insurance rules (insurance mathematics, statistics) are considered non-discriminatory (§ 19 para. 1 no. 2 in conjunction with § 20 para. 2 AGG). Thus, a actuarially justified premium differentiation is still possible.

Excursus on the Unisex Judgment of the CJEU of 2011

In addition to the laws, court rulings influence the legal situation, and unlike the laws, these are sometimes hardly foreseeable and occasionally change the situation surprisingly.

This happened in a ruling of the Court of Justice of the European Union: In contrast to the AGG, the Unisex judgment of the CJEU has caused a significant restriction of the actuarially justified premium differentiation. The CJEU decided on 01.03.2011 that insurers must offer Unisex tariffs and may not demand different premiums according to gender, as this discriminates against women (Case C-236/09).

A principle of European law is the equal treatment of women and men. However, there was an exception in the directive prohibiting discrimination based on gender in access to and supply of goods and services (2004/113/EC 1). The CJEU declared this exception from the basic rule of gender-neutral premiums and benefits in the insurance sector invalid as of 21.12.2012. Since then, the rule of gender-neutral premiums and benefits must be applied—and insurers must offer Unisex tariffs. The judgment affected gender-specific tariffs in pension, life, health, and motor vehicle insurance, which, for example, led to higher premiums for women in pension insurance due to their longer life expectancy.

On 25.05.2018, the **General Data Protection Regulation** (GDPR) came into force. It applies to all EU citizens and also EU companies. With it, penalties for data protection violations have been significantly tightened. Other significant changes include the obligation to appoint a data protection officer for almost all companies, the right to be forgotten, especially in social networks, and the associated obligation to delete data that is no longer needed, as well as the right of those affected to have their data released. With the GDPR, the **Federal Data Protection Act** (BDSG) has also been introduced in Germany as a national legal regulation; it regulates the handling of personal data, in particular their collection, processing and use (The Federal Commissioner for Data Protection and Freedom of Information 2022). The insurance product as an information product relies on personal and even risk-related data. Insurers process this data in connection with underwriting, policy issuance, administration, and claims settlement. If there is cooperation with legally independent partners, business-related personal and risk data must also be exchanged. This exchange requires the appropriate permission of the person concerned (§ 51 BDSG). The exchange of data in the course of claims or benefits processing in life and health insurance is particularly sensitive, as knowledge about the persons concerned is acquired.

Furthermore, insurance-specific legal norms influence product design: Firstly, the framework conditions stipulated by the EU in various insurance directives (Table 3.6) aim to create a uniform internal market, strengthen entrepreneurial freedoms and the freedom of insurers to offer, as well as greater choice for customers in terms of insurance providers and insurance products. Above all, with the transformation of the 3rd EC Directives by the Third Implementation Act/European Economic Law to the VAG of 21.07.1994, the so-called deregulation was initiated: As a result, for almost thirty years now, insurers have again had the opportunity to decide autonomously on their product and premium designs, which had been denied to them for decades by the obligation to obtain prior approval of conditions and tariffs. However, this **deregulation on the product and premium side was followed by regulations in other areas** (Theis 2015, p. 2): For example, product and communication policy are influenced by the regulation on information obligations regulation for insurance contracts (VVG-InfoV) as a result of the MiFID 1 directive with regard to certain contents to be communicated (e.g. cost disclosure, structure and contents of the product information sheet). And the distribution of insurance products is regulated by the intermediary law as a result of the IMD and IDD directive more than ever before (e.g. necessity of a register entry and permission to mediate, proof of expertise and further education, increased liability, good conduct and extensive information obligations).

National regulatory frameworks have significant implications for marketing decisions. The **Insurance Supervision Act** contains numerous regulations that directly determine market performance. The most important regulations include:

- **Responsibility for outsourcing functions:** If functions or insurance activities (e.g., sales, portfolio management, claims processing, or asset management) are to be outsourced to third parties, the insurance company remains responsible for complying with all regulatory requirements and provisions (§ 32 para. 1 VAG).
- **Requirement of separation of business lines** (§ 8 para. 4 VAG): It states that a company may not operate other insurance branches in addition to life insurance resp. substitute health insurance. Therefore, legally independent companies are required. Offering life and other lines of business under one brand thus requires the formation of a group.
- **Prohibition of non-insurance business** (§ 15 para. 1 VAG): Insurers are prohibited from conducting business that is not directly related to the insurance business. This significant restriction from a marketing perspective can, however, be lifted by forming a group.
- **Principle of equality of treatment** in life insurance (§ 138 para. 2 VAG), health insurance (§ 146 para. 2 VAG), accident with premium refund (§ 161 para. 1 VAG) and mutual insurance associations (§ 177 para. 1 VAG): Accordingly, premiums and benefits must be calculated on the same principles under the same conditions. From a pricing policy perspective, this ultimately means renouncing price differentiation measures, which are a common marketing tool in other industries.

- **Prohibition on the passing on of special allowances and commissions to policyholders** (§ 48b para. 1 and 2 VAG): This includes any direct or indirect benefit in addition to the service agreed in the insurance contract, in particular any complete or partial commission rebate, other goods or services that do not relate to the insurance service, discounts on goods or services, provided they are not of low value. This is primarily intended to prevent the intermediary from unilaterally granting price concessions to his customer.

Furthermore, the following contractual regulations of the reformed Insurance Contract Act (VVG)—changes have generally been made in favor of the customer—which came into force on January 1, 2008, significantly influence insurance products and services:

- **Information and advice to the customer and their documentation**: Insurers and intermediaries are required to provide regular advice and extensive information before and during the contract term, as well as to document these. Almost all marketing tools (except for claims settlement) are affected by this.
- **Application or invitation model**: The VVG provides for the application model (or alternatively the invitation model). According to this, the insurer provides the contract terms, product information sheet, general insurance conditions and other information mentioned in the VVGInfoV to the customer in good time—and unlike the once possible "Policen-Modell"—before the application is submitted (§ 7 para.1 VVG). What "in good time" specifically means is not formulated in the law and is left to the courts. In any case, the law reflects the guiding principle that a customer should be informed more thoroughly than before in order to make informed decisions (regardless of whether they will do so).
- **Distance selling**: Distance selling contracts according to § 312c BGB are particularly contracts that are concluded using exclusively remote communication means (telephone, internet, letter, etc.). Remote communication means are therefore those that can be used to initiate or conclude a contract without the contracting parties being physically present at the same time. It is not considered distance selling if the sale does not take place "within the framework of a distribution or service system organized for distance selling". Therefore, if a representative or broker mediates an insurance product via telephone or internet and this is not the only distribution method, it is not considered distance selling. In terms of information obligations, distance selling has the advantage that the insurer must immediately transmit the contract information after the conclusion of the contract if the communication medium used does not allow information in text form before the policyholder's declaration of contract (§ 7 para. 1 VVG). The obligation to provide advice and documentation is waived (for insurers) in distance selling if the customer waives it in text form (§ 6 para. 3 VVG). These regulations are important in connection with direct sales.
- **Contract terms**: In property & casualty/accident insurance, the customer is bound to an insurance contract for a maximum of three years (§ 11 para. 4 VVG). This means

for insurers to replace the previously contractually conditioned customer loyalty with a "voluntary" one, which further increases the already high importance of customer loyalty as a marketing task.

- **Possible reduction of benefits (pro rata reduction) by the insurer in case of gross negligence**: In the case of gross negligence, the customer can claim at least a reduced benefit in proportion to the severity of his fault (§ 26 para. 1 VVG). In the case of slight negligence, however, customers often also receive reduced benefits and not—as before—the full benefit without discussion, as they bear the burden of proof for the absence of gross negligence in this case.
- **Divisibility of the premium**: In the event of an early termination of the contract, the customer does not have to pay contributions until the end of the current insurance year, but only pro rata (§ 39 para. 1 VVG). This promotes contract forms with short, e.g., one-month notice periods (and thus also competition).
- **Surrender value and profit participation in life insurance**: The VVG prescribes transparency regarding the procedure, the current amount, and deviations from the initial model calculations (§§154, 155, 169 para. 3 and 5 VVG). It also requires the even distribution and corresponding allocation of closing and distribution costs at least over the first five contract years and a guaranteed minimum surrender value, which corresponds to the coverage capital minus the distributed closing and distribution costs (§ 169 para. 3 VVG). These regulations better inform customers, allow them to continuously monitor the success of their product, and exit the contract with fewer losses if necessary. On the other hand, there is the risk of premature termination, which is disadvantageous from the customer's point of view. Moreover, this regulation is at the expense of long-term retirement provision and those who do not cancel their retirement provision prematurely, as guarantees are known to incur costs and thus reduce the return. Regardless of the ambiguous assessment from the customer's point of view, it should be noted that this regulation undoubtedly represents a far-reaching intervention in the product design freedom of providers.
- **Participation in hidden reserves in life insurance**: Furthermore, the policyholders are to be involved in the valuation reserves in addition to the ongoing/annual surpluses and the final surpluses at the end of the contract according to § 153 para. 3 VVG. The insurer has to determine these annually and allocate them computationally according to a causation-oriented procedure and pay out half of the amount to be determined at this point in time to the policyholder at the latest when the contract ends. This creates for the first time a civil law claim to surplus participation (incl. valuation reserves), which can only be waived in total (total exclusion). However, explicit declarations in the GIC are necessary for this; mere non-mention of the surplus participation in the contract does not meet the requirement for their waivability. Exclusion examples are insurance contracts in which a surplus participation was expressly excluded. This regulation also represents a far-reaching intervention in the product design freedom of providers, as paid out, therefore realized valuation reserves, are no longer available to the insured collective.

Although **life and health insurance** have always been heavily regulated by the VAG and VVG, the government as a **legislator** has intervened even more in the design freedom of providers by adjusting both laws over the last 10–15 years:

In private health insurance, the **Act to Amend the Financial Investment Intermediary and Asset Investment Law** of 06.11.2011, in its Art. 22, reduced the acquisition commissions in substitute health insurance (full health insurance) to a maximum of nine monthly premium contributions (§ 50 para. 1 VAG). Furthermore, the liability for cancellation was extended to five years (newly regulated in § 49 para. 1 VAG). Both led, as intended, to a limitation of commission excesses and conversions. Particularly noteworthy, however, is that the industry practically asked politics for intervention at the time. The Association of German Private Healthcare Insurers (PKV) expressly welcomed the decision of the Bundestag. Apparently, the industry had not been able to prevent such misdevelopments in the interest of consumer protection on its own. This was impressively underscored by the following statement by CDU member of parliament *Klaus-Peter Flosbach* in the Bundestag debate at the time: "I think this was one of the most important steps to achieve a clean market for the mediation of private health insurances, and the insurance industry is grateful to us for intervening in the market and eliminating this abuse" (Mahmoodi 2012).

Shortly thereafter, this circumstance caught up with the industry again when it came to possibly also introducing a commission cap in life insurance at the end of 2013 and 2014.[4] The economically justified argument against politics not to interfere too much in the decision-making freedom of life insurers was refuted by the latter with reference to the wish of private health insurers for a political decision.

And the subsequent interventions in the area of life insurance were extensive. First, with the **VVG reform**, a minimum participation of customers in the valuation reserves in the (fixed-interest) capital investments of life insurers was written into the VVG in the event of early cancellation. However, this inevitably led to an outflow of funds to departing policyholders and was at the expense of the remaining group of insured persons. At the same time, this endangered the solvency requirements, which are also legally required. In addition, the existing low-interest environment meant that life insurers had to deal with the fact that they had to service high obligations to service old contracts—the guaranteed interest rate in the portfolio of life insurers averaged 3.2% in 2014—at consistently low capital market interest rates in the following years. This prompted politics to pass the **Life Insurance Reform Act** (LVRG), which came into force on August 7, 2014. Understood as a package of measures to stabilize the entire life insurance sector in Germany (Federal Ministry of Finance 2014), it regulated the reduction of the maximum actuarial interest rate from 1.75 to 1.25%—it is now only 0.25%—the differentiated participation of departing policyholders in the valuation reserves, the higher

[4] The discussion about a possible commission cap was still taking place on the part of BaFin in 2021/22.

participation of policyholders in risk surpluses with 90 instead of previously 75%, the possible dividend block against shareholders in the event of a threat to the rights of policyholders determined by BaFin, the introduction of the effective cost statement in the form of the effective cost rate (Reduction in Yield) and the reduction of the maximum Zillmer rate from 40 to 25 per mille.

There is no doubt that these measures increase the stability and the **security of benefits for life insurance policyholders**. The **meaningfulness and** the **effects of individual regulations** in terms of fairness towards all life insurance policyholders, i.e., those leaving and those remaining in the collective, as well as towards other stakeholder groups such as shareholders, are more difficult to assess and have been **controversially discussed** in the professional world. Regardless of this, from a business perspective, it must be stated that the further regulation of the minimum participation of customers in the valuation reserves, the increased profit participation in risk surpluses to 90%, the possible dividend ban on shareholders imposed by BaFin under certain circumstances, and the reduction of the accounting recognition possibility of acquisition costs from previously 40 to now 25 per mille (on the savings premium portions of the total premium) represent significant interventions in entrepreneurial freedom of decision. These are to be critically assessed, as they were accompanied by a little differentiated and substantiated argumentation with regard to the necessary improvement of benefits for life insurance policyholders. At the same time, the life insurance business model has become increasingly unattractive for equity providers: the chances of profit have been reduced, in the investment area by sustainably (until 2022) low interest rates and in the risk area by regulation. The entrepreneurial decision on appropriate acquisition costs and sales compensation was also restricted—albeit only indirectly—by the recognizability of only 25 per mille. On the other hand, the increasingly legally demanded transparency is to be welcomed: It has (at least theoretically) strengthened the market parties and enabled competition, as policyholders can decide for themselves, given appropriate transparency, whether they want to finance certain acquisition costs or which providers make them attractive offers.

Currently, the so-called **EU Retail Investment Strategy** is being discussed at the European level. With its adoption, even more rules and restrictions would come to life insurance. This involves, on the one hand, the sometimes considerable expansion of information obligations, suitability and appropriateness tests, supervisory and steering requirements, marketing regulations, and professional requirements. On the other hand, commission regulations and commission bans are to be introduced for the first time, and member states are to be obliged to take measures to promote the financial competence of retail investors (see excursus).

Excursus on the EU Retail Investment Strategy

The EU Commission believes that retail investors are not fully exploiting the benefits that capital markets offer them. They too often rely on products that generate only a small return, or do not take advantage of the opportunities of the capital markets at all. Therefore, as part of its **Retail Investment Strategy** presented on May 24, 2023, the Commission published a whole package of regulatory measures. It formulates the **objectives** of creating the necessary conditions for stronger capital market participation by retail investors, strengthening their position in the investment process, and ensuring "better and fairer market outcomes".

The Commission states that retail investors in the EU are not exploiting the potential of the capital markets. It sees the **reasons** for this as a lack of financial knowledge, a lack of trust in the capital markets and the advisory service for investment products, as well as problems in the investment process, such as the difficulty for retail investors to obtain "relevant, comparable and easily understandable information about investment products". In addition, it sees **risks** due to misleading or unrealistic marketing communications about financial products, especially when they are disseminated via digital channels. Furthermore, it propagates—as it has for over a decade—(still) existing conflicts of interest that would result from the payment of commissions. Finally, the Commission sees the price-performance ratio (value for money) of some investment products as not being maintained (European Commission 2023, p. 2 f.).

The **main content** of the retail investment strategy includes adjustments and additions to already existing regulations, which were introduced in Germany in 2018 with the implementation of the IDD (Sect. 13.5) as well as some new aspects (see European Commission 2023, especially pp. 67–100; Eckhardt 2023). With reference to the insurance industry, these are:

- **Information obligations**, these concern risk warnings (insurance-based investment products, short IBIP), digital disclosures (all insurance products), cost disclosure and annual cost overview (IBIP), the transfer of information obligations from the Solvency II Directive to the IDD (all insurance products) and a new information sheet for life insurance products (life insurance);
- **Commission regulations**, these concern a ban on commissions for independent advice (IBIP), a ban on commissions for the sale of insurance investment products without advice (IBIP), the introduction of the "best interest test" as a replacement for quality improvement and non-disadvantage tests (IBIP), the concept of non-tied advice (all insurance products) and possible facilitations for independent or non-tied advice (IBIP);
- **Suitability and appropriateness tests**, these concern the explanation of the purpose of the suitability or appropriateness assessment and warnings, collection of information for suitability or appropriateness assessment and a negative appropriateness assessment vis-à-vis the customer (all for IBIP);
- **Supervisory and steering guidelines**, these concern the tightening of the product approval process (all insurance products), a new pricing process for product manufacturers and for product distributors (IBIP), reporting obligations due to the new pricing process (IBIP), recording obligations (IBIP) and the development of benchmarks (IBIP);
- **Marketing regulations**, these concern the definition of marketing communications and methods, labeling and assignment of marketing communications, content of marketing communications and methods, responsibility for marketing communications, reporting obligation for marketing communications and methods, new powers for supervisory authorities and new recording obligations (all for all insurance products);
- **Professional requirements**, these concern uniform requirements for professional knowledge and skills, knowledge and skills for sustainable investments, the obligation to provide evidence and certification of knowledge and skills as well as training and further education (all for all insurance products);
- **Promotion of financial literacy**, this concerns an obligation of the member states to promote measures to strengthen financial literacy.

With **reference to insurance marketing**, the regulations on commission, supervisory and steering guidelines as well as marketing are particularly relevant. These will therefore be briefly presented.

The Commission proposal envisages **new commission bans** for insurance and insurance intermediaries in relation to the insurance distribution of insurance investment products—there is currently no commission ban in the IDD:

- **Ban in the case of independent/non-tied advice on IBIP**: Insurers or intermediaries distributing insurance investment products should in future—analogous to the regulation for securities firms—no longer be allowed to accept or retain commissions if they inform their customers that their advice on the products is "independent" or "non-tied". However, they should explicitly continue to be allowed to accept or retain commissions if they do not advertise the advice as independent or non-tied. In addition, intermediaries who are neither employed by an insurer nor contractually bound to it may call themselves non-tied intermediaries, even if they receive commissions from the insurer.
- **Ban on the sale of IBIP without advice**: Insurers or intermediaries who design or distribute insurance investment products may in future no longer pay or receive commissions to a third party—i.e. in particular the distributors of the products for the sale of the products without advice—except if the third party is the customer himself. Exceptions only exist for minor non-monetary benefits (under €100 per year) under specific conditions as well as for payments or benefits necessary for the provision of services (e.g. administrative fees) or which by their nature cannot conflict with the obligation to act in the best possible interest.

These commission prohibitions are flanked by the newly introduced so-called **best interest test**. This stipulates that insurers and intermediaries must meet the following three conditions in order to act **in the best possible interest of their customers** when advising on insurance investment products. They must

1. base their advice on the evaluation of an appropriate selection of IBIPs,
2. recommend to their customers, after determining the most suitable IBIPs for them, the IBIP from comparable IBIPs that is most cost-efficient for the customer, and
3. recommend to their customers, from the IBIPs classified as suitable, at least one IBIP that does without additional features (e.g., capital guarantees or structured products with hedging elements) that are not necessary for achieving the investment objectives and that cause additional costs.

With regard to the marketing tool of product design (related to insurance investment products), certain innovations in the area of **supervisory and steering guidelines** are particularly relevant.

The **product approval process** (POG) should in future also include a "**price formation process**" if it is a IBIP. In this context, insurers and intermediaries (as "**manufacturers** of the products) must identify and quantify all costs and fees associated with the IBIP, check whether the costs and fees, among other things with regard to performance, are justified and proportionate (value for money), and compare the identified costs, fees and performance with reference values published by EIOPA. They must carry out additional tests and evaluations to check whether the costs and fees of the designed products are justified and proportionate, if the comparison with the reference values of EIOPA shows a deviation from these reference values. A product may not be approved if the insurer and intermediary cannot demonstrate that the costs and fees are justified and proportionate.

Also, the "**product distributors**", who distribute IBIPs to retail investors, must in future identify and quantify the distribution costs and other costs and fees not taken into account by the product manufacturer, assess whether the total costs and fees are justified and proportionate, and compare the costs and performance with EIOPA's reference values. They too must carry out tests and evaluations to check whether the costs and fees of the offered, recommended or distributed products to retail investors are justified and proportionate, if these deviate from the reference values. A product may not be offered, recommended or distributed if the distributor cannot demonstrate that the costs and fees are justified and proportionate. Moreover, the distributor must inform the manufacturers of the products about the results of his conducted price formation process and alert him if he has not fully taken into account certain costs and fees in his conducted price formation process.

The manufacturers of the IBIPs must also report information on costs and fees to their supervisory authorities (**reporting obligations**), including any distribution costs and commission payments, and provide them with data on the characteristics of the products (including information on performance and risk level of the products). Product manufacturers and product distributors then have to document the evaluations and tests to check whether the costs and fees for the products are justified and proportionate (**documentation obligations**).

Finally, the Commission also tightens up the **marketing regulations** in the retail investment strategy; these are particularly important for the marketing tool of communication policy and mainly apply to insurance investment products.

"**Marketing communications**" are defined as all disclosures promoting or advertising investments in insurance products or insurance investment products. "**Marketing methods**" are all strategies, tools or techniques aimed at disseminating marketing communications or improving their reach and effectiveness. This includes methods of the **insurers or intermediaries** themselves as well as **third parties** who use them on their behalf and receive a remuneration of monetary or non-monetary nature for this; these include, for example, Finfluencer, i.e., influencers who are typically active on social media and generate and disseminate financial content on behalf of financial service providers.

In the **marketing of IBIP**, marketing communications must be **clearly identifiable** as such and clearly **attributable** to the sender. Marketing communications and methods must be developed, designed, and provided in such a way that they are **honest, clear, and not misleading**. The presentation of benefits and risks should be **balanced** and **appropriate** for the targeted audience. In all marketing communications, the essential features of the advertised products must be **visually highlighted** and **concisely presented**. The main characteristics and the main risks of the products must be presented in a way that is **easy to understand** for retail investors. The **responsibility** for the content lies with the manufacturer of the IBIP, while the responsibility for the use of the marketing communication lies with the distributor. If a separate marketing communication is created for financial instruments or insurance investment products of third parties because they are offered or recommended, the insurer or intermediary is responsible for the content and use. Furthermore, there will be a future **reporting obligation** for marketing communications and methods to management bodies once a year. Finally, a new **record-keeping obligation** is added: manufacturers and distributors should keep records of all their marketing communications, regardless of whether they have provided these themselves or made them accessible via third parties.

The **criticism of the Commission's proposal** for a retail investment strategy is substantial and affects the majority of the regulations. Since the proposal has not yet gone through the trilogue and will probably undergo some changes before its adoption, only the most important aspects are addressed below.

On the **positive side**, the approaches to digitizing information provision, efforts to strengthen the financial competencies of retail investors, facilitations for professional investors, and the inclusion of third parties (e.g., finfluencers) can be mentioned. In contrast, there are **serious objections** to the intensity and depth of regulation (e.g., with regard to marketing communications and product presentations), the unnecessary restriction of competitive freedom (interventions in almost all marketing tools; price formation regulations; prohibition of commissions) as well as the—for the effects achieved—overall much too high additional burden due to information, reporting, product presentation, notification and record-keeping obligations and the establishment of new procedures (price formation procedures, best interest test) (Eckhardt 2023, p. 31).

Some proposals are **more than questionable from a regulatory policy perspective**. For example, the now proposed partial bans on commissions are to be rejected solely because of the excessive interference with entrepreneurial freedom, for the justification of which there is no reliable evidence. The criticism of the commission cuts and bans is extensive and refers to many other, justified arguments (Eckhardt 2023, pp. 14 f.; Lach 2023a, pp. 482 f.; Lach 2023b, pp. 516 f.), which are by no means new. It is noteworthy that the Commission already attempted the commission ban in the IMD2 draft of 2014 with almost identical justifications and formulations. Even then, there was extensive and justified criticism (Köhne 2014, pp. 261–264; see also Sect. 13.6.5). Apparently, however, there is no reflection and insight on the part of the EU Commission in this respect, possibly it is acting more ideologically driven in this respect (Lach 2023b, pp. 516 f.). The new best interest test is also criticized as illogical, patronizing, too cost-focused, distorting competition, and one-sided. Similarly, the mandatory cost comparison with reference values developed by EIOPA and the determination of criteria by the Commission for justifiable and proportionate product costs come very close to state cost control, and such interference in free price formation in a market economy is questionable. This is particularly true in financial and insurance distribution, which is characterized by intense competition (Eckhardt 2023, pp. 16; 22 f.).

In addition, there are many **further points of criticism**. For example, the new obligations to consider portfolio diversification in the appropriateness assessment are not very practical. The disclosure of information about costs, incidental expenses, and third-party payments can indeed facilitate investment decisions and strengthen competition. However, it is unlikely that small investors will show interest in such granular cost information and that they can correctly classify this information and consequently make better investment decisions (Eckhardt 2023, p. 31). Further criticism is directed at the causes identified by the Commission for the insufficient use of capital markets by small investors, which according to the Commission are primarily due to a lack of trust in the capital markets, the need for improvement in investment product advice, and the difficulty for small investors to access relevant, comparable, and easily understandable information about investment products. For example, national market access in Germany fails rather due to the passivity of small investors, which results from a strong need for security and corresponding high risk aversion. In addition, there are knowledge deficits, which the Commission also acknowledges and wants to change. The numerous, no longer manageable information for a small investor also acts as a market entry barrier. All of this requires qualified intermediaries who support the customer in his decision-making process, separate the important from the (many) unimportant, explain legal technical terms in the customer's language, and help with filling out forms. This actual advisory service to customers is made more difficult or even impossible by the many additional regulations, but not improved. The intended "relevant, comparable, and easily understandable information about investment products" is contradicted. Finally, the obstacles in the cross-border market access repeatedly pursued by the Commission are not really with the insurance companies and intermediaries. The lack of offer and the hardly given cross-border comparability for small investors result rather from language barriers on the customer and intermediary side, which are critical especially for credence goods. Even more serious in the cross-border market are the national tax regulations and the nationally shaped pension systems from statutory, occupational, and private pension provision, which are not harmonized across borders (Lach 2023a, p. 480 f.).

Two sobering findings on the Commission's draft of the EU retail investment strategy must be noted: First, it seems quite obvious that it will not achieve the intended goals overall, but—on the contrary—will even have a counterproductive effect if the Commission's ideas should prevail in the end. The **majority of regulations make it more difficult** for **small investors to access the**

capital market. Second, it represents a **re-regulation of unprecedented scale** in the area of insurance investment products—and thus almost all life insurance products—which **interferes further in marketing than** it **even did before the deregulation 1994**. Affected are product policy (product approval procedures, product presentation, product contents with waiver of additional services and product alternatives), pricing policy (price formation procedures, reference values for costs), distribution policy (detailed information, consulting, documentation, reporting, and auditing obligations; prohibition of commissions) and even communication policy (regulations on marketing communications and methods).

The EU retail investment strategy is—regardless of the (for now postponed due to very extensive and strong protest) waiver of blanket commission bans—another initiative of the Commission that will pose enormous challenges to the financial industry and also the insurance sector. How strong this will be depends on the changes made in the further legislative process.

Interim conclusion: The insurance market for private customers is heavily regulated and this also influences insurance marketing

Private customers demand insurance coverage to secure their private (family) sphere and their consumption. The legal framework conditions influence the private customer business of insurance companies and the corresponding marketing to a very far-reaching extent. In essence, they define the "playing field". Politics and thus legislation are very much shaped by the consumer protection model throughout Europe and in Germany: The European Union creates competition and transparency in many areas to strengthen the position of consumers (deregulation). At the same time, attempts are made to curb excesses of competition through re-regulation (e.g., own funds and risk monitoring in Solvency II, licensing requirement for insurance intermediation, cap on commissions in private health insurance, EU retail investment strategy, etc.).

References

Altemeyer-Bartscher, M./Hohenstein, J./Ketzler, R./Theis, A./Wiener, K. (2019): Kosten und Nutzen der Regulierung, in: Volkswirtschaftliche Themen und Analysen, Nr. 9, Ed. by GDV, Berlin, 2019.

Aschoff, D./Heitmann, J. (2020): Klassische Risiken im Überblick, in: Mahnke, A./Rohlfs, T. (Eds.), Betriebliches Risikomanagement und Industrieversicherung, Erfolgreiche Unternehmenssteuerung durch ein effektives Risiko- und Versicherungsmanagement, Wiesbaden, 2020, pp. 89–114.

Bätscher, R. (1989): Financial Services für den privaten Haushalt – Entwicklung, Funktionen und konzeptioneller Ansatz im Lichte des Service-Gedankens, Dissertation, St. Gallen, 1989.

Becker, J. (2019): Marketing-Konzeption: Grundlagen des ziel-strategischen und operativen Marketing-Managements, München, 11. edn., 2019.

Boemke, B./Ulrici, B. (2014): BGB Allgemeiner Teil, Heidelberg, 2. edn., 2014.
Bundesministerium der Finanzen (Ed.) (2014): Eckpunkte des Lebensversicherungsreformgesetzes, Mitteilung vom 14. Juni 2014, Berlin, 2014.
Crane, D.B./Froot, K.A./Mason, S.P./Perold, A.F./Merton, R.C./Bodie, Z./Sirri, E.R./Tufano, P. (1995): The Global Financial System, A Functional Perspective, Boston/Massachusetts, 1995.
Der Bundesbeauftragte für den Datenschutz und die Informationsfreiheit (Ed.) (2022): Datenschutz-Grundverordnung – Bundesdatenschutzgesetz, Texte und Erläuterungen, BfDI-Info Nr. 1, Bonn, 2022.
Deutsche Bundesbank (Ed.) (2023): Finanzierungsrechnung Juni 2023, Frankfurt a. M., 2023.
Deutsche Rentenversicherung (Ed.) (2023): Die Digitale Rentenübersicht: Fragen und Antworten, o. O., 2023.
Eckhardt, P. (2023): Die neue EU-Kleinanlegerstrategie. Viel Schatten, wenig Licht, CEP-Studie, Ed. by Centrum für Europäische Politik, Freiburg, 2023.
Eisen, Roland (2017): Versicherungsmarkt, in: Gabler Versicherungslexikon, Eds. von Fred Wagner, Wiesbaden, 2. edn., 2017, pp. 1010–1013.
Europäische Kommission (Ed.) (2023): COM (2023) 279, Vorschlag für eine Richtlinie des Europäischen Parlaments und des Rates zur Änderung der Richtlinien (EU) 2009/65/EG, 2009/138/EG, 2011/61/EU, 2014/65/EU und (EU) 2016/97 im Hinblick auf die Unionsvorschriften zum Schutz von Kleinanlegern vom 24. Mai 2023, o.O., 2023.
Farny, D. (2011): Versicherungsbetriebslehre, Karlsruhe, 5. edn., 2011.
Gal, J. (2019): Rechtliche Rahmenbedingungen eines Versicherungsmarketing, in: Reich, M./Zerres, C. (Eds.), Handbuch Versicherungsmarketing, Berlin, 2. edn., 2019, pp. 97–119.
GDV (Ed.) (2021a): Anbieterlandschaft: Mehr Stabilität als Wandel, in: Makro und Märkte kompakt, Nr. 38, 2021.
GDV (Ed.) (2023a): Statistiken zur deutschen Versicherungswirtschaft 2023, Berlin, 2023.
GDV (Ed.) (2023b): Fokus Digitalisierung. Grünes Licht statt Rotstift: IT-Jobs in der digitalen Versicherungswirtschaft, Nr. 10, Berlin, 2023.
Haller, M. (1982): Risiko- und Versicherungsprobleme des privaten Haushalts – aus Sicht der Privatversicherung, in: ZVersWiss, Jg. 71, 1982, Nr. 3/4, pp. 383–437.
Haller, M. (1986b): Risiko-Management, in: Jacob, H. (Ed.), Schriften zur Unternehmensführung, Band 33, Wiesbaden, 1986, pp. 7–43.
Hermann, R. (2009): Üeberlebenswichtig oder überflüssig? Marketing für Firmensachversicherungen sichert langfristig das Marktpotenzial, in: VW, Jg. 64, 2009, Nr. 19, pp. 1.498–1.504.
Hohenstein, J./Theis, A./Wiener, K. (2020): Versicherungsschutz der Deutschen: Potenziale nicht ausgeschöpft, in: Volkswirtschaftliche Themen und Analysen, Nr. 10, Ed. by GDV, Berlin, 2020.
Homburg, C. (2020): Marketingmanagement, Strategie – Instrumente – Umsetzung – Unternehmensführung, Wiesbaden, 7. edn., 2020.
Köhne, T. (1997): Die Wirkungsversicherung im Privatkundengeschäft – Implikationen für eine kundenorientierte Marktleistungsgestaltung, St. Gallen, 1997.
Köhne, T. (2014): Ökonomische Aspekte der neuen IMD2 vom 26.02.2014, in: ZVersWiss, Jg. 103, 2014, Nr. 3, pp. 243–268.
Kotler, P./Armstrong, G./Harris, L.C./He, H. (2022): Grundlagen des Marketing, Halbergmoos, 8. edn., 2022.
Kühlmann, K./Wolf, H.-P./Wallenwein, C./Swoboda, U. (2003): Marketing und Vertrieb, Funktionsorientierte Qualifikationen, Karlsruhe, 2. edn., 2003.
Lach, H. (2023a): Die EU-Kleinanlegerstrategie – zum Wohle des Verbrauchers oder Zuviel des Guten? (I), in : ZfV, Jg. 74, 2023, Nr. 17, pp. 480–483.

Lach, H. (2023b): Die EU-Kleinanlegerstrategie – zum Wohle des Verbrauchers oder Zuviel des Guten? (II), in : ZfV, Jg. 74, 2023, Nr. 18, pp. 516–518.

Lohmann, C./Sowietzki, S./Gewand, P. (2020): Industrieversicherer im Marktumfeld der Industrieversicherung, in: Mahnke, A./Rohlfs, T. (Eds.), Betriebliches Risikomanagement und Industrieversicherung, Erfolgreiche Unternehmenssteuerung durch ein effektives Risiko- und Versicherungsmanagement, Wiesbaden, 2020, pp. 319–353.

Mahmoodi, O. (2012): PKV, Bundestag ratifiziert Provisionsdeckelung, in: procontra online vom 02.04.2012.

Maslow, a. M. (1970): Motivation and Personality, New York, 2. edn., 1970.

Meffert, H./Burmann, C./Kirchgeorg, M. (2015): Marketing, Grundlagen marktorientierter Unternehmensführung, Konzepte – Instrumente – Praxisbeispiele, Wiesbaden, 12. edn., 2015.

Meffert, H./Burmann, C./Kirchgeorg, M./Eisenbeiß, M. (2019): Marketing, Grundlagen marktorientierter Unternehmensführung, Konzepte – Instrumente – Praxisbeispiele, Wiesbaden, 13. edn., 2019.

Monopolkommission (Ed.) (2022): Wettbewerb 2022, XXIV. Hauptgutachten, Bonn, 2022.

o. V. (2023a): Die 50 größten Lebensversicherer nach gebuchten Bruttobeiträgen, in: ZfV, Jg. 74, 2023, Nr. 16, pp. 431.

o. V. (2023b): Die 50 größten Schadenversicherer nach gebuchtem Bruttobeitrag, in: ZfV, Jg. 74, 2023, Nr. 22, pp. 639.

Statistisches Bundesamt (Ed.) (2023a): Haushaltsgrößen, in: https://www.destatis.de/DE/Themen/Gesellschaft-Umwelt/Bevoelkerung/Haushalte-Familien/Tabellen/1-2-privathaushalte-bundeslaender.html, Accessed: 02.01.2024.

Statistisches Bundesamt (Ed.) (2023b): Volkswirtschaftliche Gesamtrechnungen, Hauptaggregate der Sektoren, Vierteljahresergebnisse ab 1999, Stand: November 2023, o.O., 2023.

Surminski, M. (2023a): Die PKV im Jahr 2022, in: ZfV, Jg. 74, 2023, Nr. 19, pp. 526–545.

Surminski, M. (2023b): Die großen Kompositversicherer wachsen schneller als der Markt, in: ZfV, Jg. 74, 2023, Nr. 22, pp. 538.

Tchoumta, J.-M. (2002): Allfinanz aus der Sicht der Assekuranz: eine vergleichende Studie, Frankfurt a. M., 2002.

Theis, A. (2015): Regulierung und Versicherungswirtschaft: Chancen und Herausforderungen aus ökonomischer Perspektive, in: Volkswirtschaftliche Themen und Analysen, Nr. 7, Ed. by GDV, Berlin, 2015.

Theis, A./Wiener, K. (2018): Anbieterlandschaft am Versicherungsmarkt: Ein Ausblick, in: Volkswirtschaftliche Themen und Analysen, Nr. 8, Ed. by GDV, Berlin, 2018.

Theoretical Basics of Insurance Demand by Private Customers

4

The customer orientation required in both classical and modern marketing understanding necessitates a fundamental understanding of the relationships and influencing factors of insurance demand. Thus, insurance customers with their needs and behavior are a central reference point of (empirical) marketing research. Before their approaches and methods are presented (Chap. 5), the demand behavior of private insurance customers is first discussed theoretically. Although many of the theoretical explanations presented subsequently apply to private, commercial, and industrial customers, the focus of interest here is on a better understanding of the insurance demand of private customers.

Although all theoretical models do not provide a clear picture of insurance demand because human behavior in reality is too complex, their added value lies in explaining basic principles and structures of decision-making processes and creating a corresponding understanding of the associated possibilities and limitations. This applies to decision-theoretical models (Sect. 4.1) characterized by rational decisions as well as to behaviorally economic approaches (Sect. 4.2) that are more psychologically influenced. What is important for insurance marketing is which objective and subjective factors influence the demand behavior of insurance customers (Sect. 4.3).

4.1 Decision-theoretical Analysis of Insurance Demand

> "It is hardly to be assumed that most housewives have read Schumann's microeconomic book and, while they go shopping at Aldi, formulate their 'Lagrange function' to maximize their utility. Does this now mean that demand theory has nothing to offer? Certainly not! The main point is that economic theory can only describe basic principles and structures of decision-making processes and does not provide fixed rules." (Schlesinger 1994, p. 113)

T. Köhne, *Insurance Marketing*, https://doi.org/10.1007/978-3-658-47345-7_4

The model-theoretical analysis of insurance demand outlined below is based on the explanations of *von der Schulenburg* and can be studied in depth there (see Schulenburg and Lohse 2014, pp. 278–327; however, without references).

4.1.1 Assumptions of the Model

The basis is the **decision theory under uncertainty** and a model that belongs to the class of state-preference theory and goes back to the Nobel laureates *Kenneth Arrow* and *Gerard Debreu* (cited in: Schulenburg and Lohse 2014, p. 278). In this case, a stochastic (probability-distributed) variable takes on a certain value depending on the state of nature. The random variable takes on discrete values, whereby—to enable a graphical representation—it is assumed that there are only two states of nature (loss or no loss). "State preference" means that market participants value goods or payments in the individual states differently: there are thus good and bad states. As is usual in microanalytical considerations, a representative demander is considered, i.e., a demander from whose individual economic demand function the market demand function can be derived. This demander is risk-averse and tries to maximize his expected utility.

The following **assumptions** underlie the microeconomic demand model:

- Expected utility maximization: The policyholders choose from the offered insurance contracts the one that maximizes their expected utility.
- Avoidance of loss-making transactions: Only those insurance contracts are offered that do not cause a loss.
- Market equilibrium: Equilibrium on a competitive insurance market prevails when it is no longer possible for any insurance company to sell further insurance contracts and thus make a profit.
- Consideration of an individual decision situation: Only the decision situation of a single, representative individual is assumed and his behavior is transferred to all other individuals.
- No contagion and accumulation risks: The risk (probability of loss and amount of losses) of all individuals is independent of each other.
- Identical individuals: All individuals have the same resource endowment, the same preferences, and the same probability distribution.

So, a situation of uncertainty precedes the possible decision of the individual to insure.

(1) The individual strives for the highest possible wealth w at the end of the period. In contrast to the situation with certainty, there are multiple states of nature; they evoke a probability distribution of the end-of-period wealth w. The result of an action is therefore not a fixed, but a stochastic wealth. The random variable w is distributed according to the probability function $p(w)$. For all $p = p(w)$: $0 \leq p < 1$.

(2) The random variable w without insurance coverage has only two outcomes, namely w_1 in the case of no loss and w_2 in the case of loss. They occur with the probability p_1 and p_2 respectively, where $p_2 = 1 - p_1$. Therefore, for the probability of loss, simply p can be used, so the probability of being free of loss is $(1 - p)$. The wealth w thus depends on the occurrence of one of the two environmental states and on whether and to what extent the individual has sought insurance coverage.

(3) In return for the payment of a premium $P(I)$, the insurer takes over an insurance benefit $I(L)$ in the case of a loss L. The relationship between the loss L and the insurance benefit I is $I = \alpha \cdot L$ (proportional deductible). The amount of the premium depends on the amount of the agreed reimbursement in the case of a loss. Thus, $\alpha = 1$ represents a full insurance contract and $\alpha < 1$ represents a proportional deductible contract.

The **decision situation from the policyholder's perspective**, i.e., how much insurance the individual should buy, can be depicted in a result matrix, where w^a is the initial wealth (Table 4.1).

(4) The premium calculation by the insurance company is based on the agreed loss payment I in the case of loss L. The premium rate π is proportional and determines how much premium is to be paid for a unit of insurance benefit. Formally expressed: $P(I) = \pi \cdot I$.

(5) Furthermore, a symmetric information distribution is assumed: The insurance company assumes the same probability of loss p as the policyholder. It takes this probability of loss p into account in the premium calculation. Initially, the premium rate π is set proportional to the probability of loss p: $\pi = (1 + \beta) \cdot p$. Here, β is the so-called loading, the amount of which depends on further costs and surcharges (e.g., distribution, administration and claims handling costs, profit surcharges).

4.1.2 Model Statements

The **calculation of the premium** can now be summarized as follows:

$$P(I) = \pi \cdot I = \pi \cdot \alpha \cdot L = (1 + \beta) \cdot p \cdot \alpha \cdot L$$

Table 4.1 Assets in the case of no loss (w_1) and case of loss (w_2) with and without insurance. (Schulenburg and Lohse 2014, p. 280)

	No loss (1 – p)	Loss (p)
No insurance	$w^a{}_1 = w^a$	$w^a{}_2 = w^a - L$
Insurance	$w_1 = w^a - P(I)$	$w_2 = w^a - L - P(I) + I$

with

I = agreed loss payment (I: Indemnity)
$P(I)$ = insurance premium
π = premium rate
α = coverage ratio: proportion with which the insurance company replaces the damage
L = loss amount (L: Loss)
β = (cost and profit) surcharge
p = probability of loss.

The loss amount L and the probability of loss p are exogenously given in this model, the surcharge β is determined by the insurance company and α by the insurance demander. The policyholder is free in the choice of insurance coverage α or his deductible quota (1 – α). The other sizes, such as the insurance benefit in the case of loss and the premium to be paid, result from this.

Now, the **optimization problem of the policyholder** can be formulated and mathematically solved.

The optimal insurance coverage α is given by:

$$\max E(U(w)) = p \cdot U(w_2) + (1-p) \cdot U(w_1)$$

under the constraints

$$w_1 = w^{\mathrm{a}} - P(I)$$

$$P(I) = \pi \cdot I = (1+\beta) \cdot p \cdot I$$

$$I = \alpha \cdot L$$

$$w_2 = w^{\mathrm{a}} - L - P(I) + I$$

After substituting the constraints into the objective function (optimal condition), the following results:

$$\max E(U(w)) = p \cdot U(w^a - L - (1+\beta) \cdot p \cdot \alpha \cdot L + \alpha \cdot L) + (1-p) \cdot U(w^a - (1+\beta) \cdot p \cdot \alpha \cdot L)$$

The first order condition for an optimum is obtained by differentiating the objective function with respect to the only decision variable α (1st derivative) and setting the result equal to 0. Some transformations make it easier to interpret this condition (see Schulenburg and Lohse 2014, p. 282).

As a result, the following equation is obtained:

$$\frac{U'(w2)}{U'(w1)} = \frac{(1 - p + \beta - p \cdot \beta)}{(1 - p - p \cdot \beta)}$$

From this, **two important conclusions** can be drawn:

(1)If the surcharge $\beta = 0$, then:

$$\frac{(1 - p + \beta - p \cdot \beta)}{(1 - p - p \cdot \beta)} = 1$$

From this it follows:

$$U'(w_2) = U'(w_1)$$

resp.

$$w_2 = w_1$$

This condition is only achieved with full insurance, when $I = L$ or $\alpha = 1$.

Conclusion: If the surcharge is equal to 0, i.e. the insurer demands a premium that exactly matches the expected value of the loss payment, it is optimal for the insured to fully insure. If the premium equals the expected loss payment or the gross premium equals the net premium, it is referred to as a fair premium.

(2) If the surcharge β is greater than 0, the following applies to the right side of the optimal condition:

$$\frac{(1 - p + \beta - p \cdot \beta)}{(1 - p - p \cdot \beta)} > 1$$

From this follows (for explanation see Schulenburg and Lohse 2014, p. 284):

$$U'(w_2) > U'(w_1)$$

resp.

$$w_2 < w_1$$

This condition can only be achieved with partial insurance when $I < L$ or $\alpha < 1$.

Or in other words: If the wealth in the case of loss is less than in the case of no loss, the individual has obviously not requested full insurance coverage ($\alpha < 1$).

Conclusion: If the surcharge is greater than 0, i.e., the insurer demands more than the expected value of the insurance benefit, it is optimal for the policyholder to request partial insurance, i.e., not to fully insure.

In addition to this algebraic derivation of the optimal insurance demand, it can also be graphically understood (Fig. 4.1): A so-called **insurance line** is derived, whose points represent all coverage levels from no insurance through partial, full to over-insurances and whose slope (**marginal rate of transformation**) indicates the ratio in which the wealth in the case of loss (w_2) can be increased by insurance while simultaneously reducing the wealth in the case of no loss (w_1).

Point A denotes the state of non-insurance ($\alpha = 0$). In this case, the initial wealth w^a is reduced by the financial loss L in the event of damage. Point B shows the alternative of full insurance ($\alpha = 1$). In the case of full insurance, $I = L$, therefore the end-of-period

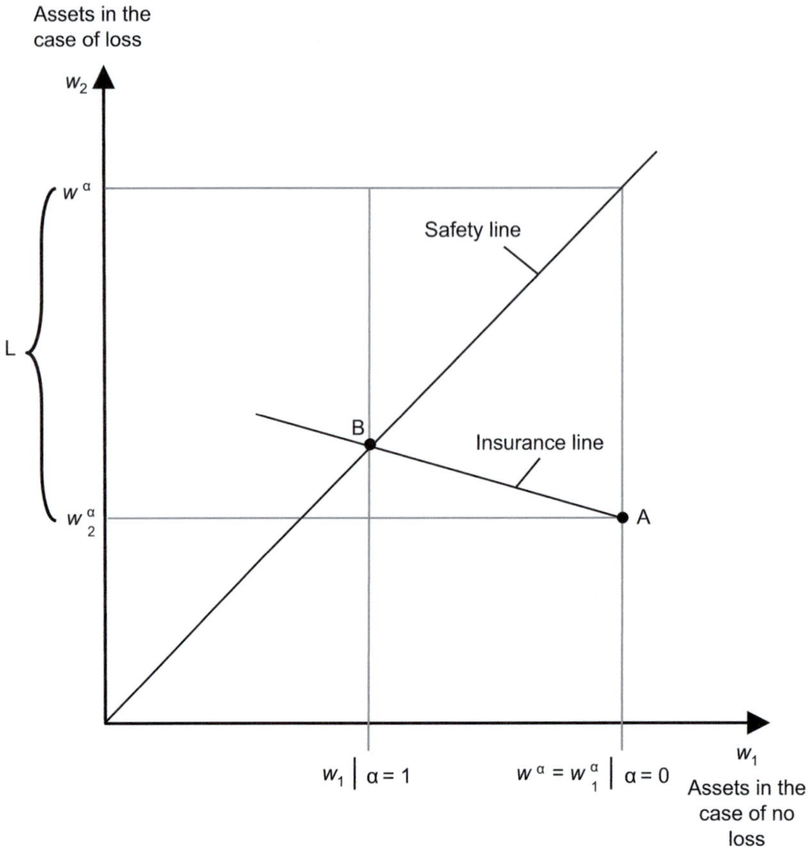

Fig. 4.1 Insurance line. (Based on Schulenburg and Lohse 2014, p. 286)

wealth is the same regardless of the state that occurs. This wealth distribution is therefore on the 45° line (safety line). The position on the safety line depends on the premium amount *P*(*I*). In addition to full and non-insurance, other coverage levels, i.e., underinsurance variants, are selectable ($0 < \alpha < 1$). In the case of proportionality of premium and coverage level, the insurance line AB results as the geometric location of all achievable wealth distributions with variable coverage levels. Points on the insurance line to the left of point B mean over-insurance.

Whether and to what extent insurance is demanded depends primarily on the preferences of the individual. According to the **expected utility theorem**, an individual will make decisions that maximize his expected utility. Here, the expected utility is the subjective evaluation of the probability distribution of outcomes resulting from an action. w_1 is preferred or considered equivalent to w_2 if and only if the utility from the asset value $U(w_1)$ is greater than or equal to the utility $U(w_2)$. If an individual can subjectively evaluate different values of end-of-period wealth, the expected utility allows the evaluation of a complete probability distribution of end-of-period wealth values according to the rule already listed above:

$$\max E(U(w)) = p \cdot U(w_2) + (1-p) \cdot U(w_1)$$

According to the assumptions of the model, rational action under uncertainty implies **expected utility maximization**. The individual's risk preferences are expressed in the utility function U, and it becomes apparent that risk aversion is constitutive for the existence of insurance, i.e., the certain expected value of a wealth distribution is preferred over the probability distribution of wealth values. The utility function of an individual can be represented as an indifference curve, which is derived from the total differential of the expected utility function. Along such an indifference curve, the utility for the individual does not change (Fig. 4.2).

The slope of the indifference curve is defined by the **marginal rate of substitution**, i.e., by the willingness to forego a unit of wealth in the case of no loss in order to gain insurance coverage in the case of loss (for derivation see Schulenburg and Lohse 2014, p. 288). How high this willingness turns out depends crucially on the perceptions of the probability of loss: If the individual estimates this probability as low, it will demand a higher net reimbursement amount per unit of premium payment. Therefore, the absolute

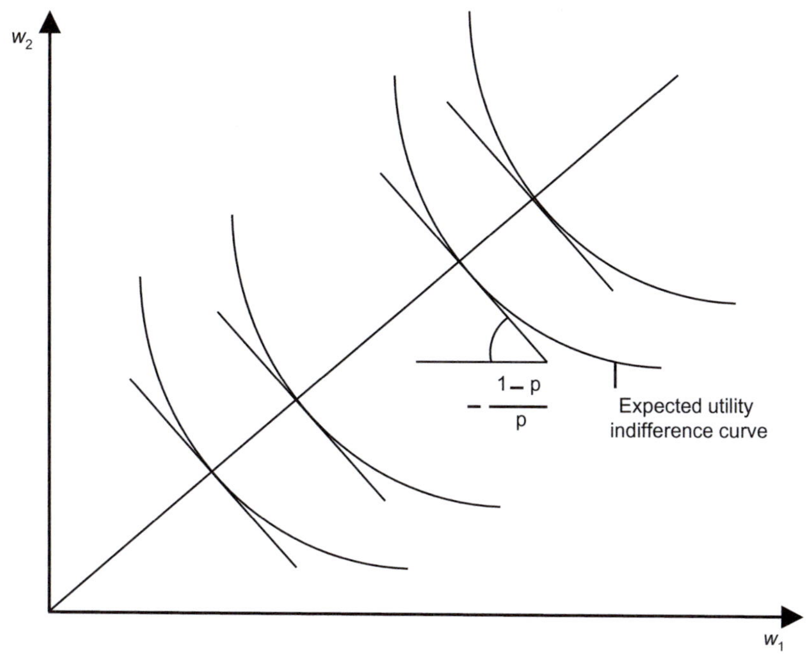

Fig. 4.2 Expected utility indifference curve system. (Based on Schulenburg and Lohse 2014, p. 288)

value of the slope of the indifference curves is greater, the lower the probability of loss p is.

From the preferences of the individual given by the expected utility function and its indifference curves, and the insurance possibilities given by the insurance line, the **insurance optimum** can now be derived. It lies at the tangential point M of the highest achievable indifference curve and the insurance line (Fig. 4.3). The maximum expected utility is therefore where the marginal rate of substitution equals the slope of the insurance line (marginal rate of transformation, for its derivation see Schulenburg and Lohse 2014, p. 286 f.):

$$-\frac{1-p}{p}\cdot\frac{U'(w1)}{U'(w2)}=-\frac{1-\pi}{\pi}$$

The optimal coverage ratio is characterized by the quotient AM/AB. Given certain preferences, it depends on the slope of the insurance line, i.e., the height of the premium rate π. Due to the convex indifference curves, the individual will choose a higher coverage ratio α the lower the premium rate π is. Full insurance is only chosen when: $p = \pi$, because only on the security line at $w_1 = w_2$ is the marginal rate of substitution (slope of the indifference curve) equal to the marginal rate of transformation (slope of the insurance line). If, on the other hand, the premium rate π is greater than p and thus the slope

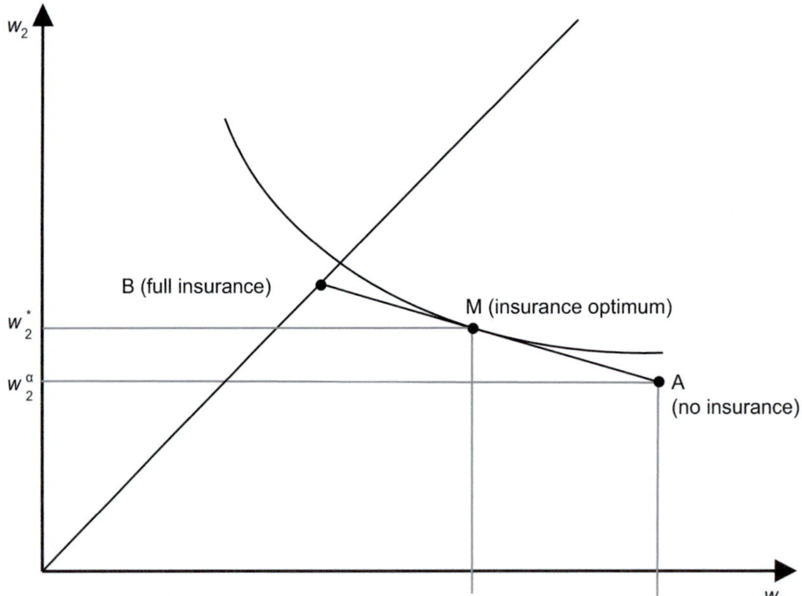

Fig. 4.3 Insurance optimum from the demander's perspective. (Based on Schulenburg and Lohse 2014, p. 290)

of the insurance line (absolute) is smaller than the slope of the indifference curve, the optimal coverage ratio is less than 1, i.e., the insured person wishes to have a deductible contract. Full coverage of his risk is not considered optimal. This case is graphically represented in Fig. 4.3.

The result just derived goes back to the economist *Jan Mossin* and is therefore referred to as the **theorem of *Mossin***: If the premium exceeds the expected loss, it is not optimal to demand full insurance coverage. Or in other words: If the proportional premium surcharge $\beta \geq 0$, then the risk-averse expected utility maximizer decides for full coverage ($\alpha = 1$) when $\beta = 0$, and for partial coverage ($\alpha < 1$) when $\beta > 0$ (Mossin 1968). *Schlesinger* modified part 2 of the theorem: (…) for full or partial coverage ($\alpha \leq 1$) when $\beta > 0$ (Schlesinger 1994, p. 121 f.).

From the model presented here, further theorems can be derived by making some modifications and additional considerations (Schulenburg and Lohse 2014, pp. 290–293):

Theorem of *Arrow* In the presence of moral hazard, it can be rational for the insured to demand full insurance coverage despite surcharge calculation, and it can be optimal for the insurer to offer no insurance coverage at all.

Theorem of ***Shavell*** If the proportional premium surcharge $\beta = 0$, then a risk-averse expected utility maximizer with moral hazard will choose full insurance coverage ($\alpha = 1$) and no loss prevention if the costs of loss prevention are too high, partial coverage ($\alpha < 1$), and certain loss prevention measures if the costs of loss prevention are low enough (Shavell 1979). Schlesinger also modified the second part here: (…) or he chooses either full or partial coverage ($\alpha \leq 1$) when the costs of loss prevention are low enough (Schlesinger 1994, pp. 124–126).

▶ **Moral Hazard** refers to the unobservable change in the behavior of an insurance policyholder after the conclusion of the insurance contract, insofar as he becomes more negligent and reduces or even stops loss prevention measures and loss limitation activities.

Theorem of *Pauly* With fixed surcharges, it is optimal for the policyholder to either fully insure or not insure at all.

Theorem of ***Rothschild* and *Stiglitz*** In a competitive insurance market with adverse selection and two types of consumers, either the quantity of self-selecting separate contracts will be the (Nash-) equilibrium, or no equilibrium will exist (Rothschild and Stiglitz 1976).

Excursus on Adverse Selection

Adverse Selection characterizes a negative risk selection due to asymmetric information distribution between insurer and policyholder. This is further intensified by insurance seekers with a high probability of loss trying to feign a lower probability of loss. The ignorance of the true risk class of the policyholders prompts insurers to make a mixed calculation, which in turn leads to good risks migrating. The insurer's average tariffing results in too high premiums being charged to good risks and too low premiums to bad risks. As a result, good risks demand too little and bad risks too much insurance coverage (Schulenburg and Lohse 2014, p. 315).

The aforementioned sentences and their derivation, as well as further findings of the theory of insurance demand, are referred to in detail in the literature; here it should only be clarified that decision theory—despite its sometimes restrictive and unrealistic assumptions—is capable of explaining rational purchase decisions by policyholders and thus contributing to the understanding of insurance demand.

Interim Conclusion on the Explanatory Contribution of Decision Theory

According to traditional economic theory, people are rational agents, often also referred to as Homo Oeconomicus. As such, they try to maximize their long-term well-being by using all available information. As rational agents, they choose the solution that brings them the most benefit; they are utility maximizers. In situations with uncertain outcomes, they maximize their probability-weighted utility (expected utility). For example, if someone can choose whether to win € 5000 with a 10% chance or € 2000 with a 50% chance, they choose the 50% option (expected value of € 1000 = 50% × 2000 instead of € 500 = 10% × 5000). Furthermore, rational decision-makers are risk-averse. If they can choose whether to win € 100 with 100% certainty or € 300 with a 50% chance, most choose the € 100, even though the expected value of the second alternative, with € 150, has a higher expected value. In other words: people are willing to sacrifice an uncertain higher result for a certain lower one. And because rational decision-makers are willing to pay to avoid risks and uncertainties, they are also willing to purchase insurance.

4.2 Behavioral Economic Explanations for Insurance Demand

> "Utility maximization is neither a necessary nor a sufficient condition to draw conclusions about who will purchase insurance." Nobel laureate Herbert Simon (literally translated from: Simon 1986, p. 216)

In reality, most people behave contrary to the assumption of decision theory that long-term utility is maximized in their decision-making process. In numerous experiments, researchers have found that behavior systematically disregards the theoretical framework and underlying assumptions of a rational decision-making process. In these cases, traditional economic theory cannot explain the decision-making process of demanders. In contrast, it is the merit of behavioral economics to show these limits of rationality and to take into account that emotions, concerns about fairness, and cognitive biases play an important role in people's decision-making process. Behavioral economics is a positive (as opposed to normative), evidence-based approach that is based, among other things, on the theory of cognitive bias and the New Expectation Theory (SwissRe 2013, p. 12).

4.2.1 Explanatory Contribution of Cognitive Bias

It is widely recognized and often confirmed by research in the field of psychology and behavioral economics that cognitive biases hinder rational decisions.

▶ **Cognitive Bias** is a cognitive psychological collective term for systematic (not random) erroneous tendencies in perception, memory, thinking, and judgment. They usually remain unconscious.

Cognitive biases often result in cognitive heuristics, such as judgment heuristics. According to Duden, a **Heuristic** is the doctrine of the procedures for solving problems, or also a methodical instruction or a directive for gaining new insights (Duden2023). However, it is also associated with simplification: "Technically defined, a heuristic is a simple procedure that helps us find adequate, albeit often imperfect, answers to difficult questions" (Kahneman 2014, p. 127), or more simply put, a rule of thumb (Kroeber-Riel and Gröppel-Klein 2019, p. 24; Gaedeke 2021, p. 1). Thus, the heuristic offers a shortcut in the decision-making process, enabling people to solve their problems and make a quick and effective assessment. It is helpful in many situations, but it can also lead to a worse outcome. A judgment heuristic is also not motivational (such as through wishful thinking or sanctions) and not emotionally conditioned, but is systematically used to facilitate decision-making and save time. In the context of behavioral economics, the unconsciously used heuristics are of particular interest, not the consciously and transparently used simplification tools. However, such judgment heuristics sometimes lead to serious, systematic errors (Tversky and Kahneman 1974, p. 1130 f.). If insurers understand how these biases influence the decision-making process, they can better align their marketing mix with the demanders. Some of the most important cognitive biases when buying insurance are now explained (see SwissRe 2013, pp. 15–18; Table 4.2).

Procrastination and Status Quo Bias Difficult decisions are often postponed because they are frequently associated with unpleasant discussions and/or considerations. The voluntary delay of an intended action, despite knowing that the situation could worsen as a result, is referred to as procrastination (Steel 2007). This can also be associated with loss aversion insofar as sometimes a decision is postponed to avoid the emotional stress and responsibility for a potentially wrong decision. This phenomenon represents a significant hurdle in reality for the acquisition of insurance. Because customers do not

Table 4.2 Selected cognitive biases. (Based on SwissRe 2013, p. 17)

Bias	
Procrastination	Refers to the replacement of more important actions with less important ones or doing something that brings pleasure, which is why pending tasks are postponed.
Status quo bias	Tendency to want things to stay as they are as much as possible.
Time-inconsistent preferences (hyperbolic discounting, shortsightedness)	Tendency of people to prefer an imminent payout to a later one, with the tendency increasing the closer both payout dates are to the present.
Framing	Drawing different conclusions from the same information, depending on how and by whom the information is conveyed.
Mental accounting	People implicitly assign money to different "mental accounts" and do not think too much about how they should spend the money in this basket.
Overconfidence	Tendency to be overly optimistic and to overvalue positive and pleasing results.
Risk perception	Once the probability of an event falls below a certain threshold, people behave as if the event could never occur.
Availability bias	Tendency to overestimate the probability of an event that is more present in memory; how recent the memory is or how unusual or emotionally charged it is can affect this tendency. People reassess their risk assessment as soon as certain events occur; e.g., more property insurance policies are taken out after an earthquake.
Herd behavior and social norms	A strategy for dealing with complexity and search costs (information overload). Imitating the actions of other people or like-minded individuals. The motto is: If it makes sense for them, it's good for me too. Can be efficient and rational under certain circumstances.

fully understand the purchasing process, and it requires a lot of knowledge from them. Moreover, the purchasing process is often lengthy, especially when the conclusion of insurance (in personal insurance) is accompanied by a medical risk assessment.

Time-Inconsistent Preferences In questions like "Would you rather have one euro today or three euros tomorrow?" or "Would you rather have one euro in a year or three euros in a year and a day?" a significant portion of respondents choose the lesser amount today, but in a year they would wait another day to receive the higher amount. In short: people apply "hyperbolic discounting", where the perceived value decreases very rapidly with short delays and slowly with longer delays (Thaler 1981, p. 201–207). However, this phenomenon can also be exploited in favor of customers, as shown by the "Save More

Tomorrow" pension concept developed in 2004: With this program, employees commit in advance to channeling part of their future pay raises into the pension savings plan. The program had a significant and lasting impact on savings rates (Thaler and Benartzi 2004). Such self-commitments could also be incorporated into life insurance policies.

Framing The Framing refers to how and by whom options are presented. People are influenced both by their decision-making environment and by how an option is presented (Kroeber-Riel and Gröppel-Klein 2019, p. 27). There are always multiple ways to present, explain, or describe something. Information in connection with another piece of information can be influenced by it, or in other words: positive and negative associations of the second piece of information influence the perception of the first piece of information (Tversky and Kahneman 1981, p. 453–458). The art now lies in choosing the most appealing presentation option. Framing is therefore a concept that can be used for sales purposes.

Experiments found strong signs of a framing effect on the attractiveness of pension products. Both negative framing of pension products and framing of pension products as investment rather than insurance instruments had a negative impact on the perceived attractiveness of the pension products (Agnew et al. 2008; Brown et al. 2008). The latter is particularly relevant in light of the still perceived low return and the skepticism of large sections of the population towards life insurance based on this.

Standard options can provide an extremely effective framework. Doing nothing is easier than examining various options and then making a decision (which also has to do with information overload and procrastination). This leads to a strong inclination towards the status quo and explains why a large part of the population currently invests their money in risk-free but also low-yield products such as bank accounts, instead of dealing with higher-yield investment alternatives. In this context, for example, the spread of insurance can be increased by providing a clever standard option and giving people a free or low-cost exit option.

Exaggerated Self-Confidence A person's subjective confidence in their own abilities is sometimes greater than they are objectively pronounced. Some people, for example, believe that they are more likely to experience good things than others and that bad events will affect them less than others (Kahneman 2014, p. 26). Exaggerated self-confidence can lead to misjudgments regarding the usefulness of insurance for risk minimization.

Risk Perception People particularly struggle to deal with very low probabilities. Many simply ignore the risk that they could die young. They assume that this will not happen and therefore forego the purchase of insurance that could be of great benefit to their dependents in the event of their early death. The same applies to liability risk and the assessment of the importance of private liability insurance.

Availability Bias Recent experiences also play a demonstrably important role in distorting risk perception, whether these are personal experiences in one's personal environment (family, circle of friends or acquaintances, work colleagues) or perceived events. Both sharpen risk perception and lead to the overestimation of risks with a low probability of occurrence that have just emerged. For example, more property insurance policies are taken out after an earthquake, and more life insurance policies after events like the terrorist attack on September 11, 2001. The Corona pandemic has influenced the perception of health insurance among a large part of the population.

Information Overload It refers to the quantity and complexity of information (Eppler and Mengis 2004, p. 328). Contrary to a widespread view, more information does not necessarily mean that consumers can make better decisions. Empirical studies have rather shown that too much information can lead to an "information overload" and make it difficult to evaluate the available options. The human brain is quickly overwhelmed when it has to process an excess of information without being influenced and/or deterred by irrelevant details (e.g., Kroeber-Riel and Gröppel-Klein 2019, p. 542). Therefore, people simply become incapable of action when they have too many or too complex choices (Chewning and Harrell 1990, p. 527; Eppler and Mengis 2004, pp. 325–332). There is ample empirical evidence that a person's willingness to purchase a product is lower if they have to make a selection from a multitude of options. A common reaction to information overload and dealing with it is herd behavior. That is, people copy the behavior of their peers to conform to social norms. A decision-making process based on herd behavior and social norms can be rational if the individual assumes that his peers have similar preferences and better information, or if he fears that the few who deviate from a social norm will not be supported by the wider society that sets this social norm. Even in the case of insurance, consumers are more likely to consider purchasing if their friends, family members, and work colleagues own it and share their positive experiences (SwissRe 2013, p. 18).

Table 4.2 (see above) already contains some known cognitive biases. However, the number of phenomena of cognitive bias and use of heuristics in decision-making behavior documented in the literature is much larger. On a related internet platform alone, about 190 cognitive biases are described (https://www.visual-literacy.org/bias-list/). Notwithstanding this, the three "main representatives" of the **judgment heuristics with regard to probabilities and outcomes** are representativeness, mental availability, and anchoring and adjustment (Tversky and Kahneman 1974, p. 1124; Theil 2002, p. 56).

Representativeness refers to the extent to which an object, person, situation, or condition is considered representative of an entire class. It is often determined by stereotypes, and a-priori probabilities, sample size, randomness, and limits of predictability are disregarded. Instead, people are subject to the illusion of the validity of their stereotype-based assessment—even when they receive new, contradicting facts—as well as a misunderstanding of statistical regression (Tversky and Kahneman 1974, pp. 1124–1127).

The heuristic of representativeness refers to probability judgments and thus also comes into play in insurance decisions, in different directions: On the one hand, events with high loss potential (accidents in nuclear power plants, plane crashes) are overestimated and not put into relation to everyday, smooth operation. The same applies to events with personal experience in one's own environment. In both cases, the probabilities of occurrence are disregarded. Conversely, everyday risks, e.g. in the household or in road traffic, are underestimated and not considered representative of one's own situation. The latter may be due to the comparatively lower extent of loss or to the higher probability of occurrence, which brings about a kind of habituation effect. Personal loss experience also leads to distortions in the assessment of probability: It is widely believed that positive and negative events balance out over time and therefore two loss events do not follow each other directly. Loss experiences could then—at least according to theory—lead to initially foregoing insurance coverage afterwards. More plausible and also observable in reality is the reverse correlation, that loss experiences trigger the demand for insurance coverage. The representativeness heuristic also explains the distortion in the assessment of loss extents; the range of actually possible loss extents remains unnoticed due to narrowing down to averages or maximum losses. It should be noted that the unequal treatment of causes and consequences influences all kinds of risk policy decisions and thus both risk analysis and the search and selection of suitable risk policy measures (Theil 2002, pp. 63–65).

The **mental availability** is the second significant judgment heuristic related to probabilities and associated outcomes. This means that some information is easier to imagine, remember, and retrieve than others, and therefore influences judgments more strongly. For example, it is easier to remember elements of larger groups or groups closer to a person (heart attacks in friends and acquaintances) than those of smaller groups or groups less close to a person (heart attacks in dermatologists). More frequent events are easier to imagine than rare ones, and associations are stronger when events occur together. Accordingly, the mentally available information is not context-independent. The availability heuristic appears in three basic types:

1. Distortion due to retrievability of comparable cases from memory;
2. Distortion because some situations are easier to imagine than others;
3. Distortion because supposed correlations between events are established.

The availability heuristic also includes the distortion that one's own characteristics or those of acquaintances are significantly overestimated in relation to those of outsiders (egocentric bias). This is accompanied by the view that one is less exposed to everyday dangers (e.g. in the household through the use of hammer, knife, lawnmower etc. or in road traffic) than others (illusion of control). Risk assessments are also strongly influenced by mental availability: For example, drivers behave more cautiously after they have seen an accident. Furthermore, correlations are assumed that do not exist (illusory correlation), e.g. between a win in the casino and a certain date like Friday the 13th

(Tversky and Kahneman 1974, p. 1127 f.; Tversky and Kahneman 1982, pp. 163–177; Theil 2002, pp. 66–68; Kahneman 2014, pp. 164–176).

The availability of information also influences insurance decisions. Two cases are particularly noteworthy in this regard: First, risk assessments are influenced by information that has nothing to do with the frequency or extent of the occurrence of the event; second, insurance primarily concerns risks that do not occur frequently. Studies on the estimation of the frequency of causes of death underline that rare causes of death are significantly overestimated, while estimates for common reasons are too low (Kahneman 2014, p. 174). The second problem of the availability heuristic relates to the low probability of insured events: Especially in the context of larger, memorable events (natural disasters such as earthquakes or floods), studies have shown that those affected perceive the risk only to the extent that they have corresponding loss experience. That available information about risk causes can even deceive experts into overlooking possible other causes is illustrated by studies on professional risk analysis using incomplete fault trees. Finally, it is shown that particularly vividly presented risks are mentally more readily available and thus lead to a higher demand for insurance than if they are presented or formulated abstractly (Theil 2002, pp. 69–77). Distortions due to mental availability can provide various clues for communication with policyholders, be it in terms of creating personal involvement or illustrating risks in the course of personal communication by insurance intermediaries or in terms of educating about probabilities of occurrence through sales promotion materials.

The **anchoring and adjustment** is the third significant judgment heuristic related to probability estimates. The anchoring effect occurs when people consider a certain value for an unknown size before they have estimated this size: The estimated values are close to the number that was presented to the people beforehand. For example, when considering how much they should pay for a house, people are influenced by the original price demand (list price). The list of such anchoring effects is endless, and estimates are demonstrably also influenced by anchors that have nothing to do with the probability to be assessed. Anchoring is an example of one of the most reliable and robust findings of experimental psychology. Adjustment means that one adjusts one's estimate gradually starting from the anchor. However, the adjustment usually ends early because people are sustainably influenced by the anchor (Tversky and Kahneman 1974, p. 1128 f.; Kahneman 2014, p. 152 f.). Anchoring effects also affect experts, they depend less on the background of experience than on the problem situation. No learning processes can be observed with regard to anchoring effects. The most significant are anchoring effects encountered shortly before the assessment (recency effect), regardless of the relevance of the information (Theil 2002, p. 79).

Insurance decisions are typically characterized by a mental anchoring to the status quo; the current state is used as a starting point for assessing future deviations. In addition, loss experiences can act as an anchor in assessing a risk, and despite later absences of loss occurrences, the assessment of the probability of loss is not corrected downwards. It also only marginally helps the estimate if probabilities of occurrence of similar risks are used as a basis. Findings also suggest that there may be a competitive relationship between anchoring and mental availability (Theil 2002, pp. 90–92).

The aforementioned **judgment heuristics** not only influence insurance decisions in isolation, but also **overlap**. Instead of processing all relevant information together, insurance decision-makers unconsciously try to simplify the decision-making process. In doing so, they apply, among other things, representativeness and availability heuristics at the same time. Moreover, their appropriate decisions are also complicated by the fact that insurance conclusion, premium payment, and potential claims payments are temporally separated. Against this background, representativeness heuristics lead to a lower demand for insurance because potential frequencies of loss occurrence and loss amounts are underestimated. In addition, certain types of damage can generate attention and others can therefore be neglected. Finally, the demanders may feel that they are involved in the damage despite taking out insurance, i.e., they do not get full insurance, which is basically always the case because the insurance does not or cannot cover all consequences of damage. At the same time, availability heuristics increase the attractiveness of taking out insurance because current (extreme) incidents in media reporting or in the circle of acquaintances, friends, or family increase attention (mental availability). The same applies to frequently occurring damages. But the sensitivity to extreme events decreases over time, and the decision-makers gradually return to their overly optimistic assessment of the risk situation. The preference observed among decision-makers for immediate payments instead of future ones also has two sides: Ignoring the time value of money (money illusion) leads to an overestimation of future payments compared to their actual present value, thereby promoting insurance demand (today's premium payment in exchange for later unnecessary loss payments). At the same time, however, frequencies of loss are underestimated because future loss events are uncertain. As a result, the aforementioned effects lead to suboptimal decisions regarding insurance demand. These heuristics, particularly applied in the private customer business, explain the high importance of personal sales. This can (and must) correct unjustified doubts about the need for insurance due to the exclusion of causes of loss, misinterpretation of probabilities of occurrence, or lack of awareness of loss (extents) distribution, recall loss events and make them "available", and take the initiative to think about risks and their loss potentials at all and thus counter overly optimistic thinking. Finally, in retirement provision, it is particularly important to illustrate present value and compound interest effects in order to establish mental availability (Theil 2003, p. 152 f.).

4.2.2 Explanatory Contribution of the Prospect Theory

The New Expectation Theory—internationally known under the name Prospect Theory—is generally considered the best available description of how people assess risks and make decisions in situations of uncertainty. It is also used to analyze the decision-making process of consumers in relation to insurance (Theil 1998, 2002).

The Prospect Theory was developed by *Tversky* and *Kahneman*. For their work in the field of judgment and decision theory, *Daniel Kahneman* received the Nobel Prize in 2002 (*Amos Tversky* had died six years earlier). Both developed the Prospect Theory to provide a theoretical foundation for empirically observed decision-making behavior. The theory is thus a descriptive decision theory. The term "prospect" refers to an arrangement of outcome heights and associated probabilities of occurrence, such as (100, 0.5; 150, 0.5) as an equal chance of winning 100 or 150 units of money (Theil 2002, p. 119).

The main postulates of this theoretical approach are reference dependence, loss aversion, diminished sensitivity, and probability weighting (Kahneman and Tversky 1979; Tversky and Kahneman 1986):

1. **Reference Dependence**: The Prospect Theory assumes that people make their decisions based on gains or losses relative to a reference point, often the status quo (see Fig. 4.4). This means that in reality, people act short-sightedly or with a narrow perspective when their decisions are based on deviations from their current utility or wealth, and thus differently than assumed in traditional economic theory. Their perspective is therefore short-term and not long-term.
2. **Loss Aversion**: An individual's utility is more susceptible to losses than to gains of equal magnitude (in Fig. 4.4: $v(-x) > v(x)$). Losses hurt about 2 to 2.5 times more than gains (Kahneman et al. 1991). Loss aversion can be seen as a natural survival tactic that protects people from risking all their possessions for the sake of survival. Therefore, people usually prefer small, certain gains to large, but unlikely gains.
3. **Diminished Sensitivity to Gains and Losses**: Utility increases with gains, but each additional gain has a slightly lesser positive effect on utility, i.e., the marginal utility of gain decreases; the utility function is concave in the gain area. Similarly, a loss reduces utility, but with each additional loss, utility decreases less than proportionally, i.e., the negative marginal utility of loss also decreases; the utility function is convex in the loss area (Fig. 4.4). From the diminishing sensitivity, it follows that people are risk-averse in the gain area: They prefer a certain gain to a higher uncertain gain. In the loss area, it is the opposite: People are more likely to take a risk by tending to speculate on a probable, high loss and thus risk an even greater loss. This is also contrary to classical economics, which assumes that sensitivity to losses increases.
4. **Probability Weighting**: According to Prospect Theory, people do not weight outcomes according to objective probabilities, but rather according to transformed probabilities or decision weights. They are only limited in their ability to realistically assess the probability of extreme events. Therefore, highly unlikely events are overweighted, while events with a high probability are underweighted.

The third postulate can be better understood when considering the underlying **Fourfold Pattern of Risk Behavior** (Tversky and Kahneman 1992):

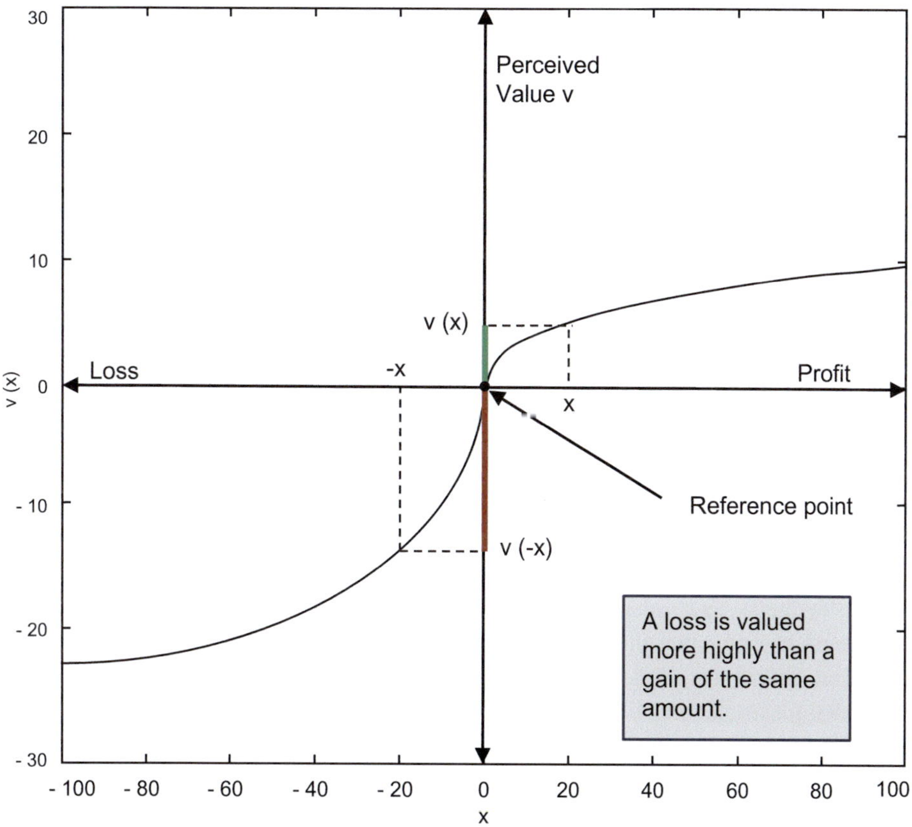

Fig. 4.4 Value function of Prospect Theory. (Based on Barberis 2013, p. 176 and Bender-Scheel 2012, p. 71)

1. In the context of gains, most people prefer a certain gain of € 9500 to a 95% chance of € 10,000, as they are fundamentally risk-averse when it comes to gains.
2. However, when there is a small chance of a large gain, they act risk-seeking and prefer a five percent chance of € 10,000 over a certain € 500. There is more to gain.
3. In the context of losses, on the other hand, most people would act risk-seeking and take the risk of suffering a loss of € 10,000 with a 95 percent probability in order to preserve the chance of avoiding a certain loss of € 9500. There is not much (more) to lose.
4. With large, but unlikely losses, they would be risk-averse: They accept a certain loss of €500 to avoid a higher, but much less likely loss of € 10,000 with a probability of five percent.

According to Prospect Theory, people's attitudes towards risk are determined by the reference dependencies, loss aversion, diminished sensitivity, and probability weighting just described. The theory was developed, parameterized, and tested in a test environment and provides interesting insights into human behavior. Like all theories, it does not provide a comprehensive explanation of purchasing decisions in the insurance sector as observed in the real world (Kahneman and Tversky 1979, p. 286). However, it does provide new explanatory contributions for observable behaviors of private customers.

Theil has examined the **potential applications of Prospect Theory in explaining insurance demand**—more specifically, its explanatory contributions to the risk assessment of policyholders as their decision-making basis for insurance demand—and has gained the following insights (Theil 2002, pp. 205–260):

In principle, it appears that Prospect Theory has a number of degrees of freedom that make its use attractive. However, there are both potential **gains in knowledge** and **various challenges**. The agreement of probabilities estimated by policyholders with actual probabilities is rather low. At the same time, the erroneous judgments are associated with an inappropriate confidence in their own estimate, which can be traced back to anchoring and adjustment heuristics. This is different for learned estimates as a result of frequent use (as in the case of underwriters), which is not the case for policyholders.

Another challenge and restriction is the transformation of verbal into numerical probability statements, as regularly occurs in the formation and communication of probability judgments. It shows that the sometimes widely scattered evaluations are mainly due to individual differences of the subjects and their interpretation differences take on a magnitude that makes generalizing statements practically impossible.

However, the study also shows that it seems sensible in the course of framing to distinguish between sum and interest insurance (indemnity insurance), i.e., to assume different forms of framing. In the course of simplification through framing, decision-makers assume interest insurance for indemnity insurance, i.e., they assume that the entire risk is transferred or the entire loss is compensated. In the case of sum insurance, the decision problem is reduced to the comparison of premium and sum insured. As a result of these empirically verifiable framings, the value function of Prospect Theory gains relevance (Theil 2002, pp. 232 f., 256). In the field of property insurance, the theory can also explain over-insurances of low risks, e.g., the tendency to low deductibles in home contents insurance (Sydnor 2010).

There is no clear confirmation for the assumption of diminishing sensitivity to losses; the results of the analysis of the value function for insurance problems are not clear. It is conceivable that decision-makers consider results and probabilities of occurrence simultaneously and thus exclude high loss potentials due to their low probability of occurrence. However, the classic Prospect Theory can explain this phenomenon if a perception threshold for probabilities is assumed and a jump point is assumed in the transition from an impossible to an uncertain event. This perception threshold results in an either-or constellation of the insurance decision: If the probability of loss from the decision-maker's point of view falls below this threshold, no insurance is necessary. If it is above, it is even overweighted according to Prospect Theory as a still comparatively low probability and insurance is demanded.

The latter is explained by the already mentioned four-part division of risk behavior: According to this, people behave risk-averse in the face of the risk of large, existential threats (with small probabilities of occurrence) and prefer to pay a comparatively low premium for insurance in order to be covered in the case of loss.

In terms of risk behavior, however, in addition to the distinction between losses and gains and their respective amounts and probabilities of occurrence, other influences also play an important role. The so-called "Cushion Effect" describes that people take more risk to achieve a certain goal when a minimum goal is already secured or a buffer is available. This explains, among other things, the popularity of guarantee products for retirement provision, which increase their equity quota just enough that a certain minimum goal is not endangered (Knoller 2016).

As an immediate contribution to knowledge, the Prospect Theory provides **numerous empirically confirmed indications of misjudgments** that occur when deciding on a particular risk policy measure such as the demand for insurance. However, the hope of being able to correct these errors through learning or the provision of additional information is low (Theil 2002, p. 258 f.). Moreover, the Prospect Theory can be applied to a wide range of questions in finance and insurance (Barberis 2013; Richter et al. 2018, p. 29).

At least, the use of certain heuristics can lead to **shaping information differently** and thus achieve effects, e.g., against the background of the simplification of the decision field postulated by the theory by the policyholder. Such a simplification on the customer side could also explain the proven lack of influence of price presentation (price optics, i.e., offering different price models; price bundles, i.e., individual versus total price) of guarantees on the assessment and demand for life insurance (Huber et al. 2015). A practical application of behavioral economic findings can be found at the highest level in the context of EU requirements: The (quite far-reaching) regulations for the design of product information sheets are based on behavioral economic findings and are intended to simplify the decision field on the part of the policyholder (European Insurance and Occupational Pensions Authority 2017, p. 20).

A second exemplary approach arises from the fact that heuristics are fundamentally based on **comparisons between different elements**: This could be taken into account when designing risk information (loss extents, types of damage, probabilities of loss occurrence, causalities, etc.) or information about the insurance (insured risk, premium, additional services, etc.). For example, a risk for which an insurance contract is offered but which is not perceived by demanders could be presented in relation to a similar risk for which there is a corresponding insurance demand, e.g., the occupational disability risk in the context of the risk of death (Theil 2002, p. 259 f.). However, the hurdle of subjectively shaped understanding of probabilities must be overcome again according to the theory, as well as the herd instinct ("Everyone has a term life insurance, but I don't know anyone who has a disability insurance").

In the areas of life insurance and retirement provision, the Prospect Theory also provides a possible explanation for the so-called "Annuity Puzzle" mainly through the inclusion of a reference point and loss aversion: The investor converts none or only a very small part of the wealth saved for retirement into a pension. Because if he annuitizes his wealth at 65 and dies at 66, this represents a very large loss. Since the annuitized wealth serves as a reference point, almost everything is lost in this case. In the reverse case of a long life, he does achieve a large gain—however, loss aversion causes the losses to be rated much more heavily and therefore the negative effects subjectively outweigh. This effect is supported by the distortion of probability (overweighting of the early mortality probability), which leads to a heavily weighted "total loss" of the invested wealth. Both effects explain at least part of the low attractiveness of annuitization (Hu and Scott 2007; Gottlieb 2012). As a finding, it can be deduced from this to make annuitization options more attractive for the customer by, for example, offering guarantees that reduce the very high losses in the event of early death (Richter et al. 2018, p. 30).

Excursus on the Benefit of a Capital Investment in Prospect Theory

To determine the benefit of a capital investment, one would usually set the distribution of the final wealth in relation to the invested wealth or a predetermined target wealth (reference point). Accordingly, the subjective benefit for the customer is determined only by the distribution of the final wealth, and interim value developments and value fluctuations have no influence on it. However, various scientific studies show that investors tend to evaluate their investment regularly, suggesting that people also regularly adjust their reference point and always evaluate their investment with respect to the current reference point. With roughly the same profit in the first year and loss in the second year, the negative effects of the loss in the second year outweigh due to the described loss aversion of the Prospect Theory. *Benartzi* and *Thaler* (1995) incorporate this perspective in their theory of "**Myopic (short-sighted) Loss Aversion**". With this, they can explain the according to economic theories too high difference between the returns of stocks and comparatively safe investments, such as government bonds: Specifically, the differences present in the market are the result of an annual evaluation and an overweighting of losses with a factor of about two.

In the area of retirement provision, the question is interesting as to why certain retirement provision products are popular and others are not. For example, LifeCycle funds (Graf 2017), lifecycle models in fund policies and annual guarantee forms (Ebert et al. 2012) are very popular—according to the expected utility theory and even the Prospect Theory they should not be demanded. However, both theories do not take into account the regular control of the value and value changes of the capital investments by the customers. Therefore, Ruß and Schelling—based on the Prospect Theory and myopic loss aversion—have proposed the "**Multi Cumulative Prospect Theory**" as a further development of the Prospect Theory, which takes into account that customers already include the subjective benefit of future annual value fluctuations in their decision when selecting a product. This can explain, among other things, the high popularity of LifeCycle funds (Graf et al. 2017) and of annual guarantee forms in private retirement provision (Ruß and Schelling 2017).

(Richter et al. 2018, p. 30 f.)

The numerous studies on judgment heuristics provide **no uniform, in the sense of a theory in itself closed explanatory model** for the risk assessment of policyholders, but only indications of individual distortion phenomena, which sometimes reinforce, sometimes counteract each other. Some effects, such as the judge's own experience, are very individual. Or as *Theil* puts it: "(…) situation (…), that not only representativeness and mental availability are in the ambivalent relationship of mutual reinforcement or competition, but the process of anchoring and adjustment only leads to a consolidation of a predestined attitude. Which value is anchored may depend on a representativeness or availability judgment, and this in turn may go back to an individual situation" (Theil 2002, p. 96). Thus, the studies on judgment heuristics underline that an absolute correlation in the sense that a certain risk is always perceived and processed in a predictable way is not to be expected. And they illustrate the considerable difficulties in dealing with uncertain situations, whether it is the mere estimation of individual probabilities or the holistic understanding of causal relationships. Therefore, complex decision-making processes such as insurance demand are very difficult to grasp, and this is further intensified by the high number of possible "shortcuts". But they are subject to typical (systematic) distortions of probability and result estimation and are therefore not rational. They are also influenced by the situational context and therefore only partially predictable.

Apart from this general insight, the **studies** on judgment heuristics **provide** further **clues**. For example, the significance of the memorability of a risk can be a guideline for the design of framing: vivid messages in advertising or a significant simplification of the decision situation would be possible measures in this regard. Simplifications can refer to all sizes relevant for the assessment, including loss extents, types of damage, or premiums. Apparently, high and typical loss events are preferably used as a basis for the assessment; risks are not described statistically, but based on their threatening extent. Another insight is that people often base their decision on a dominant assessment dimension of the problem and neglect the others. In the case of insurance, the compatibility of the assessment scale requires a focus on sizes measurable in money. If the scope of services cannot be measured in concrete monetary units due to their legal, abstract formulations incomprehensible to laypeople, and the loss extents used as a substitute (and simplifying) are more difficult to estimate due to the associated probabilities of occurrence, the decision between two insurances may be reduced to the premium amount (Theil 2002, pp. 96–98). Finally, the observed simultaneous application of the representativeness and availability heuristic in combination with particularly long planning horizons in personal insurance explains the great importance of personal sales (Theil 2003).

Behavioral economics thus contributes—also and especially in the insurance industry—to better **understanding** the **behavior of consumers**. An important insight is that a change in the environment in which decisions are made, and the way information is conveyed, has a major influence on consumer behavior. It has been shown that seemingly insignificant details, e.g., the type of formatting or structuring of a letter, can significantly affect consumer behavior (Adams and Hunt 2013). These are interesting and important insights, but they also confirm that many aspects of behavioral economics are very context-specific and cannot be generalized (see also for a current application in the insurance industry the marketing highlight of Versicherungskammer Bayern in Sect. 14.2.5).

Behavioral economics also has **political and societal relevance**. Some insights have already been applied in guiding consumers towards solutions that are beneficial for both the individual and society. Examples include higher savings contributions as a standard option in pension plans or programs for healthier behavior (e.g., warning labels on tobacco products, nutritional information on food packaging). In connection with retirement provision products such as life insurance, the political goal should be to reduce the coverage gap inevitably resulting from demographic development in order to increase the well-being of the individual and that of society. In this regard, behavioral economics provides important insights into how citizens can be helped to overcome their reservations and make better decisions in dealing with their risk potential (SwissRe 2013, p. 19). A good example is the aforementioned "Save More Tomorrow" pension program from 2004, which has had a significant and lasting impact on savings rates (Sect. 4.2.1). In the field of non-life insurance, the also already mentioned EU requirements for the uniform and simple design of product information sheets are to be mentioned.

Interim Conclusion on the Explanatory Contribution of Behavioral Economics

Behavioral economics contributes—also and especially in the insurance industry—to better understanding the behavior of consumers. It shows and explains that and how a change in the environment in which decisions are made, and the way information is conveyed, has a major influence on consumer behavior. The complex decision-making processes in the course of insurance demand are very difficult to grasp, and this is further intensified by the high number of possible "shortcuts" (biases). They are also influenced by the situational context and are therefore only partially predictable, i.e., many statements of behavioral economics are very context-specific and cannot be generalized. But behavioral economics makes it clear that insurance policyholder decisions are subject to typical (systematic) distortions of probability and outcome estimation and are therefore not rational. Nevertheless, it provides numerous clues for influencing and possibly even overcoming typical perception distortions through the marketing tools of an insurer and also for political regulatory approaches.

4.3 Determinants of Insurance Customers' Demand Behavior

In the sense of a comprehensive analysis of insurance demand, all essential influencing factors that affect the selection process and the purchasing decision must be recorded. Starting from the degree of direct influence on the purchasing decision, these are psychological, personal, social, and cultural influencing factors (Fig. 4.5).

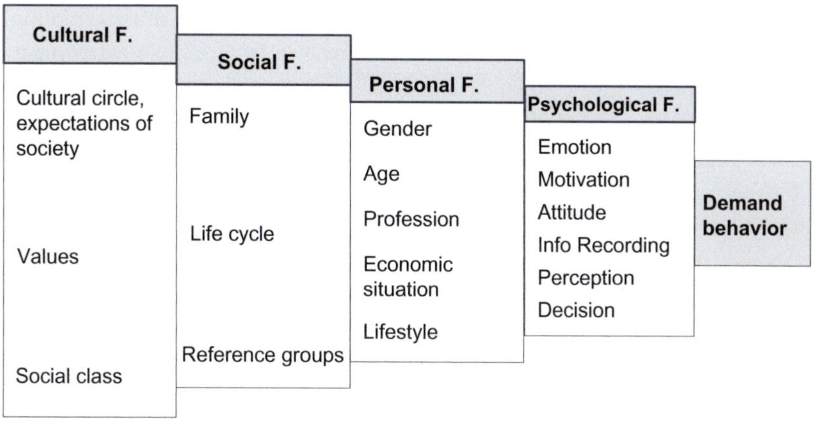

Fig. 4.5 Factors influencing insurance demand. (Based on Kotler et al. 2022, p. 255; Köhne 1997, p. 59)

4.3.1 Psychological Factors Influencing Insurance Demand

The **psychological influencing factors** of insurance demand cause individual behaviors (even within a customer group). They are largely responsible for the fact that even members of the same customer group, despite largely similar segmentation criteria, behave differently or individually.

Internal psychological processes can be both activating and cognitive processes: **Activating processes** are associated with internal excitations and tensions. They drive behavior and are thus human driving forces responsible for behavior occurring at all. These include emotion, motivation, and attitude. Cognitive processes are those through which the individual recognizes himself and his environment. These are processes of cognitive information processing.

▶ **Emotions** (and drives) are internal excitation processes that are experienced as pleasant or unpleasant and are more or less consciously experienced.

▶ **Motivation** stands for emotions that are associated with a goal orientation for behavior.

▶ An **attitude** is a motivation that is linked to a—cognitive—object assessment.

(Kroeber-Riel 1992, p. 50)

To simplify, one can also say that emotions are directed inward to one's own experience, motivations to action, and attitudes to an object. How similar these three facts are can be seen when the terms are related to a specific stimulus. The stimulus consists, for example, in the sight of a fast car. This sight is experienced as pleasant (emotion), triggers the desire to drive it (motivation), and is expressed in a positive assessment of the car (attitude) (Kroeber-Riel 1992, p. 50 f.).

Emotions influence the decisions of insurance demanders (see research window). Apart from general emotional states, the private insurance customer is primarily influenced by feelings of security and insecurity; behind these are fear, sorrow, excitement and surprise as well as relief and satisfaction (Görgen 2007, p. 28 f.). The emotionally shaped expectations of customers towards insurance companies inevitably lead to disappointments when a loss occurs. This is contributed to by the occurrence itself, which the insurance should protect against, but also the sober, impersonal treatment of the claimant during the claims settlement phase contradicts the expectations of a protective ("motherly") hand in case of misfortune. Finally, the pursuit of profit (and not security for the customers) disillusion the emotionally shaped policyholder (Köhne 1997, p. 62–66).

Research Window: Influence of Emotions on Insurance Decisions

Emotions can have a systematic influence on the decisions of insurance demanders and can therefore—like the cognitive biases already discussed in Sect. 4.2.1—have a distorting effect. *Wiersich* (2013) has developed a theoretical model that structures the influence of emotions on insurance behavior. Various experimental studies have been conducted to investigate how the emotion of affection influences the willingness to pay for insurance and whether emotions change over time.

The **results of the study** confirm the influence of emotions on insurance behavior:

1. The effect of affection influences the willingness to pay for insurance coverage and thus affects the perception of results and risk. However, the type of risk moderates this effect: The effect of affection does not influence the willingness to pay for insurance in risk situations, but only in situations characterized by uncertainty. The reason for this are differences in information processing and decision-making. Decision-makers tend to be analytical in risk situations and actively incorporate the given information into the decision-making process, while they make their decision intuitively in situations of ambiguity. In such a situation, affection can influence insurance behavior.
2. Current emotions such as fear and concern also influence insurance behavior: The more fear or concern a decision-maker feels at the time of decision, the more he is willing to pay for insurance. Current emotions are in turn influenced by the factor of time: As a potential loss event approaches in time, both concern and the willingness to pay for insurance coverage decrease. It seems that the decrease in willingness to pay is due to a reduction in concern.
3. Finally, positive anticipated emotions influence insurance behavior. The more positive anticipated emotions a decision-maker associates with the idea of having insurance in the case of loss, the higher his willingness to pay for this insurance.

However, the willingness to pay for insurance decreases the more positive anticipated emotions the decision-maker associates with the idea of not having taken out insurance in the case of no loss. Women and men differ in their insurance behavior: Women are more risk-averse than men and are willing to pay significantly more for insurance coverage, which seems to be due to a different emotional experience of women and men. Women apparently associate more intense positive anticipated emotions with the idea of having insurance in the case of loss than men. The result is a higher willingness of women to pay for insurance coverage.

From these findings, various **implications for insurance marketing** are derived. For example, insurance companies should specifically offer insurance coverage for objects to which an insurance customer has an emotional relationship or affection, because these objects are in high demand for insurance coverage by customers. In communication policy, insurers should avoid communicating objective probabilities of loss occurrence. Otherwise, decision-makers would integrate the additional information into the decision-making process, resulting in a lower willingness to conclude. Furthermore, the intensity of positive anticipated emotions associated with the idea of having insurance in the case of loss should be promoted. Since especially women associate intense positive anticipated emotions with this idea, they should be the target group of a corresponding communication policy. In the area of pricing policy, the emotional value of an object or the affection for an object could be used for price differentiation by differentiating the premiums depending on the importance of an object to the insurance customer by product groups. However, the compatibility with the legally required principle of equality of treatment in life insurance premium calculation would have to be checked. Finally, there are implications for sales policy: In the consultation, it should therefore be explicitly asked which objects are important to a customer in order to offer targeted insurance coverage for these (Wiersich 2013).

Further research on the influence of emotions on insurance decisions:

- Huber and Schlager 2011.
- Papon 2008.

The **motivation** includes an activation component on the one hand and a cognitive component of goal-directed behavior control on the other. The activating motivational components include the emotions and drives underlying a motivation. They activate behavior and direct it in a certain direction. The cognitive motivational components are perception and interpretation of the action situation as well as considerations of the goal-means relationships. In this respect, motivation can be described as a conscious striving for goals, as a will to do something. Two influencing variables are to be considered (as with most cognitive models) (Kroeber-Riel 1992, p. 135–140; Meffert et al. 2019, p. 106 f.):

- the subjectively perceived goal-means relationship,
- the subjectively expected value (satisfaction value) of the goal.

According to the considerations made, motivation can be divided into drive component (I.) and cognitive component (II.): With regard to the **drive-related classification (I.)**, the **motivation hierarchy of *Maslow*** (Need pyramid), which ranks human motivation according to its different urgency for behavior, represents a widely used approach. Accordingly, the essential needs or layers of needs are (Maslow 1970; Meffert et al. 2019, p. 107 f.):

1. Physiological (biological) needs such as food, sleep and preservation of health
2. Security needs, e.g. preservation of employment and retirement provision
3. Social needs, e.g. needs for affection, love, sociability
4. Striving for self-esteem and recognition by others (desire for prestige)
5. Striving for self-actualization, i.e. development of personality and creativity in the broadest sense.

The first four layers represent deficit needs, which are the result of a lack of need-reducing stimuli. The fifth, "highest" need represents a growth need, which is characterized by an active striving of the individual with the ultimate goal of individual realization. Growth goal refers to the phenomenon that the desire for further self-actualization is stronger the more the original self-actualization need is satisfied. The human motivation resulting from these needs becomes effective in a hierarchical order.

Central to *Maslow's* motive theory is the **principle of relative priority in need actualization**: All superordinate motives of the hierarchy are only activated as goals when the respective subordinate goals are fulfilled according to a certain level of demand. The level of demand is dependent on society and the immediate environment of the buyer. The experiences of past purchase decisions also flow into the demands, so that the demand levels are dynamic sizes. However, this is an ideal-typical view, because firstly, the motivation ranking is differently pronounced in many people and secondly, a motivation does not always have to be completely fulfilled before a higher-ranking motivation can become effective. However, if one accepts the hypotheses of this dynamic motive model despite the objections and takes into account the situation of increasingly freely available income, conclusions can be drawn especially for product policy and advertising: With increasing prosperity, the upper layers of the need or motive hierarchy are to be addressed, as they are considered particularly relevant to behavior (Kroeber-Riel 1992, p. 141 f.; Meffert 1986, p. 151).

In relation to insurance, *Haller* investigates the question of in which layers of needs the lack of security manifests itself (Haller 1975, p. 19). Essential parts of external security are found in the layer of existential needs (protection against illness, disability, and similar threats). Further external security needs emerge with increasing prosperity: They arise from the danger that existing conditions could deteriorate. The pursuit of security thus increasingly asserts itself in the area of social and ego needs. The growing importance of social and ego needs also affects the pursuit of internal security: The more a person frees himself from existential worries, the more he turns to his relationship with others and himself. It can be stated that with increasing prosperity, the desire for security—and thus for security services—increases. Security is therefore, in contrast to *Maslow's* theory, a fundamental human need that encompasses all layers of needs (Köhne 1997, p. 69).

In addition to the **classification** of motivation according to the drive component, the **classification according to the involved cognitive components (II.)** is conceivable: A distinction based on the extent of product knowledge results from the fact that product knowledge is required for purchase motivation on the one hand, and is responsible for its divergent occurrence in products that require explanation or do not require explanation on the other hand. Insurance is one of the products that require explanation.

The analysis and classification of motivation according to product knowledge can be carried out using the so-called **laddering concept**; it serves to make visible the subjective knowledge that causes a product to be linked with basic emotions in such a way that a concrete motivation to purchase the product arises. Such analyses should focus on the benefits that the offered products have for the customer, and not on the objective product characteristics (Kroeber-Riel 1992, pp. 143–145).

However, the concept of motivation is not to be equated with that of motive. The motive as the basic drive of behavior underlies motivation as an actualized reason for action. The needs form on the original level of motivation into an inner drive or desire for a specific action. With the addition of means of satisfaction, the phenomenon of need shifts to the level of conscious and volitional decision making (which are dealt with in connection with cognitive variables) and is thus transformed into a demand, i.e., an object-oriented intention to act. The same applies to the concrete **insurance need**: It is understood as the actual demand for insurance services in the market, which is a general **insurance need** that is endowed with purchasing power and has been concretized (actualized) in terms of its satisfaction (Krüger-Barvels 1971, p. 91).

Insurance needs can almost exclusively be traced back to the fundamental need for security. In relation to life insurance, further or more differentiated needs may be survivor protection, one's own old-age provision, the securing of contractual obligations, savings and wealth accumulation, and the achievement of tax savings. Needs regarding property & casualty insurance, on the other hand, primarily relate to the protection or preservation of property and assets (Krüger-Barvels 1971, pp. 84 f.; Wähling et al. 1993, p. 174; Kremer 1994, pp. 69, 78–81; Haller and Ackermann 1995, Part 3, p. 8; Puschmann 2003, pp. 123–125).

In relation to the need for insurance, it is important to point out the **phenomenon of the prospective reduction of future potential needs** (see also under availability heuristic and overly optimistic assessment in Sect. 4.2.1). The sales success of an insurance company depends crucially on the fact that insurance needs maintain a certain degree of immediacy. This means that future needs gain relevance when they are highly likely to occur and are perceived as an acute threat. The challenge lies in convincing potential policyholders of the urgency of taking out insurance before they have learned from damage (Krüger-Barvels 1971, p. 89). In all branches (except life insurance on survival or some variants thereof such as marriage or education insurance), the policyholder receives a visible return for his premium payment only under a condition that is very unpleasant for him, namely the occurrence of an insured risk such as fire, burglary, accident, illness, etc. The insurance company thus sells a monetary benefit in the case of a loss, which the customer actually does not want (Farny 1961, p. 132). At the same time, many customers perceive the benefit of insurance according to the loss concept (see Sect. 2.2.2). Consequently, the insurance cannot score points if the loss does not occur.

> **Note** The central need underlying the **demand for insurance** is the **need for security**. With increasing prosperity, which can be observed in German-speaking countries, the need for security also increases, especially the **desire for inner security**. However, it must be taken into account that many private customers use decision heuristics because they are subject to cognitive biases (see Sect. 4.2.1) and sometimes even have irrational ideas about the insurance product when their purchase is actually based on the desire to eliminate the danger as such, i.e., to escape fate (Pesendorfer 1982). On the other hand, there is the widespread belief that the performance of the insurance consists in its payment of losses, and therefore one should receive at least as much money from the insurance as one has paid in premiums.

The **attitude** as the third activating process was defined as the link between motivation and cognitive object assessment. This view is based on the goal-means analysis of attitudes. Accordingly, attitudes can be described as the subjectively perceived suitability of an object to satisfy a motivation. It is noteworthy that the object assessment is based on entrenched (stored) views. *Meffert et al.* describe attitudes as "internal predispositions of an individual to consistently react positively or negatively to certain stimuli in the environment" (Meffert et al. 2019, p. 108).

The construct of attitude is most often used to explain buyer behavior. Because it is **proven that attitudes measured today determine tomorrow's behavior**. In purchase behavior predictions, it can therefore be assumed that the probability of purchase increases with the increasing strength of a positive attitude towards the product (Kroeber-Riel 1992, p. 165).

In the interpretation and analysis of attitudes, three components are distinguished (Kroeber-Riel 1992, p. 165; Kroeber-Riel and Gröppel-Klein 2019, p. 208 f.):

1. The **affective** component; it contains the emotional assessment of an object associated with an attitude (this is the attitude in the narrower sense).
2. The **cognitive** component; it includes the thoughts associated with an attitude. This refers to the consumer's subjective knowledge about the object.
3. The **conative or intentional** component; it describes a tendency to act associated with the attitude (intention to act, readiness to buy).

From this tripartite division, it follows that on the one hand, the intention to act can be related to the object-related concept of attitude, and on the other hand, the connection between the affectively defined attitude and its cognitive basis can be established.

It is critical to note that despite these correlations between the attitude towards a specific brand and the willingness to buy, there are often significant deviations. The characteristics that determine the attitude towards a product are not necessarily identical to those factors that justify the attitude towards an action (Meffert 1986, p. 153). A remedy here can be the **inclusion of typical influences of the buying situation**. In relation to the insurance industry, this means that the customer's risk situation comes into play alongside activating factors such as emotion, motivation, and attitude. It determines the intensity of the insurance need and thus the demand (Kroeber-Riel 1992, p. 170; Krüger-Barvels 1971, p. 91; Kroeber-Riel and Gröppel-Klein 2019, pp. 211–213).

The buying behavior of private customers can only be partially explained by emotions, motives, and attitudes alone, as activating processes are always more or less accompanied by cognitive processes (recognition and consciousness processes). These can be described as thought or rational processes. Through them, the individual gains knowledge of his environment and of himself. **Cognitive processes** serve the mental control and voluntary steering of customer behavior. They include information intake, perception including judgment, and decision-making (Kroeber-Riel 1992, p. 218).

The **intake of information** includes the processes that lead to the adoption of information into the central processor, i.e., into the short-term or working memory. The findings of information research are of great importance, especially for advertising issues. But also with regard to product design and sales policy, the process of information intake is insightful (Kroeber-Riel 1992, pp. 261–264; Kroeber-Riel and Gröppel-Klein 2019, pp. 282–340):

1. The correlation applies that the drive to seek additional information is stronger, the **greater the perceived purchase risk** is. However, one should not overlook the motivational function of perceived risk in such considerations. Because to what extent information is actually sought depends on the selection of available risk reduction strategies. In the insurance sector, the majority of private customers are exposed to an increased purchase risk due to the increasing variety of products and the associated lack of clarity in the market, which necessitates increased information search.
2. Personal communication plays by far the largest role in information procurement, while mass communication plays a relatively minor role. The superiority of personal information through sellers, acquaintances, etc., is based on its adaptation to the specific information wishes of individual private customers. In addition, personal information accommodates the customer's convenience, as he can take over pre-digested information as well as ready-made opinions and evaluations (see also availability heuristic in Sect. 4.2.1). This fact is of constitutive importance for the insurance industry: The success of insurance companies and the trust in the use of intermediaries is based on this.

Information intake is examined and explained in the context of marketing theory using various models of consumer behavior (see in depth Meffert et al. 2019, pp. 104–131; Homburg 2020, pp. 57–112). With regard to insurance as an information product, information economics is particularly suitable for this (Nickel-Waninger 1987, pp. 1–162; see also Sect. 10.2.2, Research Window Product Concepts).

The possibilities of information intake have significantly increased in the internet age and have improved enormously both qualitatively and quantitatively. At least potentially, this has reduced the information asymmetry between insurance companies and intermediaries on the one hand and customers on the other, or shifted it in favor of the demanders. As mentioned, the interest of private customers in information about insurance topics in general is low (Sect. 1.1.1). Precisely for this reason, intermediaries, but also the immediate personal environment, play a crucial role in the context of information intake, as customers can shorten the (annoying) process of information intake through them.

The cognitive process of **perception and evaluation** also influences the demand behavior of private insurance buyers through subjectivity, activity, and selectivity of perception. It is not the objective offer that determines the demand behavior, but the subjectively perceived one. It is not enough to offer objective services. These services must also be perceived by the (potential) customers. The consumer mainly perceives stimuli that correspond to his needs and desires. Perception is largely based on experience and is the result of learning processes. A distinction must be made between conscious and unconscious perception. The focus here is primarily on conscious perception, which includes active and selective information processes and depends significantly on subjective knowledge, the expectations derived from it, and subjective motivation (Kroeber-Riel 1992, p. 266–271; Bittl and Vielreicher 1994, p. 194; Meffert et al. 2019, p. 95 f.).

The **hypothesis theory of perception** can be used as a descriptive and explanatory approach for individual demand for insurance coverage. It also simultaneously provides a theoretical foundation for the demand to focus on the customer and his individual needs in the context of customer orientation. Individuals are therefore constantly exposed to various risks, which they initially perceive differently depending on their own, subjective risk attitude. In addition to the individual risk attitude, life situations in which a person finds themselves also influence their **risk perception and risk awareness**. The risk perception, which is thus dependent on the situation, in turn leads to individual insurance needs (Bittl and Vielreicher 1994, p. 195 f.).

While the type and extent of assets (which can be more objectively determined) are also important risk characteristics for the individual risk situation: Only those who have something to insure at all feel a lack of security if they do not have insurance coverage. However, in all cases where the occurrence of loss is affected by the subjective behavior of the policyholder, the subjective risk must be recorded separately: Because first, the personal assessment of the individual risk situation can deviate from the actual one (incorrect risk assessment). Second, the actual danger situation can be reacted to differently depending on individual risk tolerance (different risk behavior). Both lead to a higher objective risk due to a higher subjective risk (Krüger-Barvels 1971, p. 95).

The different **risk acceptance** mentioned in the second aspect is (empirically proven) determined by various pairs of characteristics (Zweifel and Pedroni 1988, p. 33):

1. **Voluntary/involuntary**: The most important evaluation criterion is whether one takes a risk voluntarily or whether one is involuntarily exposed to a danger. The former significantly increases risk tolerance.
2. **Familiar/unknown**: Getting used to a danger reduces fears of it.
3. **Danger to oneself/to society**: If an individual is threatened by a risk, it shows a lower risk tolerance than if it were threatened by this risk as part of society.
4. **Low/high number of endangered**: A disaster with many injured or dead is perceived as worse (lower risk tolerance) than if the same number of injured/dead occurs over the course of a year ("Flying is more dangerous than driving a car").

These examples show that the **actual states of consciousness** of the customer are **not rational in most cases**. A "mature" insurance consciousness thus represents the ideal case in which perception is not subjectively distorted. However, it is emotionally comprehended by few.

Individuals strive for internal consistency of their information. They try to protect themselves from too much information about a risk. The number of everyday risk situations is so large (information overload) that an unrestricted amount of risk information would overwhelm the individual and render them incapable of action. Therefore, mechanisms of repression and selection are used. A **faulty risk anticipation due to repression, isolation, or selective perception** leads to a conscious or unconscious (see also representativeness heuristic, Sect. 4.2.1) misjudgment of the probability of loss occurrence and the extent of loss. If the latter two factors are greatly underestimated, there is usually a lack of motivation for a problem-conscious risk behavior (Müller-Reichart 1993, pp. 195–197).

Many policyholders are not aware of their risk situation or do not understand the benefits of different types of insurance: Because an accident as a result of sporting activity, as well as the onset of disability, are considered rare events (probability of loss), the risk is underestimated and a corresponding insurance need is denied. This attitude is even more pronounced with regard to liability risk. It is overlooked that the occurrence of damage can have such severe financial consequences (extent of loss) that a single occurrence is enough to ruin the uninsured. On the other hand, more frequently occurring damages with affordable sums are more present in the customer's consciousness (see also availability heuristic, Sect. 4.2.1), and therefore he seeks insurance coverage here.

According to these assessments, product and service evaluations by customers are distorted. Contrary to the assumptions of classical decision theory (Sect. 4.1), the **vast majority of private customers are thus unable to correctly assess the product benefit**. Due to the rather unusual contract content, customers easily have false ideas about the product. In addition, the time-relatedness of the insurance contract intensifies this, as the insured's ideas about the contract content often change during the (usually long) term. This leads to the customer perceiving a quality that does not satisfy him, although the insurer's performance has remained the one that the customer acquired when the contract was concluded. It is worth mentioning in this regard the customer behavior observed in reality of individual policyholders who consciously waive certain risk inclusions at the time of contract conclusion, but then expect full coverage in the event of a claim (Stremitzer and Ennsfeller 1994, p. 387 f.).

> **Note** It should be noted regarding the **risk perception by private customers** that an objectively and subjectively large risk can lead to a relatively low insurance need due to individual misjudgment and/or risk-loving behavior; conversely, relatively small risks can generate a comparatively large demand due to overestimation and/or a pronounced desire for security.

Finally, the cognitive process of **decision-making** is important for the demand behavior of private insurance customers: It is interesting that the **product choice only in exceptional cases** is based on decisions that have been made **consciously and deliberately**. Consumer research therefore considers the conscious decision as a special case of product choice. Often, the product choice is thoughtless and rather random or it is dominated by strong emotions—in the case of impulsive buying. If one wants to examine the various behaviors of private customers, they can be represented on a scale from "very strongly cognitively controlled" to "very weakly cognitively controlled". Very weakly cognitively controlled is the stimulus-driven, impulsive behavior of the demander, who reacts largely automatically to a product presentation. In habitual behavior, the demander follows already actively defined behavior plans (product loyalty). Only when the consumer weighs the pros and cons of a product choice are there "real" decisions.

In this context, it is important to note the relationships between involvement (interest, inclusion) and purchasing behavior, from which typical purchasing decisions are derived. The **classic purchasing decisions** are therefore **extensive, rational, habitual, and impulsive** decisions (Table 4.3). Extensive decisions are characterized by detailed, comprehensive information gathering from as many different sources as possible and a differentiated decision preparation. They tend to require more time and are often used for

Table 4.3 Purchasing behavior and involvement. (Based on Kroeber-Riel and Gröppel-Klein 2019, p. 391)

Involvement		Purchasing behavior
Cognitive	Emotional	
Pronounced	Pronounced	Extensive decision
Pronounced	Not pronounced	Rational decision
Not pronounced	Pronounced	Impulsive decision
Not pronounced	Not pronounced	Habitual decision

more complicated, expensive and/or long-term binding purchases (e.g., house purchase with financing and security; retirement provision). Rational decisions are based on a targeted and time-saving decision preparation. Once the buyer has received the first offer that meets his wishes, he stops the search process and decides to buy. Further search is considered not beneficial by the time-benefit ratio (e.g., relatively rare replacement purchases of a light bulb, screw, battery). Due to the limited time commitment, they are also referred to as limited decisions. Habitual decisions are based on habit. The product, the place where it is available, and its price are known. These are simple, less time-intensive purchasing decisions (e.g., cigarettes, daily newspaper, other everyday goods). Impulsive decisions are characterized by spontaneous actions triggered by a stimulus or impulse. They are due to a momentary need, hence rarely rational because they are unprepared, but also require little preparation time (e.g., souvenirs on holiday trips, food when thirsty or hungry).

For the **insurance industry**, a (so far) **mostly not pronounced cognitive involvement** has been noted (Farny 2011, p. 429 f.). Emotional involvement, on the other hand, often exists—as described above—although it tends to distort perception. The **purchase decision** then, according to the classification in Table 4.3, tends to have an **impulsive character**. The many contracts concluded through the intermediary, which result from personal conversation, seem to confirm this statement. If customers are neither cognitively nor emotionally involved in insurance matters, but still buy insurance coverage because the relationship with an intermediary was decisive for the conclusion (relationship sale), this corresponds to a habitualized purchase decision; not the insurance company or the product characteristics are in the foreground, but the intermediary. The **habitualized buying behavior** is likely to be **still very widespread** in the private customer business today. However, if one argues that for the sale of a "quality product", where quality is the decisive buying factor, at least a cognitively involved demander and thus a rational decision is necessary, this explains the demands of consumer protection and regulation advocates regarding information and transparency, which should promote an enlightened, informed demander. This is also provided with comprehensive information through new media. The **proportion of rational purchase decisions** with pronounced cognitive involvement and rather low emotional involvement is therefore likely to **increase**. Nevertheless, purchase decisions with low cognitive involvement will continue to make up a large part of private insurance demand, because insurance is and remains a classic low-interest product and because people's ability to absorb information is limited: The consumer uses only a small part of the offered information for his decision, and three to five impressions explain more than 80% of the judgment variance (Kroeber-Riel 1992, p. 319 and 399).

Interim Conclusion: Psychological Factors Have a Significant Impact on the Buying Behavior of Private Insurance Policyholders

It can be concluded that activating and cognitive processes usually occur together and both determine the demand behavior of private customers. They do this in a person-specific weighting, which is also influenced by the specific situation in which the customer currently finds himself. For example, a customer who has recently experienced the death of a close friend, whose family is inadequately provided for financially, will approach the topic of retirement provision emotionally and rationally differently than a customer who has not yet had direct contact with this topic.

4.3.3 Personal Factors Influencing Insurance Demand

The buyer's decisions are influenced not only by psychological factors but also by **personal characteristics** such as demographics (age, gender), profession, economic situation (income and wealth), lifestyle, or personality (Kotler et al. 2022, pp. 266–279). These lead to the psychological needs for individual security being concretized into an individual need for insurance (Bittl and Vielreicher 1994, p. 196).

The **age** and thus the demographic development have a direct influence on the demand for insurance: Depending on their age, consumers have different attitudes and needs towards insurance services. In life insurance, age is used to calculate premiums because it affects the intensity of the need for protection. Moreover, structural demographic developments mean changes in needs. The low birth rate, later entry into professional life, and the increasingly higher life expectancy of retirees change the demands on security services. By 2035, approximately 19.8 million citizens, i.e., 24% of the population, will be over 67 years old, which is one in four citizens. After deducting those under 20 years old, this is almost one in three customers of a intermediary (Federal Statistical Office 2021, Table 11, p. 164).

Closely related to this issue is the question of gender. In personal insurance, the **gender** leads to different needs for insurance coverage due to various risk constellations, e.g., women can become pregnant once or several times. Moreover, they live longer on average than men, which reduces their mortality risk compared to men but increases their pension risk.

It is undisputed that the **profession** also has a significant influence on the buying behavior of customers. This becomes particularly clear when considering the different situations of self-employed, employees, or civil servants—especially regarding life and health insurance.

The **economic situation** of the policyholder is also important for the intensity and especially for the scope of the insurance demand. High incomes correlate with correspondingly generous budgets for insurance expenditures. Insurance is among the goods that are demanded disproportionately to the general income development. By the way, income plays a dual role in determining needs: Where it is about securing the standard of living, it becomes a substantive component of the needs analysis. But it also determines the demand potential, as only needs equipped with sufficient income (purchasing power) lead to demand.

The customer's economic situation is determined by income and wealth: The larger the wealth, the greater the fear of losses and the potential for loss. The increase in tangible assets in private households necessitates an increase in insurance coverage. Private households have increasingly larger assets (see Sect. 3.2.3).

The **personal lifestyle** stands for a pattern of a person's way of life, which is reflected in activities, interests, and attitudes. It encompasses more than the social class and the personality of a customer, as the social class disregards individuality and the personality does not say much about the actual activities, interests, and opinions of this individual. The lifestyle is therefore essentially a personal influencing factor resulting from the interaction of various psychological (especially behavior-related), personal (especially those concerning the economic situation), and social (social class) influencing factors. As an action profile, it determines the demand behavior.

4.3.4 Social Factors Influencing Insurance Demand

While psychological and personal factors cause intrapersonal influences on demand behavior, **social** aspects are interpersonal **influencing factors** (Meffert et al. 2019, p. 93). Social factors include the family, various reference groups from the immediate environment, and the life cycle phase in which one finds oneself.

The **family** or family members are the primary group most strongly influencing purchasing behavior. The family shapes customer behavior in two ways: On the one hand, the parents' family influences attitudes towards religious, political, and economic issues as well as feelings such as personal ambition, self-esteem, etc. On the other hand, one's own family with spouse and children is important for daily life.

Of the private households, those households consisting of families are of the greatest importance. This refers both to the number (quantitative) and to the problematics of family decisions (qualitative). However, the number of families is decreasing, whereas single-person households (singles) are increasingly coming into focus. They already accounted for 41% of all households in 2022 and are expected to increase to between 42 and over 44% by 2035, depending on the forecast (Federal Statistical Office 2023c). With regard to the influence of the family on individual purchasing behavior, three profound changes should be highlighted:

1. the trend towards the nuclear family (and singlehood);
2. the increased employment of women and
3. the increasing influence of reference groups outside the family.

The employment of women and the weaker kinship relations emanating from the nuclear family have led to a significant increase in social influences on family members from outside. The importance of family members for individual and joint purchasing decisions is therefore decreasing (Kroeber-Riel 1992, p. 452).

▶ **Reference Groups** are communities of people who exert a direct, immediately personal, or an indirect influence on the attitudes, behaviors, and ultimately purchasing decisions of an individual.

The behavior of a person is influenced by numerous other **reference groups** apart from the family. Groups with direct influence can be divided into primary groups with frequent and constant contacts between the members (family, circle of friends, neighbors, colleagues, certain social networks) and secondary groups with more formal relationships (religious community, professional associations, trade unions). The potential primary groups have numerically increased due to the greatly grown influence of social media (see also Sect. 14.2.5) because these media have created numerous, mostly new, social networks.

In a broader sense, idols and opinion leaders as well as influencers are also to be counted as reference persons here. Membership in a group enables group discussion. In the course of this communication, an exchange of information and opinions takes place, in which the individual group members usually accept information with trust (Kotler et al. 2022, pp. 261–264).

The social environment is also influenced by the **life phase** in which one finds oneself (life cycle). Accordingly, the **life cycle concept** is based on a socio-demographic segmentation: It assumes that despite all individuality of private individuals, a common need for provision and financial services can be derived from the respective life circumstances, which changes with the position of the customers and their interests in the life cycle (Bruhn et al. 2019, p. 230 f.) (see Sect. 8.2.3.2).

4.3.5 Cultural Factors Influencing Insurance Demand

The **cultural circle** determines a person's desires and behaviors, as human behavior is largely learned. During growth, one acquires certain fundamental values, ideas, preferences, and behaviors that are shaped by the cultural circle. Within certain tolerance limits, a conforming behavior of the society members is established (Görgen 2007, p. 23–25). According to the extent of this behavioral leeway, must, should, and can norms can be distinguished: Consumption-relevant must expectations are based on prohibitions and commands. An insurance-specific example is liability insurance when buying a car. Should and can expectations, on the other hand, establish more general behavioral standards and ensure a larger behavioral leeway.

Cultural and subcultural **norms are the most important social behavior determinants**. A look at lifestyle helps to uncover cultural and subcultural behavior patterns, as lifestyle is shaped by the values at a higher level in addition to attitudes. And it is precisely these values—ideas of desirability and fundamental goal concepts—that determine the motives, attitudes, and behaviors of people. Thus, cultural differences are particularly evident in the value attitudes of citizens. Cultural values are partly constant if they are based on firm beliefs and value concepts. Partly, however, they are subject to dynamic changes and thus shape the cultural circle in a differentiated way. Changes in people's image of themselves and their fellow human beings, their attitude towards organizations, society, nature, and the universe and religion can be observed (worldwide and also in Germany) (Kotler et al. 2022, p. 179–182). Looking at Germany, it is noticeable that in recent years or decades a relatively profound **change in values** has taken place, which is characterized by the following tendencies (Köhne 1997, p. 99–102; Görgen 2007, p. 17, 35 f.; Meffert et al. 2019, p. 136–142; Kotler et al. 2022, p. 159–164, 179–182):

- Education explosion among the population part that participates in education and further training,
- therefore, a widening gap in the level of education between the educated population and those who dropped out of the education system early,
- a changing concept of family with altered role models within the family,
- Increase in migration and resulting, among other things, in ethnic diversity in the population,
- increasing sense of entitlement,
- Individualization, associated with the search and choice of diverse options (multi-option society) and associated with a divided consumer consciousness that allows luxury orientation and extreme price orientation at the same time (hybrid customer behavior),
- related to this, the loss of importance of certain values such as religious faith values, solidarity, consideration, or renunciation in favor of others, but at the same time also
- Postmaterialistic consumer behavior, i.e., ethical orientation, strong environmental and health awareness, and a tendency to consume collectively (see Sect. 3.2.3).

Every culture also contains numerous, smaller **subcultures** or groups of people who share a value system based on common life experiences and circumstances. Classic examples are nationalities, religions, ethnic groups or regional subcultures, but also groups oriented towards leisure activities (hobbies) such as bodybuilders, motorcyclists or mountain hikers as well as nerds, gamers or silver agers. If these are characterized by special, common needs for products or services, they should be addressed from a marketing perspective. For example, the "**young at heart seniors**", the market segment "55+", are interesting for insurers because they represent a large and increasing proportion of the population and have about two and a half times as much available means as the 16- to 34-year-olds, i.e., they have higher incomes and assets. In addition, they have a subculture: They are open to new things (brand change), health-conscious, travel-affine, much more active and mobile than before. And they are increasingly digital: Two thirds use the internet, almost half own a smartphone and a third are active in social media (Kotler et al. 2022, p. 255–258). Basically, the empirically recognizable differences of the generations also count here, so that the baby boomers, Generation X, Y (Millennials), Z and α also have their own subcultures.

Apart from the cultural circle, the **social class** can also influence insurance demand. Social classes exist in almost every cultural circle. The term "social class" describes groups of people whose societal contributions are valued approximately equally, whose prestige and social status do not differ greatly from each other. Social classes show clear product and brand preferences, so that a company's marketing efforts can focus on certain classes. At the same time, they demand different ways of communication: An insurer can, for example, sell insurance products to certain customer segments—in terms of social class, e.g. lower, middle and upper class—via certain, like-minded types of intermediaries. This happens in practice, but more due to mutual affinities than conscious control.

Interim Conclusion on the Explanatory Contributions of Theoretical Approaches to Private Customer Insurance Demand

It is not possible to comprehensively explain insurance demand in a theoretical model because human behavior in reality is too complex and is influenced by too many (sometimes situational) conditions. However, the added value of theoretical approaches lies in explaining basic principles and structures of decision-making processes and creating an understanding of the associated possibilities and limitations. Thus, decision-theoretical models explain rational decisions under economic utility aspects, which are at least aimed at by a—however large—part of the demanders or whose argumentation at least flows into the decision-making process. The more psychologically influenced behavioral economic approaches explain the numerous cognitive biases that stand in the way of a purely rational decision. They too undoubtedly flow into the decision-making process. Finally, consumer behavior research systematizes all actually given objective and subjective influencing factors of the purchase decision and thus provides various starting points for insurance marketing, be it for understanding the peculiarities of marketing research in the insurance industry (Sect. 5.4) or of customer value (Sect. 8.3.2.1) and as a basis for target group marketing (Sect. 8.3.1.2), for the design of the deductible and the product documents (Sect. 10.2), of the advisory and intermediary approach (Sect. 13.6) and of personal communication (Sect. 14.2.3).

Further Reading Recommendations for Chap. 4

- Barberis 2013.
- Dolan et al. 2012.
- Kahneman 2014.
- Kotler et al. 2022, Sects. 3.3 and 5.3.
- Latzel 2020.
- Schulenburg and Lohse 2014, Chap. IV.
- Spreer 2021.
- Theil 2002.
- Zweifel and Eisen 2012, Chap. 3.

References

Adams, P./Hunt, S. (2013): Encouraging Consumers to Claim Redress: Evidence from a Field Trial, in: Financial Conduct Authority (Ed.), Occasional Paper, Nr. 2, London, 2013.

Agnew, J.R./Anderson, L.R./Gerlach, J.R./Szykman, L.R. (2008): Who Chooses Annuities? An Experimental Investigation of the Role of Gender, Framing, and Defaults, in: American Economic Review: Papers & Proceedings, Vol. 98, 2008, No. 2, pp. 418–422.

Barberis, N.C. (2013): Thirty Years of Prospect Theory in Economics: A Review and Assessment, in: Journal of Economic Perspectives, Vol. 27, 2013, No 1, pp. 173–196.

Benartzi, S./Thaler, R.H. (1995): Myopic loss aversion and the equity premium puzzle, in: The Quarterly Journal of Economics, Vol. 110, 1995, No. 1, pp. 75–92.

Bender-Scheel, M.S. (2012): Die Satisfaction-Profit Chain in der Logistikdienstleistungsbranche, Eine Längsschnittanalyse, Wiesbaden, 2012.

Bittl, A./Vielreicher, P. (1994): Individuelle Wahrnehmung und Versiche rungsnachfrage, Konsequenzen für Produktgestaltung und Unterneh menskommunikation von Versicherungsunternehmen, in: ZVersWiss, Jg. 83, 1994, Nr. 1–2, pp. 193–217.

Brown, J.R./Kling, J.R./Mullainathan, S./Wrobel, M.V. (2008): Why Don't People Insure Late-Life Consumption? A Framing Explanation of the Under-Annuitization Puzzle, in: American Economic Review, Vol. 98, 2008, No. 2, pp. 304–309.

Bruhn, M./Meffert, H./Hadwich, K. (2019): Handbuch Dienstleistungsmarketing. Planung – Umsetzung – Kontrolle, Wiesbaden, 2. Aufl., 2019.

Chewning, E.G./Harrell, A.M. (1990): The Effect of Information Load on Decision Makers' Cue Utilization Levels and Decision Quality in a Financial Distress Decision Task, in: Accounting, Organizations and Society, Vol. 15, 1990, No. 6, pp. 527–542.

Dolan, P./Elliott, A./Metcalfe, R./Vlaev, I. (2012): Influencing Financial Behaviour: from Changing Minds to Changing Contexts, in: Journal of Behavioural Finance, Vol. 13, 2012, No. 2, pp. 126–142.

Duden (Ed.) (2023): Heuristik, in: https://www.duden.de/rechtschreibung/Heuristik, Accessed: 29.12.2023.

Ebert, S./Koos, B./Schneider, J.C. (2012): On the optimal type and level of guarantees for prospect theory investors. Paris December 2012 Finance Meeting EUROFIDAIAFFI Paper.

Eppler, M.J./Mengis, J. (2004): The Concept of Information Overload: A Review of Literature from Organization Science, Accounting, Marketing, MIS, and Related Disciplines, in: The Information Society, Vol. 20, 2004, No. 5, pp. 325–344.

European Insurance and Occupational Pensions Authority (EIOPA) (Ed.) (2017): Draft Implementing Technical Standards concerning a standardised presentation format for the Insurance Product Information Document of the Insurance Distribution Directive, EIOPA-17/056, o.O., 2017.

Farny, D. (1961): Die Versicherungsmärkte, Berlin, 1961.

Farny, D. (2011): Versicherungsbetriebslehre, Karlsruhe, 5. Aufl., 2011.

Gaedeke, O. (2021): Vertriebseffizienz mit Behavioral Economics und Entscheidertypen steigern, Select Typen in b4p Mediaanalyse und -planung, Sirius Campus-White Paper vom 16.08.2021.

Görgen, F. (2007): Versicherungsmarketing, Strategien, Instrumente und Controlling, Stuttgart, 2. Aufl., 2007.

Gottlieb, D. (2012): Prospect theory, life insurance, and annuities. The Wharton School Research Paper, No. 44, University of Pennsylvania, 2012.

Graf, S. (2017): Life-cycle funds: Much ado about nothing?, in: The European Journal of Finance, Vol. 23, 2017, No. 11, pp. 974–998.

Graf, S./Ruß, J./Schelling, S. (2017): As you like it: Explaining the demand for lifecycle funds with multi cumulative prospect theory. Working paper IFA Ulm, 2017.

Haller, M. (1975): Sicherheit durch Versicherung? Gedanken zur zukünftigen Rolle der Versicherung, Bern, 1975.

Haller, M./Ackermann, W. (1995): Versicherungswirtschaft – kundenorientiert, Zürich, 1995.

Homburg, C. (2020): Marketingmanagement, Strategie – Instrumente – Umsetzung – Unternehmensführung, Wiesbaden, 7. Aufl., 2020.

Huber, C./Schlager, T. (2011): To Buy or not to Buy Insurance? The Antecedents in the Decision-Making Process and the Influence of Consumer Attitudes and Perceptions, Working Papers on Risk Management and Insurance, No. 90, St. Gallen, 2011.

Huber, C./Gatzert, N./Schmeiser, H. (2015): How Does Price Presentation Influence Consumer Choice? The Case of Life Insurance Products, in: JoRI, Vol. 82, 2015, No. 2, pp. 401–431.

Hu, W.Y./Scott, J.S. (2007): Behavioral obstacles in the annuity market, in: Financial Analysts Journal, Vol. 63, 2007, No. 6, pp. 71–82.

Kahneman, D. (2014): Schnelles Denken, langsames Denken, München, 7. Aufl., 2014.

Kahneman, D./Tversky, A. (1979): Prospect theory, An analysis of decision under risk, in: Econometrica, Vol. 47, 1979, No. 2, pp. 263–291.

Kahneman, D./Knetsch, J./Thaler, R. (1991): The Endowment Effect, Loss Aversion, and Status Quo Bias: Anomalies, in: Journal of Economic Perspectives, Vol. 5, 1991, No. 1, pp. 193–206.

Knoller, C. (2016): Multiple reference points and the demand for principal-protected life annuities: An experimental analysis, in: Journal of Risk and Insurance, Vol. 83, 2016, No. 1, pp. 217–255.

Köhne, T. (1997): Die Wirkungsversicherung im Privatkundengeschäft – Implikationen für eine kundenorientierte Marktleistungsgestaltung, St. Gallen, 1997.

Kotler, P./Armstrong, G./Harris, L.C./He, H. (2022): Grundlagen des Marketing, Halbergmoos, 8. Aufl., 2022.

Kremer, M. (1994): Das Nachfrageverhalten von Versicherungs- und Bankkunden aus ganzheitlicher Sicht – Konsequenzen für den Finanzdienstleistungsgedanken, St. Gallen, 1994.

Kroeber-Riel, W. (1992): Konsumentenverhalten, München, 5. Aufl., 1992.

Kroeber-Riel, W./Gröppel-Klein, A. (2019): Konsumentenverhalten, München, 11. Aufl., 2019.

Krüger-Barvels, R. (1971): Marketing im Versicherungsbetrieb, Freiburg i.B., 1971.

Latzel, C. (2020): Verhaltenssteuerung, Recht und Privatautonomie, Berlin, 2020.

Maslow, A.M. (1970): Motivation and Personality, New York, 2. Aufl., 1970.

Meffert, H. (1986): Grundlagen der Absatzpolitik, Wiesbaden, 1986.

Meffert, H./Burmann, C./Kirchgeorg, M./Eisenbeiß, M. (2019): Marketing, Grundlagen marktorientierter Unternehmensführung, Konzepte – Instrumente – Praxisbeispiele, Wiesbaden, 13. Aufl., 2019.

Mossin, J. (1968): Aspects of Rational Insurance Purchasing, in: Journal of Political Economy, Vol. 79, 1968, pp. 553–568.

Müller-Reichart, M. (1993): Risiko-Management privater Haushalte, in: Brunner, W.L./Vollath, J. (Eds.), Handbuch Finanzdienstleistungen, Stuttgart, 1993, pp. 191–201.

Nickel-Waninger, H. (1987): Versicherungsmarketing, auf der Grundlage des Marketing von Informationsprodukten, Karlsruhe, 1987.

Papon, T. (2008): The Effect of Pre-commitment and Past-Experience on Insurance Choices: An Experimental Study, in: The Geneva Risk and Insurance Review, Vol. 33, 2008, No. 1, pp. 47–73.

Pesendorfer, B. (1982): Zur Theorie von Angst und Gefahr, Sicherheit und Versicherung, Einige theoretische Grundlagen zum besseren Verständnis der Haltungen von privaten Versicherungsnehmern, Arbeitspapier, St. Gallen, 1982.

Puschmann, K.-H. (2003): Praxis des Versicherungsmarketing, Karlsruhe, 2. Aufl., 2003.

Richter, A./Ruß, J./Schelling, S. (2018): Moderne Verhaltensökonomie in der Versicherungswirtschaft, Denkanstöße für ein besseres Verständnis der Kunden, Wiesbaden, 2018.

Rothschild, M./Stiglitz, J.E. (1976): Equilibrium in Competitive Insurance Markets: The Economics of Markets with Imperfect Information, in: Quarterly Journal of Economics, Vol. 90, 1976, pp. 111–125.

Ruß, J./Schelling, S. (2017): Multi cumulative prospect theory and the demand for cliquet-style guarantees, in: Journal of Risk and Insurance. https://doi.org/10.1111/jori.12195.

Schlesinger, H. (1994): Zur Theorie der Versicherungsnachfrage, in: ZVersWiss, Jg. 83, 1994, Nr. 1/2, pp. 113–136.

Schulenburg, J.-M. Graf von der/Lohse, U. (2014): Versicherungsökonomik, Karlsruhe, 2. Aufl., 2014.

Shavell, S. (1979): On Moral Hazard and Insurance, in: Quarterly Journal of Economics, Vol. 93, 1979, pp. 541–562.

Simon, H.A. (1986): Rationality in Psychology and Economics, in: The Journal of Business, Vol. 59, 1986, No. 4, Part 2: The Behavioral Foundations of Economic Theory, pp. 209–224.

Spreer, P. (2021): PsyConversion, Wiesbaden, 2. Aufl., 2021.

Statistisches Bundesamt (Ed.) (2021): Ausblick auf die Bevölkerungsentwicklung in Deutschland und den Bundesländern nach dem Corona-Jahr 2020, Erste mittelfristige Bevölkerungsvorausberechnung 2021 bis 2035, o.O., 2021.

Statistisches Bundesamt (Ed.) (2023c): Vorausberechnete Privathaushalte, in: https://www-genesis.destatis.de/genesis/online?sequenz=tabelleErgebnis&selectionname=12421-0100#abreadcrumb, Accessed: 02.01.2024

Steel, P. (2007): The Nature of Procrastination: A Meta-analytic and Theoretical Review of Quintessential Self-regulatory Failure, in: Psychological Bulletin, Vol. 133, 2007, No. 1, pp. 65–94.

Stremitzer, H./Ennsfeller, K.C. (1994): Gedanken zur kundenorientierten Qualität von Versicherungsdienstleistungen, in: Hesberg, D./Nell, M./Schott, W. (Eds.), Risiko, Versicherung, Markt, Festschrift für Walter Karten zur Vollendung des 60. Lebensjahres, Karlsruhe, 1994, pp. 381–399.

SwissRe (Ed.) (2013): Lebensversicherung – Fokussierung auf den Konsumenten, in: Reihe sigma, Nr. 6, Zürich, 2013.

Sydnor, J. (2010): (Over)insuring modest risks, in: American Economic Journal: Applied Economics, Vol. 2, 2010, No. 4, pp. 177–199.

Thaler, R.H. (1981): Some Empirical Evidence on Dynamic Inconsistency, in: Economic Letters, Vol. 8, 1981, No. 3, pp. 201–207.

Thaler, R.H./Benartzi, S. (2004): Save More Tomorrow: Using Behavioural Economics to Increase Employee Saving, in: Journal of Political Economy, Vol. 112, 2004, No. 1, pp. 164–187.

Theil, M. (1998): Prospect Theory's Approach to Insurance Decisions; Aspects and Challenges, in: Association Internationale pour l'Etude de l'Economie de l'Assurance (ed) Etudes et Dossiers, 1998, Nr. 220, pp. 55–72.

Theil, M. (2002): Versicherungsentscheidungen und Prospect Theory, Die Risikoeinschätzung der Versicherungsnehmer als Entscheidungsgrundlage, Wien, 2002.

Theil, M. (2003): The Value of Personal Contact in Marketing Insurance: Client Judgments of Representativeness and Mental Availability, in: Risk Management and Insurance Review, Vol. 6, 2003, No. 2, pp. 145–157.

Tversky, A./Kahneman, D. (1974): Judgment under Uncertainty: Heuristics and Biases, in: Science, Vol. 185, 1974, No. 4157, pp. 1.124–1.131.

Tversky, A./Kahneman, D. (1981): The Framing of Decisions and the Psychology of Choice, in: Science, Vol. 211, 1981, No. 4481, pp. 453–458.

Tversky, A./Kahneman, D. (1982): Availability: A Heuristic for Judging Frequency and Probability, in: Kahneman, D./Slovic, P./Tversky, A. (Eds.), Judgment under Uncertainty: Heuristics and Biases, Cambridge, 1982, pp. 163–178.

Tversky, A./Kahneman, D. (1986): Rational Choice and the Framing of Decisions, in: Journal of Business, Vol. 59, 1986, No. 4, pp. 251–278.

Tversky, A./Kahneman, D. (1992): Advances in prospect theory: Cumulative representation of uncertainty, in: Journal of Risk and Uncertainty, Vol. 5, 1992, No. 4, pp. 297–323.

Wähling, S./Trumpfheller, J./Schulenburg, J.-M. Graf von der (1993): Die Nachfragemotive nach Kapitallebensverischerungen und ihre Struktur, Eine empirische Analyse, in: VW, Jg. 48, 1993, Nr. 3, pp. 173–180.

Wiersich, M. (2013): Der Einfluss von Emotionen auf Versicherungsentscheidungen, Dissertation, Nürnberg, 2013.

Zweifel, P./Eisen, R. (2012): Insurance Economics, Heidelberg, 2012.

Zweifel, P./Pedroni, G. (1988): Chance und Risiko. Messung, Bewertung, Akzeptanz, Basel, 1988.

5 Marketing Research for Procuring Information Basics for Insurance Marketing

In the preceding chapters, the actors in financial services and insurance markets as well as the financial service products traded there (Chap. 3) and then the theoretical foundations of insurance demand (Chap. 4) have been presented. A concrete understanding of these markets, the private customers operating there, and the impact of the marketing activities carried out in the markets and with the customers then requires empirical studies and thus the application of marketing research and its methods. The most important aspects of marketing research are to be presented in three sub-chapters: First, the conceptual foundations are created and the areas of investigation and tasks of marketing research are briefly introduced (Sect. 5.1). Then, the most important methods of data collection (Sect. 5.2) and data evaluation (Sect. 5.3) are described. The presentation of marketing research is deliberately kept short because the methods and procedures in the insurance sector hardly differ from those in other industries—this rather applies to the content and objects of investigation (Sect. 5.4). The minor industry-specific features do not change the fact that the process and methods of marketing research are indispensable in academic marketing education:

1. Decision-makers in companies come into contact with marketing research information to a large extent. They must be able to interpret this, and in case of queries, they must be able to communicate with marketing research specialists.
2. In the course of academic education and further training, knowledge of these methods is often indispensable when carrying out one's own research work.

For both reasons, marketing research should at least be briefly addressed; moreover, references to further literature will be given.

T. Köhne, *Insurance Marketing*, https://doi.org/10.1007/978-3-658-47345-7_5

5.1 Concept, Subject of Investigation, Tasks and Stages of Marketing Research

Modern marketing research is characterized by numerous changes that go hand in hand with digitalization, as well as—in times of high uncertainty—by a decreasing predictability of competitive environments.

On the one hand, the central **advancements in information technology** have an impact on both information gathering and data evaluation. Nowadays, customers transmit almost infinite amounts of data in real time via various channels, and digital technologies such as smartphones make this data ubiquitous. The volume, diversity, distribution across various sources (e.g., smartphone apps, emails, social networks) and dynamic change of this data make it difficult to impossible to evaluate it in its entirety; this phenomenon is also referred to as **big data**. Data is ubiquitous and is considered the "new oil" of the digital economy. Therefore, the flood of data in most companies has continuously increased over the past decades. At the same time, the costs of data collection have often decreased, as many data, such as transactions, customer browsing behavior on the internet or the use of apps, can be automatically recorded. Accordingly, an interdisciplinary data evaluation has become necessary, which has given rise to the so-called **data science**, a science that generally deals with the generation of knowledge from all kinds of data. In addition to the growing availability of data, the possibilities for evaluating these data volumes are also increasing. The increasingly data-driven culture in many companies and increasing computing capacities allow new automated data analysis methods such as **machine learning**. Learning here refers to algorithms that recognize patterns and regularities from existing data and derive generalized knowledge from them (Homburg 2020, p. 272 f. and the literature cited there; Meffert et al. 2019, pp. 170–172). An impressive overview of the further development of data (quantity, quality, timeliness) and methods of their evaluation is shown in Fig. 5.1.

On the other hand, a growing **market dynamism** and an increasing **unpredictability of changes in the corporate environment** can be observed. Alongside a globally increased political and economic uncertainty, there is a reduced predictability of the micro and macro environment of companies due to the globalization of the world economy, rapid technological developments, and increasingly shorter product life cycles. The possible **disruption of business models** by innovations as a factor of uncertainty for companies is more pronounced than in the past. Within the markets, there are also more fragmented consumer needs, higher transparency, and thus a high bargaining power of the demand side, as well as low entry barriers. At the same time, organizational adjustments (e.g., through mergers or acquisitions) and increasingly frequent changes in legal conditions have increased complexity within companies (Homburg 2020, p. 274).

Modern marketing research can help to identify these developments early and to react to them, and can thus support entrepreneurial agility, i.e., the ability of companies to respond quickly to environmental changes and identify new opportunities for growth. Against this background, intuition and experience alone are no longer sufficient

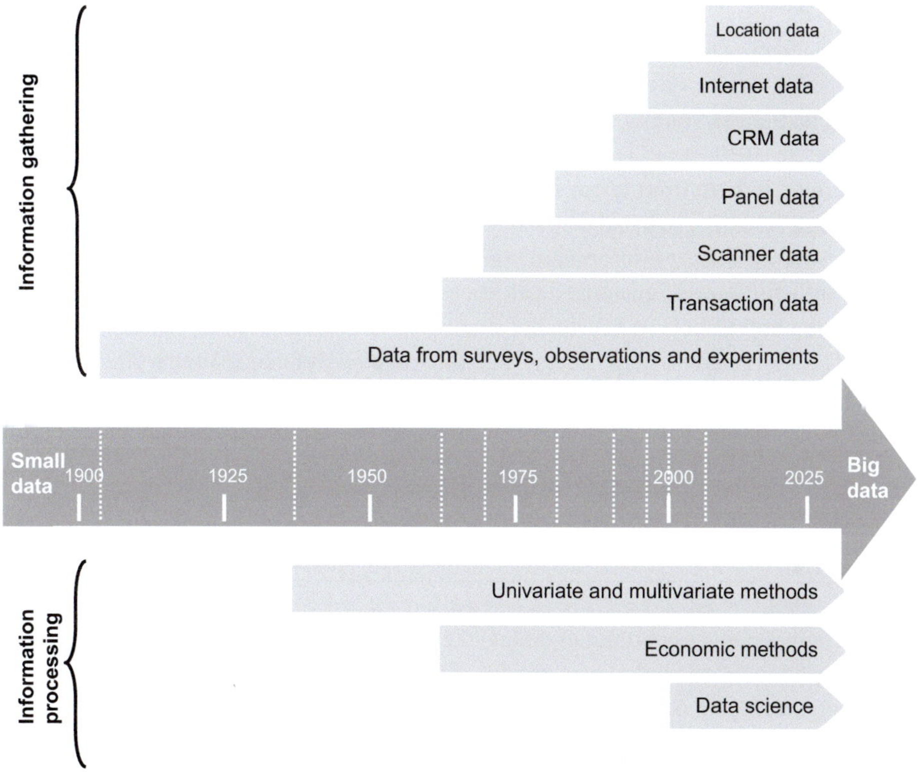

Fig. 5.1 Development of marketing research. (Based on Meffert et al. 2019, p. 169)

to prepare marketing decisions. The risk of misjudgments, incorrectly assessed market conditions, and neglected interactions is too great. Rather, in addition to these undoubtedly important skills, well-founded information is needed, which can only be obtained through consciously conducted marketing research.

▶ **Marketing Research** stands for the systematic collection, processing, analysis, and interpretation of data and information about markets (customers, competitors, market structure)—strictly speaking, this is market research as part of marketing research—and about the impact of marketing measures (e.g., product improvement, commercial, introduction of a new distribution channel); all for the purpose of substantiating marketing decisions.

(adapted from Homburg 2020, p. 270, and Meffert et al. 2019, p. 173 f.)

The data and information relevant for assessing the marketing situation refer to various, typical **areas of investigation**: These include market development (market potential, market volume, framework conditions; with reference to the insurance industry in particular the legal framework conditions), market participant behavior (behavior of demander, competitor, intermediary), market reaction functions for marketing tools (determination of the effect of the marketing tools) and finally company-related marketing factors (sales volume, market share, marketing budget, contribution margin etc.) (Meffert et al. 2019, p. 173). **Insurance-related** particularly interesting in this regard are **customer information** about the number of potential customers, customer characteristics, risk situation, risk and demand behavior as well as already achieved coverage of needs (insurance density), information on **competitor and intermediary behavior** and **market information** on quantities and prices of insurance transactions. With regard to the **instrumental effects**, the insurance marketing is interested in the reactions to product changes, the price elasticity of demand, the frequency of cancellations after premium increases, the satisfaction with the claims settlement or the consequences of sales-related competitions (Farny 2011, p. 695 f.), as well as the quick recognition of emerging unwanted instrumental effects such as delay, carry over, decay and spill over effects of individual marketing tools (Köhne and Lange 2020, p. 183 f.; see also Chap. 15).

The information obtained through marketing research is intended to (Kotler et al. 2022, p. 203),

- identify marketing opportunities and marketing problems,
- design and improve marketing activities,
- measure marketing performance, and
- understand marketing and markets.

Central **tasks** are assigned to marketing research: From the abundance of information, the aspects relevant to marketing decisions are to be identified, then procured and processed (selection function). The information supply addressed in this way promotes the understanding of market conditions and market developments (structuring function) and thereby reduces decision uncertainty (uncertainty reduction function). However, this requires at the same time to condense only the decision-relevant information and thus to curb the flood of information. Furthermore, marketing research allows the uncovering of the causes of success or failure of marketing decisions (control function). Market research—as part of marketing research—targets the market as a reference point for information gathering and observes customer and competitor behavior. This provides clues for future innovations and their evaluation (innovation function). At the same time, early information about trends and changes allows an equally early response, i.e., market research can also perform the task of an early warning system (early warning function) (Meffert et al. 2019, p. 173–176).

Systematic marketing research is based on scientific research methods and a planned **research process**. Ideally, this process goes through various stages (Table 5.1).

The determination of the research design and the data collection method (and thus the classic instruments of data collection) as well as the data analysis and interpretation (and thus the classic instruments of data evaluation) will now be briefly explained.

Table 5.1 Process of marketing research. (based on Homburg 2020, p. 275)

Marketing research stage	Central question
Problem formulation	What is the goal of the study? (e.g., analysis of customer satisfaction)
Determination of the research design	With which type of study can the goals be achieved? (descriptive, recognizing, explanatory)
Determination of the executor	Who should conduct the study? (own department, external service provider)
Determination of the data collection method	Which form of data collection is appropriate? (primary or secondary collection)
Sample selection	With which procedures is the sample to be identified, and what size should it have? (conscious or random selection, full or partial survey)
Design of the data collection instrument	How should interview guidelines, questionnaires or experiments be structured? (scaling, type of questions)
Execution of data collection	What should be considered during data collection? (instructions for interviewers or observers)
Editing and coding of data	How can the data be processed with (numerical) codes?
Data analysis and data interpretation	Which analysis methods are to be applied?
Presentation of results	How can results be meaningfully presented? (complexity, depth)

The **research design** describes which type of study is used (Homburg 2020, p. 282):

- Descriptive (= describing): The facts (variables) relevant to the study are recorded and described, but relationships between these are not investigated.
- Exploratory (= recognizing): The research topic should be understood and structured, relationships between variables should be recognized, i.e., they should only emerge through the study and not be formulated in advance as hypotheses.
- Explanatory (= explaining): This is about explaining cause and effect and the relationships between variables. Pre-formulated hypotheses (which, for example, were derived and formulated from the exploratory study) should be confirmed or rejected.

In determining the **data collection method**, the focus is on selecting an appropriate form of data collection. However, this is not trivial, as a variety of methods are generally available (see Sect. 5.2). In practice, various of these methods are often combined to gradually penetrate the subject of investigation: For example, an (exploratory) preliminary study (e.g., group interviews or in-depth interviews) is first carried out to explore the facets of the topic, followed by a broad main study (e.g., telephone survey).

In the stage of **data analysis and data interpretation**, it is about the insights to be drawn from the data, which can be descriptive, explanatory, but also exploratory in nature. If the type and scope of the data allow it, complex and often unmanageable amounts of data are converted into meaningful information using statistical analysis methods in order to evaluate the data collected during the data collection (see Sect. 5.3).

5.2 Information gathering through Primary and Secondary Data Collection

In marketing research, a basic distinction is made in connection with the collection of decision-relevant data (information gathering) between primary and secondary surveys.

▶ **Primary Survey** (Field Research) refers to the initial collection of data, i.e., data that has not yet been available on a topic and that is also tailored to the individual information needs in connection with the question to be investigated.

▶ **Secondary Survey** (Desk Research) is, in contrast, the collection and processing of information relevant to the question to be investigated from existing information sources that were collected for other purposes. Therefore, they are usually not completely tailored to the individual information needs in connection with the question to be investigated.

When deciding between primary and secondary surveys, a basic trade-off between informative value and cost must be made. The **primary survey** is therefore particularly suitable when certain information is of central importance for the marketing decision to be made and thus also the quality of this information, but this information cannot be obtained at all, not in sufficient quantity or not up-to-date enough from existing data and information material. The disadvantage of the primary survey lies in the high methodological requirements and as a result in comparatively high costs and the required time frame. Due to the required resources and the necessary knowledge, primary surveys are often carried out by specialized market research institutes.

In contrast, data and information in the case of the **secondary survey** can be obtained comparatively easier, cheaper and faster—the internet has significantly reduced the search costs in this regard. However, it can prove difficult that the secondary data were not collected for the question of interest and therefore were not prepared accordingly or are no longer up-to-date. This is also risky if they have to be purchased for a fee without being able to assess their informative value beforehand. Apart from that, there are also data that exist, but their existence is not known or they are not accessible (Homburg 2020, p. 285 f.).

The main methods of data collection can be structured in an overview (Table 5.2).

The essential methods of primary data collection include surveys, observations, test procedures (experiments), and panels (multiple surveys). These methods require test or informant persons, also referred to as subjects. Internally, a financial service provider

Table 5.2 Overview of important data collection methods

Primary surveys	
Interview with	
a) Open questions	Expert interview
	In-depth interview
	Group discussion
b) Predefined questions	Oral survey
	Written survey
	Telephone survey
	Online survey
Observation	Participatory
	From outside
Experiment	Laboratory experiment
	Field experiment
Panel	Consumer panel
Secondary surveys	
Internal data	
External data	Publicly available data
	Commercially available data

has employees from the back-office and salesforce as well as its own customer surveys available for this purpose. External sources are insurance customers, the population, and competitors.

In the case of **surveys**, open, i.e., flexible in terms of the questions and aimed at a rather limited number of respondents, approaches such as expert, in-depth, and group interviews can be distinguished from standardized survey methods aimed at as many respondents as possible (Berekoven et al. 2009, p. 87–92).

▶ **Expert and in-depth Interviews** are personal conversations with open, semi-structured questions based on an interview guide with the aim of allowing the interviewee to speak as comprehensively and freely as possible in order to

- in the case of the expert interview, obtain important technical information and gain deeper insights into the subject of investigation, and
- in the case of the in-depth interview, explore the interviewee's ways of thinking, feeling, and acting, and in the case of employees, aspects of the company culture reflected therein.

In-depth interviews in particular require a high level of methodological and psychological competence from the interviewer. However, they provide important insights into spontaneous impressions, emotional states, and basic attitudes of the interviewee. With their help, sensitive customer information can be obtained, such as the population's attitude towards insurance, the behavior of respondents in insurance matters, the use of certain insurance products, or the image of a particular insurer.

In contrast to expert and in-depth interviews, a group discussion aims to provide as comprehensive an overview as possible of the opinions and ideas of several people.

▶ **Group Discussion:** It is a one to two-hour discussion within a small group of up to 20 people (focus group) led by a trained moderator, where a deliberately chosen topic (e.g., road safety) is discussed with the aim of capturing as many opinions and aspects as possible without influencing them.

(Kühlmann et al. 2003, p. 112)

Due to their exploratory nature, group discussions serve, for example, to identify needs and usage patterns in advance of the new or further development of insurance products, accompanying services, or distribution channels.

In contrast to the aforementioned, rather open survey methods, standardized surveys—whether in written, telephone, oral, or digital form—allow for the direct comparison of the answers of a large number of respondents. The data obtained through them are accessible to quantitative methods of data analysis (see Sect. 5.3)—hence these survey methods are also referred to as quantitative surveys (as opposed to the qualitative, open survey methods discussed above). Depending on the research situation, one or the other variant may be appropriate.

Written surveys have the advantage that they are relatively inexpensive, are not influenced by an interviewer, can be conducted without time pressure, and can reach a large number of recipients. However, customers appreciate them less due to the time involved and often ignore them due to a lack of urgency, leading to low response rates. They are more suitable for surveying one's own sales force (Kotler et al. 2022, p. 212).

Oral surveys, on the other hand, increase understanding and reduce the refusal rate through the possible interaction between the interviewer and the interviewee, but they are more expensive and subject to a certain influence by the interviewer. Due to the higher commitment through direct, personal contact, they are preferable to written surveys for private customers. Telephone surveys offer high temporal flexibility, can be evaluated quickly, are relatively cost-effective, and allow for understanding questions through their interactivity. Depending on the complexity of the survey and the accessibility of certain target groups, however, representativeness is at risk. Moreover, at least the same applies to their popularity among private customers as for written surveys. Finally, online surveys impress with their low costs, high reach, and the relatively quick achievement of large case numbers. However, the quality of the answers is more at risk due to the high level of anonymity than with the other survey methods: Insufficient information about the total population and its representativeness support this phenomenon (Homburg 2020, p. 295 f.; Meffert et al. 2019, p. 195).

All mentioned standardized survey forms are also used in the insurance industry for consumer, customer, intermediary, or employee surveys. Table 5.3 illustrates various types of questions (direct/indirect; closed/open) using an insurance-typical example.

The second important method besides the survey is the **observation**. With it, perceptible facts, behaviors, and characteristics are systematically recorded. This can be done through self-observation, independent third parties (external observation), or by devices (instrumental observation). Although this allows behavior to be directly observed, the reasons and motivations behind it cannot be.

Advantages of observation are the sometimes unique insights (e.g., eye tracking in advertising research), the sometimes affordable options (e.g., user behavior on websites), and the lack of influence by the interviewer. On the other hand, the disadvantages of observation include the observation effect (when the observed person behaves atypically due to the observation), the lack of repeatability, and the possible exclusion of aspects from perception and memory by the observer. Apart from observing shopping behavior, the internet in particular offers a variety of affordable opportunities to observe surfing behavior, for example by identifying the paths taken and typical correlations between visited websites or when using smartphone applications (Homburg 2020, pp. 293–296).

Insurance companies use observation in connection with the training of consultation talks during the training of their sales force, at assessment centers in the context of personnel recruitment and development, in the case of skin resistance measurement when

Table 5.3 Examples of different types of questions. (Based on Kühlmann et al. 2003, p. 123)

Type of question	Example
Direct question	Do you have accident insurance?
Indirect question	Can you imagine recommending a friend to conclude an accident insurance? (→ Respondent's interest in conclusion)
Closed questions	
a) Alternative variant	Do you have accident insurance? o Yes o No
b) Selection variant	Which features do you think best characterize the accident insurance you have? o Flexibility o Scope of insurance coverage o Affordable price o Good image of the provider o Other
Open questions	Why did you take out accident insurance? What do you think of accident insurance?

viewing commercials, and to analyze behavior on their websites (especially in direct sales) or the handling of offered apps by the recipients.

Furthermore, experiments and panels appear as mixtures between surveys and observations.

▶ **Experiment:** This involves repeatedly running through an experimental procedure under controlled environmental conditions, changing one factor of the experimental setup (cause) from one experiment to the next in order to measure its influence on dependent variables (effect) using survey and observation techniques. The aim is to recognize cause-effect relationships.

(Homburg 2020, p. 302)

Often, surveys and observations are combined in the **experiment**. The laboratory experiment takes place under artificial conditions in a kind of experimental setup; this is suitable, for example, when using instrumental observations in advertising research. The field experiment is conducted in a natural environment, i.e., in the normal environment of the test subjects. To keep the test subjects as unbiased as possible, they are usually not informed about the experiment. The quality of the test results is higher in terms of largely missing interference effects in the laboratory experiment, on the other hand, in terms of generalizability due to the greater proximity to reality in the field experiment.

Such test procedures play a significant role in insurance advertising and occasionally in the design of sales promotion materials. They control the effect (memory activation, image influence), conception (credibility), and design (visual prominence, attention effect of an advertisement or flyer) of communication measures.

The **panel**, unlike the survey methods discussed so far, captures changes over time, as it involves multiple surveys at different times and thus enables longitudinal analyses.

▶ **Panel** refers to a specific, constant group of recipients, from whom surveys on the (in principle) same subject of investigation are conducted at regular intervals.

(Homburg 2020, p. 315)

Its establishment and maintenance are correspondingly time-consuming and costly and are therefore usually operated by market research institutes, which can then use the panel for various studies and clients. This generates synergy effects. A good example is so-called omnibus surveys, in which companies participate with specific questions in an already financed survey with existing questions.

In relation to financial services, for example, there is the Income and Consumption Sample (EVS) of the Federal Statistical Office, with the help of which statements about the financial behavior of private households are collected (see excursus to the EVS Sect. 3.2.3).

In contrast to the primary surveys presented, **secondary surveys** use existing data (Berekoven et al. 2009, pp. 39–42; Kotler et al. 2022, pp. 206–208): Companies can use both internal and external secondary data. Company-internal data relevant to marketing include sales statistics by customers, divisions and distribution channels, customer statistics, data recorded in branches and directorates, internal service and sales force reports, customer complaints, but also data from cost accounting (e.g., contribution margins of products, distribution costs) or older data from previous primary surveys.

External corporate data either comes from public sources, i.e., it is publicly and freely accessible, or it must be purchased (commercial data). Both types of data sources are continuously growing in number. The internet has contributed to a drastic increase in the amount of data and information over the past two decades; the positive effect is that important, current, statistical data—often available for free—are now available, which in the past would not have been available at all or only with great effort. Of interest to insurers, for example, are data sources from public-law institutions (e.g., from supervisory authorities), associations, institutes, other insurance companies, financial services, consulting and market research companies, specialist literature, online portals or databases (Table 5.4).

Databases, in particular, are playing an increasingly important role as a source of information. Many of them can be accessed virtually from anywhere via the internet. Depending on the provider, these are sometimes of very high quality both qualitatively and quantitatively. Numerical databases primarily contain statistical information, whereas text databases offer documents or references to such: As reference databases, they refer to the title, location, and time of publications and a few related keywords; as fact databases, they summarize information; as full-text databases, they store complete articles and essays and allow a full-text search.

Secondary surveys in the insurance industry have a good data and information base: The numerical processing of insurance business transactions by BaFin, GDV, and the annual reports of the insurers is qualitatively and quantitatively advanced. Ratings and rankings from rating agencies and other information service providers are also helpful in relation to company data (Farny 2011, p. 696).

▶ **Tip** Databases—especially text databases that contain information on specialist books and articles—are very suitable for literature research not only for companies but also for (prospective) academics in the course of preparing and writing (scientific) papers.

5.3 Information Evaluation through Data Analysis and Data Interpretation

The objective of information or data evaluation is either verification (= confirmation) or falsification (= refutation) of the suspected statement about a fact (= hypothesis) or the recognition of facts. The task in the evaluation phase is to organize, check, analyze, and interpret the multitude of data and then condense it to a meaningful level for decision-making.

Table 5.4 External data sources for insurance companies

Data source	Examples
(Semi-)Official national sources	Federal Statistical Office and State Offices; Statistical Offices of Cities and Municipalities; Federal and State Ministries; Deutsche Rentenversicherung; Chambers of Commerce and Industry
European Central Bank; Deutsche Bundesbank	Information on economic issues and capital markets; e.g., monthly reports
European Insurance Supervision (EIOPA); German Insurance Supervision (BaFin)	Supervisory information and regulations; statistics on insurance markets
Associations	e.g., GDV; PKV Association; BDVM; BVK; GVNW; Insurance Europe; BIPAR
Economic research institutes	e.g., German Institute for Economic Research, Berlin; Institute for the World Economy, Kiel; Institute for Economic Research, Munich
Insurance companies; other financial services companies (company websites)	Brochures, published by the research departments; annual reports; investor relations; PR information
Consulting firms; market research institutes	Studies (often for a fee)
Specialist literature	Specialist books; dissertations; encyclopedias
Specialist journals	e.g., Versicherungswirtschaft; Zeitschrift fü Versicherungswesen; Versicherungsmagazin; AssCompact; Versicherungspraxis; VersicherungsVermittlung; German Journal of Risk and Insurance; Geneva Papers on Risk and Insurance; Versicherungsjournal (online).
Economic newspapers	e.g., Wirtschaftswoche; Capital; Handelsblatt; Börsenzeitung
Specialist conferences, congresses	Lecture information
Online portals	Sales statistics, product or price comparisons
(Online) Databases	e.g., Business Source Ultimate, Database Information System (DBIS), DACH Information, EconLit, Entrepreneurial Studies Source, Euromonitor Passport, SpringerLink, Statista, WISO, AZ Direct Analytical Services; GBI-GENIOS

If the collected data is suitable for statistical evaluations in terms of type and scope, there are numerous (statistical) methods of data analysis. These will only be outlined and structured here. For a deeper engagement in preparation for the application of these methods, the relevant specialist literature is referred to (see references at the end of the chapter).

The methods for data analysis can be divided into uni-, bi-, and multivariate methods according to the number of variables included in the analysis. An alternative classification according to the objective of the methods distinguishes between descriptive and inductive methods (Table 5.5).

Descriptive methods provide information about the existing data set, i.e., about the structures found in a sample, such as the average age of the people in the sample. In contrast, inductive (= inferential) methods based on probability theory allow conclusions to be drawn from the sample to the entire population. An example on the subject of age: If an average age of 28.3 years is observed in a sample, the hypothesis would then be formulated that the average age in the entire population is 28 years, and it is determined that this hypothesis is not rejected with a probability of error of 5%, in short, it is 95% likely to be correct (Homburg 2020, p. 355).

In relation to its application in marketing research, it is important to note the **cross-tabulation** as a method of association analysis, which, at a nominal scale level (i.e., textual rather than numerical statements), indicates the frequencies of all possible combinations of the characteristics of two features. For example, one could ask whether there is a correlation between belonging to a customer segment (e.g., demanding delegator) and brand preference for certain insurers.

The **bivariate regression analysis** examines the effects of an independent variable on a dependent variable (requirement: metric or quasi-metric scale level): For example, the relationship between the price and the sales volume of a product can be analyzed if the same product is offered at different prices at different locations (via different distribution channels) and the corresponding sales figures are compared. Insurance tariffs are generally less suitable for this analysis due to their low transparency for the customer. The principle of equal treatment in life and health insurance also has a restrictive effect. However, (perceived as such) standard products such as travel health or luggage insurance or a car protection letter could be examined for price effects with regression analysis.

Table 5.5 Overview of uni- and bivariate data analysis methods. (Based on Homburg 2020, p. 356)

Descriptive	Univariate	Frequency distributions
		Parameters of frequency distributions: Location, dispersion, shape, concentration parameters
	Bivariate	Association analysis or correlation analysis
		Regression analysis (linear, non-linear)
Inductive	Univariate	Tests related to distribution parameters: Mean value test
		Tests related to distribution: X^2-Test adjustment test
	Bivariate	Tests related to distribution parameters: t-Test, single-factor analysis of variance
		Tests related to distribution: X^2-Test of independence

Multivariate analyses refer to three or more variables and their relationships. **Dependence analyses** examine the effect of an independent variable on a dependent variable and thus directed dependencies, interdependence analyses only their mutual influences, without distinguishing between independent and dependent variables. The high importance of multivariate analyses is due to the fact that considering only one or two variables can easily lead to false conclusions, as too many other influencing factors are neglected.

Interdependence analyses include factor analysis and cluster analysis. In **factor analysis**, a group of (indicator) variables is examined for its underlying structure with the aim of reducing a large number of indicator variables to a few basic factors and reducing complexity through this feature condensation. In the case of exploratory factor analysis, neither the number nor the assignment of the factors is predetermined, as these are to be discovered through the analysis. In contrast, both are specified in advance in the so-called confirmatory factor analysis and then checked for consistency with the data material of the existing sample.

Factor analysis is used, for example, in the creation of personality profiles in the study of consumer behavior, when it reduces the numerous research variables (personality traits) to a few underlying factors (e.g., in the identification and description of customer types). In product policy, it is about positioning different products or brands in the context of various product characteristics; the numerous product characteristics are to be condensed into a few underlying evaluation dimensions (Homburg 2020, p. 389).

The **cluster analysis** reduces the complexity of a data set by grouping objects (e.g., customers) into groups or clusters (e.g., customer segments). While factor analysis thus groups variables, this is done in cluster analysis with reference to objects. The central field of application is market segmentation, i.e., the division of a heterogeneous (= non-uniform) overall market into homogeneous (= uniform) sub-markets with the intention of carrying out differentiated market development (Meffert et al. 2019, p. 207).

Significant methods of dependency analysis include (multiple) regression analysis and conjoint analysis. The **multiple regression analysis**, as one of the most widely used analysis methods in marketing research, examines the influence of several independent variables on a dependent variable. For example, in a marketing context, it investigates which performance parameters (e.g., coverage scope, goodwill in claims settlement, premium level, etc.) influence customer satisfaction, what customer loyalty depends on, or which influencing factors promote the decision to conclude a contract. The so-called **conjoint analysis** also takes into account the benefit from the customer's perspective: It examines how individual characteristics or feature expressions of a product contribute to its overall benefit from the customer's perspective. It determines how customer preferences change when individual product features are adjusted. The dependent variable is the overall benefit, the independent variables are the individual product features. Conjoint analysis is a significant analytical instrument in product policy: It provides valuable insights when it comes to new or the revision of existing insurance products or the pricing of performance components or performance enhancements (Homburg 2020, p. 410, 440).

5.4 Specifics of Marketing Research in Insurance

The specifics of marketing research in the insurance industry relate less to the methods and more to the questions and the object of knowledge of the insurance service.

From the service element, the relevance of employees in customer contact for the perception of service quality by insurance customers follows. Therefore, the behavior of employees and the underlying skills and motivation of **people with customer contact** is an **important subject of investigation**, which ultimately affects the marketing tools of sales, care or service, and claims settlement policy. To investigate employee behavior in customer-related areas, observation using the silent shopper analysis, also called **mystery shopping**, is suitable. The goal is to derive training measures to increase customer-oriented behavior from the observations, if necessary. In this method, the mystery shoppers pose as customers and do not reveal themselves as actual marketing researchers in order not to influence the actual employee behavior towards customers (Homburg 2020, p. 300 f.; Bruhn et al. 2019, p. 377). In the insurance industry, this method is used by some insurers to observe internal and external service employees in customer contact. For some time now, it has also been increasingly used by journalists—albeit with questionable motives—and recently even by BaFin (Grischuk 2021) to uncover malpractices for consumer protection issues. For this purpose, the alleged customers (mystery shoppers on behalf of the broadcaster or BaFin) request consultation talks through insurance intermediaries and record them without their knowledge. In the media processing of the journalistic contributions, those examples that underline the postulated grievances are then broadcast. The representativeness of the results is, however, questionable with such a procedure. However, this does not preclude using the method properly for research purposes to identify possible malpractices in insurance advice, if a neutral market research institute is commissioned and the positive cases are also documented, as can be assumed in the case of application by BaFin.

Furthermore, **studies of the demand and communication behavior of insurance customers** serve the purposeful design of customer communication along the service or care process. They help, for example, in the customer-oriented implementation of the consulting process and the goal-oriented improvement of the sales conversation to increase the closing rate (proportion of contracts concluded in relation to the consulting conversations). An interesting application of purchase behavior observation is the **collaborative filtering** used on the Internet, in which visitors to a website are assigned to already identified customer segments whose members show similar behavior or similar preferences and attitudes. They are then recommended products and services that were preferred by members of the same segment (Ansari et al. 2000). This method is known from online bookstores, although it is now used by most online retailers. Particularly attractive is the possibility to automate marketing research and the implementation of marketing research results when customer segments are automatically formed and served. Automation also makes research and implementation dynamic and timely. However, the application potentials in the insurance sector are likely to be lower than in retail:

insurance products are less frequently demanded and also considered individually, rarely as product bundles. In the case of personal insurance, they are often associated with very personal information, in the case of life insurance alone they are very individual to assess from a tax perspective. In the case of annex sales—i.e. in combination with other products—for simple insurance products, however, collaborative filtering could be insightful.

Another characteristic of insurance services is their immateriality. This goes hand in hand with an abstract benefit from the customer's point of view. The **customer assessment of the insurance service** can therefore only be indirectly captured through **image, satisfaction, and complaint analyses**. The results serve on the one hand as indicators for future purchasing behavior (new conclusion, extension or termination), and on the other hand they provide starting points for the design of marketing tools and their success measurement.

The non-storability of the insurance service requires an ever-present readiness to perform. With regard to the constant **availability in the course of customer care**, this requires, for example, the establishment of internal or external call centers. These must master the challenge of ensuring consistently high availability while at the same time maintaining only as much staff as necessary, i.e. reconciling service and cost orientation. Since the temporal distribution of demand is not constant, this requires corresponding **customer frequency analyses** that identify the volume, distribution over months, weekdays and hours, and their volatilities (fluctuations) (Meffert et al. 2018, pp. 109-111).

While low insurance know-how, lack of customer interest, and negative industry image on the part of private customers do not exactly facilitate customer surveys. But from the importance of employees and especially intermediaries for the provision of the insurance service follows a chance for marketing research to compensate for this shortcoming a little: Through an **employee survey**, the **customer interactions can be assessed from the employee's perspective**. Especially the own agents are in direct, personal contact with customers and receive detailed customer data and differentiated knowledge about customer behavior and customer requirements. Thus, they can record the intensity of customer loyalty (number of contacts and visits) and recognize through customer statements (observation) or direct questioning the customer satisfaction with the overall performance or certain partial performances, possibilities for improvement, additional needs as well as upcoming needs (house construction, car purchase etc.).

Guest Contribution

Dr. Oliver Gaedeke (Founder and Managing Director of Sirius Campus GmbH)

Customer Orientation and Behavioral Economics—Proven and New Approaches to Market Research in Insurance

1. **Market Research in the Insurance Industry**

As in other industries, the most important market research projects focus on the following topics (in order of their importance):

1. Customer Satisfaction and Customer Loyalty Research
2. Innovation and Product Research
3. Brand and Advertising Media Research
4. Market Development, Target Groups and Customer Journey

Despite identical topics, market research in the insurance industry differs significantly from other industries.

This article presents the most important peculiarities and new approaches in insurance market research. It does not claim to provide a detailed presentation of methods, which can be found in standard works on market research.

2. **Insurance is a low-interest product**

Only five percent of insurance customers fully agree that they regularly review their existing insurance policies in terms of price and performance. Another 21% somewhat agree with this statement (Sirius Campus 2019a). Even young people from GenZ, despite the high availability of information on the internet, do not have higher, but lower competence in insurance matters than older people (Sirius Campus 2023a). The search and decision-making effort before taking out insurance has been consistently low for years. It can only be temporarily increased by intensive advertising for seemingly simple products—such as motor vehicle insurance.

The following five causes can be named as the main **reasons** for the low interest in insurance:

1. **Hedonism**: A positive attitude towards life and self-presentation prevent serious engagement with negative life events.
2. **Availability heuristic**: Probabilities of occurrence and costs or consequential costs of accidents, burglaries or illnesses are underestimated due to lack of everyday experience.
3. **Mental Convenience**: People's mental convenience seeks simple and quick problem solutions, which the textual insurance conditions fundamentally do not offer.
4. **Intangibility**: The intangibility of insurance prevents a sensory experience of the product. None of the five senses are directly addressed. Only cognitive processing allows a psychological evaluation of the offer. Indirectly—e.g., through the brand, letters, websites or intermediaries and their offices—the sensory perception of customers can be addressed.
5. **Trust characteristics**: Services from insurers in the form of claim settlement or pension payments usually lie far in the future. Before the contract is concluded, customers usually only have trust in the performance promises. Only the price or the stated return are search characteristics that customers can subjectively orient themselves by. Objectively, however, these also depend on the trust that they will not change to the customer's disadvantage after the contract is concluded.

Nevertheless, most customers find a coverage and provision that satisfies them. For this purpose, heuristics are used. These are practiced cognitive approaches to solve problems despite obstacles such as lack of information, inaccessible knowledge or little time. These heuristics are increasingly moving into the center of customer-oriented market research (see also Sect. 4.2.1).

3. **Control the collection and activation of respondents specifically**

The willingness of both private and business customers to participate in an interview on the subject of insurance is significantly lower than for other topics. To ensure the representativeness and validity of the sample, insurance market researchers typically use the following measures:

- Random selection: As in all studies, a random draw from the total population is to be made and, if necessary, adjusted by subsequent weighting based on known structural data (e.g., sociodemographics). Especially in the case of efficient surveys in an online panel, weighting along market-specific behavior, e.g., a known psychographic market segmentation, is recommended.
- Transparency: Openness about the survey objective and disclosure of the client significantly increase the willingness to participate. For this reason, a postal announcement or an authorization fax is used in b2b interviews.
- Incentivization: Raffles of shopping vouchers are the most common choice of monetary incentive for survey participation. However, this is almost only used in postal-written, personalized online or b2b surveys.
- Cooperation partners: The choice and communication of scientific or media partners are other possible motivators.
- Insurance decision-makers: Focusing on decision-makers and co-decision-makers for insurance matters in households or companies ensures that the interview is conducted with the people who make the decisions in real life.

Especially with low-interest topics, there is a high risk that only platitudes without value for the development of market strategies will be collected. Therefore, the quality of the survey must be ensured by various measures: In quantitative questionnaires and qualitative guidelines, the rule is generally to ask "from the general to the specific". An overall impression of providers or products is at the beginning of a survey, followed by an evaluation of individual performance areas down to very factual questions about individual service or product aspects (Sirius Campus 2022a). This prevents rationalizations and generalizations that only describe the self-image of a test person along an ideal Homo Oeconomicus, but do not allow behavioral predictions.

The deeper an interview goes into detail, the more specifically the questions focus on the actual behavior in previous contacts and experiences with the research object (e.g., advertising, consulting, product, service). This has two advantages: On the one hand, respondents are introduced to the topic, thus activating memories and hidden thoughts. On the other hand, these customer reports bring the actual perceptions, considerations, and emotions of the test persons to light.

This event-related approach highlights a further peculiarity of the insurance market: Many customers have only infrequent contact with their company. Interviews about claims from five years ago are not only deeply buried in the respondents' memories, but they also no longer provide any statements about the current service quality of the claims department. Quality questions about advice or claims settlement should be raised with a "timestamp" (e.g., in the last 12 months) or as part of timely customer feedback (e.g., up to three months after the event). Insurers should be able to record customer data in a customer contact history differentiated by contact occasions. If this is not possible, an elaborate screening in the survey is necessary.

And finally, the clear and understandable formulation of the questions is of great importance. Clear language increases the interest of the test person in the interview and enables or motivates him to give clear answers. This seemingly trivial requirement is often one of the biggest challenges in market research projects. Insurance companies' specialist departments rarely succeed in translating product benefits or process steps into a language understandable to the customer. It is advisable to formulate the topic strictly from the customer's perspective and, if necessary, to make it transparent with examples.

4. **Select target groups and methods correctly**

Due to the high importance of personal sales, intermediaries should also be considered as a target group in innovation and product research in addition to customers. Pure broker insurers have so far even focused only on the broker as the "first" customer for satisfaction and product development research.

In many studies, benchmarks—comparisons to the advertising, products, or service of competitors—are essential to obtain a correct assessment of one's own strengths and weaknesses (Sirius Campus 2022b). Thus, customers or intermediaries of competitors are another target group that can be integrated into satisfaction or sales studies, for example. As a rule, smaller samples are sufficient for the target groups affiliated with the competitor (at least n = 100 for private customers and n = 30 for intermediaries or b2b customers). The selection of competitors to be included in the benchmark should be based on similarities in distribution channels, mix of insurance lines, and possibly company size. In addition to this external benchmark, the time series development from previous surveys and—if possible—an internal comparison between regions should be evaluated as far more meaningful comparison values.

As already mentioned, decision-makers and co-decision-makers should be specifically selected for the surveys. In qualitative creative workshops, a certain extroversion is also taken into account in order to achieve the highest possible group dynamics.

The selection of methods along the question is very similar in market research for insurance products to other industries. Explorative and open questions up to the exploitation of a creative potential from the target group are appropriately collected with qualitative methods. In detailed analyses (e.g. in a customer journey study), personal individual interviews are conducted. On the other hand, advertising materials or product concepts can be better evaluated in a focus group, where the intensive interaction of the participants quickly brings the essential experience and evaluation spaces to light. In order to be able to carry out representative surveys with statistical analyses, quantitative surveys with fixed questions and answer formats are conducted.

In addition to the form of data collection, the measurement and analysis method is also becoming increasingly important. There are only low to moderate correlations between attitudes and behavior. Nevertheless, to be able to derive action-oriented measures from research projects, non-reactive methods are used. They provide insights into psychological motives and mechanisms of action in decision-making and opinion-forming processes. Depending on the research topic, different methods can be used to ensure the effectiveness of management recommendations (Table 5.6).

5. **Designing decision processes with Behavioral Economics**

In recent years, behavioral economics has gained importance for customer-oriented communication, consulting, and offer design (see also Sect. 4.2). The focus is on the "last mile" before the purchase or conclusion, to analyze the previously often underestimated or at least not systematically considered influencing factors in the decision-making process. Thus, preference formation can be multiplied by a multi-stage and simply arranged offer portfolio (Sirius Campus 2019b). Possible situational influencing factors such as anchoring, framing, or decoy effects are already collected in a hypothesis-like manner in service and product design and are usually experimentally investigated in accompanying research through choice tasks or within the framework of a conjoint analysis.

Furthermore, heuristics, i.e., rules of thumb for dealing with complex tasks, are taken into account. For the insurance market, four decision patterns are considered, which result in a market segmentation called Select Types (Sirius Campus 2022c, see also: www.select-typen.de):

- **Partners** delegate and seek a trustworthy intermediary in their vicinity to be fully advised by them. They are looking for long-term reliable and individual service in insurance matters.
- **Optimizers** focus on certain services that can give them an advantage. They are looking for something new, unique, or cost-benefit advantages that they cannot get elsewhere.

Table 5.6 Research topics, target variables, and examples of non-reactive measurement or analysis methods

Research topic		Quantitative methods		Qualitative methods	
		Target variable	Procedure/Method	Target variable	Procedure/Method
1.	Customer satisfaction and customer loyalty research	Overall satisfaction, customer loyalty, willingness to recommend (NPS)	Correlation, Multiple Regression, LMG	Enthusiasm triggers	Exploration of events in experience chains
2.	Innovation and product research	Design of products and offer portfolios, price willingness	Price sensitivity meter, Conjoint analysis, Maximum-Difference-Scaling	Innovations in services	Exploration of experience spaces and need structures
3.	Brand and advertising media research	Relevant Set, First Choice, purchase and price willingness	Correlation, Multiple Regression, LMG	Brand attractiveness/Reason Why	Laddering or projection techniques
4.	Market development, target groups and customer journey	Behavioral preference (e.g. preferred sales points)	Choice tasks, tests, Maximum-Difference-Scaling	Target group approach	Biotic interviews, lifestyle and mentality exploration

- **Cautious** reduce the decision-making effort and orient themselves towards simple recommendations without wanting to delve too deeply into a subject. They are looking for security, not to be taken advantage of.
- **Independents** like to take the scepter into their own hands and independently search the internet for suitable insurance solutions and conclude them there after thorough analysis and consideration. They are ultimately looking for savings opportunities for good coverage.

The Select Types are already included in numerous market studies such as the market and media analysis "best for planning" as well as in the associated mds-online-counting-machine of Axel Springer Publishing. In addition, the Select Types can be specifically identified in quantitative and qualitative surveys. Aligning service and product designs along the core expectations of the four Select Types offers great opportunities for higher customer orientation. Based on AI with learning samples, an insurer's CRM can also be enriched with the Select Types, thus optimizing the approach in letter or consulting design based on previously collected target group-specific results.

Sources:

- Sirius Campus 2019a.
- Sirius Campus 2019b.
- Sirius Campus 2022a.
- Sirius Campus 2022b.
- Sirius Campus 2022c.
- Sirius Campus 2023a.

Interim Conclusion: In the Insurance industry, the Object of knowledge of Marketing research is Special, not the Methods

The established methods of marketing research can in principle also be applied well to insurance-specific questions. The peculiarities of marketing research in the insurance industry relate less to the methods to be applied, but rather to the way they are applied and their weighting. The object of knowledge of the insurance service is a low-interest product, which is sometimes concluded over long periods, but where customers rarely come into contact with the provider. Due to the low interest and at the same time low product competence, most policyholders (unconsciously) apply heuristics (rules of thumb) to facilitate decision-making; moreover, their willingness to participate in surveys is even lower than usual. Consequently, market research has to control the survey and activation of respondents specifically and select target groups and methods correctly. Finally, industry-specific heuristics on the customer side need to be uncovered and taken into account.

Further Reading Recommendations for Chap. 5

- Backhaus et al. 2021.
- Berekoven et al. 2009.
- Finn 2001.
- Hassler 2017.
- Herrmann et al. 2008.
- Homburg 2020, Chaps. 6 and 7.
- Keller et al. 2019.
- Koch et al. 2016
- Kuß et al. 2018.
- Kromrey 1988.
- Meffert et al. 2019, Chap. 3.
- Sarstedt and Mooi 2019.

References

Ansari, A./Essegaier, S./Kohli, R. (2000): Internet Recommendation Systems, in: JoMR, Vol. 37, 2000, No. 3, pp. 363–375.

Backhaus, K./Erichson, B./Gensler, S./Weiber, R./Weiber, T. (2021): Multivariate Analysemethoden, Eine anwendungsorientierte Einführung, Berlin, 16. edn., 2021.

Berekoven, L./Eckert, W./Ellenrieder, P. (2009): Marktforschung, Methodische Grundlagen und praktische Anwendung, Wiesbaden, 12. edn., 2009.

Bruhn, M./Meffert, H./Hadwich, K. (2019): Handbuch Dienstleistungsmarketing. Planung – Umsetzung – Kontrolle, Wiesbaden, 2. edn., 2019.

Farny, D. (2011): Versicherungsbetriebslehre, Karlsruhe, 5. edn., 2011.

Finn, A. (2001): Mystery Shopper Benchmarking of Durable Goods Chains and Stores, in: Journal of Service Research, Vol. 3, 2001, No. 4, pp. 310–320.

Grischuk, P. (2021): Mystery Shopping, in: BaFin Journal, Dezember 2021, pp. 18–21.

Hassler, M. (2017): Web Analytics: Metriken auswerten, Besucherverhalten verstehen, Website optimieren, Frechen, 4. edn., 2017.

Herrmann, A./Homburg, C./Klarmann, M. (Eds.) (2008): Handbuch Marktforschung – Methoden, Anwendungen, Praxisbeispiele, Wiesbaden, 3. edn., 2008.

Homburg, C. (2020): Marketingmanagement, Strategie – Instrumente – Umsetzung – Unternehmensführung, Wiesbaden, 7. edn., 2020.

Keller, B./Klein, H.-W./Tuschl, S. (2019). Zukunft der Marktforschung: Entwicklungschancen in Zeiten von Social Media und Big Data, Wiesbaden, 2. edn., 2019.

Koch, J./Gebhardt, P./Riedmüller, F. (2016): Marktforschung, Grundlagen und praktische Anwendungen, Berlin, 7. edn., 2016.

Köhne, T./Lange, M. (2020): Marketing und Vertrieb von Versicherungs- und Finanzprodukten für Privatkunden, Fach- und Führungskompetenz für die Assekuranz, Karlsruhe, 4. edn., 2020.

Kotler, P./Armstrong, G./Harris, L.C./He, H. (2022): Grundlagen des Marketing, Halbergmoos, 8. edn., 2022.

Kromrey, H. (1988): Empirische Sozialforschung, Modelle und Methoden der Datenerhebung und Datenauswertung, Opladen, 8. edn., 1988.

Kühlmann, K./Wolf, H.-P./Wallenwein, C./Swoboda, U. (2003): Marketing und Vertrieb, Funktionsorientierte Qualifikationen, Karlsruhe, 2. edn., 2003.

Kuß, A./Wildner, A./Kreis, H. (2018): Marktforschung: Datenerhebung und Datenanalyse, Wiesbaden, 6. edn., 2018.

Meffert, H./Bruhn, M./Hadwich, K. (2018): Dienstleistungsmarketing, Grundlagen – Konzepte – Methoden, Wiesbaden, 9. edn., 2018.

Meffert, H./Burmann, C./Kirchgeorg, M./Eisenbeiß, M. (2019): Marketing, Grundlagen marktorientierter Unternehmensführung, Konzepte – Instrumente – Praxisbeispiele, Wiesbaden, 13. edn., 2019.

Sarstedt, M./Mooi, E. (2019): A concise guide to market research: The process, data, and methods using IBM SPSS statistics, Berlin, 3. edn., 2019.

Sirius Campus (Ed.) (2019a): Entscheidertypologie im Versicherungsmarkt, Köln, 2019.

Sirius Campus (Ed.) (2019b): Erfolgsfaktoren für Kundenberatungen zur Berufsunfähigkeitsversicherung, Köln, 2019.

Sirius Campus (Ed.) (2022a): Strategien für den digitalen Kundenservice in der Assekuranz, Köln, 2022.

Sirius Campus (Ed.) (2022b): Erfolgsfaktoren im Ausschließlichkeitsvertrieb. Benchmark-Untersuchung zur Zufriedenheit, Motivation und Bindung im Versicherungsaußendienst, Köln, 2022.

Sirius Campus (Ed.) (2022c): Kundenmonitor Assekuranz, Köln, 2022.

Sirius Campus (Ed.) (2023a): Versicherung der Zukunft – Was sind Erwartungen junger Menschen an die Versicherung von morgen?, Köln, 2023.

Part III

Analysis of the Initial Situation as Part of the Insurance Marketing Conception

6 Analysis of the Marketing Situation of the Insurance Company

A crucial component of the insurance marketing conception is the analysis of the marketing situation. It is in a reciprocal relationship with the determination of marketing objectives: On the one hand, these cannot be set completely independently without considering the initial situation, as they would otherwise most likely miss the market, the customers and/or the company's own possibilities. On the other hand, they are derived from the overarching company objectives and are not determined "on the green field" solely from the findings of the analysis of the marketing situation. Thus, certain target ideas can also lead to certain analyses. The same basically applies to the marketing strategy and the individual marketing tools: Their design should indeed serve to achieve the previously determined marketing objectives—insofar as an analysis of the initial situation has preceded them—but they often require an updated or more detailed analysis of the marketing situation tailored to their object area. In terms of the interaction with the other components of the insurance marketing conception, the analysis of the strategic starting situation must therefore be distinguished from the ongoing analysis of the marketing situation: The former is the **basis of strategic marketing and thus also of operational implementation** (and is therefore treated as the first component in most textbooks and also here). The latter is due to market dynamics and specific information needs in the course of further development of the other components.

The basis of strategic and operational insurance marketing is information, some of which have a closer relationship because they directly affect the relevant market of the insurance company (**micro-environment** of marketing), some have a more distant relationship because they affect the framework conditions of the relevant market that influence it as a whole (**macro-environment** of marketing). The analysis of the marketing situation therefore includes the recording of the global environment and its essential framework conditions with influence on the insurance market (Sect. 6.1). In addition, the relevant market itself must be examined, i.e., the market characteristics of the relevant market (market analysis), its demanders (demander and customer analysis),

T. Köhne, *Insurance Marketing*, https://doi.org/10.1007/978-3-658-47345-7_6

its competitors (competition analysis) and last but not least the most important other stakeholder groups (Sect. 6.2). To capture the strategic starting position, the situation of the company itself in this market must also be taken into account (company analysis) (Sect. 6.3). Finally, all analyses together result in the SWOT analysis (Sect. 6.4) (Homburg 2020, pp. 504–506).

6.1 Analysis of the Macro-Environment of Insurance Companies

Above all, the design of the marketing strategy is influenced by the global corporate environment in terms of its scope for action. Sometimes opportunities arise from environmental developments, but often they also limit strategic possibilities. The scope for design depends specifically on **societal, macroeconomic, political, legal, technological, and ecological framework conditions and developments**. Especially in times of digitalization, globalization, and internationalization, the analysis of the macro-environment is becoming increasingly important. For better structuring, the PESTEL analysis (Political, Economic, Social, Technological, Ecological, Legal Factors) is also used (Bruhn 2022, p. 15). In the insurance industry, the legal and political framework conditions, as already explained, play a major role, which is also increasing (reregulation) and now appears to be more overarching, similar to digitalization, compared to the other framework conditions. Law and politics are closely related because politics is responsible for legislation, and should therefore be considered together (Sect. 6.1.1). Also relevant according to the PESTEL order are macroeconomic (Sect. 6.1.2), societal (Sect. 6.1.3), technological, foremost digitalization (Sect. 6.1.4), as well as ecological and health (Sect. 6.1.5) framework conditions.

The methods for analyzing the global corporate environment, however, are not specific to the insurance industry. They include early warning and early detection systems, forecasting methods, and scenario techniques (for further reading, see e.g., Homburg 2020, pp. 510–514 and the literature cited there).

6.1.1 Political and Legal Framework Conditions and Developments

Political developments, e.g., changes in social, health, tax, consumer protection, or environmental policy, usually result in legal developments such as **the introduction or changes of laws and regulations**. The financial services sector has always been affected by this, but in recent years the frequency and scope of regulations have increased (see Sect. 3.4.2). More and more often, this process is initiated at the EU level by new directives that bring far-reaching consequences and also requirements for national legislation, as well as national laws and regulations: Specifically, about ten years ago, 80% of the laws passed and adopted in the German Bundestag were based on European law and legislative initiatives from Brussels, Strasbourg, or Luxembourg (Friedrich 2013, p. 11). Politics and legislation throughout Europe and in Germany are strongly influenced by the **principle of consumer protection**: The European Union creates competition and transparency in many areas to strengthen the position of consumers (deregulation). At the same time, attempts are made to curb excesses of competition through reregulation (Theis 2015, pp. 8–12), and transparency requirements are accompanied by comprehensive reporting obligations, most recently as part of the Corporate Sustainability Reporting Directive (CSRD). The **increasing regulation** challenges insurers (not only in Germany) (GDV 2023c; The London Institute of Banking & Finance 2023, p. 7). In any case, insurers today and in the future have to deal with many legal regulations that significantly limit their decision-making freedom and also tie up considerable resources that are therefore not available for actual entrepreneurship and marketing.

> **Note** The legal framework conditions thus particularly influence the private customer business of insurance companies and the corresponding marketing to a very large extent. In essence, they define the "playing field" for strategic marketing and for shaping the marketing strategy.

Above all, **personal insurances** are **strongly affected**. The business model of private health insurers depends almost entirely on the political situation: Depending on the government coalition, it is confirmed and strengthened in one extreme case, and completely questioned in the other.

The business model of life insurance is also significantly influenced by politics and legislation: Firstly, the tax treatment of products in the context of promoting retirement provision determines their attractiveness. Until December 31, 2004, endowment insurances were particularly attractive due to their non-taxable capital payout. However, the interests in promotion can change: With the Retirement Income Act (AltEinkG) effective from January 1, 2005, the promotion shifted from endowment insurances to annuity insurances, which significantly contributed to the former being demanded much less and the latter much more. In addition, the interests in promotion do not develop uniformly across Europe: In the UK, the opposite path was taken before and ten years ago, privileging the capital payout of pension funds. Since then, savers can withdraw the entire accumulated wealth at the start of retirement in a lump sum without tax burden (o. V. 2014a, p. 205). In addition to the tax, other legal framework conditions influence the business model of life insurance, such as regulations on calculation, profit participation, capital investment, accounting, or solvency. These regulations are increasingly shaped by consumer protection aspects. The Life Insurance Reform Act (LVRG) of 2014 is evidence of this (see Sect. 3.4.2).

Other personal insurances such as accident, occupational disability, or long-term care insurance are currently (still) less in focus, but their market potential already indirectly depends on the provisions of statutory social insurance today.

In the **life and health insurance** sector, political and legal developments are directly **relevant to the viability of the business model**. At the beginning of this millennium, opportunities were seen from the political environment, resulting from the increased withdrawal of the state from statutory social insurance in the form of benefit restrictions, the deregulation of 1994, and state support programs of the Retirement Savings Act (AVmG) of 2001 and the AltEinkG of 2004 (Görgen 2007, p. 18). Currently, the mindset in politics has changed—possibly as a result of corresponding consumer protection demands and their media dissemination, and not least motivated by the banking crisis. Many politicians see the taming of unbridled economic forces as a task of politics against this background and the state as the fairer, more moral institution for shaping social and financial security. The regulatory and socio-political idea behind the Riester pension as a cooperative service of the state, economy, and individual has only partially borne fruit. Rather, the political belief in the necessity of increased regulation is growing—currently, this seems to be more the case at EU level than in Germany—from which **potential dangers for insurers** result:

1. The individual benefit of each policyholder becomes more important than the comparatively abstract risk compensation in the collective (**threat to the insurance principle**).
2. Consumption is economically more noticeable and desired than saving or old-age provision with compulsory saving (**threat to the idea of old-age provision**).
3. It is easier to realize short-term wishes today than to consider long-term wishes of future generations that still appear abstract today (**threat to intergenerational justice**).

The outlined trends are thus highly relevant for the development of marketing strategies, but at the same time difficult to control and partly hardly predictable or plannable. This explains why insurers see mastering the **multitude of different regulatory requirements** as **one of the greatest challenges of the future** (The London Institute of Banking & Finance 2023, pp. 7, 15 f.).

Property and wealth insurance is comparatively little affected by political conditions. Legislation influences the risks insured there and thus the calculation and product design, at least the marketing mix. However, the direct impact on the entire business model of property & casualty insurers is less. Exceptions confirm this rule: For some time, politics has been dealing with the question of whether natural hazard insurance should become compulsory insurance as in some European countries. The background is the observation that it is difficult to impossible to obtain insurance coverage against natural hazards in some particularly endangered locations. Advocates speak of market failure (which is very often used as a justification for regulation, sometimes prematurely), opponents of a (further) disproportionate intervention in competition and product freedom. The insurance industry prefers a bundle of measures and, with regard to the insurance solution, no compulsory insurance, but an opt-out model, albeit with exemption from liability (GDV

2021c). In any case, compulsory insurance seems to be effective only in combination with risk-appropriate premiums (Osberghaus 2021; Fuest and Thum 2021). The topic will remain on the political agenda.

6.1.2 Macroeconomic Framework Conditions and Developments

The potentially severe and lasting impacts of macroeconomic, but also purely financial developments, became clearly evident in the **global economic crisis of 2007** and the subsequent years. The **interconnection of international markets** led to a initially national real estate financing problem of a speculatively inflated real estate market (especially subprime market) in the USA first dragging the entire global financial market into its wake, and this development then spilled over to the real (= goods economic) economic markets. The beginning of the financial crisis is dated August 9, 2007, because on this day the interest rates for interbank finance loans jumped sharply. The crisis reached its peak with the collapse of the US major bank Lehman Brothers on September 15, 2008. The financial crisis prompted several states to secure the existence of large financial service providers through capital increases and recapitalizations of enormous magnitude, primarily through state debt capital, but also equity capital. Some banks were nationalized and later closed. Insurers were comparatively less affected, with the exception of the American Insurance Group (AIG), which the USA had to support with extensive financing. The already high public debt of many countries increased sharply due to the crisis, especially in the USA. Further "legacy burdens", e.g. companies that were well positioned in terms of real economy, but had speculated financially, partly high corporate debts, partly long-existing but not reduced overcapacities (e.g. in the automotive and banking industry), had a crisis-enhancing effect. These phenomena demonstrate the particular explosiveness of global networking and the associated **danger of escalating upward and downward developments**. That such economic "shocks" also influence the relevant market in all its facets requires no further explanation (GDV 2008, pp. 8–11; BaFin 2010, pp. 9–21).

Even and especially in recent times, exogenous shocks have strongly influenced the macroeconomic framework conditions and developments. While these have been quite stable in Germany for many years with the gradual overcoming of the economic crisis of 2007 and have enabled moderate growth, the Corona pandemic has "shaken" the world economy in 2020 and 2021, and **currently the financial system must face major** challenges such as the war of aggression against Ukraine, the energy crisis and high inflation **head on**. Accordingly, the **indicators for systemic stress in the European financial system** have **risen** sharply in the short term in 2022 (Fig. 6.1). In addition, the ECB and Bundesbank note market, credit and liquidity risks due to reduced economic growth and more restrictive financing options. In the past two years, (not only) Germany has experienced an unusually rapid increase in inflation. After the long-term low interest rate environment, the **interest rate hikes** by the central banks in 2022 and 2023 led to

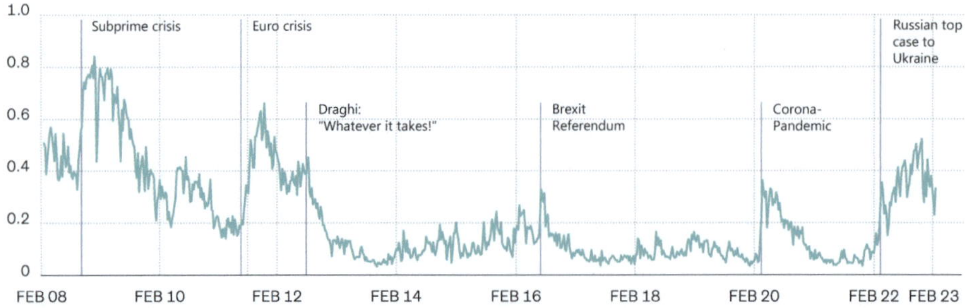

Fig. 6.1 Composite Indicator of Systemic Stress (CISS) of the ECB. (Seemann and Theis 2023, p. 2)

a rapid and substantial increase in the level of interest rates in the markets. Even though the financial system has so far proven to be resilient, substantial stability risks remain: On the one hand, the deteriorated financing conditions and reduced real incomes only fully take effect with a delay—for example on the real estate markets. On the other hand, the downside risks for economic development—such as a renewed intensification of the energy crisis or the need for further monetary policy measures to combat inflation—remain high (Seemann and Theis 2023, pp. 2–5).

The EIOPA assesses the **risk situation for insurers** using a so-called **Risk Dashboard.** Due to the deteriorated overall economic outlook and high inflation, the supervisory authority rates macroeconomic risks—as has been the case since the Corona crisis in 2020—as high. The **market risks** for insurers have also been rated high by the EIOPA since July 2022, among other things due to high volatility in the financial markets (Fig. 6.2). In addition, further potential risk factors are highlighted, specifically the negative effects of high inflation on property & casualty/accident insurers, particularly due to the sharp increase in claims payments in some areas, **liquidity risks for life insurers** in the event of further abrupt increases in interest rates, if this would lead to a large number of contract cancellations, as well as increased **market and credit risks from assets** with lower credit quality or illiquid assets. Last but not least, the digital transformation of the financial system means that **cyber risks** are becoming one of the most important potential stability risks. Conflicts such as the war in Ukraine exacerbate this risk (Seemann and Theis 2023, pp. 5 ff.).

Apart from the various overall economic crises to which the economy and thus insurers are exposed, macroeconomic key figures such as the size of an economy or its economic development—independent of crises—influence the business potential of insurers. The **economic development** of the overall economy influences customer demand behavior.

In **retirement provision**, as in other sectors, sales resistance is much higher in downturn phases than in upturn phases, when one can rather put something aside (Kühlmann et al. 2003, pp. 37 ff.). The interest rate and thus real wage development, as well as relief payments such as the inflation adjustment premium and the advance payment for natural

Fig. 6.2 EIOPA Risk Dashboard 2023. (European Insurance and Occupational Pensions Authority 2023a, b)

gas and heat in December 2022, expand the scope for retirement provision and thus for the demand for life insurance; at the same time, savings flow into other interest-bearing deposits at higher interest rates, and the uncertain amount of expected additional costs due to increased energy costs is likely to prompt many households to prefer liquidity.

Looking ahead to 2024, uncertainty could decrease and a certain habituation to the new inflation environment could contribute to people returning more to their usual consumption and saving habits (Berenberg-Gossler et al. 2023).

The development in **private health insurance** (PHI) is initially dependent on the annual adjustments of the annual salary limit and the contribution assessment basis for health and long-term care insurance, and thus also on wage development and benefits in statutory health insurance (SHI). In addition, there is the cost development for treatment costs and (sometimes expensive to import) medicines. Looking ahead to 2024, the discussion about further premium jumps or benefit cuts will remain current in view of a further worsening financial deficit of the SHI. This could positively influence the balance of changes and thus the stock in the PHI. The trend to supplement the insurance protection of the SHI with private supplementary insurance will also continue. Furthermore, the shortage of skilled workers and thus the goal of becoming more attractive for employees and binding them in the long term will promote company health insurance and long-term care insurance from the employer's perspective. For employees too, this will become more attractive due to the rising costs of their own insurance and the overall rising cost of living (Berenberg-Gossler et al. 2023).

The **property & casualty insurance** is also affected by economic development. The sensitivity to secure oneself against financial losses is even higher in phases when one believes they cannot afford these losses. However, in these phases, there is a risk for the same reasons that the number of damage cases will increase. In phases of economic boom, private customers are more relaxed in both areas (conclusion of insurance contracts, assertion of damages) (Kühlmann et al. 2003, pp. 37 f.). The premium volume in property & casualty insurance is heavily dependent on the development of costs and the resulting premium adjustments. For example, the high repair and especially replacement part costs currently influence the claims expenses in motor vehicle insurance, the long-rising prices for construction services influence the claims expenses in buildings insurance, and the inflation-related necessary sum adjustments in home contents insurance affect their premium level. In credit insurance, there is a close connection because economic downturns often lead to payment defaults (Berenberg-Gossler et al. 2023).

Furthermore, the **income structure** plays a role in the demand for insurance coverage (see also Sect. 3.2.3). In the area of retirement provision, the demand behavior is, among other things, dependent on the budget available to customers. The distribution of net incomes of private households shows that a large part of the German population is able to finance at least small amounts for insurance coverage and retirement provision (Federal Statistical Office 2023d). The savings rate (savings formation in relation to available net income) is also important, which in Germany in 2023 is at 11.3%, roughly at the level of the previous year's period—a high rate compared to other industrialized countries. A savings rate of 11.3% means that private households saved an average of €11.30 for every €100 of available income (Federal Statistical Office 2023e). The development of income and the savings rate suggest an increasing demand.

6.1.3 Societal Framework Conditions and Developments

Insurance companies are also exposed to societal and **demographic trends**: The declining population development and the changing age structure are of great importance for marketing planning due to their demand effect. Especially for retirement provision products, the combination of declining birth rates, increasing aging, and reversal of the population pyramid is extremely relevant. In 2020, the total quotient (proportion of those under 20 or over 67 years of age to those between 20 and under 67 years of age) was 61.2%, in 2035 it will be between 75.6 and 77.1% depending on the migration balance, i.e., for every four people from predominantly working age groups, there are three from predominantly non-working age groups. The old-age quotient (proportion of those aged 67 and older to those between 20 and under 67 years of age) increases in the same period from 31.5 to 41.3 to 43.2%; one thing is certain, the proportion of seniors will significantly increase (Federal Statistical Office 2021, p. 11; Kotler et al. 2022, pp. 154–164).

In addition to marketing to the **target group of "young at heart seniors"**, activities should be more consistently aligned with lifestyles such as single and two-person households, which already accounted for 75% of all households in 2022 and are expected to increase to about 77% of all households by 2035 (Federal Statistical Office 2023c). This is accompanied by a continuing **change in values**, which was expressed in the 1990s in the pursuit of self-fulfillment and self-realization, a correspondingly greater willingness to take risks, a higher orientation towards experiences, a greater sense of entitlement, and a stronger environmental awareness among consumers. At the beginning of the 21st century, more prudent consumer behavior and community-oriented, familial behavior with social responsibility, and correspondingly, charitable organizations and volunteer work come to the fore. Behavior towards fellow human beings is characterized by people making fewer arrangements with others and often spending time at home (cocooning). In behavior towards organizations, there is a more frequent demand for meaning and applied methods, and many employees are less loyal, seeing their job not as a source of satisfaction, but as a source of income to finance their leisure activities. Their "work-life balance" is more important to them than their career. Finally, an emerging national consumer patriotism is evident in attitudes towards society, with consumers hoping to obtain higher quality and secure local jobs by purchasing local products. These developments have been accompanied in recent years by the establishment of ethnic subcultures as a result of increasing migration and post-materialistic consumer behavior (ethical, environmentally and health-conscious, and shared consumption) (see Sect. 3.2.3; Kotler et al. 2022, pp. 161–163, 255–265; Meffert et al. 2019, pp. 136–138).

A strong influence on this change in values is the technological development around **digitalization**. A quantum leap was made here in the late 90s and the beginning of the new millennium with the internet, the use of which has now reached a dimension with smartphones and social media that has also **permanently changed the entire communication behavior**. In this context, we speak of the cohorts of Generation Y, Z, and α, which include people who grew up with smartphones and social media (Digital Natives). Generations Y and Z are very similar in their consumption and communication behavior. However, representatives of Gen Z make the digital world more their domain, where they develop personal relationships, maintain them, and learn new things. In addition, compared to other generations, they learned early on how to deal with information surpluses and are highly capable of multitasking. Millennials already have a high information acquisition competence; Gen Z is also credited with being very quick to switch between different devices and channels when acquiring information—both online and offline (Meffert et al. 2019, p. 152).

The term "Generation D" (Digital) is somewhat broader and includes, in addition to the Digital Natives, Baby Boomers and also Generation X, i.e., all those for whom the use of digital media has become a matter of course in everyday life—it is therefore a cross-generational group that defines itself more by its (communication) behavior than by age. They already use products and services on a daily basis that bring a high degree of convenience, simplicity, and speed, and are used to buying books, electronics, music, travel, and many everyday necessities online on the computer and/or via smartphone. The benefit of these applications is seen as a personal enrichment across generations. With the widespread use, the social behavior of society changes, boundaries shift, and thus old market structures. The **consumer behavior becomes more individual,** the **multi-option society** (Bruhn 2019a, p. 542) thus becomes a reality. As a result, users initiate new processes and accelerate the societal change in values themselves (Blum and Weller 2013, pp. 48 f.; Richter 2014, p. 48).

The use of new media creates an information society capable of obtaining comprehensive and cross-offer information and—with appropriate commitment and interest—gaining an advantage over the provider (**information asymmetry in favor of the customer**). This applies at least to the educated citizens, who also increasingly engage in lifelong learning. These societal developments lead to a displacement competition for more demanding customers and require new and more flexible services as well as emotional appeal. At the same time, the proportion of the population that does not participate in this "education competition", is temporarily or even for a long time without work and/or has little interest in insurance offers, is growing. It demands its own and differently structured marketing measures.

Also, changed lifestyles determine the need for insurance coverage: For example, in certain parts of Germany, there has been a rural exodus for several years, which is accompanied by an increase in the conurbations around large cities (urbanization). This development has a direct influence on the risk development in motor vehicle insurance, but also on the concentration of values and real estate price development and thus the need for residential buildings and home contents insurance. The increasing number of single households (especially in the conurbations) leads to a changed need for survivor protection and—with the opposite sign—for care services in old age.

6.1.4 Technological Framework Conditions and Developments

Since the mid-90s, the technologically initiated **digitalization** has had significant effects on the micro and macro environment of companies. The currently available computer capacities, large customizable data volumes and their networking (big data) as well as their mobile acquisition and use lead to new business and market-related effects (Kollmann 2019). These include network effects and the associated exponentiality, the new and recombination of information in real time, the zero marginal cost phenomenon and the overcoming of human-machine interaction boundaries. The associated increasing inclusion of customer-related data allows for more individual and faster response to customer wishes. Digitalization does not refer to one industry, rather it represents a cross-industry key technology. Therefore, its significant effects on companies are also classified as the **fourth industrial revolution** (Meffert et al. 2019, p. 217).

The **online and offline worlds are increasingly merging**. The change in consumption patterns and media usage behavior of internet users (of all age cohorts) as well as the increasing reduction of digital transaction costs with increasing convergence of web-based information and communication technologies noticeably change people's daily professional and private lives. At the same time, the economic opportunities of providers are taken to another level because their technical infrastructure conditions fundamentally change. For example, email text messages as well as digital documents can be delivered to their recipients in a few seconds—simultaneously and globally. Similarly significant are the developments of Web 2.0. This technology has also significantly expanded the scope of action for companies. Added to this is the increasing **networking of everyday objects** that communicate with each other and provide people with greater benefits in everyday life. The respective technologies are integrated as flexibly as possible into the environment and daily actions of people ("internet of things"). This enables new (digital) business models, especially in the area of (mobile) internet services (very early and in detail at Oberholzer 2003; see also Meffert et al. 2019, p. 74).

The **insurance industry** as a **highly data-driven industry** is a significant player in Germany's digital economy. According to a GDV survey, IT expenditures in 2021 again amounted to over 5 billion €. This corresponds to a ratio of 2.4% in relation to total gross premium income. Compared to other industries, this is a high level; for example, the OECD estimates cross-industry IT investments in Germany for 2019 at 1.4% of gross domestic product, and the Kreditanstalt für Wiederaufbau (KfW) reports digitalization expenditures for the German SME sector in the same year at about 0.9% of total sales (GDV 2023b, p. 2). The **digitalization has long since encompassed all areas of the insurance value chain**. There are already industry-specific application fields of new technologies in data acquisition and data analysis (artificial intelligence, big data, internet of things), in data storage (blockchain, cloud computing) and in the communication and sales area (mobile devices with apps, chatbots, robo-advisors, social networks, online video applications, websites) (Eling and Lehmann 2018; see also Nicoletti 2021). Mobile devices, social networks, Wi-Fi, sensors, and machines generate mass data at high speed, and experts estimate that the volume of digital data doubles every two years. For companies and insurers, it is therefore interesting to effectively transform these large amounts and different sources of data with high complexity into usable knowledge. The availability of large amounts of data is referred to as **big data**, and the improved possibilities of using this data could be attributed to artificial intelligence. When both phenomena are used together in the financial system, methods of machine learning are usually applied. Algorithms are used that learn from existing data and then apply what they have learned to new data (BaFin 2018, p. 7). Big data is thus a holistic approach that generates detailed knowledge from large and complex data sets using various technologies. An example of such a technology is blockchain technology, on which Smart Contracts (e.g., for flight cancellation or weather insurance) are based (Eling and Lehmann 2018, p. 364). The big data approach accesses both internal and external data in different formats and structures.

The **applications** of big data and artificial intelligence are diverse. Traditional insurance companies can capture new valuable data through the use of big data and AI technologies, which could complement the standardly captured data of the insured and their claim data (Wedlich 2019). **In the field of insurance marketing**, such analyses help, for example, in product development, customer behavior analysis, cancellation prevention, market research, or sales support. However, compliance, security, and not least data protection requirements must be observed (BaFin 2018, pp. 95–134; Amerirad et al. 2023). After all, the use of the latest technologies is also subject to supervision, and the BaFin, for example, has already outlined principles for the use of algorithms in decision-making processes (BaFin 2021). A prominent application example for the retail business are usage-based motor vehicle insurance products based on **telematics technology** (Pay-as-you-drive, Pay-how-you-drive). The recording of driving-related data, which is transmitted to a mobile network operator and then evaluated, is technologically carried out via an app on the smartphone in combination with a retrofittable black box with GPS tracking, a plug or sensor, or directly via the technology installed in the car. The technology is primarily used by car manufacturers to offer customers more information and safety services, but it is also very suitable for the price calculation of motor vehicle insurers (Grüner and Hiebl 2014, pp. 60–62; Petrovs 2016; BaFin 2018, pp. 122 f.). Likewise, in the course of problem-solving service bundles, so-called **Smart-Home technologies** are increasingly being offered together with home contents and buildings insurance (Barb et al. 2018).

Digitalization leads **on the customer side** as mentioned to customers coming into contact with a multitude of touchpoints from companies in the pre-purchase, purchase, and post-purchase phases (see Sect. 2.2.4, excursus on Customer-Dominant Logic) and thereby changing their communication behavior. In addition to classic offline communication and sales channels, **new digital touchpoints** have been added (e.g., display banners, company websites, or review portals). This is associated with **new purchasing behavior patterns**: Demanders can search for information and purchase a service in different sales channels (Research Shopping). In showrooming (also referred to as Research offline, Purchase online, or RoPo), they purchase in an online channel, while the information search takes place offline. In webrooming, they purchase offline after having previously informed themselves online. Apart from research shopping, **demanders** can now **interact with each other** and become producers of their own content (User-generated Content), which they can spread on social media platforms; they can also use this to exchange information about companies' services. Thus, consumer experiences in the form of Electronic-Word-of-mouth can be made accessible to a large number of other consumers (Meffert et al. 2019, pp. 136–146; Homburg 2020, p. 83).

Digitalization **thus changes the communication and purchasing behavior** of the population and thereby also affects **core areas of insurance marketing**: Insurance is both a classic service and an information product. Both characteristics are responsible for the fact that the purchase of insurance by customers requires trust in the future performance (in the event of a claim). Before and during the contractual relationship, the insurance business essentially consists of information and information exchange. Developments around the internet, electronic commerce (incl. mobile payments), social media, multimedia (Web 2.0) as well as big data and artificial intelligence influence the **possibilities of this information exchange along the entire service process**, and this for both providers and demanders (Eckert et al. 2022). The information and comparison possibilities of the customer increase quantitatively and qualitatively, while the information costs decrease at the same time. Decreasing transaction costs open up new intermediaries, appearing beneficially (e.g., portals and FinTech or InsurTech companies). But also the providers benefit from the internet. Their access possibilities to existing and potential customers become more diverse, more flexible in terms of time and content, and more cost-effective. The same applies to product or coverage design (BaFin 2018, pp. 95–108; Nicoletti 2021, pp. 101–104). Therefore, insurance companies need professional digital communication (see Sect. 14.2.5).

Excursus on InsurTechs

The term FinTech is used in connection with the founding of financial services-based start-up companies and is an abbreviation of the German term Finanztechnologie as well as the English words Financial Services and Technology. Thus, it serves as a collective term for the application of modern technologies in the financial services sector. Limited to the insurance industry, we speak of **InsurTechs** (**Insur**ance and **Tech**nology Start-ups; tech-based companies in the insurance industry). The term is predominantly used when describing the business models of start-up companies and/or their financing with venture capital. These—**technology and mostly web-based business models**—try to challenge established financial service providers through the intelligent use of technologies, either through independent, competing business models or as new cooperation partners. They are customer-centric and offer customer-related mobile service. Their advantages over established insurers: They are specialists in new technologies, have no legacy IT, their business models are fully tailored to the new technologies and typically only focused on a small part of the value chain, their corporate culture is characterized by flexibility and error tolerance, and the employees are predominantly "Digital Natives" (Nicoletti 2021, Chap. 15). In retrospect, they have also benefited from very favorable financing conditions for many years due to the EU's low-interest policy (Wiener and Theis 2017, p. 2; Eling and Lehmann 2018, p. 371). The most important FinTech application areas include banking, insurance, lending, payment, and trading. Insurance-related InsurTechs can now be located along the entire value chain. The first InsurTechs to enter the German market were, among others, Friendsurance (P2P and group insurance), Clark (insurance manager with commission participation) or WeFox (broker software).

Current market studies (Oliver Wyman and policen direct 2021, p. 33) confirm that a lively InsurTech scene has developed in the entire DACH region[1] that has become an integral part of the insurance industry. On the contrary: InsurTechs are a **driving force of the digital transformation of the insurance industry** and take on a kind of catalyst role. The maturation process of the market has continued, the founding boom has flattened, the number of active start-ups has even slightly decreased. In 2021, there are 149 active start-ups in the insurance sector in Germany, 16 in Austria, and 44 in Switzerland. Many of these InsurTechs are not so young anymore, some have been active for ten or more years. New start-ups and market entries are also expected in the coming years, but not with the same dynamics as in the past. The first InsurTech start-ups with BaFin license have been on the market for about five years: So far, seven InsurTech start-ups have received such a license as insurers, i.e., risk carriers, six property & casualty/accident insurers, and one health insurer. Some of the shareholders are also traditional insurers. These seven InsurTech insurers make up half of all new non-life insurers between 2017 and 2022; however, their share of the premium income remains negligible at about 0.03% (Theis 2023). The relevance of innovative, technology-driven products and services will continue to rise. InsurTechs benefit from this. The COVID pandemic has further accelerated the digitalization of the insurance industry, which benefits both B2C InsurTechs and those with B2B2C models. Start-ups with a valuation of more than one billion US dollars—so-called "unicorns"—now exist in Germany, Austria, and Switzerland. They are mainly found in the areas of FinTechs (neobanks and crypto) as well as the logistics and travel industry. In the insurance industry, WeFox is so far the only unicorn (Oliver Wyman and policen direct 2021, pp. 33 f.).

The term "InsurTech" was in the past a clear distinguishing feature because the start-ups in the insurance industry wanted to position themselves as an **antithesis to everything established**. However, this has been **only partially successful**. One reason for this may lie in the challenges of insurance marketing presented in this textbook, which result from the peculiarities of the insurance market, its products, and the demand for insurance. These also apply to InsurTechs, and their management is not a matter of course. In addition, with the increasing cooperation and investment relationships between traditional insurers and InsurTech start-ups, as well as the digital in-house start-ups of insurers, the boundaries are blurring. It can therefore be assumed that the digitalization driven by InsurTechs will increasingly merge into the overall digital transformation of the industry. In other words: InsurTechs accelerate the digitalization of the insurance industry, but do not generate disruptive business models or market shifts.

Further reading for in-depth study:

- BaFin 2018.
- Braun and Schreiber 2017.
- Nicoletti 2021.
- Oliver Wyman and policen direct 2021.
- Stöckli et al. 2018.

[1] DACH stands for Germany (D), Austria (A), and Switzerland (CH).

Further technological developments such as in genetic technology, microelectronics, laser technology, robotics, bio- or nanotechnology, or in other areas (Homburg 2020, p. 508) also affect insurers, provided these represent the risks assumed or change the risks assumed by insurers, whether directly in industrial business or indirectly with commercial and private customers. They thus offer new business potentials through the coverage of novel or changed risks, but at the same time also challenges in terms of calculation (risk of error and risk of change). Novel risks due to technological advances are one of the main drivers of product innovations in property & casualty insurance (Köhne and Kopp 2007, pp. 227 f.). An example is cyber coverage. With digitalization and its applications, new risks have emerged such as data theft or the use of mobile services such as location or recording without the user's consent, and much more.

6.1.5 Ecological and Health Framework Conditions and Developments

The consideration of a company's natural environment is becoming increasingly important, as the protection of the environment and health will remain one of the most important issues for companies and the public in the long term (Kotler et al. 2022, pp. 167 f.).

The central ecological development is **climate change**. The associated risks affect all societal areas and all (nature-related) ecosystems, which with their diverse structures and services represent the basis of life. Therefore, the development of risk prevention and adaptation capacities is a societal task to which insurers can and must also contribute. Limiting global warming and its impacts represents the **central political challenge of the 21st century worldwide**; it is a crucial prerequisite for achieving the goals of the UN Agenda 2030 for sustainable development. As early as 2008, the German government presented the first German Adaptation Strategy to Climate Change (DAS) and has been continuously developing it since then. Its overarching goal is to reduce the vulnerability of ecosystems and society to the effects of climate change and at the same time to increase the resilience and adaptability of these systems. Since 2021, the German government has been intensifying the political control of climate adaptation through a federal law, a preventive climate adaptation strategy with measurable goals, and the anchoring of a joint financing of measures by the federal and state governments (Federal Environment Agency 2023, p. 12).

It cannot be denied that **climate changes are already evident in Germany**. In recent years, Germany has repeatedly faced heatwaves, droughts, flash floods, and floods. The temperatures of air, water, and soil continued to rise, and with them, the impacts on humans, the environment, the economy, and infrastructures also intensified. Particularly noticeable are the extreme events: In July 2021, the **low-pressure area 'Bernd'** brought extreme rainfall in various parts of Western Europe. In the region around the rivers Ahr and Erft in Rhineland-Palatinate and North Rhine-Westphalia, the flash floods and floods resulted in catastrophic damage and losses with over 180 fatalities in Germany.

This resulted in insured property damage to residential buildings, home contents, and businesses amounting to €8.1 billion, the highest damage expenditure in property insurance for natural hazards to date. The 'World Weather Attribution' (WWA), an international association of scientists, concluded that the probability of such extreme rainfall events has increased 1.2 to 9 times due to climate change. The DAS monitoring report shows: **Heavy rainfall and floods** as well as **heat and drought** with all their consequences have measurably arrived in Germany. Summers with strong heatwaves and the highest recorded air temperatures to date are becoming more frequent; for example, in July 2022, a temperature of over 40°C was measured north of the 53rd parallel for the first time. The heatwaves in the years 2018, 2019, 2020, and most recently 2022, particularly challenged the population in large cities. Between 2018 and 2020, about 19,300 additional people died as a result of heat.

Heatwaves and drought also brought about **functional restrictions on infrastructures and waterways**: Due to high water temperatures, there was not enough cooling water available on the one hand, and on the other hand, coal could only be delivered by ship to a limited extent due to low water levels. The consequences were technical obstructions in freight and passenger traffic as well as significant restrictions on power production in nuclear and coal-fired power plants. The hot summers, in conjunction with insufficient rainfall, led to severe droughts in some regions, resulting in massive losses in the water balance between 2018 and 2020. From 2019 to 2021, record lows of long-term groundwater levels were recorded in many places, and the effects of the drought years have not yet been compensated for in 2023. Consequences included, among other things, **yield losses in agriculture**, a significant increase in crown thinning in forests, a sudden **increase in tree mortality rates** for all tree species, a significantly **increased incidence of forest fires**, and—despite the drought—at the same time, extreme floods in the summer half-years, in which the long-term average high water discharges were exceeded many times over in some places. The apparent contradiction between drought and extreme floods can be resolved: On the one hand, warmer air absorbs more moisture, increasing the risk of heavy rainfall; on the other hand, dry periods increase. The dried-out soils can then not absorb and store the water during heavy rainfall, so the rainwater runs off on the surface and the rivers rise quickly (Federal Environment Agency 2023, p. 13).

Naturally, there are direct **interdependencies between ecological developments and the market performance of insurance**. Climate events (and their increase in the course of climate change) have a strong, often immediate influence on many risks and the associated damages, e.g., floods on buildings, business, and motor vehicle damage, storms and hail on motor vehicle and crop damage, or heat and drought on mortality, health, or crop failure. Climate events thus influence the demand on the customer side, but also the insurability, the coverage design (Sect. 10.2.2) and the price determination (Sect. 11.2).

Interdependencies also exist between the various developments in the macro-environment of the company. For example, **ecological developments** have prompted politics to adjust the **legal framework conditions**: Findings about the increasing acceleration and the dimensions of climate change have led to the (international) politics making the issue one of their main concerns and increasingly involving the economy and the companies in the responsibility to counteract or align their activities more sustainably (see excursus).

Excursus on the anchoring of environmental and ESG goals in the regulation of insurance companies

Sustainability has become the top issue of any regulatory efforts through the stylization of the **Green Deal** propagated by the President of the European Commission. The EU-wide regulatory requirements include the Disclosure Regulation and the Taxonomy Regulation, an adapted Insurance Distribution Directive (IDD), a changed Markets in Financial Instruments Directive (MiFID 2), and the already existing Corporate Sustainable Reporting Directive (CSRD); they are intended to flank the ESG sustainability criteria within the framework of the Green Deal with supervisory law and bring them into the markets with regulatory pressure.

A significant basis of the sustainability considerations with reference to the financial services and insurance industry are the EU **Taxonomy Regulation** (Regulation (EU) 2020/852 of 18 June 2020 on the establishment of a framework to facilitate sustainable investments and amending Regulation (EU) 2019/2088) and the EU **Disclosure Regulation** (Regulation (EU) 2019/2088 of 27.11.2019 on sustainability-related disclosure obligations in the financial services sector; Sustainable Finance Disclosure Regulation, SFDR) in combination with the Delegated Regulation on the technical regulatory standards of the Disclosure Regulation (Delegated Regulation (EU) 2022/1288 of the Commission of 6 April 2022).

As a dogma of the taxonomy regulation, it is stipulated that any economic activity must serve at least one of the sustainability goals defined by the EU and at the same time must not contradict any of these goals. In the first step, the taxonomy regulation focuses on the area of ecological sustainability (**E**nvironment), while also defining minimum standards for labor and human rights as sustainability goals. In addition to ecological sustainability goals, expectations of socially and societally (**S**ocial) correct as well as ethical (**G**overnance) corporate governance are also included.

So-called 'European Sustainability Reporting Standards (ESRS)' as standards for key figures, which are to be provided from 2024 for the sustainability reporting envisaged according to the Corporate Sustainability Reporting Directive (CSRD) and Corporate Sustainability Due Diligence Directive, are being developed by the European Financial Reporting Advisory Group. From the perspective of the current, ecological focus, the EU defines **six primary goals of ecological sustainability** (Art. 9 Taxonomy Regulation):

- Climate protection
- Adaptation to climate change
- Sustainable use and protection of water and marine resources
- Transition to a circular economy
- Prevention and reduction of environmental pollution
- Protection and restoration of biodiversity and ecosystems.

In particular, the financial industry had to comply with the **Corporate Sustainable Reporting Directive (CSRD)** for the first time in 2022 and publish data on how many of their assets they hold in industries for which environmental criteria are defined in the taxonomy. Against this background and due to the confusing regulations on sustainability, BaFin has drafted a **guideline on dealing with sustainability risks** (see BaFin 2020). Broken down to the insurance industry, it calls on **insurance companies** to identify, analyze and manage risks that can result from a deficient handling of ESG criteria. According to BaFin, these are "events or conditions from the areas of environment, social or corporate governance, the occurrence of which can actually or potentially have negative effects on the assets, financial and earnings situation as well as on the reputation of a supervised company" (BaFin 2020, p. 13).

The BaFin guideline formulates the supervisory expectations for the sustainability management of the financial services industry in Germany and provides assistance in the supervisory understanding of sustainability. There are also some **examples of ESG-risks**. The listed **environmental risks** (Environment) refer to the six primary goals mentioned in the taxonomy regulation. Sustainability risks in the areas of climate and environment are divided into physical risks and transition risks: **Physical risks** arise both with regard to individual extreme weather events and their consequences (e.g., heat and dry periods, floods, storms, hail, forest fires) and in relation to long-term changes in climatic and ecological conditions (e.g., frequency and amounts of precipitation, weather instability, sea level rise, increase in average temperatures). Physical risks can also have indirect consequences (e.g., collapse of supply chains). Since 2023, companies have been forced to conduct a risk analysis of their own supply chain through the **Act** on Corporate Due Dilligence Obligations in Supply Chain (LkSG). This means, for example, for industrial insurers, to investigate ecological risks along the supply chains of policyholders: The insurability of these companies must then be assessed on the basis of this risk analysis. **Transition risks** are those that arise in connection with the transition to a low-carbon economy, for example the increase in cost and/or shortage of fossil energy sources or excessively high investment costs due to necessary renovations of buildings and facilities.

The BaFin deliberately does not limit the term "sustainability risk" to a clear definition, as the direct, physical risks from the ESG areas and the associated indirect transition risks for adapting to the changed risk world are of a complex nature and can by no means be limited to a few, exemplary risks. Rather, the BaFin provides examples in the guideline for dealing with sustainability risks within the framework of the IKS-risk nomenclature given according to VAG (in reference to §§ 26, 29 VAG):

- **Credit risk/Counterparty default risk**: An insurance company underwrites the bond of a company whose business model is significantly affected by political decisions on ESG topics (e.g., production of weapons, use of child labor).
- **Market (price) risk**: An insurance company invests in companies that demonstrably neither operate sustainably nor use the invested funds for the sustainability transition. The disclosure of this lack of consideration of sustainable criteria leads to devaluations of the market title.
- **Liquidity risk**: A life insurer is overwhelmed with cancellations of its policy portfolio due to a dubious reputation.
- **Operational risk**: Natural disasters or pandemics impair the processes of insurance companies.
- **Underwriting risk**: In the area of building insurance, damages increase, for example, as a result of storm, floods, hail, or snow pressure. Natural disasters or pandemics lead to insured losses in business interruption insurance according to insurance conditions. Insurers have to take into account the (increasing) frequency of loss and/or average amount of losses in their tariff calculation and in the actuarial valuation of technical provisions, as well as the fact that they can be affected financially (active side) and in terms of loss reserves (passive side) by a sustainability risk.
- **Strategic risk**: An insurance company focused on insuring stationary trade must drastically reduce its new business due to the growing online trade.
- **Reputation risk**: An insurance company insures a retail chain that sells products from a well-known manufacturer with a clothing factory in East Asia, or the clothing factory itself. Due to insufficient national guidelines regarding safety standards and lack of self-provision, the

building burns down, hundreds of workers die, the case goes through the media mentioning the investors and insurers. In addition, in the currently sensitive societal perception, investing in only seemingly sustainable financial products ("greenwashing") can pose a high reputation risk for ESG-conscious stakeholders.

- Compliance with ESG guidelines will become a **governance criterion** from a regulatory perspective and thus the main task of the responsible compliance function.

The regulation of the insurance industry in terms of sustainability takes place in many areas and through various levers, not just through the two mentioned regulations. Since January 1, 2023, the **technical regulatory standards for the implementation of the Disclosure Regulation** have been applied (Delegated Regulation (EU) 2022/1288 of the Commission). According to the **IDD** (Delegated Regulation (EU) 2021/1257 of the Commission), since August 2, 2022, insurance companies must actively track and determine the sustainability preferences of their policyholders when distributing funded pension products. Because this is difficult due to some still unclear terminology and incomplete data, EIOPA has published further guidance on implementation (European Insurance and Occupational Pensions Authority 2022). With the **Delegated Regulation 2021/12565** amending the Delegated Acts on Solvency II, sustainability risks have had to be integrated into risk management and the ORSA (Own Risk and Solvency Assessment, i.e., the company's own assessment of the risk and solvency situation) since August 2, 2022. Finally, the issue of sustainability is also part of the **Solvency II review**: A long-term climate scenario analysis is to be implemented within the framework of the ORSA, which was explicitly mentioned in the EU Commission's Renewed Sustainable Finance Strategy and proposed by the EU Commission. The national supervisory bodies have already taken this up by taking sustainability requirements into account in advance of an EU-wide determination; BaFin has included this in its guideline (see BaFin 2020, p. 33). The industry has reacted to this: The GDV published a comprehensive information paper to support its member companies at the beginning of 2022 and has already presented an updated and expanded new version of the "Approaches for Climate Change Scenarios in the ORSA" in 2023 (GDV 2023c).

In addition to the mentioned global regulatory elements, there are indirect influences on the insurance business activity in the sense of a regulatory sustainability obligation. For example, the **Energy Saving Regulation** issued by the EU and already implemented in the nation states indirectly influences sustainable action when insurance companies have to carry out the reconstruction or repair of a property in an environmentally friendly manner according to this regulation after a damage event.

(Müller-Reichart and Graumann 2022; BaFin 2022)

The extensive and increasing regulatory requirements for sustainability demand a lot from insurers.

In the **area of capital investment**, sustainability is discussed under the keyword "sustainable finance": As part of the Europe-wide Green Deal efforts, European companies have been asked since 2022 to record the negative impacts of investment decisions on ecological and social factors. The insights gained in this process will in turn flow into a revised Disclosure Regulation. This is intended to address the sustainability aspects of capital investment in particular—a significant requirement for the asset management of insurance companies.

The **EU Disclosure Regulation** already differentiates capital market funds according to their sustainability criteria in Articles 8 and 9. While Article 8 funds can only be described as tending towards sustainability, Article 9 funds ensure full sustainability. According to Articles 8 and 9 of the Transparency Regulation, it must be demonstrated for sustainable financial products to what extent investments that take into account at least one of the environmental objectives of the **Taxonomy Regulation** (see excursus in this chapter) are included in the capital investment portfolio underlying these products. For the part of the capital investment portfolio that does not meet these environmental objectives, it must be published that these investments do not meet the EU criteria for environmentally sustainable economic activities. Furthermore, it must be informed to what extent the individual investments within a financial product represent an environmentally sustainable economic activity and which environmental objectives they pursue according to the Taxonomy Regulation. The social and corporate ethical criteria have not yet been specified. As soon as this is the case, their compliance will also have to be demonstrated in the course of a sustainable investment policy (Müller-Reichart and Graumann 2022, p. 421).

The **insurance industry** has already responded to EU efforts with a **sustainability positioning**, explicitly committing to sustainable and climate-friendly capital investment. It is also stipulated that insurance companies aim for greenhouse gas neutrality of their capital investments by 2050. More and more insurers are also engaging in voluntary initiatives, such as the "Principles for Responsible Investment" (PRI), and insurers representing more than 55% of the sector's capital investments are members of the Net Zero Asset Owner Alliance (NZAOA), which is committed to aligning their investment portfolios with climate neutrality by 2050. Considering that the German insurance industry currently holds around **2 trillion Euros in capital investments**, this shows both the importance of the insurance industry as a capital pool and the **challenge of shifting this investment volume into climate-neutral assets** (GDV 2023d, pp. 3 f.).

In the **field of insurance advice and intermediation**, sustainability has become a mandatory topic in the consultation on insurance investment products with the adaptation of the IDD. Intermediaries and insurers must ask their customers how much value they place on ecological and social aspects as well as good corporate governance, i.e., the so-called ESG criteria. Insurance intermediaries must also inquire about the sustainability preferences of their clients during the consultation and advise them accordingly with appropriate expertise on sustainability.

In this context, the intermediary is even required to conduct a **suitability test** to determine whether the insurance or investment product is suitable in light of the expressed sustainability preferences (suitability assessment), and this test must be repeated regularly (see in detail Sects. 13.5.1 and 13.5.3). The intermediary is responsible for identifying and exposing potential 'greenwashing products' (label fraud of supposedly sustainable products), as he is not allowed to recommend these. Thus, a corresponding sustainability expertise is assumed on the part of the sales organs. However, despite possible training and support measures, a sound sustainability consultation in insurance sales is by no means guaranteed—on the contrary, it seems hardly feasible due to the already demanding consultation and numerous information, consultation and documentation obligations. This is even more true in online sales or via aggregators—a simple "tick box" is unlikely to suffice.

In order to meet the required sustainability consultation, sustainability aspects must inevitably be incorporated into the internal **product approval process** of an insurance company (Sect. 10.3). The POG guidelines (Product Oversight Governance) will therefore have to be consistently expanded to include sustainability elements in order to take these into account already in the product conception (Müller-Reichart and Graumann 2022, p. 422). The question arises whether, as a last resort, it should be determined in the context of target group definition that the respective insurance product is not suitable for customers who violate sustainability criteria; however, this would significantly limit the customer base, regardless of whether in the industrial, commercial or private customer segment.

In addition to ecological factors, **health conditions and developments** also influence the market-oriented scope of action of insurers. Three different constellations are evident:

1. The healthcare system with its actors and infrastructure as a healthcare "framework" has effects on the consequences and spread of diseases as well as on healthcare costs and thus influences in particular health and life insurance.
2. The previously outlined climate change has demonstrable health effects on the population.
3. Other events such as pandemics have demonstrable health effects on the population.

To connect to the previous explanations on climate change, the **health effects of climate change** (2.) are first considered. Global warming can affect health both directly and indirectly. The **indirect effects** include an extended pollen flight season or the multiplication and spread of vectors (pathogens). Allergies caused by pollen will occur much more frequently and intensely in the future, leading to severe respiratory diseases such as asthma; on the one hand, the periods in which the plants bloom will be significantly longer due to mild temperatures, on the other hand, new types of pollen can emerge. In addition, the amount of pollen increases due to the increased temperature and the increased fine dust pollution in the atmosphere. The rising temperatures also promote the spread of vectors such as ticks or mosquitoes and thus the spread of the infectious diseases they transmit.

Direct health effects result from UV radiation and heatwaves. UV radiation carries health risks such as cataracts or skin cancer. Heatwaves have even more far-reaching health effects. They increasingly lead to various diseases or even death. In Germany, densely built-up cities are particularly affected by heatwaves, as they heat up quickly and strongly and store the heat, but cool down slowly at night. Heatwaves can have various effects that go far beyond the typical cardiovascular weaknesses, such as chronic stress, increased water loss, which can lead to dehydration and the well-known circulatory collapse, as well as increased heart attacks or heat strokes. Moreover, people can be weakened or even die from anemia and oxygen deficiency in the internal organs, cell death, inflammation, or organ failure. Heatwaves generate so-called excess mortality, i.e., a difference between the course of observed mortality and the estimated course of mortality without a heatwave. In conjunction with general global warming, they rather lead to excess mortality in summer (see Mahnke and Schmidt 2022, pp. 251–253 and the literature cited there).

Apart from climatic changes, **other events** such as **pandemics** also have health effects (3.). The example of the Corona pandemic shows that these are naturally immediate when a virus results in death or long-term effects (Long COVID). In addition, the risk of infection as an underwriting risk is as pronounced as never before in pandemics, as not even an international risk equalization works. Additional effects with relevance for insurers are added: The COVID-19 pandemic can transfer significant psychological perception effects and compare the changes in risk assessments with the effects of other disaster events. For example, pandemics make the potential dangers they pose visible to the public. However, the population only focuses on current risks. The development of fear only increases temporarily after the occurrence and then falls back to the pre-crisis level after a few years (Eichner et al. 2023). The COVID-19 pandemic has also caused significant economic damage. The value-added losses (in the national accounts) can be quantified at several hundred billion euros, although the long-term effects on the growth potential in Germany can only be estimated. The long-term effects include educational losses, the increase in the state quota, or the loss of life years due to the lockdown measures, but also effects on social cohesion or societal cohesion (Hüther 2023).

Finally, the **healthcare system** with its actors and infrastructure forms a significant health framework condition (see for economic importance: Federal Ministry for Economic Affairs and Climate Protection 2023). It affects the consequences and spread of diseases, think for example of the capacities in the intensive care units, as well as the healthcare costs and thus particularly influences health and life insurance.

6.2 Analysis of the Micro-Environment of Insurance Companies

The micro-environment of insurance companies is referred to as the **relevant market**. Unlike the macro-environment, this can indeed be influenced by one's own marketing strategy. Its investigation concerns the external market environment of the insurance company: Such information includes details about the company's immediate sales market, statements about the market structure and market dynamics (Sect. 6.2.1), about existing and potential customers (Sect. 6.2.2), the offer and strategies of existing and potential competitors (Sect. 6.2.3) as well as the expectations of other stakeholder groups (Sect. 6.2.4).

6.2.1 Market Analysis

In the course of market analysis, it is about the **collection of general market characteristics**. These include the market volume, current and future market growth, purchasing power in the market, potential profit margins, and prevailing competitive forces. These aspects provide insights about the current and future attractiveness of the relevant market.

Market Indicators

Market capacity expresses the turnover a sector could achieve in a market in a period if all potential customers both had the need or interest in acquiring a product offered and the means to acquire it. For example, one can calculate the market capacity in the motor vehicle third-liability insurance business for private customers in Germany by considering all citizens over 18 years of age and multiplying the number by the average premium income.

Market potential on the other hand, is the turnover of a sector in a market in a period with those customers who actually both have a need or interest in acquiring a product offered and the means to acquire it. In the same example, the market potential in motor vehicle third-liability insurance for private customers in Germany is calculated by considering all citizens over 18 years of age who own or want to acquire a car and can finance it, and multiplying the number by the average premium income.

Market volume represents the actual sales of a sector in a market in a period and is thus a part of the market potential. From the ratio between the market volume and the market potential, the **market saturation** or the degree of saturation can be determined: If both are the same size, the market is saturated. In the case of motor vehicle third-liability insurance in the private customer market, the market volume is determined by the actual premium income of a reporting period, provided the corresponding data is only available for the private customer segment, i.e. without the shares in the commercial and industrial fleet. In the case of motor vehicle third-liability insurance, the degree of saturation is very high, i.e. the market potential is almost exhausted, as this insurance is compulsory insurance, without which a car may not be driven.

Market share of a provider is its share of the market volume, i.e. the actual sales of the provider in a market in a period in relation to the entire sector (see for further reference sizes of the market share Sect. 7.2.2). Accordingly, the market share of motor vehicle third-liability insurers can be determined.

To assess the attractiveness of a market, the **model of the five competitive forces** (five forces model) by *Porter* can be used: According to this, attractive markets are those with low competitive intensity and high willingness to pay of the demanders. Therefore, to assess market attractiveness, the prevailing competitive forces in this market must be examined. The *Porter* model considers the current competitive intensity, i.e. the rivalry among existing providers, as well as four factors that influence this. These include supplier and buyer power (e.g. due to concentration), the entry of potential new competitors from other markets, and the threat of substitute products (= replacement products for existing products) (Porter 1980, 2004, p. 4).

The model of the five competitive forces provides a structuring approach for strategic market analysis. It helps to identify not only the current market structures but also to consider possible influencing factors of market development and change. From a strategic point of view, this is essential and therefore must be taken into account when formulating the marketing strategy.

The application of this model in the insurance industry can provide a general understanding of developments in the insurance market. Examples: "Hard" reinsurance markets (supplier power), market saturations on the private customer side (buyer power), substitute products by banks in the area of pension provision and new competitors such as car manufacturers in motor vehicle insurance can increase the intensity of competition in the industry. A comprehensive and industry-wide application of the model can be found in *Ehrler* (Ehrler 1999, pp. 82–106). However, as mentioned, the model can also be applied situationally to submarkets or market segments.

In the course of market analysis, another model by *Porter* is helpful: The **model of strategic groups** classifies competitors into strategic groups that pursue similar competitive strategies and are characterized by similar strategic characteristics and behaviors. This is associated with lasting profitability differences because the respective strategies are differently promising. Due to mobility barriers, a short-term switch to another, more promising group is however difficult (Porter 1980). A meta-analysis of empirical studies identified mobility barriers in market-related aspects (e.g., product structures, distribution channels), in peculiarities of the industry-typical value creation (e.g., cost degression possibilities in certain value creation areas) as well as in structural features of the individual company (e.g., degree of vertical integration, organizational structure). The model also explains the competitive behavior of individual companies: Within the strategic group, there is intense competition and similar reaction patterns to environmental changes, while the competition between the strategic groups follows different rules, and the intensity depends on the market interdependence between the groups (Homburg 2020, pp. 245 f. and 526 f.).

In the insurance-related (marketing) literature, the approach of the strategic group is not widely spread, although it can also be used there to gain insights. The thesis of polarization tendencies in the insurance market goes in this direction to some extent, postulating the orientation of insurers into the two extremes based on various criteria (product quality, price level, range, company size, number of business fields, customer groups, business regions, distribution channels) (Farny 2011, pp. 526–530; Krausz 2002, pp. 200–284). However, the approach of the strategic group goes further, as it uses more than two criteria to determine the group and is therefore more meaningful. **With regard to the German insurance market**, for example, at least four strategic groups could be identified based on size, range, product variants, price, and distribution channels as well as their respective common target market, which are similarly positioned and behave within themselves, but differ from group to group in this respect:

1. Large all-branch corporations (**All-rounders**): high turnover, wide range of products, many product variants within an insurance branch, higher price level, multichannel distribution and orientation towards the overall market.
2. Large all-branch corporations with process focus (**Standardizers**): high turnover, wide range of products, few product variants within an insurance branch, lower price level, focus on few distribution channels and orientation towards the overall market.
3. Medium-sized insurers with range focus (**Specialists**): high turnover, narrow range of products, few product variants within an insurance branch, medium price level, multichannel or pure broker distribution and orientation towards the overall market or target groups.
4. Medium-sized direct insurers (**Direct distributors**): medium turnover, small to medium range of products, few product variants within an insurance branch, low to medium price level, direct sales plus distribution cooperations. They are often focused on the business field of motor vehicle insurance.

InsurTechs could also represent a strategic group insofar as they behave similarly in the criteria size (start-up), range (limited), product variants (limited) and distribution channel (mostly online via portals, direct sales or brokers); however, they serve very different business fields along the entire value chain and therefore only compete directly with each other to a limited extent and thus do not form a strategic group as a whole.

In the course of market analysis, it is not very productive to collect the mentioned market characteristics and competitive forces across the entire industry. Rather, they should be calculated and identified for the submarkets of the insurance market that the insurer wants to investigate. This applies, for example, to the concentration in the insurance market, as not the same and equal number of providers and demanders appear in every insurance sector. And the competitive forces are also differently pronounced in customer- or product-related differentiated submarkets, such as in the industrial and private customer sector or in the motor vehicle and accident insurance sector.

At least it can be determined across the industry that the concentration process in the insurance sector is moderate overall (see also Sect. 3.4.1). Moreover, in the **private customer sector**, a **buyer's market** can be assumed, as the supply far exceeds the demand. After all, the general public demands and competition enforces the **search for customer-oriented overall services**, which is also increasingly observed. Thus, in the sense of functional thinking (see Sect. 2.2.4), some providers have organized the offer of "Allfinanz" solutions around various financial services functions. Care strategies also bundle various functions such as supply, assistance, service provision, and organization of the whole (originally mainly Swiss insurers like Zurich and Winterthur). Recently, German providers are also increasingly pursuing such approaches in cooperation with other service partners in so-called ecosystems (see excursus in Sect. 9.2).

6.2.2 Demand and Customer Analysis

This involves the examination of current and potential customers in the relevant market. The starting point is the question of who appears as a **demander in the relevant market**. It needs to be clarified whether and, if so, which customer segments can be distinguished here. Of great importance for the marketing strategy are also the basic needs of the customers (see Sect. 3.2) and the customer behavior (see Chap. 4) in the relevant market—both in the status quo and with regard to future development (Homburg 2020, pp. 515 f.). For insurers, it is interesting to know, for example, how different types of customers express themselves in terms of their usage behavior when obtaining information or their attitudes towards intermediaries, in order to be able to react accordingly.

With regard to the needs and behavior analysis, one's own customers must be distinguished from potential demanders in the relevant market: Information of a more general nature about all demanders of the relevant market can be found in public statistics (e.g., Federal Statistical Office, Deutsche Bundesbank, BaFin, Deutsche Rentenversicherung, etc.), those of a more special nature are to be developed by market research (see Chap. 5). Information about one's own customers can be collected by a company through direct surveys, evaluation of complaints, or through the sales force. Customer base analyses are also possible: For example, customer types and their share of the customer base can be identified based on personal characteristics, and needs, attitudes, and behaviors can be derived from this. With regard to potential new customers, customer types to be targeted can be determined accordingly and the product design can be adapted to these.

The insurance market consists of a multitude of current and potential insurance customers, who have quite different needs in terms of their risk coverage and retirement provision. In order to meet these needs in a customer-oriented manner, insurers must segment the market, i.e., divide the total market into submarkets using certain characteristics of the demanders, which are homogeneous within themselves, but heterogeneous in comparison to each other. This allows them to better meet the different needs of the market segments through appropriate market services. The **market segmentation** is thus a useful method of a differentiated demand analysis. In a broader sense, it includes both market identification (information side) and market development (action side), in a narrower sense only the market identification (Meffert et al. 2019, pp. 215 f.). In the course of the demand analysis, only the market identification or information side should be the subject of market segmentation; market segmentation in the broader sense is understood here as target group marketing. The associated target group-related market development is the subject of the marketing strategy and the marketing mix.

Excursus on clarification of the term insurance customer

In the insurance industry, there are various contexts in which the insurance customer can be associated with the insurance company. In life insurance, up to four roles are even distinguished, the policyholder, the premium payer, the insured person, and the beneficiary:

- **Policyholder** (PH): The PH is the contractual partner of the insurer and thus the holder of all rights (design and disposal rights) and obligations arising from the contract.
- **Premium payer**: If the premium payer and PH are not identical, the premium payer does not acquire any rights from the contract solely through the payment of premiums. He merely takes over the payment. Even the reminder in case of payment default must be made to the PH. In practice, this occurs, for example, when grandparents take out an education insurance policy for their grandchildren and the parents or one parent are the policyholders.
- **Insured person** (IP): The insured person is the one on whose life the insurance contract was concluded. However, she does not acquire any rights from the life insurance contract, nor any obligations. In addition, there can be a co-insured person, for example, if the wife is entitled to receive a pension in addition to the husband. If IP and PH are not identical, this is referred to as third-party insurance.
- **Beneficiary or entitled person**: The beneficiary receives the contractual benefit upon maturity, which can become due in the event of death and/or survival.

A person assumes all four forms at the same time, for example, when a single person takes out a pension insurance for himself: Then he is PH, premium payer, IP and in the event of survival the beneficiary through the pension payment. However, four different people can also be involved in a contract, for example, when the father (PH) takes out a term life insurance for his daughter as the beneficiary in the event of the mother's (IP) death, which is paid by the grandmother. In this respect, the policyholder is always directly the insurance customer. However, other participants can indirectly be added as customers.

(Ronsdorf et al. 2009, pp. 380–385)

In principle, all the determining factors of the demand behavior of insurance customers presented in Sect. 4.3 can be used as segmentation criteria for the formation of market segments, in the case of multivariate segmentation also combined with each other (Kotler et al. 2022, pp. 348 f., 356–359). However, it is advisable to refrain from this solely for reasons of complexity, and it seems sensible to determine the essential factors that contribute to the formed market segments being as uniform as possible in terms of their needs and demand behavior, while at the same time being as different and distinct from each other as possible.

Market segmentation can fundamentally be pursued in two ways: If the insurer is interested in customers with favorable risk characteristics, the design parameter of market service is the price (**Risk segmentation**). Examples of this are non-smoker policies in life insurance or risk-based premiums in motor vehicle insurance (single driver tariffs). If the insurer is interested in customer needs, the essential design parameter is the product (**Needs segmentation**). Table 6.1 characterizes the two approaches.

Table 6.1 Different approaches to market segmentation

Market segmentation approach	Data basis	Marketing tool
Risk segmentation	Damage data and risk characteristics	Price or premium policy
Needs segmentation	Market research data	Product policy

The demand analysis can in principle focus on both risk and needs segments. However, if the insurance market is to be segmented in order to better understand demand and ultimately design market performance more in line with needs, customer needs and their segment-specific characteristics are of interest, i.e., market segmentation according to customer needs.

In the case of **needs segmentation**, the effectiveness depends on various factors which the customer segments fulfill and to which the **segmentation criteria** should contribute (Meffert et al. 2019, pp. 221 f.):

- **Relevance** of the segmentation criteria: The chosen segmentation criteria for determining target groups must be demand and/or behavior determining and influence the customer's purchase decision.
- **Measurability** of the segments: This is a prerequisite for determining the size and purchasing power. Accordingly, the chosen segmentation criteria must allow for clear measurement.
- **Distinctiveness** of the segments (heterogeneity): The segmentation criteria must contribute to a clear assignment and must not lead to an overlap of the different target groups.
- **Minimum size** of the segments (substance): The resulting market and customer segments must be lucrative enough for segment-specific processing to be worthwhile.
- Effective **reachability and serviceability** of the segments: The determined customer segments must first be identifiable, i.e., the customers specifically belonging to the predetermined target groups must be identifiable. In addition, these customers must also be reachable, i.e., they must be addressable with marketing and communication measures.
- **Data basis**: The insurer must have a sufficient data basis and a correspondingly large customer base or address this via an external service provider—in contrast to risk data as the basis of damage calculation, a cross-company cooperation is neither desired for antitrust reasons nor by competitors in the case of market segmentation.
- **Stability** of the segments: The once selected, demand-relevant segmentation criteria should remain relevant in their informative value over time, as otherwise adjustments of the criteria and the market segments become necessary, which is very complex.

The requirements mentioned here for market and customer segments and the underlying segmentation criteria show that ultimately compromises are necessary both for the target groups and for the criteria. Neither can all criteria be fulfilled at the same time, nor will the chosen segments be able to fulfill all criteria equally well.

6.2.3 Competitive Analysis

In a market economy, the economic activities in the insurance company and thus the strategic and operational marketing are strongly determined by the activities of competitors in individual markets. The desired differentiation from the competition requires knowledge of the market services offered, i.e., products and services. Therefore, with the help of competitive or competitor analysis, the **current and potential competitors** in the market need to be **identified** and their behavior **and** marketing strategies **observed**. In the insurance industry, established competitors observe each other very closely. Due to the lack of patent protection and comparatively short development times, a very similar product policy is often even noticeable—real differentiations are rather rare. However, this does not change the fact that there is competition in the insurance industry, in some business areas even very intense. The general competitive behavior is therefore of interest for the formulation of the marketing strategy. With increasing competitive intensity, the question arises whether one wants to face a looming premium decline in terms of pricing policy or promotes differentiation based on other criteria. One response to increasing price competition is direct sales, which comes with an independent, cost-oriented business model. And with regard to product policy, competitor observation leads, for example, to quickly reacting to product innovations with promising market launches with adapted products.

In terms of marketing decisions, competition on the **procurement markets** mainly affects the search for qualified personnel and insurance intermediary services. The high importance of intermediaries leads to competition for and poaching of intermediaries in often saturated markets, which can, however, subsequently also result in a reshuffling of contracts. However, this game of customer retention and customer poaching is economically (and also from the consumer's point of view) questionable.

On the **sales markets**, it is essentially about the market offers of German and international competition from all-branch and specialist insurers. New competitors are often foreign financial service providers and insurers who want to gain a foothold in the German market. Furthermore, insurance companies compete with social insurance carriers when customers have the free choice between these and individual insurers, such as increasingly in the area of supplementary health insurance. In addition, current and potential competitors come from industries with pronounced customer contact (client owner), whose product is somewhat related to the purchase of insurance coverage, e.g., associations or car manufacturers, or whose product competes with insurance coverage (e.g., banks or fund companies). In addition, InsurTechs attack established insurers (see excursus in Sect. 6.1.4). In the industrial customer sector, self-insurance companies (captive insurers) also appear as competitors, which have been founded by large companies to insure certain risks "themselves" as company or group-owned insurers (Farny 2011, pp. 100 f.).

The **competitive analysis** refers both to the entire relevant market and to individual competitors (Homburg 2020, pp. 516–518):

In relation to the entire market, it needs to be clarified

- what characterizes the competitive behavior in this market and whether it will change,
- to what extent the entry of new competitors or the exit of existing ones is to be expected and what this would cause,
- who the competitors are,
- who are the best competitors in the relevant market,
- how strong the position of these individual competitors is and whether it is changing.

In any case, the **competitive forces** and **strategic groups** identified in the context of market analysis must be **taken into account**, as they reflect the market-wide competitive situation (and therefore belong to both market and competitive analysis). The tool of **benchmarking** is also suitable for market-wide competitive analysis. A benchmark is a reference standard for assessing one's own performance and identifies potential for improvement. In benchmarking, functional areas (e.g., sales), processes (e.g., application processing), or products of one's own company are compared with other (competing) companies, ideally with the (industry) leaders who are considered leading in the area under investigation. After a quantitative measurement of the performance gap to the best-practice companies, a qualitative investigation of the reasons follows. The goal of benchmarking is to improve performance by closing the identified gaps.

In insurance, benchmarking takes place where information about the competition is sufficiently accessible, for example in product and, increasingly, in pricing through comparison portals. Internal data, such as process qualities and durations, are hardly obtainable and such benchmark comparisons, which include at least some companies, are reserved for management consultants. A possible obstacle to even broader application in the insurance industry is that the benchmarking process reaches its limits in complex contexts. It remains to be seen to what extent a sector-wide standardization of processes, as has been initiated for many years by the industry initiative for process optimization (BiPRO), will lead to a more extensive use of process benchmarking in the future (Meffert et al. 2019, p. 422; Görgen 2007, p. 63).

The competitive analysis refers not only to the overall market but also to the **most important competitors**. The aim is to assess individual competitors in terms of their market position, strategy, strengths and weaknesses, and the resulting development of the market position (Kotler et al. 2022, p. 853):

- Who are the relevant competitors today and tomorrow?
- What are their goals?
- What strategy do they pursue?
- What particular strengths and weaknesses can be attributed to individual competitors?
- What are their usual patterns of reaction?

To answer these questions, it is helpful to look more closely at the products, the product range and the associated prices, product contents and services, the target groups addressed, the distribution channels used, the communication messages, and sales figures (e.g., new business, cancellations, growth in existing business). With regard to the market behavior of competitors, for example, the sales methods (soft or hard selling), the underwriting policy and portfolio policy (sales, profit orientation, restructuring and goodwill policy), and the innovation behavior (innovator, imitator) or the behavior towards competitors (confrontation, cooperation, evasion, adaptation) can be observed.

In particular, the direct competitors with similar target groups and market services may require reactions. A consistent collection of information about offers from these insurers, advertising material and advertisements, radio and advertising spots, contributions from daily newspapers or trade publications, and via the internet provides information about market position, market appearance, and marketing strategy.

6.2.4 Stakeholder Analysis

In modern—as well as in the insurance-related marketing definition used here—the aim is to create customer benefits in order to create value for the insurance company and its stakeholders. This broad understanding of marketing in terms of stakeholder orientation is in line with socially responsible marketing, the so-called "sustainable marketing" (as a further development stage after the product, sales, and marketing concept), which also takes into account the environment and social aspects. In this context, marketing decisions are made in accordance with the wishes and long-term interests of customers, the goals of the company, and the long-term interests of society. This goes hand in hand with the demand for companies to act responsibly voluntarily, even where it is not already enforced by more restrictive legislation, and to offer only those products and services that not only offer a short-term incentive, but also provide long-term benefits for the customer (Kotler et al. 2022, pp. 81 f. and Chap. 20).

Traditionally, the stakeholders include the immediate market actors such as customers and competitors, who have already been analyzed, as well as insurance intermediaries on the sales side and reinsurers on the procurement side. Furthermore, the owners (shareholders) are also a stakeholder group—in the case of a mutual insurance association (VVaG), these are the association members as customers of the VVaG, who thus represent two stakeholder groups at the same time. In addition, there are other groupings of the public who have a more or less concrete, current or potential interest in corporate action due to societal claims and who directly or indirectly influence corporate objectives or the manner in which they are achieved. These include the internal public (employees, works council, executives and managers) as well as the external public with local interest groups (municipalities, residents), the general public (population), trade unions, associations, citizen initiatives, media, the legislator and politics (Kotler et al. 2022, pp. 153 f.; Meffert et al. 2019, pp. 66–68; Farny 2011, p. 349).

The stakeholder analysis pursues several objectives: It should help to identify the relevant stakeholders, clarify their respective importance for the company and provide information or ideas about their demands and needs. Possible expectations of selected stakeholder groups are exemplarily shown in Table 6.2.

The stakeholder analysis provides indications of what a company should pay attention to when positioning itself vis-à-vis its stakeholders. Often, interests will diverge, so that tension fields can always be expected, which need to be balanced out by certain action strategies. The analysis can be very insightful, for example, when it is noticed that expectations of stakeholders are distorted and not very realistic, or it becomes clear that the company's own stakeholder management sets wrong priorities because too much attention is paid to stakeholders with little influence or who can hardly be influenced (Müller-Stewens and Lechner 2016, pp. 156, 163).

Table 6.2 Expectations of stakeholder groups. (Based on Müller-Stewens and Lechner 2016, p. 160)

Stakeholder group	Expectations
Shareholders	Control/Power, Information, Value Increase, Investments, Tax Rate, Dividend, Capital Gain, Loyalty
Supervisory Board	Control/Power, Delegation of Tasks, Competencies, Responsibility, Information, Competence/Performance, Loyalty, Relationships
Employees	Income, Job Security, Status, Social Relationships, Meaning, Self-Realization
Representatives	Income, Sales Support, Product Quality, Price Worthiness, Image, Loyalty
Customers	Purchasing Power, Product Quality, Price Worthiness, Financial Strength, Flexibility, Image
Business Partners	Power, Purchase Security, Sales, Conditions
Government & Politics	Taxes, Task Relief, Compliance with Legal Regulations, Solvency, Jobs, Macroeconomic Function (Capital Pool)
Public	Jobs, Macroeconomic Function (Securing of Activities), Donations, Infrastructure Financing, Preservation of Societal Values (Ecology, Social, Sustainable Corporate Governance (ESG))

Insurance marketing thus has to consider not only the needs of the demanders, but also the diverse demands of other stakeholders. The negative image spiral mentioned in Sect. 1.1.3 due to the interaction of consumer protectors, media, and politics is an example of how important the observation and as far-reaching as possible consideration of the interests of important claim groups is for the company image.

6.3 Company Analysis

The company analysis deals with the situation of the insurance company in relation to all demanders in the market, towards its own customers, and in the competitive environment. In each case, the current state, differences in individual market segments, and changes over time must be recorded (Homburg 2020, pp. 529–531).

Guiding questions in the analysis of the marketing situation of one's own company

1. Situation of the company with demanders and its customers in the market (Analysis of the current situation, segment-specific differences, and changes over time)
   - What image do the insurance company and its products/brands have among demanders?
   - What level of awareness do the insurance company and its products/brands have among demanders?

2. Situation of the company with its customers
   (Analysis of the current situation, segment-specific differences, and changes over time)
   - How satisfied are customers with the services of the insurance company?
   - How loyal are customers to the insurance company?
   - To what extent does the insurance company penetrate its customers in terms of the sales potential there ("customer penetration")?
   - What is the customer-related profitability of the insurance company, and what profits are made with individual products (with different customers)?
3. Situation of the company in the competitive environment
   (Analysis of the current situation, segment-specific differences, and changes over time)
   - What (absolute or relative) market share does the insurance company have?
   - What strengths and weaknesses does the insurance company have in comparison to the competition?
   - To what extent does the insurance company have a lasting, customer-relevant, and customer-perceived competitive advantage?

The **market position against all demanders** is supported by the level of awareness and the image. Corresponding deficits suggest considering a more offensive market approach. Positive values among non-customers indicate sales increase potentials that can be tapped by increased new customer acquisition. Thus, especially well-known and trustworthy or sympathetic insurance brands have advantages in direct sales or sales through cooperation partners from other industries.

The **market position against its own customers** is closely related to customer satisfaction and customer loyalty. High customer satisfaction is not a guarantee for corresponding customer loyalty. But it at least does not prompt customers to look for alternative offers on their own. High customer loyalty, on the other hand, makes customers relatively resistant to attempts to poach them and strengthens the market position of the provider. In connection with one's own customers, the sales potentials with these customers must be identified and possibly cross-selling initiatives must be started. In this context, the customer equity must also be determined (see Sect. 9.1) in order to be able to specifically court valuable customers. The analysis of one's own customers is thus the basis for systematic Customer Relationship Management (CRM).

The **market position in the competitive environment** largely depends on the extent to which the company can benefit from competitive advantages. Competitive advantages result from a superior performance in comparison to the competition, which creates customer benefits, which the customer perceives accordingly, and which cannot be quickly imitated by the competition. As part of the marketing strategy, such competitive advantages must be developed and expanded. Typical competitive advantages of insurers can, for example, result from a strong sales organization, high financial strength, large market shares and thus large portfolios, a strong brand, or innovative power.

Competitive advantages are based on a company-specific strengths-weaknesses profile. This involves financial, personnel, intellectual, and technological resources, capabilities, and know-how. Success in the market is co-determined by internal resources and competencies, which vary from company to company. Therefore, the internal resource analysis attempts to determine what the company can strategically do in light of its current and future resource situation. To do this, a resource profile must first be created, then the strengths and weaknesses of the company in this regard must be identified. Finally, the specific competencies of the company that are important for a sustainably successful market launch and for building and maintaining competitive advantages according to the **Resource-based View** (RbV) must be derived (Meffert et al. 2019, pp. 272 f.; detailed in: Müller-Stewens and Lechner 2016, pp. 194–207).

Relevant variables in the **resource profile of an insurer** include, for example, the absolute (on the entire business field) and relative market share (in relation to competitors), employee potential, rationalization potential, IT equipment, innovative power, service intensity, and investment volume (Schradin 1994, pp. 116 f.). *Farny* adds the current and future capacity to process the chosen business field(s) in terms of underwriting capacity depending on equity, reinsurance capacities, underwriting and claims settlement know-how, and existing intermediary and customer preferences of the insurer (Farny 2011, pp. 518 f.).

In the context of the **strengths and weaknesses of insurers**, corporate culture has a particularly formative effect in both positive and negative directions. It often manifests in specific, historically grown thought patterns and problem-solving patterns, traditions in leadership behavior, established business practices, and organizational structures. Corporate culture is reflected in the values and behaviors of the executives and thus determines entrepreneurial action. On the one hand, it is confirmed and consolidated by economic successes. On the other hand, this carries the risk that necessary changes are not perceived. Insurers are sometimes very strongly influenced by their company-specific cultures, some of them unfortunately also restricted by them (Kühlmann et al. 2003, p. 100).

Methods that can be usefully employed in the course of company analysis include answering guiding questions (see overview above) and creating a resource profile. Often, the **analysis of the value creation chain** is cited as another method, following the value chain analysis by *Porter* (Homburg 2020, pp. 531–533; Kotler et al. 2017a, pp. 43 f.; Görgen 2007, pp. 75–77). Its contribution to the situation analysis of the insurer is to identify sources of customer benefit and thus potential competitive advantages in individual value creation activities and at the interfaces to other companies. Each value creation activity has the potential to either contribute to cost reduction or to differentiation from the competition in terms of performance. The value chain thus provides a systematic approach to identifying actual or potential sources of competitive advantages (Porter 1985, pp. 33–61).

The value creation of an insurance company is also the result of various value creation activities (Fig. 6.3). The primary value creation activities of an insurance company

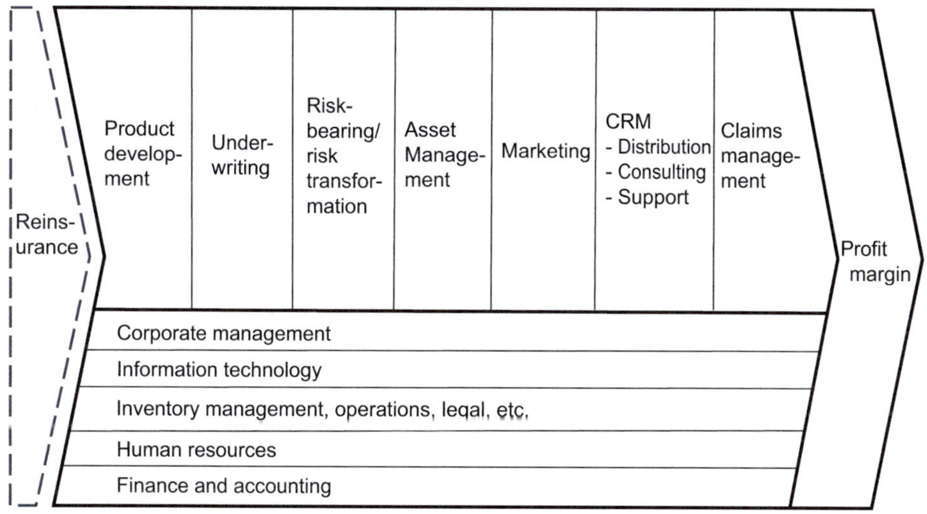

Fig. 6.3 Value creation chain of a (primary) insurance company. (Based on Köhne 2006, p. 261)

that occur in this context relate to the physical creation and sale of the insurance service. The secondary value creation activities support the primary activities of the entire chain. In addition, the profit margin is recorded, which results from the difference between the created value and the incurred costs. The value creation activities of various insurers and various insurance branches (e.g., motor vehice, home contents, legal expenses, life, or health insurance) can also be assigned to this generic value chain, although these activities are based on different business processes in detail because they are designed differently from company to company or are simply branch-specific (see Köhne 2006, pp. 260–264 for this and the following).

The **primary value creation activities of the insurer** include product development, underwriting, risk bearing and transformation, asset management, claims management, marketing, and direct customer contact activities (sales, consulting, and customer service). Each of these can be assigned further sub-processes:

- The **product development** includes the phases of the product development process (see Sect. 10.1).
- The **underwriting** includes both the risk assessment within the underwriting guidelines and the underwriting of specific insurance policies (contract processing). Subprocesses include application processing, standardized and complex underwriting processes, policy issuance, and commissioning.
- **Risk-bearing and risk transformation** are the subject of risk policy. The insurer organizes risk equalization in the collective (and over time). Essentially, this is the production of insurance coverage: "The combination of factors for insurance

production can only be economically meaningful in the collective; for a single insurance, the required quantities of the production factor claims compensation are completely indeterminate and a priori unknown" (Farny 1965, p. 12).

- The **asset management** (investment business) is a separate business area, which is predominantly caused by the insurance business and at the same time contributes value to it: On the one hand, the insurance business enables investment through the prepayment of premiums (in all insurance branches) and the handling of savings processes (in life insurance) as well as the uncommitted equity capital. On the other hand, investments are production factors for the insurance business when they secure technical obligations. Value-creating sub-processes of asset management include strategic and tactical asset allocation, the development of investment products, and the determination of individual investments.
- Particularly relevant, value-creating sub-activities in the **marketing** of insurance companies are marketing research, brand management in the area of strategic marketing, and the design of insurance products, communication (especially sales promotion, advertising), and centrally conducted customer contacts in the area of operational marketing.
- The central value creation activities in direct customer contact can occur together and separately, refer to the initiation of contact, the **consultation**, the **sale** as such, the **customer care over time** (in the course of contract adjustments or additions and in the event of a claim) as well as contract termination in the sense of Customer Relationship Management along the entire service process (see Sect. 2.2.1) and use various communication and distribution channels.
- The **claims management** or the actual claims processing consists of the five sub-activities claims acceptance, claims examination, claims settlement in the form of financial service provision, post-claims processing and claims controlling, as well as the cross-functions fraud detection and information forwarding.
- The **reinsurance** is purchased as an important production factor and flows as a (pre-) service into the value creation activities of product development, underwriting, and risk transformation.

The **secondary value creation activities** support individual, several, or all primary value creation activities. These include operations, inventory and data management, law, IT management, human resources management, finance and accounting, and last but not least, corporate management.

The challenge in practice is to determine and allocate the costs of the individual value creation activities and especially the corresponding distribution of the created value, i.e., the profit margin, to these activities. It becomes even more difficult to consider and compare with competitors, as adequate information about them cannot be obtained (Köhne 2004b, p. 345; Görgen 2007, p. 77).

As **sources of information for corporate analysis**, internal company sources and secondary statistical sources are used (internal accounting and controlling, annual financial statements and benchmarks with other companies, organization charts, job and process descriptions, internal correspondence and mail traffic, internal presentations, marketing and sales controlling statistics, etc.). Other important information is of a qualitative nature, such as the attitude and know-how of employees, the service behavior of employees with customer contact, or the corporate culture. Their collection and documentation require a qualitative evaluation by the insurer's executives and possibly internal or external consultants.

As a result of the corporate analysis, it should be noted in which business fields, product areas, primary and secondary value creation activities, customer segments, and distribution channels the insurer is positioned in terms of its strengths and weaknesses profile. Ideally, important competencies or even real **core competencies can be derived** from resources, abilities and know-how, which should then be built upon in the marketing strategy. This shows the interplay between the Resource-based View, from which the core competency approach has developed, and the Market-based View, which theoretically underpins the market orientation essential for the marketing strategy.

▶ **Core Competency** is a competency based on a bundle of abilities and technologies that, in their interaction, enable a company to provide its customers with a certain, subjectively perceived benefit. A core competency must first provide a significant additional benefit to the customer, secondly be suitable for differentiation from the competition or be resistant to imitation and substitution, and thirdly have the ability to expand into new markets, i.e., open up a broad spectrum of application possibilities in various company services.

(Prahalad and Hamel 1990; Hamel and Prahalad 1995)

In principle, **insurers' core competencies cannot be generalized**, but can only be assigned to specific insurers. Each insurer has differently pronounced resources, abilities, and know-how, and thus certain competencies. However, real core competencies according to the (demanding) definition are rare. Across the industry, however, it can at least be stated which services and value creation areas could potentially provide above-average value in terms of sustainable customer benefit—and thus also company benefit. Insurers' (core) competencies can then, for example, be a strong brand, stable customer relationships, specialist knowledge, a lived target group orientation, a sophisticated, well-controllable sales system, a needs-oriented consulting system or a holistically integrated consulting approach, or the combination of creating innovative service bundles and professional cooperation management. Certain value creation activities such as product development, underwriting, portfolio management, capital investment, and claims processing are only core competencies if they contain distinctive specialist knowledge or can be carried out particularly economically. These activities are indeed close to the actual core business "insurance" and require insurance-specific knowledge, in short, core abilities or competencies. But in themselves, they are relatively quickly imitable and are usually very product-related (for further information, see Köhne 2006, pp. 264–269).

6.4 SWOT Analysis as an Integrative Bracket

The term "SWOT analysis" (Strengths, Weaknesses, Opportunities, Threats) stands for the combined strengths-weaknesses and opportunities-threats analysis (Table 6.3). It integrates and condenses the presented analyses of the macro environment, the micro environment, and the company. The aim is to juxtapose the essential strengths and weaknesses of the company with the significant opportunities and threats from the external environment. The opportunities and threats are derived from the examination of the macro environment, the market, customer, and competitor analysis. In the step of condensation, the SWOT analysis brings together numerous detailed information from the already conducted analyses and records the most important ones to find clues for the focus of the marketing strategy. At the same time, it identifies possibly missing information that still needs to be processed. Based on the SWOT analysis, the marketing strategy can be developed in a structured way, and the decision field is narrowed down to those strategies where special competencies of the company meet market opportunities or opportunities arising in the market. The advantages of this methodology are its simplicity and integrativity; it is therefore very helpful for summarizing the analysis results of the strategic starting situation (Homburg 2020, pp. 536 f.; Meffert et al. 2019, pp. 273 f.).

In relation to insurance marketing, the methodology can be applied well. The following arbitrarily chosen examples from different areas may briefly illustrate this:

- **Opportunities-Strengths Scenario**: Consumer advocates and media are creating an increasing awareness in the population for the necessity of natural hazard insurances; the insurer is a large residential buildings insurer and is already well positioned there, but has so far acted rather passively in this segment. Recommendation for action: Improve the existing natural hazard modules qualitatively and actively market them in (own) sales.
- **Opportunities-Weaknesses Scenario**: The need for private care provision beyond statutory long-term care insurance is increasing, this is therefore promoted by the state and therefore increasingly demanded by customers; the insurer is mainly active in the composite area and in direct sales. Recommendation: Do not perceive opportunity; possibly check whether a simple care product can be produced or "purchased" to sell it via direct sales.

Table 6.3 SWOT analysis and recommendations for action

Environment Company	Opportunities (Opportunities)	Threats (Threats)
Strengths (Strength)	Use strengths to perceive opportunities	Use strengths to ward off threats
Weaknesses (Weaknesses)	Reduce weaknesses to perceive opportunities or not perceive opportunity	Reduce weaknesses or retreat

- **Threats-Strengths Scenario**: New regulatory requirements and critical reporting lead to a sharply declining acceptance of traditional life insurance; the insurer has very good life insurance products and is therefore committed to all independent sales channels and demanded by these. Recommendation: Switch to modern life insurance products with flexible guarantees and other biometric products (e.g., occupational disability), intensify sales promotion there and create compensation for declining traditional life insurance.
- **Threats-Weaknesses Scenario**: In the motor vehicle insurance market, customers are increasingly informing themselves via internet portals, becoming more price-sensitive and direct conclusion becomes the preferred purchase method; the insurer is not lean, has no direct sales, but tied agents, which is financed among other things by the motor vehicle insurance commissions. Recommendation: Discontinue motor vehicle insurance or "buy in" from third parties (fallback solution (Ventillösung) for own sales force).

Excursus on integrating analysis methods

In the literature, in addition to the most widely used and intuitively applicable SWOT analysis, other methods are proposed for an integrated analysis of the external and internal environment. For example, the **core capabilities scenario analysis** combines external business segment segmentation with the scenario technique to derive required internal core capabilities. Another approach involves game-theoretical considerations, which model the interactions between the environment and the company in the form of games. *Nalebuff* and *Brandenburger* (1996) developed a "**business game**" from this, which generates starting points with the help of which a company can improve an environmental situation in its favor. In terms of the environment, it needs to be clarified who the actors (= players), who the "audience" (e.g., media, consumer advocates), what the conditions of the "game" (demographic, legal, etc.) and who the "referees" (e.g., BaFin) are, what the "rules of the game" are and what constitutes the "playing field" (regional, industry, etc.). Starting points for the company are then, for example, the players, whose composition can be changed through acquisitions or alliances, the rules of the game, which can be influenced by a new business model, or the scope, which can be redesigned by shifting the boundaries.

A third approach that looks at the interactions between the external and internal environment of a company is the **method of networked thinking**, which can in principle be used for any problem considered to be complex. "Complex" is understood to mean that a system (including companies) is exposed to a multitude of factors that are interconnected, therefore influence each other and trigger a dynamic that gives the system a life of its own that can no longer be clearly predicted. This basically also applies to the interactions between the external and internal environment. Networked thinking takes place in five steps, which are interconnected—the first three serve to analyze the relationships, the last two deal with implementation. In the first step, the key factors are to be identified from the influencing factors collected in the individual analyses. In the second step, the relationships between the factors, their direction of effect, the effect (positive or negative) and the intensity are to be graphically represented in a network. The central cycle, which shows which chain of factors leads to profit, should be highlighted. In the third step, controllable and non-controllable factors are differentiated. On this basis, in the fourth step, using creativity techniques, alternative actions and scenarios are generated and each qualitatively and quantitatively evaluated. In the last step, developed measures are to be implemented in such a way that they allow for adaptation and further development (Müller-Stewens and Lechner 2016, pp. 207–216).

While opportunities-risks- and resources analyses are predominantly used for existing companies, another approach has been established for the evaluation of new business ideas and the establishment of new business areas or companies, the **Business Model Canvas** (BMC). It goes back to *Osterwalder* and *Pigneur* (2010) and includes the holistic analysis and description of business models. A business model describes the functional logic by which a company can achieve value creation through customer satisfaction (Osterwalder and Pigneur 2010, p. 14). It also involves a conceptual connection between overarching business strategy, corporate organization, and information technology. While the identification of visions and goals is in focus with regard to the business strategy (e.g., using a SWOT analysis), the corporate organization is about the structural and procedural implementation of the strategy and the necessary technological components such as hardware, software, and systems. The BMC consists of nine dimensions, each representing market-related (external) and company-related (internal) key factors of a successful company, some of which are in mutual relationships. The market-related dimensions include value propositions, customer segments, communication and distribution channels, customer relationships, and revenue streams, the company-related dimensions key activities, key resources, key partners, and cost structure. The BMC is now widely used. However, critics postulate that the model is very simplified, it is a generic approach and the demarcation between the individual components is sometimes difficult (Meffert et al. 2019, pp. 274–279).

Further Reading for In-depth Study:

- Gomez and Probst 2007.
- Nalebuff and Brandenburger 1996.
- Osterwalder and Pigneur 2010.
- Schoemaker 1995.
- Vester 1999.

Further Reading Recommendations for Chap. 6

- Amerirad et al. 2023.
- Braun and Schreiber 2017.
- Ehrler 1999, pp. 82–136.
- Köhne 2006, pp. 259–299.
- Müller-Stewens and Lechner 2016, pp. 126–216.
- Nicoletti 2021.
- Oberholzer 2003, Chap. 2–4.
- Porter 1980.
- Porter 1985.

References

Amerirad, B./Cattaneo, M./Kenett, R.S./Luciano, E. (2023): Adversarial Artificial Intelligence in Insurance: From an Example to Some Potential Remedies, in: Risks, Vol. 11, 2023, pp. 20–37. https://doi.org/10.3390/risks11010020

BaFin (Ed.) (2010): '09 Jahresbericht der Bundesanstalt für Finanzdienstleistungsaufsicht, Bonn, 2010.

BaFin (Ed.) (2018): Big Data trifft auf künstliche Intelligenz. Herausforderungen und Implikationen für Aufsicht und Regulierung von Finanzdienstleistungen, Studie, o. O., 2018.

BaFin (Ed.) (2020): Merkblatt zum Umgang mit Nachhaltigkeitsrisiken, o. O. 2020.

BaFin (Ed.) (2021): Big Data und künstliche Intelligenz: Prinzipien für den Einsatz von Algorithmen in Entscheidungsprozessen, o. O., 2021.

BaFin (Ed.) (2022): Nachhaltigkeit: Daran kommt niemand mehr vorbei, in: BafinJournal vom 22.12.2022, Bonn, 2022.

Barb, C./Klein, K./Kraft, M. (2018): Auswirkungen von Smart-Home-Technologien auf die verbundene Hausrat- und Wohngebäudeversicherung—Markt, Ausgestaltungsmerkmale und Preisbereitschaft, in: ZVersWiss, Jg. 107, 2018, pp. 495–516.

Berenberg-Gossler, P./Bertelsmann, T./Hanisch, M. (2023): Branchenprognose Versicherungswirtschaft: Aussichten für 2023 und 2024 hellen sich auf, in: Insurance Perspectives, Nr. 3, Ed. by GDV, Berlin, 2023.

Blum, R./Weller, S. (2013): Der Schlüssel ist der Mensch, Der Wertewandel durch neue Technologien zwingt die Versicherer zu radikalem Umdenken, in: VW, Jg. 68, 2013, Nr. 16, pp. 48–50.

Braun, A. und Schreiber, F. (2017): The Current InsurTech Landscape: Business Models and Disruptive Potential, I.VW-HSG Schriftenreihe, Vol. 62, St. Gallen, 2017.

Bruhn, M. (2019a): Qualitätsmanagement für Dienstleistungen, Handbuch für ein erfolgreiches Qualitätsmanagement. Grundlagen, Konzepte, Methoden, Berlin, 11. Edn., 2019.

Bruhn, M. (2022): Relationship Marketing. Das Management von Kundenbeziehungen, München, 6. Edn., 2022.

Bundesministerium für Wirtschaft und Klimaschutz (Ed.) (2023): Gesundheitswirtschaft, Fakten & Zahlen, Daten 2022, Ergebnisse der Gesundheitswirtschaftlichen Gesamtrechnung, Berlin, 2023.

Eckert, C./Neunsinger, C./Osterrieder, K. (2022): Managing customer satisfaction: digital applications for insurance companies, in: GP, Vol. 47, 2022, No. 3, pp. 569–602. (https://doi.org/10.1057/s41288-021-00257-z)

Ehrler, B. (1999): Kernkompetenzorientiertes Management der Versicherung—Strategien in Risiko- und Finanzdienstleistungsnetzen, St. Gallen, 1999.

Eichner, D./Fritsch, C./Kothe, G.-L./Kühner, S./Remond, Y./Warnke, J. (2023): Risikowahrnehmung durch und nach Corona, in: Arnold, R./Berg, M./Goecke, O./Heep-Altiner, M./Müller-Peters, H. (Eds.), Risiko im Wandel, Herausforderung für die Versicherungswirtschaft, Wiesbaden, 2023, pp. 35–60.

Eling, M./Lehmann, M. (2018): The Impact of Digitalization on the Insurance Value Chain and the Insurability of Risks, in: GP, Vol. 43, No. 3, 2018, pp. 359–396.

European Insurance and Occupational Pensions Authority (EIOPA) (Ed.) (2022): Guidance on the integration of sustainability preferences in the suitability assessment under the Insurance Distribution Directive (IDD), EIOPA-BoS-22-391, Frankfurt a. M., 2022.

European Insurance and Occupational Pensions Authority (EIOPA) (Ed.) (2023a): Risk Dashboard January 2023, EIOPA-BoS-23-26, Frankfurt a. M., 2023.

European Insurance and Occupational Pensions Authority (EIOPA) (Ed.) (2023b): Risk Dashboard November 2023, EIOPA-BoS-23-392, Frankfurt a. M., 2023.

Farny, D. (1965): Produktions- und Kostentheorie der Versicherung, Karlsruhe, 1965.

Farny, D. (2011): Versicherungsbetriebslehre, Karlsruhe, 5. Vol., 2011.

Friedrich, T.A. (2013): Brüsseler Steine ins Rollen bringen, Bericht über die europäische Gesetzesmaschine, in: VW, Jg. 68, 2013, Nr. 14, pp. 10–13.

Fuest, C./Thum, M. (2021): Hilft eine Versicherungspflicht für Elementarschäden?, in: Handelsblatt vom 28. Juli 2021, p. 48.

GDV (Ed.) (2008): Jahrbuch der deutschen Versicherungswirtschaft 2008, Berlin, 2008.

GDV (Ed.) (2021c): Versicherung gegen Naturgefahrenereignisse in Deutschland, Gesamtkonzept der deutschen Versicherer, Berlin, 2021.

GDV (Ed.) (2023b): Fokus Digitalisierung. Grünes Licht statt Rotstift: IT-Jobs in der digitalen Versicherungswirtschaft, Nr. 10, Berlin, 2023.

GDV (Ed.) (2023c): Klimawandelszenarien im ORSA, Ansätze zur Umsetzung der aufsichtlichen Anforderungen, Version 2.0, Berlin, 2023.

GDV (Ed.) (2023d): Nachhaltigkeitspositionierung. Der Beitrag der deutschen Versicherer zum Klimaschutz, Stand: 19.01.2023, Berlin, 2023.

Görgen, F. (2007): Versicherungsmarketing, Strategien, Instrumente und Controlling, Stuttgart, 2. Edn., 2007.

Gomez, P./Probst, G. (2007): Die Praxis des ganzheitlichen Problemlösens, Bern, 3. Edn., 2007.

Grüner, T./Hiebl, K. (2014): Bändigung gewaltiger Datenvolumina, Big Data ermöglicht Generierung von Wettbewerbsvorteilen im gesättigten Marktumfeld, in: VW, Jg. 69, 2014, Nr. 4, pp. 60–63.

Hamel, G./Prahalad, C.K. (1995): Die Zukunft gestalten—schon heute, in: HBM, 1995, Nr. 1, pp. 36–42.

Homburg, C. (2020): Marketingmanagement, Strategie—Instrumente—Umsetzung—Unternehmensführung, Wiesbaden, 7. Edn., 2020.

Hüther, M. (2023): Volkswirtschaftliche Einordnung der Pandemieschäden, in: Arnold, R./Berg, M./Goecke, O./Heep-Altiner, M./Müller-Peters, H. (Eds.), Risiko im Wandel, Herausforderung für die Versicherungswirtschaft, Wiesbaden, 2023, pp. 63–74.

Köhne, T. (2004b): Strategische Kooperationen und Unternehmensnetzwerke in der Versicherungsbranche—Möglichkeiten, Herausforderungen und Erfolgsfaktoren, in: Köhne, T. (Ed.): Strategische Kooperationen in der Versicherungsbranche: Kernkompetenzen, Wertschöpfungspartnerschaften und Unternehmensnetzwerke, Wiesbaden, 2004, pp. 325–356.

Köhne, T. (2006): Marketing im strategischen Unternehmensnetzwerk, Erklärungsmodell und praktische Anwendung in der Versicherungswirtschaft, Wiesbaden, 2006.

Köhne, T./Kopp, F. (2007): Produktinnovationen und Produktmodifikationen in der Versicherungswirtschaft: Rolle und Bedeutung nach der Deregulierung, in: ZVersWiss, Jg. 96, 2007, Nr. 2, pp. 227–259.

Kollmann, T. (2019): E-Business, Grundlagen elektronischer Geschäftsprozesse in der Digitalen, Wirtschaft, Wiesbaden, 7. Edn., 2019.

Kotler, P./Keller, K.L./Opresnik, M.O. (2017a): Marketing-Management, Konzepte—Instrumente—Unternehmensfallstudien, Halbergmoos, 15. Edn., 2017.

Kotler, P./Armstrong, G./Harris, L.C./He, H. (2022): Grundlagen des Marketing, Halbergmoos, 8. Edn., 2022.

Krausz, S. (2002): Strategische Unternehmenspolitik von Erstversicherern unter Verbindung von Zielgruppen-Marketing und Kernkompetenz-Management, Karlsruhe, 2002.

Kühlmann, K./Wolf, H.-P./Wallenwein, C./Swoboda, U. (2003): Marketing und Vertrieb, Funktionsorientierte Qualifikationen, Karlsruhe, 2. Edn., 2003.

Mahnke, L./Schmidt, J.-P. (2022): Klimawandel und Personenversicherung, in: Heep-Altiner, M./Rohlfs, T./Berg, M./Schmidt, J.-P. (Eds.), Klima- und Nachhaltigkeitsrisiken für die Versicherungswirtschaft, Wiesbaden, 2022, pp. 241–268.

Meffert, H./Burmann, C./Kirchgeorg, M./Eisenbeiß, M. (2019): Marketing, Grundlagen marktorientierter Unternehmensführung, Konzepte—Instrumente—Praxisbeispiele, Wiesbaden, 13. Edn., 2019.

Müller-Reichart, M./Graumann, K.V. (2022): Nachhaltigkeit der Finanzdienstleistungswirtschaft auf der Grundlage der EU-Taxonomieverordnung, in: ZfV, Jg. 73, 2022, Nr. 13–14, pp. 419–423.

Müller-Stewens, G./Lechner, C. (2016): Strategisches Management, Wie strategische Initiativen zum Wandel führen, Stuttgart, 5. Edn., 2016.

Nalebuff, B./Brandenburger, A. (1996): Coopetition—kooperativ konkurrieren. Mit der Spieltheorie zum Unternehmenserfolg, Frankfurt a. M., 1996.

Nicoletti, B. (2021): Insurance 4.0: Benefits and Challenges of Digital Transformation, Cham, 2021.

Oberholzer, M. (2003): Strategische Implikationen des Ubiquitous Computing für das Nichtleben-Geschäft im Privatkundensegment der Assekuranz, Karlsruhe, 2003.

Oliver Wyman/policen direct (Ed.) (2021): Die Zukunft von InsurTech in DACH, Der InsurTech-Radar 2021, o. O., 2021.

Osberghaus, D. (2021): Staatliche Fluthilfe: Kurzfristig notwendig, aber keine nachhaltige Lösung, in: ifo Schnelldienst, Jg. 74, 2021, Nr. 11, pp. 3–6.

Osterwalder, A./Pigneur, Y. (2010): Business model generation, Hoboken (New Jersey), 2010.

o. V. (2014a): Radikalreform der britischen Altersvorsorge, in: ZfV, Jg. 65, 2014, Nr. 8, p. 205.

Petrovs, V. (2016): Telematik-Produktmodelle für die deutsche KFZ-Versicherung, Köln, 2016.

Porter, M.E. (1980): Competitive Strategy, New York, 1980.

Porter, M.E. (1985): Competitive Advantage, Creating and Sustaining Superior Performance, New York, 1985.

Porter, M.E. (2004): Competitive Strategy, New York, Neuaufl., 2004.

Prahalad, C.K./Hamel, G. (1990): The Core Competence of the Corporation, in: HBR, Vol. 68, 1990, No. 3, pp. 79–92.

Richter, C. (2014): Digital versichert—Wie die Assekuranz ihre Geschäftsprozesse der Zukunft neu denkt, in: ZfV, Jg. 65, 2014, Nr. 2, pp. 48–51.

Ronsdorf, K./Rossmann, S./Schlinck, P. (2009): Vorsorgekonzepte im 3-Schichten-Modell, Karlsruhe, 2. Edn., 2009.

Schoemaker, P. (1995): Scenario Planning: A Tool for Strategic Thinking, in: Sloan Management Review, Vol. 36, 1995, No. 2, pp. 25–40.

Schradin, H.R. (1994): Erfolgsorientiertes Versicherungsmanagement, Karlsruhe, 1994.

Seemann, K./Theis, A. (2023): Finanzsystem trotz widriger Umstände resilient, Financial Stability Perspectives 2023 Q1, Ed. by GDV, Berlin, 2023.

Statistisches Bundesamt (Ed.) (2021): Ausblick auf die Bevölkerungsentwicklung in Deutschland und den Bundesländern nach dem Corona-Jahr 2020, Erste mittelfristige Bevölkerungsvorausberechnung 2021 bis 2035, o. O., 2021.

Statistisches Bundesamt (Ed.) (2023c): Vorausberechnete Privathaushalte, in: https://www-genesis.destatis.de/genesis/online?sequenz=tabelleErgebnis&selectionname=12421-0100#abreadcrumb, Accessed: 02.01.2024

Statistisches Bundesamt (Ed.) (2023d): Hauptwohnsitzhaushalte: Deutschland, Jahre, Haushaltsgröße, Haushaltsnettoeinkommensklassen, Tab. 12211-0300, 2022, in: https://www-genesis.destatis.de/genesis//online?operation=table&code=12211-0300&bypass=true&levelindex=0&levelid=1704284458136#abreadcrumb, Accessed: 28.12.2023.

Statistisches Bundesamt (Ed.) (2023e): Zahl der Woche Nr. 43 vom 24. Oktober 2023, in: https://www.destatis.de/DE/Presse/Pressemitteilungen/Zahl-der-Woche/2023/PD23_43_p002.html, Accessed: 03.01.2024.

Stöckli, E./Dremel, C./Übernickel, F. (2018): Exploring characteristics and transformational capabilities of InsurTech innovations to understand insurance value creation in a digital world, in: Electronic Markets, Vol. 28, 2018, pp. 287–305.

The London Institute of Banking & Finance (Ed.) (2023): Insurance Banana Skins 2023, The CSFI survey of the risks facing insurers, London, 2023.

Theis, A. (2015): Regulierung und Versicherungswirtschaft: Chancen und Herausforderungen aus ökonomischer Perspektive, in: Volkswirtschaftliche Themen und Analysen, Nr. 7, Ed. by GDV, Berlin, 2015.

Theis, A. (2023): InsurTech-Startups: Eine Zwischenbilanz, in: Economic Research, Insurance Flash, Ed. by GDV, Nr. 2, 2023.

Umweltbundesamt (Ed.) (2023): Monitoringbericht 2023 zur Deutschen Anpassungsstrategie an den Klimawandel, Bericht der Interministeriellen Arbeitsgruppe Anpassungsstrategie der Bundesregierung, Dessau-Roßlau, 2023.

Vester, F. (1999): Die Kunst vernetzt zu denken. Ideen und Werkzeuge für einen neuen Umgang mit Komplexität, Frankfurt a. M., 1999.

Wedlich, F. (2019): Digitalisierung, Robotic Process Automation und Künstliche Intelligenz in der Versicherungsbranche, Potentiale und Möglichkeiten im Schadenmanagement, in: ZfV, Jg. 70, 2019, Nr. 14, pp. 436–440.

Wiener, K. and Theis, A. (2017): InsurTech(s): Zwischen Konkurrenz und Partnerschaft, in: Makro und Markte kompakt, Ed. by GDV, Nr. 9, 2017.

Part IV

Strategic Marketing as Part of the Insurance Marketing Conception

7 Marketing Objectives of the Insurance Company

In business administration, the discussion of objectives has increasingly come to the forefront with decision theory. Initially, the focus was somewhat one-sidedly on the higher corporate objectives, while the functional area objectives were only considered later with the development of the individual functional area doctrines. It is noticeable that the marketing objectives are discussed more closely in the newer, German-language marketing presentations, while the American marketing literature—otherwise often a model and pattern for modern German-language marketing teaching—does not contain differentiated representations of corporate and marketing objectives (Becker 2019, p. 13).

Consistent entrepreneurial action undoubtedly requires a purpose and goal orientation: The starting point of thc management process is the definition of objectives in the sense of desired states or positions. These must be based both on the entrepreneurial task (corporate purpose) and on the external and internal conditions of the company. Therefore, the marketing objectives must also be oriented towards the corporate objectives (Sect. 7.1) as well as the findings of the marketing analyses (Sect. 7.2) (Becker 2019, p. 11). In addition, the target relationships between the various objectives must be taken into account (Sect. 7.3).

7.1 Corporate Objectives of Insurance Companies

7.1.1 Concept of Objectives and Objective System in the Insurance Company

In the insurance company too, the highest corporate objectives guide the selection of action alternatives by defining what an insurance company is active for in the market and what the management is measured against. Objectives are desired states of reality of an insurance company or individual subareas. They can be specified according to their

T. Köhne, *Insurance Marketing*, https://doi.org/10.1007/978-3-658-47345-7_7

content, in the case of bundles of objectives according to their interaction (complementary, competing or independent), according to their extent, according to their time reference (By when?), according to the target group (Who is the target to be achieved?) and the responsibility (Who is responsible for achieving the objective?) (Becker 2019, pp. 19–27).

In the context of the objective extent, the desired state of reality must be quantitatively defined. The units of the chosen scale must be determined so that statements or numerical values can be assigned to the characteristics or characteristic expressions of the objectives (Scaling). This makes the achievement of objectives measurable. The objective extent is determined with increasing clarity or increasing information content:

- on a nominal scale, e.g. achievement of a profit,
- on an ordinal scale, e.g. profit increase compared to the previous year,
- on a ratio scale, e.g. profit amounting to 12% of equity capital.

Excursus on Various Scale Levels

Nominal scaling ($A = A \neq B$): Here, the characteristic values are only classified, i.e., assigned to categories or attributes. The comparison of two characteristic values is limited to the statement whether they match or not (equivalence relation). A quantitative evaluation is not possible. Examples: Gender (binary), postal codes (multiclass).

Ordinal scaling ($A > B > C$): Here, a ranking can be given between the individual characteristic values, so that a statement can be made with regard to lower, equal or higher characteristic values, but not about the distance between them (order relation). Examples: Preference and judgment statements, wind strength with Beaufort scale.

Interval scaling ($A > B > C$ and $A - B = B - C$): Here, the measurement is made in constant units, so that distance statements are possible in the form that the characteristic value of two objects (e.g., the actual target achievement and the planned target achievement) is lower or higher or exactly the same by a certain amount. The scale zero point is arbitrarily chosen (equidistant scale points). Therefore, it is also not permissible to say that the characteristic value A is a multiple higher than that of B. Examples: Intelligence quotient, temperature scale.

Ratio or ratio scaling ($A = x \cdot B$): Here, the measurement is made in constant units and with a fixed (natural) zero point, so that ratios can be given. Therefore, it is permissible to say on ratio scales that the characteristic value A is a multiple higher than that of B. Typical measurement sizes are age, income, turnover and market share.

The ratio scale has the highest scale level of the four scales mentioned. Accordingly, it is always possible to transform the characteristics to a lower scale level.

(Berekoven et al. 2009, pp. 65 f.)

It should also be noted that **objectives should meet certain criteria** in order to ignite the desired effect (Kotler et al. 2017a, p. 59):

1. **Clarity and measurability**: Clearly formulated, measurable and time-bound objectives contribute to the understanding and thus orientation for the actors and to the verifiability.
2. **Consistency** with other objectives: The individual formulated objectives should be consistent with each other, i.e., they should not contradict each other.

3. **Hierarchical order**: The consistency applies especially to superordinate and subordinate objectives, but if possible also to objectives of equal rank, in order to largely avoid goal conflicts. Determining the respective importance (prioritization) helps in this respect.
4. **Achievability**: This ensures that the employees of a company are encouraged to high performance.

The target system of a company is not a general, easily adoptable standard solution, but rather an expression of a company-specific intention and thus a creative process that must be linked to the specific conditions and possibilities of one's own company. Consequently, the target system is largely influenced by the decision-maker, i.e., dependent on the management and its subjective evaluations. Only secondarily is it determined by the decision field, i.e., dependent on the respective market and environmental constellation (Becker 2019, p. 27). For reasons of clarity, systematics, and operationalization, the target system of a company is usually represented in the form of a goal pyramid (Fig. 7.1), albeit with different classifications (Becker 2019, p. 28; Meffert et al. 2019, p. 280; Homburg 2020, p. 469).

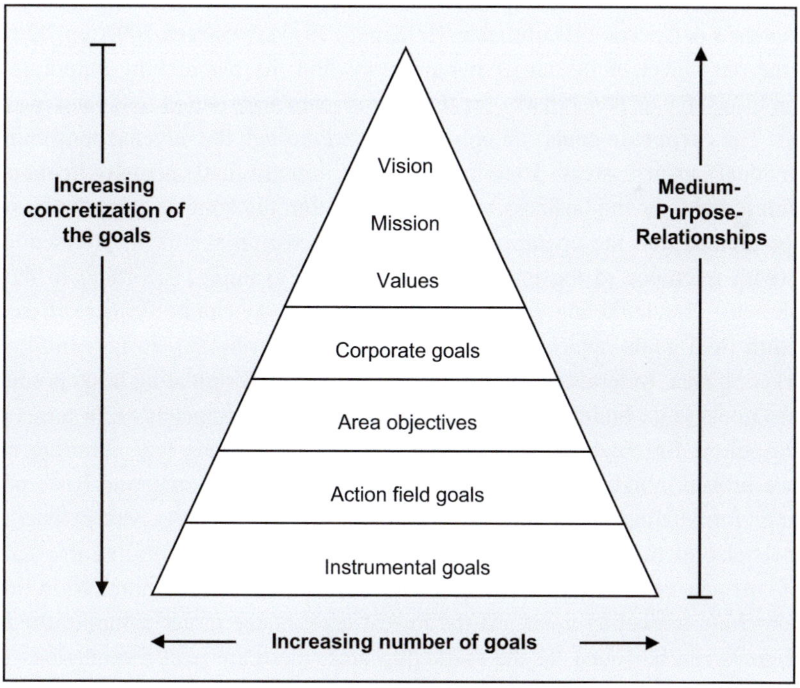

Fig. 7.1 Goal pyramid in the insurance company. (Based on Becker 2019, p. 28)

At the top are always normative guidelines of corporate policy, which are composed of the vision, mission, and values and are of a long-term nature. Short and medium-term corporate goals are linked to them. A **vision** is an image of a future reality that a company strives for. It must be meaningful, motivating, coordinate collective actions, and have an integrating effect. Insurers find this rather difficult. In contrast to the vision, the **mission** (Mission Statement, Guiding Principle) of the company defines the purpose of its actions and justifies or legitimizes its existence. It explains the contribution or the value proposition (Value Proposition) to the stakeholders. This makes it an important point of reference for marketing. Selected mission statements of insurance companies can be found in Table 7.1. The third component of the normative basis of the company are the **values**. These are (internally directed) norms for social action in the company, which are proclaimed by the management as benchmarks for employee behavior. As permanent, action-guiding maxims, they have a collective status and indicate what is considered appropriate and valuable and what is not (Müller-Stewens and Lechner 2016, pp. 217–234). Closely related to the values is the self-image or identity of a company (**Corporate Identity**); the identity is the basis for the self-presentation and behavior both internally and externally (Birgikt and Stadler 1986, p. 23). Corporate identity plays an important role in the insurance industry, among other things because it serves as a surrogate for a product and intermediary performance that is difficult to assess from the perspective of many private insurance customers and because the behavioral component of identity is so important in the industry, as it usually involves very sensitive areas from the customer's perspective (Harbrücker 1992, pp. 178–182; Görgen 2007, pp. 42 f.).

On the next level of the target pyramid, we find the overarching corporate goals, which in turn serve as benchmarks for the downstream area, action field, and instrumental goals. The **corporate goals** can only be realized through the targeted contributions of the individual business areas. Therefore, they are initially fundamentally **broken down by business fields** or the business units formed within the company. Furthermore, they are to be divided into the operational **functional areas**: procurement, production, marketing (with reference to the insurance industry, for example, according to the value chain shown). The marketing goals formulated in this way can be further differentiated into **action field goals**, which address very specific contributions to task fulfillment in the marketing area. In terms of offer policy, this involves formulating basic product performance goals (e.g., building a risk policy underwriting competence), in terms of distribution policy, formulating basic presence performance goals (e.g., limiting sales to insurance brokers), and in terms of communication policy, formulating basic profiling goals (e.g., formulating a communicative message from a marketing perspective). Action field goals also include business field-specific specifications for fulfilling the marketing tasks of customer retention and customer acquisition, which in turn must be in line with the overarching marketing goals. At the lowest level of the target pyramid, the **instrumental goals** can be found. In the marketing area, these are goal formulations that tie in with the individual marketing tools of the marketing mix. They cannot be directly derived from the overarching corporate and marketing goals, but first require appropriate

Table 7.1 Mission Statements of selected companies in the insurance industry

Allianz	Our **Purpose** is: We secure your future Since 1890, we at Allianz have been working worldwide to provide our customers with security and confidence for the future. We are actuaries, consultants and customer advisors, engineers, lawyers and IT professionals; we are daughters and sons, mothers and fathers, controllers, investors and entrepreneurs—and together as a team, we shape our industry. Because we know how important it is to have a fair partner at your side who provides sustainable, convincing offers and excellent service, we strive to do our work well—with passion, every day anew. Our **goal** is to be a trusted partner for the protection and growth of our customers' most valuable assets. Assets for us are not only the material possessions of our customers, but also human values, such as health. Our purpose and our goal can only be achieved if we keep these three promises: 1. Balance between stakeholders 2. Benchmark results on a large scale 3. High resilience in a rapidly changing world
Cosmos Direkt	**Mission Statement** Our mission is to be the first choice by delivering relevant and accessible insurance solutions • First choice: It is logical and natural that customers confirm the best offer in the market with the clearest advantages and most attractive services through their choice. • Delivering: We guarantee success and strive for the best possible result. • Relevant: Anticipate and fulfill individual life needs—tailored to the regional and personal habits of customers. • Accessible: Simple, leading and easy to find, understand and use; available at any time at a competitive price-performance ratio. • Insurance solutions: We want to offer tailor-made and thoughtful combinations of security, advice and service.
Debeka	**Corporate Mission Statement** Together for a future worth living. So that you can realize your idea of a good life.
HanseMerkur	**Our Philosophy** Innovative products, financial strength and tradition consciousness—these characteristics are appreciated by customers and sales partners at HanseMerkur. It is a financially solid medium-sized personal insurer and the only independent insurance group at the financial center Hamburg, which operates nationwide. As a "mutual insurance association", we are only obligated to our customers and employees—not shareholders or investors. This principle shapes our actions, it is part of our corporate culture and manifests itself in a clear attitude. The old Hanseatic principle of the honorable merchant is fundamental for a traditional Hanseatic insurance company like HanseMerkur. The motto "Hand in hand is … HanseMerkur" reflects this self-understanding. It is about the partnership cooperation in the house, between employees and executives as well as the members of the board, as well as the honest effort towards the customers. Our guiding idea "Hand in hand is HanseMerkur" translates the community thought into a deeply human principle. Because with mutual support—so hand in hand—everything simply works better.

(continued)

Table 7.1 (continued)

HUK-Coburg	**Company Mission Statement** 1. HUK-Coburg, a self-help institution of the public service, and its subsidiaries, which are accessible to everyone, specialize in insurance for private households. 2. HUK-Coburg, as an insurance association, operates on the principle of mutuality, as do its subsidiaries. 3. The starting point and focus of all activities are our members and customers, who are our equal partners as informed, responsible consumers. 4. The HUK-Coburg insurance group offers consumers a comprehensive range of products tailored exclusively to their needs at extremely favorable conditions in terms of performance, price, and service. 5. As a cost-effective provider, the HUK-Coburg insurance group provides consumer-friendly services at premiums in the forefront of the market. 6. Advice and support for members, customers, and interested parties are provided locally by trusted representatives, customer service offices, and by employed staff of our branches. In addition to personal contacts, we are also accessible to our members and customers via all other communication channels, such as telephone or internet. High demands on the quality of customer advice and the maintenance of cost leadership determine and limit cooperation with external sales organizations. 7. Contract conclusion, contract support, and claims processing are based on predictability, reliability, and credibility. We offer our members and customers a service that is solely oriented towards their needs and is fast. 8. We economize with the contributions of our members and customers. We consistently exploit savings potentials through technological progress and strive for cost leadership in all areas. 9. The permanent safeguarding of the company group and its independence requires a steady, appropriate earning power to create and maintain sufficient security funds; the surpluses not needed for this are distributed to the members and customers. 10. The HUK-Coburg insurance group is a fair, reliable, and attractive employer. This personnel policy ensures that qualified and motivated employees meet the requirements of members and customers with their performance.

(continued)

Table 7.1 (continued)

LVM	**LVM's Mission Statement** Security, trust, and responsibility are the central values (guiding values) that shape LVM internally and externally. They form the basis of the actions of all persons working for LVM. Associated values concretize the guiding values. They define their necessary framework and describe possible manifestations and effects into the company. How we think—how we act: • Security … (sustainability, success, loyalty, commitment) … is a promise that LVMers give to themselves and their customers. It arises from loyal and economically successful action. Security in relationships is based on commitment and loyalty. • Trust … (respect, openness, transparency, integrity, appreciation) … is the basis of a good partnership. The LVM trust culture is supported by transparency and openness, accompanied by respectful interaction. Integrity and appreciation strengthen trust. • Responsibility … (service orientation, quality, commitment, flexibility, holism, joy) … means that every LVMer contributes his or her part to the success of LVM in a service-oriented, committed, and joyful manner in the sense of the whole. LVMers think and act flexibly. Their claim is quality.
R+V	**What we stand for** Our brand is the business card of our company. It is the distinctive impression that we want to convey to you every day anew and the anchor of our thinking and actions. Since 1922, we have been the insurance expert in the Cooperative Financial Group of the Volksbanken Raiffeisenbanken. This means that behind R+V are the 18.5 million members of the German cooperative banks. The cooperative idea is a world heritage and means: standing together for each other and for the community. Fair, humane, and responsible. • Reliable partner To meet our responsibility, we want to be a reliable partner. We have been successful in this since our foundation. Because we act economically solid and forward-looking and make sustainable decisions for the company's development. We handle our financial resources and resources responsibly and prudently. Because our customers do not just buy insurance, they buy a performance promise. Customers, sales partners, and employees can always rely on our word. Because we only promise what we can keep—today and tomorrow. • Cooperative thinking Thinking cooperatively is a central attitude for us. We network, stand up for each other, and promote each other. We live partnership, respect, and appreciation and are aware of our responsibility regarding societal challenges and towards the environment. Since we are not listed on the stock exchange, our decisions are not driven by share prices, but by the goals and well-being of a strong community and its members.

(continued)

Table 7.1 (continued)

	Cooperative also means being there for each other. We meet our customers at eye level: open, fair, and cooperative. We know the needs of our customers and offer suitable and innovative offers. Whether personally or digitally: With us, the human being is at the center. Not only in our daily work but also in our commitment. In a digitalized world, we work day by day to remain the insurance company where people are most important. For more cohesion and togetherness. For a society in which everyone knows: You are not alone. • We against selfishness No matter what happens to our customers or what moves them, we do not leave them alone. In a society characterized by selfishness, demarcation, and silo thinking, we want to be the voice of reason that emphasizes the with and for each other. This cooperative credo is manifested in our brand claim: You are not alone. With this promise, we make visible what our roots are, what differentiates us, and what characterizes a multitude of our products. We celebrate togetherness and make it tangible. On a societal level. In social commitment as well as in collegial togetherness.
VGH	**Mission Statement** VGH remains true to its roots and values—for 273 years. For just as long, VGH has been the market leader in its own business area. Nevertheless, it is essential for corporate success to regularly review strategies, redefine goals, and adapt early to changes—such as on the capital market, customer expectations, the digitalization of business, or the sustainability of corporate action. New requirements of German and European legislation, innovations in the product area, and the timely modernization of communication channels also require a high degree of flexibility, foresight, and adaptability. Cornerstones of our actions: VGH is powerful, customer-oriented, and committed. These three central values form the core of our company and shape our actions both internally and externally. Whether at the level of the board, managers, or employees, whether in defining strategic goals or implementing concrete measures: Our joint action is guided by our values; our joint success can be measured by them.

Sources: Allianz SE (2024); Cosmos Direkt (2024); Debeka Group (2024); HanseMerkur (2024); HUK-Coburg (2024); LVM (2024); R+V (2024); VGH (2024)

coordination with the marketing strategies and marketing tasks, to then be finally concretized and implemented at the mix level (Becker 2019, pp. 55–60).

Insurance companies generally pursue profit goals, sales and cost goals as their sub-goals, growth goals, occasionally size goals (formulated relatively as market share goals), and the goal of meeting needs. For corporations and large mutual insurance associations (VVaG), the overarching corporate goal is to increase the company's value, the creation of so-called shareholder value, measured by the market value of equity. For VVaG's and public insurers, the overarching goal—at least at the time of foundation—was to meet needs. As a secondary goal of necessary (and not least regulatory) condition, the safety goal with the sub-goals of solvency and liquidity is added (Farny 2011, pp. 332 f.; Oletzky 1998, pp. 6–8). These economic corporate goals will be discussed in more detail below.

It should be added that insurers may pursue **additional goals** beyond the primarily economic corporate goals, which, however, are comparatively difficult to operationalize. For example, they strive for as conflict-free relationships as possible with their stakeholders (BaFin, staff, media, etc.). In addition, there is occasionally the pursuit of independence and power. Independence refers to the absence or minimal influence by third parties such as reinsurers, brokers, major customers or the state, but not least also by the capital markets or investors. A VVaG is largely immune to a takeover by third parties such as investors and is therefore in principle independent and not directly subject to capital market requirements. However, this also means that it can only obtain (additional) equity capital to a limited extent. The power goal can refer to the possible influence on both internal and external decision-makers; internal power follows from participations or takeovers and the subsequent occupation of supervisory board or board positions, external power follows from a strong position in the market (market power). Finally, ecological, socio-societal, and corporate ethical goals are increasingly being pursued (ESG-related), e.g., social responsibility towards the environment, consideration of socio-societal claims such as the working conditions of their own staff, but also in the companies within the supply chains, and adherence to ethical principles in corporate governance. These goals also relate to stakeholders, but unlike the ones mentioned above, they go beyond mere conflict avoidance because they aim for additional benefits (Farny 2011, pp. 353 f.; also Meffert et al. 2019, pp. 284 f.). Moreover, insurers are already legally required to comply with ESG criteria (see excursus in Sect. 6.1.5).

7.1.2 Meeting Needs

The goal of meeting needs is to cover the insurance needs of other economic units. A pursuit of meeting needs leads to the basic mandate for the insurer to offer general or specific insurance coverage for general or specific customers. Meeting needs takes a **dominant role** when the ones having the needs themselves establish and continue the company, **when** the **customers are also** the **company owners**. For many mutual insurance associations (VVaG's) and public-law insurers, the goal of meeting needs was at the forefront of all corporate goals at the time of foundation; however, during their lifetime, it has lost importance in relation to other goals. For many small VVaG's with high specialization, e.g., in the field of insurance by professional pension schemes, pension funds, and company-owned risk carriers (captive insurers), it remains a main goal (Farny 2011, p. 334).

Certainly, the goal of meeting needs is not sustainable in the long run without considering other goals, because sustainable economic activity requires the fulfillment of further economic goals for the existence of the insurer and thus its ability to enable the meeting of needs (Farny 2011, p. 334). Furthermore, market saturation in some insurance branches may relativize the importance of meeting needs (Oletzky 1998, p. 8). But

especially from a marketing perspective, the goal of meeting needs remains the **fundamental goal of every company**, because the need for insurance and the offer of needs-based products are necessary conditions for the demand for insurance coverage. In this respect, the argument of *Farny* also applies in reverse. And market saturation means that the market-wide need is apparently covered and it is no longer about generating offers at all. But the quality of the offers is still—and now more than ever—capable of improvement. The discussion shows that it seems appropriate to distinguish between a quantitative and qualitative goal of meeting needs. The former seems to lose importance with ongoing duration in some forms of companies and with increasing market saturation, the latter remains relevant, especially with the continued existence of the insurer and saturated markets, because it is critical to success.

7.1.3 Increasing Corporate Value

Another overarching corporate goal, which appears as an alternative to meeting needs, is the increase in corporate value. This goal is **particularly relevant for insurance corporations**, where relationships with shareholders or investors are established through organized national or international capital markets (public companies). The aim of economic activity is to increase the value of the insurance company. Consequently, entrepreneurial action is less focused on individual goals (e.g., profit, growth, security), but rather on corporate value and its increase. Generally speaking, additional corporate value is created when the generated or expected profit exceeds the risk-adjusted capital costs associated with its production. For calculation, future-oriented quantities are used, which include the (future) profit potentials. These include, for example, the future success value (based on success flows) or the discounted cash flow (based on payment flows). However, such calculations involve difficulties in forecasting future flow sizes and choosing the discount factor.

In the distribution of corporate value increases to individual stakeholders, there are **potential conflicts**, which are partly influenced by the legal form of the company. In the case of a stock corporation, shareholders can realize their share of the increase in corporate value (shareholder value) by selling their shares, which is not possible in other legal forms. The policyholders as the most important creditors only participate if the increase in value leads to better price-performance ratios or an increased security situation of the insurer; this is possible, but not mandatory. The same applies to the participation of other interest groups in the corporate value. The primary orientation of the target size "corporate value" towards the interests of the owners and equity providers can lead to conflict with customer interests; this is especially true for insurance corporations. This is a classic conflict **between equity and debt providers**: the former are interested in profit retention or profit distribution to the equity providers, the latter in benefits for the debt providers such as price reductions, performance increases or profit distributions through surplus participation. In the case of a mutual insurance association, however, the value enhancement concept is less suitable because the owners here are the members and therefore the policyholders themselves, who automatically become members of the mutual insurance association upon conclusion of the contract. They benefit from value increases only through increased security and possibly through lower cost allocations in the insurance premium. Otherwise – particullary in life and health insurance – profit participation is only regulated by law in relation to policyholders, but membership in the mutual insurance association does not result in any direct claims. Moreover, this ends without compensation at the end of the insurance relationship.

Thus, the goal of increasing corporate value is particularly relevant for large insurance conglomerates and financial conglomerates, whose individual companies or their holding companies are listed stock corporations. Although associated with possible conflicts of interest, this approach results in higher efficiency of corporate management and a **better allocation of capital and other resources** within the group (Farny 2011, pp. 346–352). Nowadays, most insurers are oriented towards this goal.

7.1.4 Profit and Profitability

The **pursuit of profit** is a system-related **fact in a market economy** and an expression of the commercial principle. Insurance stock cooperation (AG) and large mutual insurance associations (VVaG) usually pursue this corporate goal, because profit ultimately finances growth in the market, be it through the required additional liability capital or for investments, from a marketing perspective e.g., into new markets, products or sales promotion actions.

Profitability relates profit to other quantities such as sales (profit to sales) or capital (profit to equity, debt or total capital). From a shareholder's perspective, the return on equity is of particular interest.

Excursus on the Profit Calculation of an Insurance Company

The annual surplus (or annual deficit) reported in the profit and loss account (P&L) of an insurance company does not reflect the ordinary and profit generated during the fiscal year. This is because it includes extraordinary and some non-period revenues and expenses, as well as certain profit allocations or loss coverages. In relation to the profit target and profit calculation, the "**economic success**" of an insurance company is a more meaningful indicator for assessing the success situation, corrected for these result contributions. It approximates the ordinary and period-appropriate profit or loss for the fiscal year and is calculated as follows:

+/./. Annual surplus/deficit

+/./. Distributed profits/revenues from loss absorption
(Group-internal participation in annual surplus/deficit)

\+ Profit-dependent remunerations on profit-sharing capital
(Profit distribution towards capital providers)

\+ Extraordinary expenses
(Not part of the ordinary business operations)

./.	Extraordinary revenues (Not part of the ordinary business operations)
+/./.	Increases/decreases in provisions for impending losses, fluctuations and similar (Profit distribution towards capital providers)
=	**Economic profit/loss after taxes and after** **Profit participation of the policyholders**
+	Income and earnings taxes
+	Policyholder's share of profits (Insofar as not in the annual surplus)
=	**Economic profit/loss before taxes and before** **Profit participation of the policyholders**

The economic success before state and policyholder participation expresses the actual success of the business activity towards all stakeholder groups; the economic success after state and policyholder participation is, however, the more relevant size for the equity providers, as it at least approximately shows how much revenues can be achieved absolutely from the ordinary business and allows a ratio formation to the capital employed (return on equity) (based on Farny 1992, p. 179).

The **profit target** must first be **specified** in terms of type: For controlling economic activities—and this includes marketing—the internal, calculative profit is a more sensible size than the annual surplus depicted in the external annual financial statements. The calculative profit is the actually achieved or, in the context of target formulation, the profit to be achieved, defined as the sum of the performance values, including primarily the premium revenues from the insurance business and the revenues from the investment business, minus the sum of the cost values. The profit target is also to be allocated to the overall business; the served business fields of the insurer are suitable for this. It must also be determined which profit size is used as a basis (profit before/after taxes; before/after profit shares of the policyholders; absolute profit amount; relative profit (profitability) and its reference sizes (sales, capital)). Furthermore, the desired target extent must be defined: Wanting to achieve the maximum regarding the target size is rarely sensible in reality. Limited target extents such as a minimum profit, possibly even a zero profit (= cost coverage) or a restructuring (loss reduction) or an industry-average profit are more realistic—the target requirement of achievability should be considered (Farny 2011, pp. 335–338).

7.1.5 Revenue and Costs as Sub-goals of the Profit Goal

Sales revenues, i.e., the market values of the products and services sold, minus costs—in external accounting, expenses are considered—result in the profit of the insurance company. In this respect, both measures are parameters of the profit size and thus intermediate or sub-goals of the profit goal. In the insurance market, the sales target often actually has the character of a main goal. Almost all insurers define a certain absolute or relative premium income and accept cost increases or profits that are lower than expected in order to achieve this, which are thus degraded to sub-goals. According to the widespread view behind this, premium income is a central measure of importance, size, performance, image, and power of an insurer, although as a target size it does not always positively correlate with the also often proclaimed increase in company value. The high importance of the premium sales target is reflected in association statistics and media reporting, in which insurers are "ranked" accordingly. Internally, it is expressed, among other things, in the design of incentive systems in insurance sales, which are primarily oriented towards sales (see also Sect. 13.4.2). In terms of type, the sales target is thus expressed in a value size, although sales also result from quantity sizes such as the number of customers, contract quantities, or insurance sums. In terms of extent, sales targets are usually limited; otherwise, they would not be achievable.

Cost targets mean that a certain quantity of products and services should be produced and/or sold with a limited or even "minimal" amount of costs. They originate from the pursuit of efficiency as a ratio of income and expenditure. However, they can also refer to quantity specifications instead of value specifications and then express the pursuit of productivity as a ratio of output sizes to input sizes (e.g., the number of applications processed per employee). Practically relevant cost target sizes are—based on types of costs—the loss and operating cost ratios and their combination in the loss-cost ratio (Combined Ratio), which express the ratio of these costs to premiums. Even more frequently, cost targets are defined based on cost centers, which, for example, specify cost savings for a division, a department, or a group and thus represent intermediate and sub-goals of the operating cost target. Sometimes the cost targets are even superordinate goals that must be adhered to and therefore lead to other goals (especially growth) being impaired (Farny 2011, pp. 339 f.).

7.1.6 Growth

Closely linked to sales is growth. Growth targets can refer to input sizes (personnel, capital), transformation sizes (processed contract quantities), and output sizes (insurance portfolio, sales, accumulated premium sum, portfolio changes, sum of capital investments). In practice, output sizes such as sales growth or contract quantity indicators are mostly used. Growth targets can be formulated absolutely and relatively; relatively, they usually refer to a comparison with the entire industry, but can also refer to parts of it or specific competitors. The extent of the growth target is generally limited, more so in saturated markets, which include part of property insurance, than in growth markets such as private pension provision (Farny 2011, pp. 341 f.).

Growth is the expression of a certain dynamism and is generally easier to "sell" than stagnation or decline. This is especially true for corporations, whose shareholders associate growth with (future) profit opportunities. Public insurers and mutual insurance associations theoretically have less pressure to act in this regard, but here too growth targets are formulated and growth is sought. As mentioned, the insurance industry still defines itself strongly through sales and thus associated **sales growth** and size. For the new InsurTech companies entering the market (see excursus in Sect. 6.1.4), the growth target is even the overarching goal in the first years in order to build up a certain (customer) base. For most insurers, however, the profit goal is increasingly taken into account in the context of a desired increase in company value, when the goal of "**return-oriented growth**" is set; this means profit-oriented growth and thus the consideration and balancing of both goals.

7.1.7 Security, Liquidity, and Solvency

In insurance companies, the pursuit of security, i.e., the preservation of the company, plays a prominent role. The reasons for this are the risk and investment business, the comprehensive state supervision over both businesses and their risks, and—related to both—the necessary trust of customers in the sustainable performance of their insurer.

The risk business is naturally exposed to the **underwriting risk** associated with risk transfer, that the actual damage values in the insured collective could be higher than the calculated expected damage values. This industry-specific risk must be **controlled** to ensure the safe fulfillment of customer claims in the long term. In addition, the insurer is exposed to typical **investment risks** in the course of its investment business: market, price, interest, and currency fluctuations, as well as the insolvency of debtors, can lead to investments losing value or generating less income than expected. At the same time, the term transformation of both businesses is associated with industry-specific **liquidity risks**, which consist of not being able to pay due claims for damage regulation as well as capital or pension claims in the course of old-age provision because the financial resources are tied up in the investment and cannot be liquidated. Insurers therefore pursue a corresponding risk and investment policy to manage these (entrepreneurial) risks, pursuing security and liquidity objectives in this context.

In both businesses, however, the insurer essentially operates with customer funds entrusted to it for shorter or longer periods. Customers save, particularly in the areas of old-age and healthcare provision, over many years in order to be able to assert corresponding asset claims in the insured event resp. in old age. If these could not be satisfied due to a lack of security by the insurers, this would be a socio-political problem and a disaster from the perspective of the individual affected. Their **need for protection** ultimately legitimizes a **far-reaching supervision over the insurers**. In addition to the general corporate law regulations (e.g., risk management system according to § 91 para. 3 AktG), there are therefore extensive supervisory regulations: According to the basic creditor protection objective of supervision, obligations from insurance must be permanently fulfillable (§ 9 para. 1 and Chap. 2 (financial Equipment) VAG). An appropriate risk management (§ 26 para. 1 VAG), which includes, among other things, risk policy, investment management, asset liability management, and liquid funds to avoid insolvency (§ 26 para. 5 VAG), as well as an ongoing risk and solvency assessment (§ 27 VAG) are also required. Insurers must also have sufficient own funds to cover losses (solvency funds according to 89 para. 1 VAG) and must observe stricter investment regulations in the overall investment and in the area of hedging assets (§§ 124, 125 and 215 VAG).

The **security objective** can be concretized in the form of reducing the probability of the insurer's ruin to a particularly low value (e.g., to 0.5%). Based on § 97 II VAG and § 91 paras. 2 and 3 AktG, the aim is ultimately to avoid illiquidity (insolvency) and the loss of all equity (over-indebtedness). It can therefore be said that the security objective entails **two sub-objectives**, namely **liquidity at all times** and **sufficient solvency**. In practice, the security objective is usually understood as the real preservation of the company's substance. This means that the value of the equity is preserved not only nominally, but also in real terms, i.e., adjusted for inflation. In addition, relative substance preservation is sought, which means that the insurer's position or share of the industry's total performance is maintained (Farny 2011, pp. 342–345).

7.2 Marketing Objectives of the Insurance Company

The marketing objectives of the insurer should contribute to the achievement of the company's objectives and—like these—be compatible with the strengths and weaknesses of the insurer as well as opportunities and threats of the market (Sect. 7.2.1). Classic economic (Sect. 7.2.2) and "psychographic" marketing objectives, which primarily relate to the mental processes of the buyer (Sect. 7.2.3), can be distinguished. The marketing objectives must be specifically determined (Sect. 7.2.4) (Meffert et al. 2019, pp. 292–294).

7.2.1 Derivation of Marketing Objectives from Corporate Objectives and SWOT Analysis

The marketing objectives determine desired, future, market-specific target positions that are to be realized by pursuing marketing strategies, fulfilling marketing tasks, and using marketing tools. The determination of the marketing objectives is linked both to the highest corporate objectives and to the future market opportunities and existing corporate resources identified with the SWOT analysis (Becker 2019, p. 61).

The corporate objectives of an insurance company, approved by the board, thus form the basis for deriving specific marketing objectives. The highest marketing objective is already anchored in the two corporate objectives of profit-making and meeting needs: The satisfaction of customer needs, in the case of the insurance company primarily the coverage of insurance needs by providing insurance protection for general or specific customers, directly contributes to the corporate objective of meeting needs, indirectly to the profit objective, because marketing aims at market and customer orientation primarily for the purpose of profit-making.

Excursus on the contribution of marketing objectives to corporate objectives

The goal of meeting needs in particular illustrates the interplay between corporate and marketing objectives very vividly: From a corporate perspective, satisfying customer needs is more of a means to an end (profit). From a marketing perspective, it is the central marketing objective—albeit under the premise given by the corporate objectives of making a profit. Assuming that creating value for the company presupposes creating value for the customers, the role of marketing and its contribution to achieving the overarching corporate objective becomes clear: Marketing becomes the central business function for generating revenue and thus profit, and ultimately corporate value.

Doyle operationalized this, i.e., made it measurable: He first identifies the cash flows, their actual cash value, the opportunity costs of capital (risk-oriented equity costs), and the present value of marketing investments ("net present value"), which corresponds to the sum of the free cash flows generated by the investments, discounted with the risk costs, as the decisive components of shareholder value. Then he shows the relationship between various marketing target sizes, specifically the associated investments in the expansion of marketing know-how, brand strength, customer loyalty, and strategic partnerships, and the change in shareholder value.

(Doyle 2000, p. 235).

7.2.2 Economic Marketing Objectives

The economic marketing objectives **are naturally closely linked to the company's objectives**, i.e., profit, profitability, value enhancement, growth, and meeting needs are also fundamental objectives of marketing. However, they **become more specific in relation to marketing, differentiated according to business field criteria**, i.e., they are defined per division, insurance product or product bundle, region, distribution partner or target group. Thus, for example, sales and turnover increase objectives differentiated by distribution channel, regionally different market penetration and market share objectives, or target group-specific performance objectives, which concern the quality of the insurance coverage and the accompanying services. In addition to the overarching marketing objectives, contribution margin objectives also become relevant, because the **contribution margin** (= revenue minus relative individual costs) **can be determined as a market-specific contribution to success**, which, for example, refers to sales areas, insurance branches, distribution channels or customer groups. It also takes into account the fact that there may be business areas that are important to the insurer for reasons other than profit, but should at least achieve a certain contribution margin. Another central economic marketing objective is the **market share**. It reflects the degree of exploitation of the market volume and expresses the company's market position in relation to competitors in the respective business fields. Corresponding to the approach of sustainable marketing (as a further development of the marketing concept) and the corresponding company objectives, ecological, social or ethical marketing objectives may be added. They can also be sub-objectives of the objective to meeting needs if customers perceive additional benefits from a company pursuing these objectives (Meffert et al. 2019, pp. 292 f.).

Economic Marketing Objectives

- Meeting needs
- Revenue (differentiated by customers, insurance branches, distribution channels, regions)
- Growth (ditto)
- Market share (related to industry, served market, competitors)
- Contribution margin (differentiated by customers, insurance branches, distribution channels, regions)
- Profit (distribution to customers)
- Ecological, social and ethical objectives (as sub-objectives of meeting needs)

Insurers also pursue economic marketing objectives. As already indicated above, the revenue objective plays a major role in insurance marketing, as marketing activities show their effect in this respect. In addition, premium revenues are easy to formulate as a target and to control in terms of their achievement. The same applies to the transfer to marketing tools, especially sales policy. There, incentive systems often relate to sales figures, whether these are commissions for new contracts or the care of existing customers. Other marketing sub-objectives are also positively influenced by the revenue objective: In insurance practice, premium income is (still) an important benchmark for the importance and performance of an insurer.

▶ Since sales figures alone say little about the insurer's position in the competition, it makes sense to use market share. In general, if market share increases, so does the competitive position and vice versa. This is due, on the one hand, to the fact that with increasing size, scale effects should occur because the insurer can spread its fixed costs over more contracts (economies of scale). On the other hand, market power increases with market share.

▶ **Market share** of an insurer stands for the extent of company-specific sizes (quantity and/or value sizes) in relation to the total extent of the industry, the served market, several or the largest competitor.

In terms of measurement variables, the market share can be based on existing premiums, new business premiums, contract numbers, balance sheet totals or capital investments.

The **reference sizes** themselves can vary between the **total market** and a single company. In the case of the total market, the industry or its boundary needs to be specified more precisely: For example, a life insurer could see itself in the industry for term life insurance; however, it could also classify itself in the industry for all types of life insurance (including all endowment and annuity insurances), in the industry for state-sponsored retirement products (including the corresponding bank offers), or in the industry for retirement provision (including all corresponding financial services such as stocks, bonds or funds and other services beneficial to retirement provision). The management thus has a large degree of discretion and should consider to what extent customers see and treat the different retirement provision products as substitute products.

If the market share only refers to the **served market**, this is the result of a limitation to the part of the market that the insurer "serves" with its marketing program, i.e., the targeted business areas. The limitation can refer to customer groups, distribution channels, regions, or insurance branches. The reference to the served market is therefore as common in practice as it is sensible, because a company initially focuses on its immediate market, observes and expands its position in it, and then expands the served market to include new products and market areas based on this.

The reference point of the market share consideration can be further restricted, e.g., to the **largest competitors** in the industry, to which the insurer would have to react and to which it counts itself, or to the largest competitor, if the insurer itself is among the two largest providers. This results in a relative market share that only refers to a few competitors. In both cases, the market share then expresses whether the insurer is the market leader and how strong it is compared to its immediate competitors—thus, this measures the dominant position. In the German motor vehicle insurance market, the market leader HUK-Coburg had a market share of 14.1% in 2021, based on total business (motor vehicle third-liability and other motor vehicle insurances) including existing business in gross earned premiums. The following immediate competitor, Allianz, had a market share of 12.5%, almost 90% when considered as a relative market share (of the market leader's market share). The third largest motor vehicle insurer, VHV, already had only about 5.1% market share, so it was just over a third of HUK-Coburg and about 40% of Allianz. Based on the insured cars or the number of contracts, a much clearer picture emerges: HUK-Coburg has a market share of 18% with 23.57 million contracts, followed by Allianz with 13.38 million contracts and a market share of 10.2%. LVM is third with 6.83 million contracts and a market share of 5.2%, ahead of VHV with 6.23 million contracts and a market share of 4.8%. Based on the number of contracts, the market leader thus has almost twice as high a market share as its first follower (BaFin 2023a, b).

The market share is easy to calculate. Moreover, it can serve as an absolute target size of the growth target: To maintain the market share, it is therefore necessary to increase premium revenues in line with the industry average growth. The market share is thus another marketing target size that is closely related to the growth target and ultimately to the sales target.

At the same time, however, the market share expresses the (dominant) position of the insurer in the market, whether this is now related to customer segments, distribution channels, regions, or individual insurance branches. Directly connected with this is the strategic marketing scope: A large, dominating provider will position itself differently and design its marketing tools than a smaller insurer exposed to many equivalent competitors. Accordingly, the marketing strategies observed by global players and national market leaders differ significantly from those of medium-sized and smaller (niche) providers.

The cost target, as an expression of the pursuit of efficiency, is only a secondary goal of marketing; after all, it ignites indirect effect in connection with pricing policy when it increases the insurer's price reduction scope.

Indirectly, however, costs also play an increasingly important role in marketing, as profit targets at the company level lead to revenue targets for individual business areas and thus to the often postulated "profit-oriented growth" as a target specification. This makes the differentiated formulation of **contribution margin targets** according to customer groups, insurance branches, distribution channels and/or regions increasingly important in the insurance industry. The contribution margin in insurance results from the difference between the revenues from premium income and the directly attributable variable individual costs, which are essentially claims and acquisition costs. The contribution margin is calculated as follows:

+ Premium income
- Direct variable claim costs

= **Contribution Margin I**
- Commissions

= **Contribution Margin II**
- Other individual costs (e.g. acquisition costs, distribution channel or customer group)

= **Contribution Margin III**

From the customer's perspective, the general level of profit is much more interesting. This is because supervisory and competition law grant policyholders various profit-sharing rights in life and health insurance. The competition among insurers also leads to policyholders often participating in profits beyond these legally prescribed shares. For the same reason, customers also benefit from profits in property & casualty insurance, whether in the form of profit-dependent premium refunds or lower premiums.

7.2.3 Psychographic Marketing Objectives

The starting point of the psychographic marketing objectives is the empirically proven hypothesis that motives, attitudes, and images of the buyer determine the willingness to buy and thus ultimately the probability of purchase. In fact, there are close relationships between the activating and cognitive processes on the one hand and the actual buying behavior on the other hand (see Sect. 4.3.1). The psychographic marketing goals therefore target the mental processes of buyers and aim at intended, goal-conform behavior changes in the demanders (Meffert et al. 2019, pp. 293 f.).

They therefore refer to the following target or impact variables:

- Awareness,
- Attitudes,
- Brand sympathy (image),
- Knowledge transfer,
- Preferences,
- Purchase intention,
- Buyer penetration and purchase intensity,
- Customer satisfaction and customer loyalty,
- Brand loyalty.

In contrast to the economic marketing goals, the core problem is the **difficult measurability of the purchase or sales effects** as a result of changes in the buyer's psychological variables. **However, the psychological target variables themselves** can be determined and **measured** by marketing research using surveys of the population or other instruments. Their development over time can also be measured. The mental processes in buyers can be very well influenced by communication tools, especially by advertising. Thus, the psychographic marketing goals provide concrete guidelines for the design of the communication policy and its success measurement. However, the target and impact variables associated with them are usually not the result of a single marketing tool, but the result of all tools (Becker 2019, pp. 63 f.).

One of the most important (psychographic) target variables of marketing in the service sector is also **customer satisfaction**. It is the result of a complex actual-target comparison process in which customers compare subjective experiences when using the service (actual) with their expectations, goals, or norms regarding the offered service (target). If the expectations are met when using the service, customer satisfaction arises, if not, dissatisfaction. Overfulfillment can even lead to customer enthusiasm (Meffert et al. 2018, pp. 95 f.).

Empirical studies repeatedly examine the **relationship between customer satisfaction and customer loyalty** : A three-dimensional understanding of customer loyalty, which includes the customer's repurchase behavior, their willingness to make additional purchases, and their willingness to recommend, is widely prevalent. It is now considered a secure finding that customer satisfaction positively affects all three facets, although it does not generally and automatically lead to customer loyalty. Moreover, a positive correlation between customer satisfaction and customers' willingness to pay has been demonstrated, which becomes stronger with increasing customer experience (Homburg 2020, pp. 47 f. and the literature mentioned there; Meffert et al. 2019, pp. 112–114; for the insurance industry Grothe and Lohse 2003, pp. 21, 34–37 and the literature cited there). *Stauss* and *Seidel* also demonstrate the correlation between dissatisfaction and migration with simultaneous negative word-of-mouth advertising and point out that this is even more important than the one between customer satisfaction and customer loyalty and therefore complaint management offers an even greater lever than increasing customer satisfaction (Stauss and Seidel 2019, pp. 5–14).

The building of reputation (good reputation and image), awareness and ideally sympathy of the provider on the part of customers, sales and other business partners should be reflected in the building of a strong and significant corporate brand. Its building and maintenance require conscious brand management. Therefore, from the above-mentioned psychographic marketing goals, **brand building** can be derived as a central marketing goal. And according to *Kotler et al.* brand management is probably the most important marketing achievement to secure the provider's future. Brand management is also an art and the cornerstone of marketing. In a broad understanding, brand policy then forms the strategic basis for all design measures in the marketing mix. With the brand, on the one hand, the origin of the service is announced (identification function), on the other hand, a differentiation from other services is sought (individualization function) (Kotler et al. 2017a, pp. 384 f.; Kotler and Bliemel 1999, p. 689).

Also in **insurance**, the **corporate brand plays a prominent role in trust-building and identity-establishing**. Because it makes a significant contribution to overcoming the typical difficulties of service and insurance marketing: As a symbol for a performance promise, the brand makes the immaterial properties of the insurance product tangible and concretizes the abstract benefit of the insurance's long-term protection promise by conveying psychological sizes such as trust, competence and sympathy (e.g., safety, size and competence at Allianz).

The brand also signals a certain quality level and thus acts as a quality guarantee **reducing risk**, which ultimately promotes the customer's decision to conclude. However, the challenge of brand building or brand maintenance lies in ensuring the quality level expected from an established brand consistently through the service process and the various people involved with customer contact.

Another aspect concerns the **differentiation potential** of brands: Especially financial services and insurance products often have a commodity character in their core, i.e., they possess the properties of standardized and interchangeable goods. In this situation, brands can create a clear differentiation from the competition. Service products cannot be patented, (product) brands, on the other hand, can at least be protected by trademark law. This promotes the sustainability of the created market differentiation.

The (brand) image, like customer loyalty, is influenced by customer satisfaction: Empirical studies have shown the **consequence of dissatisfaction**: While a satisfied customer shares his positive experiences with an average of three people, an unsatisfied customer complains to an average of eleven people. Consequently, 75% satisfied customers with 20% unsatisfied are no longer sufficient to build a positive image in the market. Another study found that thirteen percent of unsatisfied customers complain to more than twenty people. This circumstance is exacerbated by the fact that only just under five percent of unsatisfied customers report this to the company. Thus, creating sufficient customer satisfaction is a necessary condition for sustainable business success: It certainly does not guarantee that customers will remain loyal to the company, but it is necessary in this regard (Stauss and Seidel 2019, pp. 40 f.; Homburg 2020, p. 561; Kotler et al. 2022, p. 294).

> **Note** Sufficient customer satisfaction is a necessary condition for sustainable business success, because negative word-of-mouth spreads faster and further than positive.

The high importance of customer satisfaction also arises from the fact that it is a prerequisite for customer loyalty and customer penetration in the area of psychographic marketing goals, and also influences brand building.

Psychographic Marketing Objectives

- Brand building as a top goal
  - Creating awareness
  - Creating sympathy
  - Creating preferences
  - Customer acquisition (supporting the purchase decision)
  - Creating customer satisfaction
  - Customer retention (confirmation of the purchase decision)
  - Customer penetration (up- and cross-selling, confirmation of the purchase decision)
  - Customer reacquisition (changing attitudes)

Linking economic and psychographic aspects, the marketing goals of (value-oriented) customer acquisition and customer retention can also be formulated pragmatically—these are also central marketing tasks. In insurance companies, due to the high importance of sales, (value-oriented) intermediary acquisition and intermediary retention are added.

7.2.4 Specific Determination of Marketing Objectives

Marketing objectives can be determined unlimitedly or limitedly: Unlimitedly formulated, they are e.g. maximizing sales, market share, or awareness. Limited marketing goals, on the other hand, are e.g. an increase in sales by 10%, achieving a market share of 5%, or a brand awareness in the target group of at least 70%. In reality, limited marketing goals are predominantly set, as they are more concrete and thus binding. As part of the goal determination, the period in which these are to be achieved must also be defined. This period should correspond with the short-term (e.g. weekly or monthly), medium-term (e.g. yearly) and/or long-term (e.g. multi-year) planning periods of sales control, cost accounting, and marketing strategy. Unlike corporate goals, marketing goals also have a **business field or market segment reference** (Sect. 8.2.3) and are therefore aligned with target groups that behave as homogeneously as possible (Meffert et al. 2019, p. 294). In the insurance industry, this means, for example,

- increasing the premium volume in accident insurance for private households in East Germany by 10% in the next fiscal year,
- maintaining the market share in motor vehicle third-liability insurance next year,
- increasing the contribution margin in home contents insurance by 7% by the end of the fiscal year
- increasing the awareness of the new occupational disability insurance for broker distribution among sales partners from currently 17% to at least 30% in the next two years.

7.3 Goal Conflicts and Their Resolution

The various corporate and marketing goals can complement, exclude, or be independent of each other. There are thus different types of **goal relationships**.

Goals complement each other when the realization of one goal promotes that of another, e.g. a achieved positive corporate image leads to an increase in premium income. If the achievement of one goal has no influence on that of another goal, both goals are independent of each other: The increase in market share in one insurance line in the industrial customer sector is independent of the improvement of customer retention in another line in the private customer sector (Farny 2011, p. 354; Becker 2019, p. 20).

However, natural **goal conflicts** can exist between different corporate and/or marketing goals, when the pursuit of one goal leads to a lower degree of achievement of the other goal. This is the case, for example

- between security and liquidity on the one hand and (capital) profit generation on the other,
- between demand orientation (value for the policyholders) and the creation of corporate value (value for the owners),
- between sales or even market share growth, which requires investments, and cost reduction goals, or
- between brand strengthening, which requires investments, and cost reduction goals.

If such conflict situations exist between goals, those responsible for specifying the goal system must make a **goal weighting**. This prioritization is nothing more than a formulated decision rule.

In the case of less conflicting marketing goals, a relatively balanced treatment in the form of utility maximization is conceivable. For this, a **goal relationship function** is needed, which indicates the goal combinations relevant in the concrete decision situation. The decision-making process regarding the optimal goal combination is shown in

Fig. 7.2. The optimal goal combination (Z_{11}, Z_{21}) between sales, i.e. quantity goal, and profit goal lies at point P, where the goal relationship curve just touches the goal indifference curve I_2 with the highest utility (because it is furthest to the top right) - I_3 is not reachable.

Due to the variety of goals, purposeful action usually requires a **goal hierarchy**, i.e. a ranking among the individual goals (Farny 2011, p. 333; Becker 2019, pp. 21 f.).

The distinction between **superordinate, intermediate and subordinate goals** is based on a means-end relationship and means that a certain (subordinate) goal has a means or implementation character with regard to achieving the superordinate (superordinate) goal. For example, the goal of expanding the market share in an insurance branch from 10 to 13% requires concrete goal specifications for product quality, cost level or price-performance ratio, and the control of distribution channels.

On the other hand, the distinction between **main and secondary goals** represents a goal weighting of the decision-maker regarding the priorities between the different goals. Example: In the immediate goal comparison, the company management ranks the expansion of market share as one of the main goals and thus more important than improving the brand image (secondary goal). Therefore, the insurer decides to cooperate with sales-oriented and external distribution channels, even though these may be indifferent to the company's own brand image due to their own brand strength or may even have a negative impact due to potentially high cancellation rates.

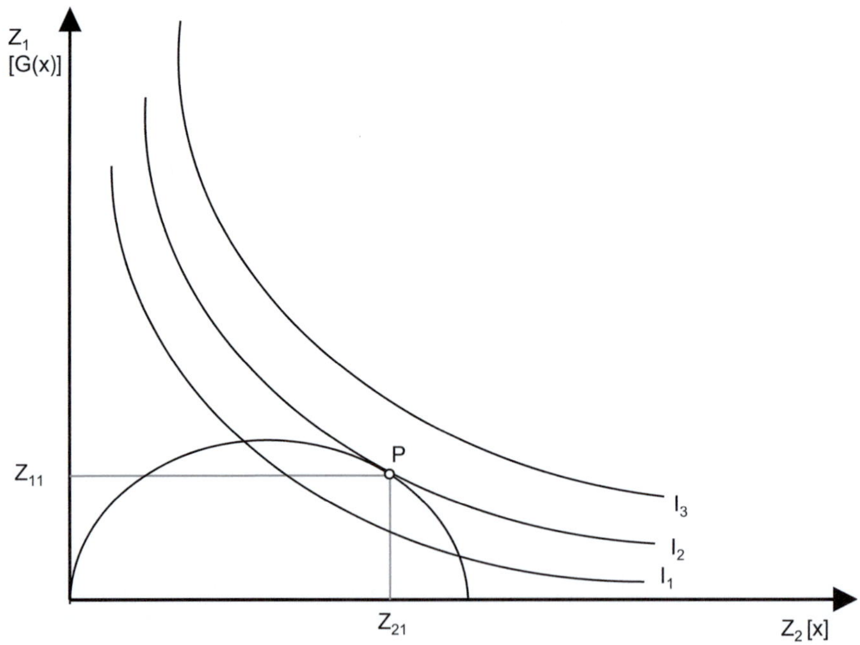

Fig. 7.2 Optimal goal combination of sales volume and profit

Finally, a weighting of the goals can be achieved through **side conditions**: The decision-maker sets a certain level of aspiration for the secondary goal, i.e. the goal is limited. The marketing manager selects from the remaining alternatives the one that has the highest degree of goal achievement with regard to the (limited) secondary goal. An example of a goal conflict between sales increase and improvement of the company image is shown in Fig. 7.3.

In the example, the aim is to improve the company's image under the constraint that the percentage market share to be achieved is predetermined. In Fig. 7.3, MA stands for the level of aspiration of the market share goal or the associated sales volume of insurance products, plotted on the Z_2 axis, Sym stands for the "sympathy value of the insurer", plotted on the Z_1 axis. If the level of aspiration for the market share is given with MA** (e.g., 3%), the goal conflict is low, and MA with the optimal sympathy value Sym_{max} is also achievable. However, if a market share of MA* (e.g., a market share of 13%) is the minimum goal, only a maximum of Sym* can be achieved, more is not achievable. The goal constraint is therefore to be seen as a strict restriction that must not be undercut under any circumstances. Exceedances are however possible.

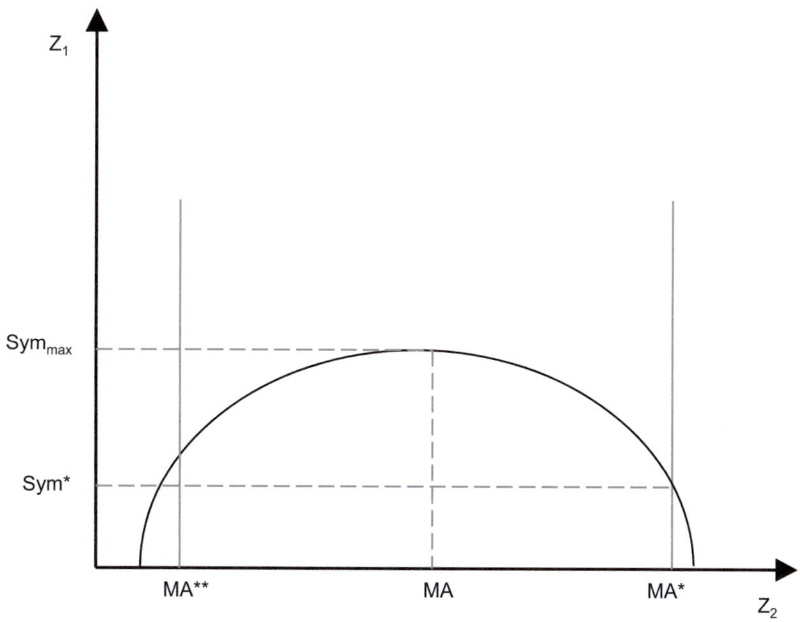

Fig. 7.3 Goal conflict between market share increase and image improvement

Goal constraints have a special significance for the solution of marketing problems in decision models because they are very common in practical reality. **Typical examples** include:

- Maximizing sales in selected branches while maintaining the given minimum return (or combined ratio),
- Increasing brand awareness and/or brand sympathy while adhering to certain marketing budgets,
- Increasing customer satisfaction while adhering to predetermined claims ratios,
- Growth through the development of new distribution channels while maintaining the existing positioning and profiling.

The resolution of goal conflicts represents a daily challenge for (marketing) management. Ultimately, goal conflicts naturally result from the necessary servicing of different stakeholder groups of the insurer. Equity providers (and analysts) demand attractive returns (profit goal), customers or policyholders good price-performance ratios of insurance coverage (coverage of needs, liquidity, quality and low costs), intermediaries the same plus attractive commissions and sufficient support, the insurance supervision and the legislator demand sufficient solvency (security). The marketing department, on the other hand, needs entrepreneurial freedoms and budgets for its goal fulfillment (coverage of needs, quality, attractive premium design).

The overarching corporate goals can be influenced little by the marketing manager. In the course of his derived functional goals, however, he must form goal hierarchies to define the scope of action given to him in terms of the goals pursued. Prioritizations help him in this, whether these are derived on the basis of mathematical functions or are the result of pragmatic selection processes based on experiences, given necessities or negotiation processes.

Further Reading Recommendations for Chap. 7

- Becker 2019, Part 1, pp. 9–134.
- Farny 2011, Chap. III 121 and 2.
- Müller-Stewens and Lechner 2016, Chap. 3.3.

References

Allianz SE (Ed.) (2024): Unser Purpose lautet: We secure your future, in: https://www.allianz.com/de/ueber-uns/strategie-werte/strategie.html, Accessed: 02.01.2014.

BaFin (Ed.) (2023a): Ausgewählte Kennzahlen der Schaden- und Unfallversicherungsunternehmen 2021, in der selbst abgeschlossenen Kraftfahrzeug-Haftpflichtversicherung, in der Rangfolge der verdienten Brutto-Beiträge, Tabelle 5631, Bonn, 2023, in: www.bafin.de.

BaFin (Ed.) (2023b): Ausgewählte Kennzahlen der Schaden- und Unfallversicherungsunternehmen 2021, in der selbst abgeschlossenen sonstigen Kraftfahrtversicherung, in der Rangfolge der verdienten Brutto-Beiträge, Tabelle 5632, Bonn, 2023, in: www.bafin.de.

Becker, J. (2019): Marketing-Konzeption: Grundlagen des ziel-strategischen und operativen Marketing-Managements, München, 11. Edn., 2019.

Berekoven, L./Eckert, W./Ellenrieder, P. (2009): Marktforschung, Methodische Grundlagen und praktische Anwendung, Wiesbaden, 12. Edn., 2009.

Birgikt, K./Stadler, M. (1986): Corporate Identity, Landsberg am Lech, 3. Edn., 1986.

CosmosDirekt (Ed.) (2024): Unsere Mission, in: https://www.cosmosdirekt.de/unternehmen/ueber-uns/leitbild/, Accessed: 02.01.2014.

Debeka Gruppe (Ed.) (2024): Unternehmensleitbild, Über den Sinn und Zweck unseres Handelns, Stand: 12/2021, in: https://www.debeka.de/ueberuns/portrait.html, Accessed: 02.01.2024.

Doyle, P. (2000): Valuing Marketing's Contribution, in: European Management Journal, Vol. 18, 2000, No. 3, pp. 233–245.

Farny, D. (1992): Buchführung und Periodenrechnung im Versicherungsunternehmen, Wiesbaden, 4. Edn., 1992.

Farny, D. (2011): Versicherungsbetriebslehre, Karlsruhe, 5. Edn., 2011.

Görgen, F. (2007): Versicherungsmarketing, Strategien, Instrumente und Controlling, Stuttgart, 2. Edn., 2007.

Grothe, T./Lohse, U. (2003): Kundenbindungsmanagement für Versicherungsunternehmen, Göttingen, 2003.

HanseMerkur (Ed.) (2024): Unsere Philosophie, in: https://www.hansemerkur.de/hansemerkur#-section_46324, Accessed: 24.01.2024.

Harbrücker, U. (1992): Wertewandel und Corporate Identity, Perspektiven eines gesellschaftsorientierten Marketing von Versicherungsunternehmen, Wiesbaden, 1992.

Homburg, C. (2020): Marketingmanagement, Strategie—Instrumente—Umsetzung—Unternehmensführung, Wiesbaden, 7. Edn., 2020.

HUK-Coburg (Ed.) (2024): So sind wir, Unternehmensleitbild der HUK-COBURG Versicherungsgruppe, Stand: 10/2017, in: https://www.huk.de/ueber-uns/unternehmen/leitbild.html, Accessed: 02.01.2024.

Kotler, P./Bliemel, F. (1999): Marketing-Management, Analyse, Planung, Umsetzung und Steuerung, Stuttgart, 9. Edn., 1999.

Kotler, P./Keller, K.L./Opresnik, M.O. (2017a): Marketing-Management, Konzepte—Instrumente—Unternehmensfallstudien, Halbergmoos, 15. Edn., 2017.

Kotler, P./Armstrong, G./Harris, L.C./He, H. (2022): Grundlagen des Marketing, Halbergmoos, 8. Edn., 2022.

LVM (Hrsg.) (2024): Leitbild, in: https://www.lvm.de/die-lvm/unternehmen/wir-als-versicherer/ueber-uns/ueber-uns-leitbild, Accessed: 02.01.2024.

Meffert, H./Bruhn, M./Hadwich, K. (2018): Dienstleistungsmarketing, Grundlagen—Konzepte—Methoden, Wiesbaden, 9. Edn., 2018.

Meffert, H./Burmann, C./Kirchgeorg, M./Eisenbeiß, M. (2019): Marketing, Grundlagen marktorientierter Unternehmensführung, Konzepte—Instrumente—Praxisbeispiele, Wiesba-den, 13. Edn., 2019.

Müller-Stewens, G./Lechner, C. (2016): Strategisches Management, Wie strategische Initiativen zum Wandel führen, Stuttgart, 5. Edn., 2016.

Oletzky, T. (1998): Wertorientierte Steuerung von Versicherungsunternehmen, Karlsruhe, 1998.

R+V Versicherung (Ed.) (2024): Leitbild, in: https://www.ruv.de/ueber-uns/unternehmen/wofuer-wir-stehen, Accessed: 02.01.2024.

Stauss, B./Seidel, W. (2019): Effective Complaint Management. The Business Case for Customer Satisfaction, Cham, 2. Edn., 2019.

VGH (Ed.) (2024): Leitbild, in: https://www.vgh.de/content/_microsites/unternehmen/ueber-uns/portrait/leitbild/, Accessed: 02.01.2024.

Marketing Strategy of the Insurance Company

8

The marketing strategy describes how and in which business areas the marketing objectives should be achieved. It sets the framework and provides the direction for the weighting of marketing tasks. In this respect, it is also a central component of strategic marketing. The marketing strategy of the insurance company (Sect. 8.1) determines the company-wide market development (Sect. 8.2) as well as the business field-related market development (Sect. 8.3).

8.1 Concept and Nature of the Marketing Strategy

The **marketing strategy** is a long-term, global behavior plan for achieving corporate and marketing goals. On the one hand, it aims to fulfill the defined marketing objectives and implement the desired profiling. On the other hand, it serves the purposeful orientation of all marketing tasks and measures in the areas of the marketing mix. The **reference level** of the marketing strategy is the **strategic business field** (Meffert et al. 2019, pp. 325 f.).

Marketing strategies are understood here with *Becker* as a distinct area and are therefore consistently differentiated from marketing goals, marketing tasks, and marketing tools. This is not always the case in both Anglo-Saxon and German-speaking marketing theory, and often instrumental strategies that concern the operational use of marketing tools, or marketing goals are addressed together with strategies, or marketing strategies are only dealt with in the context of strategic marketing planning. In this context, marketing strategies have an **important steering function** to use tasks and tools correctly and purposefully. Table 8.1 distinguishes between strategy and tactics and clarifies that the marketing strategy concerns basic regulations and **aims to do the right things**,

T. Köhne, *Insurance Marketing*, https://doi.org/10.1007/978-3-658-47345-7_8

Table 8.1 Delineation of strategy and tactics (according to characteristics). (Based on Becker 2019, p. 143)

Strategy (= Basic regulations; fundamental Predispositions)	**Tactics** (= Operational actions; ongoing Dispositions)
Characteristics: • Structure-determining (constitutive) • Real choice decisions • Medium-/long-term oriented • Delayed effect • Difficult to correct	Characteristics: • Process-determining (situational) • Routine decisions (habitual behavior) • Short-term oriented • "Immediate" effect • Easy to correct
Basic orientation: **Effectiveness criterion**: doing the right things	Basic orientation: **Efficiency criterion**: doing things correctly

whereas the marketing tools are the subject of operational actions and are subject to the efficiency postulate of doing things correctly (Becker 2019, pp. 139–143).

The **importance** of marketing strategies results, among other things, from their continuity: Medium and long-term programs are of particular relevance in marketing because certain market effects—such as the creation of preference through the establishment of awareness and image—generally require multi-period time horizons. Although there is basically no doubt about the necessity of forward-looking, potential-oriented strategy orientation, it is criticized in corporate practice that strategy determinations restrict flexibility and creativity. However, these are not opposites: Strategies define search fields within which alternative measures can be taken and situational action is possible, and this is even facilitated by the strategically formulated "**guidelines**". The same applies to creative problem solutions, which have greater chances of success if they are strategically channeled (Becker 2019, pp. 144–146).

▶ **Note** The **marketing strategy describes** at the corporate level the general market positioning and brand policy of the company as well as the selection of the strategic business areas to be worked on. It also specifies and differentiates the market development strategies in the respective business fields.

As part of its marketing strategy, an insurer must **at the corporate level** (Sect. 8.2) determine,

- **what** makes it special as a company in the eyes of the customer, i.e., find its strategic positioning (Sect. 8.2.1),
- **who** it is, i.e., concretize its corporate identity with the brand policy (Sect. 8.2.2) and
- **where** it wants to engage in the market, i.e., select its strategic business fields (Sect. 8.2.3).

In addition, the insurer must **at the business field level** (Sect. 8.3) determine,

- **how** it wants to appear in its strategic business fields towards customers, distribution partners, and competitors, i.e., define the respective market penetration strategy.

8.2 Company-wide Marketing Strategy

Company-wide and thus across business fields, the marketing strategy includes statements on market positioning, brand policy, and the selection of business fields to be worked on.

8.2.1 Company-wide Market Positioning

The **market positioning** should answer what the special benefit of the insurer's market offer is and what it stands for with the customer. The concept of positioning goes back to *Ries* and *Trout* (quoted in Kotler et al. 2017a, p. 348) and can refer to products, services, companies, and individuals. Their positioning arises in the thoughts and thus **in the mind of the prospect**. It is determined by how products, companies, etc. are perceived by customers in terms of certain properties compared to the competition. Positioning is closely related to the brand(s) formation: Not every brand is well positioned, but the best positions can only be held by a brand. If buyers can generally remember no more than seven brands of a product or industry category, positioning helps to make brands known and anchor them in memory. In insurance, positioning usually refers to the **insurer as a provider** and rarely to the individual product. The same applies to brand policy. This can be justified by the comparatively high interchangeability of most insurance products, their lack of patent protection, and their low-interest character. The positioning of corporate brands, on the other hand, is better protected.

With regard to company-wide positioning, **three strategies** are available (Kotler et al. 2011, p. 497; similarly in Kotler et al. 2017a, p. 359):

1. **Strengthening the current position**: This strategy is often suitable for market leaders who want to maintain and strengthen their successful positioning, e.g. in the German insurance market, Allianz Insurance or Deutsche Vermögensberatung (DVAG).
2. **Finding and filling an unoccupied position**: This strategy is suitable, for example, for newcomers to markets. Foreign insurers strive for this to facilitate market entry. For example, Hiscox in Germany has occupied a niche as a specialist insurer for home contents and art of particularly wealthy private customers. And the US InsurTech Lemonade has tried to acquire digital natives in the area of home contents insurance with simplified product presentations and premium calculations, thus

facilitating market entry into the German property insurance market. This strategy is also suitable for all other insurers. For example, Ideal Insurance has managed to position itself as a specialist for seniors and to expand its product range from funeral insurance to long-term care annuity insurance and accident annuity insurance.

3. **Repositioning**: This strategy is suitable for reacting to competitors' positioning and "sharpening" one's own position (soft repositioning) or for changing or reinventing one's own position (hard repositioning). An example of hard repositioning was the ERGO campaign "Insuring means understanding", with which ERGO consistently put customer orientation in the foreground about ten years ago and clearly differentiated itself from the predecessor brands Victoria and Hamburg-Mannheimer (see in detail under "Marketing Highlight" in: Köhne 2016, pp. 188–196). Repositioning is popular with InsurTechs, but usually a sign that the original business model is not working. Some start-ups started as brokers in competition with established brokers and are now their cooperation partners or started as brokers, then only provided software and are now insurance agents in some areas and insurers in others.

The insurer positions itself in the market vis-à-vis the entire corporate environment. The **desired differentiation from competitors** is a result of competition. It should be based on a comparative competitive advantage and therefore meet the following requirements (Homburg 2020, pp. 530 f.):

- **Customer benefit**: The service offered must satisfy the needs of the buyers or end customers—not those of the insurer—i.e., fulfill functions and thereby create benefits.
- **Perception by customers**: The customer benefit must be subjectively perceived and appreciated by the customer.
- **Differentiation from competitive brands**: The service offered must be associated with the generation of benefit advantages over other services for the buyers or end customers, i.e., be entirely or partially of higher quality, more flexible in design, easier to obtain and/or cheaper.
- **Competence basis**: The insurer should have the benefit-creating competencies (and the underlying abilities, resources, technologies, and knowledge).

However, it is possible that a company's competitive advantage and the desired positioning differ. The competitive advantage is based on actual strengths, the positioning on the (desired) perception by potential buyers.

Price and performance differentiation can refer to the overall market, but can also target defined market segments (niches) in order to benefit from closer customer proximity and fewer such specialized competitors. This classification of **competitive strategies** into **performance, price, or niche leadership** goes back to *Porter* (Porter 2004, p. 35). However, in general, only a few providers can succeed in gaining and maintaining price advantages over the competition in the market (see the marketing highlight HUK-Coburg in this chapter). In contrast, the possibilities of strategic positioning through general performance advantages or those for specific market segments are more diverse. The stronger the competition in an industry becomes, the more companies are even forced to realize quality and cost advantages at the same time and pass both on to the customers, i.e., to pursue so-called hybrid strategies.

Performance advantages require a consistent customer and function orientation (see Sect. 2.2.4) and thus value creation. Corresponding benefit categories are, for example (Anderson and Narus 1999):

- **Functional benefit**: It results from the basic functions of the product and its immediate use (basic benefit) and any additional benefits through further fulfilled functions. Example: Financial security through cost coverage of the repair after a car accident by the motor vehicle insurance and time and nerve relief through comprehensive organization of the repair and provision of a replacement car.
- **Economic benefit**: It is related to the costs of using the product or service. Example: Discount for self-conclusion of the insurance in direct sales.
- **Process-related benefit**: It results from the service process and can be based on convenience, speed, simplicity, and flexibility through location and time independence. Example: Fast, transparent, and uncomplicated claims settlement. Many InsurTechs start here and want to make the customer journey more customer-oriented using digital products and customer-centric processes.
- **Emotional benefit**: It results from positive feelings that arise from the service offer. Example: Relief after concluding one or more insurance contracts through the feeling of being well insured, or convenience through the takeover of the entire claims settlement and all related clarifications by the insurer after agreeing to cover the costs.
- **Social benefit**: Like the emotional benefit, it is associated with positive feelings, but these only arise in interaction with the social environment. Example: Addressing the sense of community at some VVaG's.

In the case of services, there is the possibility of **differentiation through the employees in customer contact** (Meffert et al. 2018, pp. 406 f.). However, it is difficult for insurers to differentiate themselves noticeably and sustainably in this regard. On the one hand, most competitors strive for high quality of their employees, which can be expressed in friendliness towards customers, injured parties, and potential customers, helpfulness, and professional and decision-making competence. On the other hand, despite these efforts, the quality of employees varies within the workforce of all insurers, because, for example, the use of professional competence in consulting discussions can hardly be observed and the consultation therefore (like the product itself) represents a credence good. However, in combination with appropriately designed processes, differentiation through customer-oriented consulting, support, and claims settlement can succeed if customer-oriented business processes are created through standardization of processes, use of computer expert systems, and access to central customer databases, which are then flanked by training measures on the employee side.

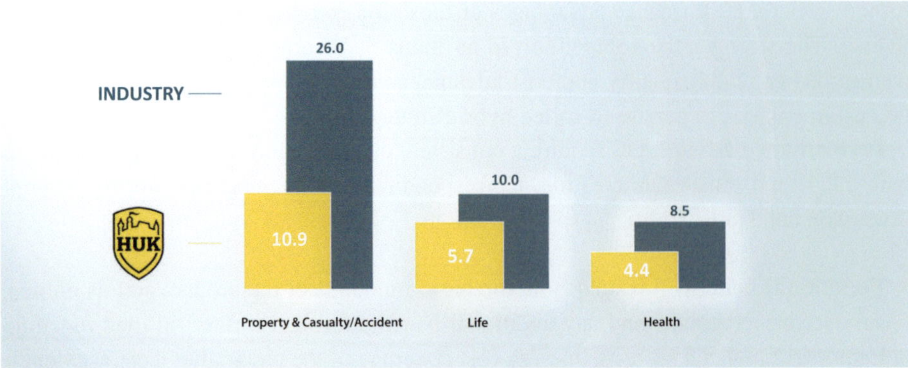

Fig. 8.1 Industry comparison of operating cost rates 2021 gross (in % of gross earned premiums) (HUK-COBURG Group, Marketing Department, based on KIVI figures, own calculations)

Marketing Highlight HUK-COBURG:
HUK-COBURG—Strategic Positioning as Price-(Performance-)Leader

1. Business Model/Strategy

HUK-COBURG was founded in 1933 as "Haftpflichtunterstützungskasse kraftfahrender Beamter V.V.a.G." as a self-help institution. The purpose of the company was—and still is today, significantly shaping the corporate culture—"the comprehensive insurance offer exclusively oriented towards customer needs at very favorable conditions with market-standard products and service quality". Over the decades, this has developed into a group that—measured by the number of customers—is leading in the property-casualty area in Germany and has very strong corporate brands in the market.

The basis of this unique positioning in the German insurance market as a price-performance leader is a very low cost ratio, which is otherwise only achieved by direct insurers—in this market segment, the HUK-COBURG group is also successful with its subsidiary HUK24 (Fig. 8.1).

The basis for these **cost advantages** are several factors:

1. Focus on private customers
2. Focused product policy with few variants to minimize complexity
3. Efficient processes through consistent digitalization
4. Utilization of scale effects due to the large number of customers (2022: 12.5 million)
5. Low distribution costs due to focus on an exclusive organization (AO), own branches as well as the headquarters (telephone) and the internet (huk.de).

Another strategic cornerstone is the focus on the motor vehicle sector—the compulsory insurance for Germans' still "favorite child"—for customer access. Here, by far the most transactions in the market take place: more than 10 million contracts in 2022, in years with "normal" motor vehicle economy even more than 11 million contracts. The motor vehicle sector thus offers the greatest potential for acquiring new customers, which HUK-COBURG has always consistently used. Through very favorable tariffs, good products and service quality as well as effective brand and product communication, the generation of active customer demand ("pull effect") is achieved.

Proof of the success of this strategy is the market leadership in motor vehicle insurance (by number of contracts and customers).

2. Pricing policy

The generally very favorable tariff level for HUK-COBURG products is based on the superior cost position in competition, and here especially on operating costs (acquisition and administration costs) (Fig. 8.1). This applies particularly to insurance lines that reflect a risk premium, such as composite and biometric products. But also capital-forming products benefit from low cost ratios in the form of higher returns.

In motor vehicle insurance, the products are priced particularly attractively due to their high importance for the business model. This ensures the high active demand on the customer side, which is essential for the functioning of the business model. The product calculation here is a mix of cost- and market-oriented pricing. Thus, the motor vehicle premiums of HUK-COBURG have significantly lower margins than the other property insurances.

3. Product policy

In principle, HUK-COBURG only offers products for private customers. These are also the same across all sales channels—both in terms of performance and premiums. In addition, no special products are offered for individual target groups or risk types. The latter are—assuming a corresponding importance in the market, either for the rating agencies or with substantial customer demand—covered by corresponding optional product components.

The products are generally positioned above the market standard in terms of performance. The standard and benchmark for this are the corresponding rating requirements—mostly from Finanztest—as 'market standard'. The aim is that HUK-COBURG's products are always among the top providers in this respect—while at the same time having a very favorable tariff positioning in the competitive environment.

In addition, as a mutual insurance association, HUK-COBURG is naturally strongly oriented towards the needs of its customers. An example of this is the buildings insurance, which now includes a general natural hazard protection due to the events in the Ahr valley. This has a high deductible of 100,000 € to keep the product competitive, but the natural hazard protection at least protects customers from total loss.

The products in motor vehicle insurance are also designed to be particularly attractive in terms of performance due to their high importance for the business model, thus supporting the active demand on the customer side and thus the pull effect in all respects.

4. Distribution policy

The sales policy of HUK-COBURG, in addition to ensuring presence in the field, also submits to the primacy of cost leadership. The channels used are the full-time and part-time exclusive organization, 38 own branches—where decentralized claims processing also takes place -, central customer service (mainly by phone and in writing including email correspondence) and the internet channel.

Cost leadership in sales is achieved on the one hand by foregoing cost-intensive channels such as brokers, banks or internet comparison portals with high commission rates. In addition, the independent agents of the AO only receive aquisition commissions. For this, the company generates the supply of a comparatively large number of actively demanding customers in motor vehicle insurance through favorable tariffs and effective communication. Thus, a HUK-COBURG agent has on average more than twice as many customer contacts as the market average. These customer contacts can then be used for cross-selling with other, also very attractive products in comparison to the competition.

In addition, HUK-COBURG is one of the few providers in the market that still relies on a significant number of part-time closing agents, thus ensuring presence in the field.

The Corona pandemic and the associated lock-down phases have led to a noticeable shift towards the more cost-effective direct channels. Here, HUK-COBURG already has a significantly higher proportion of telephone and online contracts compared to the market of service insurers.

Cost leadership, as mentioned above, also excludes presence in comparison portals. The commission figures demanded there are not compatible with the low cost rates of HUK-COBURG. The success of this strategy can be deduced from the fact that the only successful digital sales channels without portal presence are HUK24 and huk.de. Here too, the effective demand generation in motor vehicle insurance is very positive.

5. Communication Policy

In its communication policy, HUK-COBURG has been making extensive use of the tool of advertising since the late 90s, and has been successfully using TV as the main medium for generating demand in motor vehicle insurance. Meanwhile, the media mix is particularly supplemented by online moving image platforms. From the beginning, the shield, derived from the logo, was communicated as a brand symbol and accordingly sustainably anchored with consumers.

Since 2015, "Mr. Möller" has also been used as a personification of HUK-COBURG. In this way, communication takes into account the fundamental need for service insurer customers—in contrast to the self-sufficient direct insurer customers—to appreciate the possibility of personal support and advice, thus creating a relationship of trust and bonding.

In addition, the communication has unique selling points with the company color yellow and the established brand elements 'Möller' and the shield (shape of the logo), which generate a high memorability; the message "TOP-LEISTUNG, FAIRSTER PREIS" (top performance, fairest price) is in focus and corresponds to the positioning (Fig. 8.2). As a result, the effectiveness and efficiency of the corresponding investments are at the highest level (measured, for example, by the costs per percentage point of advertising recall) and in turn have a positive impact on cost leadership.

In addition, the communication has positive halo effects on the generally perceived insurance competence, which is reflected, for example, in the willingness to conclude other insurance lines up to the advice-intensive private old-age provision. This is confirmed by all corresponding market research studies.

6. Service Policy

In the service policy—in the following, 'consultation' and especially 'claims processing' are considered—the customer with his needs is at the center. The many annual awards for customer satisfaction show how well this is achieved by all involved employees in the implementation; the test seal contained in Fig. 8.2 exemplifies this. The customer satisfaction extends over all insurance lines as well as all customer contact channels. And especially the claims processing as a core service of an insurance company and thus from the customer's point of view "moment of truth" is an essential factor for the evaluation of an insurance company. And here too, HUK-COBURG has very good values.

The high satisfaction of HUK-COBURG customers is a prerequisite for their high willingness to recommend. This is an essential success factor in a market where the private environment as a source of information before concluding an insurance contract is of extraordinarily high importance, and significantly supports the business model of demand generation at HUK-COBURG.

The cost leadership in service policy arises, despite the highest perceived quality, on the one hand due to the low complexity as a result of the focus on private customers, the largely standardized product landscape, and the focused sales structure. On the other hand, the high efficiency of the processes and their high degree of digitalization make their contribution.

7. Conclusion and result of the strategy

In summary, it can be stated that the cost leadership strategy works very well: HUK-COBURG has managed to secure its customer access by generating active customer demand for the inexpensive

Fig. 8.2 Mr. Möller and the logo in shield form as established brand elements of HUK-COBURG. (HUK-COBURG Group, Marketing Department)

(yet high performing) products in motor vehicle insurance. This is not only evidenced by the contract and sales figures, but also by the willingness to buy among customers and especially non-customers (Fig. 8.3). Here, HUK-COBURG is far ahead of its competitors.

The cross-selling of other (attractive) products to existing motor vehicle insurance customers was also successfully implemented. Thus, HUK-COBURG became the market leader for private customers (by number of contracts/customers, Ipsos Financial Market Panel) in third-party private liability and legal expenses insurance and is also among the top providers in the other property insurances.

Therefore, the strategy of cost and thus price leadership can lead to success if, in addition, as a sufficient secondary condition, the other needs of the customers are met to their satisfaction.

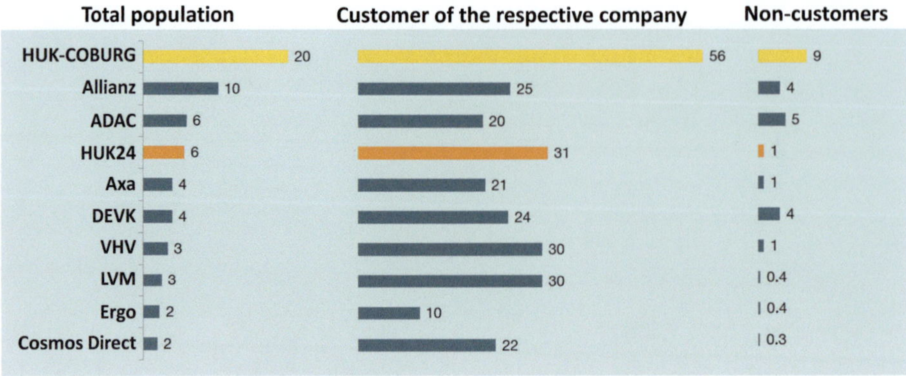

Fig. 8.3 Willingness to conclude/First Choice Motor Vehicle Insurance. (HUK-COBURG Group, Marketing Department, based on Kantar Campaign Tracking Insurance Market 2022)

Sources:

- HUK-COBURG Group, Marketing Department.

In the course of positioning, it is also necessary to clarify which and how many competitive advantages should be highlighted. When a company develops and communicates a unique selling point for a brand, this is referred to as a **Unique Selling Proposition** (USP). This could be the best quality, the best service, the lowest price, or the most innovative technology. Since it is becoming increasingly difficult—even for insurers—to be technically and functionally leading in today's competition, it makes sense to generate emotional preferences and associations of uniqueness in the buyer (Emotional Selling Proposition) and link these with the corporate brand. In relation to insurance, a (unique) brand image cannot be generated directly from the insurance product, but only indirectly through various properties associated with the insurer, such as tradition, financial strength, size, local proximity, originality, insured community, awards, etc. Moreover, several properties need to be combined, as several competitors may be considered the best for individual attributes and no sufficient differentiation can be achieved (Kotler et al. 2022, p. 382). However, in practice, it is **one of the greatest challenges of insurance marketing** to build sustainable and value-adding differentiations from the competition in customer perception. This becomes particularly clear when, following *Kotler et al.*, the following **requirement criteria** must be met for a significant **positioning difference** (Kotler et al. 2022, p. 383):

- **Important**: The difference offers the buyer a relevant additional benefit. This criterion can in principle be met, as shown above by examples.
- **Distinctive**: The difference is distinctive because the competitors do not offer anything comparable or the company does so in a unique way. This criterion poses a greater challenge for insurers—especially in the long term.

- **Superior**: The difference leads to the best solution, superior to competitive offers. This criterion is also demanding because the capabilities of insurance products and advisory services as typical credence goods are difficult for customers to assess.
- **Communicable**: The difference can be well explained and made visible. At least for the insurance product, its need for explanation complicates the fulfillment of this criterion. However, there are information surrogates such as ratings, quality seals, or corporate brands that support the communicability of performance differences.
- **Non-imitable**: The difference cannot be easily copied by the competition. Insurance products and the coverage concepts associated with them cannot be patented and thus protected from imitation. On the contrary: insurers are able to reproduce them depending on the product within weeks or months. Even accompanying services do not have patent protection, but depending on the process complexity, they are not as quickly developed as the products. However, the use of brands can at least achieve trademark protection (Haedrich et al. 2003, pp. 223–229).
- **Affordable**: The buyer can afford the offer. In relation to the insurance industry, no general statements can be made about this: the fulfillment of this criterion ultimately depends on the specific (differentiation) performance and its costs. However, it should be noted that price awareness among commercial and private insurance customers is not as high as in other industries because price transparency in most insurance branches is lower. Therefore, there are certain price ranges available.
- **Economical**: The provider can market the difference profitably. As with the last criterion, the specific individual case must also be examined here.

The mentioned criteria represent essential requirements for differentiation aspects that must be met for the differentiation to be significant or promising. The insurance industry suffers in this respect from the peculiarities of the insurance product, partly also from the product-related consulting service. At the same time, the special product characteristics such as immateriality, need for explanation, need for trust, and general disinterest on the customer side indicate that overarching communication and especially brand policy play a special role. In the insurance industry, the corporate brand as a trust-building and identity-establishing institution therefore plays a prominent role—product brands are less important in comparison because they are hardly noticed by the end customers (Köhne 1998a, p. 13, b, p. 7).

Interim Conclusion on the Positioning of Insurance Companies

Already at the level of strategic marketing, it becomes clear that product design or the consulting process alone are not very suitable for differentiating oneself as a provider in the market from competitors. Therefore, the corporate brand plays a special role when it comes to making the peculiarities of a certain insurance (service) more tangible and understandable, building trust with the provider, and arousing the customer's interest.

8.2.2 Company-wide Brand Policy

The strategic positioning should therefore also be reflected in the **brand policy** and **brand positioning**. A brand is not just a name or a symbol, but as a key element in the customer relationship, it embodies the perceptions, feelings, and attitudes of customers regarding the offered service. The actual value of a brand results from its ability to generate purchase preferences (customer acquisition) and loyalty (customer retention). Therefore, brand management is arguably the most sustainable marketing performance to secure the future of the provider (Kotler and Bliemel 1999, p. 689; similarly Kotler et al. 2017a, pp. 384 f.) and therefore also a separate marketing goal and at the same time the strategic basis for all design measures in the marketing mix.

As part of the brand policy, decisions must be made about the brand strategy and brand appearance, and finally, it must be checked to what extent the goals envisaged with the **brand strategy** have been achieved (Fig. 8.4). The brand strategy determines its reach, positioning, and architecture. The **reach** is specified geographically and can be regional, national, international, or even global. The **brand positioning** is about designing the brand core, the brand benefit, and the brand personality. The brand core stands for the identity of the brand (Who am I?), which can be formulated in the form of a concise expression or sentence (e.g., Württembergische: “The Rock in the Waves”). The brand benefit results from the promise of benefit to the customers (What do I offer?). Possible promises of benefit were already presented above in connection with positioning. A concrete example would be quick and uncomplicated help in the event of a claim. For existing customers, the insurance brand can thus be “charged” with a concrete experience in the event of a claim, which poses a challenge for new customer acquisition. Finally, the brand personality refers to human characteristics that the customer associates or should associate with the brand (How am I?). Such associations can contribute to differentiation from competitor brands. They can also create an emotional relationship and thus higher customer loyalty to the brand. HUK-Coburg, for example, manages to be perceived as “traditionally cheap”. The third part of the brand strategy is to determine the **brand architecture**. It organizes all brands of a company and defines the roles of the brands and their relationships with each other. Unlike brand reach and brand positioning,

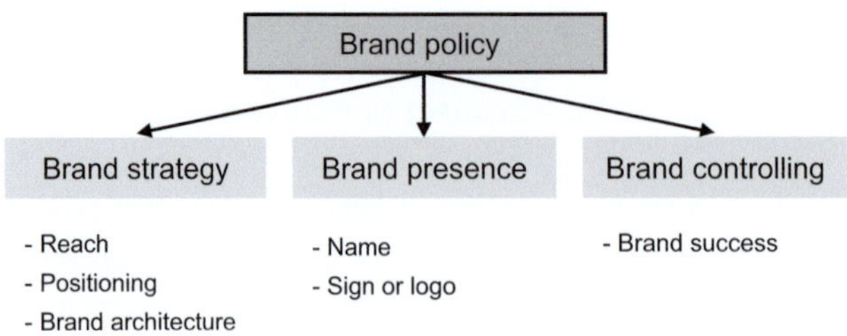

Fig. 8.4 Brand policy and its components

it does not concern individual brands, but the structure of all brands in the company (Homburg 2020, pp. 679–691).

In the context of brand architecture, **horizontal, lateral, and vertical brand strategies** are possible (Table 8.2). Horizontally, brands from providers at the same value creation level compete with each other, e.g., from manufacturers of the same insurance products, different insurance branches, or even different financial services products within the financial services group, as well as from different distribution channels within an insurance or financial services group. Vertical competition takes place between companies at different stages of the value chain. In the financial services and insurance sector, it primarily focuses on the interplay between financial service providers in the narrower sense (insurance companies, banks, building societies, credit card companies, leasing companies, etc.) and those in a broader sense (financial intermediaries, primarily

Table 8.2 Brand strategic options in horizontal and vertical competition. (Based on Köhne 2006, p. 156)

Brand strategy	Explanation and examples
Horizontal brand strategies	
Individual brand (= Product brand)	Each product or service promise is offered under its own brand. e.g. target group products of Mannheimer Versicherung such as Sinfonima, Artima, Valorima etc.
Umbrella brand	(Almost) All products or service promises of the company or financial services group are offered under one brand. e.g. Allianz, AXA
Multi-brand	A financial services group carries at least two brands in the same business field or product area. e.g. R+V with R+V and Condor Lebensversicherung, many direct sales under secondary brands (Cosmos, DA Direct, Europa)
Brand transfer	Transfer of brand images from a main brand of a certain product area to other offer categories. e.g. ADAC motor vehicle insurance (Allianz), VW motor vehicle insurance (Joint Venture VW Financial Services/Allianz)
Tandem brand	Company and product brand are combined in the sense of a double marking. e.g. Gothaer VarioRent plus fund, Mundial by Hiscox, Generali Vitality
Co-Branding	At least two different (company) brands are used side by side or combined. e.g. ERGO and DKV, Deutsche Bank/Postbank and Zurich Versicherung
Vertical brand strategies	
Sales brand	Brand that marks an financial services intermediary. e.g. MLP, DVAG etc.
Annex brand	Financial services provider is a white label supplier; the brand of the annex partner with customer access is used. e.g. Fielmann glasses insurance (HanseMerkur), Tesla motor vehicle insurance (Helvetia), ADAC motor vehicle insurance (ADAC, Allianz)

intermediaries or associations). The latter group often also uses its own strong sales or annex brands in their efforts to maintain customer contact and brand perception. Brands can also compete laterally with providers from other industries. For the insurance company, brand transfer, co-branding, using manufacturer brands, and using annex brands are sensible lateral brand strategies.

An alternative to direct brand competition is the deliberate **brand cooperation**. The use of multiple strong brands is intended to create added value. In the case of co-branding, several partners interact with the end customer. In the event of damage to a car, this could be the motor vehicle insurer and the car repair shops cooperating with him, as the example of the cooperation of various motor vehicle insurers with the company Carglass shows. In the case of a "Allfinanz" offer from Deutsche Bank and Zurich Insurance, both providers are marketed in their product categories by the respective customer advisor. In these cases, the retention of the individual brands ensures quality, as the responsibility is distributed among various partners and their brands, but also the strength of the individual company brands is used at the same time. In addition, the partners benefit from a certain brand transfer.

At the corporate level, this spectrum offers **two central paths**: The first consists in realizing brand synergies when the insurance group appears to the end customer with a dominant **umbrella brand**, such as Allianz or AXA. The second path aims to create added value from the **use of multiple strong brands**. An argument for the parallel horizontal use of different company and product brands arises from sales policy considerations: The variety of brands allows different customers to be reached and product, price and communication differentiation to be carried out. Although there is a trend in the market towards the establishment of umbrella brands and numerous traditional brands have disappeared over time, such as Nordstern, Colonia, Aggripina, Vereinte, Hamburg-Mannheimer, Victoria, Gerling, Volksfürsorge or AachenMünchener, there is an exception area where multi-brand strategies gain the upper hand: Depending on the sales channel, the same insurance branches are often marketed under their own brand in direct sales, while the umbrella brand is reserved for all other sales channels. The primary aim is to avoid "cannibalization effects" between the company's own representative sales and direct sales, whether these are actually given or only suspected, but causing unrest. Examples of such direct sales brands are Cosmos (Generali), DA Direkt (Zurich), Europa (Continentale), Bavaria Direkt (Versicherungskammer Bayern) or Berlin Direkt (HanseMerkur).

In addition to the brand strategy (reach, positioning, architecture), the **brand appearance** must be defined: It is about the question of how the brand should appear on the market. For this, the **brand name** and the brand symbol or logo (marking) must be designed. In the insurance industry, as mentioned, mainly company brands are marketed. The associated brand names can be based on the name of the company founder (e.g. Hans Gerling, Robert Hiscox), include the place of origin and first headquarters (e.g. Gothaer, Hannoversche Rück, Itzehoer, Mecklenburgische, Münchener Rück,

Nürnberger, Stuttgarter), represent an abbreviation for a meaningful designation (e.g. DEVK for Deutsche Eisenbahn-Versicherungskasse; HDI for Haftpflichtverband der Deutschen Industrie, HUK for Haftpflicht-Unterstützungs-Kasse kraftfahrender Beamter Deutschland), establish an association with the offer (e.g. Allianz, HanseMerkur) or simply be made-up names (e.g. AXA, ERGO). The **brand symbols** are either arbitrary and the result of a creative agency or industry-typical symbols for security (shield, guardian angel, castle), size (eagle) and tradition (years of foundation).

Finally, following the strategic and operational brand design is the **brand controlling**. Its object of knowledge is the **brand success** (brand equity)(Homburg 2020, pp. 694–699):

- In terms of potential, brand success depends on achieving goals that are causally upstream of (purchase) behavior of customers. It can be measured by brand awareness, brand image and brand-related attitudes among consumers.
- In terms of market success, brand success depends on achieving goals that reflect brand success based on actual customer behavior. Market success can be measured by the market share of a brand, customer loyalty to the brand, and the achievement of a price premium for the brand.
- In terms of economic success factors, brand success depends on achieving general economic goals such as the sales and profits achieved with the brand as well as the brand value, which results from the monetary quantification of the brand benefit.

Marketing Highlight Allianz:

The Allianz Brand as a Growth Driver—National Marketing within a Global Brand Management

According to the Interbrand Ranking 2023, the Allianz Group is considered the most valuable insurance brand in the world. It faces several challenges of global players in a local home market: Firstly, it is about maintaining and developing a traditional brand in times of multiple global crises, in which people are increasingly seeking trustworthy and meaningful anchor points in society and the economy (*situation*). However, global action also always requires authenticity on site. This presents marketing with special tasks and areas of tension (*complication*). Against this background, Allianz is pursuing new, modern forms of marketing and communication: the combination of unique data with empathetic creations along clearly defined success criteria (*solution*).

A. Global brand management in multinational companies (*situation*)

Background

Founded in Berlin in 1890, Allianz has developed into one of the world's largest insurers and asset managers since the 1990s through a consistently pursued internationalization strategy. In 2022, the Allianz Group is there for over 122 million customers in over 70 countries worldwide with approximately 159,000 employees and offers a wide range of insurance products, financial services, and services. In the 2022 fiscal year, the Allianz Group achieved total sales of around 153 billion euros (Source: Allianz SE 2023a).

As in all globally operating companies, it was therefore also necessary for Allianz to ensure international brand management: Until the 1990s, the business was operated with a variety of different national brands. Only about a third was under the umbrella of the Allianz brand. With the aim of creating synergies in market development, a global one-brand strategy was therefore decided and gradually implemented since 1998. Traditional companies of the Allianz Group, which were known under other brands (e.g. in Germany Vereinte Versicherung, Mondial Assistance, Euler Hermes, Allsecur), were 're-branded' to Allianz. For newly acquired companies, there is a timely re-branding to the Allianz brand. Meanwhile, the majority of the business in the insurance sector is associated with the Allianz brand. The international Interbrand Ranking reflects this continuous work with excellent placements in the circle of well-known "world brands"—Allianz has been the most valuable brand in the insurance industry for many years; its current brand value amounts to 20.85 billion US dollars and has increased by another 11% between 2022 and 2023 (Interbrand 2024).

Cornerstones of the global corporate brand

The global Allianz brand is based on three cornerstones: Firstly, an overarching self-understanding with a clearly defined value proposition, secondly, central assets that are used in all countries, and thirdly, established processes and a global organizational unit.

(1) Overarching self-understanding and value proposition

The foundation of international work with the Allianz brand is the global brand self-understanding and customer promise "We care for tomorrow", derived from the corporate purpose . Because Allianz sees its raison d'être as a global financial service provider and insurer in the triad of "shape", i.e. the active shaping of the future, "care", i.e. accompanying its customers with their plans and worries, and "deliver", i.e. the high-quality experience of protection and provision when it really matters. These three customer-oriented "experience principles" (Fig. 8.5) operationalize the brand promise.

(2) Central assets and a common brand identity

In addition, there is a uniform definition of the visual and content appearance as well as globally used communication tools: The appearance of the Allianz brand follows a clear, centrally defined logic. The aim is to ensure a global and comprehensive brand experience across all so-called touchpoints with the Allianz brand. This experience is deliberately not defined statically. On the contrary, an established iterative design process ensures the continuous further development of the 'look & feel' in the digital and analog world.

Therefore, **guidelines for the appearance** are universally prescribed for operational work with the brand. The following are the key points for operational marketing (Fig. 8.6):

- **Conciseness** (Simplicity): The focus of the appearance is on the essentials. The messages of the Alliance should be "to the point": short and concise, relevant and above all immediately understandable.
- **Logo**: The sender's identity must always be made clear. Therefore, communication with the Allianz brand always involves a basic placement of the brand logo with the lettering and the "top left" icon.

Fig. 8.5 "Experience principles" for operationalizing the brand promise. (Allianz SE 2023b)

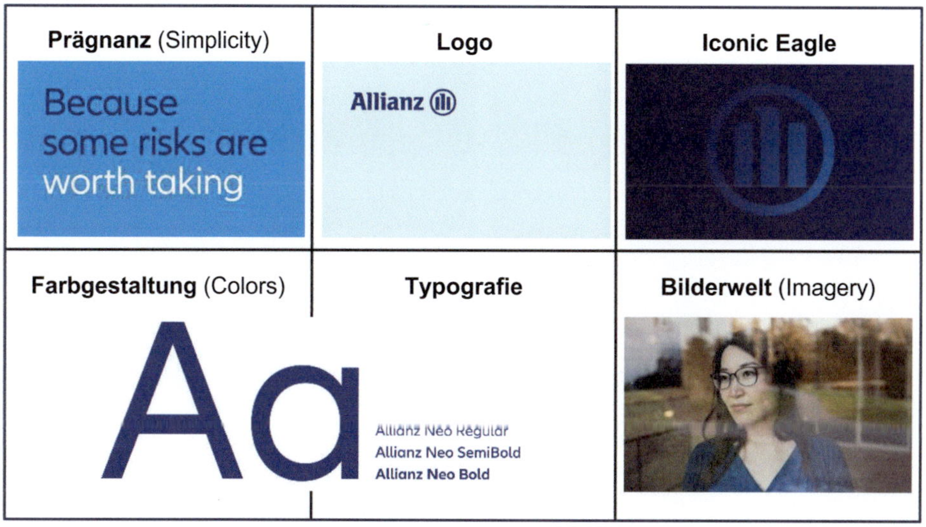

Fig. 8.6 Guidelines for the appearance of the Allianz brand. (Allianz SE 2023b)

- **Iconic Eagle**: Since its foundation over 130 years ago, the eagle has been a cornerstone in the visuality of the brand. Continually developed and increasingly stylized over the years, it now serves as an icon in many places—foremost in the logo after the Allianz lettering.
- **Color design** (Colors): The traditional central color is a dark blue. The "Allianz Blue" has a clear color definition (RAL 5013). This color identity has never been questioned throughout the entire development. However, as part of the ongoing development, the color palette has been expanded; the differentiation of the blue and additionally defined colors as a supplement give the brand a stronger vitality and thus closeness to the life of the target groups.
- **Typography**: The clearly defined typography is another element for recognition—also to ensure the desired perception. The starting point is optimal readability in both the analog and digital world. However, the goal is also empathetic, modern, and inclusive interaction with customers and stakeholders. For this, there is a specially created typography—the "Allianz Neo". It combines all the requirements mentioned above.
- **Imagery**: The imagery is probably one of the most underestimated influencing factors on the perception of communication—at all touchpoints. Current international customer analytics clearly show the high influence on the perception of customers and stakeholders and thus the importance as a central element in brand communication. Therefore, it is all the more relevant to provide this dimension with clear guidelines in international brand management: The claim to the images used in the Allianz is the reference to "real life". The right images ensure that the Allianz is perceived as it is: empathetic, competent, credible, and—in a positive sense—caring. Therefore, as often as possible, self-produced images are used in the implementation. The people shown are "perceptibly real", the situations reflect the life of the various target groups of the Allianz (Fig. 8.7).

(3) Organization and processes

In addition, coherence across central brand management and the creation of a binding set of rules (governance) for the global brand presence is important. Especially with the reach and influence of

Fig. 8.7 Examples of "authentic" imagery for better connectivity to the life situation of the target groups. (Allianz SE 2023b)

digital platforms, internationally consistent brand management is a key success factor for a globally strong brand. Therefore, global brand management at Allianz is managed by a central organizational unit. In the operational work of this team, in addition to the (further) development of the strategic guidelines described above, brand governance is also at the center. This ensures compliance with the defined standards and the necessary coherence of the brand presence at the global touchpoints.

Efficient governance design relies significantly on the support of implementation (enablement) and efficiency in daily work. Therefore, a digital marketing toolbox is a central platform of international brand management. For all units of the Alliance—and their service providers—strategy, guidelines, and best-practice applications are made transparent. For local use, there are extensive options for downloading centrally provided templates—these range from font funds and images to moving image material. This ensures both the efficiency of working with the brand and compliance with defined standards. At the same time, there is a clear definition of tasks, responsibilities, and the work processes of local teams with central brand units.

International brand management is based on a deep analytical understanding of the brand's status quo in individual countries. The content work of the central team is therefore supported by global transparency over the defined brands and perception KPIs. These key performance indicators (KPI) assist in determining the location of the Allianz markets in individual countries, tracking developments in the market and competitive environment, and deriving necessary areas of development. The decision to use an international media agency along the entire analog and digital customer journey is a crucial prerequisite. With a common taxonomy and overarching transparency, this also enables continuous development of analytics, e.g., through econometric models or the use of AI.

These three mentioned pillars—overarching self-understanding, central marketing & sponsoring assets, and a jointly supported visual identity—shape the global brand image of Allianz. At the same time, however, the brand must also appear authentic locally, i.e., in each individual country market, and remain closely linked to the respective people and their living environments. This presents brand communication with an additional complexity, namely "global" authenticity.

B. Tension between global and national *(complication)*

The challenge of balancing global brand management on the one hand and country-specific daily designs for optimal positioning in the respective competitive situation on the other hand is as old as the existence of global brands. Different paths are pursued and constantly adapted depending on the industry. In principle, a balance must always be found: On the one hand, it is important to present a "unified image" as a brand, ensure defined quality standards, and achieve efficiency. This is all the more true given the challenge of international social media platforms, where a separation between national and international is hardly possible. On the other hand, however, there is the need to meet national market conditions in order to ensure the best possible competitive position for the most sustainable business result in each country.

This applies all the more to Allianz, which in the German market must face five **challenges** with specific characteristics in its national marketing:

- **Demographics**: In Germany, as in all core European markets, marketers encounter the same situation—the large number of existing and long-term customers from the so-called Baby Boomer generation are increasingly retiring in the coming years. In the process, they fundamentally change their insurance and provision needs, which were characterized by communication via traditional media and personal care concepts. At the same time, fewer potential prospects and new customers from younger age cohorts are following, who in turn exhibit completely different consumer behavior. Customer journeys of these younger generations start digitally, and the marketing funnel is characterized by new media channels and communication formats.
- **Growth strategy**: This demographic change requires a clear priority on growth fields in three respects: Firstly, new customers need to be won, especially in younger target groups. Secondly, first-time customers with a contract must be addressed tailored to further, needs-based products, especially in special stages of life such as starting a career, starting a family, or moving. Thirdly, customers must be retained through excellent service and strengthening of the willingness to recommend, as well as actively preventing cancellations, for example through regular, also communicative customer contact.
- **Customer behavior**: Since the Corona pandemic and the associated, everyday digitalization experience in almost all B2C and consumer goods markets, as well as the subsequent high

inflation, previous consumer patterns are shifting. In the new business in the insurance market, purely price-driven offers have dominated since 2022 for the first time, which are also increasingly offered via digital channels and advertising media. On the other hand, products with a strong price-performance combination and primarily personal service and care elements—at least in the first step of a customer journey—are somewhat less important.
- **Perception of Allianz**: Allianz measures very differentiated and partly different brand attributes among interested parties, new customers, and existing customers. On the one hand, Germans uniformly reflect the image of a large, international, and very successful company. However, this positioning allows competitors with mostly regional or national positioning to present themselves subjectively "closer" and "more personal". This creates the need for Allianz to now combine its distinctly positive brand attributes with high reach with emotional closeness and reliability. Independent market research shows that long-term existing customers appreciate exactly this human and empathetic side of the Allianz brand, while non-customers have not yet been able to gather this brand experience and only the outstanding financial strength remains as a halo effect. Therefore, working on brand perception and actual brand experience becomes more meaningful.
- **Multichannel**: Both in communication and in sales, a proliferation of platforms and channels can be observed—these also have their own rules and modes of operation. The same brand spot, which was perfectly tailored to viewers of linear television, would be perceived as antiquated on new online channels and online platforms. The sequences of cuts, imagery, use of humor or irony, testimonials on public service media differ fundamentally from those on Twitch or Tiktok, for example. And at the same time, all are important. This requires completely new ways in marketing and communication in terms of staging and success measurement in the sense of "key factors for success". "One size fits all" is therefore no longer suitable for large brands with broad product portfolios.

It should therefore be noted that brand communication within the internationally binding brand guidelines must be aligned with the specific conditions of the market and competitive situation in Germany.

C. Solution approach: Analytic driven marketing (*solution*)
Allianz in Germany has faced these tasks and in recent years has completely realigned marketing and communication vertically (in relation to the global and national unit) and horizontally (in relation to national business fields and business intelligence units). The key to success was above all the combination of a (data-driven) customer understanding with the new staging of brand communication along the entire marketing funnel. This analytic driven marketing is now to be presented as an innovative solution approach (see also Lukowsky and Tidelski 2023).

As an initial organizational step, a new business division was established to evaluate Allianz (solely) from an independent and strictly data-driven customer perspective—this division is represented by the **chief customer officer (CCO)** at Allianz in Germany:

- **Function**: This unit has since been responsible for the quantitative and qualitative understanding of the different customer groups in the German insurance market and has an explicit sign-off right ("veto") for all new products and service introductions as well as for the development of new offers. For this purpose, it is responsible for all relevant market research and testing formats. The unit also continuously measures the willingness of existing customers to recommend the company using the net promoter score (NPS) or the 5-star logic. It conducts national brand and campaign tracking and measures the success of used communication tools and their efforts. For some time now, the unit has also had access to all cross-cutting customer data, thus making the development of new customers, existing customers, and customer churn transparent. The chief customer officer also sits on the executive board of Allianz Kunde und Markt GmbH (a 100 percent subsidiary of the global Allianz SE)—this company shapes the marketing, sponsoring, and communication of all German Allianz insurance companies.

- **Methods**: The CCO unit has a total of 40 qualitative and quantitative research and testing formats to support operational marketing in every development phase. An important methodological component is, for example, a representative, independent data cube on German consumer behavior at the beginning of each creation. In-depth interviews are continuously conducted with people of the domestic resident population in all age groups. The subjects of these CAPI interviews include demographics, attitudes towards life, life events, consumer behavior, brand preferences, and relevant needs of people. An important module is also the individual media behavior of people. From this, deep data-driven insights can be derived about the needs of different consumer groups, and the data cube thus provides valuable impulses for operational marketing.
- **Success measurement**. The continuous economic evaluation of the various brand, marketing, sponsoring, and communication activities of Allianz is essential. Therefore, an econometric model was developed in cooperation with the global brand unit, which economically evaluates the 'return on marketing invest' of individual campaigns. On this basis, the optimal use of budgets along the entire marketing funnel can then be controlled.

In this close-meshed systematics, the central success factors for business success are made transparent in the German Allianz. They form the basis for greater precision in marketing work and thus for higher efficiency and effectiveness. Operational marketing work is given much greater certainty of finding the right—i.e., customer- and market-oriented design—within the framework of international brand management. The detailed analytics unite a central insight and thus a call to action for marketing work: The traditional "one size fits all" no longer meets today's market situation. To exploit all sustainable growth potentials, marketing must take into account the analytically identified differences in society in terms of media consumption, preferences, purchasing power, and buying behavior.

The following are **five examples of the newly aligned marketing** at Allianz in Germany, which are oriented towards the challenges derived beforehand.

Criterion of demographics: Differentiation by target groups

In the various formats of analytics, the evaluation is now also routinely carried out according to age cohorts. The sometimes very fundamental differences between, for example, the baby boomers and Generation Z are thus made transparent on an analytical basis and form the basis for marketing planning along the entire funnel. To mention just one relevant challenge: While Allianz has extremely high brand awareness among older target groups, the picture is fundamentally different in Generation Z. Only about half are aware of the Allianz brand without prompting and additionally have a rather unclear content idea. This still puts Allianz at the top of the market, other companies are hardly or not at all known to the younger age group. To also tap into these younger target groups, it is necessary to start at the "upper end" of the marketing funnel (prompted or unprompted awareness and relevance) in order to create the prerequisites for a later product sale. A brand awareness—coupled with a fundamentally positive content perception—in Generation Z must be achieved as a starting point for the sustainable processing of this target group. The reflection of the specific media consumption behavior in communication is critical to success. This younger target group can only be reached very below average via traditional 'paid media' campaigns, especially via the traditional TV channel. It is therefore important to bring Allianz into interaction with the target group via the preferred channels. For this purpose, Allianz primarily uses social media channels.

Criterion of growth and customer retention: Differentiation by customer status

In differentiating by customer status, the objective is to achieve business success through higher individual relevance. The previous paragraph discussed the approach to new customers. However, existing customers also need to be addressed. For these customers, Allianz aims to achieve a positive experience of the business relationship and a lasting basic purchase confirmation. Within the group of existing customers, differentiation is made according to identified use cases and needs with the aim of cross-selling. An obvious differentiation is, for example, the one according to the stages of life identified in customer analytics. The online customer platform 'MyAllianz' with over 4.3 million users (as of 2023) serves as a far-reaching opportunity for specific targeting and individual interaction. The cross-selling achieved in this way then has a double lever for the business: At least as important for the existing portfolio as the additional sales is the prevention of churn (churn prevention) through increased loyalty.

Criterion of changed customer behavior: Differentiation by price

Allianz takes into account the different buying behavior. Special attention is paid to the role of price for the respective target groups and the translation into concrete information and buying behavior. In the insurance market, therefore, four different customer segments have been defined that cover the entire continuum from price-sensitive to performance- and service-strong. The starting point for marketing is the alignment of the product portfolio to these target groups, in which the different product variants reflect the respective behavior patterns. Marketing picks up on these product differences. The respective target groups are individually addressed via digital marketing with the respective product-specific value proposition. The focus is on the differentiated presentation of the price: For the target group of price-sensitive customers, the communication focuses on price competitiveness, while for service-conscious buyers, the price-performance attractiveness is particularly important.

Criterion of brand perception: Differentiation by perception clusters

The perception of Allianz in Germany is ambivalent: Extremely high awareness among the general population is accompanied by a very pointed perception as an international, very successful company with high professionalism and quality standards. The downside of this positive image, however, is the limited perception as a warm-hearted and caring organization that is there for its customers exactly when it matters, for example in the event of a claim. However, these aspects are expected in many market segments when choosing an insurance partner—especially in Generation Y and Generation Z. These target groups are the main source of future, sustainable growth. The task of marketing is therefore to unlock additional growth potential in these target groups through an improvement in perception in terms of care and community. Accordingly, marketing pays attention to avoiding the wrong "cold" perception at all touchpoints with existing customers and the market. The task of marketing is thus significantly more extensive than just "advertising". It is more about influencing the design of the many direct and indirect contact points in close cooperation with the CCO area. In addition to the production of end products, this involves a role in the overarching change process throughout the company towards even stronger customer orientation.

Criterion of channel diversity: Differentiation by digital platforms

No other criterion has had such a major impact on the development of marketing from today's perspective as the differentiation of channels and platforms—both for communication and for sales approach. This development has taken place in a relatively short time—about 15 years ago, the traditional TV-dominated world was "still in order". A target group-specific distribution of marketing messages was only very limited. Terms like 'full funnel'—i.e., the data-driven strong interlocking of communication and sales measures—were far away. However, the current media landscape with the parallel existence of traditional, digital, and social media advertising opportunities allows for a completely different marketing. Prioritized target groups and use cases can now be specifically addressed. The challenge for the marketing organization, however, is to incorporate these diverse possibilities into operational marketing work. In particular, it is important to consider how interdependent the distribution (i.e., reaching the customers), the messages (i.e., the content), and the staging interact.

D. German Beach Tour—Example of a data-driven communication campaign

In the campaign briefly presented now, many of the aspects mentioned above have been taken into account simultaneously. In particular, the described aspects of target groups, perception clusters, and the differentiated use of digital media platforms are reflected in this marketing activity.

The partnership with the German Beach Tour beach volleyball tournament series, culminating in the German Championship in Timmendorf, was developed as a key component in sustainably targeting the younger demographic (Fig. 8.8).

The positive effect on awareness and perception of Allianz in this target group was identified in various market research studies. In addition to basic awareness, the brand attributes of sympathy and trust were particularly improved as central drivers of the 'KPI relevant set'.

A key reason for the partnership was the consistent digital orientation of the Beach Tour, with an innovative mix of on-site events in the tournament cities and a parallel, wide-reaching coverage of all relevant social media platforms for the target group. Starting with streaming on Twitch, there was also intensive use of the content on YouTube, Instagram, and TikTok. As a result, interaction

Fig. 8.8 Key pillars relevant to the target group of the presented sponsorship partnership with the German Beach Tour. (Spontent GmbH 2023)

with the target group was ensured even between the actual tournaments. The strong social media focus is not only reflected in the reach achieved. The platform-appropriate, humorous presentation of the event on the various channels also gave Allianz the opportunity to present itself as a partner on an equal footing in the community.

As a result, innovative content marketing ensured a high "always-on" reach over a period of several months, particularly in Generation Z. It was particularly important to reach women within the young target group. Many alternative marketing programs and partnerships, especially in the sports environment, have a very strong focus on the male population.

Sources:

- Allianz SE 2023a.
- Allianz SE 2023b.
- Interbrand 2024.
- Lukowsky and Tidelski 2023.
- Spontent GmbH 2023.

8.2.3 Strategic Business Fields as Reference Points for Marketing Strategy

As part of the general corporate strategy, a company determines which parts of the market it wants to focus its resources on or where it wants to engage in the market. Therefore, it determines its strategic business fields. The findings of the SWOT analysis (see in detail Sect. 6.4) are incorporated into this decision.

8.2.3.1 Identification and Delimitation of Business Fields

Strategic business fields are independent, clearly distinguishable sub-fields of economic activity that serve as reference points for market success potentials and for company potentials, which are expressed in the relative competitive position as a result of special strengths or weaknesses. Market-related criteria that influence the needs and demand are suitable for their delimitation. A comprehensive and still recognized approach to the **delimitation of business fields** goes back to *Abell* (1980) (Meffert et al. 2019, pp. 302–304; see also Müller-Stewens and Lechner 2016, pp. 141–145). For him, a product is the physical counterpart of the application of a technology to solve specific problems for a specific target group. From this, he derived a three-dimensional reference framework with the dimensions customer group, function fulfillment, and technology. The customer group dimension ultimately involves the identification of target groups (target group marketing). The function fulfillment dimension picks up the already presented function thinking underlying the marketing idea: Here it is determined which basic need of the customer groups should be satisfied by the product. Finally, the technology dimension is about how these needs can be satisfied (Abell 1980).

Applied to insurance, the needs-based and target group orientation can be well implemented. The product dimension can be represented by means of insurance branches.

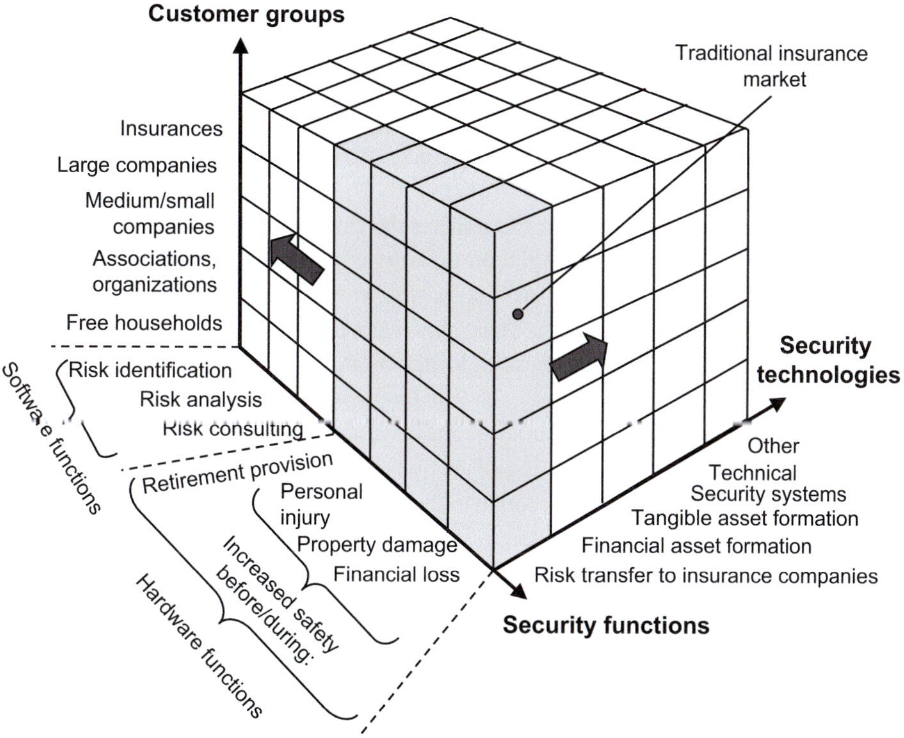

Fig. 8.9 Determination of business fields from the perspective of an insurer. (Based on Birkelbach 1988, p. 234, quoted in: Meffert et al. 2018, p. 161)

However, distribution channels also offer themselves as another component of the service for differentiation. As in other industries, the regional reference also plays a needs-determining role. The transfer of *Abell*'s approach to the insurance industry is illustrated in Fig. 8.9.[1] Instead of the "security technologies" listed there, one could use the offered insurance branches, the served distribution channels, and the spatial extent (countries, regions).

In **insurance practice**, business field delimitation is usually done **according to insurance branches**, because the permission to operate, insurance conditions, and supervision are oriented towards this and the division of the board departments follows this to some extent. Market potentials and related needs fields, on the other hand, are rather shaped by customer relationships and **customer groups**, whose risk coverage and/or pension provision needs extend beyond individual insurance branches. In

[1] An alternative classification for financial services of all kinds based on immediate and current technologies can be found in Meffert et al. (2019, p. 304).

certain cases, it may also make sense to base business fields on **distribution channels**. Because, as mentioned, distribution plays a significant role in the insurance market as a buyer's market, and the individual distribution channels require somewhat different market development strategies. Finally, in practice, **regional** business fields are formed to take into account regionally different success potentials in the German market and in the international area (Farny 2011, pp. 515–517).

In the private customer business, the **market development is generally country-specific** (see Sect. 8.2.2, Marketing Highlight on Allianz), because the political, social, tax, cultural, and economic conditions ultimately require this; basically, this also applies to the commercial customer segment. Thus, the regional spread in insurance companies is a first central criterion for business field delimitation. In other words: The regional expansion, i.e., the "**market area**", is usually determined company-wide and thus **across business fields** in the insurance industry, not within the individual business fields (Sect. 8.3.1), i.e., no further regional differentiation of market development generally takes place at or within the country level. In the insurance industry, all variants of processed market areas can be found: Small mutual insurance associations operate in very regionally limited market areas, public insurers operate in larger, but also only partial regions of Germany, national insurers target the country market, often as a result of country-specific conditions (especially in personal insurance), many insurers have implemented a market development strategy and are active in some other countries outside the home market, internationally oriented insurers are present in various countries around the globe (see Sect. 8.2.3.3), and some large, globally active insurance companies and industrial insurers are present in most countries of the world.

If, for company policy reasons, **selected criteria are to be determined across business fields**, this must be determined in the course of business field delimitation. For example, an insurer could commit to a branch (e.g., ARAG the legal expenses insurance in international business) or focus on one customer segment as a private customer insurer. Similarly, the distribution channel mix could be designed across business fields in order to realize synergy potentials when used in several business fields (Sect. 13.4.1).

8.2.3.2 Evaluation and Selection of Business Areas

After the potential business fields have been identified and delimited, the strategic business fields in which the company wants to become or remain active must be selected. The selection decision requires a **evaluation of the various business fields**. Various concepts such as portfolio, customer lifecycle, or value chain analysis are suitable for this purpose.

The **portfolio analysis** determines the opportunities and risks of the individual business fields through various determining factors. The determining factors are recorded in two main dimensions, which span a matrix along two axes, in which the individual business fields can be positioned. One main dimension summarizes factors that can be directly influenced by the company management and express the company's position in the market, e.g., market share, resource strength, product quality, relative competitive advantages. The other main dimension takes into account factors that cannot be influenced or only indirectly, which represent the market environment and company environment and allow statements about market attractiveness, e.g., market volume, market growth or market lifecycle, competitive dynamics, product lifecycle. The portfolio analysis can be theoretically substantiated in both main dimensions with the experience curve analysis (relative competitive strength) and the market or product lifecycle analysis (market attractiveness) (see excursus). Portfolio management, as a further development of portfolio analysis, now links so-called **norm strategies** to the analysis findings and provides indications of how the company should operate in its strategic business areas in the future. Investment and growth strategies require resources, while harvesting and divestment strategies save resources and reduce investments. The two most well-known portfolio concepts (analysis and norm strategies) are the four-field matrix of the Boston Consulting Group (BCG) and the nine-field matrix of McKinsey & Company (Meffert et al. 2019, pp. 312–315).

Both portfolio concepts can also be applied in insurance, although their limits must be observed (Görgen 2007, pp. 71–74). Many insurance branches already have a high market penetration. However, insurers cannot simply harvest them or let them expire according to the recommendation of the four-field matrix, as insurance represents a permanent protection promise and insurance products sometimes have very long terms. The divestment strategy does not automatically apply. On the other hand, investment decisions play an even more significant role than before under Solvency II, especially when it comes to evaluating the return-risk potentials of business fields and the corresponding allocation of equity (as an investment). The nine-field matrix takes into account more factors than the four-field matrix and also qualitative factors. Accordingly, its norm strategies are more differentiated. It is better suited to the insurance industry: In addition to market growth and market volume, customer loyalty and the technical earnings potential are suitable as determinants of market attractiveness, and the market share in an insurance branch, the technical competence, the operational rationalization potential, the sales strength and the investment potential (Schradin 1994, pp. 167 f.) as determinants of relative competitive strength. Although this model also has limits, such as the possible error in quantifying qualitative facts and the complexity of the model, it still helps to examine various business field more closely and to sensitize management to the consideration of the respective market potentials and the strengths and weaknesses of their own.

Research Window: Experience curve and market lifecycle as the theoretical basis of portfolio analysis

The portfolio analysis can be substantiated in the main dimension of relative competitive strength with the experience curve analysis and in the main dimension of market attractiveness with the market or product lifecycle analysis:

The **experience curve effect**, primarily demonstrated in the industry, consists of the real unit costs of a product decreasing on average by a relatively constant amount of 20 to 30% whenever the production experience expressed in cumulative production volumes doubles (Henderson 1974, p. 19, cited in: Meffert et al. 2019, p. 315). Strictly speaking, this effect is based only on productivity increases due to experience values and rationalizations associated with the production volume. Therefore, the term economies of scale is actually better suited to describe the decreasing unit costs with increasing production volume. Because economies of scale result from three causes: In addition to (1) experience gain, there are (2) distribution of fixed costs over several products and (3) increasing purchasing power with increasing production. The experience curve analysis allows statements about the development potentials of one's own competitive position, and from this, investment and disinvestment decisions can be derived. It also plays a significant role in marketing planning because it provides statements on the long-term forecast of cost and thus price development, long-term profit potentials, market share changes, competitors' pricing leeway, and the substantiation of make-or-buy decisions.

However, the experience curve and also the statements on economies of scale cannot be transferred one-to-one to the **insurance industry**. Although these effects apply in principle to administrative costs, as far as personnel, office equipment, and IT infrastructure are concerned. But these costs play a very subordinate role compared to the costs for claims and benefits regulation in insurance cases (varying depending on the type of insurance, but on average about 70%) and the distribution costs for intermediary remuneration, (brand) advertising, and sales promotion. **Operational size advantages** due to pure cost degression are therefore difficult to prove. Instead, they typically follow **risk-theoretical considerations**, because with increasing size of the insured collective, fewer safety surcharges are necessary, which constitute a part of the claims costs. However, the effects associated with this are less significant for insurers because they become increasingly smaller with increasing collective size and are only noticeable with too small collectives. And in these cases, reinsurance helps to keep the safety surcharges low. Despite these industry-specific obstacles to empirical proof of economies of scale, there are at least indications of **existing scale inefficiencies** as well as overall minor inefficiencies due to lack of fixed cost degression and somewhat larger inefficiencies due to improvable productivity (Köhne and Matz 2010).

The **life cycle analysis** examines growth potentials of markets or products and thus market attractiveness. It derives norm strategies of investing or skimming from the assignment of a market or product to market phases—specifically to the introduction, growth, maturity, saturation, and degeneration phase. For example, it advises on certain market entry strategies depending on the market constellation for young markets: Regarding timing, it distinguishes the pioneer, early follower, and late follower strategy, regarding the type of entry new product introduction, acquisition, and cooperation. In stagnating and shrinking markets, it advises on market assertion strategies, which largely correspond to the general marketing strategies, or—if these are no longer promising—on withdrawal or market exit strategies such as concentration and deliberate downsizing, skimming, and breaking up the business field (Meffert et al. 2019, pp. 318–324).

When applying the **product life cycle** approach to **insurance**, a longer-term perspective must initially be adopted, as contract terms are usually multi-year. This is particularly true for personal insurance lines such as life, disability, long-term care, and health insurance. Therefore, the development of new business and the associated premium income, the development of the insurance portfolio and the associated premium income including cancellations, as well as risk and operating costs over time must be analyzed. In the **introduction phase**, insurers have comparatively low costs for research and development, but do have general market development costs (training of internal and external staff, sales promotion and advertising, technological support) and possibly high risk costs due to lack of their own statistics. Therefore, the premium level tends to be high. In this phase, in the event of success, new business and premium income will increase and portfolio outflows will be low. In the subsequent **growth phase**, premium income and portfolio grow. However, insurers must expect, due to the rapid possibility of imitation by competitors, to achieve a unique selling proposition only temporarily. This applies even more so in broker distribution than in their own sales force. For long-term contracts, there is at least some protection of the portfolio, either due to prohibitive cancellation costs or due to the reluctance of policyholders to constantly deal with their insurance coverage. In the growth phase, risk costs and operating costs decrease with increasing collective size due to better resource utilization. In the **maturity and saturation phase**, the volume of new business stagnates or declines, reducing overall portfolio growth. However, the total portfolio only decreases when the number of cancelled contracts exceeds the number of new contracts. Finally, the **degeneration phase** is atypical for insurance products. The complete withdrawal of insurance products from the market takes decades, partly due to long contract terms, but mostly because customers do not cancel their old contracts (Farny 2011, pp. 416–418). However, it does happen in selected insurance lines that tariffs are closed, i.e. no longer offered in new business, and the old portfolios are transferred to other insurers or in life insurance to so-called run-off companies. In recent years, several life insurers have done this because their traditional business model—especially in the classic life insurance based on guaranteed interest rates—has come under pressure due to the prolonged low interest rate environment. Thus, at the end of 2021, seven German life insurers with a premium volume of around €3.7 billion (4% of the market) were in external run-off, i.e. they had handed this over to external run-off platforms; in addition, some life insurers have settled their closed contracts themselves (internal run-off) (Assekurata Assekuranz Rating-Agentur GmbH 2022).

The approaches of the experience curve and the life cycle are **not suitable for directly deriving a marketing strategy from them**. For example, the individual product life cycle phases are hardly clearly distinguishable in practice, and products do not statically follow the ideal-typical course during the phases. In addition, the norm strategies are too globally held to make concrete material statements about customer-, competitor-, intermediary- and stakeholder-oriented marketing strategies. Finally, the normative orientation determines the interchangeability of companies and thus counteracts the competitive differentiation intended by marketing. Nevertheless, both approaches **help** in **assessing the initial situation** and can therefore in principle be used to support the development and implementation of marketing strategies (Kotler et al. 2017a, pp. 438–449, 590; Meffert et al. 2019, pp. 324 f.). Criticisms of the product life cycle approach also apply to insurance: the cycle depends on other insurance products and cannot always be isolated when policyholders demand product bundles. The mentioned lag effect of revenues and claim payments even after the cessation of new business influences the maturity and saturation phase, and there is no degeneration phase in the classic sense. Product modifications extend the lifetime of products without causing them to lose their identity. Finally, contrary to the statements of the approach, growing insurance markets sometimes go hand in hand with high cash surpluses, and established insurance markets cause a sustainable cash need (Schradin 1994, pp. 117–119; Görgen 2007, pp. 68, 72).

Further reading for in-depth study:
On scale effects:

- Eling and Luhnen 2010.
- Holzheu 1991.
- Kaluza and Kürble 1986.

- Köhne and Matz 2010.

On the life cycle of insurance products:

- Farny 2011, pp. 416–418.
- Menhart 2003, pp. 122 ff. ◀

Due to the limited suitability of the product life cycle approach for insurance products, strategic market growth opportunities may be better identified by customer groups, so a behavior and need-oriented customer or customer group life cycle approach could be helpful. For private households, for example, the phases of foundation, build-up phase without and with children (young family household), consolidation phase without and with older children (old family household), and old age phase (decline and phase-out) could be distinguished (Farny 2011, p. 426; Görgen 2007, pp. 68 f.). The **customer-related life cycle concept** is not new: In the area of sales promotion, it can be used to develop concepts for private households to orient themselves to the social environment in various, typical life phases (life cycle). Accordingly, the life cycle concept is based on a socio-demographic segmentation: It assumes that despite all individuality of private individuals, a common need for provision and financial services can be derived from the respective life circumstances, which changes with the position of the customers and their interests in the life cycle (Meffert et al. 2018, pp. 142; Köhne and Lange 2020, p. 199). However, this approach seems to be more productive for operational marketing and less suitable for evaluating strategic business areas. Moreover, it is practically difficult to offer customers only offers when they are in a certain life phase. Apart from that, the long-observed differentiation of society with different lifestyles and life plans is often not adequately addressed with prefabricated life phase concepts.

Finally, with the **value chain analysis** (see in detail Sect. 6.3), another approach remains to evaluate strategic business fields. Using the value chain, actual and potential competitive advantages can be identified, which express themselves as a higher value of the company's performance for the customer. This means that from the customer's point of view, it is the amount of money that he is willing to pay for the total or partial services, from the company's point of view, the value of a total or partial service results from the difference between the prices achieved by the value activities and the costs they cause. Companies create value when they generate more sales than they receive in preliminary services. The entire entrepreneurial value creation is based on value creation activities, which in turn are based on a whole bundle of business processes. The contribution of considering the insurer's value chain is to show sources of customer benefit and thus potential competitive advantages in individual value creation activities and at the interfaces to other companies. Each value creation activity has the potential to either contribute to cost reduction or to performance-related differentiation from competition. The value chain thus forms a systematic approach to the **identification of**

actual or potential sources of competitive advantages (Meffert et al. 2018, pp. 148 f.). Regarding the insurance-specific value chain and the underlying business processes, refer to Sect. 6.3.

Therefore, value chain analysis helps in identifying mutual relationships between the activities of the company's own and the value chains of various other business fields, whether they are upstream or downstream or at the same value chain level. In practice, as mentioned, the determination of the values generated by individual value-adding activities proves to be extremely difficult. In addition, information about costs and values generated by competitors can only be obtained, if at all, with considerable effort. To some extent, business consultants can provide a remedy here, but the company lacks direct access to the data and is dependent on the external service provider. As already explained in connection with portfolio approaches, value chain analysis is therefore useful for obtaining a **better picture of the individual business fields and possible competitive advantages**, and should therefore be used as a supplement. However, it neither provides comprehensive insights into business fields, nor does it help in the material-content design of business field management. For this, the so-called market development strategies (Sect. 8.3) are necessary.

8.2.3.3 Country Markets as Strategic Business Field in the Case of an International Market Area Strategy

As part of an international **market area strategy**, the insurer determines the country-specific focuses of market development. In the context of opening up international country markets, it is about the specific market selection and the respective market entry strategy. The **market selection** requires an international segmentation and a subsequent segment evaluation, which contributes to the final selection of target markets and the determination of market coverage using heuristic and analytical methods.

As part of the **market entry strategy**, the forms of market entry (e.g., export, licensing, joint venture, direct investment) and the timing must be determined, which involves whether to open up several countries simultaneously or successively across countries, and whether to pursue a pioneer or follower strategy on a country-specific basis (Meffert et al. 2019, pp. 330–333; Kotler et al. 2022, pp. 110–112).

In the insurance industry, countries have generally been opened up step by step because this is easier to control and avoids cross-country flops, as products are only offered in other countries after successful introduction in one country. Insurers even apply this strategy within countries when they first introduce new products in regionally limited (test) markets. For German property & casualty/accident insurers, it has also been proven that they have become internationally active when they have reached profitability limits in their home market and have also benefited domestically from this (Altuntas and Gößmann 2015, pp. 286–288). The step-by-step opening up of countries is comparatively faster for some InsurTechs; this may be due to the higher dynamics

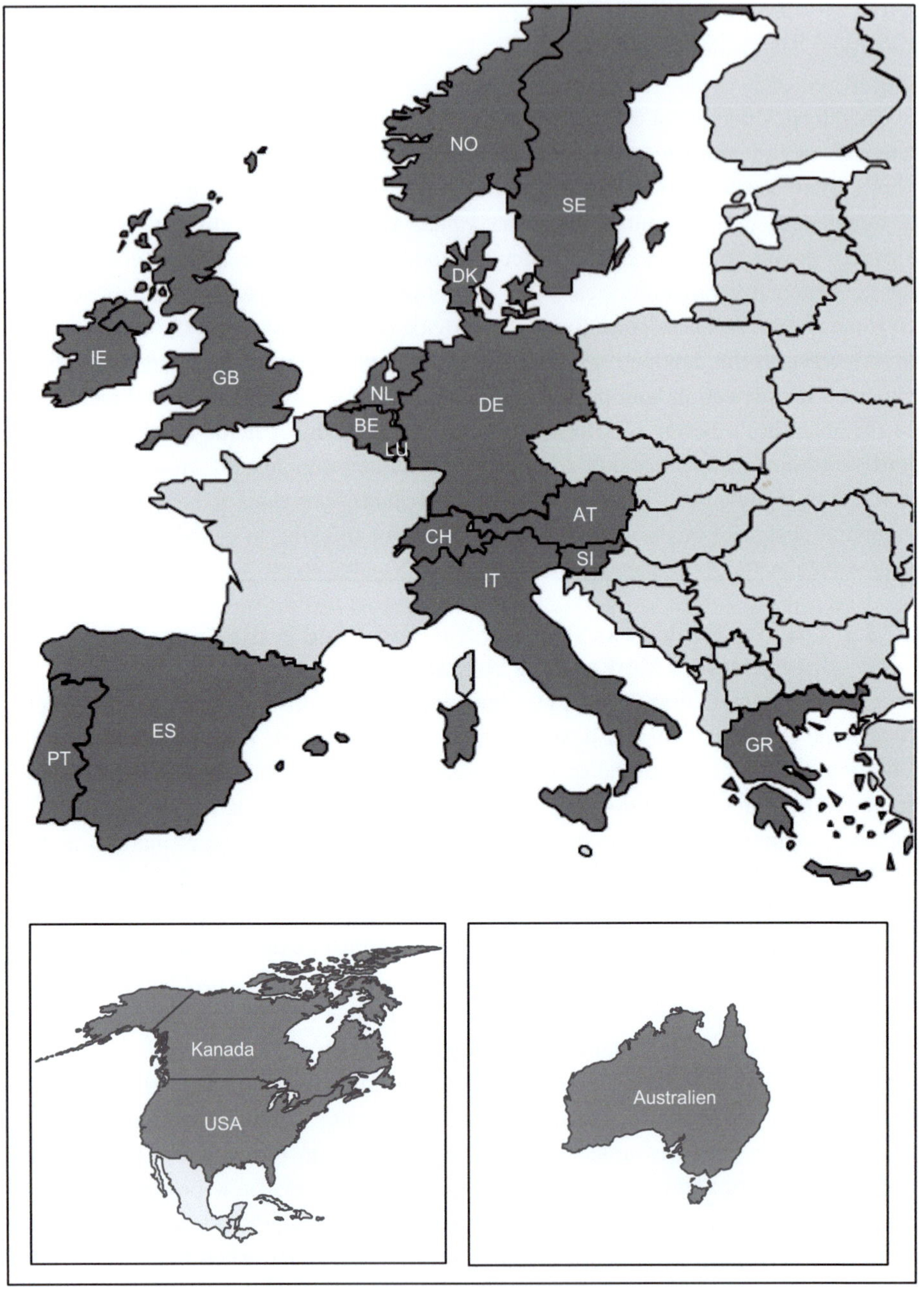

Fig. 8.10 Locations of the ARAG Group. (Based on ARAG Holding SE 2023, p. 5)

of the business models, but in many cases where success in the first country has not yet occurred, it also seems to be due to the growth story intended for investors.

Excursus on the internationalization of a family business: the example of ARAG

The ARAG Group is the largest family business in the German insurance market and the world's largest legal expenses insurer. Founded almost 90 years ago (1935) as a pure legal expenses insurer, ARAG today positions itself as an innovative quality insurer—international and independent. In Germany, in addition to the legal expenses business, it also offers products and services in the composite and healthcare branches. In addition to the cross-sector business in the German market, the company has also been specifically exploiting growth potentials in the international legal expenses business for many years: The more than 4700 employees generated a sales and premium volume of over 2.2 billion euros in 2022.

ARAG began operating outside Germany about 60 years ago. The idea was to stand by German legal expenses customers in the event of a claim internationally. However, this model was not viable on its own. However, it turned out that there was a great need for legal expenses insurance in the respective countries themselves, so that these could be opened up with new business models according to the respective conditions.

ARAG is now active in a total of 19 countries, including Germany, through branches, companies and participations (Fig. 8.10). The international legal expenses business is the largest group business area. With its more than 2500 employees outside Germany—which represents over 50% of the employees—the group generated a sales and premium volume of 907 million euros in the international business in 2022, which is 41.2%.

(ARAG Holding SE 2015, p. 13; ARAG Holding SE 2023, pp. 2, 9, 33)

8.3 Business Field-related Marketing Strategies

The marketing strategy is a conditional, global behavior plan for achieving corporate and marketing goals. It primarily refers to individual business fields and specifies their respective market development. This means that the **market development strategies** presented in the following sub-chapter need to be designed in relation to the business field and can indeed differ significantly from each other. However, the limits of differentiated market development are predetermined by the associated resource requirements and the lack of utilization of synergy potentials (as then additional opportunity costs) (Meffert et al. 2019, pp. 325–328). It is important that the development of market development strategies is oriented towards business field-related marketing goals and is aimed at their fulfillment (Sect. 7.2.4) (Table 8.3).

For each business field, the insurer must specify the two basic strategies of market choice (Sect. 8.3.1) and market participant orientation (Sect. 8.3.2).

8.3.1 Market Choice Strategy

As part of the market choice, the insurer has to make decisions about the market field and market segmentation—the market area is usually determined company-wide and thus across business fields in the insurance industry (Sect. 8.2.3).

8.3.1.1 Market Field

The **market field strategy** is based on the well-known **product-market matrix** (also *Ansoff* matrix), which provides guidance for the strategic direction of the company in the respective business field (Ansoff 1966). The company can then decide to what extent it wants to serve current and/or new markets with current and/or new products. Four strategies derive from this (Meffert et al. 2019, pp. 308–310):

Table 8.3 Systematics of market development strategies and strategic options. (Based on Meffert et al. 2019, p. 327)

Basic strategies	Strategy dimensions	Strategy contents	Strategic options
Market selection strategies	Market field	Product-market combination	• Current or new products in current or new markets • Withdrawal from existing markets
	Market area	Market or sales area	• Local, regional, national, international, multinational or global orientation
	Market segmentation	Type or degree of differentiation of market development	• Undifferentiated • Segment-oriented • Individual (One-to-One)
Market participant strategies	Customer-oriented	Market development towards customers	• Innovation strategy • Quality strategy • Brand strategy • Program/Service strategy • Price strategy
	Distribution channel-oriented	Behavior towards distribution channels or intermediaries	• Cooperation • Adaptation • Evasion/Bypass • Conflict
	Competition-oriented	Behavior towards competitors	• Cooperation • Adaptation • Evasion • Conflict
	Stakeholder-oriented	Behavior towards other stakeholder groups	• Innovation • Adaptation

1. **Market Penetration**: The strategy generally pursued first with company foundation or market entry refers to current products and markets and aims at their exploitation. The market penetration strategy requires an intensification of marketing efforts and provides the basis for all other strategies. Its approaches for market development are the increase (intensification) of product use by customers, the acquisition of competitor customers, or the acquisition of previous non-users. The insurance market is a saturated market in many areas, so the focus here is primarily on poaching customers from competitors.
2. **Market Development**: Markets are developed when current products are introduced and marketed in new markets. This can be achieved through regional, national, and international expansion or by winning new market segments, e.g., through product variants specifically tailored to certain target groups. In the insurance sector, both approaches are observable and promising.
3. **Product Development**: This strategy aims to develop new products for existing markets. This can be achieved through genuine market novelties (product innovations), but also product extensions or variants (product modifications). In the insurance sector, the second approach is easier to implement and therefore much more common (see Sect. 10.4).
4. **Diversification**: This involves developing new products for new markets. This can be achieved through **horizontal** diversification, when the existing range is expanded with products that are related in substance because they share the same technologies, distribution systems, or related sub-markets. Furthermore, **vertical** diversification is an option when the program depth is increased towards sales (forward integration) or procurement (backward integration). Finally, **lateral** diversification involves a move into completely new product and market segments, with the company breaking out of its traditional industry. In the insurance industry, the first two diversification strategies are observed. The first is very common because many insurers have made product extensions for additional sales channels and countries. The vertical strategy is pursued more by large corporations, which also include reinsurers and distribution companies. Lateral diversification is less common. This may superficially be due to the legally anchored prohibition of non-insurance business, which in fact poses no restriction for corporations. The reason is probably more likely the associated risk, as there is no direct substantive connection with the previous business, making this strategy the most opportunity-rich and at the same time the most risky.

The logical, albeit not mandatory, sequence of these four strategies results from the aforementioned numbering: First, the existing market is to be exploited, then further market potentials are to be tapped beyond its borders. Further growth opportunities then arise through additional products for existing customers. Due to the comparatively lowest synergy potentials, diversification should generally only be pursued when the previous strategies have been exhausted.

8.3.1.2 Market Segmentation and Target Group Marketing

The **market segmentation strategy** initially determines whether a business field should undergo undifferentiated, segment-oriented, or individual market processing. In the insurance sector, all three segmentation strategies are found: In industrial insurance, market processing—especially in the area of coverage design, pricing, and key account management—is traditionally predominantly individualized. In the commercial customer sector, there are market processing activities oriented towards types of businesses, and in the private customer sector, some providers pursue target group concepts. However, many providers still practice undifferentiated market processing in this customer segment.

Both private customers and smaller commercial customers seem to be predestined for target group marketing to enable segment-oriented market processing. One could argue that the target groups have already been defined at the level of strategic business fields if the business field segmentation has been oriented towards customer groups. In terms of insurance, such a division of business fields plays a role when industrial customers, commercial customers, private households, and public households are distinguished. However, the **target group marketing** only comes into play at the business field level and means differentiating and addressing target groups within the individual business field. It thus follows from the decision to process a business field in a segmented manner.

Target group marketing is carried out in three steps (Kotler et al. 2022, p. 342, with reference to insurance Köhne 1997, p. 170):

1. Market or customer segmentation
2. Concrete target group formation and selection
3. Design of products and services suitable for the target group

Regarding the first step of target group marketing, the **market and customer segmentation** taking into account segmentation criteria, reference is made to the statements in Sect. 6.2.2 (demand analysis).

The second step involves the **formation and selection of specific target groups**. The formation of target groups can basically be based on assumptions, strategic specifications and **derived hypotheses (inside-out)** or on insights gained from data about customer needs and behavior patterns (outside-in). In practice, hypothesis-based methods predominate. Many companies form target groups based on theoretical considerations and existing experiences and make statements about their insurance needs or purchasing behavior based on generally accessible statistics. An example of group formation based on internally developed hypotheses is the traditional market segmentation based on observable characteristics of individuals. Here, geographical, demographic, and socio-economic as well as behavior-related sociological and psychological characteristics and any combinations of these characteristics are used. The focus in German-speaking countries is on demographic and socio-economic characteristics, which can easily be determined due to the available data and can easily be recorded specifically for each customer.

Increasingly, sociological and psychological segmentation characteristics are also being used in the context of behavior-related type formation. Geographical data are rather used for tariffing (risk segmentation) (Meffert et al. 2019, pp. 225–234).

The determination of the characteristics to be used—and in the case of behavior-related characteristics also their situation-specific measurement—is difficult in practice. A relief in this respect is offered by so-called **customer types**. These can be oriented towards

- Lifestyles (e.g., alternative, DINKs (Double income, no kids), conservative, puritans, yuppies (Young urban professionals), etc.),
- Decision-maker types (e.g., extensive, rational or limited, habitual, impulsive),
- Customer typologies (e.g., comfortable experts, loyal representative customers, demanding delegators, price-oriented rationalists, overwhelmed support seekers, skeptically indifferent, distinguished conservatives).

In the course of customer segmentation focused on **lifestyle** as an action-oriented behavior pattern (see Sect. 4.3.2), various lifestyle approaches are used, e.g., Sinus-Milieus, Euro-Socio-Styles, or Euro-Styles (Homburg 2020, pp. 52 f., 831 f.).

As already illustrated (see Sect. 4.3.1), customer types can also be distinguished based on typical **decision patterns** in purchasing: The variants are thus extensive, rational or limited, habitual, and impulsive purchasing decisions.

Another way to distinguish customer types is based on the formation of **customer typologies**. In the past, these were derived based on a combination of psychological and personal characteristics (YouGov 2014, p. 151). A newer approach relies on the search and decision behavior of policyholders, because the "Select Types" formed in this way show large differences in all relevant behavioral levels and explain purchasing decisions better than socio-demographic characteristics (see excursus on the development of the typology of private policyholders). Partners delegate their decision to a reliable provider, optimizers focus on their advantages, cautious ones reduce their decision-making effort, and independents scrutinize offers closely (Gaedeke 2021, pp. 2 f.; Gaedeke and Müller 2023, pp. 26 f.).

Excursus on the development of the typology of private policyholders

The market research company Sirius Campus identified so-called **Select types** a few years ago as a basis for possible market segmentation, which are based on the search and decision behavior of policyholders. This can be described in a differentiated way on nine behavioral levels. These include self-management, willingness to relate, quality orientation, price willingness, dominance, decision-making effort, peer group orientation, exclusivity, and cocooning. Behind this are 18 behavioral dimensions, from which nine levels are formed based on around 100 items using a two-stage factor analysis. For example, self-management is expressed by the behavioral dimensions of online dialogue readiness (willingness to change contracts or conclude additional services online with insurer), digital orientation (willingness for insurance advice via digital media such as chat, SMS, app or social media), search activity (search and offer comparison before conclusion, attention to seals, regular review of own insurances) and decision delegation (conclusion of all types of insurance only with personal advice).

In comprehensive studies in the insurance market, four **typical heuristics in purchasing decisions** have been identified: Delegating, Focusing, Reducing, and Controlling. The customer typologies formed in this way—Partners, Optimizers, Cautious, Independents (Fig. 8.11)—differ based on four typical heuristics used as overarching problem-solving strategies, which contribute to making a decision despite apparent overwhelm. These become effective already in the search process and thus demonstrably influence search behavior, communication effect, and purchasing decision (Gaedeke and Müller 2023, pp. 22, 26).

Partners *delegate* their decision to a reliable provider. They rely on long-term relationships with a provider or advisor, as they expect high product and service quality and bring the highest price willingness for this. In the insurance market, partners prefer to delegate product selection in personal consultation meetings, so a lasting and comprehensive relationship with a personally known advisor or a regionally available provider is at the center of their purchasing heuristic. Thus, agency representatives or brokers from the vicinity are preferred. If high product and service quality is communicated and delivered, partners are very loyal. This means, for example, that only young unattached or willing-to-change partners can be successfully addressed through advertising.

Optimizers *focus* on their advantages. They are the most active of all Select types. Despite their high internet affinity, they prefer personal consultation, as they can enforce additional benefits and individual solutions through their pronounced negotiation behavior. The latter is their core motive. They are constantly looking for innovative or exclusive product offers. Here, communication can start with digital and interactive offers, e.g., in connection with telematics tariffs in motor vehicle insurance or with smart home devices in buildings insurance. In this case, a price advantage is less important than the possibility of being able to put together an individual offer from several options. However, optimizers require the most care and contract effort—even in the event of a claim, they seek optimization. They must be regularly offered performance or contract updates, but they show a slightly higher willingness to pay than the average customer.

Cautious *reduce* their decision-making effort. They shy away from more complex purchase decisions and often postpone them due to uncertainty (procrastination). Therefore, their most important purchase impulse also results from an external occasion such as a move, a claim, or

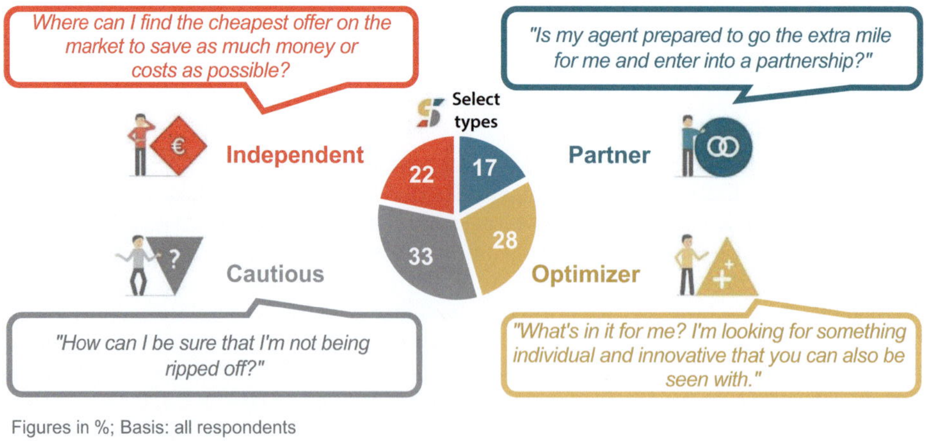

Fig. 8.11 Select types in the private insurance market 2023. (Gaedeke and Müller 2023, p. 23)

a necessary consultation. When concluding contracts, they rely on recommendations and proven methods (status quo bias). They want to reduce their perceived purchase risk and therefore often choose the medium offer in three-tier product concepts. Advertising has less effect unless proven benefits are communicated and confirmations from credible testimonials are given. Due to the passivity of the cautious, their care effort is low and their customer loyalty is very high. They are therefore a very attractive market segment in the long term; however, they should not be overwhelmed with too extensive or very innovative offers.

Independents *scrutinize* offers closely. They hardly trust providers and sales staff. In contrast, they prefer to compare different offers with a high expenditure of time before making a decision. They are convinced that they make rational decisions themselves. In fact, they are characterized by a strong savings motive. Therefore, they react disproportionately strongly positive to price advantages and negative to brands with an unattractive price image and are suspicious of recommendations from customer advisors because they want to avoid a surcharge through commissions and especially commission-driven recommendations (Gaedeke 2021).

The Select types show large differences in all relevant behavioral levels and can explain purchase decisions much better than socio-demographic characteristics. Thus, Independents and Optimizers have a significantly higher self-management in insurance matters than Partners and Cautious, who prefer to delegate their decisions. But only Independents are "intermediary-shy" and have the lowest willingness to establish a relationship. Optimizers, despite their high search activity, express the highest desire for consultation and fully-pampered-wish together with Partners, and Partners also show the highest quality orientation and price willingness. The advantage-seeking Optimizers have high performance expectations for the product and a strong image orientation. Independents, on the other hand, have the lowest quality orientation and price willingness, but the highest decision-making effort. And Cautious have a medium quality orientation and price willingness, and they are very passive with low search activity and low desire for consultation (Gaedeke and Müller 2023, p. 27).

It is also interesting to observe the development of the Select types over time (Fig. 8.12). As expected, the segmentation has been very stable since 2003, typical for the slowly changing insurance market. Nevertheless, a long-term trend is evident: The proportion of Independents is slowly increasing at the expense of the Cautious and the Optimizers. This is due to the change in the insurance market: The increase in price wars and intensive price communication, digital comparison and conclusion possibilities is a major driver of this development. Especially young customers learn to pay even more attention to the price and savings possibilities (Gaedeke and Müller 2023, p. 29).

Unlike the hypothesis-based approach, the **data-based approach (outside-in)** allows for the formation of target groups without initial hypotheses, revealing a multitude of correlations between information about the characteristics of existing or potential customers and their behaviors. The starting point is as extensive as possible data sets about the market participants to be investigated (big data). Based on these data sets, attempts are made to identify systematic correlations in the data set through statistical, computer-aided algorithms and search methods. The term "Data Mining" encompasses all methods that enable the detection of similarities in large data sets (see also Sect. 6.1.4).

Data Mining however, requires large data sets with numerous customer and contract data features. This leads to it being operated either market-wide by independent third parties, such as market research institutes with a behavioral research focus, or by companies with the corresponding data set. However, most insurers find this very difficult because

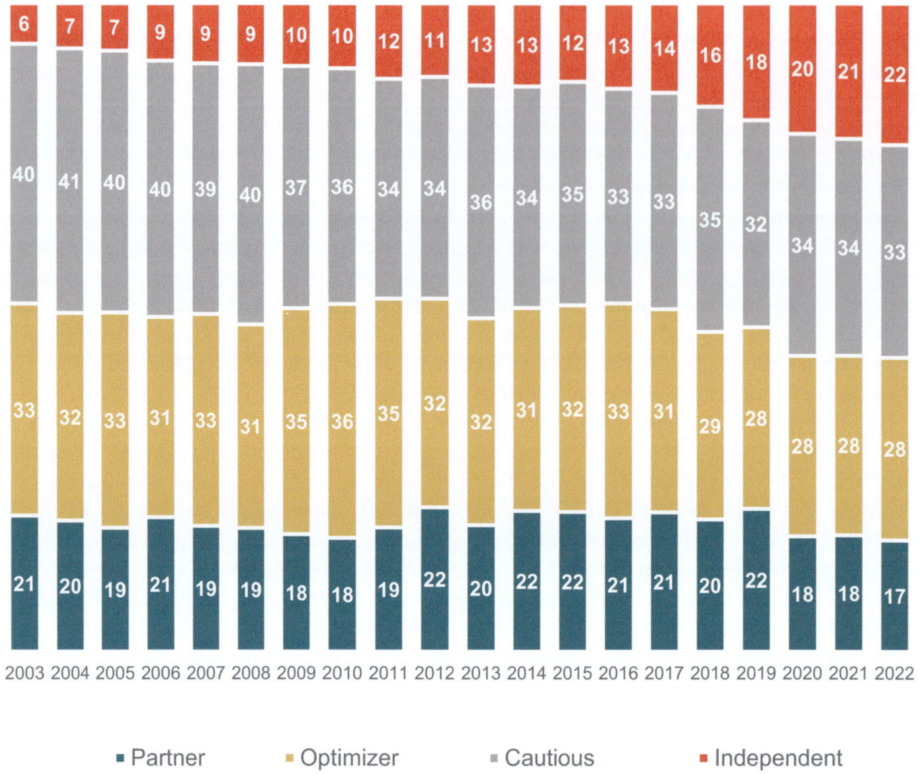

Fig. 8.12 Select types: Development from 2003 to 2022. (Gaedeke and Müller 2023, p. 29)

they have not collected the necessary data comprehensively. Direct insurers are further along in this respect. In any case, data mining is complex, and the challenge—especially in personal sales—is to transfer insights about demand-relevant correlations into concrete sales situations. When purchasing from third parties, there is also the problem of transferring the insights generated market-wide to one's own customers. With own data, the problem is that these have only been collected from existing customers and not from potential new customers. However, this method is quite suitable for selected marketing actions: Insurers use it in portfolio campains when they recognize typical behavior patterns in advance of cancellations or additional contracts and react accordingly.

With the target group formation carried out, the basis has been created to decide in the next step which market and customer segments should be worked on (**target group selection**). For this, the insurer has to consider its objectives and resources on the one hand. Because existing strategies, structures, and cultures significantly determine the possibilities for implementing a target group approach. On the other hand, the targeted **market segments need to be evaluated**: Indications are provided by the financial attractiveness of the segment (especially size and growth), its structural attractiveness, and the correlation with other segments (Kotler et al. 2022, pp. 362–370). The structural attractiveness of a segment can be determined **based on the five competitive forces** (see Sect. 6.2.1):

1. **Buyer power**: What position do the policyholders have in the relevant target market? Can they, for example, exercise power due to a monopoly-like position (merger into buyer communities)?
2. **Industry competitors**: How strong is the competition in the targeted market (in terms of sales, number, access to the target group, competitive products)?
3. **Non-industry competitors**: Which non-insurance companies can penetrate the target group with insurance-like products due to their know-how or offer the target group better market services (e.g., credit card, leasing, banking, brokerage, reinsurance or real estate companies, car manufacturers, Big Techs)?
4. **Substitute products**: Which other products can fulfill the functions of insurance products just as well or even better (e.g., credit cards, bank loans, guarantees, savings accounts, security technology, etc.)?
5. **Reinsurers**: How do reinsurers support the processing of the target group?

Once the insurer has evaluated the market segment(s) or target group(s) to be worked on and compared them with its own corporate objectives and available resources, it can decide whether and which target groups it wants to work on. In practice, these are mainly

- target groups formed according to demographic characteristics such as women, singles, families (with/without children), and age groups (young, seniors), and
- target groups delimited according to socio-economic characteristics such as wealthy individuals, single-family homeowners, vacationers, farmers, employees, academics, freelancers, civil servants, or company owners.

In the third step of target group marketing, building on the needs-oriented market segmentation and target group definition, follows the **needs-based product and services design**. This can be realized on the product side by developing insurance products and services oriented towards target groups. Communication, e.g., through advertising and sales promotion, can also be oriented towards target groups. However, such target group concepts ultimately stand or fall with the extent of their demand relevance. It turns out that objective factors of demand such as demographic and socio-economic characteristics show this demand relevance, but that demand is also determined by further subjective, situation-dependent factors in connection with psychological and sociological behavioral characteristics. Thus, target group formation creates a certain alignment with selected (rather demographic or socio-economic) characteristics, but does not replace the concrete consideration of all objective and also subjective factors relevant in individual cases. This is rather the responsibility of individual and personal communication with people at the service hotline, in consultation and sales talks or in the event of a claim.

Thus, it becomes apparent that target group marketing provides guidelines for the design of all marketing tools—and thus also allows for leeway.

8.3.2 Market Participant Strategies

Decisions about the orientation towards the relevant market participants in the respective strategic business field first refer to the (potential) customers, specifically it is about the business field-related positioning and possibly a business field-specific brand policy. With regard to sales partners, it is about their selection and how to deal with them. Finally, the orientation towards competitors and various stakeholder groups must be determined.

8.3.2.1 Business Field-related Positioning (Customer Value) and Brand Policy

Once the decision has been made in which segments a company wants to be active, it must be determined for these segments which position it wants to occupy there with its products. This **positioning in the business field** stands for a clear, desirable and sharp position of the offered product or service in the perception of the target customers and in comparison to competitive offers. To generate a competitive advantage in the target markets associated with the business field, one must offer the target groups addressed there a higher benefit than the competition (Kotler et al. 2022, p. 370). Often, this benefit already results from the company-wide, i.e., business field-overarching (brand) positioning and refers back to this (see Sect. 8.2.1). However, the business field-specific positioning also offers the opportunity to better meet the market and competitive conditions as well as customer needs of the business field and to adapt to them. In doing so, it can orient itself towards the same benefit categories that have already been introduced in the context of company-wide positioning.

In the **traditional benefit construct**, the benefit generally describes the customer's assessment of a product's ability to satisfy needs (Balderjahn 1995, p. 186). When purchasing a service, the customer has to pay a price as well as invest time and possibly further efforts. These are to be compared with the (gross) benefit. Only if the net benefit as a positive difference between expected product benefit and costs associated with the purchase is positive, there is an incentive for the buyer to make a transaction (Meffert et al. 2019, pp. 15 f.).

In addition to the traditional benefit concept, the concept of value for the customer (Customer Value) has emerged in recent decades: According to this, **Customer Value** refers to the **value created for the customer, which the customer perceives from his very specific perception**. Although it can be influenced by the provider, it is ultimately determined individually and subjectively by the customer (Lauterborn 1990, p. 26; Woodruff 1997, p. 142). In contrast to the benefit concept, the customer value concept is about all value-increasing and value-decreasing aspects in connection with the purchase of the product, i.e., about positive and negative benefits through the fulfillment of positive and negative functions, about conscious and unconscious value components as well as cognitive and non-cognitive (e.g., activating and affective) determinants. The degree of fulfillment of the functions thus directly influences the customer value (Haller 2006, pp. 745–760). For positioning, this is very significant: The value of the offered service for the customer results not only from real positive effects, but is also influenced by—mostly unconscious—mental value constructs such as emotions, motives and attitudes as activating determinants, which are also dependent on the situational context. Thus, the customer value concept has the merit of considering behavior-based variables in the determination of value from the customer's perspective in addition to the cognitive, rather rationally oriented benefit aspects when designing the positioning (Hartmann 2006, p. 77).

Looking at the insurance industry, the **customer value concept can be connected to** the already presented **specifics of the insurance service** or picks up on these: The customer value includes the cognitive and affective influencing factors as an appreciation of the insurer's product and service performance by the insurance customer (Sect. 4.3), results from the interplay of fulfilled core and additional functions and is generated along the entire service process from initial contact through consultation and mediation, support, claims settlement to termination (Sect. 2.2.4). This means that the customer value, in addition to the more rationally shaped price-performance considerations, captures the psychological aspects that are so important in insurance—*Haller* explicitly mentions the feeling of inner security as a component of the insurance service (Haller 1982, p. 398)—and also the time aspect of the insurance service. The latter results from the promise of permanent protection according to *Farny* (Farny 1995, p. 81) and the dynamics of the customer relationship due to changing customer needs over time as a result of new risk situations, motives or attitudes. Thus, the customer value is determined by a situational interplay of economic-rational, psychological, personal, social and cultural influencing factors, which also changes dynamically over the course of a customer relationship.

It is to be **appreciated** that the customer value concept integrates various marketing aspects such as functional thinking and also expands, concretizes and differentiates the customer benefit, which is too abstract in itself to design market services in a customer-oriented manner and to explain customer behavior. In addition, the customer value perspective sensitizes to view the various influencing factors of the appreciation of the service offered by the customer holistically and not to focus solely on purely rational purchase criteria. This makes the concept realistic, but from a customer perspective it hardly allows predictions through models and largely eludes concrete measurability.

The **business field-related brand policy** must also be considered in the context of the company-wide, cross-business field brand policy: On the one hand, it is conceivable that a business field is worked on with its own (corporate) brand. Then the brand policy decisions—apart from the brand architecture—are to be made at the level of the business field (and by its responsible persons), and there are great freedoms with regard to brand positioning. The decision-making facts are the same as in the case of company-wide brand policy (see Sect. 8.2.2). On the other hand, it is possible that the business field is worked on under the corporate umbrella brand. In this case, the specifications of the company-wide brand policy must be adhered to and business field-related adjustments are possible within the given scope (see also Sect. 8.2.2, marketing highlight Allianz).

8.3.2.2 Behavior Towards Intermediaries, Competitors and Other Stakeholder Groups

Due to the high importance of sales in the insurance industry, the **behavioral strategies directed at intermediaries** play the most important role in further market participant strategies. As this involves more or less strong influence on sales partners as a downstream stage in the value chain, the corresponding marketing activities are also referred to as **vertical marketing**. Basically, evasion, cooperation, conflict engagement, and adaptation are considered. Adapting to the wishes of the sales partner is the most passive variant, but in the case of power imbalances with the sales partner, such as large sales companies, banks or brokerage firms, it is pursued if it is the only way to do business with these partners. The most common variant is cooperation, combined with a more or less strong strategic orientation towards the interests of independent sales partners—these include brokers, sales companies, large exclusive representatives and non-industry companies with customer access. In this context, providers often pursue a push strategy and direct their marketing mix directly at the sales partners (e.g., pure broker insurers). In contrast to these two approaches, the variants of conflict seeking and evasion towards large sales companies, brokers or non-industry companies are to be relativized. Because a sales partnership between two parties is generally at risk if they "fight" each other in another business field with a conflict strategy. And evasion is the opposite of cooperation. However, in contrast to the competition-oriented ones, the intermediary-oriented behavioral strategies offer the additional possibility of bypassing: Firstly, the insurer can bypass the intermediary by either working with other intermediaries or operating direct sales. Secondly, he can pursue a pull strategy, i.e., direct all marketing activities directly at the awakening of needs and brand awareness among end customers with the aim of a resulting demand pull (Lach 1995, pp. 150–167; Köhne 2006, pp. 347–350).

Preceding the determination of behavior towards sales partners is the strategic **decision on the sales channel mix** (see Sect. 13.4.1). Structural changes in the sales system are only possible with considerable effort and in the long term for insurance companies. In this respect, the decision is only a choice between all conceivable sales channel constellations for new foundations—for all existing sales structures, it is primarily about constant improvement and adaptation to internal company changes or market developments. Although most insurance providers used to use only one or a few sales channels, competition for market shares in an increasingly saturated private customer market has prompted some providers to use several sales channels in parallel in order to exploit all sales potentials. This goes hand in hand with the need for multi-sales channel control, also known as multi-channel management (see Sect. 13.4.3).

The **competitive behavior strategies** encompass the same spectrum: evasion, cooperation, conflict engagement, and adaptation. With evasion strategies, companies try to avoid increased competitive pressure through innovative activities that lead to the early establishment of market entry barriers and/or the realization of specialization effects. This can be achieved, for example, through shielded market segments, new product or process technologies, or pronounced marketing efforts. In the insurance industry, this strategy is generally not very promising due to the lack of patent rights. Opportunities for application exist in selected constellations, such as an online portal like Check24, when process technologies, marketing efforts, and first-mover advantages come together. Companies pursue cooperation strategies when they do not have a clear competitive advantage or lack resources for conflict strategies, or in other words, when higher returns can be achieved through cooperation than through going it alone, because synergies can be utilized. In the case of a cooperative connection of several companies, so-called strategic corporate networks are created. In the insurance industry, cooperations play a role in many business areas, while insurance networks are still rare. One of the best known and largest is the association of public insurers (Köhne 2004a, 2006). Conflict strategies, as the third variant, aim to gain market shares through behavior that is innovative compared to competitors. In their most aggressive form, they aim to weaken or displace the competitor through a "direct attack" on main products, "encirclement" by introducing various competing products and brands, or a "flank attack" on weak points—the latter is the strategy of InsurTech companies (see excursus in Sect. 6.1.4). Such strategies are often pursued in stagnating or shrinking markets. In this respect, the insurance industry would potentially be affected in some insurance branches. However, in practice, insurers are not so easily displaced from a market, as the contract terms of insurance contracts are sometimes very long and because unique selling points, as mentioned, cannot be easily and permanently realized. Finally, the adaptation strategy aims to maintain the once achieved market position. The behavior is aligned with the reaction of the competitors. This strategy, which is not very promising in the long run in many industries, is quite widespread in the insurance industry, although it is not very creative from a marketing point of view (Meffert et al. 2019, pp. 349–353).

For the sake of completeness, the **behavior strategies towards other stakeholder groups** of the company should be mentioned at the end, which include, for example, equity and debt providers, employees, suppliers, service providers, society, and the state. The innovation variant describes a proactive attitude towards the claims of certain groups, adaptation a waiting, cautious approach, resistance the maintenance of the current (not meeting the claims) state, and evasion the attempt to evade the demands of stakeholder groups. Although the behavior towards stakeholder groups and dealing with them is also of high relevance for insurance companies, this is more a matter of corporate policy than insurance marketing and will therefore not be further deepened here (Müller-Stewens and Lechner 2016, pp. 156–165; Meffert et al. 2019, pp. 360–363).

Further Reading Recommendations for Chap. 8

- Aaker and Joachimsthaler 2000.
- Altuntas and Gößmann 2015.
- Ansoff 1966.
- Becker 2019, Part 2, pp. 135–480.
- Esch 2018.
- Krausz 2002, esp. Chap. C.

References

Aaker, D./Joachimsthaler, E. (2000): Brand Leadership, New York, 2000.

Abell, D.E. (1980): Defining the Business, The Starting Point of Strategic Planning, Englewood Cliffs N.J., 1980.

Allianz SE (Ed.) (2023a): Allianz SE Geschäftsbericht 2022, München, 2023.

Allianz SE (Ed.) (2023b): OneAllianz Creators Platform, München, 2023.

Altuntas, M./Gößmann, G. (2015): Stand zur Internationalisierung deutscher Versicherungsgruppen im Schaden- und Unfallgeschäft, in: VW, Jg. 70, 2015, Nr. 9, pp. 283–288.

Anderson, J./Narus, J. (1999): Welchen Wert hat ihr Angebot für den Kunden?, in: Harvard Business Manager, Jg. 21, 1999, Nr. 4, pp. 97–107.

Ansoff, H.I. (1966): Management-Strategie, München, 1966.

ARAG Holding SE (Ed.) (2015): Geschäftsbericht 2014, Konzernabschluss, Düsseldorf, 2015.

ARAG Holding SE (Ed.) (2023): Geschäftsbericht 2022, Konzernabschluss, Düsseldorf, 2023.

Assekurata Assekuranz Rating-Agentur GmbH (Ed.) (2022): Assekurata-Studie: Run-off in der Lebensversicherung 2022, Pressemitteilung vom 12.12.2022, Köln, 2022.

Balderjahn, I. (1995): Bedürfnis, Bedarf, Nutzen, in: Tietz, B./Köhler, R./Zentes, J. (Eds.), Handwörterbuch des Marketing , Vol. 2, pp. 179–190.

Becker, J. (2019): Marketing-Konzeption: Grundlagen des ziel-strategischen und operativen Marketing-Managements, München, 11. Edn., 2019.

Eling, M./Luhnen, M. (2010): Frontier Efficiency Methodologies to Measure Performance in the Insurance Industry, in: GP, Vol. 35, 2010, pp. 217–265.

Esch, F.-R. (2018): Strategie und Technik der Markenführung, München, 9. Edn., 2018.

Farny, D. (1995): Die Gestaltung von Versicherungsprodukten im Marketing von Versicherungsunternehmen, in: ZVersWiss, Jg. 84, 1995, pp. 79–102.

Farny, D. (2011): Versicherungsbetriebslehre, Karlsruhe, 5. Edn., 2011.

Gaedeke, O. (2021): Vertriebseffizienz mit Behavioral Economics und Entscheidertypen steigern, Select Typen in b4p Mediaanalyse und -planung, Sirius Campus-White Paper vom 16.08.2021.

Gaedeke, O./Müller, C. (2023): Erfolgreiche Kundenberatung und -betreuung mit den Select Typen, Ansätze zur wirksamen Gestaltung von Entscheidungsprozessen bei allen Kundenkontakten. Ein Handbuch für Marketing, Produktentwicklung, Vertrieb und Service, Ed. by Sirius Campus, Köln, 2023.

Görgen, F. (2007): Versicherungsmarketing, Strategien, Instrumente und Controlling, Stutt-gart, 2. Edn., 2007.
Haedrich, G./Tomczak, T./Kaetzke, P. (2003): Strategische Markenführung, Planung und Realisierung von Markenstrategien, Bern, 2003.
Haller, M. (1982): Risiko- und Versicherungsprobleme des privaten Haushalts—aus Sicht der Privatversicherung, in: ZVersWiss, Jg. 71, 1982, Nr. 3/4, pp. 383–437.
Haller, M. (2006): Funktionen-Ansatz, in: Belz, C./Bieger, T. (Eds.), Customer Value, Kundenvorteile schaffen Unternehmensvorteile, Landsberg a. L., 2006, pp. 745–760.
Hartmann, C. (2006): Customer Value im Bereich der Automobilität—empirische Analyse und strategische Implikationen für die Kfz-Versicherer als automobile Dienstleistungsanbieter, St. Gallen, 2006.
Holzheu, F. (1991): Skalen- und Verbundvorteile von Unternehmen mit besonderem Blick auf Versicherungsunternehmen, in: ZVersWiss, Jg. 80, 1991, pp. 531–559.
Homburg, C. (2020): Marketingmanagement, Strategie—Instrumente—Umsetzung—Unternehmens-führung, Wiesbaden, 7. Edn., 2020.
Interbrand (Ed.) (2024): Best global brands, in: www.interbrand.com/best-global-brands, Accessed: 03.01.2024.
Kaluza, B./Kürble, G. (1986): Die Erfahrungskurve als Instrument des strategischen Unternehmensführung in Krankenversicherungsunternehmen, in: ZVersWiss, Jg. 75, 1986, pp. 193–232.
Köhne, T. (1997): Die Wirkungsversicherung im Privatkundengeschäft—Implikationen für eine kundenorientierte Marktleistungsgestaltung, St. Gallen, 1997.
Köhne, T. (1998a): Chancen und Grenzen der Produktpolitik im deregulierten Versicherungsmarkt (Teil I), in: IVW Management-Information, St. Galler Trendmonitor für Risiko- und Finanzmärkte, 1998, Heft 4, pp. 2–15.
Köhne, T. (1998b): Chancen und Grenzen der Produktpolitik im deregulierten Versicherungsmarkt (Teil II), in: IVW Management-Information, St. Galler Trendmonitor für Risiko- und Finanzmärkte, 1998, Heft 5, pp. 2–10.
Köhne, T. (Ed.) (2004a): Strategische Kooperationen in der Versicherungsbranche: Kernkompetenzen, Wertschöpfungspartnerschaften und Unternehmensnetzwerke, Wiesbaden, 2004.
Köhne, T. (2006): Marketing im strategischen Unternehmensnetzwerk, Erklärungsmodell und praktische Anwendung in der Versicherungswirtschaft, Wiesbaden, 2006.
Köhne, T. (2016): Versicherungsmarketing. Marketing und Vertrieb im Versicherungsunternehmen in Theorie und Praxis, Karlsruhe, 2016.
Köhne, T./Lange, M. (2020): Marketing und Vertrieb von Versicherungs- und Finanzprodukten für Privatkunden, Fach- und Führungskompetenz für die Assekuranz, Karlsruhe, 4. Edn., 2020.
Köhne, T./Matz, S. (2010): Die Effizienz deutscher Kompositversicherer—Eine Untersuchung mit-tels Data Envelopment Analysis, in: ZVersWiss, Jg. 99, 2010, pp. 277–317.
Kotler, P./Armstrong, G./Wong, V./Saunders, J. (2011): Grundlagen des Marketing, München, 5. Edn., 2011.
Kotler, P./Keller, K.L./Opresnik, M.O. (2017a): Marketing-Management, Konzepte—Instrumente—Unternehmensfallstudien, Halbergmoos, 15. Edn., 2017.
Kotler, P./Armstrong, G./Harris, L.C./He, H. (2022): Grundlagen des Marketing, Halbergmoos, 8. Edn., 2022.
Krausz, S. (2002): Strategische Unternehmenspolitik von Erstversicherern unter Verbindung von Zielkgruppen-Marketing und Kernkompetenz-Management, Karlsruhe, 2002.
Lach, H. (1995): Vertikales Marketing von Versicherungsunternehmen, Berlin, 1995.
Lauterborn, B. (1990): New marketing litany—four P's passe; C-words take over, in: Advertising Age, 1990, October, p. 26.

Lukowsky, T./Tidelski, O. (2023): Datengetriebenes Marketing und Kommunikationsmanagement der Allianz; in: Krämer, A./Kalka, R./Merkle, W. (Eds.): Stammkundenbindung versus Neukundengewinnung, Marketing und Vertrieb im Spannungsfeld von "Hunting" und "Farming", Wiesbaden, 2023, pp. 357–369.

Meffert, H./Bruhn, M./Hadwich, K. (2018): Dienstleistungsmarketing, Grundlagen—Konzepte—Methoden, Wiesbaden, 9. Edn., 2018.

Meffert, H./Burmann, C./Kirchgeorg, M./Eisenbeiß, M. (2019): Marketing, Grundlagen marktorientierter Unternehmensführung, Konzepte—Instrumente—Praxisbeispiele, Wiesbaden, 13. Edn., 2019.

Menhart, M.: Innovationsdynamik und Lebenszyklen in der Versicherungsindustrie, Aachen, 2003.

Müller-Stewens, G./Lechner, C. (2016): Strategisches Management, Wie strategische Initiativen zum Wandel führen, Stuttgart, 5. Edn., 2016.

Porter, M.E. (2004): Competitive Strategy, New York, Neuaufl., 2004.

Ries, A../Trout, J. (2000): Positioning: The Battle for Your Mind, New York, 2000.

Schradin, H.R. (1994): Erfolgsorientiertes Versicherungsmanagement, Karlsruhe, 1994.

Spontent GmbH (Ed.) (2023): Review GermanBeachTour Saison, Düsseldorf, 2023.

Woodruff, R. (1997): Customer value, The next source for competitive advantage, in: JoAMS, Vol. 25, 1997, No. 2, pp. 139–153.

YouGov (Ed.) (2014): Kundenmonitor e-Assekuranz, Der Vertriebswege-Monitor, Köln, 2014.

Marketing Tasks of the Insurance Company

9

The marketing tasks connect the marketing objectives with the marketing tools and are therefore a central component of strategic marketing. They take up the specifications from the marketing objectives and the marketing strategy and concretize these by weighting customer and performance as well as innovation and preservation orientation. In this way, the marketing tasks connect the mere product orientation of the product concept and the mere market orientation of the marketing concept—customer and performance are considered simultaneously. Overall, six core marketing tasks can be distinguished (Sect. 9.1), which are incorporated into core task profiles with different weightings in the sense of an integrated approach (Sect. 9.2).

9.1 Six Core Tasks of Marketing

The four core tasks of marketing—customer acquisition, customer retention, performance innovation, and performance maintenance—as already presented, go back to *Tomczak* and *Reinecke* (1999) (see Sect. 2.2.4). From the increasingly important relationship marketing and with it the explicit orientation towards long-term business relationships, two additional marketing tasks result, partner acquisition and partner retention. Relationships with current and future or potential business and especially sales partners are to be established, developed or terminated. Consequently, the remaining tasks can not only be taken over in one's own company, but also together with or solely by business partners (Table 9.1).

The weighting of marketing-tasks provides more concrete **guidelines for the design of the marketing mix**. A clear focus on new customer acquisition (potential development), for example, requires a sales and revenue-oriented sales policy as well as innovative products, while customer retention (potential exploitation) requires product improvements and comprehensive service and claims benefits. Top management must

T. Köhne, *Insurance Marketing*, https://doi.org/10.1007/978-3-658-47345-7_9

Table 9.1 Core marketing tasks. (Further developed from Tomczak and Reinecke 1999, p. 309 and Köhne 2006, p. 160)

Core Task	Objective	Content
Customer Acquisition	Exploitation of Customer Potentials	Measures that promote a customer's first purchase from the respective provider
Customer Retention	Exhaustion of Customer Potentials	Measures that promote repeat and follow-up purchases and prevent customer churn
Partner Acquisition	Exploitation of Partner Potentials	Measures that promote the initial cooperation between two partners (especially between insurer and intermediaries)
Partner Retention	Exhaustion of Partner Potentials	Measures that promote continuous cooperation
Performance Innovation	Exploitation of Performance Potentials	Measures for the creation of new offers and enforcement in the market
Performance Maintenance	Exhaustion of Performance Potentials	Measures to promote a sustainable market presence of an offer

fundamentally deal with all core tasks, even if it can set different priorities (Tomczak and Reinecke 1999, pp. 313–315; Köhne 2006, pp. 159 f.; see also Bruhn 2022, p. 21).

The high importance of **customer acquisition** as a central lever of new business growth has always prompted insurers to generate customers through additional partnerships, e.g., through sales companies, brokers, banks, or sales cooperations with companies from other industries (annex distribution), in addition to their own sales force organizations. Especially in times of a certain market saturation in many property & casualty insurance branches and in a difficult environment for most life insurance lines, however, customer acquisition requires considerable investments in advertising, direct marketing, sales, or even portfolio acquisitions. Acquiring new customers can be up to five times more expensive than retaining current customers (Kotler et al. 2017a, p. 179). Growth through aggressive new customer acquisition thus comes at the expense of company profits. However, in growth markets and in the phase of business development, new customer acquisition is sensible and the basis for (future) profits. Despite this fact, customer acquisition plays a significant role in practice, even in more or less saturated markets.

The importance of **customer retention** for the insurance industry has been recognized at least since the studies by *Reichheld* from the 1990s and the underlying experiences of the US insurance market. Accordingly, most German insurers have now also adopted **Customer Relationship Management** (CRM). For the sake of completeness, it should be noted that customer reacquisition is also possible. Although it resembles new customer acquisition, it is often separated as a third component of CRM (Bruhn 2022, p. 112). In the context of marketing tasks and in the sense of comprehensive CRM that applies over the lifetime of the customer, customer reacquisition is attributed here to customer retention because the customers have already been won once. The need to achieve strong customer retention, however, is not only derived from developments at the macroeconomic (market saturation) and individual entrepreneurial level (formulation as a marketing goal), but also directly from the economic implications associated with good (increase in profits) and poor customer retention (increase in costs): It was recently demonstrated for the Swiss market that there is a positive relationship between customer satisfaction on the customer side and profitability and sales on the insurer side (Jahnert and Schmeiser 2022). And Reichheld (1997) showed almost 30 years ago that the customer retention rate—the quotient between the number of customers who are customers both at the beginning and at the end of a period and the number of customers at the beginning of the period—is a crucial lever for the profitability of insurance companies.

The following empirically confirmed facts are responsible for the **relationship between customer retention rate and company profitability** (generally in Kotler et al. 2017a, p. 179; insurance-related in Reichheld 1997, especially Chaps. 2 and 3):

With reference to the **individual contract**:

- More loyal customers are less price sensitive.
- The claims ratio generally decreases with the duration of customer retention.
- The productivity of the sales force increases with an increasing customer retention rate.
- The overhead costs in the administration area decrease significantly as the customer retention rate increases.
- A customer becomes profitable after four years in the portfolio.

With reference to the **customer (and all his contracts)**:

- The number of contracts increases with increasing customer loyalty duration.
- The damage loads decrease for customers with multiple contracts.
- The price sensitivity of loyal customers decreases, so that products with higher contribution margins are increasingly demanded.
- The acquisition costs decrease with each additional contract, as more and more opportunities for direct customer approach arise. This aspect is central to claims management.

With reference to the **customer's relationship potential**:

- New customers through referrals are more loyal and therefore lucrative due to the previously mentioned correlations.

- Customers gained through recommendations usually generate lower damage loads than other new customers and are less price sensitive.
- Recommendation leads to new customers being more willing to conclude multiple contracts with an insurance company.
- New customer acquisitions through the recommendation of satisfied regular customers are associated with lower acquisition costs due to the unnecessary sales effort and their openness to concluding multiple contracts.

It thus becomes apparent that with increasing customer loyalty, all components of the **Customer Lifetime Value** develop positively, i.e., the customer equity increases (see Sect. 2.2.4). Venohr (1996, p. 366) estimates the potentials of long-term customer relationships based on studies in the composite sector to be such that a 10-year customer relationship is 8 to 10 times more profitable than a 5-year one. A 2 percent improvement in the customer retention rate from 90 percent to 92 percent, according to his studies, leads to a 45 percent increase in the present value of the customer relationship with an average customer loyalty duration of 10 years. Especially in saturated insurance markets, customer loyalty is therefore essentially the central marketing task of insurance providers (even if some insurers still focus more on new customers and growth).

Customer loyalty is complemented by the marketing tasks of **performance maintenance** and **performance innovation**. These determine the direction of product and service policy. In the service sector in general and in insurance in particular, as mentioned, the process character and the time-relatedness of service provision play an important role. Therefore, in the context of the marketing task of performance maintenance, quality management is of central importance when it comes to planning, controlling, and monitoring potential, process, and result-related service quality (see research window on service quality).

Research Window: Quality management in services and insurances

The importance of **service quality** for customer satisfaction results from the psychological effects of delivered quality, or in other words: customer satisfaction results from expected or exceeding service qualities. Therefore, the service provider must formulate quality objectives that meet the expectations of the target customers regarding the service quality. But service quality is harder to define, judge, and measure than product quality. This is because the **subjective perception of the customer** about the actually delivered service has to be objectively evaluated. From the mentioned characteristics of the service such as the Uno-actu principle, the process character, and the non-storability, it results that service quality is conceptually difficult to grasp. This is also shown by the definition of Bruhn, who defines service quality as the ability of a provider to create the quality of a primarily intangible and customer participation requiring service based on customer expectations at a certain requirement level (Bruhn 2019a, p. 37). The determination of service quality therefore requires a recourse to its relevant dimensions:

These can initially be the **potential, process, and outcome dimensions**, which result directly from the aforementioned peculiarities. In the potential dimension, the quality of the provider's material, organizational, and personal performance prerequisites is then recorded, in the process dimension the process quality during service provision, and in the outcome dimension the outcome quality at the end of the service process (Donabedian 1980, cited in Meffert et al. 2018, p. 100). Furthermore, the quality dimensions can result from the customer's expectations: In this case, the **routine component** stands for all properties that are normally expected from a service. The **exception component**, on the other hand, stands for additional services that are not expected by the customer. Negative deviations from routine services are punished by dissatisfaction, fulfillment is expected and therefore does not lead to special satisfaction. The non-provision of exceptional services has no effect because they were not expected anyway, their provision leads to satisfaction or even enthusiasm because they were not expected (Berry 1986). Finally, empirical studies often use the five quality dimensions of environmental comfort (tangibles), reliability, responsiveness, credibility through performance competence (assurance), and empathy, which go back to Zeithaml et al. (Zeithaml et al. 1988). This positive correlation between customer satisfaction and service quality—expressed here in the dimensions of performance competence, individuality of financial planning, employee competence, corporate image, environmental comfort, and technology—has also been empirically confirmed for life insurance (Siddiqui and Sharma 2010).

With the help of **models of service quality**, initial starting points for quality management measures can be derived. Of the numerous models (overview in Bruhn 2019a, pp. 111–150), the **Gap model** by Zeithaml et al. (1988) should be mentioned because it has gained particularly wide distribution. It provides a comprehensive framework for determining service quality from the customer's and company's perspective and is the result of focus group interviews with customers and expert discussions with various service providers, including insurers. It shows discrepancies (gaps) between the customer's perceptions and the company's attempt to translate customer expectations into service specifications. The model defines service quality as the difference between customer expectation and performance perception (Gap 5), which results from four other occurring gaps:

1. Gap between customer expectations and their perception by management.
2. Gap between the customer expectations perceived by management and their implementation in service quality specifications.
3. Gap between the specifications of service quality and the actual performance created.
4. Gap between the actual performance created and the communication directed at the customer.

Quality management has to keep the described gaps as small as possible. In addition, it must evaluate the criteria by which customers assess the quality of the service, the expectations of the customers, and the evaluation of the current services in relation to these expectations. Ten typical evaluation criteria can be divided into result-oriented and process-oriented: The assessment of the result quality is related to accessibility, trust, knowledge or customer understanding, reliability, and security of the service provider, while that of the process quality is related to competence, communication skills, politeness, responsiveness to the customer, and ambiance (Kotler et al. 2022, p. 433).

The **measurement of service quality** can be carried out using customer- and/or company-oriented measurement approaches. Customer-oriented measurement methods include methods based on objective criteria that allow the use of third parties, such as the Silent-Shopper method (fake or test customers, also known as Mystery Shopping; see Sect. 5.4), expert observation or service tests (in the insurance sector, for example, by Finanztest or the German Institute for Service Quality). Methods based on subjective criteria include feature-oriented approaches such as multi-attribute methods (impression measurement, satisfaction measurements according to the "Confirmation/ Disconfirmation Paradigm" based on a divergence measurement between target and actual component, SERVQUAL approach by Parasuraman et al. (1985) and the Penalty-Reward-Factors approach by Berry (1986) or the very similar Kano method). The "SERVQUAL method" is a standardized, industry-independent measurement method that measures and evaluates the difference between the service performance expected by the customer and the service performance actually experienced. It uses a questionnaire, the questions of which cover the five dimensions of service quality (reliability, convenience, responsiveness, performance and social competence of employees) and ask about the target and actual state in each case. Subjective methods also include event-oriented measurement methods such as the sequential event method (blueprints) and the Critical-Incident technique (key events). Finally, problem-oriented measurement approaches such as the Frequency-Relevance Analysis for Problems (FRAP) and the complaint analysis are also part of the subjective methods. Company-oriented measurement methods then include management-oriented approaches such as the Failure Mode and Effects Analysis (FMEA) and the Fishbone Analysis (Cause-Effect Diagram) as well as employee-oriented approaches such as employee surveys and the company suggestion system (see Meffert et al. 2018, pp. 212–236; in detail at Bruhn 2019a, pp. 151–241).

In the insurance industry, two customer satisfaction systems are primarily used for measurement and control: the KUBUS satisfaction survey and the Net Promoter Score (Trautinger 2018, p. 22). In recent years, the so-called **Net Promoter Score** (NPS) has been increasingly discussed, which goes back to Reichheld (2003). It measures customer satisfaction and loyalty, specifically the willingness of customers to recommend an insurance provider to friends and colleagues. Methodologically, a representative group of customers is asked only one question: "How likely is it that you will recommend company/brand X to a friend or colleague?" The scale of responses ranges from 0 (unlikely) to 10 (extremely likely). The score is calculated by the difference between promoters, who answer with 9 or 10, and detractors, who answer with 0 to 6. Customers who answer with 7 or 8 are considered "indifferent". The advantage of the NPS lies primarily in its simplicity, as only one question is required for calculation. This is offset by methodological weaknesses (e.g., the arbitrary division into three groups) and the lack of convincing evidence of the behavioral relevance of recommendations (Bruhn 2019a, pp. 570 f.). Therefore, the NPS will not replace satisfaction measurement, but rather supplement it. The NPS only indicates a recommendation status. The analysis of the causes for the lack of recommendation must be carried out separately and is at least as important in order to draw the success-critical conclusions (Meffert et al. 2019, p. 496).

The **implementation of quality management** in service companies requires the use of various tools. A control loop is to be run through, which is oriented towards the classic management functions of planning, execution and control: 1. Quality planning; 2. Quality implementation; 3. Quality controlling; 4. Quality management presentation.

The **Q-Planning** involves measuring customer requirements (e.g., through customer and employee surveys, in insurance for example sales force surveys) and formulating quality objectives. The **Q-Implementation** includes measures and activities to achieve the defined quality objectives; these include, for example, customer orientation seminars, quality circles, appropriately aligned personnel recruitment and development, work techniques and forms, incentive systems, information technologies and, last but not least, a quality-oriented alignment of leadership style and behavior. As part of the **Q-Controlling**, the ongoing testing of processes and success is carried out; the associated instruments are the employee evaluation, complaint management, ongoing customer satisfaction surveys or observations, as well as employee tests or observations. Finally, in the last phase of the **Q-Management Presentation**, the documentation of the quality management system for internal and external communication is carried out, e.g., using manuals, certificates, statistics or audits (Meffert et al. 2018, pp. 240–245; Lehmann 1993, pp. 76–102; detailed in: Bruhn 2019a, pp. 309–418).

Further reading for in-depth study:

- Bruhn 2019a.
- Kromschröder 1993.
- Lehmann 1993.
- Lehmann 1998.
- Meffert et al. 2018, Chap. 5.
- Parasuraman et al. 1985.
- Reichheld and Markey 2011.
- Trautinger 2018.
- Zeithaml et al. 1988.

The **partner acquisition** for the development of partner potentials includes all measures of initial partner acquisition with its sub-steps of selection and evaluation of potential partners, the specific choice of partner and the subsequent contract design. It should be noted that in the insurance industry, depending on the value-added component considered, the number of potential value-added partners is still limited, as the disintegration of the value chain has only just begun at least industry-wide. In addition, the service and credence character of insurance is responsible for the fact that the long-term protection promise and all associated **services** must be **provided over a multi-year period** without any loss of quality. This results in **increased requirements for partner selection**, whether these are risk carriers, portfolio managers, intermediaries and advisors or claims adjusters. In addition, constructive and destructive effects of partner selection must be considered in the course of partner evaluation: Constructive effects are, for example, new customer potentials, increased underwriting capacities, access to risk assessment know-how, complementary products or services or cost savings. Destructive effects, on the other hand, are, for example, an expected resource dispersion with too low unit numbers, brand erosion with a lack of coherent brand policy or the negative image transfer in the case of cooperation of a customer and advisory-oriented primary insurer with a purely multi level sales organization.

Against the same background, **partner commitment** also plays a significant role. It involves the creation of factual or psychological ties (switching barriers). Factual ties initially result from relationship-specific investments and the quasi-rent to be achieved thereby, e.g., the linking of consulting, sales, and claims settlement systems with inventory systems or a product-related training of employees. In addition, contractual agreements reinforce partner commitment, which is particularly important due to its strategic significance, especially in customer-oriented distribution and claims settlement. Partner commitment results both from the inputs into a relationship (specific investments, effort, commitment, financial participation) and from the outputs (profit, distribution of relationship success, customer access). In contrast, the psychological commitment of a cooperation partner is the consequence of created trust, a strong cooperation identity, and a high attractiveness of the cooperation. For example, the pronounced common identity and the attractiveness resulting from high earning opportunities bind the employees of sales companies, just as the expected sales volume and the demonstrable success bind the primary insurers to them (e.g., at DVAG, MLP) (Köhne 2006, pp. 330 f.).

9.2 Integration into Core Task Profiles

Typical weightings of the different marketing tasks lead to so-called **core task profiles** (Fig. 9.1).

A trendsetter, for example, is characterized by customer acquisition and performance innovation, while a marketing virtuoso masters and fulfills all core tasks. In contrast to the trendsetter and virtuoso, the potential exploiter has a large customer base and an established performance offering. He focuses mainly on retaining his customers and designing his performance competitively to avoid losing his customers. Partner retention outweighs partner acquisition.

Another typical core task profile is that of the multiplier: It often goes hand in hand with franchise concepts. The multiplier exploits the potential of an idea or a business system worldwide by acquiring new customers through new sales partners, maintaining its performance quality, and binding the contributing product and sales partners. Customer retention is largely left to the partners. Finally, the brand exploiter maintains his performance, develops and broadens it through innovative products, and triggers a

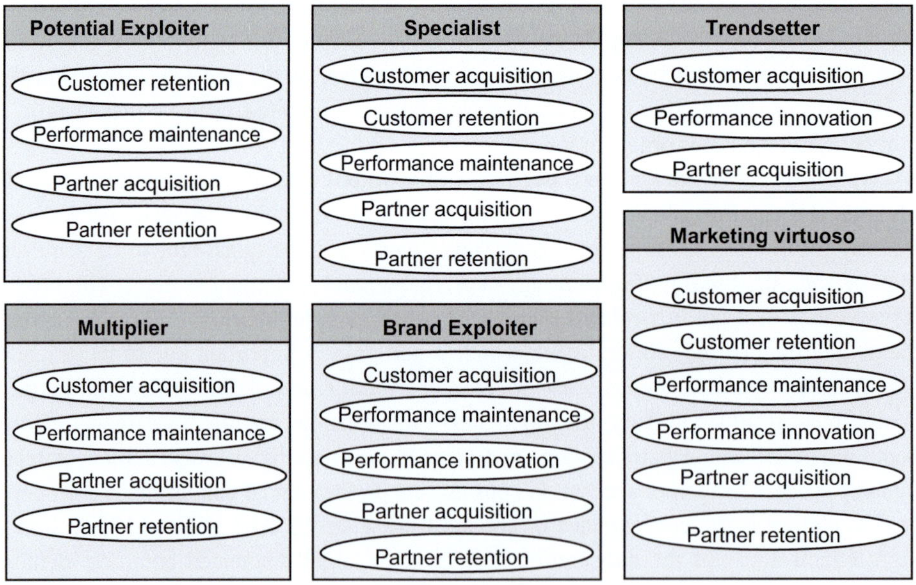

Fig. 9.1 Typical core task profiles. (Based on Tomczak and Reinecke 1999, p. 317)

demand pull through intensive end-customer marketing (product design and communication). Partner acquisition and partner retention, but also partner exchange, go hand in hand. End customer retention is done via the manufacturer's or provider's brand, but is largely left to the sales partners (Tomczak and Reinecke 1999, pp. 316 f.; Reinecke 2004, pp. 201–204; Tomczak et al. 2023, pp. 70–72).

The framework conditions of the **insurance industry**, its previous cooperation experiences, and the peculiarities of the insurance product make only selected task profiles appear sensible: Thus, the trendsetter profile (customer and partner acquisition and performance innovation) and the marketing virtuoso (all core tasks) are likely to be less promising due to the longevity of the products and the rather low interest on the customer side. In contrast, the potential exploiter profile (customer retention, partner retention, and performance maintenance), the multiplier profile (customer acquisition, partner acquisition, partner retention, and performance maintenance), and the brand exploiter profile (performance maintenance, performance innovation, partner acquisition, partner retention, and end-customer marketing) are fundamentally suitable for insurance companies.

The **potential exploiter** has a large customer base and an established performance offering. Potential exploiters are, for example, the public insurers. They focus mainly on retaining their customers and those of the savings banks (e.g., potential exploitation through cross-selling across all branches and mediation via the savings banks) and the internal division of the market (regional principle) to avoid losing their customers. Partner retention outweighs partner acquisition.

Above all, the core task profile of the multiplier seems to be suitable for insurers: The **multiplier** exploits the potential of his business system by acquiring new customer potentials through new distribution partners, maintaining his performance quality, and binding the contributing product and sales partners. Customer retention is largely left to the distribution partners. Primary insurers pursue this strategy when they implement multi-channel approaches to increase their sales.

The **brand exploiter** maintains his performance, develops and expands it through innovative products, and triggers a **demand pull** through intensive end-customer marketing (product design and communication), which also supports partner acquisition and partner retention. End-customer retention is achieved—as far as possible—via the corporate brand, but not without the participation of sales partners, who also carry out customer acquisition. In insurance, such pull marketing is difficult to implement for primary insurers due to the low product attractiveness and high importance of personal intermediary contact. Allianz may be able to achieve this to some extent when it operates with brokers, in annex distribution with car manufacturers, and in employee business of companies or associations (e.g., in the Riester pension of IG Metall ("Metallrente")). **Typical for insurance**, the brand exploiter strategy is **more likely to be found with the sales partner**. Large sales companies and large financial service brokers exploit their brand strength against product suppliers by developing their own ideas regarding performance maintenance and innovation and demanding the support of partners, binding these (product) partners and dedicating themselves primarily to customer acquisition and customer retention.

In insurance, another core task profile is the **specialist**: On the product side, this can be a target group insurer who acquires and binds customers in his target group, offers needs-based target group-specific products, and binds target group-appropriate sales partners to himself. Although he will occasionally also develop products and gain new sales partners, his focus is on customer acquisition as well as customer, partner, and performance maintenance. The specialization can also be oriented towards sales channels; typical is the broker insurer, who primarily focuses on brokers as sales partners. His focus is more on customer acquisition than customer retention, continuous performance maintenance, performance innovation in the broker market, as well as partner acquisition and partner retention.

In the implementation of certain core task profiles, cooperations with other service providers offer the opportunity to achieve quality improvements and innovations, especially in the product-related service area, and to occupy customer interfaces. So-called **ecosystems** create the prerequisite to combine various financial services products and thus create problem solutions (performance maintenance and innovation). They also enable the participation of partners who serve the customer interface (customer acquisition and retention). At the same time, they require the acquisition of the most suitable partners and sustainable cooperation with them (partner acquisition and retention). The ecosystem as a whole has the potential to act as a marketing virtuoso; the partners within the ecosystem will occupy various roles and thus core task profiles (see excursus on ecosystems).

Excursus on ecosystems in the insurance industry

Understanding markets and companies as so-called **ecosystems** entered management literature in the 1990s (Moore 1996). Since the creation of services in general and the creation of insurance-related problem solutions also face increasing complexity due to various environmental developments (see Sect. 6.1), it is advisable for providers to no longer create services alone, but **in strategic corporate networks** (Sydow 1992, with reference to insurance Köhne 2006), in which different actors bring in their respective resources and competencies. The value creation potential is particularly determined by the cooperation and innovation ability of the network partners. The incentive to participate in ecosystems follows from the fact that the involved actors (providers, demanders, and platform operators) can gain competitive advantages through **network effects** by bringing in complementary technologies and competencies (McIntyre and Srinivasan 2017). The concept of the 'Service Ecosystem' follows the Service-Dominant Logic (see excursus on Customer-Dominant Logic and its approaches in Sect. 2.2.4), according to which every company is considered a service company and service innovations take place in so-called 'Actor-to-Actor' networks. Accordingly, a service ecosystem is a autonomous and self-regulating network of mostly economically and socially connected actors who create a common value through the mutual exchange of services (Lusch and Nambisan 2015, p.161).

The ecosystem approach focuses on the relationships of actors within networks, primarily considering the cooperative and collaborative relationships of actors within networks. In this context, **Value Co-Creation** (Vargo and Akaka 2012) and the resource integration from both the provider and customer side are emphasized. This approach highlights the complex reciprocal relationships of the actors who want to realize value creation and innovation potentials together in networks (Sydow 1992). Furthermore, this perspective brings together the participants of an ecosystem in a novel way, where the place of exchange is increasingly seen as a **platform** (Bruhn et al. 2019, pp. 60 f.).

Development trends such as digitalization (Sect. 6.1.4), the international interweaving of value chains as a result of globalization (Sect. 6.1.2) and service transformation have brought about the importance and possibilities of using ecosystems for both providers and demanders. The **service transformation** signifies a shift away from the product towards process-oriented services, from standardized to individualized service creation, and from pure transaction to (long-term) customer relationships. Digitalization connects not only different actors through IT-based communication and information processes, but also the actors, products, and processes themselves. This enables new, **digital and virtual platforms as well as the development of data-driven and collaborative business models**, whose main value drivers are services and no longer physical products. Characteristic for platform providers (e.g., Uber, Airbnb, partly also Amazon) is that not only the technology is provided, but through the active management of the ecosystem of these platforms, additional services are developed, for whose execution, however, not the platform provider itself, but the participating providers are responsible (Bruhn et al. 2019, pp. 61, 321–327).

The business models of the internet giants (e.g., Google, Facebook, Amazon, Apple) create **digital ecosystems**, in which the internet giants themselves are at the center. Their platforms, apps, and content, sometimes in combination with services from the real world, shape the respective manifestation and connect these with their different user groups.

▶ **Digital Ecosystem** is a user-driven, loosely coupled collaborative environment in the interplay of hardware and software components and their networking, in which users can satisfy their individual needs (Lemke and Brenner 2015, p. 231).

Ecosystems are thus a kind of 'full-range supplier' in providing users with digital and networked offers, thereby creating a high utility value. In addition, the mostly independent users create value for the other users, but especially for the business model of the internet giants, by participating in the ecosystem (principle of utility-centeredness as a value standard). The **implementation** as digital ecosystems can be observed both **among the current internet giants** and **among emerging digital companies (start-ups)**: They combine the most diverse offers with platform bindings and app usage on the various mobile and stationary end devices. In addition, selected offers are specifically combined with the real world, and constant new or further developments lead to a constant renewal of the digital ecosystems. Through both, the degree of relevance of the content for the users and their attention can be continuously maintained and expanded (Lemke and Brenner 2015, pp. 229, 231).

The **established insurance industry** is more active in the area of digital ecosystems than one might think. As early as 2021, it operated at least 10 offer InsurTechs on the market via subsidiaries or acquisitions. The initial focus was on digital process innovation as a new playing field: On the green field, the ideal of fully digital business operations becomes a reality. The **InsurTechs used by the insurers** for this purpose operate largely separately from their parent companies with a high degree of independence to promote innovation and speed, while at the same time there is the necessary knowledge transfer when needed (Oliver Wyman/policen direct 2021, p. 6; see InsurTechs excursus in Sect. 6.1.4).

A crucial driver in the move towards ecosystems is the topic of "**Embedded Insurance**". This refers to the inclusion of insurance services in third-party offers, thus resembling product-related annex sales (Sect. 13.2.4). This could be a bundle offer, such as the offer of a new car warranty for a used vehicle by the car dealer, which he represents through an extended warranty policy. Alternatively, there could be a type of 'opt-in' model, where the customer is offered travel cancellation protection at the end of a travel booking. Both variants can be implemented more easily with digital offers than with analog ones. Moreover, new digital offers also create new risks that digital providers can cover more easily than traditional insurers. For example, this applies to liability risks in the short-term rental of an apartment through AirBnB's "Host Protection Insurance". Common to all these offer variants is the focus on value creation through a function-oriented compilation of products into a problem solution (value bundles) (see the excursus on functional thinking in Sect. 2.2.4; see the design of problem solutions in Sect. 10.2.2 and Sect. 10.5). Embedded Insurance is a significant trend in the digitalization of the insurance industry. The InsurTech Simplesurance, founded in 2012 and now grown into an international scale-up, is based on this, and traditional insurers like Allianz or AXA bundle corresponding business in globally operating business units. SwissRe is betting on this trend with its scale-up iptiQ (Oliver Wyman/policen direct 2021, pp. 6 f.; Fritzsche and Bohnert 2022, p. 819).

Another driver towards ecosystems are **sales platforms** (sales bundles). They have steadily gained importance in recent years and have even become systemically important in some cases. Sales platforms are technology-based business models that provide other providers with access to their customers for a fee. They address three customer groups: InsurTechs such as price comparators, insurance managers and financial partners target end customers, InsurTechs in the "sales platform" category target intermediaries, and InsurTechs in the "enterprise platform" category serve companies. Examples of such sales platforms can be found among the successful original InsurTechs (e.g., Acturis, Check24, Hypoport or Verivox) and most scale-ups in the sales segment (e.g., durchblicker, Clark, FINLEX, Thinksurance, Wefox or Xempus) (Oliver Wyman/policen direct 2021, p. 6).

Digitalization is an enabler of ecosystems. Although this naturally applies to digital ecosystems, thinking in terms of ecosystems is not limited to digital business models. **Ecosystems as customer-centric, cross-industry value networks** are the result of market saturation, hence increasing competition and thus increasing customer orientation. The insurance industry benefits from the fact that insurance coverage is an essential part of holistic customer solutions—e.g., around mobility, health, living and travel—and thus of ecosystems (see in detail: Jost 2022, pp. 183–265). However, it is a major challenge to build and orchestrate one's own ecosystem. This requires certain competencies and 'assets' such as foremost customer access, but also image and brand presence, financial strength and/or relevant technological and strategic capabilities. If at all, only a few insurers will be able to do this. The alternative for many insurers is to focus more on the role of the supplier of insurance coverage, coupled with the risk of completely losing the interface to the customer. At least they have the opportunity to continue interacting directly with customers in addition to participating in the ecosystem. A third option is to act on an equal footing in an ecosystem. This requires cooperation on an equal footing and thus similarly strong assets; for insurance companies, this is rather difficult compared to other industries, because as a rule, the partner with the best customer access is the focal actor. A horizontal network of various insurers with regional division of labor (e.g., association of public insurers) is possible, but in itself not yet an ecosystem (Köhne 2006, esp. pp. 379–396).

According to the trade press, it is primarily **Chinese insurers** who are demonstrating how to build an ecosystem around insurance. For instance, the insurer Zhong An sees itself as part of digital ecosystems in the areas of digital retail, consumer credit, health, mobility, and travel. The insurer Ping An, as an external partner, provides capital and services for the ecosystems of financial services, health, auto, and housing. With its "Good Doctors" platform, Ping An has created a digital ecosystem in the health sector that reaches nearly 200 million users and collaborates with 3100 hospitals and 7500 pharmacies. **Swiss and German insurers** have at least begun to build their own platforms. Broadly speaking, Baloise currently appears to be very ambitious, building ecosystems in the areas of mobility and housing through numerous partnerships and investments in start-ups. And in the field of mobility, HUK-Coburg is also very committed. For example, the "HUK-Autowelt" has four business areas: car sales in Düsseldorf, nationwide car purchases, long-term rental of new vehicles (so-called car subscription), and car repair shop service, which is now offered by HUK-Autowelt at 450 stations in Germany thanks to a minority stake in Pitstop GmbH. In addition, HUK-Coburg is building a mobility ecosystem together with the insurers LVM and HDI through the joint venture Onpier: An app store is intended to offer additional services to the 18 million drivers. Besides the two examples mentioned, there are many other initiatives of individual cooperations in the areas of housing, mobility, travel, and health. However, their success is still pending and is likely to require a long breath (Barbier 2023; o. V. 2023c).

Further reading for in-depth study:

- Accenture 2020.
- Biedebach 2023.
- Fritzsche and Bohnert 2022.
- Hein et al. 2019.
- Kapoor 2018.
- Köhne 2006.
- McIntyre and Srinivasan 2017.
- Moore 1996.
- Nicoletti 2021, esp. pp. 334–342.
- Sydow 1992.
- Torrance and Robinson 2022.
- Vargo and Akaka 2012.

However, the determination of the desired task profile serves not only to integrate the core marketing tasks, but also to design the marketing mix in a profile-appropriate manner. For example, a clear focus on acquiring new customers requires a sales and revenue-oriented sales policy, market-appropriate and ideally innovative products, as well as communicative support. Customer retention, on the other hand, requires product improvements and comprehensive services, as well as customer-oriented claims settlement (Köhne 2006, pp. 331 f.).

Further Reading Recommendations for Chap. 9

- Bruhn 2022, Sect. 5.2.
- Bruhn and Homburg 2017.
- Eckert et al. 2022.
- Eurich 2001.
- Reichheld and Markey 2011.
- Tomczak and Reinecke 1996.
- Tomczak et al. 2023, pp. 51–79.
- Trumpfheller 2005.

References

Accenture (Ed.) (2020): Ökosysteme in der Versicherungsindustrie, Potenziale und Umsetzungsstrategien, Whitepaper, 2020.

Barbier, E. (2023): Verschmelzende Geschäftswelt: Nach den ersten Ökosystem-Ausflügen der Branche macht sich Katerstimmung breit, in: Newsletter 'Versicherungswirtschaft-heute' vom 25.06.2023, 2023.

Berry, L.L. (1986): Big Ideas in Service Marketing, in: Venkatesan, M./Schamelensee, D.H./ Marshall, C.E. (Eds.), Creativity in Service Marketing, Chicago u.a., 1986, pp. 6–8.

Biedebach, M. (2023): Industrial-age Ecosystems and Digital Innovation—Implications for Structures, Roles and Value Capturing, Univ.-Diss., Kassel, 2023.

Bruhn, M. (2019a): Qualitätsmanagement für Dienstleistungen, Handbuch für ein erfolgreiches Qualitätsmanagement. Grundlagen, Konzepte, Methoden, Berlin, 11. Edn., 2019.

Bruhn, M. (2022): Relationship Marketing. Das Management von Kundenbeziehungen, München, 6. Edn., 2022.

Bruhn, M./Homburg, C. (Eds.) (2017): Handbuch Kundenbindungsmanagement, Strategien und Instrumente für ein erfolgreiches CRM, Wiesbaden, 9. Edn., 2013.

Bruhn, M./Meffert, H./Hadwich, K. (2019): Handbuch Dienstleistungsmarketing. Planung—Umsetzung—Kontrolle, Wiesbaden, 2. Edn., 2019.

Eckert, C./Neunsinger, C./Osterrieder, K. (2022): Managing customer satisfaction: digital applications for insurance companies, in: GP, Vol. 47, 2022, No. 3, pp. 569–602. (DOI: https://doi.org/10.1057/s41288-021-00257-z)

Eurich, A. (2001): Bestandskundenmarketing von Versicherungsunternehmen, Lohmar, 2001.

Fritzsche, A./Bohnert, A. (2022): Implications of bundled offerings for business development ad competitive strategy in digital insurance, in: GP, Vol. 47, 2022, pp. 817–834. (DOI: https://doi.org/10.1057/s41288-021-00244-4)

Hein, A./Weking, J./Schreieck, M./Wiesche, M./Böhm, M./Krcmar, H. (2019): Value co-creation practices in business-to-business platform ecosystems, in: Electronic Markets, Vol. 29, 2019, No. 3, pp. 503–518. (doi: https://doi.org/10.1007/s12525-019-00337-y)

Jahnert, J.R./Schmeiser, H. (2022): The relationship between net promoter score and insurers' profitability: an empirical analysis at the customer level, in: GP, Vol. 47, 2022, pp. 944–972. (DOI: https://doi.org/10.1057/s41288-021-00237-3)

Jost, T. (2022): Kundenbeziehungsmanagement in der Versicherungswirtschaft: Ein Perspektivwechsel vor dem Hintergrund der Digitalisierung und der Entwicklung von Ökosystemen, Karlsruhe, 2022.

Kapoor, R. (2018): Ecosystems: broadening the locus of value creation, in: Journal of Organization Design, Vol. 7, 2018, No. 1, pp. 1–16. (doi: https://doi.org/10.1186/s41469-018-0035-4)

Köhne, T. (2006): Marketing im strategischen Unternehmensnetzwerk, Erklärungsmodell und praktische Anwendung in der Versicherungswirtschaft, Wiesbaden, 2006.

Kotler, P./Keller, K.L./Opresnik, M.O. (2017a): Marketing-Management, Konzepte—Instrumente—Unternehmensfallstudien, Halbergmoos, 15. Edn., 2017.

Kotler, P./Armstrong, G./Harris, L.C./He, H. (2022): Grundlagen des Marketing, Halbergmoos, 8. Edn., 2022.

Kromschröder, B. (1993): Qualitätsmanagement in der Versicherungswirtschaft, Karlsruhe, 1993.

Lehmann, A. (1993): Dienstleistungsmanagement, Strategien und Ansatzpunkte zur Schaffung von Servicequalität, Stuttgart, 1993.

Lehmann, A.P. (1998): Qualität und Produktivität im Dienstleistungsmanagement. Strategische Handlungsfelder im Versicherungs- und Finanzdienstleistungswettbewerb, Wiesbaden, 1998.

Lemke, C./Brenner, W. (2015): Einführung in die Wirtschaftsinformatik, Band 1: Verstehen des digitalen Zeitalters, Berlin, 2015.

Lusch, R.F./Nambisan, S. (2015): Service innovation: A service-dominant logic perspective, in: MIS Quarterly, Vol. 39, 2015, No. 1, pp. 155–175.

McIntyre, D.P./Srinivasan, A. (2017): Networks, platforms, and strategy: Emerging views and next steps, in: Strategic Management Journal, Vol. 38, 2017, No. 1, pp. 141–160.

Meffert, H./Bruhn, M./Hadwich, K. (2018): Dienstleistungsmarketing, Grundlagen—Konzepte—Methoden, Wiesbaden, 9. Edn., 2018.

Meffert, H./Burmann, C./Kirchgeorg, M./Eisenbeiß, M. (2019): Marketing, Grundlagen marktorientierter Unternehmensführung, Konzepte—Instrumente—Praxisbeispiele, Wiesbaden, 13. Edn., 2019.

Moore, J.F. (1996): The death of competition: Leadership and strategy in the age of business ecosystems, New York, 1996.

Nicoletti, B. (2021): Insurance 4.0: Benefits and Challenges of Digital Transformation, Cham, 2021.

Oliver Wyman/policen direct (Ed.) (2021): Die Zukunft von InsurTech in DACH, Der InsurTech-Radar 2021, o. O., 2021.

o. V. (2023c): Ökosystem zum Anfassen, in: VW, Jg. 78, 2023, Nr. 5, pp. 42–44.

Parasuraman, A./Zeithaml, V.A./Berry, L.L. (1985): A Conceptual Model of Service Quality and its Implications for Future Research, in: JoM, Vol. 49, 1985, No. 1, pp. 4–50.

Reichheld, F.F. (1997): Der Loyalitäts-Effekt, Die verborgene Kraft hinter Wachstum, Gewinnen und Unternehmenswert, Frankfurt a. M., 1997.

Reichheld, F.F. (2003): The one number you need to grow, in: Harvard Business Review, Vol. 81, 2003, No. 12, 46–54.

Reichheld, F./Markey, R. (2011): The ultimate question 2.0—how net promoter companies thrive in a customer driven world, Boston, 2011.

Reinecke, S. (2004): Marketing Performance Management, Empirisches Fundament und Konzeption für ein integriertes Marketingkennzahlensystem, Wiesbaden, 2004.

Siddiqui, M.H./Sharma, T.G. (2010): Analyzing customer satisfaction with service quality in life insurance services, in: Journal of Targeting, Measurement and Analysis for Marketing, Vol. 18, 2010. No. 3/4, pp. 221–238.

Sydow, J. (1992): Strategische Netzwerke, Evolution und Organisation, Wiesbaden, 1992.

Tomczak, T./Reinecke, S. (1996): Der aufgabenorientierte Ansatz, Einen neue Perspektive für das Marketing-Management, Fachbericht für Marketing, Heft 5, St. Gallen, 1996.

Tomczak, T./Reinecke, S. (1999): Der aufgabenorientierte Ansatz als Basis eines marktorientierten Wertmanagements, in: Grünig, R./Pasquier, M. (Eds.), Strategisches Management und Marketing, Festschrift für Richard Kühn, Bern, 1999, pp. 293–327.

Tomczak, T./Reinecke, S./Gollnhofer, J. (2023): Marketingplanung, Einführung in die marktorientierte Unternehmens- und Geschäftsfeldplanung, Wiesbaden, 8. Edn., 2023.

Torrance, S./Robinson, B. (2022): EMBEDDED INSURANCE 2.0, A Multi-Trillion dollar opportunity for brands and insurers, Ed. by aperture/Embedded Finance & Super App Strategies, 2022.

Trautinger, M.-J. (2018): Kundenzufriedenheit als Steuerungsinstrument in einem Versicherungsunternehmen—nur Schall und Rauch oder ökonomisch sinnvoll?, in: ZVersWiss, Jg. 107, 2018, pp. 3–39. (DOI: https://doi.org/10.1007/s12297-017-0394-x)

Trumpfheller, J. (2005): Kundenbindung in der Versicherungswirtschaft, Eine theoretische und empirische Analyse unter besonderer Berücksichtigung des Versicherungsvertriebs über Versicherungsintermediäre, Karlsruhe, 2005.

Vargo, S.L./Akaka, M.A. (2012): Value cocreation and service systems (re) formation: A service ecosystems view, in: Service Science, Vol. 4, 2012, No. 3, pp. 207–217.
Venohr, B. (1996): Kundenbindungsmanagement als Unternehmensziel. Leitmotiv für Versicherungsunternehmen, in: VW, Jg. 51, 1996, Nr. 6, pp. 365–368.
Zeithaml, V.A./Berry, L.L./Parasuraman, A. (1988): Communication and Control Processes in the delivery of Service Quality, in: JoM, Vol. 52, 1988, No. 4, pp. 35–48.

Part V

Operational Marketing as Part of the Insurance Marketing Conception

Product Policy as a Marketing Tool of the Insurance Company 10

10.1 Basics of Product Policy

Product policy encompasses all decision-making aspects that relate to the market-oriented design of an insurer's products and services. Since the enduring fulfillment of customer needs or the generation of customer value is a prerequisite for sustainable sales and growth, product policy plays a special role in achieving corporate goals. Product policy also influences the other marketing tools (price, service, communication, and distribution), as these are usually related to the product or should be related. Therefore, product policy generally has a special significance among the marketing tools in the marketing mix, and it was even referred to as the "heart of marketing" in the past (Kotler and Bliemel 1992, p. 702; Meffert and Bruhn 1995, p. 361). However, it has already been emphasized in the introductory chapter of this book that this only applies to insurance products to a limited extent. For these—not least because of the lower customer interest and the credence good character—the sales and communication policy play an (at least) equally important role.

▶ **Product Policy** includes all decision-making aspects that are aimed at the market-oriented design of an insurance company's products and services over the entire course of the customer relationship.

Product policy includes the three dimensions of product design, product development, and product management (Fig. 10.1):

- The **Product Design** deals with the material-content and formal (i.e., concerning the external appearance) design of insurance products. It asks what the scope of performance of a product or service should look like and how the presentation to the customers should take place. It is therefore related to the design object.

T. Köhne, *Insurance Marketing*, https://doi.org/10.1007/978-3-658-47345-7_10

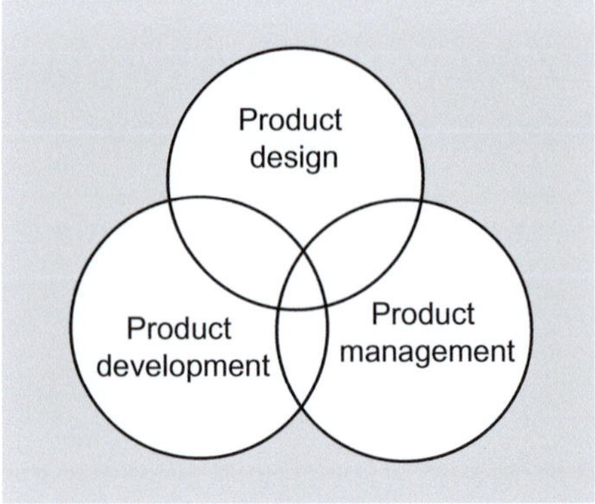

Fig. 10.1 The three dimensions of product policy

- The **Product Development** as the second dimension of product policy concerns the creation process of insurance products in the company. It asks which processes need to be run through in the course of product development and which questions need to be answered. It is related to the design process.
- **The Product Management** as the third component of product policy refers to its organization and competence allocation. It plans, executes, and monitors the product development process and coordinates the involved departments and actors. It asks how product design and product development should be organized in the company and how competencies should be distributed. It is therefore related to the design function.

Product design will be addressed in the next subchapter. As for product development, it is particularly networked in insurance and takes place across departments. Ideally, it goes through various phases in a temporal sequence, which, however, allows for feedback loops (Fig. 10.2).

The idea generation phase is heavily influenced by competition. Market research often focuses on competitor observation. The imitation of promising approaches is often preferred to an own, cost-causing and risky **product development.** The impulses from the market often come from the sales partners, be it from the own sales force or from brokers. A direct involvement of (private) customers in product development, which is known from industries such as the sports goods industry, is rare in the insurance industry. Comprehensive statistical studies on the benefit of various product features have only been used for a few years (e.g., conjoint measurement analysis; focus groups).

Customer orientation and thus marketing have gained importance in recent years, at least in larger insurance companies. Some companies also aim to develop and evaluate products consistently from the customer's perspective. Although regulatory requirements such as the required establishment of a product approval process (§ 23 VAG) are actually supposed to aim for this, they tend to be rather restrictive. Actuaries and lawyers shape the products to a considerable extent—not least because of numerous legal

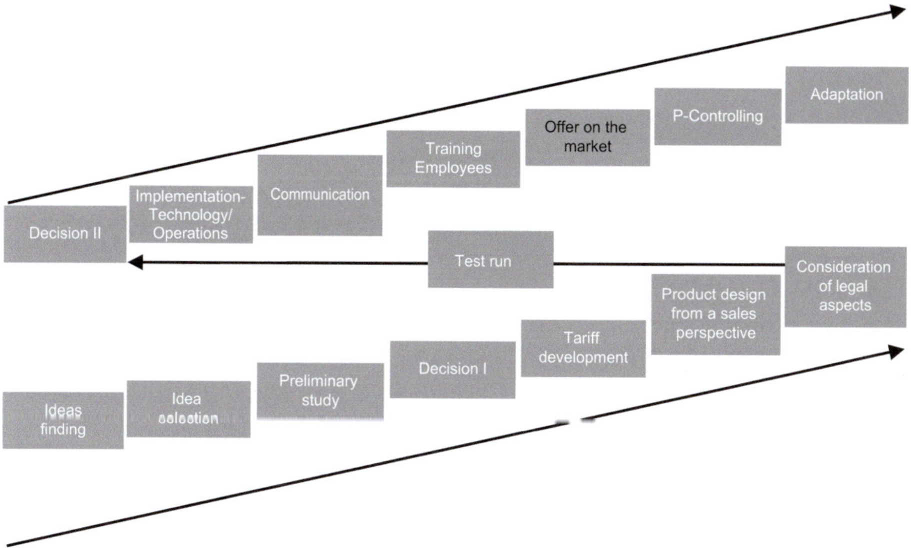

Fig. 10.2 Phases of product development in the insurance industry. (Köhne 1998b, p. 3)

regulations around the already legally formulated insurance products. Sales specialists are often (still) more influential than marketing specialists. While it does provide important impulses from the market, its customer perspective ends when customer interests contradict sales interests (see also Betschart and Mussak 2021, p. 376 f.). Other partners involved in product development are the reinsurers. They bring underwriting know-how and meaningful statistics into the development process. If they take the products to be developed into reinsurance themselves, the reinsurers are primarily interested in compliance with underwriting and legal requirements and tend to be less interested in (possibly risky) market innovations. Due to these constellations, claims departments and possibly complaint management departments in the insurance industry do not have the influence on product development that they should have from a customer's perspective. Positive impulses come from increasing competition, primarily from InsurTechs, who test new product ideas such as situational insurance or partial coverage and thus also stimulate established insurers.

The **product management** as another component of product policy is historically anchored in the insurance lines in the insurance industry. For some years now, it has been slowly but surely breaking out of these structures and taking on an increasingly independent role in companies. The need for product managers, as they are known from other industries (Kotler et al. 2017a, p. 837), was promoted not least by deregulation in 1994, which enabled independent development of insurance products, which until then had essentially taken place at association level.

Special requirements are placed on **product managers:**

- As an analyst and controller, the product manager picks up signals from the market and incorporates them into the design of the marketing mix.
- As a strategist and planner, he develops strategies for the insurance product he manages, which he breaks down into sub-plans.
- As a coordinator, the product manager coordinates a large number of internal and external functionaries in terms of content and schedule.
- As a doer, he thinks and acts entrepreneurially and ensures the implementation of product ideas.

The **institutional anchoring** of product management justifies its organizational embedding in the insurance company. In the most extreme form, this is done in a separate department with full decision-making authority. Similarly structured, but of a short-term nature—e.g. only for product development and introduction—is a project organization with a responsible project manager. For the same purpose, but with reduced decision-making competence of the product manager, the project organization can be combined with a steering committee to which the project manager reports regularly. The weakest form of competence assignment is finally a working group without decision-making authority or the formation of a staff position (see also Betschart and Mussak 2021, p. 378).

Product policy can not only be concretized on the basis of its subtasks, but also in terms of its scope, i.e. in relation to the extent of its design leeway. In addition to product design, **product range design** then comes into play. While product design focuses on an financial services product or insurance product, product range design determines in which markets the insurer appears with which combinations of financial service products and insurance products (mix of lines in the insurance coverage product range) and to what extent the provider is thus able to put together so-called financial services product bundles for the customer as a problem solution (Köhne 1998b pp. 2–4).

10.2 Design Parameters of the Insurance Product

In the case of an insurance product, the product design affects the insurance coverage and the accompanying services. The insurance product can be designed formally and materially. In addition, the insurer designs its insurance product range.

10.2.1 Formal Product Design

The **formal design** essentially involves the following

- the search for the appropriate product name or the formation of product brands,
- the design of the insurance application,

- the design of the insurance policy, the insurance conditions and the product information sheet, and
- overall, a clear presentation of the insurance products as possible.

The formal design of the insurance product usually only produces moderate (sales policy) effects. Intangible economic goods have no designable substance, apart from the carrier media, in the case of insurance coverage, the paper or digital processing (Farny 1971, p. 32).

One marketing goal is the profiling of one's own products to give them a clear distinguishing power compared to comparable services of the competition. Apart from the product contents, profiling can mainly be achieved through a convincing **product name.** Accurate factual names may have some advantages over fantasy names or abbreviations (Puschmann 2003, p. 132 f.):

- They are more likely to correspond to the truth and clarity.
- They can make the needs of the target group or the customer more recognizable (e.g., single policies, family protection, mobility protection, etc.).
- Fantasy names require exceptionally high advertising budget to make the name popular and the content understandable to the public.
- Fantasy names and abbreviations do not create product clarity and require additions or clarifying subtitles for better customer information (e.g., "Varioplan—insurance protection with automatic adjustment").

A special aspect in connection with the product name is the formation of **product brands:** Firstly, the aim of branding is primarily to create the impression of high, uniform and constant quality over time and to signal this to the market. One of the few insurers in the German market that consistently uses product brands and links them with target group products is Mannheimer Insurance. For example, it offers a brand program for jewelers under VALORIMA, and a brand program for professional musicians under SINFONIMA (Reuter 1994, pp. 55–61). The quality of an insurance product is inseparably linked to the quality of the producer, i.e., the insurance company. Therefore, company brands are generally more likely to be considered than pure product brands. Secondly, product brands are also suitable for making the long-prevailing tariff abbreviations more tangible and understandable for external business partners (e.g., brokers). For this reason, they are often used in this environment.

In addition to the product name, the previously mentioned product documents also need to be designed. From an economic and legal point of view, the **application document design** is significant, as it forms the decisive basis for the subsequent insurance conclusion, the contractual relationships and the administrative processing, in short, the subsequent policy issuance. It must fulfill the following central functions (Puschmann 2003, p. 133):

- Means of identifying needs
- Means of describing the intended insurance coverage

- Basis for data collection
- Part of the legal relationship.

Despite this multitude of tasks, the application document should be clearly designed and well visualized. In addition to readability, the content order plays a role. Furthermore, it is useful to include data that appear appropriate for later needs-based offers, e.g., marital status, profession, and ownership. In intermediating-related sales, the legally required **consultation protocol** is also a useful source of information—provided it is used sensibly.

The **design of the insurance policy** document (= policy) should be visually appealing and have a document character (similar to a classic, issued share), because insurance policy and associated insurance conditions represent the insurer's promise of performance to the customer. The policy represents the visible equivalent for the customer's premium payments. In practice, this concern is often opposed by technological reality: Many insurers still use self-developed, sometimes old policy systems that leave relatively little room for visually appealing design. At the same time, there are more and more customers (Digital Natives) who do not want a physical document at all, but even prefer digital documents. As far as the legislator accordingly accepts text form instead of paper form and digital signatures instead of manual signatures, new possibilities open up in the design, because it is no longer subject to technical limits.

In the case of comprehensive (all-round) insurance packages with legally independent insurance contracts, the application must already ensure clarity, readability and comprehensibility, and the applicant must be informed in writing and with special emphasis on the legal independence of the contracts applied for, including the insurance conditions provided for them, as well as the respective application binding periods and contract terms (§ 7 para. 1 VVG in conjunction with § 1 para. 1 No. 6 and 7 VVG-InfoV). From a marketing perspective, it should be emphasized that the prevailing practice of combining a uniform application with several insurance policies (bundling) jeopardizes the closed product presentation intended with a comprehensive offer.

Other documents that can be designed include possible insurance endorsements, premium invoices, tariff documents or product brochures. The same applies to these documents as to the applications, insurance policies and conditions, even if they are comparatively of subordinate importance (Puschmann 2003, p. 134 f.; Köhne 1997, pp. 145–148).

Since insurers have apparently not succeeded in presenting the core elements of their offered insurance coverage in relation to the individual customer relationship in a concise and understandable way, despite the use of product brochures, the legislator has obliged them to do so with the so-called **product information sheet.** The Regulation on Information Obligations in Insurance Contracts (VVG-Informationsvpflichtenverord nung—VVG-InfoV) not only prescribes the use as such (§ 4 para. 1 VVG-InfoV). The presentation of the contents and their order in the product information sheet are (uniformly throughout Europe) exactly prescribed (§ 4 para. 2 VVG-InfoV with reference to the EU Implementing Regulation 2017/1469) (Fig. 10.3). This represents a significant intervention in the formal product design. Even more serious is the obligation in life,

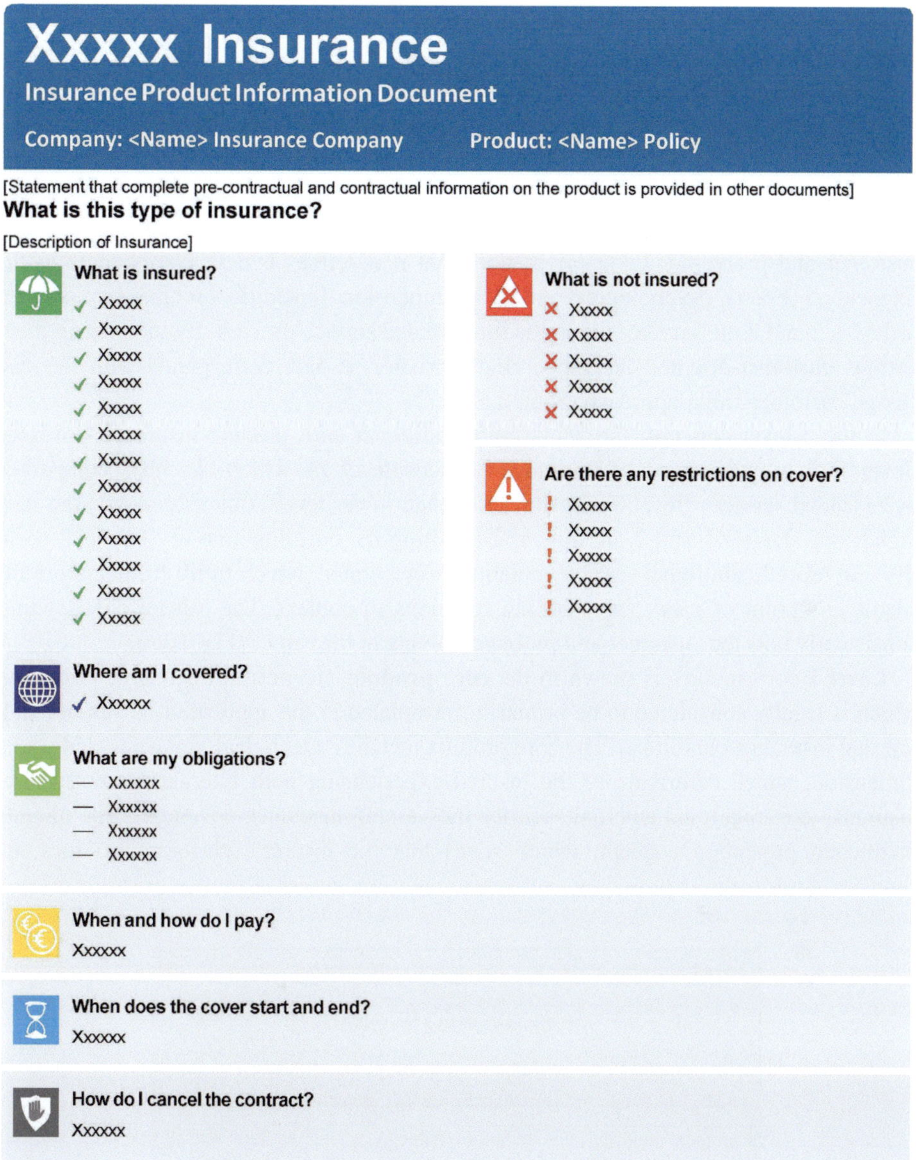

Xxxxx Insurance

Insurance Product Information Document

Company: <Name> Insurance Company   Product: <Name> Policy

[Statement that complete pre-contractual and contractual information on the product is provided in other documents]

What is this type of insurance?

[Description of Insurance]

What is insured?

✓ Xxxxx
✓ Xxxxx
✓ Xxxxx
✓ Xxxxx
✓ Xxxxx
✓ Xxxxx
✓ Xxxxx
✓ Xxxxx
✓ Xxxxx
✓ Xxxxx
✓ Xxxxx
✓ Xxxxx
✓ Xxxxx

What is not insured?

✗ Xxxxx
✗ Xxxxx
✗ Xxxxx
✗ Xxxxx
✗ Xxxxx

Are there any restrictions on cover?

! Xxxxx
! Xxxxx
! Xxxxx
! Xxxxx
! Xxxxx

Where am I covered?

✓ Xxxxxx

What are my obligations?

— Xxxxxx
— Xxxxxx
— Xxxxxx
— Xxxxxx

When and how do I pay?

Xxxxxx

When does the cover start and end?

Xxxxxx

How do I cancel the contract?

Xxxxxx

Fig. 10.3 Prescribed appearance of the product information sheet (EU Implementing Regulation 2017/1469 on the establishment of a standard format for the insurance product information sheet, Appendix)

disability and health insurance to specify acquisition and administration costs separately and in euros (§ 2 and 3 VVG-InfoV); it is to be criticized from the point of view of equal treatment compared to competitors from other sectors.

10.2.2 Material-content Product Design

The **material-content product design** refers to the contents of the insurance benefit, i.e. the insurance coverage promise and the accompanying services. From a marketing perspective, the 3-level concept of *Haller* is particularly suitable for describing the insurance product and its services from the customer's point of view (see also research window on product concepts). It integrates the principle of functional thinking and thus customer and problem-solving orientation, and it describes benefit components in the financial, technical, psychological and social dimension. In addition, it takes into account its levels 2 and 3 the services along the time-related service process. By integrating these various customer-oriented insurance characteristics, it also corresponds with the discussed customer-value-approach (Sect. 8.3.2.1).

In the **3-level concept**, the actual and traditional core product insurance coverage (level 1) is supplemented to insurance services (level 2), which can be accompanied by extended services (level 3). In this case, each lower level is integrated into the next higher one. Levels 1 and 2 are aimed at fulfilling the core function of "financial security"; in level 3, additional service contents are integrated, which fulfill further, from the customer's point of view, value-adding functions in context. The 3-level concept thus consistently puts the customer and problem-solving at the center (Fig. 10.4).

Level 1 corresponds as shown to the **core product**, the **actual insurance coverage**, which is legally considered to be primarily formulated in the application, insurance policy, and insurance conditions. The core product includes a technical, financial, and social dimension, which contribute to the insured experiencing both internal (knowledge of insurance coverage) and external security (possessing insurance coverage). The already mentioned protection concept, which states that the insurer's performance does not

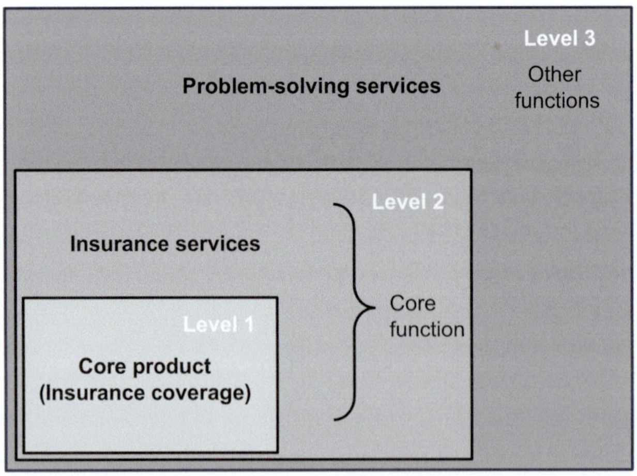

Fig. 10.4 Three levels of the insurance product according to *Haller*. (Based on Haller 1986a, p. 1108)

consist (only) in claims settlement, but in the certainty conveyed during the entire contractual relationship of being able to achieve certain financial goals despite disruptions (see excursus in Sect. 2.2.2), ties into the social dimension. From such a perspective, claims settlement appears as a guarantee service.

Level 2 supplements the core product with the immediate services to the **insurance service:** These **services directly related to the insurance product** include advice, explanation, care, and claims settlement and are thus part of the service process. On this level of consideration, the question arises as to how the product is integrated, which problems it solves, how it is expanded to comprehensive insurance service. This requires the definition of customer needs that are to be or can be fulfilled by the market performance. In the context of such customer and problem orientation, advice is therefore appropriate with regard to the problem-solving process, which ideally includes the clarification of the risk phenomenon, assistance in the security process, and the integration of insurance coverage into the problem solution. The insurance service refers in its levels 1 and 2 to the fulfillment of the **function of financial security.**

Level 3 expands the previous orientation of the insurance service to **additional functions.** This corresponds to the expanded problem-solving thinking from the customer's perspective: Because isolated insurance protection loses importance, while problem solutions and service bundles oriented towards customer functions secure the market position, because various products in combination with new services can offer similar benefits and fulfill the same functions (functional orientation). The expanded services can take place in three dimensions: A horizontal expansion in the first dimension is primarily oriented towards the trend towards connected financial services ("Allfinanz") and strives for the **combination of the protection function with other financial service functions** such as income and expenditure, asset accumulation and saving, investing and diversification (see Sect. 3.2.2). A vertical expansion, on the other hand, is less about financial aspects than about specialization and **function fulfillment in the technical area.** Services of a more technical nature can, for example, be in-depth risk management consulting with services for loss prevention and safety technology (2nd dimension). Finally, in a third dimension (diagonal expansion), **social and psychological functions** can be fulfilled when insurers meet social and emotional concerns of customers as part of so-called (total) care strategies. These include, for example, immaterial old-age services or assistance services of all kinds. Especially against the background of increasing individualization and the (social) deficits associated with it, such care services represent a **profiling opportunity for insurers**, apart from the fact that care services, by influencing customers, combine customer and profit orientation. The services of the third level enable increased product differentiation, a service bundle that corresponds to the customer's ecosystem, as well as additional fields of application for personal advice by the sales force. In general, the activities of customer contact are included in the 3-level concept, i.e., the services and behavior of the sales force are part of the product (Haller 1982, 1986a; Köhne 1997, pp. 129–134; Köhne 2008, pp. 25–27).

Research Window: Product Concepts for Describing the Insurance Product
In the context of the material-content description of insurance products, the so-called product concepts serve as the subject of product-related insurance business administration as theoretical explanatory approaches. With regard to insurance marketing, the most important product concepts are those of *Farny, Müller and Haller*—they are now presented in their basic features.

Insurance Protection Concept by *Farny*
The scientific origin of the **insurance protection concept** developed by Farny lies in the considerations of *Gutenberg,* which explicitly refer to the industrial production conditions (Farny 1965, pp. 67–129). Apart from the strong production-theoretical imprint, the insurance protection concept is at least partially influenced by the (legal) risk-bearing theory and the (risk-theoretical) product concept. *Farny* modified the production-theoretical approach for insurance business administration and developed an explanatory model of insurance production (production theory). This corresponds to the goods-economic insurance business administration, which explain the economy in the company as the production of insurance protection through the use and combination of production factors. Insurance production is thus the transformation process from input factors to the intended output, the insurance product. The latter is an immaterial economic good that is "produced" in principle similarly to material goods. The insurance product is the result of production (Farny 1995, pp. 79–83). With regard to the explanations of the insurance business, he divides it into the risk business, the savings and disinvestment business, and the service business.

In accordance with production-theoretical considerations, the insurance product represents the output of the production process and thus the result of insurance production. The insurance protection concept serves to describe this insurance product (Fig. 10.5). Accordingly, the **service of the insurance company** is an abstract **long-term protection promise,** which is fulfilled by the predominantly monetary insurance benefits after the occurrence of a precisely defined insurance case. Since the protection promise refers to the term of the insurance contract, this approach is based on the concept of a time-related protection promise (Farny 1975, pp. 169–172; Farny 1995, pp. 81–83).

The core of the insurance business is the **risk business**. Here, the potential economic results of a person's actions and thus their goal achievements are interpreted as manifestations of a random variable with the consequence that the actual economic situation deviates favorably or unfavorably from the plans. Unfavorable deviations mean economic loss. The combination of the losses with the probability of their occurrence results in the loss distribution. Assuming that risks arise because the results of human behavior are not deterministic, but distributed probabilistically, the risk business can thus be understood as the transfer of a probability distribution of losses from the policyholder to the insurer in exchange for a premium. Since an

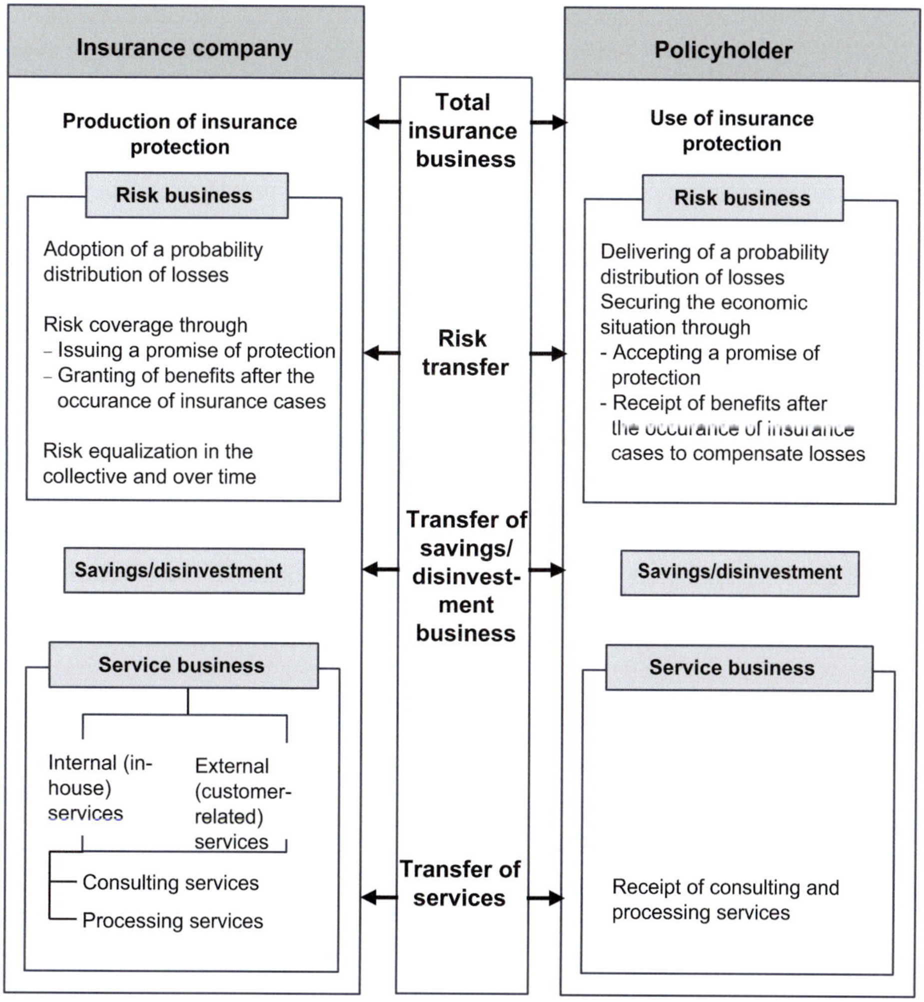

Fig. 10.5 Insurance protection concept according to *Farny*. (Based on Farny 2011, p. 23)

insurer produces a large number of risk transfers, it achieves a risk equlization in the collective and over time. The insurance product thus represents the **assumption of a damage distribution from the insurer's perspective** and a **protection promise from the customer's perspective,** in which the insurer promises the policyholder for a certain period of time to provide the assured (financial) compensation after the occurrence of a defined insurance case (Farny 2011, pp. 24–52).

In contrast, the **savings and disinvestment business** involves the implementation of regular interest-bearing savings and disinvestment processes and is therefore comparable to the active and passive businesses of credit institutions. A savings business exists when the policyholder pays one-time or ongoing savings amounts to the insurer and the insurer commits to interest the resulting savings capital and to repay it to the insured at certain times (or other conditions) in the form of a lump sum (capital) or a pension, i.e., to disinvest. Important examples of savings businesses are the main forms of life insurance, which can be interpreted as a regular savings process with insurance-appropriate coverage of the not yet achieved savings target, accident insurance with premium refund, and health insurance. The term life insurance and health insurance have savings components for another reason: In both cases, the customer is offered almost constant premiums over the contract term, although the expected loss value of the insured persons increases over time. This works because the customer, from a risk-technical point of view, initially pays too much (savings phase) and then too little (disinvestment phase) with his constant premium (Farny 2011, pp. 53–55).

The **service business** complements the abstract risk business with consulting and processing services. These include both internal services to create readiness to perform and customer-related (external) services. The latter include advising the customer on the risk business and the savings/disinvestment business in the factual and temporal context of sales, contract processing, and claims processing, as well as the handling of the risk and savings/disinvestment business in sales or contract conclusion, contract processing (initial, follow-up, and final processing), and claims processing (Farny 2011, pp. 55–57).

The basic statements of the insurance protection concept have received great attention both in the insurance business administration literature and in practice, and other concepts also refer to the insurance protection concept in their statements.

Information concept by *Müller*

The starting point of the **information concept** is the question of what function insurance fulfills or can fulfill in the decisions of the policyholder. Consequently, the theory of decision-making under risk or uncertainty (decision theory) is used, applied to studies of decisions by individual decision-makers: If a decision-maker does not have complete information regarding future outcomes of his decisions, he is in a risk situation. However, after concluding an insurance contract, the decision-maker can predict part of the future outcomes of his decision with certainty, thereby reducing the risk completely or partially, so that he is in a more favorable information situation than before. The insurer cannot reduce the policyholder's information deficit regarding the question of whether and to what extent a decision-relevant loss event will occur in the future. But the insurance company can guarantee that a certain contractually agreed state of a certain object, income, or wealth will continue to exist in the future. Therefore, by concluding an insurance contract, the insurance company provides each buyer with an insurance product in the form of a specific state guarantee for the insured's assets. The asset state guarantee includes the obligation to restore the state of assets through loss payments to the agreed extent in the event of a reduction in assets due to a contractually covered loss event (Müller 1981, p. 165; Müller 1994, p. 364).

From the **perspective of the individual decision-maker,** the insurer's state guarantee can also be understood as a forecast. There is a shift in the forecast risk regarding the future state of the insured object, which can be understood as risk transfer. The guaranteed forecast for the future state of the insured object, the **prognostic information,** represents the **actual benefit of the insurer.** Müller concludes from this that loss payments are not part of the product or the insurance service (Müller 1981, pp. 166–168).

In order to concretize the necessarily abstract characterization of the information-economic insurance product, a general model for describing insurance products has been developed (Müller 1994, pp. 364–371). The basis for this is the consideration that, according to the information concept of insurance, **every insurance product consists of a linguistically represented set of information,** which defines the type, scope, and validity conditions of the asset status guaranteed by the product. The characteristics for describing insurance products are derived from the three essential dimensions of the risk covered or insured by the state guarantee (Table 10.1):

1. The **object risk** arises from the type and quantity of the customer's or policyholder's assets for which the insurance company assumes the state guarantee (insured assets), from the possible changes in the guaranteed asset status (insured state changes), and from their causes (insured perils).
2. The **behavioral risk** is the result of the asymmetric information distribution between the insurance company and the insurance buyer about the object risk. It necessitates behavioral requirements.
3. The **financial risk** results from the amount of the loss payment to be made for the restoration of the guaranteed asset status.

The duration for which the state guarantee applies is deliberately neglected, as it has little significance for the desired objective product description. The type and scope of the state guarantee are determined by the risk dimensions, which is specifically defined for each insurance product by linguistic statements in the respective insurance conditions.

Table 10.1 Product features of the description model by *Müller* (1994, p. 367)

Risk Dimension	Product Feature
Object risk	insured perils insured assets insured state changes
Behavioral risk	insured perils
Financial risk	insured assets

The presented description model has been empirically tested using 13 sets of insurance conditions (GIC) to determine whether the described product features are necessary and sufficient for the description of insurance products. The result of the study allows two conclusions: First, all examined GIC contain partial information on each of the five product features. Second, the study has shown that all sets of conditions contain information that is not required for product specification according to the description model (Bosselmann 1994, pp. 68–71).

3-level concept by *Haller*

The **3-level concept of product policy** by *Haller* finds its conceptual origin a) in systems theory or the systemic risk concept and b) in marketing thinking.

Regarding (a): The systemic thinking is already reflected in *Haller's* **systemic risk concept:** Initially, a holistic or comprehensive thinking requires the reference to larger contexts and thus the relationship of all elements in a total system. This brings with it the necessity to consider the purpose of a system as a whole. Risks accordingly only occur in systems in which certain expectations are to be met; this can happen both through consciously set goals and through unconsciously assumed framework conditions. In addition, risks can only be captured in defined systems. Directly derived from the interdisciplinarity of systemic thinking is the consideration of various subsystems (financial, technical-economic, social, ecological). Finally, risks are a natural consequence of the dynamic world of life and the possible disturbance processes therein, which are rarely associated with a single cause or effect (process orientation). Based on systems theory, *Haller* thus defines risk as "the sum of the possibilities that the expectations of a system will not be fulfilled due to disturbance processes" (Fig. 10.6) (Haller 1986a, p. 11 f.).

The risk concept forms the basis for the 3-level concept of product policy and primarily justifies the core product insurance protection (level 1). This supports the fulfillment of the expectations set by the insured system (e.g., private customer) by

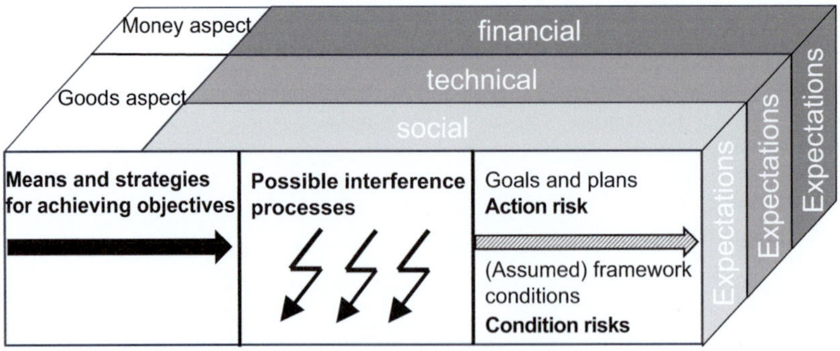

Fig. 10.6 Components of the risk concept according to *Haller*. (Based on Haller and Ackermann 1995, Part 1, p. 22)

providing certainty in social and psychological terms, under legally specified conditions, of having insurance coverage, which gives the customer inner security. In technical-economic terms, the insurance protection is expressed in the form of policy documents and in the actions of the insurer during the duration of the insurance relationship. Financially, it is expressed in precisely regulated financial services and services in return. The core product insurance protection is thus related to two aspects of customer well-being: Having insurance protection expresses the fact that insurance coverage is available. Knowing about the insurance protection expresses the customer's feeling of understanding the insurance product he has purchased and trusting the associated insurance protection. This simultaneously addresses the two dimensions of inner and outer security, because understanding and trust lead to inner security, and having leads to outer security (Haller 1982, p. 397 f.).

Regarding (b): Apart from systems theory, the 3-level concept is strongly influenced by **marketing thinking.** The product concept of *Kotler* and the functional thinking served as a basis in this respect: The distinction into three levels is based on that of *Kotler* (1. core product; 2. formal product; 3. extended product); the differentiation according to functions (insurance service with the function of financial securing versus extended services with other functions) follows the functional thinking (Haller 1986a). Among other reasons, the 3-level concept is used in this textbook and presented in the main part in terms of content and used as the basis for product design.

Benefits of the various product concepts for theory and practice

In a deregulated insurance market, a scientific insurance product design must complement the traditionally entrepreneurial product policy (inside-out) with a customer-oriented perspective (outside-in). The increasing (information) needs of customers thus require a more effect-oriented design of the insurance product. However, the (justified) orientation towards the effects on the customer side introduces a complexity-increasing, subjective component into the game. The very situational (and subjective) benefit of services makes their representation and operationalization in a general, theoretical model difficult. Therefore, it is compelling to use the insights of the various product concepts in parallel and according to their contribution to the promotion of knowledge. Or as *Karten* aptly put it:

> "The attempt to illuminate the insurance product economically cannot be an end in itself in this way, but must be directed towards economic questions. Corresponding to the different perspectives of policyholders and insurers, different aspects of the product must be illuminated for different tasks. The aim can only be to develop useful explanatory patterns—no more and no less—and to check whether they fit and prove to be knowledge-enhancing and fruitful for application." (Karten 1995, p. 57)

With reference to the product concepts presented here, this means for insurance marketing, for example,

- to use *Farny* to describe and explain the risk business as probability-distributed loss compensation;
- to interpret the resulting wealth guarantee effect with *Müller,* but also with all others;
- to use the insights into the service business from *Farny* on the company side and organizationally, and the statements on the process character of the service according to *Haller* on the customer side and marketing-oriented—they basically already describe in the 1980s the modern customer experience management with the consideration of the customer journey (see excursus in Sect. 2.2.4);
- to understand the insurance product from the customer's point of view as a problem solution that already includes emotional aspects (e.g. inner security) in the core product, is supplemented by accompanying services such as information, advice and support to become an insurance service and ultimately only becomes a comprehensive problem solution through the fulfillment of further functions (according to *Haller*)—they basically already describe in the 1980s the benefit creation through the fulfillment of function bundles and thus the basic idea of the ecosystems discussed today (see excursus in Sect. 9.2);
- to use the insights of the information concept according to *Müller* and from *Haller's* matrix representation (Haller and Ackermann 1995, Part 3, pp. 24–28) for a more customer-friendly design of insurance conditions.

The product concepts presented thus provide partly similar, partly complementary and partly contradictory explanatory contributions and thereby contribute to a deeper analytical penetration of insurance products. Their complementary use ensures the consideration of various important perspectives, namely risk-theoretical, production-economic, decision-theoretical, information-economic as well as market- and customer-related aspects. Product concepts are therefore very suitable for the economic analysis of product design in the insurance market.

Further reading for in-depth study:

- Farny 1965, pp. 5–129.
- Farny 1975.
- Farny 2011, pp. 8–11, 21–57.
- Haller 1982.
- Haller 1986b.
- Haller and Ackermann 1995, Part 3, pp. 10–34.
- Köhne 1998c (with many further references).
- Köhne 2008, pp. 10–31.
- Müller 1981.
- Müller 1994. ◀

The core product (level 1) concerns the **insurance coverage** and is described by the insurance protection features 'insurance case' (1), 'loss evaluaton' (2), and 'insurance form' (3) according to quantitative, qualitative, temporal, and spatial criteria (i.e., materially and substantively determined). The defined features determine the insured loss distribution, i.e., the insurance protection from an economic perspective. Its legal fixation is achieved through the interplay of application, consultation protocol, insurance policy, and the associated insurance conditions and clauses (Fig. 10.7) (Farny 1975, pp. 172–177; Farny 2011, p. 395 f.).

Already with the design of the insurance protection, the insurer lays the foundation for the benefits ultimately perceived by the customer. Because the offer of contemporary and above all needs-based products is mainly influenced by the ability of a flexible, individual, and transparent core product design.

The **insurance case** (1) is the cause system responsible for triggering the loss and thus for the insurer's obligation to perform. The manifestation of the insurance case is in terms of its nature; it is often referred to as "insured perils" in the property insurance lines (qualitative dimension). The counting of loss realizations as insurance cases affects the quantitative dimension: An example is the counting of several losses as one insurance case. The insurance case is also spatially defined, as the fixed location for immovable items or as a region for movable risks. The temporal dimension refers e.g. to extended insurance cases (business interruption and health insurance) or to long-term causal

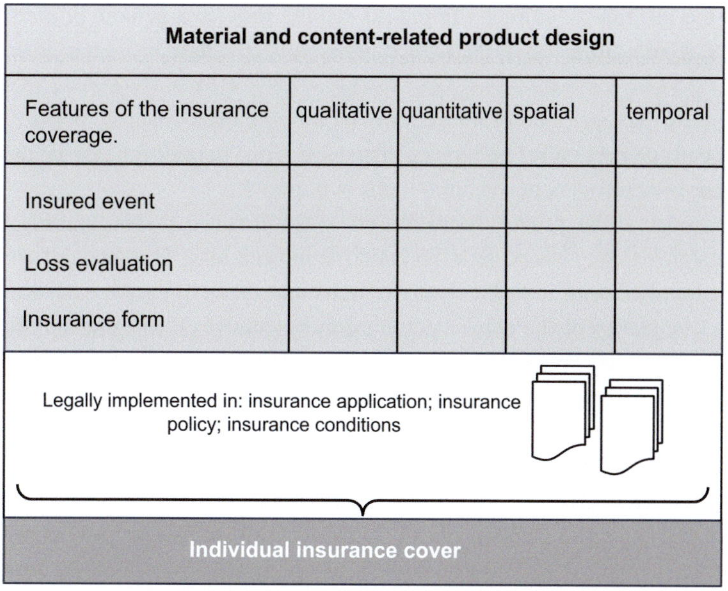

Fig. 10.7 Design features of individual insurance coverage. (Köhne 1997, p. 149)

chains (liability insurance). The contractual agreements on the insurance case finally define the facts, in the presence of which the realization of the risk is assumed (Farny 2011, pp. 396–398).

In connection with the determination of the insurance case, special attention must be paid to the **coverage principle.** Actual insurance coverage is given when the question of insurance protection (being insured) is affirmed with regard to a risk. Insurance contracts can be distinguished according to whether the coverage is defined according to the principle of universality or the specialty of perils. The distinction is immediately clear, as every insurance contract, in addition to the insured legal good or the loss potential, must also specify the type or cause of loss occurrence. Either fundamentally—i.e., unless expressly excluded—any impairment is covered regardless of the cause (universality of perils), or only the consequences of individually listed causes or damage situations are covered (specialty of perils).

Over time, a variety of coverage types have developed in practice between the two poles of specialty and universality, which have led to today's branch coverages or occur in them (Köhne 1997, pp. 151–160).

A first, widely used type of coverage is the Named-Perils-**Coverage**. This means in relation to insurance coverage that the insured perils are individually named and defined in the insurance policy or in the associated insurance conditions. The consequences of all causes or damage situations named in the contract are insured (principle of specialty).

▶ **Named-Perils-Coverage:** Here, the insured perils are individually named and defined in the insurance contract. Only if an insured loss (to a person, property or assets also named) results from one of the named perils, it is covered.

Named-Perils-Coverages therefore require clearly defined insured perils. Therefore, exclusions can (theoretically) be largely dispensed with. In addition, the declaration of a large number of heterogeneous insured items is required.

The advantage is the **precise formulation of the insured perils** (and in practice the exclusion catalog that exists despite this) and the insured loss. The scope of coverage can be clearly described with individual single limits and deductibles for each named perils. In addition, the clarity of the named perils promotes statistical insights and thus the calculation of premiums. Specialized insurance knowledge is preserved. Finally, a certain legal certainty is given, as Named-Perils conditions have established and developed over time in case law.

Disadvantages of the Named-Perils-Coverage mainly result from the customer's point of view or the perspective of private customers: If the individual modules of perils are not coordinated or if the customer is not well advised, coverage gaps as well as coverage overlaps can occur. Private customers are generally overwhelmed to understand the differentiated and quite complex relationships between named perils and insured losses. From their point of view, the many parallel and legally convoluted conditions (theoretically for each named peril) are hard to digest and mostly incomprehensible. This often results in indifference or mistrust towards the insurers.

Examples of Named-Perils-Coverage components in today's insurance branches can be found in most buildings and especially home contents insurance (listing and definition of insured perils), in partially comprehensive motor vehicle insurance (regarding theft and damage) or in accident insurance (definition of accident).

The alternative approach is the **All-Risks-Coverage** (All-Perils-Coverage): To put it simply, an All-Risks-Coverage means that **everything is covered** that is **not expressly excluded.** Therefore, an exclusion catalog—a list of excluded perils—is a constitutive feature of every All-Risks-Coverage. For underwriting reasons, the exclusion catalog is a necessary and undisputed condition for every serious All-Risks-Coverage. However, the conditions of directness, suddenness, and external occurrence do not necessarily have to be met; it is ultimately up to the insurer how far he wants to extend the coverage.

▶ **All-Risks-Coverage:** It basically covers all perils that [directly,] unexpectedly [and suddenly] [from outside] affect the insured items [persons, assets] and result in their destruction, damage or loss, unless they are expressly excluded. ([ ] = dispositive additions)

An All-Risks-Coverage therefore requires a clear definition of perils tested by case law and practice, as well as clearly defined exclusions—both for insured items (possibly also persons and financial loss) at an insurance location that is clearly recorded in a directory. The insurer needs a relatively homogeneous risk inventory of a larger number, which allows a statistical evaluation of the loss from the various covered perils and an assignment to the insurance sums for a needs-based calculation of premiums. Since the area of insured perils is not limited in the usual way in an All-Risks-Coverage, it is referred to as All-Perils-Coverages or the already mentioned principle of universality or totality of the covered perils.

The advantages of all-perils coverage can be described from the perspective of the private customer and from the insurer's perspective. From the private customer's perspective, gaps and double coverage can be avoided; this is accompanied by an increase in the feeling of security. There is also the **possibility of insuring unnamed (unless explicitly excluded) and unknown perils.** In contrast to Named-Perils-Coverage, the insurer has the burden of proof if he wants to dispute his obligation to perform. The insured only has to provide evidence of loss **(reversal of the burden of proof).** Furthermore, it is possible to simplify and reduce the conditions (improvement of transparency). This results in—with respect to insured items, persons and assets—uniform obligations of the customer, uniform replacement value regulations and the use of a common declaration. Depending on the design, the demarcation problems between the individual insurance lines or insured perils are reduced in the event of a claim. From the insurer's perspective, the range of offers can be completed in the sense of meeting customer needs, product differentiation can be achieved and additional premium income can be generated.

From the private customer's perspective, it may be perceived as a disadvantage that All-Risks-Coverage, like all standardized insurance products, includes perils that the policyholder would not have insured as non-existential after a more detailed analysis (over-insurance). All-Risks-Coverage can be expensive, especially if there are no deductibles. This is partly due to the inclusion of additional perils. Furthermore, policyholders may be misled by the misleading term All-Risk-Coverage. For the insurer, the initial disadvantage is the lack of statistical foundations. In addition, there may be uncertainties regarding the wording, especially with regard to definitions of exclusion facts. The risk of new, barely known and assessable perils lies with the insurer. Further introduction risks are the development of demand, contributions and especially jurisprudence (in connection with the reversal of the burden of proof). An exhaustive exclusion catalog is not very sales- and customer-friendly; a catalog that lists the covered perils appears much more sales-friendly.

Examples of All-Risks-Coverage approaches in today's branch products are transport insurance, life insurance, health insurance and pet insurance. In both life and health insurance, coverage is guaranteed regardless of the risk. In travel luggage insurance, the named-perils principle and the all-risks principle appear side by side in the same contract: The all-risks principle applies during the actual journey in public transport, the named-perils principle, however, for the own vehicle and the stay at the holiday destination.

Widely spread are the **conventional branch coverages,** which assign certain risks to an insurance branch and which have arisen with the historical development of the risks. Therefore, insurance companies are often still predominantly organized according to branches or certain risk categories (fire insurance, business interruption insurance, accident insurance). The formation of insurance branch serves the purpose of being able to clearly define the insured risks and the insurance coverage offered for them, both conceptually and in reality (Farny 2011, p. 371).

▶ **Insurance branch** includes those insurances and types of insurance that offer insurance coverage against the same or similar risks (Koch 1988, p. 1251).

With branch coverages, insurance protection manifestations become distinguishable from each other, and the prerequisite for calculating the risk premium is created. Administratively, the insurance portfolios are also grouped together by sector and usually managed separately from each other. In addition, the approval for business operations by BaFin is branch-oriented. For these reasons, most insurance companies have a pronounced branch orientation.

The advantages of branch coverages are their economic and legal appropriateness with regard to the following aspects:

- Legal certainty through legal opinions on the branch-related conditions,
- Calculation certainty due to the branch-related structure of the existing calculation bases and corresponding statistics,
- Branch-related training status of insurance employees and a technical infrastructure oriented towards this,
- At least a certain degree of familiarity and an associated imagination among policyholders with regard to the conventional branch products.

However, branch coverages also have some disadvantages. Each branch has its own general insurance conditions (GIC) as the basis for the rights and obligations of the contracting parties. They serve to define as clearly as possible the risk assumed by the insurer and thus as the basis for calculation. This simultaneously reduces transparency for the policyholder. This **age-old dilemma between legal clarity and practical ambiguity and difficulty to understand** (Farny 1995, p. 100) is rather increased than reduced by numerous new consumer protection regulations. Another disadvantageous consequence for the private customer is the lack of ability to evaluate two variants, the first of which is based on the named-perils principle, the second on the all-risks principle. An All-Risks coverage can be so limited by exclusions that in the end there is less insurance coverage than with a coverage that names a large number of insured perils without many exclusions. And due to the mixing of different coverage principles and even different insurance forms—e.g. in health insurance—even the classic sector products are hardly comprehensible for the private customer, let alone comparable. This does not promote his inner security.

For the insurance company, the tradition of branches is also not only associated with advantages: It goes hand in hand with relatively high administrative costs of specialization and the sector-related (often not integrated) IT infrastructure. Moreover, from a marketing perspective, it represents an obstacle on the way to the customer when customer-oriented services are to be designed in a branch-neutral way.

The second design feature of insurance coverage to be specified in terms of qualitative, quantitative, temporal and spatial aspects, in addition to the insurance case, is the **loss evaluation** (2) or the insured loss.

The provisions on loss evaluation are primarily **valuation rules in the form of value conventions.** Qualitatively, they include insured items, persons and other facts. Often, the types of damage covered by the insurance are also defined: In liability insurance, these are, for example, personal, material and pure financial losses. Quantitative characteristics of the damage are mainly determined by the valuation rules. To evaluate the insured loss, the insurable value is used in indemnity insurance. Where this is impossible or inappropriate, needs determined as subjective decision values are insured; this is done in sum insurance (especially life insurance) using the insurance sum. Further differentiations here are the replacement cost value or actual cash value of items, cost- or benefit-related values or the market value as well as minimum and/or maximum value. The spatial and temporal dimension of losses also plays a role: In the case of losses abroad, the applicable legal system and currency issues have to be regulated, in the case of pension payment in personal and liability insurance, the realization time of the 'damages' has to be taken into account (Farny 2011, p. 398).

Excursus on types of value for determining the insurable value

Replacement cost value: The amount that needs to be spent to produce or procure a similar new item (including procurement costs).

Actual cash value: New value, minus depreciation according to the condition of the item. The depreciation can result from wear and tear or possibly from the obsolescence of the items (in the case of changing fashion trends or due to technological progress).

"Gemeiner Wert": Disposal value (market value), i.e. without taking into account a personal sentimental value (affection value). For example, buildings destined for demolition, as well as home contents goods or business equipment that are no longer usable, are insured at common value.

Residual value: Value of the remaining parts of insured items after the insurance case, if they are not completely destroyed, but technically a total loss is present (e.g. due to irreparability, unworthiness of repair). The residual value is deducted from the insurance benefit.

The third and last design feature of insurance coverage to be specified in terms of qualitative, quantitative, temporal and spatial aspects is the determination of the **insured benefit** (Farny 2011, pp. 399–403).

Qualitatively, spatially, and temporally, formalities are regulated that do not require further elaboration here. However, an important design feature is the establishment of transformation rules (= **compensation rules**), with the help of which the actual amount of the (insured) loss is inferred to the amount of the granted insurance benefits (= compensation). The transformation rules are usually referred to as **insurance forms**, the two basic versions of which are sum insurance and indemnity insurance (Table 10.2).

The **sum insurance** is characterized by the fact that insurance benefits are agreed as a fixed amount of money, which is to be paid after the occurrence of the insurance case without proof of a specific loss amount (coverage of abstract needs). The amount of the benefit is independent of any loss and is already fixed in advance in the contract at the amount of the insurance sum. The staggered insurance is a subcase of the sum insurance.

Table 10.2 Insurance forms as a design feature of insurance coverage. (Based on Köhne 1997, p. 162)

	Abstract Compensation	Concrete Compensation	
Insurance Form	Sum snsurance	Full Value Insurance	First Risk Insurance
Example branches	Life insurance	Home contents insurance (HCI)	Liability insurance
Examples—product components	Daily Hospital Allowance Insurance	Fire as an insured risk in the HIC	Motor vehicle third-party liability
Insured object	Person	Object	Person/object

In it, different, but predetermined insurance benefits are due for differently defined insurance cases; this is intended to allow a better adaptation to the damage that has occurred (e.g., agreed value in accident insurance).

The indemnity insurance is characterized by the fact that the insurance benefit always depends on the amount of the loss incurred (coverage of conrete needs). In this context, we speak of compensation, which is usually limited upwards by the amount of loss and acts like a prohibition of enrichment. This was previously explicitly named in the law (§ 55 VVG older version), today it is regulated and interpreted in the context of § 74 VVG regarding over-insurance. According to the prevailing opinion, compensation for the replacement cost value of used items is not considered enrichment or over-insurance in this sense. Both losses and insurance benefits are measured by a suitable value convention that precedes the application of the insurance form. The **subtypes** of indemnity insurance are:

- Pure, **unlimited interest insurance** (e.g., unlimited property losses in liability insurance)
- **First risk insurance** (e.g., financial losses limited to the sum insured in liability insurance)
- **Full value insurance** (e.g., home contents insurance and other property insurances)
- **Fractional insurance** (e.g., burglary/theft, water damage, and storm in warehouses of commercial and trade businesses)
- **Cut-off date insurance** (similar to fractional insurance, but with a comparatively lower risk of underinsurance).

Within the framework of transformation rules, these insurance forms can be provided with **deductibles**. Their purpose is to avoid the uneconomical regulation of minor losses (money exchange transactions) below the deductible limit. For the policyholder, deductibles are associated with lower premiums. Moreover, from the customer's point of view, deductibles are sensible for rational considerations because the coverage of risks below the deductible limit does not offer him any additional benefit in relation to the premium to be paid. From the insurer's perspective, in addition to avoiding uneconomical small transactions, another goal of the deductible is to increase the customer's interest in loss prevention, thus reducing the moral risk.

There are various **types of** deductibles**:**

1. The integral deductible only excludes minor losses by having the insurer bear every damage in full above the deductible limit. However, it is practically not used except in transport insurance. It has the disadvantage that there can be disagreements between the contracting parties in the case of losses near the deductible limit.
2. The classic deductible, on the other hand, deducts the amount of the deductible from each loss. Here, one can distinguish the **absolute deductible** , which is a deductible that always has the same amount in absolute terms (e.g., € 300 in partially comprehensive motor vehicle insurance), from the relative deductible (**percentage**

deductible), which is a percentage deductible that is always the same in relative terms (e.g., 50% of dental treatment costs in cost-of-illness insurance). Closely related to the classic deductible and having the same effect is the success-independent premium refund in the case of no losses (bonus), which usually has a more favorable psychological effect on the demander.

3. The **waiting period deductible** involves the policyholder in every loss that occurs within a fixed period after the conclusion of the contract—depending on the contractual agreement, completely or with a decreasing share over time. An example of a time participation of the policyholder is the so-called waiting period in legal expenses and also in health insurance.

In addition to deductibles, the various insurance forms can be provided with **limits** (= liability limitations or liability limits). This is done, for example, in the case of cumulative risks.

The previous explanations have dealt with design aspects of the core product (level 1). However, as mentioned, the core product is supplemented by immediate services related to the insurance coverage such as information, advice, explanation, conclusion, support during the contract term, and claims processing in the event of a claim. The connection is expressed in the fact that the core product and accompanying processing services together embody the classic **core insurance service of the insurer (level 2)**, which fulfills the main function of the insured's financial protection (see excursion on functional thinking in Sect. 2.2.4).

In the context of the **total service bundle of the insurer (level 3),** the perspective is expanded from isolated insurance coverage to holistic problem solutions that fulfill further functions in addition to financial protection. Then, product design also includes associated financial services ("Allfinanz"), services of a more technical nature, as well as care services of an immaterial nature or assistance services of all kinds (function of remedying the damage or emergency situation).

Identifying customer needs proves to be difficult in the private customer sector: The service process is usually initiated in the social field and over time is fed and accompanied by social references, especially to the personal intermediary—in the event of a loss, the importance of a personal connection to the trusted intermediary or a helpful claims adjuster is psychologically even higher. **Customers thus perceive the overall performance**—in contrast to the providers—primarily **through their integration into the individual life situation** (levels 2 and 3 of the insurance product), i.e., in their ecosystem**,** only then do the cognitive (= knowledge-based, knowledge-related) components of the consultation to be recorded follow, and finally the core product (level 1 of the insurance product). In addition, the customer's environment (individual, societal or community-related, and national-cultural) influences his perception. Against this background, customers evaluate each component—consciously and unconsciously—with the result of a hardly predictable overall assessment (see in detail Sect. 4.3). In this respect, personal contact and personal communication in the course of the services of levels 2 and 3 play a significant role in product perception by customers.

The development of problem-solving capacities is closely related to an insurer's range of products. Therefore, considerations in connection with level 3 inevitably lead to product range policy.

10.2.3 Product Range Design

The **product range design** of the insurer includes the systematic compilation of an attractive program of insurance, investment and other service products, which is determined depending on the positioning aimed for by the insurer in the strategic business fields and the target groups addressed therein (Sect. 8.2.3).

The **insurance product range** is expressed in the number and type of insurance branches and product variants offered, ranging from high specialization (= one insurance branch, one product variant) to high generalization (= all insurance branches, all (usual) product variants). It also needs to be designed in terms of its depth and breadth: The **range depth** describes the number of product variants or types of insurance to be offered within a product line or insurance branch. On the other hand, **range breadth** refers to the fact of how many different product lines or insurance branches are operated.

The **ideal-typical cases** of insurance product ranges are as follows (Farny 2011, p. 368 f.):

1. Narrow and shallow range: An insurer offers only one insurance branch with few variants, e.g., a foreign health insurer that only offers supplementary health insurance in Germany, or an insurer specialized in travel health insurance that offers this worldwide.
2. Narrow and deep range: An insurer offers only one insurance branch with many product variants, e.g., a specialized health insurer that offers health insurance in all usual variants.
3. Broad and shallow range: An insurer (insurance group) offers many insurance branches, each individual insurance branch, however, only in one or a few variants, e.g., an insurer focused on private customer business that offers only a few, but competitive product variants in the operated insurance branches.
4. Broad and deep range: An insurer (insurance group) offers many insurance branches in many variants.

In the **investment product range,** the insurer determines the number and types of investment products (funds, home savings contracts, mortgage loans, credits etc.) offered on the market and decides to what extent it creates an "Allfinanz" product range. This is needed if it wants to supplement insurance products with extended services in the financial dimension (according to level 3) to problem solutions.

The same applies to the other **service product range.** This is also a logical consequence of the strategically planned product design in terms of problem solutions. In the private customer sector, such a range includes, for example, consulting services for risk management, investment and wealth accumulation, survivor's provision or loss prevention, healthcare services (diagnosis, therapy, rehab, cures), funeral services as well as all kinds of assistance services (emergency and support services) (see Chap. 12).

However, it should be noted that product range policy cannot be carried out independently of supervisory law. Because the separation of branches according to § 8 para. 4 VAG and the prohibition of non-insurance business according to § 15 VAG must be taken into account in product and range design.

10.3 Legal Framework Conditions of Product Policy

The extensive deregulation of the conditions and tariff design in 1994 created regulatory framework conditions for free product and tariff design in Germany after many decades of regulation. This allowed product policy as a marketing tool an entrepreneurial freedom that had never been known before. However, the European and German development in this millennium is characterized by consumer-oriented legislation and jurisprudence. In this respect, one can observe a re-regulation—also in the area of product policy.

Most of the current **regulatory frameworks** (see Sect. 3.4.2 in detail) only partially influence product policy: The requirement to separate branches and the prohibition of non-insurance business have always had to be taken into account. However, both can be well managed through group structures. More serious is the involvement of a responsible actuary in life, substitute health, and accident insurance. The responsible actuary must ensure the proper calculation of premiums and mathematical provisions, as well as verify the ongoing fulfilment of obligations. He also has to propose to the board an appropriate profit participation for the policyholders and justify this (see §§ 31, 141 para. 5, 156 para. 2 VAG). All in all, the actuary thus serves to secure price-performance ratios in certain long-term insurance businesses and strongly influences product and price design in these insurance branches. Also, capital investments—insofar as they are related to capital investments in the insurer's security assets—cannot be made arbitrarily, but must be guided by VAG regulations (§§ 125–131, 215 VAG; for smaller insurers, the Investment Ordinance also applies).

However, the solvency system anchored in the VAG **(Solvency II)** with its required risk-based determination of solvency capital has far-reaching effects on product design: On the one hand, entering new product lines may allow the exploitation of diversification effects and thus reduce capital requirements. On the other hand, any risks contained in existing and newly developed insurance products require solvency capital. In life insurance, therefore, existing products, some of which are equipped with capital-intensive options (e.g., increase in death benefit, cancellation, premium exemption, premium dynamics, capital choice right, etc.) and guarantees (e.g., minimum interest rate, surplus participation, annuity factor), have either been "streamlined" or priced risk-adequately.

In addition, new business at most insurers has been focused on unit-linked, guarantee-free life insurance, and some old portfolios with guarantee products have been partially or completely outsourced to run-off companies. Also in non-life insurance, the necessary solvency capital (target capital) under Solvency II is calculated differently: Relevant are not only expected loss values, but also volatility, susceptibility to major losses, cumulative loss intensities and correlations in the loss area, as well as investment risk. Consequently, new products with risk exclusions, extended deductibles and/or risk-adjusted premiums have also emerged here.

Furthermore, as a result of the EU Directive on Insurance Distribution (IDD) of 2016, the so-called **product approval process** (Product Oversight Governance, or POG for short) has also been implemented in German law (see also Sect. 13.5.1). According to § 23 para. 1a VAG, insurers must maintain, operate and regularly review a product approval process for the internal release for distribution of each individual insurance product or any significant change to existing insurance products. This means that for each insurance product, before it is distributed to customers, a specific target market must be defined and all relevant risks for the specific target market must be assessed. The intended distribution strategy must then correspond to the specific target market. This must be ensured within the framework of appropriate business organization. Although these regulations do not bring with them any direct content-related requirements, they do prescribe the product development process very precisely. It is clear that this involves further documentation and testing effort; however, it is unclear whether the products will materially change in terms of better fit for customers.

The design of insurance coverage is significantly influenced by **regulations of the VVG,** whose general part applies to all types of insurance (Part 1, Chap. 1) and for all branches of indemnity insurance (Part 1, Chap. 2) and which also contains special regulations for individual insurance branches (Part 2) in the specific part. Some regulations relevant to product design, which were added with the VVG reform of 2008 to the numerous regulations already existing before, are as follows (see in detail Sect. 3.4.2):

- Information, consultation and documentation obligations towards the customer
- Abolition of the policy model and instead admissibility of the application model
- Special information and consultation regulations for distance selling
- Limitation of the permissible contract terms in property & casualty/accident insurance to a maximum of three years
- Abandonment of the all-or-nothing principle
- Elimination of the principle of indivisibility of the premium
- More transparency regarding the procedure, the ongoing amount and deviations from the initial model calculations for the surrender value and the policyholder's profit participation in life insurance
- Expansion of profit participation beyond surrender value and surplus participation in life insurance from the ongoing/annual surpluses and the final surpluses to the valuation reserves

- Requirement of an even distribution and corresponding allocation of closing and distribution costs at least over the first five contract years and a guaranteed minimum surrender value
- Additional information imposed on the policyholder by the Regulation on Information Obligations for Insurance Contracts (VVG-InfoV), such as cost disclosure, structure and contents of the product information sheet.

Product design must also not violate the prohibition of discrimination according to the **AGG.**

Some branches of insurance are also confronted with **special laws** that further specify the framework conditions for product design through additional regulations. For example, the minimum insurance coverage for motor vehicle third-party liability insurance is legally determined (§ 4 PflVG). The laws in the area of old-age provision with consequences for life insurance go much further. There, the AltEinkG and the AVmG provide binding rules, among other things, for the design of tax-advantaged products and for the tax effects at the time of premium payment and benefit payout. The LVRG introduced in 2014, among other things, the differentiated participation of departing policyholders in the valuation reserves, the higher participation of policyholders in the risk surpluses, the introduction of the effective cost disclosure and the reduction of the maximum Zillmer rate to 25 per mille (with effects on the amount of the surrender values).

The legal framework conditions of product design are also significantly specified by the **jurisprudence.** This applies almost continuously to the interpretation of the mentioned legal regulations and the contract-related insurance conditions. Every now and then there are supreme court rulings with very far-reaching effects on product design. For example, the BGH has repeatedly called on life insurers to formulate their terms and conditions and the explanations of the surrender value more understandably for customers.

In one regulatory area—**commercial legal expenses**—it is the other way around: Here it even happens that the non-regulation is disadvantageous for product design or innovation promotion. Because for product design and especially for product innovation, the lack of exclusive rights is a hindering factor: Insurance products are not protected by patent, copyright or competition law and are therefore easy to imitate. Their production method and the necessary know-how even support this fact. At most, trademark law offers limited protection, which, however, only refers to the designation. Thus, sustainable competitive advantages through the creation of new insurance coverages are hardly possible (Nordemann 1995, pp. 129–137; Gal 2019, pp. 102–107).

10.4 Product Innovations and Product Modifications

From a business perspective, innovations (= renewals) arise in the market or through internally introduced qualitative changes to existing thought content and behaviors. Innovations can be distinguished according to the aspects of the innovation object, the novelty of the innovation, and the degree of innovation (Schröder 2008, p. 311 f.).

The **innovation object** (= subject of the innovation) describes what the renewal refers to. Thus, the opening up of new procurement and sales markets is referred to as market innovation. Process innovations describe improved production methods or new technical processes that improve operational processes and thus the production of goods. Finally, the term product innovation stands for the development, production, and enforcement of new products and product qualities. While product innovations result in an improvement in effectiveness (= better achievement of risk coverage), process innovations tend to lead to efficiency gains (= cheaper risk coverage). Often, and especially with services, the introduction of a product innovation is associated with a process innovation. Both can hardly be separated from each other. Thus, in the insurance industry, a new product also results in a change in process characteristics, because the insurance service is provided in a service process (Schütze 1972, pp. 27–29; Menhart 2003, pp. 59, 79).

The **criterion of novelty** as another aspect of an innovation indicates what the actual renewal consists of. This raises the question, on the one hand, for whom a renewal exists (subjective view), and on the other hand, what is new about the service (content view). In the subjective view, company novelties can be distinguished from market novelties. A company novelty exists when an insurance company brings a product to the market that was not included in its previous product portfolio. From an (external) market perspective, this insurance product is not necessarily innovative if it has already been available on the market. The market novelty and thus the relevant market of a new service is, however, more suitable as a criterion of novelty. According to the content view, a novel purpose-means balance between supply and demand should be sought, i.e., either existing purposes can be fulfilled with new means or new purposes with existing means or both together. The criterion of the novelty of an innovation must therefore be oriented towards the customer(-benefit) and lead to a higher or different kind of satisfaction of needs (Köhne 1998b, p. 4; Müller-Reichart 2002, p. 17 f.).

Finally, product-specific product innovations can be distinguished from product modifications according to the **degree of novelty** of the innovation. Product innovations are based on new benefit components. This means, in insurance terms, the generation of a new insurance line or sub-line or at least fundamental changes to the existing insurance coverage. A customer-oriented innovation also exists when a function expected by the customer, such as financial security in the event of an insurance claim, can be solved better or more satisfactorily than before (process innovation), e.g., through the integration of financial derivatives, or when a novel, meaningful function from the customer's perspective can be performed, which meaningfully complements the financial risk provision as a core function (product innovation), e.g., technical risk provision or care services in the event of a claim as services supplementing the core product. In contrast, mere changes or adaptations of existing things are product modifications (Schütze 1972, pp. 28 f.; Köhne 2008, pp. 3 f.).

▶ **Product innovation** of an insurance product incl. its processual characteristics in the service process (levels 1 to 3) exists when it has not yet been offered on the relevant market with regard to the satisfaction of the need for financial risk provision or other needs related to it in a function-oriented context and is therefore a market novelty. A product innovation at level 1 thus requires a content renewal of the insured area or the core product.

▶ **Product modification** refers to (all other) changes to existing insurance products that only represent adjustments, additions, and flexibilizations of the insured area resp. the core product and also do not fulfill any new functions compared to the original product.

▶ **Product renewal** can occur in the form of a product innovation or a product modification.

With regard to the core product and the insured area, this can be concretized as follows (Vielreicher 1995, pp. 10–16):

Product innovations (without market predecessors) result from

(Köhne 2008, p. 5)

1. the **creation of an entirely new insured area,** i.e., new insured persons, objects, or interests (e.g., nuclear insurance), new insured risks (e.g., natural hazard insurance, dread disease insurance, cyber insurance against hacker attacks) as well as new insured loss (e.g., IT insurance against data loss due to defective data storage devices).
2. from the fact that at least one **element** of the insured risks, the insured persons, objects, or interests, and the insured loss is extracted from an existing insured area and **offered in a new context** as an independent product on the market (e.g., the managers in D&O insurance).

Product modifications (with market predecessors), on the other hand, are changes in the scope of an existing insured area by adding, reducing, or varying elements of the insured persons, objects, or interests and/or the insured risks and/or the insured damages. This includes both changes in the insured area, such as changes in the coverage scope (e.g., key loss insurance or increase in the insurance sum for financial losses in liability insurance), and changes in the tariff system through tariff innovations as well as the offer of deductibles.

Product modifications also include **both variations and differentiations of the coverage scope** of an insurance product.

▶ **Product variation** is the further development of individual benefit components to increase attractiveness for the policyholder, e.g., by introducing secondary risks into standard products such as marten bites in partially comprehensive motor vehicle insurance.

▶ **Product differentiation** is the flexibilization of existing coverage, e.g., in target group marketing, when existing coverage concepts are to be aligned with new customer target groups or new regional markets.
(Köhne 2008, p. 4 f.)

The role of product renewals in the insurance industry is generally discussed from the perspective of the insurance company. However, it is also determined from the perspective of intermediaries and insurance customers (Farny 1995, p. 96; on this and the following Köhne and Kopp 2007, pp. 233–238).

From a **company perspective**, product renewals are first to be assessed in terms of their contribution to achieving the formal company goals (profit, sales, costs) (Sect. 7.1):

In terms of sales striving, product innovations in the form of customer-oriented problem solutions can reduce the cancellation probability and increase the probability of repeat purchases. Product modifications at least support new business (growth target). In this respect, both can cause an increase in sales in terms of quantity. The price component of the sales target is mainly influenced by product innovations, as they allow the extraction of monopoly profits from the time of market introduction.

The costs associated with the development and introduction of product innovations and modifications result once from increasing operating costs as a result of the product development work carried out, necessary marketing, and the adaptation of existing systems. However, modern, modular product components—especially in modifications—could provide a remedy, as they support product innovations through their flexibility and at the same time reduce product development and IT costs due to standardization. In addition to operating costs, particularly in the case of product innovations, higher security capital costs are usually incurred because the underwriting risk is higher due to less experience in estimating the damage distribution (Solvency II).

The profit goal is therefore only supported if new products really provide customer benefits or are associated with lower administrative costs.

On the other hand, new needs-based products naturally directly serve the goal of insurance companies of meeting needs. However, this goal must not be at the expense of the profit or value creation goal. But this danger exists with product innovations, as generally low monopoly profits of product innovators (so-called first movers) due to lack of exclusive rights are opposed by high entrepreneurial risks of an acturial nature and lack of customer interest.

The security objective as an important secondary condition for the company goals of profit or coverage of needs also plays a role in product renewals: On the one hand, high security as a quality feature influences the assessment of product quality by customers, specifically in the form of rating results. On the other hand, insurers are naturally more risk-averse and thus less innovation-friendly due to the high (legally induced) security requirement.

In addition to the stated corporate goals, product renewals promote customer-related psychological goals such as the company image. Needs-based products contribute to an image enhancement of the innovating companies, which is perceived by both the policyholder and the competition and not only affects the new product, but also the existing product program. This also supports economic goals, as a positive company image influences the attitude of customers and makes it easier for the intermediary to approach (potential) customers. Finally, product innovations in particular promote the corporate culture—they demand and promote flexibility among employees.

▶ **Note** From a company's perspective, product renewals aim to improve the company's competitive situation by supporting the overarching, formal company goals.

For **intermediaries,** product renewals have a different meaning, as brokers have their own perspective on it. Their guiding interest is characterized by achieving income, which in turn is strongly linked to sales and commission. Furthermore, they try to keep the costs associated with achieving income goals as low as possible. This primarily includes optimizing the time spent on preparing and following up on customer visits and on their own qualification, as well as reducing administrative costs (Lach 1995, p. 115, 140–142).

From a intermediary's perspective, product innovations are attractive when they are easy to sell because customer demand is very high (and competition offers are lacking), and when the associated monopoly profits lead to particularly high commissions. In this case, the additional costs associated with product innovations and additional qualification efforts are overcompensated.

Product modifications are also attractive for intermediaries, as they require comparatively less training effort and offer the intermediary arguments for customer visits from a marketing perspective. But product modifications generally do not allow for large premium increases and therefore no commission concessions to the intermediaries. And it should be noted that with an increasing number of product variants due to frequent product modifications, the costs of complexity increase: Intermediaries then have to know and distinguish more and more product and tariff variants and manage them. The same applies to the normally desired marketing support and the associated sales competitions: If several competitions accompany various product modifications during their market introduction or later sales-increasing measures within one business year, this triggers counterproductive effects.

Intermediaries, in turn, play an important role in product renewals: They have direct customer contact and regularly find out to what extent the offered insurance products meet customer needs. They are therefore—and in reality will be—intensively involved in product development (Lach 1995, pp. 232–236).

▶ **Note** From a intermediary's perspective, product renewals are generally desired, and they serve to strengthen customer loyalty and new business, as long as they remain manageable in terms of number and timing.

Finally, the **customer's perspective** also plays a decisive role in the insurance industry in connection with the importance of product renewals. Essentially, insurance customers themselves determine (and are responsible for) this importance through their demand behavior. On the one hand, they provide the raison d'être for insurance companies because they do not take care of the financial consequences of loss events themselves, but transfer them to insurers. This actually obliges insurers to use the freedoms created by deregulation to solve customer-specific risk situations and to develop new products again and again (Bittl 1998, p. 729 f.). The ongoing public criticism from the media and consumer protection, the intensification of image problems, and the increasingly consumer-oriented legislation and case law can ultimately be interpreted as circumstances that practically force product renewals. On the other hand, the effect of product renewals is often limited. Private policyholders are becoming more demanding and, above all, more spoiled due to competition offers. A classic evidence for this are the increasingly extensive or cheaper offered assistance services, which as emergency service services are a cheap part of many insurance products. At the same time, short-term contracts and interesting competitive products make it easier for intermediaries of competitive offers to encourage customers to switch. Customers therefore only partially reward product renewals.

Research Window: Product Innovations from 1996 to 2017

With the deregulation in 1994, the product design options for insurers significantly improved, and insurers regained entrepreneurial freedom in product policy. Against this background, two studies—based on publicly available information from trade journals—examined how deregulation has affected the product renewal behavior of insurers in the German private customer market.

The subject of **the first study** were the **insurance products** that appeared new in the German insurance market within the period **between 1996 and 2005.** The focus was primarily on the number of product innovations and product modifications, the ratio between the two categories, and their distribution among the three insurance branch groups property & casualty/accident, life and health, and among the 177 affected or innovating insurance companies.

The study showed that even in the period after deregulation, both product innovations and product modifications have taken on a manageable number and that this volume has hardly changed in the ten years under consideration—after adjusting for politically and legally motivated adjustment necessities. In terms of absolute numbers, product innovations played a minor role with 2.4 product concepts per year compared to product modifications (63 modifications per year), so that the **implementation of innovative product policy in insurance was mainly through product modifications.** But their importance is probably also to be relativized, as it was indicated that 69% of all insurers have only developed up to four product renewals in ten years and 27% have only developed one new product. Apparently, deregulation initially only resulted in the abolition of the obligation for prior approval and association product policy, but hardly changed the role of product renewals in the German insurance industry. It was also confirmed that product renewals are mainly dependent on newly emerging risks or legal changes: About one third of the identified product innovations were related to newly emerging risks, the rest to benefit-based ideas for service improvement. Legal changes, on the other hand, influenced a large part of the product modifications in the life and health insurance sector.

The **second empirical study**—following the first survey—examined the further development of **product renewals** in the German insurance market for private customers **between 2006 and 2017.** It identified 1457 product renewals, of which 79 were product innovations and 1378 were product modifications. Thus, the number of product renewals has significantly increased compared to the earlier period and almost doubled from an average of 65 to 121 products per year. There were still significantly more product modifications than product innovations, accounting for almost 95% of product renewals. In both life and health insurance, a large part of the product renewals was still caused by political and legal impulses. Traditional life insurance products with guaranteed interest rates have increasingly been replaced by alternatives without guarantees. In property & casualty/accident insurance, product renewals were often technology- or risk-induced.

Thus, the **product renewal behavior of insurers** in the German private customer market in the second decade after deregulation has obviously **increased compared to the first decade, and this in all insurance branch groups,** albeit at a moderate level. It was also confirmed that a large part of the product renewals in life and health insurance is caused by political and legal impulses. In property & casualty/accident insurance, there are comparatively more real product innovations, and these are often the result of new technologies or risks.

Further reading for in-depth study:

- Köhne and Kopp 2007.
- Köhne and Melashenko 2019.
- Kopp 2008. ◀

Interim Conclusion on Product Renewals since Deregulation in 1994

Deregulation and intensification of competition have led to insurers increasingly having to differentiate themselves from each other through their product policy, and this has become a central competitive policy instrument, although this is mainly done through product modifications and less through real innovations.

10.5 Approaches to Customer-oriented Product Design

An important aspect from the customer's perspective at **level 1** (core product) is the **degree of product customization** (standardization degree). This corresponds to the market segmentation strategy determined in the course of the marketing strategy (Sect. 8.3.1.2), which—if present and formulated—is the guideline for product policy as a marketing tool.

From a product design perspective, on the one hand, there is **standardization.** It is characterized by aligning the sales efforts of the insurance company to the average demands of a large number of insurance customers, by providing services for an anonymous clientele, by offering a uniform product, and by foregoing customer involvement and the resulting possibility of production before selling. This reduces the costs of service provision and sales. A standardization strategy makes sense when little personal interaction is needed, i.e., with regard to insurance products in many areas of private customer business, especially in direct sales (see Sect. 13.2.8) and annex distribution (see Sect. 13.2.4). However, it can also support sales through intermediaries because it facilitates training and enables faster and simpler customer advice. The opposite pole to standardization is **individualization:** Its characteristics are the offer of tailor-made products, the extreme alignment of the insurance company's sales efforts to the individual customer, their involvement in the service provision process, and the noticeable difference in service for the policyholder or a group of policyholders compared to other policyholders. This segmentation strategy promotes sales opportunities by individually adapting insurance coverage to the actual risk situation of the customer. Due to the associated effort, it is primarily pursued in industrial and upscale private customer business (Farny 2011, p. 404 f.).

The following presents **three** possible **customer-oriented approaches to product design,** which create more customer-friendly coverage by combining standardization and individualization and which are also suitable for the commercial and general private customer segment (Köhne 2016, p. 273 f.).

A first customer-oriented approach that combines standardization and individualization is the **offer of target group products**. They result from the consideration that, on the one hand, uniform processing of a heterogeneous (= multi-layered) market leads to significant scattering losses because standard products do not satisfy the specific needs of customers. On the other hand, customer-specific product design, as mentioned, reaches efficiency limits, and private customers are generally not willing to bear the associated costs. The compromise now consists in defining certain target groups, whose members are characterized by similar demand structures, and then designing insurance products for these demand structures.

Thus, in the insurance market, there are target group products that are oriented towards

- Life phases of customers (e.g., children's accident policies, education insurances, senior products),
- Professions (e.g., doctors, lawyers, craftsmen, etc.) or
- Fields of need (e.g., around the car or around the travel).

However, a distinction must be made between genuine target group products with corresponding coverage forms and those that are merely marketed in a new, supposedly customer-oriented form, although they are actually just a bundling of conventional standard products. Both exist in the market (Köhne 1997, pp. 170–173; Hertel and Sartorius 1994, pp. 53–55; Müller 1994, pp. 3–11).

A second customer-oriented approach that combines standardization and individualization is so-called **modular products**. Theoretically—in the case of offering the smallest possible modules or partial services and not just the bundling of entire products (bundle products)—they offer high coverage flexibility and combine standardized modules (cost aspect) with individual insurance products composed of these (aspect of meeting needs). Assuming the calculability or the tariff assignment of as parcelled individual services as possible, each customer would have the opportunity to assemble individual, relevant modules as desired. The modular composition of insurance coverage also largely avoids the risk of overdimensioned products that exists in the case of target group products. However, modules require appropriate calculation, integration in the insurer's entire process system, and the necessary IT support—implementing these requirements is a major challenge in practice. Therefore, most modular products offered in the market are not based on small, finely defined risk modules, but draw on entire branches or insured risks as a module. They thus promote not coverage flexibility, but at best cross-selling (Köhne 1997, p. 176–180; Wagner 2001a, b).

A third customer-oriented approach that combines standardization and individualization are **multi-level product offers**: These are predefined insurance packages from one insurance branch (e.g. home contents insurance), each with a different scope of coverage (Multi-level product). For example, the packages Basic, Compact and Premium—insurers choose different names for this in practice, but mean the same thing—are offered, with Compact including more comprehensive insurance coverage than Basic; Premium accordingly offers more than Compact. The difference to traditional, standardized branch products is that the customer can choose between different (each standardized) variants when concluding the contract. He can therefore make an individual selection, but cannot link parts of the relevant insurance packages together. Consequently, these offers cannot be combined into truly individually adapted insurance solutions.

Overall product design is inseparably linked with actuarial aspects of calculation and thus with premium design (Chap. 11). Because a novel coverage can only be offered if it is based on a serious calculation; otherwise, strictly speaking, it is "gambling". The design of coverage is influenced by actuarial requirements on the one hand, and has effects on the calculation on the other. Consequently, it can be assumed that in the course of more customer-oriented coverage, insurers' calculation will evolve from a branch-oriented to a customer relationship-oriented calculation.

At **level 2** (insurance service), the question arises as to how product and services can be integrated in a customer-oriented manner and how the core product can be adapted to the customer's risk situation within the framework of its coverage flexibility. Customer-oriented advice and support affects the entire security process. The individual consulting steps in the consulting and concluding phase have even been anchored in the VVG since 2008 (see § 61 VVG). Subsequently and during the entire customer relationship, it is necessary to keep an eye on the necessary adjustment need of the various security, financing or pension provision measures and to ensure customer-oriented support in the event of a claim.

It turns out that both consulting and support services in the course of mediating insurance coverage (see in detail Sect. 13.6.3) as well as those in the course of ongoing customer care and claims processing (see in detail Chap. 12)—in other words, the interactions during the entire customer journey—are components of the insurance service and must be coordinated with the product design or receive specifications from it.

In **level 3** (Complete Problem Solving), the insurance product can be expanded in three dimensions by additional services (see also Sect. 10.2.2):

1. An expansion in the financial dimension primarily follows the trend towards linked financial services ("**Allfinanz**") and aims to combine various functions of financial services, such as the protection function (risk transformation function) with the functions of earning and spending (liquidity function), financing, wealth accumulation and saving, as well as diversifying.
2. An expansion in the technical-economic performance dimension, on the other hand, takes place through additional **services in the technical area,** for example in the form of in-depth risk management consulting, services for loss prevention and safety technology, and technical damage repair. A holistic (= comprehensive) risk management consultation for private customers (consultation in the broad sense) covers all risk management measures as a mix of self-retention, risk reduction, shifting and risk avoidance, of which insurance is only one measure in the course of shifting. In the sense of ongoing advice, this also includes safety consultations following damage events with the aim of adjusting precautionary measures. Managed care services in health and accident insurance, as well as services for technical damage repair, are also part of this. In home contents and buildings insurance, smart home technologies are offered to provide prevention and quick response before, during or after a damage event (Barb et al. 2018). The services described here fulfill the function of technical securing and/or technical repair.
3. Finally, the expansion in the psychological-social dimension offers the opportunity to meet social and emotional customer concerns in the sense of (Total-)**Care-Strategies.** These include, for example, immaterial old-age services or assistance services of all kinds.

An insurer can differentiate itself sustainably from competitors if it offers comprehensive problem solutions that go far beyond the conventional products and services of insurers, which are typically associated with negative connotations. The sustainability of such benefit-oriented problem solutions, however, depends on whether consciously articulated or latent, unconscious customer needs can be satisfied better, faster or cheaper due to the core competencies available at the insurer than by competitors, in short, whether customer value (see Sect. 8.3.2.1) is generated.

> **Note: Problem solving is more attractive to customers than an abstract insurance protection promise** Although the insurance product enables the execution of various risk-related activities and thus has a benefit-generating effect, it is predominantly associated with negative connotations, as it derives its benefit from the potentially conceivable occurrence of damages. This also applies in comparison to other financial services. While these usually at least directly promote consumption or wealth accumulation, most insurance products only support the preservation of wealth by promising financial compensation for certain losses. To circumvent this circumstance, insurers are increasingly marketing their function as active problem solvers in the customer's ecosystem. For most policyholders, this is much more tangible than the comparatively abstract insurance protection promise.

Insurers traditionally take a market-driven (outside-in) approach, as they (must) react to market and competitive observations, even if the customers themselves drive the development of services less due to generally low interest.

As outlined, customers do not only use the best possible factual-rational solution to a financial and insurance problem as a benchmark for their quality assessment, but are also influenced by psychological and social factors (Sect. 4.3). This means in connection with the **search for beneficial problem-solving offers,** on the one hand, to use articulated customer wishes only as initial points of reference (and not conclusively) and on the other hand, also from the provider's perspective (inside-out), to offer the customer (and his advisor) multifunctional choices through the development of problem-solving capacities or ecosystems (Sect. 9.2). Consequently, an active positioning of innovative, interactive, and individual problem solutions is required. Consider, for example (Fig. 10.8):

- Security services of all kinds to fulfill technical-economic functions
- Provision services of a financial nature to fulfill financial functions
- Provision services of a social-psychological nature to fulfill care functions
- All-round offers around need fields or events (graduation, car purchase, wedding, family foundation, relocation, death, etc.) or around life worlds (mobility, living, health, travel, etc.).

The creation of beneficial problem solutions requires a radical alignment of the customer interface towards the customer, who is becoming increasingly demanding. Many insurers already offer a mix of personal and digital services, products, and channels to cover as many variants and contexts as possible for events in the customer's life. Soon, there will be no reason for customers to forego thrilling overall experiences in favor of good products or trustworthy brand values, as there will be more and more providers offering both—within and outside the insurance industry. The problem solutions thus start with the **customer's life world,** the environment that individuals (or groups) perceive

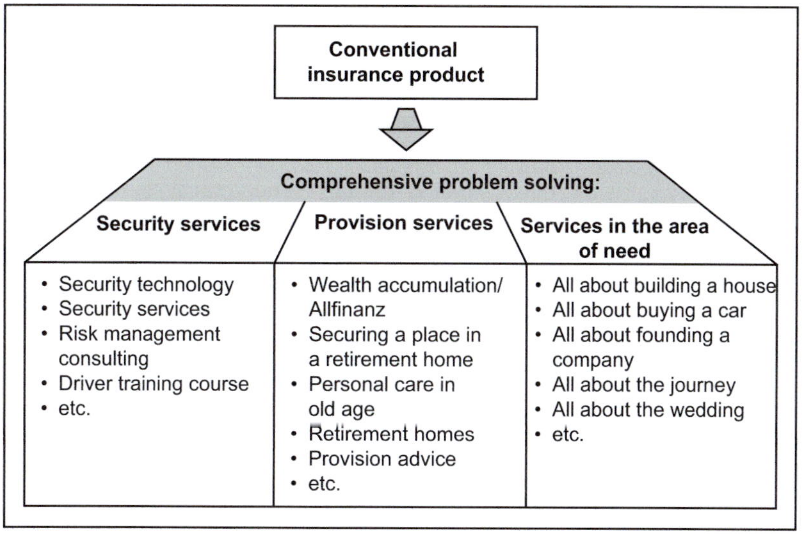

Fig. 10.8 Approaches to comprehensive problem solutions. (Köhne 2006, p. 337)

and move in everyday life. They are therefore designed holistically. At the same time, they have a certain vagueness because they can overlap and, depending on the situation or perspective, merge into each other (Accenture 2020, pp. 8–16).

10.6 Product Policy Strategies

The product policy as a marketing tool receives its **strategic guidelines from the marketing strategy** (Chap. 8) **and the chosen marketing task profile** of the insurer (Sect. 9.2).

The **company-wide positioning and brand strategy** sets the broad framework for product design. The **business field-specific marketing strategy** becomes more concrete in this respect: It gives as a rough direction the market field to be worked on, geographically the market area, the degree of market segmentation, and the positioning towards the (potential) buyers in the respective business field. The product policy should therefore support current or new products in current or new markets or the withdrawal from existing markets. Furthermore, it should be oriented locally, regionally, nationally, or—depending on the insurance product—internationally. It should be undifferentiated, segment-oriented, or individual. Finally, it is determined whether the differentiation towards the (potential) buyers should be achieved through innovation, quality, brand, program diversity, service, or price. Product-related, the whole is condensed by the marketing task profile, thus weighting the importance of service maintenance (product modifications) and service innovation (product innovations)

Even the business field-related positioning has effects on product policy: In the case of a cost and price leadership strategy, product renewals are rather unsuitable, as they are associated with additional costs. The only exception is when the product renewals directly reduce the product costs or the premium, as in the case of coverage exclusions, deductibles, or standardizations, which are associated with lower process costs. A differentiation strategy, on the other hand, is directly supported by new products: product innovations are the instrumental implementation of a differentiation strategy at the product level; with product modifications, at least an attempt is made to communicate the differentiation and uniqueness of the modified product via marketing (and the intermediaries). Finally, product renewals are a means to implement niche strategies. These require the performance to be tailored to specific market niches, e.g., target groups. To implement target group products, coverage differentiations are often necessary—hence product modifications are particularly in demand.

Further clues for the product policy are obtained from the marketing tasks and the **marketing task profile** chosen by the insurer. For insurance companies, the potential exploiter profile (customer retention, partner retention, and performance maintenance), the multiplier profile (customer acquisition, partner acquisition, partner retention, and performance maintenance), the brand exploiter profile (performance maintenance, performance innovation, partner acquisition, partner retention, and end customer marketing), and last but not least, the specialist profile (customer acquisition, customer retention, partner retention, and performance maintenance) appear to be sensible task profiles.

The **potential exploiter** has a large customer base and an established range of products and services as well as a large market share. Acquiring new customers is much more complex than further exploiting the existing customer base. However, the customer base must be defended against competitors. To do this, the sales partners must be bound. Customer and sales partner retention require a product policy that meets market developments, primarily product modifications.

The **multiplier** exploits the potential of its business system by opening up new customer potentials via new distribution partners, maintaining its service quality, and binding the contributing sales partners. Customer retention is left to the partner companies, at least for independent sales partners. Even with this multi-channel strategy pursued by many insurance companies, service maintenance and differentiation, and thus product modification with its two manifestations of variation and differentiation, play a significant role, whereas product innovations are rather subordinate.

The **brand exploiter** maintains his service program, develops and broadens it through innovative products, and triggers a demand pull through intensive end-customer marketing (product design and communication), which also supports partner acquisition and partner retention. End customer retention is achieved—as far as possible—via the company brand and product quality, partly with the participation of sales partners, who also carry out customer acquisition. The brand exploiter relies on product modifications and product innovations because his high-quality service program should contribute to or pay into the brand value. In this strategy, product policy plays a central role.

Finally, the **target group specialist** also focuses on his target group from a product perspective; the development and maintenance of needs-based target group-specific products is important, occasionally supplemented by genuine product innovations for the target group. The distribution channel specialist must have product modifications ready to meet the differentiated market needs of his distribution channel and market dynamics; product innovations are also good sales arguments for the sales partners, especially in the fiercely contested broker market.

Shaped and determined by marketing strategy and marketing tasks, insurance companies respond to customer needs within the framework of customer-oriented product strategies: combined products, tiered products formed from modules (basic, compact, premium), target group products, all-risks coverage, and traditional branch products with special customer-oriented elements are various approaches derived from these strategies at the core product level. However, the resulting variety of coverage and tariffs increasingly leads to a lack of transparency and thus to the overburdening of insurance customers. This increases the need for information services from consumer protection agencies, rating agencies, and scientific institutes. As a result, in addition to the customer, intermediaries, consumer protection, and rating organizations have increasingly become the addressees of product policy.

Ultimately, however, it is still the customers who reward innovative insurers through demand or switching insurers, and who can punish less innovative insurers with outdated insurance coverage through migration and negative word-of-mouth. A look at the sales volume and sales increase of insurance companies that have introduced product innovations does not seem to unreservedly underline this behavior of insurance customers. Rather, it is widely recognized that insurance products are low-interest products and that customer interest in insurance matters (involvement) is generally very low. This means that even truly innovative insurance products require a great deal of marketing effort to be noticed by the majority of potential insurance customers at all. In addition, there is another finding: For the vast majority of customers, competence in terms of insurance products is even declining, so that typical psychological mechanisms become effective, such as complexity reduction by excluding information (Sirius Campus 2019a). This circumstance is further exacerbated by the decreasing transparency on the customer side due to the increasing number of product modifications and differentiation attempts on the provider side.

Interim Conclusion on the Marketing Tool of Product Policy

Insurance customers, due to their largely lacking interest in insurance products, contribute little to promoting the role of product renewals, which is important from their point of view, from the demand side. Instead, product development in large parts of the insurance market is rather driven by competition and intermediaries.

Further Reading Recommendations for Chap. 10

- Betschart and Mussak 2021.
- Farny 1995.
- Fritzsche and Bohnert 2022.
- Grösch 2020.
- Köhne 1997, Chap. 3.
- Köhne 2008.
- Müller-Reichart 2002.
- Riege 1990.
- Schütze 1972.
- Vielreicher 1995.

References

Accenture (Ed.) (2020): Ökosysteme in der Versicherungsindustrie, Potenziale und Umsetzungsstrategien, Whitepaper, 2020.

Barb, C./Klein, K./Kraft, M. (2018): Auswirkungen von Smart-Home-Technologien auf die verbundene Hausrat- und Wohngebäudeversicherung—Markt, Ausgestaltungsmerkmale und Preisbereitschaft, in: ZVersWiss, Jg. 107, 2018, pp. 495–516.

Betschart, A./Mussak, P. (2021): Steuerung der Produktentwicklungsprozesse, in: Junglas, A./ Schradin, H./Wiegard, M.: Steuerung von Versicherungsunternehmen, Stuttgart, 3. Aufl., 2021, pp. 359–390.

Bittl, A. (1998): Vertrauenserwerb durch innovative Problemlösungsangebote, in: ZfV, Jg. 49, 1998, Nr. 24, pp. 727–735.

Bosselmann, E.H. (1994): Versicherungsmakler und deregulierte Versicherungsmärkte, Karlsruhe, 1994.

Farny, D. (1965): Produktions- und Kostentheorie der Versicherung, Karlsruhe, 1965.

Farny, D. (1971): Absatz und Absatzpolitik des Versicherungsunternehmens, Karlsruhe, 1971.

Farny, D. (1975): AVB unter dem Gesichtspunkt der „Produktbeschreibung“, in: ZVersWiss, Jg. 64, 1975, Nr. 2, pp. 169–184.

Farny, D. (1995): Die Gestaltung von Versicherungsprodukten im Marketing von Versicherungsunternehmen, in: ZVersWiss, Jg. 84, 1995, pp. 79–102.

Farny, D. (2011): Versicherungsbetriebslehre, Karlsruhe, 5. Aufl., 2011.

Fritzsche, A./Bohnert, A. (2022): Implications of bundled offerings for business development ad competitive strategy in digital insurance, in: GP, Vol. 47, 2022, pp. 817–834. (DOI: https://doi.org/10.1057/s41288-021-00244-4)

Gal, J. (2019): Rechtliche Rahmenbedingungen eines Versicherungsmarketing, in: Reich, M./ Zerres, C. (Eds.), Handbuch Versicherungsmarketing, Berlin, 2. Aufl., 2019, pp. 97–119.

Grösch, M. (2020): The impact of product variety on customers’ default acceptance and company perception. Experimental studies for the insurance industry, in: ZVersWiss, Jg. 109, 2020, pp. 377–398. (doi: https://doi.org/10.1007/s12297-020-00458-w)

Haller, M. (1982): Risiko- und Versicherungsprobleme des privaten Haushalts—aus Sicht der Privatversicherung, in: ZVersWiss, Jg. 71, 1982, Nr. 3/4, pp. 383–437.

Haller, M. (1986a): Funktionen-Marketing—zur Bewältigung der „Financial Services (R) Evolution"? in: Belz, C. (Ed.), Realisierung des Marketing, Festschrift zum 60. Geburtstag von Prof. Dr. H. Weinhold-Stünzi, St. Gallen 1986, pp. 1.097–1.124.

Haller, M. (1986b): Risiko-Management, in: Jacob, H. (Ed.), Schriften zur Unternehmensführung, Band 33, Wiesbaden, 1986, pp. 7–43.

Haller, M./Ackermann, W. (1995): Versicherungswirtschaft—kundenorientiert, Zürich, 1995.

Hertel, A./Sartorius, B. (1994): Innovatives Zielgruppenmarketing für Versicherungen ab Juli 1994, Karlsruhe, 1994.

Karten, W. (1995): Versicherungsproduktgestaltung—ökonomische Grundlagen, in: ZVersWiss, Jg. 84, 1995, Nr. 1, pp. 57–77.

Koch, P. (1988): Versicherungszweige, System und übrige Sparten, in: Farny, D./Helten, E./Koch, P./Schmidt, R. (Eds.), Handwörterbuch der Versicherung (HdV), Karlsruhe, 1988, pp. 1.251.

Köhne, T. (1997): Die Wirkungsversicherung im Privatkundengeschäft—Implikationen für eine kundenorientierte Marktleistungsgestaltung, St. Gallen, 1997.

Köhne, T. (1998b): Chancen und Grenzen der Produktpolitik im deregulierten Versicherungsmarkt (Teil II), in: IVW Management-Information, St. Galler Trendmonitor für Risiko- und Finanzmärkte, 1998, Heft 5, pp. 2–10.

Köhne, T. (1998c): Zur Konzeption des Versicherungsproduktes—neue Anforderungen in einem deregulierten Markt, in: ZVersWiss, Jg. 87, 1998, Nr. 1/2, pp. 143–191.

Köhne, T. (2006): Marketing im strategischen Unternehmensnetzwerk, Erklärungsmodell und praktische Anwendung in der Versicherungswirtschaft, Wiesbaden, 2006.

Köhne, T. (2008): Produktinnovationen in der Versicherungswirtschaft—Theoretische Grundlagen zur Analyse aktueller Praxisentwicklungen, in: Köhne, T. (Ed.), Produktinnovationen in der deutschen Versicherungswirtschaft, Theoretische Analyse aktueller Praxisentwicklungen, Karlsruhe, 2008, pp. 1–39.

Köhne, T. (Ed.) (2008): Produktinnovationen in der deutschen Versicherungswirtschaft, Theoretische Analyse aktueller Praxisentwicklungen, Karlsruhe, 2008.

Köhne, T. (2016): Versicherungsmarketing. Marketing und Vertrieb im Versicherungsunternehmen in Theorie und Praxis, Karlsruhe, 2016.

Köhne, T./Kopp, F. (2007): Produktinnovationen und Produktmodifikationen in der Versicherungswirtschaft: Rolle und Bedeutung nach der Deregulierung, in: ZVersWiss, Jg. 96, 2007, Nr. 2, pp. 227–259.

Köhne, T./Melashenko, I. (2019): Produktinnovationen und Produktmodifikationen in der Versicherungswirtschaft zwischen 2006 und 2017, in: ZVersWiss, Jg. 108, Nr. 3–4, 2019, pp. 275–305.

Kopp, F. (2008): Produktneuerungen in der deutschen Versicherungswirtschaft nach der Deregulierung—Eine empirische Untersuchung des Zeitraums zwischen 1996 und 2005, in: Köhne, T. (Ed.), Produktinnovationen in der deutschen Versicherungswirtschaft, Karlsruhe, 2008, pp. 41–76.

Kotler, P./Bliemel, F. (1992): Marketing-Management, Analyse, Planung, Umsetzung und Kontrolle, Stuttgart, 7. Aufl., 1992.

Kotler, P./Keller, K.L./Opresnik, M.O. (2017a): Marketing-Management, Konzepte—Instrumente—Unternehmensfallstudien, Halbergmoos, 15. Aufl., 2017.

Lach, H. (1995): Vertikales Marketing von Versicherungsunternehmen, Berlin, 1995.

Meffert, H. /Bruhn, M. (1995): Dienstleistungsmarketing, Grundlagen—Konzepte—Methoden, Wiesbaden, 1. Aufl., 1995.

Menhart, M.: Innovationsdynamik und Lebenszyklen in der Versicherungsindustrie, Aachen, 2003.

Müller, H. (1994): Marktsegmentierung im Privatkundengeschäft von Versicherungsunternehmen, Karlsruhe, 1994.

Müller, W. (1981): Das Produkt Versicherung, in: Jung, M./Ralph, L./Seifert, W. (Eds.), Geld und Versicherung, Festgabe für Wilhelm Seuß, Karlsruhe, 1981, pp. 155–171.
Müller, W. (1994): Informationsökonomische Grundlagen und empirische Überprüfung eines Beschreibungsmodells für Versicherungsprodukte, in: Schwebler, R. (Ed.), Dieter Farny und die Versicherungswissenschaft, Karlsruhe, 1994, pp. 363–379.
Müller-Reichart, M. (2002): International orientierte Produktinnovationspolitik globalisierter Versicherungsunternehmen, Karlsruhe, 2002.
Nordemann, W. (1995): Innovationsschutz für Versicherungsprodukte, in: ZVersWiss, Jg. 84, 1995, Nr. 1, pp. 129–137.
Puschmann, K.-H. (2003): Praxis des Versicherungsmarketing, Karlsruhe, 2. Aufl., 2003.
Reuter, F. (1994): Markenartikel in der Versicherungswirtschaft, in: Mehring, H.-P./Wolff, V. (Eds.): Fesetschrift für Dieter Farny zur Vollendung seines 60. Lebensjahres, Karlsruhe, 1994, pp. 55–61.
Riege, J. (1990): Das Versicherungsprodukt, in: ZVersWiss, Jg. 79, 1990, Nr. 3, pp. 403–470.
Schröder, H.-H. (2008): Technologie- und Innovationsmanagement, in: Corsten, H./Reiß, M. (Eds.), Betriebswirtschaftslehre, Band 2, München, 4. Aufl., 2008, pp. 307–438.
Schütze, U. (1972): Probleme der Produktgestaltung in der Versicherungswirtschaft unter besonderer Berücksichtigung der Produktinnovation, Karlsruhe, 1972.
Sirius Campus (Ed.) (2019a): Entscheidertypologie im Versicherungsmarkt, Köln, 2019.
Vielreicher, P. (1995): Produktinnovationsmanagement in Versicherungsunternehmen, Wiesbaden, 1995.
Wagner, F. (2001a): Gestaltung von Versicherungsprodukten nach dem Bausteinprinzip, in: VW, Jg. 56, 2001, Nr. 11, pp. 818–822.
Wagner, F. (2001b): Gestaltung von Versicherungsprodukten nach dem Bausteinprinzip, in: VW, Jg. 56, 2001, Nr. 12, pp. 916–920.

Price and Premium Policy as a Marketing Tool of the Insurance Company 11

11.1 Basics of Pricing in Insurance Markets for Private Customers

As in other markets, the logic of a **price-sales function**, which determines the relationship between supply and demand, also applies in the insurance market. The price-sales function of an insurer indicates which quantities of insurance coverage *x* can be sold at alternative price demands *p* in new business and—with some restrictions, because other aspects also play a role—can be maintained in the portfolio. Since premium revenues (= sales) are the product of sales quantities and prices, a revenue function can also be represented in addition to the price-sales function.

The **double-kinked price-sales function** goes back to *Gutenberg,* and it illustrates that providers can vary their prices in a certain price range without significantly changing sales (monopolistic leeway). In the classic private customer branches, a falling price-sales function can be assumed, which runs more or less steeply depending on the competition of a branch, i.e.: The lower the prices, the higher the sales volume. Generally, it also applies that above a certain price threshold (pain threshold), customers increasingly migrate to the competition. Conversely, below a certain price threshold—e.g. at a price that promotes a product in the ranking among the three cheapest products and thus attracts ranking-focused customers—disproportionate customer access can be achieved; in practice, this benefits especially the comparators, online comparison portals, where demanders can compare insurance offers in terms of price and then also conclude. Between these is a (depending on the branch more or less) large premium leeway with comparatively low price elasticity, i.e., with equal price changes, the quantity changes are smaller (Farny 2011, p. 709 f.; Krüger-Barvels 1971, pp. 161–167). This phenomenon is attributed to information deficits and information costs and can also be justified theoretically: In oligopolistic competition and specific customer preferences,

T. Köhne, *Insurance Marketing*, https://doi.org/10.1007/978-3-658-47345-7_11

the autonomous (monopolistic) price range increases with the costs of a provider change and the search costs resulting from incomplete customer information (Schulenburg and Lohse 2014, pp. 364–366).

▶ **Price elasticity** of demand expresses the ratio of the relative change in new business volume to the relative price change. An elasticity of 0 means no influence on the demand quantity, an elasticity of 0 to −1 a below-average influence, an elasticity of −1 a proportional influence and an elasticity of less than −1 a disproportionate influence. In the last case, there is a high price sensitivity among demanders, i.e., they react disproportionately to price changes.

Figure 11.1 illustrates this graphically: A double-kinked price-sales function can be seen, where above the price p_0 relatively strong portfolio outflows (range between 0 and x_0) and below the price p_u relatively strong portfolio inflows (range from x_u) are recorded. In these two areas, the price elasticity is higher than with the classic (not kinked) price-sales function.

Based on the now presented price-sales function, *Farny* has introduced a simple **model for pricing policy in new business** that has explanatory power for various pricing policies found in insurance practice (Fig. 11.2). The model shows at which prices p which new business volumes x of a certain insurance branch are concluded and which

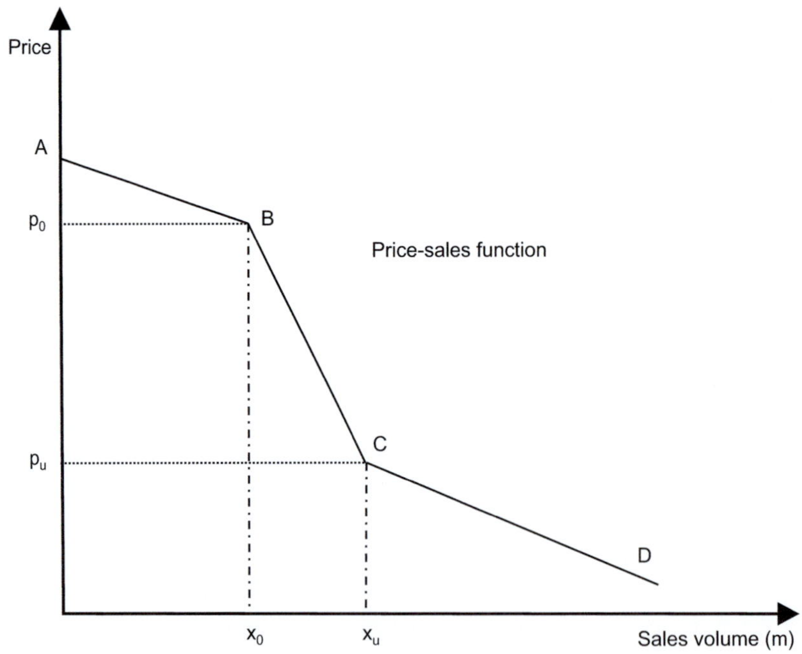

Fig. 11.1 Double-kinked price-sales function

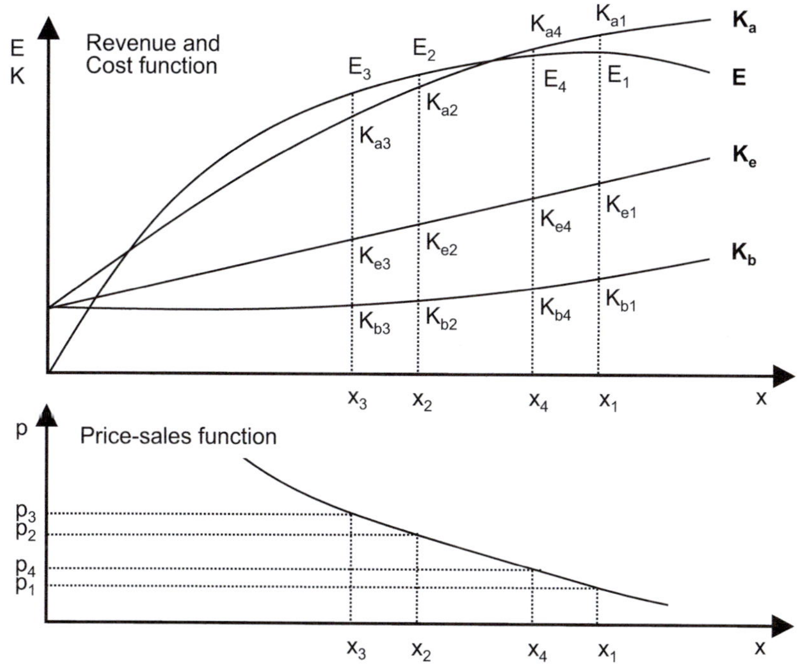

Fig. 11.2 Pricing model for new business. (Based on Farny 2011, p. 722)

premium revenues E are achieved from it. In addition, the total costs K for the achievable new business volume x are known. The damage costs contained therein are modeled not only with their expected value (K_e), but also with alternative positive (K_b in case of under-damages) or negative (K_a in case of over-damages) deviations, in order to take into account the randomness underlying the insurance business on the cost side in the pricing calculation (Farny 2011, pp. 721–724).

The model very clearly illustrates how the insurer's pricing decision is influenced by its corporate goals and the sales targets derived from them (see Chap. 7). A revenue-oriented insurer will demand price p_1 at which the revenue is maximum. At the same time, he risks a loss in the event of a randomly poor claims experience amounting to $K_{a1} - E_1$. A profit-oriented provider will always demand a higher price. However, due to the randomness of the claims costs, the profit is a random variable, which means that the insurer must make its pricing decision under risk and this is therefore dependent on its risk appetite. A risk-neutral provider is guided by the expected claims costs K_e and optimizes the profit at p_2. A risk-averse insurer assumes K_a and therefore optimizes his profit at p_3 ($E_3 - K_{a3}$). In the event of an expected claims experience, however, he will make less profit than the risk-neutral insurer because he has foregone business ($x_2 - x_3$). Finally, the risk-loving provider is guided by the most favorable claims experience K_b and sets the price at p_4. As a result, he will make less profit than the risk-neutral insurer in the event of an expected claims experience and will even realize a loss in the event of a poor claims experience.

The model can well explain the **pricing situation in practice:** Sales increases through new business are often achieved with battle premiums—but at the expense of profitability. The most expensive insurer with p_3 is the pessimistic one. In reality, too, there are many insurers for whom profit security is the top priority and who therefore tend to be high-priced and less growth-oriented. A stronger focus on returns is accordingly associated with more risk—the optimistic insurer is betting on good years and trying to win new business in these. However, this already reduces profits (and returns) in the event of an expected claims experience and even leads to losses in the event of a poor claims experience. This phenomenon is particularly known from industrial insurance. However, there are also providers in the private customer segment who write losses in insurance branches where their competitors are making profits at the same time. Thus, the conflict of objectives between sales, profit and security is illustrated.

However, it should be noted that the model **only represents the basic logic of the market.** In reality, many other factors play a role, and the insurer cannot rely solely on this simple model. For example, competitive situations reduce the scope for action, and new business can only be achieved with tightly calculated premiums. The same applies to the start-up phase of a branch: only a rapid minimum portfolio size allows for the coverage of fixed costs. Another very crucial factor is the effects of a price change on the existing business.

The effects of price decisions in new business on existing business depend on many legal and factual characteristics of the insurance transactions in the portfolio as well as on the behavior of the insurer and its existing customers. In a model-like manner, it can at least be shown that a price increase in new business affects the new business according to the existing price elasticity of demand and the effects on prices, quantities and premium revenues in the existing business are determined by the extent of the price increase, the extent of the application to the existing premiums and the resulting cancellation behavior (Farny 2011, p. 727).

11.2 Price resp. Tariff Components in the Insurance Business

In the private customer business, a generally designed premium policy prevails—for reasons of economic efficiency alone. In this context, the term used in practice is the tariff premium or tariff design, often abbreviated to just the tariff. The tariff design is rather long-term, sets the intended (actuarial) premium differentiation, is the basis for handling large volumes of business and is therefore standardized.

▶ **Tariff** stands for a binding list of premium amounts for certain insurance coverage components or a guideline for premium calculation based on given characteristics. It includes the accounting of accompanying services.

In **indemnity insurance,** the premium or tariff calculation is based on a breakdown of the total premium into individual parts. As a rule, interest effects are neglected, but possible investment returns that an existing insurance portfolio generates from prepaid premiums (interest bearer) are taken into account. In **sum insurance** (especially in life and health insurance), risk and savings premiums are not calculated separately, but in combination. Interest effects are taken into account within the framework of a present value model, because the bilateral payment flows can be well estimated in terms of amount and timing. For the discount rate, supervisory law provides for a maximum value that is below the average return on capital investments achievable in the market, so that there are generally significant premium refunds (profit participations) to the policyholders.

The so-called **premium-cost model** illustrates the components that make up the total premium for insurance coverage in indemnity insurance (Table 11.1). The pure risk premium—also called net risk premium—for own account represents the contribution margin for the expected loss value of the primary insurer. The premium share for the reinsurer corresponds to the expected loss value of the transferred risk plus the reinsurer's safety, operating costs, and profit surcharges. The safety surcharge covers the costs of taking on the underwriting risk, namely the possible collective excess losses for own account., i.e. again only the share of the primary insurer, as well as the costs for the provision of safety capital (equity costs). The latter are also lower when reinsurance is taken. Pure risk premium for own account, reinsurance premium, and safety surcharge result in the gross risk premium (Farny 2011, pp. 60–64).

The **tariff calculation is based** primarily and fundamentally **on the calculation of the pure risk premium.** This calculation is done in the indemnity insurance sector with a focus on the expected loss value without interest effects, in the life and health

Table 11.1 Premium-cost model in indemnity insurance. (Based on Farny 2011, p. 63)

	Total Costs	Gross Premium	
Risk costs	Damage costs for own account (Expected value)	Pure risk premium for own acccount	Gross risk premium
	Reinsurance costs (Risk premium, surcharges)	Premium share for reinsurer	
	Safety capital costs for possible excess losses for own account	Safety surcharge	
Operating costs	Acquisition costs	Operating cost surcharge, possibly also installment surcharge	
	Administrative costs		
	minus capital investment returns	minus capital investment returns	
	Fire protection tax	Fire protection tax	
	Profit or equity costs	Profit surcharge	
	Insurance tax	Insurance tax	

insurance sector with a focus on present values of inflows and outflows over the entire (long-term) contract term.

The calculation of the pure risk premium in **indemnity insurance** is roughly outlined by determining the expected frequency of loss and the expected amount of loss; when considering insurable values in property insurance, a risk premium rate is first calculated, which expresses how large the proportion of the expected loss is to the insurable value (= average percentage loss spread), and therefore only needs to be multiplied by the desired insurable value, however it may be, to calculate the specific risk premium.

▶ **Note: Basic logic of calculation in indemnity insurance** Pure risk premium = Expected frequency of loss x Expected amount of loss

Application example: Building fire insurance

The number of insured buildings in the portfolio is 400,000, with a total insurable value of 140 billion €. On average, this portfolio experiences 4,000 insurance cases per year due to fire, totaling 28 million €. The expected value of the frequency of loss is 0.01 (= 4000/400,000) and the expected value of the average percentage of loss spread is 0.02 or 2%. This is derived from the calculation of the proportion of the average loss amount (= total loss amount/number of insurance cases, in the example 28 million €/4000 = 7000 €) to the average insurable value (= total insurable value/number of insured buildings, in the example 140 billion €/400,000 = 350,000 €). If you now multiply the expected frequency of loss (0.01) by the expected percentage of loss spread (0.02), you get the risk premium rate of 0.2 per mille. Accordingly, the insurer could offer the fire risk component for a building with an insurable value of 500,000 € at a pure risk premium of 100 € (plus various surcharges).

Recommended for further study: Radtke 2008. ◀

The calculation of the risk premium in **life insurance** is based on the premise that, according to the principle of equivalence, the present value of the future premium payments of the policyholder (= discounted income) must correspond to the present value of the future benefits of the insurer (= discounted expenses) and—to take into account interest effects—all cash flows must be discounted or compounded to the same point in time. The calculation of the net premium is based on the mortality table and the actuarial interest rate—both values can be combined in a calculatory mortality table (e.g., mortality table of the German Actuarial Association, DAV).

▶ **Note: Basic logic of calculation in life insurance** Present value of the policyholder's benefits (including net premiums ongoing or one-time) = Present value of the insurer's benefits (death and/or survival benefits); solved for the net premium.

Application example: Single premium term life insurance

Assumptions: The policyholder is male, 35 years old, the sum insured is 100,000 € and the insurance period is five years. According to the DAV mortality table 2008—there are now also newer mortality tables—for men and with a discount rate of 1.75% (now 0.25%), this would mean that the present value of all insured persons, which results from the single premium *P* and the number of living 35-year-olds in the first period, must correspond to the present value of the insurer, which results from the number of deceased in the five-year period (i.e., between 35 and 39 years) and the sum insured discounted over five years at 1.75%. Rearranging the equation for *P* means that the number determined for the present value of the insurer must be divided by the number of living 35-year-olds to arrive at the net premium or pure risk premium (in the example 483 €).

In life insurance mathematics, cumulative values are used for simplification, which discount the number of living and deceased (instead of the sum insured) and cumulatively add up these numbers over the years. Accordingly, in the given example, the net premium can be easily derived from the mortality table, which starts from a fictitious initial stock of 1 million people, and its cumulative values:

$$P = (M_{35} - M_{40}/D_{35}) \cdot VS$$

which means that the number of discounted deceased between 35 and 39 years (according to the mortality table equal to the difference between 263,714.263 (M_{35}) and 261,148.580 (M_{40})) is to be divided by the number of discounted living at the age of 35 (according to the mortality table: 531,198.585) and this value is then to be multiplied by the sum insured (100,000 €). If you insert the values, you get 483,- Euro.

Recommended for further study: Schulenburg and Lohse 2014, pp. 137–148. ◄

The **operating cost surcharge** covers the acquistion costs (e.g., advertising, sales force compensation) and administrative costs (internal service compensation, operating resources, auxiliary and operating materials, imputed or effective rents, costs of external services) proportionally. Likewise, proportional capital returns can be deducted from these costs (cash flow underwriting, see Sect. 11.4). Premium payment during the year causes higher collection, i.e., settlement costs, and interest losses, so a corresponding installment surcharge is justified. Since this item is freely selectable by the customer on an individual contract basis, it can possibly be added individually and is therefore listed separately. In the case of comprehensive buildings insurance and comprehensive home contents insurance, an additional contribution margin is required for the owed fire protection tax. The profit surcharge is intended for the interest on equity—if it is already included in the cost of equity capital, no separate allocation is required. Finally, the insurance tax must be shown and collected separately as a service owed by the customer and thus a pass-through item.

11.3 Legal Framework Conditions of Premium Policy

For the premium policy, as for the product policy, since deregulation in 1994 through the abolition of the obligation to obtain prior approval for premiums and tariffs, there is greater entrepreneurial freedom with regard to this marketing tool. Nevertheless, there are some **general clauses of insurance supervision** to be observed (see also Sect. 3.4.2), which influence the pricing policy:

- General legal and financial supervision with the **goal of appropriate premiums** with regard to the interests of the policyholders as creditors and debtors (e.g., in the course of approving business plans).
- The **major and minor branch separation** make it difficult or impossible to have cross-divisional mixed prices that would take into account appropriate risk diversification.
- The prohibition of special remuneration to policyholders (= **prohibition on the passing on of commissions**) and of preferential contracts deprives intermediaries of the opportunity to make price concessions themselves or to negotiate their own advising and intermediating price in competition for the customer.

In **life, health, and accident insurance with premium refund** (APR), pricing policy is subject to further **restrictions**, which is justified by the special need for protection of private customers in these premium-intensive and long-term binding insurance branches:

- The **principle of equal treatment of policyholders** applies in life, health, and accident insurance with premium refund as well as in mutual insurance associations and requires that premiums and benefits be measured only according to the same principles under the same conditions. On the one hand, it is thus understood as a **mandate for actuarial premium differentiation;** according to this, each policyholder should pay a premium corresponding to his expected loss value (= individual actuarial equivalence principle). On the other hand, this ultimately means for these insurance branches the renunciation of classic price differentiation measures in the sense of marketing, which would aim to set regionally or customer-specific different prices for risk-technically identical insurance coverage in order to fully exploit the different purchasing power and willingness to buy.
- In health insurance, there are also **information obligations** regarding the calculation of premiums in substitute health insurance (§ 146 para. 1 no. 6 VAG) as well as **provisions for aging reserves** for a premium reduction in old age (§ 149 VAG).
- The **participation of a responsible actuary** is required in the **premium calculation** in life insurance (§ 141 VAG), correspondingly operated health insurance (§ 156 VAG) and APR (§ 161 para. 1 VAG).

- The **participation of a trustee** is additionally required for **premium adjustments** and changes in profit participation in old stocks. of life insurance (§ 142 VAG), in health insurance (§ 155 VAG) and the APR (§ 161 para. 1 VAG).
- Finally, there are supervisory regulations for the **implementation of profit-sharing systems** in life (partly limited to old stocks), health, and APR insurance.

The premium policy and tariff design is particularly affected by the **Unisex judgment of the CJEU** from 2011. It results in a significant restriction of the actuarially justified premium differentiation. Since this point, the rule of **gender-neutral premiums** and benefits must be applied, and insurers must offer unisex tariffs. The ruling has affected gender-specific tariffs in pension, life, health, and motor vehicle insurance and has led to higher safety surcharges to catch the newly created **risk of adverse risk selection** by too many men or women in the collective.

All in all, a look at the legal environment of insurers' price and premium policy shows that there are various restrictions, but especially in property & casualty insurance, there are **definitely pricing leeways.** And even in the personal insurance sectors, there are pricing opportunities despite consumer-oriented guidelines, as will be shown later.

11.4 Approaches to Market- and Customer-oriented Pricing

Decisive factors for pricing include, among other things, market conditions. For example, customers and their behavior play a role: well-informed, perceptive, evaluative, and rationally acting customers are more price-sensitive than others. Furthermore, market transparency is responsible for whether price levels can be assessed at all. Another factor is the already mentioned term of the contracts. With short-term contracts (e.g., in motor vehicle insurance), the risk of poaching by cheaper competitive offers is much higher. The provider's product range also plays a role: price reductions (discounts) when concluding several contracts are only possible with a corresponding range of products.

The most important design parameter of sales market-related pricing policy is the gross premium presented in the previous section, which represents the total price of insurance coverage for the customer. In the course of **gross premium design,** the main focus is on determining the extent of the actuarial differentiation of risk premiums. In competitive markets, the application of the equivalence principle is necessary to a certain extent to counter the risk of adverse selection, which consists of attracting only bad risks because they are priced too favorably or must be priced (see above for unisex judgment). Different risk characteristics (e.g., construction class in buildings insurance, annual mileage in motor vehicle insurance) can be taken into account through surcharges or discounts. In addition, there is a margin of discretion regarding the amount of safety surcharges (depending on the risk propensity or the company's objectives).

Another important component of the gross premium concerns the investment results. If they do not result from the savings contributions and thus serve the customer's surplus participation, they can be used to reduce the gross risk premium. If investment returns are already included in the risk premium and reduce it accordingly, this is referred to as so-called **cashflow underwriting**.

Furthermore, the choice of the type and extent of acquisition costs (e.g., advertising budget, sales cost budget) and their allocation to a specific insurance product offers pricing leeway. The same applies to administrative cost surcharges: Here, with reference to overhead costs, a varying degree of allocation is possible, so that, for example, in the case of a low-price strategy, rewarding customer loyalty, or for the purpose of cross-selling, a deliberate cross-subsidization between different tariffs can be operated **(discount design).** Finally, the remaining safety capital or profit surcharge—depending on the ownership structure and owner objectives to varying degrees—is designable.

Pricing policy in existing business requires corresponding prior contractual agreements or an agreement with the customer, especially in the case of premium increases. In industrial business, premium increases occur to eliminate loss situations in individual contract developments (restructuring). In private customer business, individual contract premium negotiation would be too costly. Therefore, **variable premium systems** are more suitable here, which are based on various facts and are applied in a standardized way for all similar contracts (of one type of insurance) (Farny 2011, p. 716):

1. Premiums are based on the loss development of the insurance contract (experience rating):
   This includes the established bonus-malus system, which is used in motor vehicle and health insurance. In the case of a good loss development (absence of losses), premium shares are refunded to the customer on an individual contract basis (= independent of success—because **dependent on loss development–premium refund**).
2. Premiums are based on the total profit or the profit in partial stocks:
   This mainly involves the refund of unused safety and administrative cost surcharges (settlement profits). In life insurance (with savings/disinvestment business), the refund usually takes the form of an addition to the accumulated retirement capital (provision fund). In this premium system, the insurer takes in more premium than it needs and pays out the reserves built up with it, if they are not needed, to the customer later as profit participation (= **success-dependent premium refund**).
3. Premiums are based on changes in the expected loss values over time:
   For this, **premium adjustment clauses** are necessary, which must be agreed upon in the contract already at the conclusion and can be linked to different indices in different insurance branches. In life and health insurance, the adjustment fact must be determined by independent trustees. It should be noted that the policyholder has a right to extraordinary termination in the event of each premium increase, if the insurance coverage does not change, as well as in the event of each reduction of the insurance coverage with a constant premium (§ 40 VVG).

In conclusion, it can be stated that **premium design in the insurance industry is more challenging than in other industries** because the underlying calculation is not deterministic, but stochastic: Future expected loss values and their dispersion parameters are calculated on the basis of past loss histories by forming loss distributions in order to calculate future premiums. Despite the associated collective calculation, premium design in the sense of an **individual premium-risk equivalence is possible:**

- Rates can be designed to be risk-appropriate because the tariff characteristics are continuously developed and revised.
- Deductibles reduce risk and also administrative costs, thus enabling premium reductions.
- Premium refunds result from the pre-financing effect of premiums and their tendency to be set too high according to the principle of prudence. They are therefore important for the final price determination of insurance coverage.
- Premium adjustments take into account changed loss distributions.

Research Window: Huge Price Differences in the Motor Vehicle Insurance Market

A nationwide study conducted annually between 2010 and 2018 on behalf of an insurer also found enormous price differences of up to 234% for motor vehicle insurance in the German motor vehicle insurance market for the **year 2018:** The gap between the most expensive and cheapest offer averaged €1311.

The market study was based on 33,837 tariff calculations across 20 regions in Germany and ten model customers, making it representative. The calculation of the tariffs was done using the NAFI calculator, an independent analysis tool for determining motor vehicle insurance tariffs.

Key findings: The tariff landscape in the German motor vehicle insurance market is very diverse. There is a multitude of tariffs, the calculation of which is also based on a varying number of customer characteristics. Accordingly, it was shown across the 200 examined model cases that the price adjustments at that time did not turn out equally strong in all regions, and they even varied more depending on the model customer. The same applies to the determined price differences, which can vary between individual model customers and regions (Fig. 11.3). The pricing policy of motor vehicle insurers is therefore differentiated according to risks and regions. This corresponds to the search for risk-appropriate premiums according to the individual actuarial equivalence principle; however, this also reduces the necessary transparency, and it is difficult for insurance customers to find the suitable and additionally cheapest tariff.

The study also identified the fundamentally **huge price differences between the offers of the approximately 100 motor vehicle insurers in the German insurance market.** These existed both in cities and in rural regions. For the same model customers, however, the premiums in the city are generally more expensive than in the countryside. The largest price difference was found in Berlin: Here, the differences

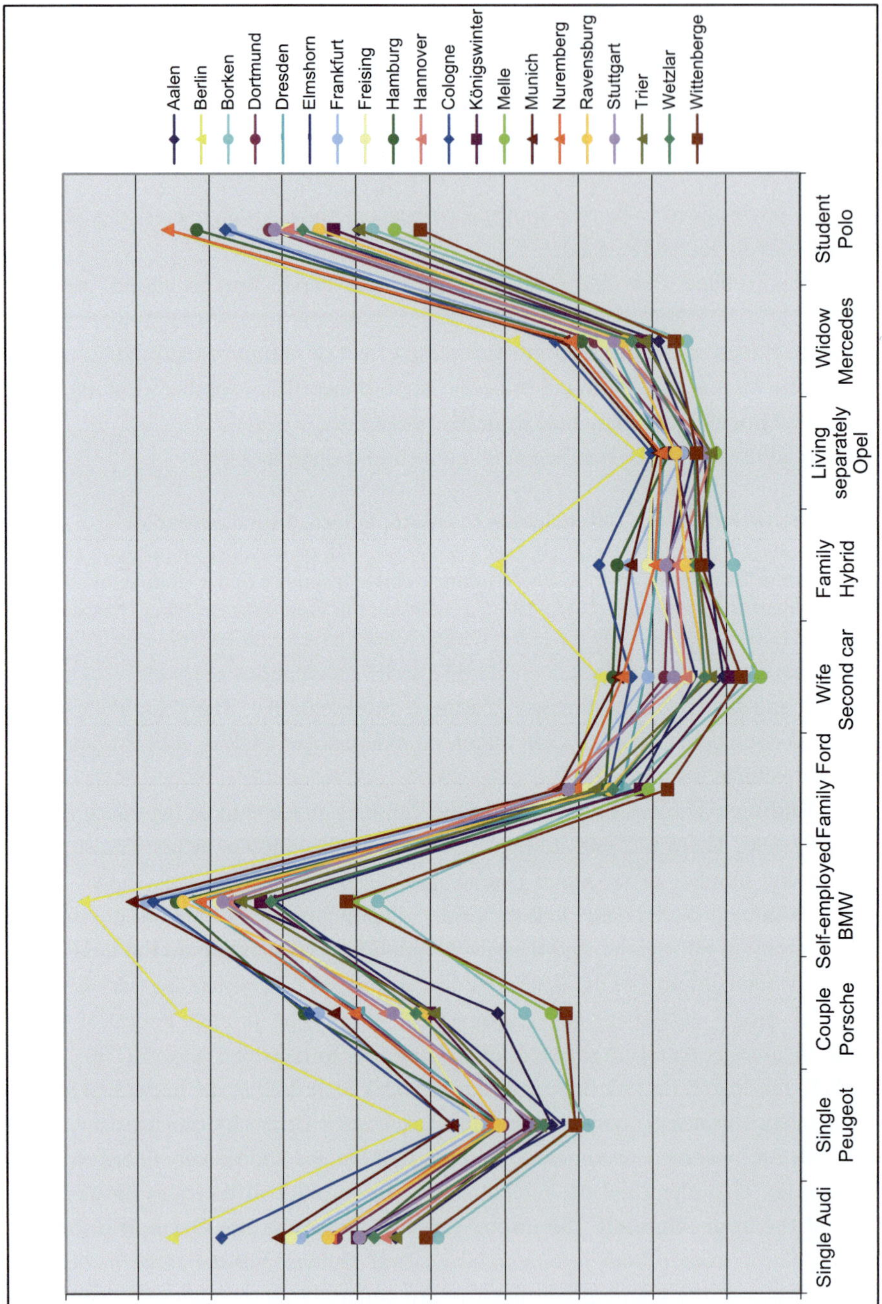

Fig. 11.3 Price differences by model customers and regions in Euro. (Köhne 2018, p. 57)

between the most expensive and the cheapest offer averaged €1629. In the rather rural Wittenberge, on the other hand, the price difference was the smallest: Here it was on average €1092. There are also differences between the individual model customers. In the worst of the 200 cases, the determined price difference was 234% between the most expensive and the cheapest provider. The minimum price difference was 108% between the cheapest and most expensive offer, i.e., the latter was still 2.08 times as high as the former, thus more than twice as high.

Since the insurance tariffs differ greatly in terms of services, the price differences were also particularly considered for **two groups of product offers:** The first group includes tariffs with a rather low coverage scope, which are therefore also cheaper on average. The second group includes tariffs with a larger coverage scope, i.e. those where the entered customer requirements are met to over 88 or 91%. However, this has changed little in the basic findings.

In order not only to compare the most expensive with the cheapest offers, the **price difference between the cheapest offer and the average price was additionally determined,** which represents an indicator for a quite **realistic saving potential:** Even the smallest difference determined in this way among all 200 sample cases was still an absolute 281 € (average of 626 €, cheapest premium of 345 €), thus around 45%. Across all cases, the cheapest offer—viewed relatively—was between 31 and 50.3% below the average value. Figure 11.4 shows the average realistic saving potential of the various model customers across all regions.

Overall, large price differences between the offers of different insurers could also be determined for 2018. These can be attributed to different scopes of services offered, different risk assessments by insurers, and different pricing policies, i.e., cost situations.

Source and further literature for in-depth study:

- Köhne 2013a.
- Köhne 2018.

In some insurance branches, significant price differences can be observed (see research window). Since the premiums or actual prices—among other things due to the design options mentioned above—are not very transparent, policyholders have great difficulties comparing the premium offers of different insurers (Nickel-Waninger 1987, p. 230 f.). Against this background, the price awareness of private and commercial policyholders has traditionally been low; however, it has been increasing for several years due to increasing media reporting, consumer protection policy statements, and the increased importance of comparison portals.

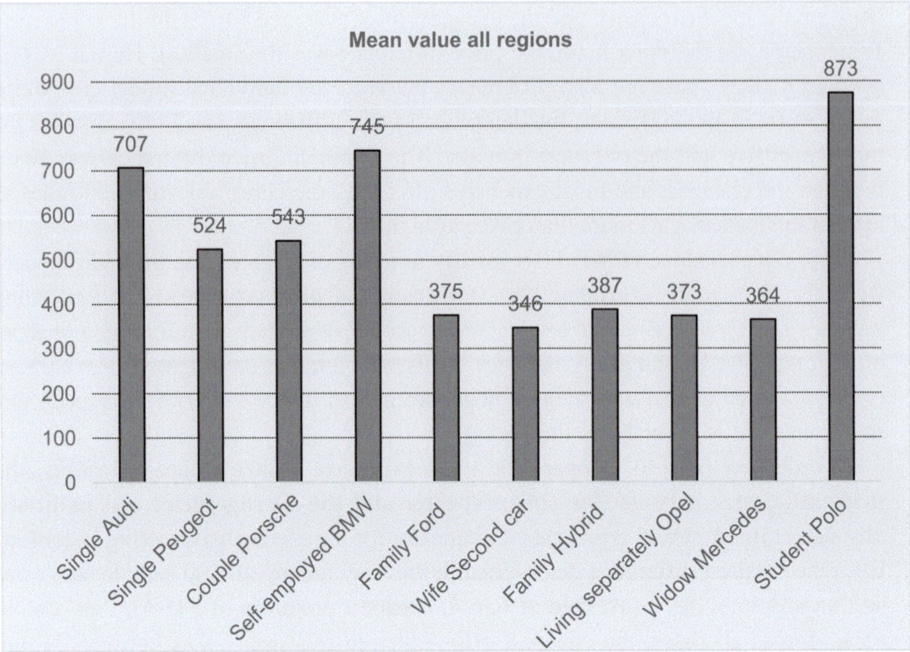

Fig. 11.4 Realistic saving potential of the model customers across all regions, in Euro. (Köhne 2018, p. 7)

11.5 Pricing Strategies

In pricing policy, insurance companies must take into account that product and price are perceived as a unit from the customer's perspective. The basic pricing policy setting is a marketing strategic decision and is—like product policy—already **predetermined** by the **positioning** of the provider in the business fields being served (see Sect. 8.3.2.1). Basically, if the price is to promote the image, there are only two basic profiles: Either the insurer pursues a low-price strategy and must accordingly align its prices with the price leaders and be able to reflect a significantly below-average price level (price leadership). Or it does not position itself via the price, but via alternative differentiation features in the area of products and services (quality leadership).

Also of a fundamental nature is the decision whether to pursue **active or passive pricing policy** (Farny 2011, p. 719 f.): A passive approach means to **orient oneself** to **foreign premium decisions**—this is still a popular strategy among some insurers in practice—or to align premiums with factual (e.g., actuarial bases such as mortality tables, claims statistics) and legal requirements. Such behavior can certainly have economic advantages, as resources for price wars are conserved. Moreover, it leads to "safe" profits when competition is weak. However, it does not allow any conclusions about the dynamics of competition: Because it can be a sign of weak competition if sufficient profits can still be achieved despite passive behavior, but also a sign of strong competition and high market transparency if higher prices than those of competitors could not be enforced at all. Such behavior is problematic from a competition policy perspective when it involves agreements aimed at avoiding competition.

Active pricing policy, on the other hand, is characterized by the fact that the **price decision is autonomously derived from company-specific data.** Pricing is then based on the company's own strategy, estimated price ceilings on the customer side, and calculated costs as a price floor. Such an approach is probably more entrepreneurial and creative, but also involves more risks. The flexibility in pricing is higher, which allows for price differentiation and thus a corresponding attention effect on the customer side. The risk is higher because in the event of a misjudgment, not all providers are affected to the same extent and because the pioneer must possess the necessary competencies in accounting and premium calculation.

Two other pricing approaches are **cost- or market-oriented pricing** (Kühlmann et al. 2003, p. 174–178). Often, cost-oriented pricing, which calculates the effective costs of service provision and sales and adds a profit margin to determine the price (inside-out), is contrasted with market-oriented pricing. The latter takes into account not only costs but also the market constellation including the number and behavior of competitors and demanders as well as their price awareness (outside-in). This does not mean that market-oriented pricing ignores the cost situation and tolerates deficit prices. Rather, it proceeds in a differentiated manner (in the sense of marketing) and aims for a profit over the entire customer relationship. This can mean offering an entry-level product with high market and price transparency at or even below the cost limit in order to generate new business at all, but subsequently selling the customer more margin-rich products that are not subject to price transparency (cross-subsidization). However, it is important that the insurer consistently controls this strategy and does not only sell the bait products. Another reason for less profitable prices may exist if a market does not allow higher prices, but still provides contribution margins for the overhead costs of the head office or at least the branches.

Another pricing decision is the **degree of price differentiation**. The insurer can pursue a general pricing policy that affects the entire range and applies equally to new and existing business, or it can pursue a differentiated pricing policy, whether risk- or market-oriented or according to new and existing customers.

The **differentiation** can, from the actuarial perspective—according to the reverse conclusion from the equal treatment requirement of the VAG, that unequal facts must be treated unequally, and thus quite VAG-compliant—**be oriented towards risk characteristics** and thus follow the actuarial equivalence principle.

From a **marketing perspective,** it can also refer to customer segments, business areas, insurance branches, companies in the group, and distribution channels and **be justified with differences in operating costs**. The aim is then to take into account the respective purchasing power and context-specific demand behavior through different prices in different contexts in order to achieve the maximum possible profit margin in each case. However, a purely purchasing power-related price differentiation is likely to contradict the equal treatment requirement and cannot be justified by operating costs. Possible and compatible with the equal treatment requirement is however the **use of multi-level product offers** (Sect. 10.5). These demonstrably increase the price willingness on the customer side. An empirical study among interested parties and current policyholders of a BU insurance (18 to 40 years, n = 500) showed that compared to the situation with one offer, the closing interest (take-rate) increased from 52 to 93% and the price willingness from 39 to an average of 52 € with a three-level offer (Sirius Campus 2019b).

It also needs to be determined whether and how to differentiate between **new customer and existing business.** Equal treatment means dissatisfaction among existing customers in the event of a premium increase and possibly higher cancellation rates; a premium reduction results in lower contribution margins for the insurer. Differentiation leads to a premium increase or reduction only in new business. However, the effect is limited if, for example, premiums are increased for restructuring reasons, but only the comparatively small part of the new contracts is affected. A premium reduction can be made for competitive reasons in order to generate new business at all. If it is noticed by existing customers, they demand the same premiums or even switch to the competition out of disappointment. It is evident that there is obviously no royal road. For this reason, insurers often try to combine premium differentiation with new products or coverage variants so that it is not obvious.

As a **basis** for the pricing policy decisions just described, insurers need **internal and external price information** (Meidan 1984, p. 59 f.; Nickel-Waninger 1987, p. 232 f.):

- Information about the willingness to pay and the price elasticity of demand in a business field;
- Information about the prices of competitors for the corresponding insurance products in a business field;
- Information about their own costs for determining short-, medium- and long-term price floors;
- Information on the aforementioned legal framework conditions.

Interim Conclusion on the Marketing Tool of Pricing Policy

Despite some regulatory requirements, pricing policy has several design options and offers various strategic action options. It is closely linked to product policy. The great challenge with both tools is that changes not only affect new customer business, but also existing customer business, and thus have far-reaching effects, among other things, on the insurer's earning power and on the actuarial risk in the insurance portfolio.

Further Reading Recommendations for Chap. 11

- Ebner 2010.
- Huber et al. 2015.
- Jahnert et al. 2022.
- Musiol and Steul-Fischer 2017.
- Musiol and Steul-Fischer 2019a.
- Störmer 2014.
- Zweifel and Eisen 2012, p. 206–241.

References

Ebner, M.D. (2010): Preispolitik in der Kompositversicherung, Dissertation, Karlsruhe, 2010.

Farny, D. (2011): Versicherungsbetriebslehre, Karlsruhe, 5. Aufl., 2011.

Huber, C./Gatzert, N./Schmeiser, H. (2015): How Does Price Presentation Influence Consumer Choice? The Case of Life Insurance Products, in: JoRI, Vol. 82, 2015, No. 2, pp. 401–431.

Jahnert, J.R./Schmeiser, H./Schreiber, F. (2022): Pricing strategies in the German term life Insurance market: An empirical analysis, in: Risk Management and Insurance Review, Vol. 25, 2022, pp. 19–34. (https://doi.org/10.1111/rmir.12202)

Köhne, T. (2013a): Preisdifferenzierung in der deutschen Kfz-Versicherung—unverändert enorme Preisunterschiede, in: ZfV, Jg. 64, 2013, Nr. 3, pp. 81–84.

Köhne, T. (2018): Zur Preissituation im deutschen Kfz-Versicherungsmarkt, Studie im Auftrag der Verti Versicherung AG, Berlin, 2018.

Krüger-Barvels, R. (1971): Marketing im Versicherungsbetrieb, Freiburg i.B., 1971.

Kühlmann, K./Wolf, H.-P./Wallenwein, C./Swoboda, U. (2003): Marketing und Vertrieb, Funktionsorientierte Qualifikationen, Karlsruhe, 2. Aufl., 2003.

Meidan, A. (1984): Insurance Marketing, Leighton Buzzard, 1984.

Musiol, A./Steul-Fischer, M. (2017): The psychological effects on tariff choices for car insurance, in: ZVersWiss, Jg. 106, 2017, pp. 525–538. (https://doi.org/10.1007/s12297-017-0395-9)

Musiol, A./Steul-Fischer, M. (2019a): Price framing and consumers' purchase intention on pay-how-you-drive tariffs, in: ZVersWiss, Jg. 108, 2019, pp. 407–419. (https://doi.org/10.1007/s12297-019-00440-1)

Nickel-Waninger, H. (1987): Versicherungsmarketing, auf der Grundlage des Marketing von Informationsprodukten, Karlsruhe, 1987.

Radtke, M. (2008): Grundlagen der Kalkulation von Versicherungsprodukten in der Schaden- und Unfallversicherung, Karlsruhe, 2008.

von der Schulenburg, J.-M. Graf/Lohse, U. (2014): Versicherungsökonomik, Karlsruhe, 2. Aufl., 2014.

Sirius Campus (Ed.) (2019b): Erfolgsfaktoren für Kundenberatungen zur Berufsunfähigkeitsversicherung, Köln, 2019.

Störmer, T. (2014): Essays on risk differentiation and price transparency in the insurer's pricing process, Univ.-Diss. St. Gallen, Meiningen, 2014.

Zweifel, P./Eisen, R. (2012): Insurance Economics, Heidelberg, 2012.

Service and Claims Settlement Policy as Marketing Tools of the Insurance Company

12

12.1 Significance of Service and Claims Settlement Policy in Insurance Companies

Ongoing service and claims management are two central components—alongside the product and distribution—of insurance services. Since they are very closely linked, and claims settlement is a—very central—part of the service policy, they are presented together in this chapter, even though they are essentially two different marketing tools.

Service and claims settlement policies contribute to the perception of service quality over time by customers and **directly determine** their (dis)satisfaction. Creating sufficient **customer satisfaction** is, as shown, a necessary but not yet sufficient condition for sustainable business success: It does not guarantee that customers will remain loyal to the company, but it is necessary in this regard (see also Sect. 7.2.3). This insight is of immediate importance for the service and claims settlement design, which can both contribute to customer satisfaction and thus customer loyalty, as well as to dissatisfaction and termination. If we believe current customer surveys, additional services influence the contract conclusion for more than every second German (61%) (Müller-Reichart et al. 2023, p. 326). These two marketing tools therefore play an important role in achieving the goals of insurance companies.

The role of services is already evident in (financial) services from the designation itself, if one equates service with service provision. In this respect, financial services in general and insurance in particular are essentially pure service products, or at least very strongly influenced by them.

The **interplay between point-in-time and period-related service provision by the insurer** is constitutive for the insurance service: Its service content extends to all potentially realizable possibilities of creating benefits in customer contact (customer touchpoints) over the entire service process (customer journey). From a marketing perspective,

T. Köhne, *Insurance Marketing*, https://doi.org/10.1007/978-3-658-47345-7_12

this ideally involves contributing to the positive well-being of the customer, taking into account his possibilities. This involves—in line with the understanding of customer value (see Sect. 8.3.2.1)—providing solutions to factual problems as well as technically easy and reliable processes, and also making mental and emotional contributions. Thus—at least outside of direct sales—**"human" services and exchange relationships** become the central service content. Thus, with every customer contact with the insurer, a "Moment of Truth" can be identified, which influences the overall relationship of the customer with the insurer: In insurance, such moments of truth and thus tests of endurance are specifically the initiation of contact, information, advice, contract conclusion, subsequent customer care through information and communication during the contract period, claims settlement, complaint handling, and termination processing. Over the entire service process, these various **"Moments of Truth"** develop into a "**Process of Truth**" (Fig. 12.1).

This process of truth is thus another aspect of insurance marketing design—complementing the insurance product and its pricing: The product is supplemented by customer interaction, thereby taking into account the Uno-actu principle (coincidence of production and consumption in the so-called "Prosumer"). At the same time, the point in time (moments of truth) is linked with the period of time (process of truth) (Lehmann 1989, pp. 306–309). Finally, the process of truth illustrates the points of connection and the interplay of service and claims settlement policy as marketing tools, as well as

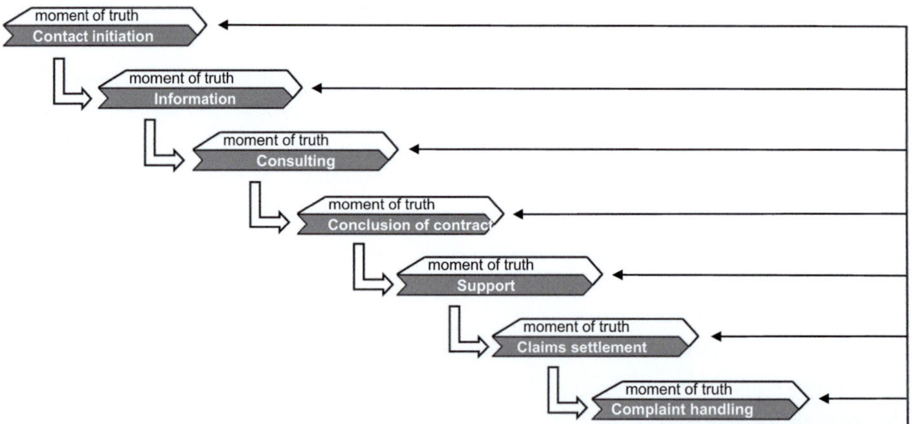

Fig. 12.1 Insurance service: From "Moment of Truth" to "Process of Truth". (Further developed from Lehmann 1989, p. 308)

their different temporal perspective: **Service policy shapes the entire process of truth, Claims settlement policy a (very central) moment of truth.**

Excursus on the design of claims settlement as a product component from a theoretical perspective

From a marketing theoretical perspective, the relationship between product and claims settlement design and other marketing tools can best be illustrated using ***Haller's*** **3-level concept of the insurance product** (see Sect. 10.2.2), which puts the customer and problem-solving at the center:

Level 1 corresponds, as shown, to the core product, the actual insurance coverage. The objective framework conditions for claims settlement are already laid down in the core product: The insurance contract (policy and insurance conditions) constitutes the insurance coverage and thus any claims payment and accompanying services in the event of a claim. In this respect, customer-oriented product design can create scope for needs-based, problem-solving-oriented services around claims payment.

Level 2 supplements the core product with services directly oriented towards the basic function of (financial) securing, which include advice, explanation (both tasks of sales policy), care (task of service policy) and claims processing. At this level of consideration, the question arises as to how product and services can be integrated in a customer-oriented manner and how the standardized core product can be individualized. Advisory and support services in the course of claims processing are thus components of the insurance service. This also includes safety advice following damage events, as they correspond to the advisory process in terms of risk management and to the ongoing adjustment (of precautionary measures) in terms of the service process, thus serving to fulfill the securing function. The claims settlement, which aims to "reduce negative implications of damage events or improve the risk exposure of those affected" (Jara 2000, p. 52), is thus explicitly part of the product and service of insurance companies. The claims settlement includes advisory, support and remedial measures following damage events as well as preventive activities to reduce the frequency of damage or the average damage of potentially affected persons. At level 2, direct relationships between product design and the marketing tools of sales and claims settlement design become visible, all of which constitute the average benefit of insurance.

Level 3 extends the orientation of the insurance service to the securing function to other functions. The extended services can develop in three directions: A horizontal extension is primarily oriented towards the trend towards combined financial services ("Allfinanz"). A vertical extension takes place through specialization in the technical area. Services of a more technical nature can include in-depth risk management advice with services for damage prevention and security technology. Finally, in a diagonal extension, care strategies can meet the social and emotional concerns of customers. These include, for example, all kinds of assistance services. Especially in the event of a claim, some of these additional services are offered: They can contribute sustainably to customer satisfaction and customer loyalty and at the same time provide starting points for cross-selling or new customer acquisition (referral business). Level 3 is designed in product policy, but touches on service, claims settlement and sales policy and is partly implemented by these (Köhne 2003, pp. 74–77).

The provision of **claim settlement** represents a very **critical success factor,** if not the most significant **care service,** because from the customer's perspective, it is ultimately *the* moment of truth in which it becomes apparent whether the policyholder has purchased the credence good insurance from the right provider. Moreover, the claim event is one of the few opportunities—apart from the consultation phase during the conclusion of the contract—to come into personal contact with the customer or the injured party (Fig. 12.2).

Both the importance of individual service touchpoints (moments of truth) and that of the cross-channel coordinated service process (process of truth) have been empirically proven, e.g., for the positive influence of services after contract conclusion on the one-year cancellation rate in life insurance (Jayswal and Brahmbhatt 2013) or for the positive influence of cross-channel coordinated services on customer loyalty (Cassab and MacLachlan 2009).

12.2 Customer-oriented Service Design along the Process of Truth

To concretize and systematize the service elements of insurance, it is advisable to separately address the contents of services (= service as a product) and the points of contact of services in the entire customer relationship (= services as a process).

▶ **Service policy** includes all decisions regarding the strategy-compliant implementation of insurance services and extended services of a company.

The concrete specification of service benefits is closely related to the (material-content) product design (see Sect. 10.2.2). Services can therefore be divided into immediate services in connection with the application and processing of insurance coverage (level 2) and extended services that are intended to provide additional benefits beyond financial security (level 3).

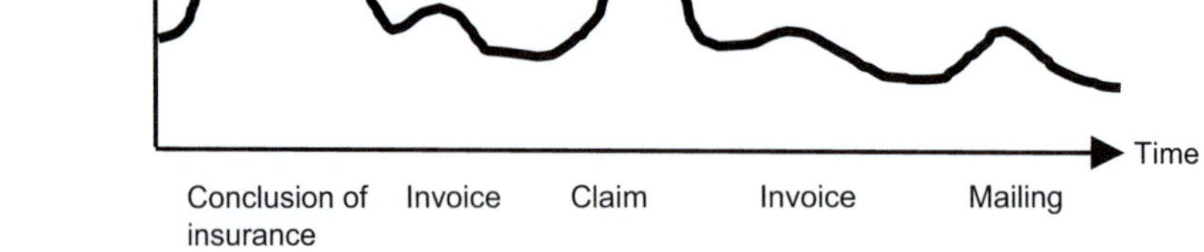

Fig. 12.2 Time-contact intensity diagram. (Based on Joho 1996, p. 133)

The **immediate services** include the consultation, explanation, and mediation of insurance coverage, the ongoing care during the contract term, the care and regulation in the event of a claim, and the care and possibly consultation in the event of cancellation. In the sense of the marketing concept, customer needs initially form the starting point of product design. These customer needs must be recognized and met in their context. In the case of insurance issues, this is about the entire security process of the private customer and the corresponding insurance coverage.

The fundamental service in the course of mediating insurance coverage is thus comprehensive advice based on the recording of the customer-specific risk and security situation (see Sect. 13.6.3). The design of services in connection with the recording of the risk situation and the explanation of insurance coverage can be supported person-related through employee qualification and training in internal and external service, as well as document-related through the preparation of information material—a task of sales promotion (see Sect. 14.2.2).

Service measures can be divided according to the phases of the service process, i.e., before and during contract conclusion, during the contract term, and in the event of an insured case (pension provision or claims settlement). They can also be systematized according to the life phases of the customer. Finally, they can be structured according to whether they supplement the function of financial security horizontally, vertically, or diagonally as product-accompanying services (level 3) with further function fulfillments (see Sect. 10.2.2) (Kühlmann et al. 2003, p. 189 f.).

Based on the **classification according to the service process,** the following specific services provided by insurers can be exemplified (Farny 2011, p. 789 f.):

Services **before and at the time of contract conclusion** include, for example, customer advice on risks and the impact of insurance, the analysis and evaluation of customer risks, advice on technical loss prevention, customer-friendly explanation of insurance products using sales support tools (flyers, expert systems, etc.), the provisional coverage commitment, and the issuance of documents such as the Green Card in motor vehicle insurance.

During the contract term, from a service perspective, it is about, for example,

- continuously informing the customer about important contract-related developments (tariff changes, residual value, surplus development, fund development, etc.),
- informing him early about important changes,
- advising him in case of changed risk situation and adjusting insurance coverage accordingly,
- relieving him as much as possible in case of contract adjustments (e.g., address changes due to relocation),
- implementing simple complaint options and taking customer complaints seriously,
- providing uncomplicated assistance in emergency situations, and
- being easily accessible when needed.

Services **in the case of an insured event** refer to all services related to pension provision or claims settlement (see Sect. 12.3).

All mentioned services can be offered in a wide range: In one extreme case, this means that the customer is left to his own devices and must drive the process forward himself. In the other extreme case, the insurer takes care of almost everything, drives the process forward and prepares the initial situation together with the customer (risk, income and asset, pension situation, damage situation). For example, the procurement of specific documents, receipts or letters can be imposed on the customer or largely taken off him.

The **extended services** fulfill additional functions besides or instead of financial security or pension provision (in life insurance) and thus provide additional benefits (level 3). In the sense of a comprehensive overall service or a problem solution from the customer's perspective, they embody the service idea par excellence. Since they go beyond the insurance business, they are usually provided by external service providers. Nevertheless, the insurer can specify the content and scope of the services and thus shape the overall performance. For possible financial, technical-performance-economic, social and psychological product additions, see Sect. 10.5.

From a service perspective, the so-called **assistance services** should be highlighted here. A customer-oriented design of the insurance service finds its consistent complement in the offer of meaningful—the function of financial security—supplementary assistance services.

▶ **Assistance services** are (often globally) offered services for customers who have gotten into an emergency situation (emergency, help or assistance services) or who are simply seeking support in certain life situations (leisure, home, travel).

The ultimate goal of assistance and at the same time the benefit for the customer is support in coping with an emergency situation or other predefined life situations or events, whether by maintaining or creating health, a sense of security, time saving, flexibility or convenience. Classic assistance services are emergency, help or assistance services of a technical, medical, legal and tourist nature. Modern assistance services include care (nursing, senior services) or support services (home, job, leisure service). The examples of specific assistance services from the mentioned areas are so numerous that they cannot be listed here due to the scope (see in detail at Esser 2004).

However, mastering such crisis situations requires increased organizational efforts: The service network may need to be globally oriented, the employees multilingual trained, and the IT platform designed for (global) data exchange between network partners. For these reasons, **assistance companies are usually specialized providers** in their own legal form, some of which are independent and some of which have insurance companies as owners. Figure 12.3 shows the possible relationships between the actors involved in the assistance business. The insurer offers its customer the assistance service and then bears the costs towards the assistance organization, who coordinates the actual

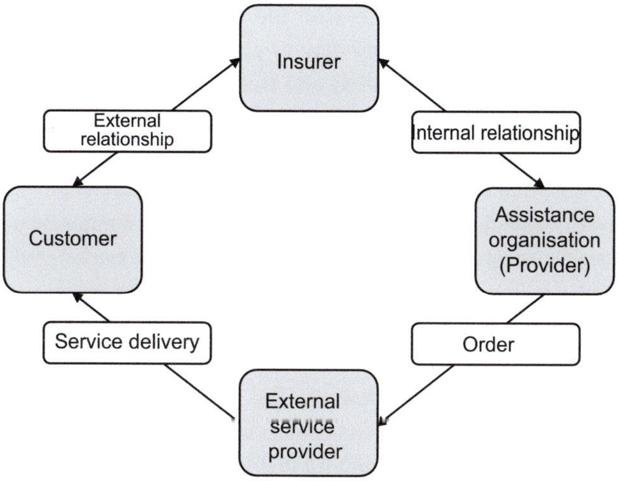

Fig. 12.3 Relationship between the actors involved in the assistance business. (Based on Lange et al. 2013, p. 177)

provision in the case of an insured event, and usually an external service provider provides this service or work performance.

With reference to the insurance benefit, it should be noted that assistance services, like all services, make the abstract product insurance tangible and emotional for the customer. **Help in an emergency leaves** more lasting **impressions** than a promise of a certain, legally defined coverage. Assistance offers are particularly popular in the areas of mobility, travel, and motor vehicles: As early as 2015, one in three (34%) had used such services. In the event of mobility disruptions, the willingness to delegate to service providers is particularly high, due to a greater feeling of being overwhelmed in unfamiliar territories and unusual situations (o. V. 2015). The importance of the service idea in the German population has been increasing over the last decade and is now at a high level: After all, in general, 94% expect services as a product added value from their service providers, specifically 63% do this from insurers. Service, assistance, and support have thus reached the status of an expected basic benefit. Citizens are also willing to pay for this: While only 38% are willing to pay for general service promises, this value doubles for specifically described, imaginable services such as obtaining a second opinion in health assistance or pointing out craftsmen in home and family assistance to 76%. Thus, particularly for benefit-generating support, a material appreciation of (assistance) services can be observed (Müller-Reichart et al. 2023, p. 323 f.).

Originally, assistance services were closely causally related to an insurance (damage) case, e.g. the car protection letter with towing service or the foreign travel protection letter with repatriation in case of accidents or illnesses. However, they have increasingly detached themselves from the actual damage case and offer support services in many everyday life situations. Strictly speaking, these were always additional services (level

3), as they have little or nothing to do with the original task of insurance—either the financial compensation of losses or retirement provision. On the other hand, they **are in a functional problem-solving context** and **therefore fit so well with the insurance service**. From a differentiation perspective, it should be noted that assistance services make insurance products more interesting and customer-oriented and are actually indispensable from a service perspective. Although they thus provide good sales arguments, it should not be overlooked that a **unique selling proposition** cannot be achieved through assistance services, as these—for cost reasons alone—are always offered as an additional service by several service providers. Moreover, they are, as mentioned, **increasingly expected** by customers.

The **procedural design of the service policy** encompasses the entire contractual relationship and thus the entire service process. The most significant, customer-perceptible service activities take place in direct, i.e. personal customer contact and often with the intermediary. However, customer contact is not limited to one opportunity, but can occur during contact initiation, information, consultation, explanation, sales as such, customer care over time in the event of a claim, in the course of contract adjustments or additions and in the event of a complaint, and even at the end of the contract. In addition or instead, service can also be provided during these moments via other communication (e.g. telephone, letter, internet) and distribution channels (call centers, customer or contract departments, claims departments, claims inspectors, assistance organizations, contract partners, etc.).

Consequently, designing the entire service chain is a complex and demanding task. This requires professional **service controlling**, which systematically records, standardizes, and measures the central service performances to increase customer benefit, possibly improves them, and thus ultimately controls the entire process chain; nowadays this is called Customer Experience Management (see Sect. 2.2.4). It first has to identify the critical contact points where customers assess the service quality of the provider. Then, in the sense of process management, the identified service processes, their sub-steps, and results have to be defined and continuously measured (Kühlmann et al. 2003, p. 185). Of course, digitalization, in connection with direct customer access via apps, the automatic use and linking of data, and AI applications, now supports both a fast, error-free, and largely automated service provision and the measurement data generated in the process to check the quality. Most processes can be implemented digitally, and in some business models and customer situations, this is already working (Nicoletti 2021, chapters 5 and 9). But—especially in insurance matters—many citizens still trust in personal contact (Sect. 5.4 and 4.3.1), and a large part of communication takes place between people. However, people are far less controllable by the insurer than technology. Therefore, tools for contact analysis, quality controlling, and measurement of customer and employee satisfaction are needed (Kühlmann et al. 2003, p. 185 f.).

A well-known tool for contact analysis is **blueprinting**, a graphical representation of the various customer contact points (Touch Points), starting from the initial contact to the end of the contract (Bruhn 2022, p. 231). Key processes with customer contact along the service process are typically:

- Customer consultation in the initiation phase (usually by the intermediary, also call center),
- Application processing and policy issuance (by the internal service, automated),
- Contract changes (by internal service/call center or sales force),
- Contract correspondence (information letters, customer's address change notifications) (by internal service/call center, automated),
- Premium invoices (automated),
- Ongoing advice and support (by internal service/call center or sales force),
- Claims or service processing (by internal service/call center, claims field service, possibly sales force, partly automated),
- Customer complaints (usually by internal service/call center, possibly sales force),
- Information events for customers and potential customers (by sales force together with sales promotion specialists, automated),
- Conclusion of further insurance contracts (by sales force, partly internal service/call center).

After recording the relevant service processes, these are to be described. A **service manual** can be helpful in this regard, which shows what expectations customers have in the individual phases of the contractual relationship and how they are to be met. It should describe how employees should behave in specific customer situations and define as clear standards as possible (i.e., service standards). If this is successful, the benefit lies firstly in sensitizing the employees, and secondly, service quality becomes measurable and verifiable. However, the continuous review and possibly further development of the guidelines together with the affected employees is important.

Further consideration should be given to **service guarantees**. They serve to define clear service goals, continuous measurement of goal achievement, measurability of service deficits and the costs caused by them, as well as the optimization of internal processes for the benefit of the customer or injured party. These promises are communicated to the customer and, in the event of non-compliance, lead to payouts to the customer. The injured party receives a consideration in case of service deficiencies and it is made clear to them that their objections are taken seriously and pursued. Service guarantees also support market profiling by drawing the customer's or injured party's attention to services that can distinguish the provider from the competition. Apart from the external profiling effect, service guarantees have an internal effect: Provided they are not determined without the employees' knowledge, they promote motivation and thus also service quality. They may even be linked to incentive systems if the amount of variable wage components corresponds to the compliance with service guarantees (Peill and van Eck 1997).

Already about 35 years ago, cross-industry studies (PIMS studies) confirmed the positive influence of a higher service quality compared to the competition on company profits. It has also been shown that good quality management does not automatically mean always and everywhere striving for the highest service quality (Bruhn 2019a, p. 12, 15). Rather, the aim is to achieve a **market-oriented**, differentiated by target group (and thus relative) **service quality**. Consequently, the service dimensions decisive for the customer's purchase decision are to be developed and quality objectives derived from them (Lehmann 1993, p. 75).

The postulate of customer orientation uses individual customer perception as the standard for satisfying needs. Thus, customer satisfaction and satisfactory service quality only arise when the actual experiences with a service at least meet the previously existing expectations (see Sect. 7.2.3).

Note: Evaluation of service quality from the customer's perspective
Customer expectation ≤ Customer experience → good service quality (possibly enthusiasm if exceeded)
Customer expectation > Customer experience → poor service quality (disappointment)

Customer expectations are always **subjective in nature** in relation to the individual case, because objective determinants (age, education, horizon of experience, wealth status, place of residence, chosen contact medium, chosen distribution channel) are supplemented by many subjective (= person-dependent, individual) circumstances (emotion, motivation, attitude, knowledge and skills, personal experiences, influence by family environment or other persons). These lead, on the one hand, to people with equally pronounced objective determinants still having different expectations of service performances. On the other hand, subjective circumstances are responsible for the fact that these expectations are not even necessarily stable, but can change situation-specifically over time (Sect. 4.3). Customer expectations are thus influenced, among other things, by past experiences, their individual needs, personal word-of-mouth propaganda (e.g. from family or acquaintances) and only partly by marketing communication (Chap. 14).

Since it is not economically feasible in the private customer business to inquire about customer expectations in individual cases and to design the service performance accordingly, **standardized surveys** are conducted and conclusions for the design of the service are drawn from them (standardized). In addition, customer expectations should at least be differentiated according to target groups insofar as recipients of service performances, apart from end customers, are numerous other business partners who stand as recipients or intermediaries between the provider and insurance customers (= policyholders) or as third parties involved (e.g. insured persons, injured parties, sales force, brokers, loss adjusters, employers, assistance organizations etc.) and who have different expectations related to business. In addition, statistical methods (e.g. factor and cluster analysis, see Sect. 5.3) can be used to identify which groups within the private customer business can be formed in terms of their service expectations, e.g. depending on the chosen contact and distribution channels.

The specific **customer experiences** refer to three service-typical quality dimensions, the evaluation of which naturally depends on the respective (conscious or unconsciously existing) expectations: The **result quality** describes the degree of factual fulfillment of expectations and thus refers to the end result of the service; its evaluation is based on the question of what service the customer has actually received. The **process quality,** on the other hand, refers to the perception of all activities in customer contact, i.e., the manner of service provision. It is based on the question of how the customer experienced or perceived the service. Finally, the **potential quality** describes the quality of the factual, organizational, and personal performance prerequisites of the provider. Its evaluation is based on how well the service provider presents itself to the customer, whether and how quickly he can be reached.

In relation to insurance services, **examples** of service result qualities are the comprehensibility and content quality of information and contract documents, the accessibility and help in case of need, the duration until feedback, the content quality of statements, the reliability of promises or in the event of loss, the duration and scope of claims settlement. Examples of service process qualities relate to the pleasantness of the visible environment (rooms, staff), the willingness and speed in solving the customer problem, and the politeness, trustworthiness, and empathy of the staff. Examples of service potential qualities are accessibility abroad and the sufficient and qualified staffing of claims hotlines and claims settlement departments, especially during times of major damage events such as hailstorms or heavy rain, which affect many customers at the same time.

As mentioned, service controlling also includes the **measurement of service quality.** This can be done by surveying customers, as is known from hotels. Customers are asked to weight various predefined quality dimensions and evaluate their degree of fulfillment using a form. The "Servqual method" developed in the USA aims in the same direction. In the insurance industry, the Net Promoter Score and the KUBUS satisfaction survey are mainly used (see research window in Sect. 9.1).

Another way of measuring service quality is the relative comparison with the most successful competitors (**benchmarking**) or—if these cannot be identified—with the relevant competitors. Measurable quality indicators can then be, for example, customer satisfaction as the overarching measure (e.g., using NPS), result-related indicators such as error rates, cancellation rates, and rating results, as well as process-related indicators such as processing times, complaint analyses, or friendliness determined through customer reviews. Such measurements are usually carried out by external service providers (rating or market research institutions, scientific institutes, consulting firms) who can collect and compare cross-company data anonymously.

In the procedural design of services, **complaint management** plays an important role. The importance of complaint management is explained by the empirical observation (also in insurance companies) that customers whose complaint was handled to their full satisfaction often show higher loyalty to the provider afterwards than before (Hart et al. 1990; Stauss and Seidel 2019, p. 47–51; Homburg 2020, p. 1027). In addition, 77% of dissatisfied customers communicate their negative experiences intensively to third parties, while only 48% of dissatisfied customers do so if they have complained to the company (Blodgett et al. 1995). However, it is also problematic when customers are dissatisfied and do not complain at all. These are then latently at risk of churn, and customer loyalty decreases. And for every articulated complaint, there are far more unarticulated complaints. Across all industries in Germany, the proportion of non-complainants is extraordinarily high and, depending on the industry, goes up to over 90%. Two surveys of customers of an insurance company also confirmed that among existing customers, 55% of the annoyed customers did not complain and 86% of the annoyed customers who had already cancelled did not complain (Stauss and Seidel 2019, p. 41 f.).

▶ **Customer complaints** are articulations of dissatisfaction towards the company. They are raised when the customer subjectively considers the experienced problems to be serious (Bruhn and Hennig 1993, p. 222; Stauss and Seidel 2019, p. 26 f.).

▶ **Complaint Management** is a system of measures to encourage the articulation of customer dissatisfaction, to assess it, and to initiate activities to remedy the causes of dissatisfaction (Meffert et al. 2018, p. 228).

From a marketing perspective, various **objectives** are pursued with systematic complaint management (Meffert et al. 2018, p. 229):

- Achieving high (complaint) satisfaction
- Avoiding customer churn and negative word-of-mouth
- Improving the company's image
- Gaining information as a basis for service improvements, service modifications, and service differentiations (cross-reference to product policy)
- Increasing service quality through reduced error costs.

In this context, complaint management according to *Stauss* and *Seidel* (2019) has to go through **various phases** (Fig. 12.4): The first phase is complaint stimulation by setting up easily accessible complaint channels. This is followed by complaint acceptance, which aims at the complete recording of the complaint and where customer dissatisfaction can already be reduced through appropriate behavior. In the subsequent complaint processing, it is about who does what by when and in what order and documents it. In the next phase, the complaint response takes place, i.e., problem-solving through an official apology, information or explanation, and possibly material or financial compensation. Here too, in addition to the result quality, the process quality plays a major role: For example, a timely receipt confirmation or telephone response, the general handling of the complainant, and empathy in communication, as well as regular information about the processing status, influence the customer's perception of the complaint processing. Finally, in the concluding complaint processing, it is about possibly drawing structural, informational, and/or personnel consequences from the complaint and maintaining a functioning complaint system that combines a complaint culture, adequate IT-based complaint systems, and enough appropriately trained employees (Stauss and Seidel 2019, pp. 62–65).

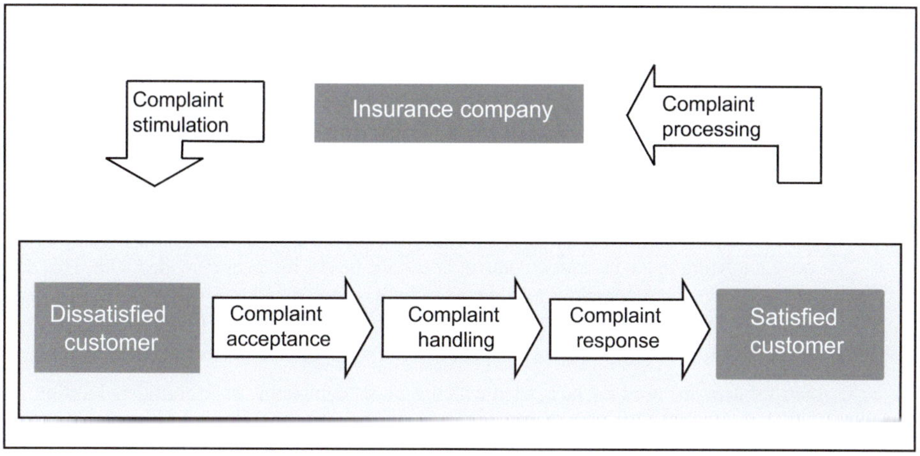

Fig. 12.4 Phases of the complaint management system. (Based on Meffert et al. 2018, p. 229; Stauss and Seidel 2019, p. 62)

In insurance, the establishment of systematic complaint management has been **demanded by the insurance supervisory authority** for over ten years. Based on § 23 para. 1 VAG, BaFin has issued Circular 3/2013 on "Minimum requirements for complaint handling by insurance companies". In this, it prescribes far-reaching requirements for complaint management, which affect the various phases of the complaint management system (see excerpt from the BaFin Circular of 2013). The central reporting system required by BaFin has led to a standardization of definition, recording, and controlling of complaints by group-wide complaint departments. However, there is a risk that due to the regulation, the complaint management, which is so important from a marketing point of view, degenerates into a complaint bureaucracy with a lot of documentation, rather than actually providing improvements and lean customer communication. On the other hand, the circular at least obliges all insurers to do something that is fundamentally welcome from the customer's point of view, and the regulations should not prevent any insurer from operating professional complaint management with corresponding customer satisfaction (Fleck and Herrig 2015, pp. 88–94).

Excerpt from BaFin Circular 3/2013 on "Minimum requirements for complaints-handling by insurance undertakings"

A. Preliminary remarks

(…)

B. Minimum requirements for complaint handling by insurance companies

B.1. General—Definitions

(…) A well-functioning and transparent complaints-handling system including appropriate documentation is one of the basic compenents of an effective risk management system. (…) If the minimum requirements for complaints-handling include principle-based objctives, these are to be met taking into account the risks specific to the undertaking, the nature and scope of the business operations as well as the complexity of the insurance undertaking's business model. Generally speaking, these minimum requirements aim to secure a certain (consumer) protection level for the insured parties/policyholders, which must be maintained.

The following indicative definitional apply to the minimum requirements listed in this circular:

a) Complaint

Complaint means a statement of dissatisfaction adressed to an insurance undertaking by a person relating to the insurance contract or service he/she has been provided with. This definition also includes complaints addressed to insurance undertakings with reference to an insurance intermediary. Complaints-handling should be diffentiated from claims-handling as well as from simple requests for execution of the contract, information or clarification.

Such statements need not be headed with the word "complaint" to be considered a complaint.

b) Complainant

Complainant means a person who is presumed to be eligible to have a complaint considered by an insurance undertaking and has already lodged a complaint, e.g., a (potential) policyholder, insured person, beneficiary or injured third party.

B.2. Internal complaints management policy

(…) The internal policy should include processes for the following areas, to the extent possible:

a) Lodging complaint: (…)

b) Complaints-handling: (…)

c) Training: (…)

d) Compliance with the internal policy: (…)

The afore-mentioned minimum requirements do not affect the freedom of insurance undertakings to internally implement/apply the internal policy in the specific manner they choose.

B.3. Complaints management function

(…), insurance undertakings are to establish a complaints management function which enables complaints to be investigated fairly and in a legally correct manner and potential conflicts of interest to be identified, avoided or managed as well as possible. In doing so, undertakings are to appoint one or more experienced person(s) directly beneath board level, if possible, to bear responsibility for proper performance of complaints-handling duties. (…)

The complaints management function may be centralised or decentralised; however the required analysis (B.6. sentence 1) may only be performed centrally. The responsibilities and individual tasks are to be clearly defined. The compliance management function should be structed in such a way that it is free of conflicts of interest as far as possible.

B.4. Registration

(…)

B.5. Information obligation

(…), insurance undertakings must submit a complaint report to the Federal Financial Supervisory Authority (Bundesanstalt für Finanzdienstleistungsaufsicht - BaFin).

They are also expected to use their influence to obtain knowledge of complaints lodged with their tied agents within the meaning of section 34d (4) of Industrial Code (Gewerbeordnung - GewO), which they should also enter into their own internal complaints system and of which they are also to notify BaFin. Only in this manner can complaints be fully documented and comprehensive complaints-handling ensured regardless of whether complaints are lodged with the agent or with the insurance undertaking.

B.6. Internal follow-up of complaints-handling
Insurance undertakings are to analyse the complaints-handling data on an ongoin basis (complaints analysis) to ensure that recurring or systemic problems and potential legal and operational risks are identified and remedied. The following measures are to be taken into account: (…)

B.7. Provision of information
The insurance undertaktins shall

a) inform the complainant, upon request or when acknowledging receipt of a complaint, about the complaints-handling process, in writing if the complainant so desires; (…)

B.8. Procedure for responding to complaints
The insurance undertakings shall

a) seek to gather and investigate all relevant evidence and information regarding the complaint;
b) communicate in plain language, which is clearly understood;
c) provide a response without any unnecessary delay; (…)
d) when providing a final decision that does not fully satisfy the complainant's demands, include a thorough explanation of the insurance undertakings's position on the complaint and set out the complainant's option for maintain the complaint (e.g., the option of approaching an ombudsman, BaFin, availability of an alternative dispute mechanism, etc.). Such decision should be provided in writing if the complainant so desires.

The service policy must first justify the basic service philosophy from the strategic guidelines (positioning, business areas, marketing task profile), then determine differentiated service expectations with a focus on the various target groups and business areas, in order to derive the necessary service standards from this and finally to continuously measure and possibly adjust these in the sense of professional service controlling.

Interim Conclusion on the Marketing Tool of Service Policy
The service policy applies along the entire service process and (almost) all customer contact points; it must prove its quality in several, certainly differently important moments of truth of the customer relationship. Thus, it influences the entire customer journey, which in the case of insurance services rather embodies a process of truth. This includes the definition of services to be provided (content service design) and their differentiated distribution to the various phases of the service process (processual service design).

12.3 Customer-oriented Design of Claims Settlement in the Moment of Truth

The **claims management** in the insurance company performs **various functions** (see also Guttenbacher et al. 2021, p. 477):

1. As a **risk policy tool**, it aims to control and possibly reduce claims costs.
2. As a **tool of process organization**, it designs claims settlement and optimizes claims settlement costs.
3. As an **actively designable marketing tool**, claims management deals with the customer-oriented design of claims settlement (Claims settlement policy).

The following is about claims management as a marketing tool. It is about nothing less than the fulfillment of the permanent protection promise that was sold to the customer at the time of contract conclusion, so that financial security is provided in the event of a claim (core function of insurance). At the time of consultation and conclusion, the customer cannot really assess the quality of the insurance service. Result and potential quality cannot yet be assessed, the process quality initially only with regard to these contact phases. In the event of a claim, the **provision of the claims service** as **from the customer's perspective** is by far the most important support service and due to the necessary advance of trust, the **moment of truth**, in which it becomes apparent whether the trust placed in the insurer was justified.

Therefore, it is not surprising that both a disappointment and the enthusiasm in the case of a particularly good fulfillment of the claims service leave a **lasting impression on the customer or the injured party**. To recall: A disappointment of the customer damages the image (by notification to up to eleven other people) and weakens customer loyalty. Conversely, a customer-oriented claims service supports the achievement of marketing goals (Chap. 7) and marketing tasks (Chap. 9), namely the following (Joho 1996, p. 238 f.; Jara 2000, pp. 91–94, 100–103; Farny 2011, p. 677; Guttenbacher et al. 2021, p. 478):

- Need orientation through problem solutions,
- Image improvement through positive word-of-mouth propaganda,
- Customer loyalty through high customer satisfaction and opportunity costs when changing providers with the potential for cross-selling,
- Customer (re)acquisition as a result of referral business with new customers or with injured third party who were once customers.

In addition, the claim event is **one of the few opportunities**—apart from the consultation phase during the conclusion of the contract—to come into **personal contact** with the customer or injured party. The market figures collected by the GDV give a first rough impression of this marketing potential (GDV 2023a, p. 65): In motor vehicle third-party liability insurance alone, there were around 3.4 million customer contact opportunities with injured third parties in 2022, after deducting their own customers, still a considerable contact potential. The claim-related customer contact and customer loyalty opportunities with their own customers in comprehensive motor vehicle insurance amounted to just over 5 million. In all insurance branches of property & casualty/accident insurance, there were 22.7 million claims, which expresses a considerable contact, customer loyalty, and probably also cross-selling potential.

A customer-oriented claims service design is initially based on the consideration of customer needs and the functions underlying them. In research and practice, there are numerous surveys and studies on the needs of insurance customers and the importance of various aspects of claims services—these are usually based on surveys. From this, the following **expectations of customers** towards insurers regarding the claims service can be derived (Jara 2000, p. 109):

- Speed of payment commitment and payment initiation,
- Correctness of the financial benefits, preferably a complete assumption of the damage costs,
- Friendliness towards injured parties,
- Unbureaucratic approach,
- Transparency regarding the procedure and the claims for the injured parties.

In addition, 89% of policyholders want specific emergency aids (assistance services) as an additional service to pure claims coverage. And for 68% the organization of repair measures for damage elimination is very important or important (Müller-Reichart et al. 2023, p. 324).

Such market research results, however, need to be supplemented by conceptual considerations and by the **use of further research methods** such as observation in focus groups, as they only apply with certain limitations. Firstly, the respondent's environment at the time of the survey does not match that at the time of the decision or the damage event. This is particularly true for the actual needs of injured parties following damage events, which arise, for example, due to psychological stress and the novelty of the situation (Laakmann and Rahlf 2019, pp. 413–417). Another limitation of the aforementioned studies is that they predominantly orient themselves towards existing structures and derive the characteristics to be queried from them. They assume the role of the insurance industry to essentially make financial compensation for contractually fixed damage events. Possible additional value-adding services in the course of damage processing cannot be captured at all because the respondents have no ideas about them and therefore cannot articulate such wishes.

Against this background, it seems promising to additionally ask proactively and benefit-oriented with *Haller*: "**What would my customer want if he knew what he needed?**" (Haller and Ackermann 1995, Part 3, p. 5) and to answer this question function-oriented.

The assistance organizations have impressively done this and developed a number of possible emergency and independent support services (see Sect. 12.2). Some of these are also suitable in the context of providing damage services to turn this into a comprehensive problem solution.

The **damage services** can be aligned with their **basic functions** (Jara 2000, p. 124):

1. Compensation for the financial consequences of damage events,
2. Relief of injured parties from transaction costs of restoration after damage events,
3. Support of the injured parties in the social and psychological damage coping and extensive restoration of inner security.

Against the background of this functional view, the results of studies (using conjoint measurement analysis and its preceding workshops) are easy to understand, which have found a **wide acceptance of comprehensive problem solutions** that largely relieve injured parties from dealing with the repair of the damage, e.g. in the form of replacement or the organization of repair measures (psychonomics/avanturo 2002; Müller-Reichart and Schäfer 2014, p. 223).

From the insurer's perspective, this context refers to **active claims management**, which has become increasingly widespread over the last ten to 15 years (Farny 2011, p. 679 f.; Jeßnitzer 2008, p. 1618; Lange et al. 2013, p. 169 f.; Guttenbacher et al. 2021, p. 498–501). The elimination of actual damages is not part of the insurer's contractual obligations, which generally only compensates for economic loss through insurance benefits in the form of money. The **elimination of actual damage** is the responsibility of the policyholder, in the case of liability claims even that of the injured third party. However, both parties do not have the experience of damage elimination, the insurer can generally implement this more cost-effectively, either because it can realize scale and network effects, or because it is not exposed to the moral risk of settling the claim at higher than justified costs. Through active claims management, the insurer can either influence the damage elimination by the policyholder by advising him and supporting him in the selection of service providers and the monitoring or taking over these for the policyholder, e.g. by using partner repair shop networks for motor vehicle damage. Or the insurer takes over the damage elimination from the outset and uses further (external) service providers and controls and monitors these. The boundary between both variants is as fluid as the transition between damage elimination services and assistance services. The shorter the time span between the occurrence of damage and the reporting of damage, the easier customers and claimants can be referred to their own repair shop, rental car, lawyer, and craftsman networks. Therefore, it is important for insurers—just like for car manufacturers because of the steering into their own brand repair shops—to be the first point of contact as soon as possible after the damage event. This calculation explains the battle of various industries for access to the emergency hotlines and the control of the emergency calls sent from the electronic security system in the motor vehicle (see also Breuer and Zimmermann 2019, p. 619 f.; Guttenbacher et al. 2021, p. 498–501).

Apart from the fact that through **active claims management** both the pure damage costs and the claims settlement costs can be reduced, it is from a marketing perspective a very suitable **approach to convince the customer as a problem solver** and thus bind him sustainably (see also Guttenbacher et al. 2021, p. 478). Instead of a cash benefit, customers and claimants are offered solutions to the specific damage elimination and procurement problems that arise from the damage event in the customer ecosystem. Customers and claimants benefit from faster regulation through simplified and standardized processes as well as the guarantee of service levels and value-added services of the service providers. Practical examples are the mediation of rental cars and repair shops in the event of car accidents, craftsmen in the event of storm and building damage, lawyers in the case of legal expenses, doctor's offices and hospitals or the sale of wrecks via residual value exchanges. However, it should be noted that the customer is simultaneously deprived of the autonomy to decide on the use of the insurance benefits. This will trigger reservations if the customer feels at the mercy of the damage elimination process or even has to fear receiving a damage elimination that is not free of complaints. Therefore, it is the task of communication to convince the customer that he has a clear benefit advantage overall if the insurer solves his problems.

From a marketing perspective, the classification of claims services into **minimum and profiling services** is also very helpful (Jara 2000, p. 126–135, 285–287). Minimum service therefore include, for example, the correct and transparent financial payment, accessibility, a certain degree of speed, and a minimum level of friendliness and information towards the injured party.

Differentiating services are, on the one hand, minimum services that exceed expectations, i.e., particularly fast regulation or a pronounced degree of empathy and communication skills, and on the other hand, pronounced problem solutions, e.g.

- a total financing of the emergency situation, which provides financial support (in the form of a short-term free loan) beyond the payment of covered loss events,
- comprehensive physical support in the course of damage repair by taking over the coordination of the entire restoration and replacement through replacement, by measures to prevent damage extensions, and by relieving injured parties of other tasks to be completed during the repair of the damage case,
- comprehensive psychological-social support in coping with damage events through visitor services, care services, or rehabilitation facilities,
- future-oriented measures following the damage repair, resulting from insights of the specific damage case during the damage repair, which strengthen the inner security of the injured party and lead to an improvement of the risk situation.

The situation with minimum and differentiating services is as described by *Berry* in relation to service quality regarding routine and exception components already in 1986 (Berry 1986; see also research festival in Sect. 9.1): Financial compensation, accessibility, and a minimum level of friendliness are simply expected and taken for granted during claims settlement. Therefore, **minimum services** do not lead to a surprise of customers and to differentiation, but at most to their **dissatisfaction in case of non-delivery**. On the other hand, non-delivered differentiating services have no negative impact on marketing goals because they are not expected at all. But goodwill services, the complete takeover (financing and organization) of damage repair, and relief services can—in contrast to minimum services—positively surprise customers and differentiate the provider in the market against the competition (Fig. 12.5).

In practice, minimum services are usually (still) in the foreground of consideration. Service offers in the German insurance industry often only correspond to minimum

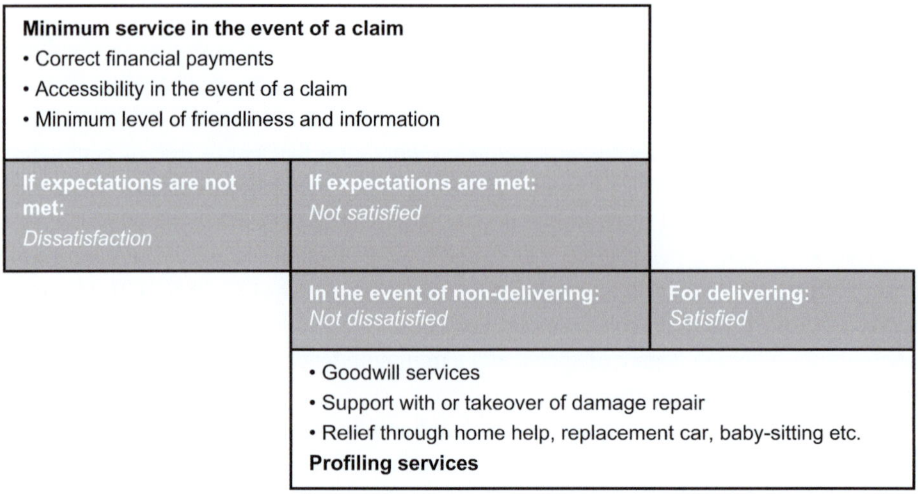

Fig. 12.5 Differentiation through claims settlement. (Based on Jara 2000, p. 287)

services, when lean, so-called no-frills offers provide high-quality core products with only absolutely necessary service features (Gericke 2001, p. 68). As mentioned, market research has determined that customers expect minimum services to be fully met. And their high-quality fulfillment results in (possibly) cost savings and the avoidance of customer dissatisfaction. From a marketing perspective, however, minimum services can only actively lead to negative consequences such as damage to the image and customer churn if they are not satisfactorily provided.

The situation is different with **profiling services**: They are not as widespread as the minimum services and often fall victim to cost-cutting. Unprovided profiling services also have no negative impact on marketing goals because they are not expected at all. But because they are not expected, they can—in contrast to the minimum services—lead to customer satisfaction or even customer enthusiasm and thus actively contribute to image improvement, customer loyalty and possibly even to new customer acquisition. Initial practical examples from the German-speaking insurance market for such service services in the event of a claim are

- the organization of the repair—in cooperation with selected partner repair shops—while providing a replacement motor vehicle as part of the motor vehicle insurance,
- comprehensive services around the coordination of craftsmen in the event of building damage,
- a prevention service as part of the independent occupational disability insurance, which can be used in case of problems in the psycho-social area,

- the assumption of the entire funeral with all necessary clarifications in connection with a burial insurance, a service that relieves the bereaved in the event of death (damage event),
- the referral of selected drying companies in the event of water or moisture damage at the customer's request as part of the home contents insurance.

However, the importance of fulfilling minimum services should not be underestimated: Their non-fulfillment leads to dissatisfaction and thus to decreasing customer loyalty and possible customer migration. Exciting non-dissatisfied customers with profiling services, in contrast, only has an indirect effect and maintains or increases customer loyalty. On the other hand, customer expectations are also raised, and it becomes more difficult over time to surprise and excite customers again and again. In addition, there is the greater reach of negative word-of-mouth propaganda by dissatisfied customers compared to the reach of positive statements (Sect. 7.2.3). Therefore, the lever in avoiding dissatisfaction is generally greater than in creating enthusiasm (Stauss and Seidel 2019, pp. 5-14).

A central implementation aspect of customer-oriented claims management concerns the associated behavioral and qualification requirements for employees in the claims department. The **importance of the person-based care and service component** is particularly high in connection with the claims service, because in the event of a claim, the emotional involvement on the customer or injured party side and thus their state of mind is much greater than in the rest of the service process.

Certainly, the result quality in the form of the actual quality of the claims service still plays an important role, whether it is the extent of financial compensation, the speed and comprehensibility of this process, or the package of other service benefits (replacement car, safety advice, damage limitation measures, etc.). The potential quality is also important to ensure accessibility and thus at least the tacitly assumed minimum performance and to avoid dissatisfaction. In crisis situations such as widespread hail or storm damage, the potential quality can also contribute to profiling: In 2013, two major insurers were able to successfully regulate severe mass damage caused by flooding and hail by quickly setting up a crisis center, bundling all their own forces and resources, and calling in external service providers, thereby achieving image gains and customer satisfaction (Schmidt-Kasparek 2013, p. 62). Furthermore, the process quality is important to enable the process quality, e.g. when there are sufficient personnel resources in terms of quantity and quality. Because at the time of the claim, the performance quality is at least as important: The treatment of the customer or injured party influences how they experience the claims service. It is influenced by the manners of the claims handlers, their friendliness, empathy, in short, their social competence (see also Laakmann and Rahlf 2019, p. 418 f.). Therefore, the **process quality of the claims service** offers excellent opportunities for insurance companies to stand out from the competition and **can**

significantly contribute to customer loyalty. However, the existing corporate culture sometimes stands in the way of process quality (Fig. 12.6).

An (now older) US study by Mercer Management Consulting has shown that **customer orientation in claims departments** played a subordinate role in practice there and states: Many companies lack personal contact in the event of a claim with the injured party or customer—especially internal claims staff behave more as auditors than as problem solvers (Fopp 2002, p. 80). This situation was also similar for insurers in Germany. However, this has now been recognized, and in most companies, claims settlement has become much more customer-friendly compared to the past. Call centers and especially internal customer centers with trained telephone operators have the necessary communication skills and are—at least in the case of standard cases—technically able to handle these cases conclusively.

Another possibility is to **transfer claims settlement**—at least in selected areas and up to certain claim amounts—to their own **agents**, i.e. to grant them claims settlement powers. In the event of a claim, the customer then sees his agent, who also takes care of him otherwise, and this agent handles everything for the customer, records the claim and possibly gets a picture on site. For the agents, this has been proven to have an impact on their business success, because the claims settlement is a major driver of overall customer satisfaction. Typical lines of business for sales force regulation are comprehensive home contents and comprehensive buildings, glass, partially or fully comprehensive motor vehicle, accident and third-party private liability insurance—experience shows that about 50% of all claims are suitable for regulation by the sales force. The

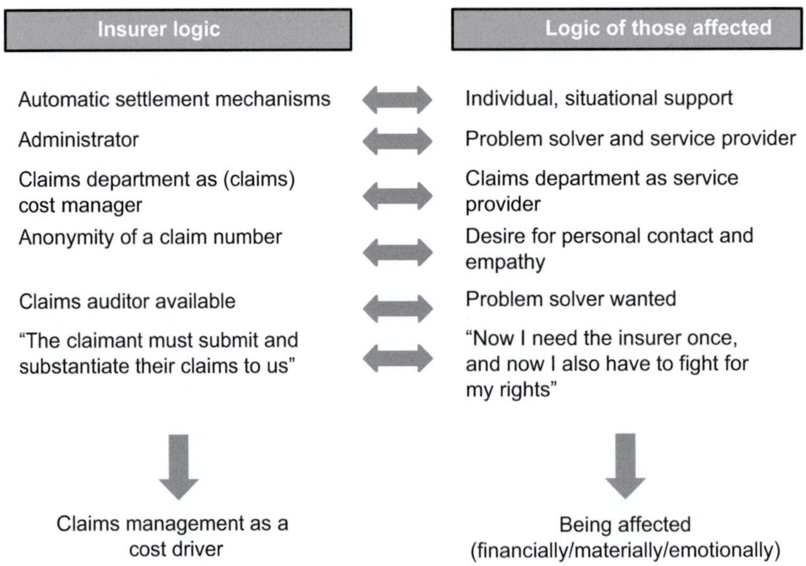

Fig. 12.6 Insurer versus victim logic in claims settlement. (Köhne 2003, p. 86)

insurers' regulation powers relate to small claims and are—depending on the company, sometimes depending on the agency size and sometimes with increases in the event of major events—different, e.g. 500, 1500, 3000 or even 5000 € (Kühl and Ramezani 2008, pp. 95–98; Lange et al. 2013, p. 167; o. V. 2014b, pp. 54–56).

In addition, the **digitalization** has already affected claims settlement. In recent years, more and more claims have been digitally and automatically regulated directly (**dark processing**); this applies at least to simple, standardized and lower-value claims settlements. And the development continues: Artificial intelligence, big data, and drones technically enable a complete claims processing, at least for certain property damages, e.g. in the automotive sector (Reich and Braasch 2019, pp. 297–302).

From a marketing perspective, this is **ambivalent**: The automatic, customer-initiated claims settlement will ensure customer satisfaction, and may even increase it in some cases. Because it brings result quality (payment) and process quality (speed and simplicity). Whether it leads to customer enthusiasm is questionable, especially as this is increasingly expected by customers and thus becomes a minimum service. At the same time, the personal, emotional, and social component of interpersonal communication and the corresponding personal contact with the customer or injured party are lost. This at least offers the chance for empathy and trust-building, but carries the risk of poor execution and also costs more. **Insurers should** therefore **proceed in a differentiated manner**: Where it only depends on payment, simple processing and speed, and the customer or injured party is not exposed to emotional sensitivities, a highly automated, self-triggering claims settlement process (of course with control mechanisms against insurance fraud) is suitable, e.g. for the recurring settlement of cost reimbursement receipts in private health insurance or for settlement via the insurer's service partners (repair shops, craftsmen, etc.). When it comes to rare, emotional and/or larger damage events such as flood damage in buildings insurance, burglary offenses in home contents insurance or more serious personal injuries in accident insurance, personal conversation should be chosen, the problem solution addressed and the corresponding message communicated that the insurance is there and helps when needed.

The claims settlement policy, like the service policy, specifically ties in with the strategic specifications (positioning, business fields, marketing task profile); as part of the service process, it is subject to the basic service philosophy, corresponding service expectations and service standards of the service policy and the associated service controlling.

12.4 Interim Conclusion on the Marketing Tool of Claims Settlement Design

Claims settlement represents the (central) moment of truth, in which it becomes apparent from the customer's perspective whether he has rightly acquired the credence good insurance. The result quality will influence his satisfaction; if no or only a small compensation occurs, i.e. less than expected, he will be dissatisfied. The process quality (speed, simplicity, in the case of a personal service provision additionally empathy and solution orientation) has an additional effect. In the case of simple, little clarification requiring damages and automated processing, it will at best confirm the perception of the result quality, in the case of inadequacies lead to dissatisfaction, in the case of personally regulated damages it applies at best that it can compensate for inadequacies in the result (i.e. less payment than expected) and generate understanding or in combination with a result quality corresponding to expectations (i.e. full payment) can even trigger enthusiasm, because also social and psychological concerns of the customer or injured party are satisfied. The provision of (expected) minimum services is absolutely necessary to avoid dissatisfaction and its spread. Profiling services can additionally increase customer satisfaction, customer loyalty and his willingness to recommend.

Further Reading Recommendations for Chap. 12

- Bruhn 2019a.
- Bruhn 2022, Chap. 6.3.
- Esser 2004.
- Guttenbacher et al. 2021.
- Jara 2000.
- Kromschröder 1993.
- Lehmann 1989.
- Lehmann 1993.
- Stauss and Seidel 2019.
- Trautinger 2015.
- Wedlich 2019.
- Wiedmann et al. 2009.

References

Berry, L.L. (1986): Big Ideas in Service Marketing, in: Venkatesan, M./Schamelensee, D.H./ Marshall, C.E. (Eds.), Creativity in Service Marketing, Chicago u. a., 1986, pp. 6–8.

Blodgett, J./Wakefield, K./Barnes, J. (1995): The Effects of Customer Service on Consumer Complaining Behavior, in: Journal of Service Marketing, Vol. 9, 1995, No. 4, pp. 31–42.

Breuer, W./Zimmermann, K. (2019): Werkstattmanagement—Schadensteuerung im Spannungsfeld zwischen Kunde und Versicherung, in: Reich, M./Zerres, C. (Eds.), Handbuch Versicherungsmarketing, Berlin, 2nd ed., 2019, pp. 615–624.

Bruhn, M. (2019a): Qualitätsmanagement für Dienstleistungen, Handbuch für ein erfolgreiches Qualitätsmanagement. Grundlagen, Konzepte, Methoden, Berlin, 11th ed., 2019.

Bruhn, M. (2022): Relationship Marketing. Das Management von Kundenbeziehungen, München, 6th ed., 2022.

Bruhn, M./Hennig, K. (1993): Selektion und Strukturierung von Qualitätsmerkmalen, Auf dem Weg zu einem umfassenden Qualitätsmanagement für Kreditinstitute, Teil 1, in: Jahrbuch der Absatz- und Verbrauchsforschung, Jg. 39, 1993, Nr. 3, pp. 214–238.

Cassab, H./MacLachlan, D.L. (2009): A consumer-based view of multi-channel service, in: JOSM, Vol. 20, 2009, No. 1, pp. 52–75.

Esser, M. (2004): Assistance in der Versicherungswirtschaft. Ein marketingorientierter Ansatz zur Unternehmenswertsteigerung, Karlsruhe, 2004.

Farny, D. (2011): Versicherungsbetriebslehre, Karlsruhe, 5th ed., 2011.

Fleck, J./Herrig, C. (2015): Das "neue" Beschwerdemanagement—ein Erfahrungsbericht aus der Praxis, in: ZfV, Jg. 66, 2015, Nr. 3, pp. 88–94.

Fopp, L. (2002): Schadenmanagement aktiv gestalten, Die Combined Ratio drastisch senken mit Value driven Claims Management, in: VW, Jg. 57, 2002, Nr. 2, pp. 80–81.

GDV (Ed.) (2023a): Statistiken zur deutschen Versicherungswirtschaft 2023, Berlin, 2023.

Gericke, S.H. (2001): Customer Relationship Management in der Assekuranz unter besonderer Berücksichtigung neuer Verfahren und moderner Informationstechnologie—Ziele, Nutzen, Inhalt und Umsetzung, Karlsruhe, 2001.

Guttenbacher, S./Steinbrück, P./Waschkowitz, A.B. (2021): Steuerung der Schadenbearbeitungsprozesse, in: Junglas, A./Schradin, H./Wiegard, M.: Steuerung von Versicherungsunternehmen, Stuttgart, 3rd ed., 2021, pp. 475–514.

Haller, M./Ackermann, W. (1995): Versicherungswirtschaft—kundenorientiert, Zürich, 1995.

Hart, C./Heskett, J./Sasser, W. (1990): The Profitable Art of Service Recovery, in HBR, Vol. 68, 1990, No. 4, pp. 148–156.

Homburg, C. (2020): Marketingmanagement, Strategie—Instrumente—Umsetzung—Unternehmensführung, Wiesbaden, 7th ed., 2020.

Jara, M. (2000): Zielorientierte Neugestaltung des Schadenmanagements in Versicherungsunternehmen, St. Gallen, 2000.

Jayswal, M.M./Brahmbhatt, A.C. (2013): Exploring the Impact of Post Purchase Services by Bancassurance on First Year Policy Lapsation Rate in Life Insurance Selling, in: IJBIT, Vol. 6, 2013, No. 2, pp. 94–101.

Jeßnitzer, A. (2008): Auf zur Champions League der Schadenbearbeitung (I), in: VW, Jg. 63, 2008, Nr. 19, pp. 1.615–1.619.

Joho, C. (1996): Ein Ansatz zum Kundenbindungs-Management für Versicherer, Bern, 1996.

Köhne, T. (2003): Schadenmanagement als Marketinginstrument oder: Kundenorientierung im "Moment of truth", in: El Hage, B./Jara, M. (Eds.), Schadenmanagement, Grundlagen, Methoden und Instrumente, Praktische Erfahrungen, St. Gallen, 2003, pp. 67–90.

Kromschröder, B. (1993): Qualitätsmanagement in der Versicherungswirtschaft, Karlsruhe, 1993.

Kühl, H./Ramezani, S. (2008): Schadenregulierung durch den Außendienst: Königsweg oder Sackgasse?, in: VW, Jg. 63, 2008, Nr. 2, pp. 94–98.

Kühlmann, K./Wolf, H.-P./Wallenwein, C./Swoboda, U. (2003): Marketing und Vertrieb, Funktionsorientierte Qualifikationen, Karlsruhe, 2nd ed., 2003.

Laakmann, M./Rahlf, C. (2019): Customer Journey am Beispiel des Schadenprozesses in der Versicherungswirtschaft, in: Reich, M./Zerres, C. (Eds.), Handbuch Versicherungsmarketing, Berlin, 2nd ed., 2019, pp. 401–422.

Lange, M./Robold, M./Berthold, C. (2013): Schaden- und Leistungsmanagement, Sachversicherungen für private und gewerbliche Kunden, Fach- und Führungskompetenz für die Assekuranz, Karlsruhe, 2013.

Lehmann, A. (1989): Dienstleistungsmanagement zwischen industriell-orientierter Produktion und zwischenmenschlicher Interaktion, St. Gallen, 1989.

Lehmann, A. (1993): Dienstleistungsmanagement, Strategien und Ansatzpunkte zur Schaffung von Servicequalität, Stuttgart, 1993.

Meffert, H./Bruhn, M./Hadwich, K. (2018): Dienstleistungsmarketing, Grundlagen—Konzepte—Methoden, Wiesbaden, 9. Aufl., 2018.

Müller-Reichart, M./Schäfer, M. (2014): Mit Assistance auf dem Weg zu einem service- und vertriebsoptimierten Finanzdienstleistungsangebot, in: ZfV, Jg. 65, 2014, Nr. 8, pp. 222–226.

Müller-Reichart, M./Haisch, D./Graumann, K.V. (2023): Versicherungs-Assistance als Voraussetzung einer „Customer Journey", in: ZfV, Jg. 74, 2023, Nr. 11, pp. 322–327.

Nicoletti, B. (2021): Insurance 4.0: Benefits and Challenges of Digital Transformation, Cham, 2021.

o. V. (2014b): Wo Schaden zum Erlebnis wird, Vermittler engagieren sich immer stärker bei der Schadenregulierung, um sich von Billig-Anbietern abzuheben, in: VW, Jg. 69, 2014, Nr. 3, pp. 54–57.

o. V. (2015): YouGov: Reise- und Mobilitäts-Assistance sind gefragt, in: Versicherungswirtschaft-heute.de, Tagesreport vom 03.07.2015.

Peill, E./van Eck, R. (1997): Kundenbindung durch Service-Garantien, in: VW, Jg. 52, 1997, Nr. 15, pp. 1.071–1.073.

psyconomics AG/avanturo GmbH (Ed.) (2002): Aktives Schadenmanagement aus Kundensicht, Eine Untersuchung der Akzeptanz alternativer Modelle der Schadenregulierung, Köln, 2002.

Reich, M./Braasch, T. (2019): Die Revolution der Prozessautomatisierung bei Versicherungsunternehmen: Robotic Process Automation (RPA), in: Reich, M./Zerres, C. (Eds.), Handbuch Versicherungsmarketing, Berlin, 2. Aufl., 2019, pp. 291–305.

Schmidt-Kasparek, U. (2013): Regulierung und Vertrieb verzahnen, Gleich bei zwei Veranstaltungen stand das Schadenmanagement im Fokus, in: VW, Jg. 68, 2013, Nr. 24, pp. 62 f.

Stauss, B./Seidel, W.: Effective Complaint Management. The Business Case for Customer Satisfaction, Cham, 2. Aufl., 2019.

Trautinger, M.-J. (2015): Der Moment der Wahrheit—Eine empirische Untersuchung zu Zufriedenheitsfaktoren im Versicherungsschadenfall, in: ZVersWiss, Jg. 104, 2015, pp. 289–309.

Wedlich, F. (2019): Digitalisierung, Robotic Process Automation und Künstliche Intelligenz in der Versicherungsbranche, Potentiale und Möglichkeiten im Schadenmanagement, in: ZfV, Jg. 70, 2019, Nr. 14, pp. 436–440.

Wiedmann, K.-P./Seegebarth, B./Reuter, M. (2009): Reputation als strategischer Erfolgsfaktor in der Assekuranz: Herausforderungen im Beschwerdemanagementprozess für ein zukunftsorientiertes Reputationsmanagement, in: Institut für Marketing & Management (Ed.), Schriftenreihe Marketing Management, Hannover, 2009.

Sales Policy as a Marketing Tool of the Insurance Company 13

13.1 Basics of Sales Policy

The characteristics of the insurance product and the often low interest of private customers in insurance matters are responsible for the great importance of (person-related) sales. Although the basic need for security is present, the specific insurance need in individual cases usually has to be aroused by intermediaries. Hence, an old wisdom applies: insurances are *sold,* rarely actively *bought.* This also results in the importance of sales policy as a marketing tool.

▶ **Sales Policy** includes the design, control and development of the overall sales system in accordance with company-specific objectives, with the subtasks of selecting sales resp. distribution channels, determining task sharing, acquiring and retaining suitable intermediaries, and the ongoing control (= planning, coordination and control) of the sales channels.

In this respect, the location of customer contact in the insurance service is even more critical to success than in services anyway. The sales organs are to be interpreted as value creators who, throughout the entire service process, fulfill the respective **functions of customer contact** desired from the customer's perspective (Trinkhaus 1955, pp. 17–23; Farny 1971, pp. 93–96; Zietsch 1985, pp. 40–45; Hielscher 1993, pp. 31–34; Köhne 1997, p. 323; Farny 2011, p. 746):

- **Contact Function:** It is supported by all activities aimed at making contact with the customer. The contact function extends not only to the phase of contract initiation, but to the entire contract duration. Apart from possible changes to the contracts (overlap with advice, information and support), additional contracts can be concluded during a customer relationship (cross-selling). Regarding the initial contact, for example, sales

T. Köhne, *Insurance Marketing*, https://doi.org/10.1007/978-3-658-47345-7_13

cooperations with companies from other sectors (annex distribution) are possible, which only establish contact with the insurer as tipsters or act as intermediaries; the boundaries are sometimes fluid. For example, the optician Fielmann sells the glasses insurance of HanseMerkur Versicherung.
- **Information and Consultation Function:** Ideally, the identification of customer needs and their coordination with insurance coverage is achieved by eliminating information deficits. The effect of information and advice on the customer can relate to the phase before contract conclusion, the contract term, and the phase after termination of the contract.
- **Acquisition Function:** The function of sales channels, which is often central from the provider's perspective, is the conclusion (sale, distribution) of insurance contracts. The acquisition function is of central importance in the private customer sector because, as mentioned, insurances are usually sold and not bought.
- **Support Function:** It is perceived by the intermediary's measures for customer support after contract conclusion and in the case of claims settlement. It includes the emotional sub-function of psychological-social support derived from the basic function of securing, and thus person-related activities in connection with the communicative coping with fear, conveying inner security and immediate reassurance in the event of damage or complaints.

In contrast to product and pricing policy, insurers have always been free to choose their distribution channels and were not subject to any supervision. Accordingly, the **diversity and** the **competition between the numerous different distribution channels** was and is pronounced: They include company-owned, company-tied, and company-independent distribution channels, which differ based on their legal and economic dependence on the insurer (Table 13.1) (see also Farny 2011, p. 744 f.).

The classification under commercial law (Commercial Code, HGB) follows this logic: Because the three original types of intermediaries—employed sales force, single-company or group-tied agents (= exclusive agents) and insurance brokers—have always been distinguished by their commercial law status, whether they are employees according to § 59 HGB legally and economically dependent on the insurer, whether they are tied agents corresponding to the commercial agent (§§ 84 ff. HGB) contractually bound to one or more companies and thereby legally independent but economically dependent, or whether they are acting as legally and economically independent brokers corresponding to the commercial broker (§ 93 HGB).

▶ **Commercial Agent** "A commercial agent is a self-employed intermediary, who has continuing authority to negotiate transactions on behalf of another entrepreneur (the "principal") or to conclude transactions in the latter´s name. A person is self-employed if he is essentially able to arrange his activities freely and to determine his working hours." (§ 84 para. 1 HGB)

Table 13.1 Distribution channels in the insurance industry

	Distribution channels		
	Company-owned	Company-tied	Company-independent
Form of cooperation	Hierarchy	Cooperation	Market
Dependence	Legally and economically dependent	Legally independent, economically dependent	Legally and economically independent
Characteristics	• Directorate • Branch office • Employed sales force (inspectors) • Direct sales	• Single-tied agents • Group-tied agents • Multi-tied agents • Sideline agents • (Sales companies)	• Multi-company intermediaries • Insurance brokers • Insurance advisors • Policyholder-owned/-affiliated intermediaries • Associations, clubs, organizations • Bank distribution • Companies from other sectors (annex distribution) • Employers • (Sales companies)

▶ **Commercial Broker** "Whoever, on a commercial basis, undertakes on behalf of others the negotiation of contracts concerning the purchase or sale of goods or securities, or concerning insurance, carriage of goods, chartering of ships or other commercial matters, without having continuing authority to do so by virtue of a contractual relationship, shall have the rights and duties of a commercial broker." (§ 93 para. 1 HGB)

With reference to the insurance industry, both types of intermediaries have been defined for the first time in the new Insurance Contract Act since the VVG reform of 2007.

▶ **Insurance Agent** in the sense of this law is "anyone contracted by an insurer or an insurance agent to arrange or conclude contracts of insurance on a commercial basis." (§ 59 para. 2 VVG)

▶ **Insurance Broker** in the sense of this law is "anyone who contracts to arrange or conclude contracts of insurance for a client on a commercial basis without having being contracted to do so by an insurer or an insurance agent." (§ 59 para. 3 VVG)

However, the **insurance broker** has significantly distanced himself from the commercial broker (Trinkhaus 1955, pp. 129–133). Unlike the commercial broker who operates on a case-by-case basis—e.g. the real estate broker—it is recognized by the **jurisprudence** that the insurance broker is the **fiduciary of his client** and thus enters into a long-term obligation (fiduciary judgment of the BGH of 22.05.1985, BGHZ 94, 356 (359)). This includes both pre-contractual and during the contract term information, advice and activity obligations, i.e. the obligation to cover recognized risks. The broker is in a dual legal relationship with the client, who obliges him by broker contract, and with the insurer, whose interests he also has to safeguard to a certain extent.

With the new intermediary law, **insurance mediation** has generally become a **licensed business activity** since 2008 (§ 34d para. 1 GewO). Various variants of the licensing obligation now also entail a differentiation according to the Trade Regulation Act (GewO), which does not coincide with the commercial law classification in all cases.

The Intermediary Act generally only affects professionally active, independent insurance intermediaries. A professional activity is one that is permanent and aimed at making a profit and exceeds a trivial limit not further specified in the law. Also excluded are activities that are not classified as insurance mediation. This includes the activity of the so-called **tipster,** who merely provides contact evidence to potential insurance interested parties, but does not advise and inform about insurances himself. Also not considered as insurance mediation is, for example, the activity of car repair shops that participate in claims settlement.

Anyone who wants to act as an insurance broker or insurance agent on a commercial basis requires a **permission** according to § 34d para. 1 GewO from the responsible Chamber of Commerce and Industry (IHK) and must register immediately after starting the activity in the intermediaries register set up according to § 11a GewO. However, the GewO provides for various **exceptions:**

- **Exemption from permission on application for product accessory agents and brokers** (§ 34d para. 6 GewO):
  A agent or broker who mediates insurance as a supplement to the goods or services provided as part of his main activity (product accessory sales, also referred to as **annex distribution**) can apply for exemption from the permission if he proves that he carries out his activity as an insurance intermediary directly on behalf of one or more insurance intermediaries who are license holders, or one or more insurance companies, that he has professional liability insurance or an equivalent guarantee, and that he is reliable and adequately qualified and does not live in disordered financial circumstances. The principal can provide the proof or the qualification obligation. These intermediaries must therefore apply to their responsible IHK for an exemption from the permission, presenting the mentioned proofs. The product accessory nature is to be interpreted narrowly: If a bank mediates a residual debt insurance for a granted loan, this is product accessory, but if it mediates a home contents insurance, this is not product accessory, because the home contents insurance is not an annex product to the credit.
- **Exemption from permission** (§ 34d para. 7 GewO):
  An insurance agent who exclusively mediates on behalf of one **(single-tied agent)** or several insurers whose insurance products do not compete (false multi-tied agent,

e.g., **group-tied agent** with several agency contracts with the group companies) does not require a permission if the insurer(s) is (are) fully liable for him. The unlimited liability goes beyond the existing liability for assistants (§§ 278, 831 BGB). It is explained by the fact that an insurer registers the agent in the intermediaries register, whereas the intermediary requiring a permission or exempted from the permission on application is registered by the responsible IHK.

- **No permission requirement when limiting the intermediating activity to certain product accessory insurances** (§ 34d para. 8 GewO):
  Exempt from the permission and registration requirement are intermediaries who cumulatively meet all the conditions mentioned in § 34d para. 8 GewO. Firstly, this concerns the product accessory mediation of **travel and warranty insurances** as a secondary activity, if the premium does not exceed an amount of 600 € on an annual basis when calculated on a pro-rata basis, or deviating from this, the premium per person does not exceed an amount of 200 €, if the insurance is an additional service to a service mentioned at the beginning with a duration of a maximum of three months (practical examples: travel agency, optician with glasses insurance). Secondly, it concerns **residual debt insurances** calculated into building savings contracts by building societies and building savings intermediaries. Thirdly, it includes **residual debt insurances** that are concluded **to secure goods financing** and up to 500 € premium (practical example electronics market, where a television is purchased on credit, into which a residual debt insurance is calculated).

The **relationship between the classification** of insurance intermediaries **under institutional aspects, Commercial Code and Trade Regulation Act** is shown in Fig. 13.1. It shows that direct sales are institutionally a company-owned sales channel, which is not covered by HGB and GewO because no intermediaries are involved. Tipsters are a sales channel neither by institutional aspects, HGB, nor GewO because they do not sell insurance. The employed intermediaries are institutionally insurance-owned sales persons, commercial employees in the sense of § 59 HGB and not covered by GewO because they are not working on a commercial basis (i.e., there are not independent). The agents, on the other hand, are institutionally company-tied, commercial agents in the main or secondary profession under commercial law, and insurance agents under GewO, who depending on the constellation are either subject to a permission or are exempt from the permission if registered by their insurer, as product accessory tied agents for certain types of insurance mentioned in the GewO are not subject to the permission requirement from the outset, for the rest only exempted from the permission upon request. Finally, the insurance brokers are institutionally company-independent sales channels, commercial brokers under HGB with industry-specific characteristics, and independent insurance brokers under GewO, who are normally always subject to a permission; only in exceptional cases as product accessory brokers can they—like the product accessory agent—be exempted from the permission requirement.

It should also be noted that the **classification under HGB and GewO do not coincide in all cases:**

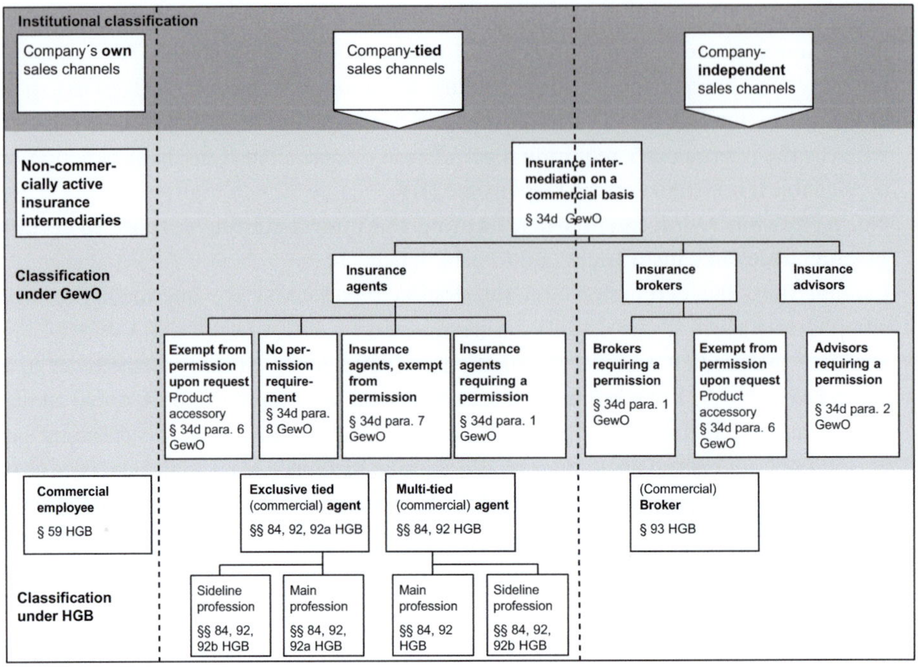

Fig. 13.1 Classification of sales channels according to institution, GewO and HGB. (Further developed from Beenken 2010, p. 19)

- Exclusive tied agents according to § 84 HGB can both be registered by the insurer in the intermediaries register as license-free tied agents according to § 34d para. 7 GewO and obtain their own commercial trade permission according to § 34d para. 1 GewO and registration by the IHK.
- Sub-agents of an insurance broker are indeed insurance agents according to §§ 84, 92 HGB, but - according to GewO - they need a permission as insurance brokers because they have to implement his consulting basis as vicarious agent.
- Multi-tied agents can be registered as "pseudo" multi-tied agents with several agency contracts with non-competing insurers as product partners by an insurer as a license-free tied agent. "Real" multi-tied agents with competing insurers as product partners must obtain a commercial trade permission according to § 34d para. 1 GewO.
- Sideline commercial agents have fewer rights than full-time ones (no compensation claim according to § 89b HGB, no notice periods increasing with the duration of activity, no obligation to secure a minimum income). In contrast, sideline agents are not treated differently than full-time agents under GewO. This means that the same trade law requirements must be met for sideline commercial agents as for full-time ones, e.g. regarding proficiency examination and ongoing further education.

Since the introduction of the intermediaries register, the number of intermediaries differentiated according to the Trade Regulation Act can be read directly from this, as well as the development over time. The largest number are the tied intermediaries registered by the insurer, followed by insurance brokers and insurance tied agents with a permission requirement. The brokers include all intermediaries of the brokerage company, even if they are commercial agents (of the brokerage company) according to Commercial Code, such as all independent intermediaries of MLP; the tied agents requiring a permission include the exclusive tied agents who not want to be or have not been registered by the insurer, as well as multi- tied agents and their independent tied-agents, such as all independent intermediaries of Swisslife Select (Table 13.2).

Over the past few years, the total number of registered intermediaries has been steadily declining; while the number of brokers is increasing, especially the insurance tied agents registered by the insurer are decreasing.

Excursus on insurance brokerage from an information economic perspective

Information economics, as well as the principal-agent approach as approaches of the so-called New Institutional Microeconomics, assume limited rationality, opportunistic behavior, and sometimes existing long-term business relationships between business partners; therefore, they are suitable for examining the relationship between insurers or intermediaries and insurance customers (e.g., Hax 1991, p. 56).

From an **information economic perspective,** insurance intermediation is a credence good, the quality of which cannot be determined before or at the time of purchase, but only (much) later, e.g., in the event of a claim and its settlement, or not at all (Kaas 1990, p. 543; Karten 2002, pp. 47, 49). The information missing to the policyholder about the quality of the intermediation service creates an asymmetric information distribution between him and the intermediary. This can result in a sustainable deterioration in quality and market failure across the market in the worst case (Akerlof 1970), but at least adverse selection, if, for example, informed customers choose good intermediaries, and/or moral hazard, if intermediaries exploit their information advantage (Bosselmann 1994, pp. 134–138; Traub 1995, p. 117 f.; Cummins and Doherty 2006, p. 383; Eckhardt 2007, pp. 113, 121; Eckhardt and Räthke-Döppner 2010, p. 670). As a rule,

Table 13.2 Number of registered insurance intermediaries, as of: 01.01.2024. (German Chamber of Commerce and Industry (DIHK) 2024)

Types of intermediaries according to GewO	Number
Exclusive agents (§ 34d para. 7 GewO)	103,796
Insurance agents with permission (§ 34d para. 1 GewO)	27,964
Insurance brokers (§ 34d para. 1 GewO)	46,383
Product accessory agents (§ 34d para. 6 GewO)	5,007
Product accessory brokers (§ 34d para. 6 GewO)	186
Insurance advisors (§34d para. 2 GewO)	319
Total number	183,655

policyholders cannot directly observe the intermediation service and the intermediary's behavior either ex ante or ex post, so they have to accept it despite uncertainties about quality and behavior. In detail: Ex ante, they can hardly assess the quality of the intermediation service in relation to their advisory needs (meeting needs) as well as the intermediary´s performance (qualification) and the willingness to perform of the insurance intermediary. Ex post, they cannot objectively evaluate the service result. Furthermore, the intermediary has behavioral leeway and the opportunity to exploit this opportunistically (Höckmayr 2012, pp. 71–76).

One of the essential characteristics of **insurance intermediation** is that it—like the insurance product—represents a **credence good**. The policyholder cannot assess the quality of the mediation and advisory service at the time of its provision and must rely on it. Rather, the broker has information advantages regarding his qualification, intentions, characteristics, and behaviors, and resulting behavioral leeway towards his customer. This creates the potential danger that he will exploit these to his advantage. This situation is inherently systemic in the relationship between the intermediary and the customer. Even though most intermediaris in practice work in the interest of their customers and not against them—after all, they usually have a long-term relationship with them on a personal basis and therefore have an interest in maintaining this—critics from the media, consumer protection, and politics address the (potential) **risk of conflicts of interest** from this fundamental information asymmetry.

13.2 Distribution Channels and their Evaluation from the Insurer's Perspective

From a sales policy perspective, the characteristics of the various distribution channels as well as their strengths and weaknesses, which they bring into the insurance service, are of interest.

13.2.1 Exclusive Tied Agents and Multi-Tied Agents

The exclusive tied agents has always been and still is the **dominant distribution channel** in the private customer business in German-speaking countries. From a company perspective, distribution takes place indirectly and decentrally through the use of a sales force. The customer contact is initiated by the intermediary and is predominantly characterized by direct, personal communication between the two. Specialization in certain sectors makes it easier for the intermediary to provide competent advice, but often exclusive tied agents have to or want to advise and sell the entire range of insurance products plus selected financial services products. Sometimes they also take on other tasks such as in- and out-payment, parts of the claims settlement, and support for the policyholder in the event of a claim.

For the collaboration between insurance companies and insurance agents, both the §§ 84 ff. HGB (commercial agents) and the **agent contract** (also: agency contract) are of particular importance. The **exclusive tied agent** appears both as a main and a secondary profession. Moreover, he may only mediate for one or more providers (exclusivity clause)—in the latter case, however, only for one provider per insurance line (= non-genuine multi-tied agent). The **multi-tied agent** can also mediate for several providers per insurance line (= genuine multi-tied agent), but is then no longer an exclusive tied agent because the strict competition ban otherwise listed in the agent contract is missing. Nevertheless, he remains a tied agent who is equipped with several agency contracts and has thus assumed obligations towards the insurers, which distinguishes him from the broker.

The **characteristics of the commercial or insurance (tied) agent** are therefore (Farny 2011, p. 749; see also Trinkhaus 1955, pp. 38–128)

- the constant entrustment, in the insurance industry through the agent contract,
- the activity for another entrepreneur, who can be an insurance company, but also another insurance intermediary (insurance agent or broker),
- the activity of mediating or concluding in the name of the principal, the latter only being possible for an insurance company and rather rare (there are some so-called underwriters ("Assekuradeure") who have an extended conclusion authority of an insurance company),
- Independence, which is characterized by essentially free activity and work schedule design. This means that the agent must have entrepreneurial decision-making freedom, e.g., to choose the location of his activity, the procedures used, the organization of work, and the working hours. Above all, the agent must not be bound by instructions. However, constraints that result from the organization and processes of the insurer must be taken into account, e.g., compliance with acceptance guidelines and marketing specifications. Also, the freedom of activity and work schedule design can be temporarily restricted if the agent contract is at risk due to lack of success.

The insurance agent has a number of **duties to observe** towards the insurer according to § 86 HGB:

- **Duty of effort:**
  The insurance agent must strive to mediate or conclude insurance contracts. He does not owe a specific mediation or conclusion success, but only the effort to do so, e.g., through sufficiently frequent acquisition appointments.
- **Duty to represent interests:**
  In his efforts to mediate or conclude insurance contracts, the insurance agent must represent the interests of the principal. This includes observing professional instructions, careful selection of customers and risks, or supporting business decisions externally.
- **Duty to inform:**
  The insurance agent must give the principal "the necessary messages, in particular to inform him immediately of each business mediation and each business conclusion". In the case of new mediations or conclusions, this is in the absolute interest of the insurance agent, because without submitting the application he cannot expect any

commission. But the agent is also obliged to pass on other messages and information, e.g., cancellations, amendment requests, or contract-relevant information on risk increases.

- **Duty of care:**
  The insurance agent "has to fulfill his duties with the care of a prudent businessman". This means, for example, that he carefully stores documents, data, and other information entrusted to him and protects them from unauthorized access.
- **General duties of consideration** (§§ 241 para. 2, 242 BGB):
  According to the general rules on the duties arising from the obligation, the insurance agent is obliged to "take account of the rights, legal interests, and other interests" of the principal and has" a duty to perform according to good faith, taking customer practice into consideration". This includes, for example, the duty to maintain silence about trade secrets.

In addition to the duties, the insurance agent has the following **rights** (§§ 86a, 87, 87c, 89b HGB):

- **Provision of necessary documents by the insurer:**
  Samples, drawings, price lists, advertising materials, terms of business: In the case of the insurance agent, these are primarily the necessary tariff documents, product descriptions, insurance conditions, and contract information.
- **Access to information:**
  The insurer has to inform about acceptance or rejection of the mediated contracts or about their non-execution or significantly lower execution than expected.
- **General duties of consideration on the part of the principal** (§ 241 para. 2 BGB).
- **Payment of a commission:**
  The prerequisite is that an insurance contract has been concluded, the first or one-time premium has been paid, and the conclusion is attributable to the activity of the agent. The insurer has to create a monthly statement and a book extract from which the facts relevant for the calculation of the commission emerge.
- **Payment of a compensation claim:**
  This claim exists after termination of the agent contract under certain further conditions. It compensates for the benefits remaining with the insurer, insofar as this is fair. This includes in particular the waiver of commission with the termination of the contract through the usual commission waiver clause.

The aforementioned rights and obligations are recorded in an agent or agency contract. This is usually designed according to the **main points of the GDV** and contains general contract provisions as well as usually an appendix with the commission reversals, i.e., detailed provisions on the amount of commission and ancillary conditions of commission payment (GDV 2000; Federal Association of German Insurance Brokers 2020).

With regard to marketing tools, the agent or agency contract prescribes a **multitude of vertical ties** (Lach 1995, pp. 184–186; Puschmann 2003, p. 161), namely

- a relative **regional** tie, which allows the agent to conduct intermediation transactions outside the agreed business area, provided they involve new customers or existing customers of the representative;
- a vertical **customer tie** via the given acceptance guidelines, which show the agent on the one hand which risks and customer types the insurer prefers or rather rejects, but on the other hand also provide planning security regarding the accepted risks;
- a vertical **product tie,** which results from the fact that the agent may only offer products of the company/companies he represents, i.e., he cannot independently change their coverage concepts and conditions;
- a vertical **range tie,** which results from the exclusivity clause and means that the agent may only sell the products from the range of the insurer he represents, in the case of multi-tied agents, he is limited to the ranges of the insurers he represents;
- a vertical **premium tie,** as the agent must adopt the fixed prices set by the insurer and is simultaneously (still) prohibited from passing on parts of the commission to the customer (prohibition on the passing on of commission). Although there are discount possibilities, these are also set by the insurer;
- a vertical **tie** regarding the use of **sales promotion materials,** as agents must use the sales promotion materials of their insurer or insurers and cannot simply design these themselves; the same applies to logo use and the corporate style guide.

However, this is offset by **certain rights regarding marketing activities,** such as more or less extensive territorial protection promises on the part of the insurer, protection of the agents's customer base or at least for extensions and renewals of mediated contracts, or by using a fallback solution (Ventillösung) the possibility of providing customers with products from other insurers that are not offered by the insurer if required. Furthermore, discount authorizations, but also claims settlement authorizations, increase the agent's flexibility in dealing with customers. Finally, the agent benefits from professionally designed sales promotion measures and a company brand created through advertising.

For the **assessment of the insurance agent from a company perspective,** the strengths and weaknesses of this distribution channel must be compared and weighed in the context of the marketing strategy and marketing task profiles (see also: Farny 2011, p. 761 f.; Lach 1995, pp. 121–128).

The strengths and **advantages** of the exclusive tied agent are based primarily on personal contact with the customer and the possibility of building trust. Personal communication takes place during consultation, ongoing support, and in the event of a claim. From the customer's perspective, the intermediary becomes the partner for concerns with the insurer and the central contact person. Furthermore, the exclusive tied agent has cross-branch product competence because he is tied to an insurer and is therefore trained accordingly by this insurer, and the amount of information to be mastered is limited to the services of this provider. From a company perspective, the initiative of the exclusive tied agent is added, as he actively approaches people and awakens the latent need for security. Exclusive tied agents, as self-employed individuals, are not bound by instructions in terms of their work and time allocation, but are nevertheless particularly closely tied to the interests of the insurer, obligated to the marketing mix specifications, and therefore easier to steer in line with the strategy. Furthermore, a high level of portfolio security (low cancellation susceptibility) and the great influence on the qualification of the intermediary speak for exclusivity.

The **disadvantages** are primarily the relatively high costs associated with this approach, which are borne by the customer for building the organizational structure, training, and fixed remuneration components. In contrast, the variable remunerations are, for example, below those of the insurance broker.

Furthermore, the quality of advice from intermediaries is not always guaranteed: Not all intermediaries active in the market have the same level of expertise. The required proof of expertise and ongoing training introduced across the board with EU intermediary law will fundamentally improve the situation; however, not all intermediaries will operate at the same high level.

Finally, it should be noted that the initiative, which is positively evaluated from a company's perspective, also forms a point of attack: With appropriate remuneration, the intermediary—which is not to be blamed on him, but rather on the insurer's incentive system—may consider the mere conclusion of a contract more important than the optimal solution to the customer's risk situation.

The **(genuine) multi-tied agent** is very similar to the exclusive tied agent in many respects. However, unlike the latter, he represents several, independent providers. In extreme cases, he is able to mediate a large part of the providers active in the insurance market because he has concluded representation contracts with correspondingly many companies. Basically, the same applies to the assessment as with the exclusive tied agents. In contrast, the multi-tied agent has a larger product range and potentially higher economic independence from individual providers. He can, but does not have to, use this for a better product selection. At the same time, with an increasing product selection (range and depth), it is comparatively more difficult to ensure his product knowledge and the controllability from the perspective of the individual product partner decreases. Therefore, in practice, you often find some preferred product partners in each branch or product.

13.2.2 Insurance Broker

In person-related sales, the broker is the second important sales channel compared to the agent. He is legally and economically independent of the product providers and is closer to the customer than to the product providers. While the agent represents one or more providers, the insurance broker, as already mentioned, is the fiduciary **of the customer** (according to the fiduciary judgment of the BGH of 22.05.1985): His related activities essentially include independent risk assessment, education and advice of the customer, urging for a needs-based insurance, mediation, support including assistance in the event of damageand ongoing control of the conformity of the concluded contracts with the needs of the customers and the market situation as well as independent action when he has identified an acute insurance need.

The legal obligation is also more pronounced towards the customer than towards the insurer: The broker concludes with the customer explicitly by contract or implicitly by action a **brokerage contract** for the mediation of insurances as well as advice, support, administration as ancillary services of the mediation activity. In addition, there are listed duties such as examination of insurance needs, investigation of the insurance market and selection of the suitable coverage offer, mediation of the insurance contracts deemed necessary, administration, monitoring and ongoing support of the insurance contracts and possibly adjustment of the insurance coverage as well as support of the customer in the event of damage. In addition, a brokerage order is agreed, i.e., a power of attorney from the customer to the broker, with which the latter is legitimized to act on behalf of and for the account of the customer towards the insurers **(power of representation).** With the brokerage contract with the customer, the insurance broker according to § 93 HGB, unlike the commercial broker, usually enters into a **long-term obligation** — unless he expressly agrees otherwise with the customer in individual cases (Farny 2011, p. 750 f.; Wagner 2017, p. 1008. f.).

Between the broker and the insurer, there is a contract-like relationship, the **commission agreement,** with which the insurer promises the broker the payment of a commission in the event of a (non-obligatory) insurance mediation. Therefore, one also speaks of a dual legal relationship of the broker. However, an insurer cannot be obliged to make a commission promise, not even if a broker takes over existing insurance contracts from this insurer by brokerage order into his administration and notifies the insurer of this. The insurer must then, however, treat the broker as a correspondence broker, i.e., send him copies of the correspondence with the customer, so that the broker can fulfill his contractual obligations, which he has entered into towards the customer.

The **characteristics** of the broker from the insurer's perspective are first and foremost that he also represents an indirect and decentralized distribution channel. The initiative comes either from the intermediary or from the customer. The broker's communication with the customer predominantly takes place directly at the customer's location or that of the intermediary. Brokers come in various forms: there are small one-person businesses up to internationally active, very large brokerage companies (AON, Marsh McLennan, Willis Towers Watson) in various legal forms, generalists and specialists for reinsurance, industrial, commercial and private customer insurance, target groups or certain insurance branches such as company pension schemes (Farny 2011, p. 763).

The broker has the following **duties** towards the **customer:**

- Information about his activity,
- Safeguarding interests, especially observing the customer's instructions and independently covering identified risks within the scope of the power of attorney granted by the customer,
- Duty of care,
- General duties of consideration,
- Possibly further duties that can arise from the brokerage contract.

The most important **rights** of the broker are:

- Possibly fee payment: Deviating from the case of commission payment by the insurer, the customer can also be the debtor of the remuneration if this was agreed, e.g. in the case of determined net tariffs.
- Further rights can arise from the brokerage contract; these include information rights that the customer has to fulfill, but above all also the brokerage order with the corresponding powers of representation, with which the broker is authorized to act on behalf of the customer, e.g. to conclude and terminate his insurance contracts.

However, under current German law, it is expressly not the broker's duty to provide so-called Best Advice, which is required in the UK for the mediation of capitalization products, including life and pension insurance, i.e. to mediate the cheapest or best insurance product. In Germany, the so-called **Suitable Advice** applies, i.e. the obligation to mediate suitable insurance that meets the customer's needs (see in detail Sect. 13.5.3).

The broker is also obliged to exercise care and generally safeguard interests towards the **insurer**, and he has to provide him with necessary information about the insurance risk. The role in the context of risk assessment justifies the traditional payment of the broker by the insurer with the commission (Cummins and Doherty 2006, p. 361 f.). The broker's most important rights vis-à-vis the insurer consist on the one hand in the claim to commission payment after successful mediation—this is the standard case in which a fee payment was not agreed with the customer—and on the other hand result from the brokerage contract with the brokerage order, which authorizes the broker to act on behalf of the customer, i.e. to conclude and terminate insurance contracts.

From the insurer's perspective, this results in the following **strengths and weaknesses** of this distribution channel: The insurance broker, as a personal distribution channel like the agent, has a high level of initiative. In addition, brokers usually have a very high qualification for the businesses to be mediated, are often even drivers of innovation when they negotiate their own broker conditions (or coverages). Customers appreciate the independence of the broker; however, in the private customer business, he is not yet as widespread as the agent. From the insurer's perspective, it should also be noted that brokers are liable for advisory and execution errors, take over a large part of the customer and contract-related tasks and independently develop customer potentials. This has its price: Brokers charge their acquisition and consulting activities with sometimes high commissions. The independence also means a low controllability for the product provider, which tends to result in a higher susceptibility of customers to change and a lower bundling rate (number of contracts with one insurer). In addition, brokers are demanding business partners and—above all the industrial brokers—are on par with the insurers in terms of underwriting know-how (Farny 2011, p. 763 f.; Lach 1995, p. 125–131).

13.2.3 Insurance Advisor

In addition to the broker, there is another type of intermediary unrelated to the insurance company, the **insurance advisor** (§ 59 para. 4 VVG), who is legally and economically independent of the product providers and is closer to the customers than to the product providers.

The regulations concerning him are formulated in § 34d para. 2 GewO as follows:

"Insurance advisor is someone who, without receiving an economic advantage from an insurance company or being dependent on it in any other way,

1. advises the client legally in the agreement, amendment or review of insurance contracts or in the assertion of claims from insurance contracts in the event of insurance,
2. represents the client out of court against the insurance company, or
3. takes over the mediation or conclusion of insurance contracts for the client.

The insurance advisor may only be paid for his services by the client. He may not accept any benefits from an insurance company in connection with the consultation, especially as a result of mediation following the consultation. (...)"

The latter is even further specified; if several insurance offers are equally suitable, those that can be obtained without a benefit (e.g., commission) from the insurance company should be offered. And if an insurance with benefit components is mediated, the insurance advisor must immediately arrange for the payout of the benefits by the insurance company to the policyholder according to § 48c para. 1 VAG (pass-through requirement).

In essence, the insurance advisor does the **same as the broker,** his activities also essentially include independent risk assessment, customer education and advice, urging for adequate coverage, mediation, support including assistance in the event of damage and ongoing control of the conformity of the concluded contracts with the needs of the customers and the market situation, as well as independent action when he has identified an acute need for insurance. The same advisory duty applies to both according to § 61 para. 1 VVG (§ 68 VVG). In the private customer sector, the **main (and only) difference** is in the **remuneration:** While the broker—whether usually through the insurer's commission or in the case of net tariffs through fees from the customer—is only paid in the event of successful mediation, the insurance advisor is only paid by the customer and only through a fee, may not receive any remuneration from the insurer, but receives the fee from the customer even for mere advice, if there is no mediation.

Or as the Federal Association of Insurance Advisors (BVVB) puts it on its website: Insurance advice by an insurance advisor is neutral and independent advice on all insurance matters—without sales or mediation intent. Unlike the fee-based advisor, the term insurance advisor is a protected term. To ensure the necessary objectivity, independence and neutrality, he must avoid any risk of conflicts of interest. His advice is (legally required) exclusively on a fee basis (Bundesverband der Versicherungsberater (BVVB) 2024a). Regarding costs, the BVVB further states that the insurance advisor is only paid by his clients in the form of a time fee or according to the Lawyers' Remuneration Act (RVG) based on the value of the subject matter—according to the complexity and content of the advice—and that the framework conditions are generally determined before the start of the consultation through a corresponding advisory agreement. A success-dependent remuneration is rejected for reasons of objectivity. It is also stated that the customer "regularly achieves cost advantages" because the information about necessary insurance protection no longer comes from the insurance industry, but from their own advisor and insurance costs can usually be reduced (Bundesverband der Versicherungsberater (BVVB) 2024b). This largely hits the nail on the head. However, it should be critically noted that a success-dependent remuneration would certainly be in the customer's interest and therefore a specification of what is meant by "reasons of objectivity" would be necessary. In addition, the statement is incorrect that insurance advice regularly leads to cost advantages; for less well-off customers, it is rather more expensive than mediation via agents or brokers (Sect. 13.6.5).

Evaluation From the insurer's perspective, the advantages of working with insurance advisors include their potential to build trust with customers as a personal sales channel and, like brokers, they usually have a very high qualification for the businesses they mediate. In addition, the insurance advisor—comparable only to the company-tied intermediary—cannot be accused of being biased due to compensation from the insurer. Furthermore, like the broker, he is liable for advisory and execution errors. However, in Germany, this sales channel—although it has existed in principle for many decades—is not widespread with only about 300 players nationwide; strictly speaking, it plays no economic role from the insurer's (and also the customer's) perspective. Disadvantages include the low controllability for the product provider, which tends to result in a higher susceptibility of customers to change and a lower bundling rate (number of contracts with one insurer). In addition, the insurer must have net tariffs, because the legally required alternative of calculating the mediation remunerations from the usual gross tariffs and crediting them to the respective customer's account (pass-through requirement) is not justifiable from a business perspective due to the low number of cases.

13.2.4 Annex Distribution

Another form of external sales is distribution through companies in other sectors (= **annex distribution**):

1. In this case, an insurer can use the other company's sales channels directly to sell its own insurance products **(sales connection).** Typical examples from practice are the sale of life insurance through bank counters and credit card providers, insurance through supermarkets or coffee traders, and through mail order companies.
2. Or the insurance products serve to round off the other company's range of products, so they are **product-bound** (= product accessory). Corresponding examples are motor vehicle insurance in connection with motor vehicles, travel and travel insurance, leasing contracts and property insurance, product manufacturer guarantees and product warranty insurance, as well as loans or building society mortgages and residual debt insurance.

▶ **Annex distribution** refers to the sale of insurance products through companies in other sectors by "attaching" the insurance product to the product or sales channel of the other company.

Regarding the **characteristic manifestations,** the picture in annex distribution is **inconsistent,** as the business models are very different: Indirect and decentralized sales are predominant, except for centralized sales in mail order and credit card organizations. The initiative for business and the types of communication depend on the business model and are inconsistent. The quality of insurance advice is generally low. The acquisition costs tend to consist of variable commissions, but this too ultimately depends on the business model and is handled inconsistently (Farny 2011, pp. 765–767).

Therefore, annex distribution can hardly be evaluated uniformly. It seems particularly suitable for mediating insurance in existing ecosystems; insurers are then more suppliers than controllers of the ecosystem. It is also suitable for digital business models in the context of embedded insurance, it is basically even the same (see excursus on ecosystems in Sect. 9.2). However, its evaluation always depends on the specific manifestation in the individual case: Both successful and failed business models have been implemented. Some cooperations have been going on for a very long time, and insurers have accordingly adapted to their annex partners (see marketing highlight in this section). This applies, for example, to specialized travel insurers and their cooperation with tour operators and travel agencies. In any case, if the insurance product is attached to another main product, it is also just an "appendage"—the insurer must adapt to the business logic of the partner. In the case of mere use of the sales channel, this may be less compelling. For this, the insurance product must have something special so that the customer accepts this sales channel.

Marketing Highlight HanseMerkur:

Annex Distribution as an Important Pillar of HanseMerkur Versicherung

As an independent mutual insurance association with nearly €2.6 billion in revenue in 2022 and approximately 2300 employees and commercial agents, the HanseMerkur Insurance Group is a (large) medium-sized insurer. Annex distribution, as sales through cooperation partners from other industries, play a significant role at HanseMerkur: For example, over 100,000 additional insurances have been sold since 2004 through Haspa, Germany's largest savings bank, and millions of zero-tariff glasses insurances have been sold through Fielmann, Germany's largest chain of opticians, since 2005. In total, annex distribution accounted for nearly a quarter of new business in 2022. Corresponding to the importance of health and travel insurance in the insurer's product portfolio, sales through cooperation partners play a significant role in both business areas. In health insurance, annex distribution mainly refer to supplementary health business through statutory health insurers and account for a smaller share of new business, while in the travel insurance sector, it is all the more significant. HanseMerkur has achieved above-average market growth in recent years—among other things, with the help of its annex distribution.

Annex distribution in health insurance using the example of cooperation with DAK-Gesundheit

Since 2004, HanseMerkur, as a private health insurer, has been cooperating with the statutory health insurance company DAK-Gesundheit. Customers of DAK-Gesundheit can choose from over 20 additional insurance tariffs from HanseMerkur and supplement their statutory insurance coverage with them. Since the beginning of the cooperation, over one million DAK customers have concluded additional insurance. The background to the cooperation was the health reform of 2004, which reduced benefits in statutory health insurance, but which the SHI providers were allowed to compensate for by mediating additional tariffs from private health insurers. The subject of these additional tariffs are, in particular, cost reimbursement for dental prostheses, dental care, glasses, hearing aids, outpatient services, elective doctor treatment and single or double rooms in the hospital, loss of earnings, and foreign travel health insurance (Fig. 13.2).

In the following years, a multi-channel distribution approach was developed: Today, HanseMerkur's additional insurances are sold online via the websites of DAK-Gesundheit and HanseMerkur, via social media and digital newsletters, as well as offline via mailings (postal mail), the service centers of DAK-Gesundheit, and via the customer magazine of DAK-Gesundheit. Customers can also obtain information, receive advice, and request offers via a special service hotline from HanseMerkur. In addition, the tariffs are mediated via the personal selling in the nationwide service centers of DAK-Gesundheit through sales partners of HanseMerkur.

The cooperation can be described as very successful for both cooperation partners. By now, a large number of DAK customers have concluded additional insurance through DAK-Gesundheit with HanseMerkur. It can be assumed that the conclusion of the additional insurances has increased the customer loyalty of the DAK insured. Over time, HanseMerkur's additional insurances have been awarded several times by independent testing institutes. And last but not least: The cooperation has been in existence for almost 20 years.

However, such extensive cooperation does not run by itself. The requirements of a cooperation partner are diverse: For example, DAK-Gesundheit expects affordable and powerful tariffs as well as their stable premiums and guaranteed performance security; at the same time, they should sensibly supplement the DAK services. Finally, a solid financial basis, low administrative costs, and customer-oriented service according to agreed quality standards (service level agreements) are demanded from the private health insurer. This also involves challenges: The interests of both cooperation partners should be represented and implemented in a balanced manner, legal restrictions of a health insurance fund as a public-law corporation should be observed, and sales measures

Fig. 13.2 Sales brochure additional insurance PlusGesundheit SPECIAL 01/2023. (HanseMerkur)

should be continuously innovatively optimized. An additional challenge is to highlight the gap in statutory health insurance coverage and the associated need for additional coverage for the customer, without diminishing the services of the statutory health insurance (SHI). Active SHI member acquisition by the PHI is also part of the cooperation. The cooperation of both insurers can be used to develop and introduce new, innovative tariffs that are not yet available on the market.

The central success factor of a SHI/private health insurance (PHI) cooperation is first and foremost the partnership-based cooperation with mutual trust. Then it is necessary to define concrete goals and pursue them together. Culturally, there is a need on both sides to be willing to go new ways together and to overcome the traditional SHI/PHI system boundaries. Finally, the customer benefit should be put in the foreground, and it is necessary to think and act from the customer's point of view.

Annex distribution in the tourism market

HanseMerkur Reiseversicherung is a traditional travel insurer since 1977 and with a turnover of over 250 million euros in 2022, it is one of the largest providers in the German travel insurance market. In annex distribution, it works with numerous tour operators, travel agencies, and travel intermediaries. These include, for example, AIDA Cruises, Condor, DERPART travel agencies, Eurowings, FTI, Lufthansa City Center travel agencies, Reiseland travel agencies, and TUI Cruises (HanseMerkur Reiseversicherung 2023). On the product side, it mainly involves insurance for travelers (e.g., travel cancellation insurance, travel guarantee through travel interruption insurance, travel health, emergency, travel accident and travel luggage insurance, flight ticket and rental car protection) as well as insurance for tour operators and travel agencies (e.g., liability insurance for the travel agency and the activity as a travel intermediary, tour operator liability insurance, financial loss liability insurance for tour operators and travel intermediaries, business contents insurance, insolvency insurance for customer money protection) (Fig. 13.3).

Fig. 13.3 Contents of the premium protection for the partner Wolters Tours 08/2023. (HanseMerkur Reiseversicherung)

The cooperation partners primarily pursue sales objectives with the sale of travel insurance. The weak margins in tourism make additional sales necessary. Furthermore, the (good) protection of their own customers has a direct influence on the (perceived) quality of the tourist product. HanseMerkur also pursues sales objectives: It is about profitable growth as well as securing and expanding brand awareness in the travel insurance market. Strategically, the focus is placed on the B2B business and cooperation with organizers, travel agencies, online partners, airlines, and cruise companies is sought. Primarily, sales are made directly through these. In addition, direct sales take place via hansemerkur.de and hmrv.de. The annex distribution in the travel insurance sector can also be considered successful: The proportion of insurance premiums concluded via annex distribution currently accounts for more than two-thirds of HanseMerkur Reiseversicherung's total turnover.

However, the requirements of the partners are high: These include a high, market-appropriate remuneration at marketable premiums, very good products, preferably confirmed by an independent body (e.g., Stiftung Warentest), advice and support regarding the products and their distribution across all channels, fast and accommodating claims processing, and a good image of the insurance company. Challenges for the travel insurer include legal regulations (EU Intermediary directive, tax legislation), disasters with global characteristics or impact, the economy in Germany and worldwide, general tourist consumer behavior, and not least the intense competitive situation. Key success factors in the travel insurance market are the flexible and seamless integration of offers and the offer process into the booking systems of cooperation partners, good and easy-to-communicate product benefits, a globally functioning service network, and a simple and functioning handling of the application and billing process.

Conclusion
The example of HanseMerkur shows that annex distribution can be successfully operated. However, the insurer must consistently and comprehensively adapt to its sales partners. In addition, the products of both partners must match each other. Attempts at annex distribution often fail at these points.

Sources:
HanseMerkur Insurance Group, Sales and Marketing Department.

HanseMerkur Insurance Group, Travel Sales Germany Department and Cooperations Department.

HanseMerkur Reiseverischerung (2023).

13.2.5 Bank Distribution

All in all, the most significant distribution channel in terms of annex distribution is **bank distribution:** This means that insurance products are sold to bank customers via the bank or its employees, and the insurer is the product provider (Bancassurance). Particularly in pension provision, there is a close connection between product and distribution, and there are therefore many financial services-related points of contact for the bank employee. In the life insurance sector, banks or savings banks mediate about a third of new business. Due to its high importance and proximity to the insurance business, bank distribution is discussed and evaluated separately here.

Characteristics of bank distribution: Bank distribution is also an indirect sales channel to the customer; in this case, the bank or its employees stand between the insurer and the customer. Moreover, this distribution channel is decentralized, whether through branches or mobile bank advisors. In the course of "Allfinanz" efforts, both **complementary** (= mutually supplementing) network relationships, such as in financing security for mortgages or loans, and **substitutive** (= mutually replacing) **network relationships** can be formed in pension provision. Like intermediary distribution, bank distribution is usually an intermediary-active sales channel, i.e., bank employees approach the customer on insurance topics, less often the customer approaches the bank employee. Communication with the customer is predominantly direct and takes place in the bank branch; nowadays, the offer of insurance products is often also integrated into online banking or bank portals as well as bank-operated or used financial services apps. This is particularly suitable for "simpler" insurance products (Kottmann 2018, p. 54 f.; Kallerhoff 2018, p. 346 f.). Banks mainly specialize in life insurance and a few selected other insurance branches in retail business, increasingly also in commercial business. They sometimes operate regionally. The savings banks and Raiffeisen and Volksbanks offer comprehensive product ranges with almost all insurance lines through their affiliated insurers (Farny 2011, p. 767).

The **evaluation** of bank distribution from the insurer's perspective initially reveals some potentials: Insurers are particularly interested in distribution via banks or savings banks because they hope to tap into a high customer potential that they would otherwise not have access to. In addition, this distribution channel appears relatively inexpensive as it mainly or even only incurs variable costs depending on the design. An image transfer from one established financial service provider to another is also possible. In digital bank distribution, insurers also benefit from the already widespread use of online banking and access to digitally affine target groups (especially for simpler products). On the other hand, the challenges of qualifying and—anyway only indirect—control of bank employees are eliminated.

In the traditional, person-bound bank distribution, which still clearly dominates in complex pension consultations, it should be noted that bank employees are generally not insurance experts and find it particularly difficult to deal with property & casualty insurance. Therefore, person-bound bank distribution is not equally suitable for all products. Apart from that, there has been a decline in bank branches for years. From a distribution policy perspective, the difficult control of banks and savings banks by insurers is another drawback. And finally: If the insurer still rates the opportunities higher than the restrictions, it faces a limited and quite manageable number of potential partners. Most major banks as well as the savings banks and Raiffeisen and Volksbanks already have fixed cooperation partners. Consequently, this leads to a displacement competition, which makes bank distribution more costly.

13.2.6 Distribution via Associations, Clubs, and Organizations

Another form of utilizing non-insurance sales channels is distribution via associations, clubs, and organizations. In this case, their members are collectively addressed in cooperation with the respective institution. Similar to annex distribution, the cooperation partner can offer access to its members and thus act more as an **insurance company's distribution channel** or understand itself more as a **procurement organization for its members** and search for special products or rates for them. In any case, group insurances are suitable for this distribution channel due to the similar structure of the member clientele.

Examples of this type of distribution include insurances of all kinds for members of sports and other clubs, for members of trade unions as well as for members of professional and economic associations and automobile clubs. For instance, the potential of an ADAC with its approximately 21.5 million members is so large that Allianz Insurance operates its own motor vehicle insurance together with the ADAC. And products of occupational pension schemes, life and accident insurances are suitable for pension schemes for company employees (staff business). Finally, special personal and financial loss liability insurances are offered for members of professional associations (e.g., also insurance brokers).

Characteristics of this form of distribution are indirect and decentralized sales, predominantly indirect communication between customers and the respective organization, and a strong specialization either on customer groups or products.

Evaluation Depending on the role understanding, this distribution channel is either similar to the annex distribution or to that of the policyholder's own or tied insurance intermediaries. The sales potential through associations, clubs, and organizations is attractive, the profit margins depending on the institution are also attractive, but sometimes rather low. In addition, there is often a lack of direct contact between the insurer and (potential) customers (Farny 2011, p. 764 f.).

13.2.7 Distribution via Policyholder-owned or -affiliated Insurance Intermediaries

Policyholder-owned intermediaries are legally and economically dependent on the policyholder, i.e., employees in insurance purchasing departments of industrial or corporate customers. **Company-affiliated intermediaries** (fvV) are typically outsourced insurance departments that operate as legally independent insurance brokerage companies (usually as brokers according to § 34d para. 1 GewO) owned by a large economic enterprise. In addition to procuring insurance coverage and managing contracts, they often undertake more comprehensive risk management tasks.

▶ **Policyholder-owned or -affiliated insurance intermediaries** (= Captive Broker, Company-affiliated intermediaries) are procurement organs of industrial or larger commercial customers who purchase insurance coverage in the market for them.

Examples of fvV include DVA Deutsche Verkehrs-Assekuranz-Vermittlungs-GmbH (Deutsche Bahn), Mercedes-Benz Insurance Service GmbH (Mercedes), Airport Assekuranz Vermittlungs-GmbH AAV (Fraport), Albatros Versicherungsdienste GmbH

(Lufthansa Group), VVK Versicherungsvermittlungs- und Verkehrskontor GmbH (Siemens) or PALLAS Insurance (Bayer).

Such companies do not violate the prohibition on the passing on of commission(§ 48b para. 3 VAG). In terms of commercial law, fvV can assume the status of a broker, while that of an agent would lead to conflicts of interest (Maier and Faßbender 2020, p. 286 f.). Even though company-affiliated intermediaries economically represent a procurement organ of the customer, they are nevertheless a distribution channel that is legally and economically very close to that of the broker. Depending on their design, they procure insurance coverage to cover the risks of their company (as industrial customers) and/or mediate insurance products to their staff (private customer business). The latter is also referred to as **Worksite-Marketing** and stands for the sale of financial products at the customer's workplace with or without active involvement of the employer. The idea of staff business is similar to the business model of distribution via associations, clubs and organizations. However, in distribution via organizations such as the employer, there is no involvement of an fvV, who—whether as a department or independent brokerage operation—has specialized employees with insurance expertise and thus differs from associations, clubs and organizations.

Evaluation from the insurer's perspective: For the insurer, cooperation with company-affiliated intermediaries mainly means variable acquisition costs. In the course of worksite marketing, potentially lucrative business potentials can be tapped. However, the company-affiliated intermediaries are themselves interested in potential profits from the staff business. With regard to the company risks to be insured, these intermediaries or purchasers are a demanding clientele who know their risks very well and grant the insurer as little margin as possible. Relationship business plays a major role here. From a sales policy perspective, it should finally be noted that company-affiliated intermediaries can be controlled the least, as they are in a certain sense mediating their own risk.

13.2.8 Direct Sales

Compared to the distribution channels explained so far, direct sales represent a relatively independent, i.e., different sales approach.

▶ **Direct Sales** refers to the direct sale of insurance products from the insurer's headquarters to customers without the involvement of further (decentralized) sales persons or intermediaries by mail, telephone and/or internet.

Characteristics This involves direct and central sales. In contrast to intermediary sales, the initiative in new business always comes from the interested party, in existing business from the insurer or the customer, and communication only takes place indirectly via media. In direct sales, advertising plays a very large role because it—instead of people—should activate the interested party. Moreover, this sales channel requires initiative, insurance-interested and media-savvy customers, thus only addressing a certain customer group. The comparatively impersonal way of communication leads to the fact that not all products are equally suitable for direct sales (Farny 2011, p. 773).

In direct sales of insurance business, the insurer essentially has the same duties of conduct, advice, and documentation as intermediaries (§§ 1a, 6 para. 1, 6a VVG). The information obligations can be fulfilled according to the communication tool used (§ 7 para. 1 VVG). In addition, he has the general information obligations before the conclusion of the contract according to § 7 para. 1 VVG.

The following **ideal-typical prerequisites** make direct sales promising (Farny 2011, p. 771):

with the customer

- Knowledge and interest in insurance issues (Involvement)
- Action pressure
- Openness to telecommunications and digital media
- Price sensitivity

with the product

- Known standard products
- Low need for adjustment over time
- Low frequency of loss and uniform types of loss

with the insurance company

- Level of recognition
- Image as a low-cost provider
- Low operating costs
- Technological infrastructure for handling mass business

on the markets

- Transparency about providers, products, and prices.

Evaluation from the insurer's perspective: Although direct sales still have a small market share overall, they are an interesting distribution channel in certain situations. In price-sensitive markets with standard products and relatively significant premium differences, such as in the motor vehicle insurance market, direct sales have achieved considerable turnover (Table 13.3). It also benefits from digitalization, whether technologically (e.g., through advances in customer service through modern call center concepts and CRM applications (Nicoletti 2021, Chap. 5)) or in terms of changing customer behavior (e.g., in situational insurance). From a company's perspective, direct sales are also attractive because of their direct and quick controllability. It also offers an alternative to the lengthy process of building a sales force organization for newcomers from abroad (see also Nicoletti 2021, pp. 160–163).

Table 13.3 Top-selling direct insurers in property & casualty/accident insurance 2021. (BaFin 2023c)

Rank	Direct Insurer	Gross Earned Premiums 2021 (in million Euro)
1	HUK24 Versicherung	1,039
2	Verti Versicherung	368
3	Cosmos Versicherung	335
4	DA Deutsche Allgemeine Versicherung	279
5	Europa Versicherung	217
6	ERGO Direkt Versicherung	171
7	DFV Deutsche Familienversicherung	155
8	Allianz Direct Versicherungs-AG	137
9	BavariaDirekt Versicherung	137
10	R+V Direktversicherung	127

As indicated, direct sales are not promising in every situation. They demand a lot from the provider, above all competitive products and tariffs. Because of the—especially on the internet and in price comparison portals—high transparency and comparability, only the top-ranked have any chance of new business in this business model. Apart from that, with direct sales, you will only ever be able to acquire a part of the total market, as the customer has to become active in this sales channel and many customers will not deal with insurance on their own in the future. The costs of direct sales are to be assessed differently: At first glance, they seem to be significantly lower due to largely missing commissions than the effort for building and maintaining an agent system and the acquisition costs with brokers or sales companies. However, the setup costs of the technical infrastructure and especially high advertising costs, which go hand in hand with the necessary image building and maintenance as well as the ongoing activation of interested parties, are significant.

13.2.9 Sales Companies

A significant special form of distribution is represented by sales companies. They have their own legal personality—sometimes one or more insurers are involved, or the sales company is owned by others and is independent of insurers.

▶ **Sales Company** is a legally independent company with a usually very large number of intermediaries, which specializes in the mediation of selected or many financial services to private customers and is often, but not always organized in the form of a multi level marketing.

▶ **Multi Level Marketing** (MLM) means that the distribution is *organized* in a many-tiered, hierarchical structure, in which the upper level earns from all hierarchically subsequent levels, i.e., participates in the commission for each product sold.

The **essential characteristics of a sales company** include its consistently oriented organizational structure and incentive systems for the mediation of financial services products and insurances; this can take the form of a multi level sales organization, but also follow a classic sales system. Its legal independence, the high number of intermediaries, and the focus on the private customer market distinguish it from a sales policy perspective from (usually smaller) classic brokers, multi-tied agents, agents or exclusive tied agents. However, these can develop into a sales company, as in the case of a legally independent large tied agent organization like Allianz Beratungs- und Vertriebs-AG or in the case of a large insurance broker with many connected intermediaries like MLP. In this respect, the transitions between classic sales systems and sales companies are fluid. According to HGB und GewO, however, it does not represent a sales channel of its own kind—it can assume the status of exclusivity (e.g., DVAG, ERGO Pro), a multi-tied agents (e.g., Swisslife Select, OVB) or a broker (e.g., MLP).

In this respect, a sales company is not really anything new, a multi level sales organization is. Because it basically embodies a very consistent orientation (of a sales company) towards sales or acquisition in terms of organizational structure and incentive design.

Organizational Structure in a multi level sales organization In MLM sales, new employees always start at the lowest hierarchical level, but can rise in the hierarchy according to a fixed career plan. This is the same for all intermediaries and is characterized by high transparency. Every intermediary has basically the same chances, as only the mediation successes are decisive. The multi-level hierarchy system is created by associated intermediaries forming a structure with newly recruited intermediaries, which further "branches out" when the new intermediaries then recruit and "build up" further intermediaries. However, reaching a first leadership level is necessary for building up own employees, which ultimately serves quality assurance, as intermediaries have to prove themselves first.

Incentive System in MLM Basically, the commission paid by the product provider for the conclusion of an financial services product or an insurance policy is divided. On the one hand, it is distinguished whether parts of the commission are allocated for the conclusion or for other activities such as motivation, coaching and employee management, training, and sales planning, control, and monitoring. On the other hand, it is taken into account at which level a intermediary is located. At each level, it is then regulated what proportion of an acquisition commission the intermediary receives for contracts sold by himself (own commission) and what proportion of an acquisition commission he receives from the acquisition commissions of the intermediaries hierarchically following him (share commission). The commission rate for mediated business increases from level to level, thus compensating for the acquisition commissions increasingly missed by the respective intermediaries or managers due to the other activities taken over, in short, the opportunity costs. The participation of the upper hierarchy levels in the selling successes of the lower levels also ensures that managers have a vital interest in the progress and promotion of their recruited employees. In addition to the financial, there is a social incentive: Each hierarchy level is associated with a special title that expresses the (improved) position compared to the other participants. The social recognition associated with this should not be underestimated in terms of its incentive effect.

Figure 13.4 shows the principle: An employee sells a life insurance policy. Of the 35 per mille acquisition commission, he himself receives 12 per mille, his district director 3 per mille, his regional director 5 per mille, his director 7 per mille, and the board member responsible for him 8 per mille. In practice, other titles exist, the commission rates are—despite LVRG—higher, and large multi level sales organizations have more than five levels. In addition, there are also several structures side by side in the latter, because the construction of structures across all levels and thus the promotion of intermediaries to the top level is in principle possible at any time.

However, the way to the top is long and only achievable for comparatively few intermediaries. Many new intermediaries initially strive for contracts by approaching their relatives and acquaintances. From the company's point of view, this is also desired, as it provides access to new addresses. However, once these contacts have been worked through, personal initiative is required to open up other customer groups. Many newly

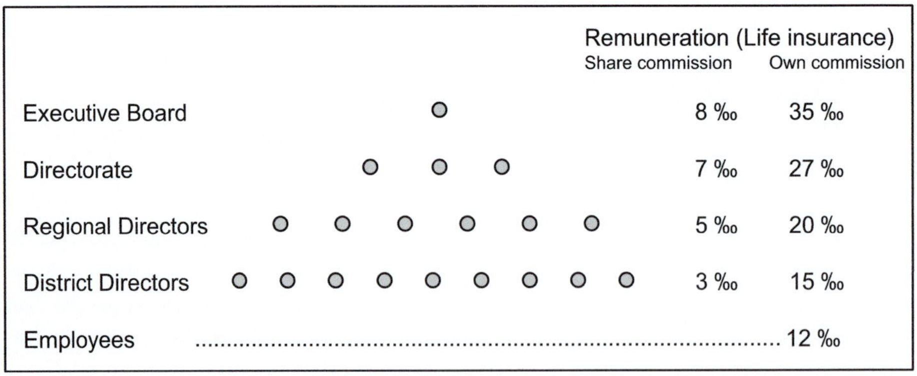

Fig. 13.4 Structure of a multi level sales organization

acquired intermediaries struggle with this, and if they fail to acquire new customers, their business basis will be withdrawn sooner or later, and they will drop out. Due to this typical mechanism for MLM, the turnover rate is rather high, especially at the lower levels. It is obvious that this also increases the risk of cancellation for customers acquired from the circle of relatives and acquaintances.

The **manifestations of sales companies** range from the tied monoliner with a few selected standard products (ERGO Pro) to the independent broker with a wide product range (MLP). The multi-tied agent is most common. The largest sales company in the German market is Deutsche Vermögensberatung AG (DVAG) with €2.2 billion in sales from commission revenues in 2022, around 8 million customers, and approximately 18,500 full-time independent financial advisors (Table 13.4).

Evaluation From the insurer's perspective, the high sales potential of MLM in new business is noteworthy. Therefore, this sales approach is also an interesting alternative for new entrants to the market. Especially with the more closely tied multi level sales organization, their share of the provider's new business is so large that there is practically no alternative to this sales partner. They thus have a pronounced own marketing potential, their intermediaries prefer direct customer contact and are extremely proactive (Lach 1995, pp. 131–133).

On the other hand, the challenges are the high turnover among intermediaries at the lower levels and the often above-average cancellation rate associated with it, the sometimes low qualification of the intermediaries with corresponding image effects for the provider, and the risk of misincentives due to the promotion of non-needs-based intermediation. In addition, this form of distribution is associated with high acquisition costs

Table 13.4 The ten largest financial sales organizations in Germany. (Cash Online 2023)

Rank	Financial Sales Organization	Commission Revenues 2022 (in million Euro)
1	DVAG	2,204.60
2	MLP AG	842.40
3	Swiss Life Holding GmbH	680.70
4	OVB	331.90
5	Telis Finanz	174.20
6	Dr. Klein	135.00
7	Global Finanz	66.74
8	Bonnfinanz	47.80
9	Finum Gruppe	34.69
10	Formaxx/Mayflower	32.44

due to above-average commissions, which ultimately represent the price for the closing strength (appreciated by the provider). The new 25 per mille accounting rule for acquistion costs created by the LVRG and the increased observation of these costs by BaFin mean that in the future, not as high closing commissions can be paid in life insurance as in the past. As a result, the multi level sales organizations are under pressure and will have to look for new sources of income in the future.

From the customer's point of view, the work of sales companies is to be welcomed when they actively draw consumers' attention to security and provision gaps that they would not have recognized or suppressed otherwise, advise them appropriately in this regard and contribute to (partial) solutions through intermediation, in short, when they really practice the repeatedly propagated ideal of a needs-based, customer-oriented and serious ("Allfinanz") consultation and mediation. The flip side of the coin is the unscrupulous, non-needs-based intermediation, which is essentially based on the desire for acquisition commissions and takes advantage of the customer. The risk of such behavior is particularly high in multi level sales organizations because they work so consistently towards closing.

The reputable financial sales organizations have long recognized this and are trying to counter this danger: with appropriate qualification of their employees, consideration of the cancellation rates in the remuneration and supplementing the purely closing-oriented structures with care units or agencies that continue to look after customers after the initial closing and generate follow-up business.

13.3 Economic Importance of Distribution Channels

The importance of the various distribution channels in the insurance market results from the **acceptance and actual use by customers** and is also reflected in their respective **share of new business.**

A first indication of the potential of individual distribution channels is their respective **customer acceptance** (Fig. 13.5). When asked to what extent they like the respective distribution channels—now or for the future—to conclude an insurance, the following picture emerges: Since 2010, the 'branch' (office, agency, branch) has had the highest approval, with 78% of respondents approving this distribution channel in 2023. In second place is the agent at the customer's home (62%), still very accepted, but has fallen from over 80 to 62% in almost two decades. The broker follows with 50%. Meanwhile, direct sales via the insurer's website is already in fourth place in customer acceptance with 43%, having increased enormously from 28% in 2013. In contrast, sales via banks have lost acceptance in recent years and are (only) still at 37% and are therefore only about as accepted as comparison portal sales (36%), which has increased significantly from 23% in 2013 to 36% today. Finally, the acceptance of direct sales via post (33%) and telephone (23%) has remained similar over the past almost twenty years.

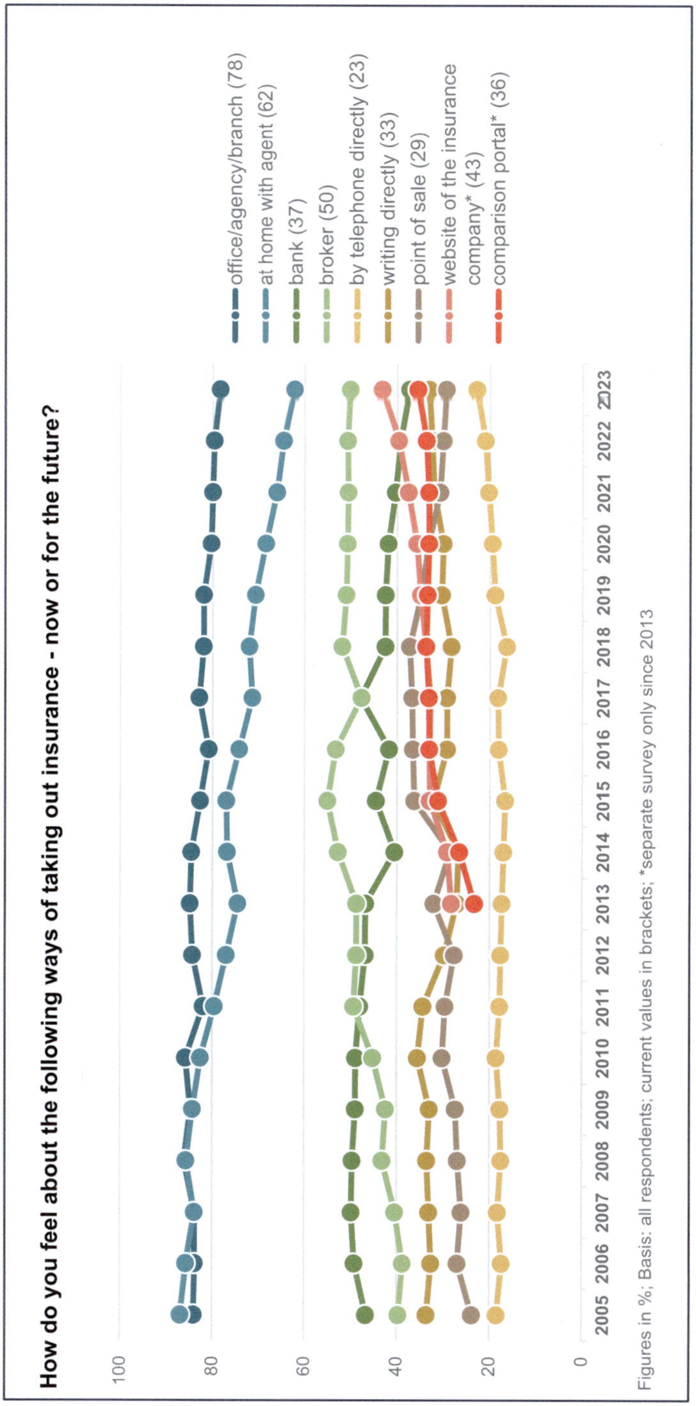

Fig. 13.5 Acceptance of distribution channels: Development 2005–2023. (Sirius Campus 2023b, p. 16)

Another indication of the importance of different distribution channels is the **actual use by customers;** this is determined by the question of which of the presented distribution channels they have already used to conclude an insurance policy (Fig. 13.6). Compared to customer acceptance, the use of the respective distribution channels is characterized by a significantly higher commitment, as opinions and assessments often differ from actual behavior. It is noticeable that only the traditional distribution channel via the agent at home passes this "test of endurance" and the actual use with 58% almost corresponds to the basic, but non-binding acceptance. However, the importance of distribution via agents in their offices or agencies is also noteworthy; with 59%, this distribution channel has been used by the most customers so far. The representative distribution still dominates in terms of actual use—and quite strongly. With a significant gap, the next most used distribution channels are the broker and the bank, both with 23% each. While bank distribution has remained relatively unchanged since 2005, the use of brokers has developed comparatively stronger upwards, specifically from 8 to 23%. Direct sales (written and by phone) have grown slightly over the same period and are at 10% each in 2023. Finally, it is noteworthy that online direct sales via insurance company websites have increased comparatively strongly and were used by 21% of respondents in 2023, i.e. every fifth person, and thus even before the use of comparison portals (16%).

The importance of different distribution channels is also largely dependent on the turnover they generate. With regard to the **share of new business,** it is noticeable that the importance of the distribution channels varies depending on the insurance branch or line (Table 13.5).

However, the **distribution channel allocation** at GDV is somewhat **unusual:** It should be noted that both full-time and sideline tied agents according to § 84 HGB as well as employed sales persons are assigned to single-company and group intermediaries; the former are listed as intermediaries working on a commercial basis in the intermediaries register according to the Trade Regulation Act, but the employees are not. In addition, brokers and multi-tied agents are grouped together under multiple intermediaries, even though the former as brokers are independent and are on the customer´s side and the latter as tied agents are bound (thus economically dependent) vicarious agents of the insurer or insurers represented. The division of credit institutions in conjunction with other sales channels does not correspond to the classification according to the Trade Regulation Act. Finally, direct sales include new business mediated via comparison portals, which usually does not represent direct sales because the comparison portals mostly act as intermediaries.

The new business shares listed in Table 13.5 from the year 2022 nevertheless provide insights and allow some conclusions to be drawn: In **life insurance,** the single-company or group intermediary dominates over the multiple-company intermediaries and credit institutions, which in turn play the largest role in this insurance branch due to their proximity to their own pension products. One could also say that the agent distribution with 41.9% is ahead of the broker (26.9%) and bank distribution (20.0%). It is noticeable that multi-tied agents in life insurance have their largest share of new business at 7.6%;

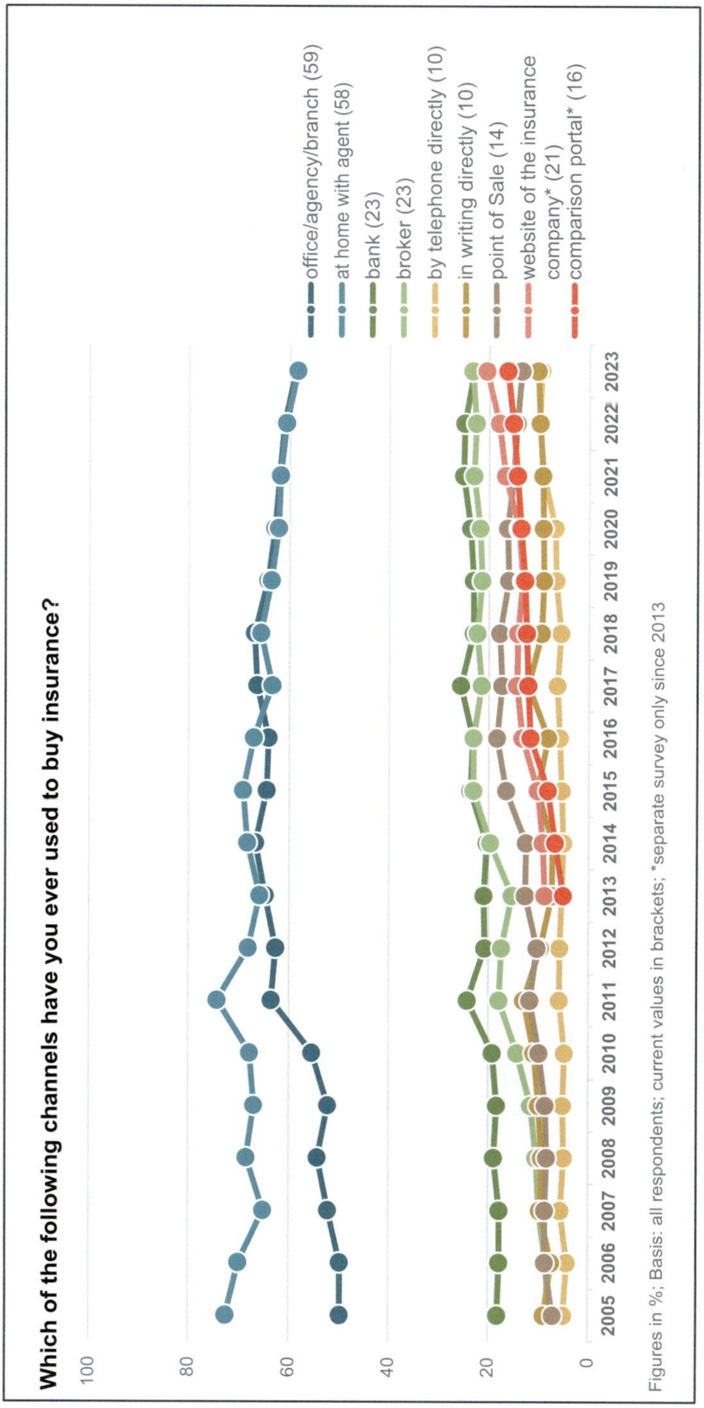

Fig. 13.6 Use of distribution channels: Development 2005–2023. (Sirius Campus 2023b, p. 17)

Table 13.5 Shares of distribution channels in the new business 2022 of the insurance industry. (GDV 2023a, p. 13)

Distribution Channels	Life Insurance[2]	Private Health Insurance[3]	Property/ Accident/ Liability Insurance[4]	Motor Vehicle Insurance[4]	Legal Expense Insurance[4]
single-company or group intermediaries	39.3	54.2	42.6	46.3	57.3
full-time	33.7	35.0	39.4	42.6	53.9
sideline	0.6	0.8	0.8	1.9	1.0
employed sales force	4.9	18.4	2.4	1.8	2.4
multi-company intermediaries	34.5	30.9	43.5	27.2	23.6
brokers	26.9	27.8	39.8	24.8	20.8
multi-tied agents	7.6	3.1	3.7	2.4	2.8
credit institutions (banks)	20.0	3.7	6.3	3.1	7.9
as a single-company intermediary	13.0	2.2	3.8	1.9	5.4
as a multi-company intermediary	7.0	1.5	2.5	1.2	2.5
direct sales[1]	3.0	8.5	3.1	18.5	7.9
other sales channels	3.3	2.7	4.5	4.9	3.3

[1]including comparison portals, [2]according to mediated premium sum, [3]according to mediated monthly premium, [4]according to mediated annual premium
all values in percent

this is due, among other things, to some multi level sales organizations that operate as multi-tied agents. Direct sales play a comparatively minor role in this product segment, which is likely to refer more to term life insurance. Also in **private health insurance,** single-company or group intermediaries dominate (even with 54.2%), with the comparatively high share of the employed sales force of 18.4% being noteworthy; this is due to the specialist knowledge required for sales and advice in private health insurance, which is often brought into the consultation by employed "specialists". It is also striking that the share of direct sales is high, which in turn is likely to be due to (comparatively simpler) supplementary health insurance products.

In the insurance branches **property, accident and liability,** broker distribution (39.8%) and distribution via exclusive tied agents (39.4%) are predominant. In **motor vehicle insurance,** the largest share of new business (still) comes from full-time exclusive tied agents (42.6%); this is surprising insofar as there is traditionally strong (price) competition here and the commissions are rather low. The same applies to brokers (24.8%). It is less surprising that direct sales have their greatest importance here with 18.5%. Other sales channels are also more strongly represented with 4.9% than in other insurance branches, probably as a result of the annex distribution of car manufacturers and car dealers. Finally, in **legal expenses insurance,** the full-time exclusive tied agents is as dominant as in no other sector, accounting for 53.9% of new business. This is followed by brokers (20.8%). It is striking that the comparatively high share of banks, which are only more significant in life insurance, and of direct sales (each 7.9%).

It should be noted that the distribution channels vary greatly depending on the insurance branch and are widespread, but ultimately all distribution channels have their justification for existence.

13.4 Design and Control of the Distribution System

13.4.1 Determination of Distribution Channels and Task Allocation (Distribution Strategy)

The distribution strategy of an insurance company refers to the determination of the distribution channel mix and the cooperation or task allocation. This applies both across business fields and within a strategic business field.

In relation to a country market, the **determination of the distribution channel mix** in insurance practice is usually a **cross-business** strategic **decision:** Firstly, the majority of insurers are historically burdened, i.e., they have been working with certain distribution channels for many years and decades. Strategically, but also structurally, process-wise, and culturally, this effectively means a strong bond that cannot be easily dissolved and possibly reactivated later. Secondly, the different distribution channels require different content, personnel, and technological support, so they are associated with significant investments that should therefore be coordinated across business fields; particularly with company-tied intermediaries, there are synergy potentials when used in several business fields. Thirdly, distribution systems are a sensitive construct because insurance intermediaries are people who have emotions and sensitivities. In a business field division according to insurance branches, it can happen that the same intermediaries are distribution partners of the insurer in several business fields; then the behavior towards these should also be coordinated and processes, remuneration modalities, contact persons, and appreciation should be as uniform as possible.

At the same time, the determination of the distribution channel mix is also a **business field-related** strategic **decision:** In international insurance companies, it will differentiate country-specifically because the distribution channels and distribution systems are differently pronounced. But as already shown (Sect. 13.2), the distribution channels are also differently predestined with reference to various customer segments and insurance branches. For example, it may make sense to operate in the industrial, commercial, and private customer segments with different distribution channels or combinations of distribution channels. Similarly, for example, in life insurance, bank distribution plays a much larger role than in full health insurance.

The design of the distribution channel mix is one of the most important tasks in marketing and sales policy. Although in principle all mix variants are conceivable, **three basic models** can be distinguished (Farny 2011, p. 786 f.):

1. Distribution channel **concentration:**
   Only one distribution channel is used, whether it is the sales force, the broker, the bank, a distribution company, or direct sales. There are pure direct and pure broker insurers and an insurer that only sells its products through a distribution company. The background to this model is the concentration of forces on the needs or requirements of the chosen distribution channel.
2. Distribution channel **focus:**
   One distribution channel is used as the main sales method, several or all other distribution channels are used additionally, but with less importance. This model is often favored by financial services providers and insurers who can access a strong sales channel (e.g., bank branches or sales force) and do not want to completely leave other sales opportunities unused.
3. Distribution channel **dispersion** (Multi-Channel-Management):
   Several or all significant distribution channels are used more or less equally alongside each other. This is intended to enable a high exploitation of sales potentials and thus market penetration as well as a differentiated business field policy. In practice, especially large (often internationally oriented) financial services and insurance groups pursue multi-channel strategies.

When an insurer is newly founded (e.g., start-ups) or enters the market as a foreign insurer, it has comparatively more freedoms in choosing the distribution channels to be used than an established insurer. However, the latter can also further develop (evolve) its distribution channel mix, i.e., restrict or expand it.

The concrete **evaluation and** subsequent **selection of distribution channels** and the distribution partners associated with them should then—taking into account the cross-business framework conditions—be made against the background of the marketing strategy (Chap. 8) and the marketing task profile (Sect. 9.2) of the insurer and can therefore differentiate quite well in the business fields. From a marketing perspective, the evaluation of the individual distribution partners is primarily about their respective marketing potential with regard to the implementation of the marketing specifications (goals, strategies, tasks, tools).

The **marketing potential of a distribution channel** can generally be determined by criteria such as

- Image
- Position in the market (e.g., market share, growth dynamics)
- Structures (e.g., marketing and procurement structures)
- Behavior (e.g., in distribution channel competition)

- Economic efficiency in relation to achievable sales volumes and distribution costs
- Control and steering capability
- Modifiability, i.e., adaptability of the distribution system
- Environmental situation: competitors' distribution channels
- Potential of the distribution channel in terms of capacity, ability, and willingness of the employees.

Based on such aspects, with *Lach,* the marketing profiles of important intermediary types can be determined (Lach 1995, pp. 121–133):

The **small agent,** who has one or a few employees and a small number of customers, therefore has a low marketing potential, relies on experiential knowledge instead of marketing research knowledge, and primarily pursues privately determined, safety-oriented goals. He operates not strategically, but regionally limited and in his social environment, focusing on specific products, demand generation, and application processing.

In contrast, the **large agent,** who has several employees and a large insurance portfolio, has a larger (though limited by exclusivity to his insurer) marketing potential. He relies on marketing information from his insurer, knows and mediates its entire range, and tends to act based on existing business. He deals with multi-tied agents and medium-sized brokers, relies on service readiness, and actively uses the sales promotion tools of his insurer (e.g., portfolio marketing actions).

Compared to the large agent, the **medium-sized broker** has a larger marketing potential, as he works with various insurers and can therefore create different problem solutions for his selected target groups—these are predominantly commercial customers or better-off private customers. Due to his broker liability (suitable advice), he needs comprehensive information, so marketing research is of central importance to him. His goal of maximizing commissions is counterbalanced by his striving for independence and the contractual obligation to achieve particularly favorable price-performance ratios for the customer. He pursues combat strategies against his main competitors (multi-tied agent) by poaching customers with better offers. Although the broker can charge fees to commercial customers and all customers for the mediation of net tariffs due to his consulting service, the commission payment by the insurer for the business mediated to him is common. Communicatively, the broker puts his operation and his consulting service in the foreground, on the performance side he seeks horizontal cooperations for quality assurance. Broker pools with their services are particularly helpful to him.

The **industrial broker** operates in another, very demanding business field from the customer's point of view, namely in the target group of large industrial and corporate customers who demand individually designed insurance protection for their complex, often internationally extended risks. He employs many, sometimes highly qualified employees. His marketing potential is large in terms of the insurable protection that can be mediated and small in terms of the number of customers. In order to be able to advise and insure these internationally, the industrial broker needs comprehensive information about foreign markets, local insurance providers, reinsurance and primary insurance capacities, and the risk exposure of his customers. This is not possible without international broker networks. Likewise, the design of complex insurance solutions requires cooperation with various primary insurers, sometimes reinsurers. Sales targets and thus the search for large industrial customers with corresponding insurance needs dominate, as do follow-up commissions to cover the high fixed costs (see also Cummins and Doherty 2006). Competitors are mainly company-affiliated intermediaries, whose advantage of greater customer proximity (better risk knowledge and lower margins) can only be offset by better risk solutions and high-quality risk management consulting services or direct cooperation. The marketing solutions are very customer-specific: this affects the coverage design and the corresponding risk carriers involved, the personal contact with the customer, and the communication (Pahl et al. 2020, pp. 301–304).

The **sales company,** in contrast to the industrial broker, is primarily active in the private customer business, and to some extent also in the commercial customer business. It has a very large number of employees and accordingly customer relationships (marketing potential). It receives important information about the potential for new customers from its product partners and its intermediaries. Its strength lies in the marketing task of acquiring new customers, so the initial objective is to achieve maximum acquisition commissions by acquiring as many new customers as possible. However, this also results in a considerable potential for existing customers (up- and cross-selling) with corresponding follow-up commissions. Competitors are all agents and medium-sized brokers. Depending on their focus and business model, sales companies sell one or more products or even the entire financial services needs of customers and carry out sales promotion measures on a large scale.

Banks and savings banks have a large number of employees with relatively regular customer contact and therefore have a large marketing potential, especially in the area of retirement provision. Their marketing goal is to generate contribution margins for the fixed costs associated with the branches and to round off the range of services. Their competitors are essentially insurance agents and sales companies, and in the upscale private customer business also medium-sized brokers. On the product side, banks and savings banks can represent the combination of variable deposits and withdrawals as well as reinvestments of retirement provision amounts in the sense of combining different financial services functions and thus create added value. The point of sale shifts to the branch or the banking app, communication takes place personally and also at the customer's request. In the area of property & casualty and health insurance, bank sales are much more difficult—the more typical insurance distribution via insurance experts in or outside the branch is therefore used as a supplement (Kallerhoff 2018, p. 343, 355).

From the insurer's point of view, the next step after the basic selection of the distribution channels to be used is to determine the **division of tasks between the provider and the distribution channel.** This is basically open and is based on cost-benefit considerations. Alternatively, the business processes of the insurer and those of the distribution partner can be placed side by side and compared. This reveals the relationships and potential duplications as well as design and optimization possibilities. With regard to the distribution system, this means, for example, investigating the following questions (Köhne 2006, p. 348):

- What are the core competencies of the distribution partner, e.g., establishing contact, consulting, closing, support, claims settlement, or reinvestment/extension?
- Which distributive partial services are central factors of his service provision, e.g., sub-processes that lie behind the mentioned competencies, such as in the case of closing as a value-adding activity the sub-processes of offer creation, application recording, risk assessment and underwriting as well as policy issuance?
- In which functions is capital tied up that can easily be reduced (e.g., in fixed cost blocks of regional directorates that can either be relocated to the head office or outsourced to the intermediary)?
- Can the distribution partner be comprehensively relieved (e.g., in the information, consulting and application recording process)?
- Which are labor-intensive and which are knowledge-intensive partial services?
- In which functions does the distribution partner have little know-how and how should this be dealt with?

The transfer of additional subtasks to intermediaries (e.g., handling customer inquiries, calculating offers (tariffing), electronic application recording, underwriting and risk selection, (partial) policy issuance, collection, modification of direct debit, address and similar data, electronic claim notification, claim settlement)—also called **function relocation or function outsourcing**—can improve the overall quality of service. This is because customer satisfaction and loyalty increase as a result of faster contract and claim processing, more flexible responses to customer requests, and improved customer data on the part of the intermediaries. However, with the additional function takeovers, the requirements for qualification, IT support, and the time spent on support services (opportunity costs due to lost acquisition time) increase, thus increasing the dependence on the insurer. The insurer must compensate for these contributions from the sales partners through incentives, e.g., through special commissions, subsidies, participation in investments in the form of technological equipment, training or start-up financing, as well as the transfer of entrepreneurial responsibility. It is also advisable to support the intermediaries via support or service centers (call centers) in order to keep the time spent on the additional activities as low as possible (Kutz 1997, pp. 8–44; Kendl 1997, pp. 50–52 and 186–200; Helten 1998, p. 93). Finally, the increasing digitalization of products and processes enables a new division of labor between insurers and intermediaries (Nicoletti 2021, especially pp. 154–158).

Research Window: Digitalization of Insurance Distribution

Digitalization is on everyone's lips. In the **insurance industry,** it is primarily addressed and discussed in the context of process optimizations, new risks, products and business models (InsurTechs), current developments such as artificial intelligence (AI) or blockchain, changed customer communication up to new sales methods and sales channels (see Sect. 6.1.4). In dealing with insurance services, the advancing digitalization has for several years led to an increased use of digital information and communication technologies by insurance companies. On the **customer side**, it leads to higher service requirements, increasing flexibility and performance expectations, as well as changes in purchasing behavior in a digitalized world.

Thus, digitalization **inevitably also captures** the **insurance distribution** and thus the insurance intermediaries. In recent times, insurance companies have been driving the use of digital technologies by insurance intermediaries—the Corona pandemic has certainly played into their hands. The goal is the consistent integration of insurance agencies into an omnichannel approach in order to pick up the (hybrid) customer at the right place, to be able to offer suitable solutions and to interact more frequently with the customer (online or offline), which is flexibly possible in terms of time and location with new digital technologies (Birkner 2017, pp. 21–24; Hauri 2018, p. 245). Insurance intermediaries must therefore in the future offer both classic offline and suitable online solutions for a conclusion and generate a multimedia customer experience in the personal sales process, as this is supposed to significantly increase the probability of conclusion (Schmidt-Gallas et al. 2018, pp. 10–12). For the digitalization on the part of the intermediary, this means: The **interactive involvement of the customer in the sales process** requires the use of mobile devices (tablets, laptops, smartphones), and even less demanding customer concerns can be handled via digital solutions in the form of apps and chatbots—and even by the customer himself.

In the technical literature and also in sales practice, the intended **objectives of the use of digital technologies** are primarily discussed: Through the "self-service" of the customer, the administrative activities for the intermediary are reduced, which is supposed to gain more time for important care, consulting and sales processes. A successful interplay of the classic sales channel with digital technologies is supposed to create dynamic synergy effects. At the same time, new digital contact and sales opportunities arise in intermediary sales. In sum, digitalization is supposed to bring increased productivity, more efficiency and ultimately more profit—also for the insurance intermediary (Vetter and Möbius 2019, p. 515 f.; Wiswesser 2018, pp. 114–125; Eckert et al. 2021, p. 135).

The **actual use of digital technologies by insurance intermediaries** and associated **negative effects such as digital stress** have so far been little researched. Therefore, the Institute for Insurance Economics at the Berlin School of Economics and Law (IVW Berlin) has conducted **two empirical studies** among insurance intermediaries to determine the actual use of digital technologies and the perceptions associated with them.

The first survey took place in June/July 2020, and the responses of 1006 intermediaries could be evaluated (see Köhne and Wendland 2022 for details). The second survey took place in September/October 2021, and the responses of 104 intermediaries could be evaluated (see Köhne 2022a for details). Both surveys were able to capture the two most important types of intermediaries, exclusive representatives and insurance brokers. The main findings are briefly outlined below.

Use of individual technologies: The first study conducted (with 34 technologies queried) shows the following (Fig. 13.7): Almost all intermediaries use email, stationary and mobile phones, printers/scanners/faxes, laptops and to a lesser extent also stationary computers and—presumably related to this—internet and wireless connections as underlying "infrastructures". The second survey confirms this usage behavior. Thus, the usage behavior of insurance intermediaries largely corresponds with observations in other industries (Gimpel et al. 2018); in this respect, the finding can also be confirmed that the most common digital technologies across industries and types of activities are those that establish a bridge function between the digital and physical world (e.g., printers, scanners, fax). The same applies to the rare use of trendy technologies (e.g., artificial intelligence, internet of things).

Comparing the results of the first study with other industries (Köhne and Wendland 2022, pp. 16–19), it can be seen that the average number of frequently used technologies is very high compared to other industries. It also shows that insurance intermediaries use technologies for communication, interaction, and collaboration such as systems for social interaction and collaboration, document and knowledge databases, and real-time communication systems more frequently than in other industries. One explanation for this may be the timing of the surveys and the associated Corona-related intensifications of use. On the other hand, this can certainly be explained by the information-based character of insurance products and the mediation and consulting activity as well as the status of the intermediaries as independent entrepreneurs. Thus, it can be seen that industry-specifically 87.8% of intermediaries frequently use customer care software (e.g., consulting, application recording, inventory management, claims settlement software). It can therefore be stated that insurance intermediaries are comparatively "digitally on the move" and—with the exception of trendy technologies—use a large part of many digital technologies.

In the second study, which mainly surveyed insurance brokers and asked about a reduced number of digital technologies, the values were similarly pronounced, sometimes even stronger. However, there are also differences between the usage behavior of agents and brokers (Fig. 13.8): The use of text, table and presentation software (e.g., MS-Office, Word, Excel, PowerPoint) is much more pronounced among insurance brokers at 94.2% than among insurance agents (67.7%), and the use of document and knowledge databases (e.g., intranet, blogs, wikis) is at least more pronounced (77.9% to 63.5%). Both may be related to the fact that insurance brokers do not (can not) limit themselves to the application and expert systems provided by the insurance companies, but have to provide for themselves as more independent entrepreneurs.

Different potential exploitation of digital technologies: In the second study, not only the frequency of use, but also the assessment of the potential exploitation of the respective technologies in the course of work support in insurance sales was queried. Tendencies have shown that the answers were similar, i.e., technologies that were frequently used were found to have a high potential exploitation, while rarely used technologies were found to have a low one. However, some interesting exceptions can be observed: With customer service software (e.g., consulting, application recording, inventory management, claims settlement software) and text, table and presentation software, usage is higher than potential exploitation, i.e., there are indeed some users who believe that they do not exploit the potential. In the use of typical end devices such as PC, laptop or tablet, the potential exploitation is rated even higher than the already rather high use, or in other words, their use and non-use, i.e., their mix, seems to be deliberate and in terms of potential rather exhausted. Finally, a similar relationship applies to statistics and analysis as well as graphics and design software and content management systems, but at a lower level of use. This can mean on the one hand that even with a lower frequency of use, the potential is exploited disproportionately, so these technologies in insurance sales seem to have comparatively less potential. On the other hand, it can also result from the fact that non-users can assess the potential of these technologies less well.

Importance of digital technologies for insurance intermediaries in the context of the Corona pandemic: The Corona pandemic has led to adjustments in the way most intermediaries work. However, some brokers did not feel any major changes in their work situation. In the agent area, more work steps were digitalized due to Corona than in the broker area. Many brokers stated that they had already digitalized many work steps before. The intermediaries predominantly experienced digital support of their way of working in coping with the challenges. However, digitalization required a change in the way of working and an induction, which about a third of all

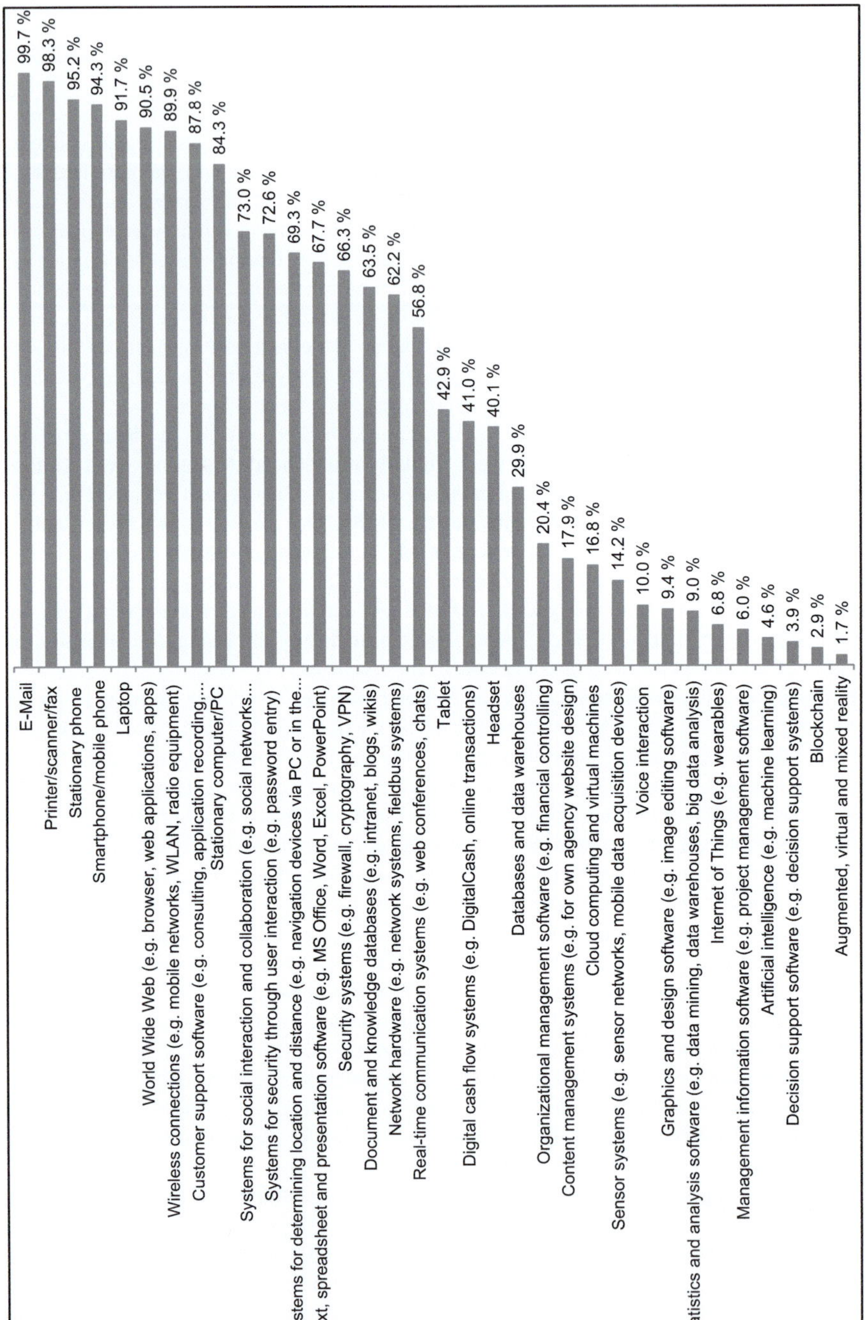

Fig. 13.7 Use of digital technologies by insurance intermediaries. (Köhne 2022a, p. 680)

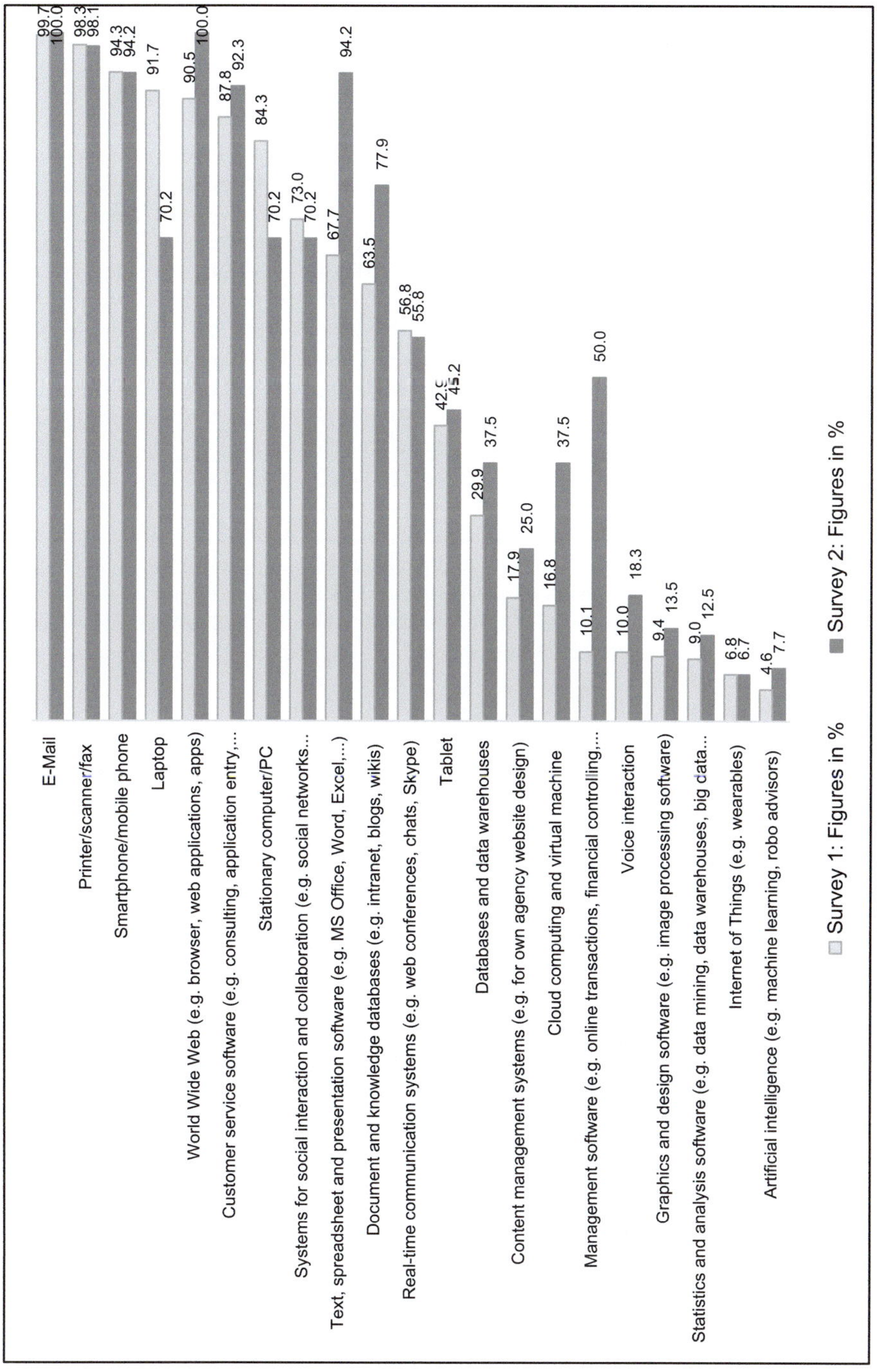

Fig. 13.8 Use of digital technologies—results of both intermediary surveys. (Köhne 2022a, p. 681)

intermediaries found strenuous. It is certainly remarkable that the intermediaries seem to have coped quite quickly and well with the change in the way they work. With regard to the benefit of digital support in this phase, it is finally noteworthy that the vast majority of the surveyed insurance intermediaries perceived that they were able to cope well with the challenges in the Corona pandemic thanks to digital support, as about 86% saw it completely or at least partially this way (Köhne 2022a).

Digital stress in insurance intermediaries: This was also empirically investigated for the first time with the two studies of the IVW Berlin. Digital stress, often also referred to as technostress, is the stress caused by the use and application of digital technologies in situations where a person's resources are insufficient for adequate and healthy handling of digital technologies, and which leads to this person's experience of stress (Hasenbein 2020, pp. 158–163). The latter manifests itself, among other things, as a subjectively unpleasant state of tension and can affect individual behavior and the emotional, cognitive and somatic level, with short-term and long-term (chronic) stress consequences to be distinguished. Consequences of unmanaged or mitigated stress-relevant situations can relate, among other things, to health, learning, memory and attention processes and to working life (e.g., loss of productivity) (Köhne and Wendland 2022, pp. 2, 8 f. and the literature cited there).

In research on digital stress, various so-called stress factors are often at the center of the investigation. The two surveys of the IVW Berlin examined the digital stress factors in insurance sales based on stress factors that are recognized in stress research and are based on *Tarafdar,* namely omnipresence of digital technologies, overload of digital technologies, complexity of digital technologies, uncertainty in dealing with digital technologies and job insecurity due to digital technologies (Tarafdar et al. 2007, pp. 301–328). The manifestations of these digital stress factors—a higher value stands for a higher perceived manifestation—do not seem to be particularly high among insurance intermediaries at first glance (Fig. 13.9).

The seemingly low values for the digital stress factors and the average of these factors of 2.68 in the first survey and 2.51 in the second survey, however, need to be put into perspective: Firstly, 1.0 or 0% would mean that the five examined digital stress factors would have no significance at

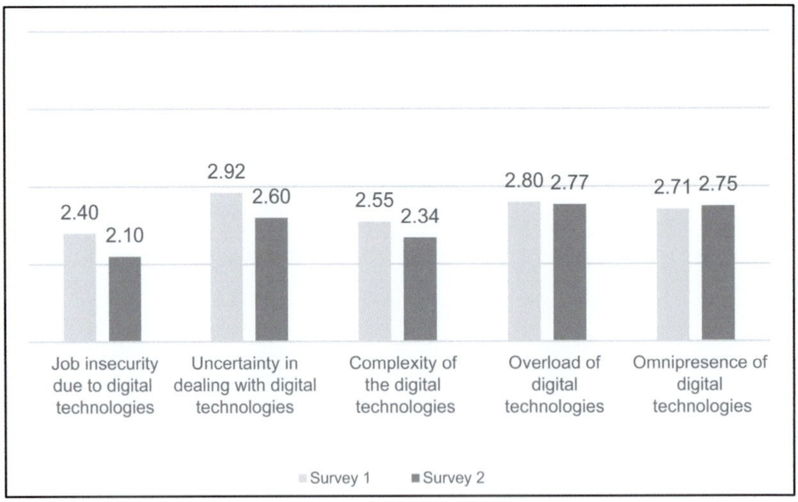

Fig. 13.9 Manifestation of digital stress factors of insurance intermediaries. (Köhne 2022b, p. 715)

all; accordingly, 2.68 stands for 42% and thus for a partial manifestation of the digital stress factors on average among all respondents. Secondly, in the 2020 survey, about 30% of the intermediaries showed a value of > 3.0 and thus stated an above-average to strong digital burden. Thirdly, the values from both surveys—with the exception of one stress factor in the second survey—are higher among insurance intermediaries than the values determined in other industries. Thus, it can be concluded that **the phenomenon of digital stress is indeed present and noteworthy among insurance intermediaries.**

In the two surveys conducted by IVW Berlin, **different manifestations of individual stress factors** can be identified. In the first survey, uncertainty in dealing with digital technologies (2.92) dominates, followed by overload (2.80) and omnipresence (2.71). In the second survey, however, overload (2.77) dominates, followed by omnipresence (2.75). Overload and omnipresence are thus comparatively strongly pronounced in both surveys, so they apparently significantly shape the activities of insurance intermediaries. In the second survey (focus on brokers), the complexity of digital technologies and the uncertainty in dealing with them are less pronounced than in the first survey (focus on exclusive tied agents). Taking this into account, it can be concluded that brokers apparently tend to feel less complexity and uncertainty. This may be due to the higher optimism of brokers identified in the second survey, the fact that they have to take care of their digitalization independently and have had to do so in the past, or the fact that they had more digital routine in 2021 than in 2020, shortly after the outbreak of the Corona pandemic (Köhne 2022b, p. 715 f.).

It should be noted that insurance intermediaries are comparatively "digitally on the move", and—with the exception of trendy technologies—they use a large number of digital technologies. This makes them one of the professional groups that use digital technologies the most in a comparison of industries. The high usage may partly be due to the requirements associated with the Corona pandemic, but it also results from the information-based character of insurance products and the mediating and consulting activity, and it can be explained by the status of intermediaries as independent entrepreneurs. All in all, the digitalization of insurance intermediation seems to be more advanced than it is sometimes said to be.

Further reading for in-depth study:

- Eckert et al. 2021.
- Gimpel et al. 2018.
- Köhne and Wendland 2022.
- Nastjuk et al. 2023.
- Rayburn et al. 2021.
- Tarafdar et al. 2007.
- Tarafdar et al. 2019.

13.4.2 Acquisition and Management of Sales Partners

Based on the strategically envisaged selection of distribution channels and the corresponding selection criteria, the task now is to acquire individual sales partners and subsequently manage them in line with company objectives.

In the course of **sales partner acquisition and retention,** the insurer can pursue a push strategy and direct its marketing mix directly at the sales partners or, through a pull strategy, carry out a direct alignment of all marketing activities towards arousing demand and brand awareness among end customers, with the aim of a resulting demand pull. The targeted influence on sales partners requires consideration of their goals, which relate to revenue-related compensation payments and marketing activities, cost-related the assumption of sales promotion, advertising and training costs as well as the desire for technological equipment. Social goals such as prestige, recognition and social benefits must also be taken into account. To acquire and retain partners, the insurer must find an adequate combination of incentive instruments and communication with the partner. The more independent the sales partners are, the more important pull marketing becomes, and thus in the financial services sector, especially the provider brand.

The optimal incentive-contribution structure towards distribution partners ultimately depends on the peculiarities of the different sales channels and their respective marketing profiles. In this context, the **compensation design**—of course in addition to contractual coordination instruments such as the agency contract discussed earlier or the granting of exclusive rights (own product, own brand etc.) to intermediaries—plays a central role. Basically, compensations related to calendar time such as salary, fixed income, fixed amount, commission guarantee, subsidy or cost reimbursement—all predominantly fixed acquisition costs—can be distinguished from performance-related compensations, which predominantly lead to variable acquisition costs. The latter are particularly suitable for sales control, as they create the incentive to fulfill the insurer's sales targets and receive high compensations through certain sales performances. Examples are commissions and bonuses. Finally, there are one-time, usually performance-related reward compensations (incentives) for the fulfillment of certain predefined goals, combined with competitions (Farny 2011, pp. 777–781).

Commissions are success- and result-dependent compensations that result in a participation in value and quantity sizes of insurance transactions. In insurance practice, numerous types of commissions (one-time, initial, follow-up, renewal, super commissions etc.) are used in various weights depending on the respective company goal.

The predominantly **individual performance-related** types of commission in practice are one-time commissions for newly concluded transactions (acquisition commission) and repeated commissions for existing transactions (follow-up commission). High acquisition commissions are particularly relevant in the personal insurance lines. On the other hand, in some property & casualty insurance lines, such as motor vehicle insurance, there is a more balanced weighting of acquisition and follow-up commissions. In addition to these control-related commissions, there are a number of processing-related commissions that compensate for ongoing customer service and readiness to serve existing customers (portfolio maintenance commission), the assumption of certain administrative activities (administrative commission) or premium collection (collection commission) or the assumption of other basic functions in addition to mediation (e.g. claims settlement).

In addition to the individual performance-related commissions, **total performance-related** commissions are used. They are based on the total (responsible) sales performances of a person such as the net increase of the (responsible) concluded new business and/or existing business or the corresponding loss ratio or the contribution margin achieved. Such compensations are common for sales executives (e.g. branch manager, regional or district director, branch manager), as they are based on their goals and tasks.

The advantage of commissions lies in their direct influence on the activities of the distribution partners. Their main disadvantage, however, is their low flexibility. While commission agreements with brokers and framework contracts with financial services companies, sales organizations and banks are ultimately subject to market rules and can be terminated at least for new business in case of non-agreement, changes to commissions promised in the agency contract are only permissible if the insurer has reserved corresponding rights contractually. Otherwise, changes must be accepted by the distribution partners and cannot be enforced by instruction. This leads to problems especially with commission reductions. This fact is noteworthy insofar as the majority of private customer business is still served by agents.

From the perspective of the sales partners, commissions are positively evaluated because they are directly assessable and influenceable and—in the case of tied agents—also form the basis for the calculation of the **compensation claim** in the event of the sales partner's departure. However, the negative aspect is the asymmetric sharing of fate between insurer and distribution partner associated with commissions in the event of cost reductions: In contrast to the symmetric or proportional participation of both partners in sales growth, premium reductions due to reduced claims costs, lower administrative costs or reduced profit surcharges lead to a reduction of the absolute compensation of the sales partners, without their tasks and costs changing.

In contrast, bonus systems or **bonuses** (compensation premiums) serve the one-time compensation of achieved predefined performance levels (target agreements). From the insurer's perspective, bonus systems are **significantly more flexible;** they can firstly be linked to goals other than purely sales-dependent ones (e.g., net inventory growth, expansion and/or renewal business, number of contracts concluded, non-cancellation rates, loss ratio, non-fluctuation rate, etc.), and secondly, they can be varied at any time as unilateral promises by the insurer. Business-specific or regional conditions can be taken into account, as the minimum or target performances must be adapted to the individual's sales opportunities. Apart from brokers, who are mainly paid commissions, bonus systems can essentially be used with all distribution partners. In addition to quantitative target specifications, bonuses offer the opportunity to set incentives for qualitative goals that are important to the insurance company but are not rewarded by a sales-related compensation system. Examples include bonuses for activities that increase customer loyalty, such as contract renewals, conversion to newer insurance conditions, cross-selling quotas, cancellation and dunning quotas, customer satisfaction quotas, etc. Bonuses or similar fees can also compensate for activities in the insurer's interest, such as claims settlement compensation.

From the distribution partner's perspective, there are disadvantages to the design freedom of bonuses: Firstly, there is less planning security compared to commissions. Secondly, not all bonified facts can be influenced by the sales partner (e.g., portfolio losses due to death). And from the tied agent's perspective, thirdly, compensation premiums (as non-components of the agency contract) are not used to achieve the compensation claim.

Another important performance-related compensation instrument besides commission and bonus are **competitions**. They are to be aligned with individual topics (branches, individual products, regions, customer groups, distribution channels) or combinations thereof and are time-limited, thus showing high flexibility. They are associated with the achievement of certain specifications, so they can be aligned thematically and take into account different conditions of competing subgroups, such as regionally different sales markets.

The success relevance of the behavior of customer-oriented distribution partners requires the insurer to manage the sales partners in line with their objectives (see also Hambach and Hiendlmeier 2021, pp. 394–398):

- **Objective conformity** means a basic sales policy orientation resulting from the marketing strategy, which among other things determines the weighting between business field portfolio, customer acquisition and customer retention, choice of distribution system, and task distribution between provider and distribution partners.
- And **manage** then means using coordination instruments in a targeted manner and, for example, reflecting the sales policy objectives in the commission system through an appropriate mix of commission types. In the case of tied distribution channels, longer-term contracts such as (usually lifelong) agency contracts, which establish the basic commission regulations, are to be used in addition. Therefore, all activities that can be designed flexibly are then rather to be compensated through target agreements in combination with bonuses. In addition, competitions can be used to set relatively flexible product-, time period-, or distribution channel-related additional impulses.

Ideally, the insurer succeeds in achieving an **alignment of interests** with the use of its coordination instruments, in the sense of the principal-agent theory, so that the distribution partners automatically (due to aligned interests) pursue the insurer's objectives. In some cases, the insurer's and the sales partner's objectives are identical, such as when it comes to maximizing sales through new business and portfolio growth. However, in other areas, the sales partners may have different interests than the insurer: These include, for example, taking on as few tasks as possible besides the actual mediation, focusing on commission-strong products, achieving a high secured income base, or an accomodating claims settlement towards their own customers. Here, it is important to achieve a broad alignment with the insurer's objectives.

This will be concretized using the **example of function relocation:** Proximity to customers and profit arguments lead to an increasing delegation of activities to intermediaries. However, this results in separate management challenges. For example, if parts of the claims settlement (minor claims) are transferred to the intermediary, there is a risk that the agent will exploit his information advantage in connection with customer proximity in the context of claims settlement to his advantage, if he—now also responsible for claims settlement—"buys" contract extensions (follow-up commission) and new contracts in the event of a claim through accomodating regulation. Aligning interests in this example means agreeing on bonus-malus regulations dependent on the loss ratio.

It turns out that a differentiated and complete remuneration system should contain both compensation payments for assumed, cost-causing activities and control payments for the target-compliant control of the sales partner (Kutz 1997, p. 186–205; Hambach and Hiendlmeier 2021, p. 399 f.).

Excursus on the design of remuneration in exclusive distribution

The **basic protection** of the exclusive tied agent is to be realized through commissions for initiation and conclusion, piece-rate remuneration for processing activities (e.g. application recording) and claims settlement, as well as portfolio-dependent service remuneration.

In addition, **control elements** are to be used via profit-specifically different commissions per product and customer category, target-oriented bonuses and participation in the portfolio-specific contribution margin, in order to influence all activities of the sales partner in the sense of the insurer's profit target. This means linking the commissions and especially the bonuses with the implementation of business plans and sales targets.

In addition, **time-dependent remunerations** for auxiliary activities towards the insurer (e.g. participation in product development, information transmission for market research) can be used.

On this basis, **bonuses** finally serve for fine control in order to bring about targeted improvements, e.g. portfolio maintenance to reduce cancellation rates and increase cross-selling rates or more thorough underwriting to improve the loss ratio (Kutz 1997, p. 206–209; Hambach and Hiendlmeier 2021, p. 399 f.).

Further literature on the topic:

- Damm 1993.
- Krauß 2009.
- Lange 1995.
- Schareck 2005, pp. 236–288.
- Trinkhaus 1955, esp. pp. 170–294.
- Wagner 2006.

If the incentive design nevertheless only brings about a conditional alignment of interests—as is partly the case, albeit for different reasons, with brokers, banks or sales companies—a more consistent monitoring of the sales activities of the partners **(sales controlling)** is required.

13.4.3 Multi-channel Management in the Distribution Channel Mix

With multi-channel distribution, insurers aim to increase sales, reduce distribution costs and/or diversify risks due to the strong dependence of individual sales channels on market and regulatory developments (Dahmen 2004, p. 97).

▶ **Multi-Channel-Management** (Multi-channel distribution) means the design, control and development of a distribution channel mix, which consists of several or all significant distribution channels, by a provider (here: insurer).

Within the multi-channel approach, two extreme variants can theoretically be distinguished, the focused and the coordinated multi-channel system (MCS); in practice, however, one often finds (hybrid) MCS that combine both approaches (Dahmen 2004, p. 96–114).

In the **focused MCS,** the insurance group uses various distribution channels under separate brands to independently address and acquire different target groups. Channel conflicts are low in this approach, while flexibility in response to market changes is high. However, the costs of this approach are comparatively high because few synergy effects can be realized. Moreover, it is more difficult to serve customers across different distribution channels from a single source. Generali Insurance has consistently pursued this approach in Germany for a long time: The traditional agent and broker distribution were operated under their brand. In addition, their traditional clientele was served via a—generally employed—sales force under the Volksfürsorge brand. In the multi level distribution, insurance products were exclusively sold through the DVAG sales company under the risk carrier and the Aachen-Münchener brand. In the broker and bank distribution, they worked with the risk carrier and the Dialog brand, and in direct sales, Generali is active with its own risk carrier under the Cosmos brand. After the already long-standing integration and dissolution of Volksfürsorge and the recent abandonment of the Aachen-Münchener brand and its replacement by the Generali brand, the MCS is now only partially focused; besides Generali (tied agents, multi level distribution), the two brands Dialog (broker) and Cosmos (direct sales) remain.

In the **coordinated MCS,** the insurance group controls the various distribution channels under one group brand. This realizes brand synergies, and the customer will—regardless of the contact channel—always communicate with the same company and the same company brand. The aim is high customer penetration (cross-selling) and customer loyalty. However, coordination is quite complex and must resolve channel conflicts. Moreover, the structure (processes, IT) is not easy to adapt, so stable market conditions are advantageous for this approach. In reality, therefore, rather large, resource-strong insurers pursue a coordinated MCS; nationally, for example, R + V does this, internationally AXA, and in recent years also Allianz.

The advantages and disadvantages of both MCS systems are further illustrated in Fig. 13.10.

Presumably, in the choice between focused and coordinated MCS, the **brand policy** is ultimately the **decisive criterion.** Building and maintaining a strong brand are very advertising- and thus cost-intensive; here, the synergy effects of the coordinated MCS are compelling. A second brand can only be justified if it characterizes a business model that is not compatible with the main brand and leads to cannibalization effects, e.g., direct sales with significantly cheaper tariffs, a comparison portal distribution with "special" commission agreements, or a multi level distribution with a worse image than the main brand. Alternatively, the choice of the focused MCS is easier if the company brand(s) is rather weak or not much is invested in it.

In general, the more distribution channels are used in parallel, the more complex their control becomes. A number of aspects need to be decided (Schögel 1997, p. 117 f.; Schareck 2005, p. 290 f.):

- Are all distribution channels treated equally or differently in terms of products, tariffs, commissions, portfolio protection, and sales promotion support?
- Are various distribution channels run under the same, independent company brands, or under a mix of both (double brand)?
- Do all distribution channels have the same tasks or are these differentiated?

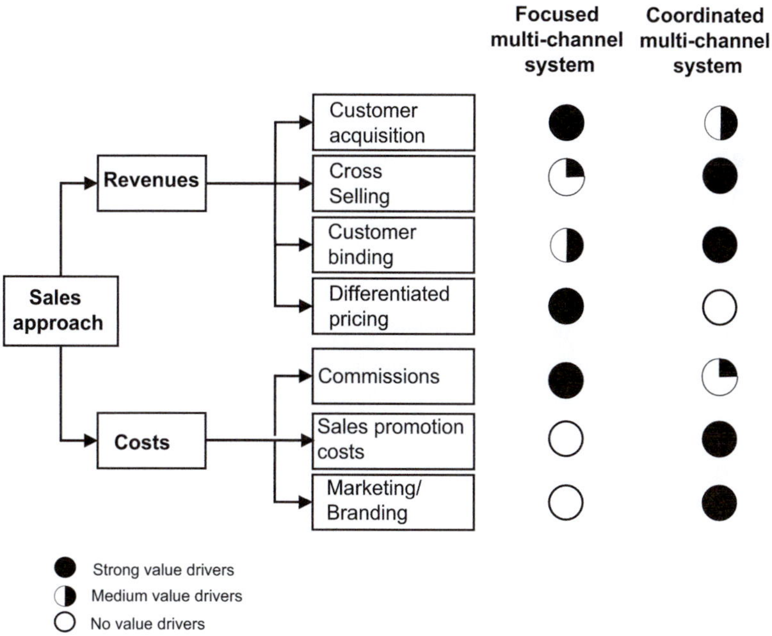

Fig. 13.10 Key value drivers of the focused and coordinated MCS. (Based on Dahmen 2004, p. 113)

- Do the distribution channels work hand in hand or uncoordinated during the service process?
- Are there common or separate board responsibilities?

Evaluation Multi-channel management is associated with opportunities on one hand: Since different distribution channels reach different market and customer segments, their simultaneous use can result in increased market coverage (effectiveness). Moreover, depending on the type of insurance, individual distribution channels are differently suitable or in demand (Sect. 13.3). The option for the customer to choose their channel throughout the entire service process, especially at the conclusion, is also very needs-oriented. If resources are used specifically and distributed across the distribution channels, achieving synergies through shared use, multi-channel distribution increases efficiency. Finally, providers can achieve reduced dependence on individual distribution channels and thus spread risk.

On the other hand, multi-channel distribution can also contribute to customer confusion if they are approached by different distribution channels at the same time or are offered different services or conditions via different distribution channels. This can lead to conflicts between the sales channels and poaching from one distribution channel to another (cannibalization). In any case, the complexity increases with the number of different distribution channels, with this the requirements for control and its costs up to a possible loss of control on the part of the provider. There is also a risk of neglecting the sales channel-appropriate support as a result of the uniform control of all distribution channels, i.e., not fully exploiting the possibilities of sales promotion, and thus not consistently using the differentiation potential based on their peculiarities.

13.5 Legal Framework Conditions in Insurance Distribution

13.5.1 Strong Influence of EU Regulation on German Insurance Distribution Law

The legal foundations in intermediary law have changed comprehensively and incisively in Germany with the implementation of the two EU directives IMD (Insurance Mediation Directive of 2002) in 2007 and IDD (Insurance Distribution Directive of 2016) in 2018. The new intermediary law influences the rights and obligations between insurer, intermediary and/or customers and is therefore of great importance for sales policy (see Teichler 2018; Reiff 2018).

The goal of the EU is to improve consumer protection when purchasing insurance of any kind, directly from the insurer or indirectly through an intermediary. Therefore, the IDD has significantly expanded the **scope** beyond the previous IMD to **all insurance distributors,** including insurance companies and their employees as well as internet-based business models, explicitly comparison portals. This also corresponds to the claim to create equal competitive conditions between the distributors in the sense of a "level playing field".

The **implementation of EU intermediary law** in Germany is carried out for insurers via the **Insurance Supervision Act**, for insurance intermediaries still in the **Trade Regulation Act**, for both parties also in the **Insurance Mediation Regulation** as well as in the **VVG** and the **VVG Information Obligations Regulation** (see also Sect. 3.4.2).

The predominantly civil law professional practice rules anchored in the VVG have been supplemented by the IDD, among other things, with very far-reaching **rules of conduct** for insurers (§ 1a para. 1 sentence 1 VVG) as well as insurance intermediaries and advisors (§ 59 para. 1 sentence 2, para. 4 sentence 2), which require them to always act honestly, fairly, and professionally in the best possible interest of policyholders in their sales activities. These rules of conduct also apply to remuneration and incentive policies: insurers (§ 48a VAG) and insurance intermediaries (§ 14 para. 2 VersVermV) may not use sales remuneration, sales targets, or other incentives that could induce the incentivized person to recommend a product other than the one that is best for the customer. Furthermore, the insurance intermediary must state the type of remuneration and the debtor of the remuneration in his **initial information to the customer.** However, there is currently no prohibition on commissions. Since the IDD is a minimum harmonization directive, the **national legislators** can adopt more extensive regulations, some of which are explicitly addressed in EU law (so-called member state options). In the area of remuneration, Germany has done this several times: thus, in 2012 a cap on commissions in substitute health insurance (§ 50 VAG), in 2018 the prohibition on the passing on of special allowances and commissions (§ 48b VAG) and the obligation to pass on of commissions to customers for insurance advisors (§ 48c VAG), and in 2022 a cap on commissions in residual debt insurance (§ 50a VAG) were introduced.

Directly from the **IDD** come **further requirements** such as mandatory standards for distribution without advice combined with optional advice, for cross-selling (distribution of product packages from insurance and other products) ("cross-selling") as well as for ensuring target group-appropriate product and distribution concepts (so-called product approval process). Moreover, the IDD has brought with it some further regulations for insurance investment products, some of which were taken from the MiFID directive with the aim of treating capital investments and insurance-like investments equally (see possible tightening in the course of the EU retail investment strategy excursus on this in Sect. 3.4.2). In advice and intermediation, however, this means that different regulations apply to various life and pension insurances, depending on whether they are classified as insurance investment products (e.g., endowmennt insurance, pension insurances) or as other life insurances (e.g., term life insurances).

However, the IDD is not exclusively addressed to the member states and to be implemented by them into their national law, but also contains authorizations with which the European Commission can issue **direct legal requirements for all insurance distributors** via so-called delegated regulations and technical standards—so to speak bypassing national law. Thus, they must observe the Delegated Regulation (EU) 2017/2358 with regard to product oversight and government requirements (this concerns the aforementioned product approval process), the Delegated Regulation (EU) 2017/2359 on information requirements and business rules as well as the Regulation (EU) 2019/2088 (Transparency Regulation) and following from it the Delegated Regulation (EU) 2021/1257 of the Commission (see also excursus in Sect. 6.1.5): Insurance distributors must, among other things, disclose whether they offer sustainable capital investments within the framework of **insurance investment products** or avoid sustainability-related risks. In addition, intermediaries must be able to provide information about their sustainability strategy and sustainability risks in the context of their remuneration, insurers have to prepare pre-contractual information for passing on to customers in this regard. Both actors have to take into account the sustainability preferences of customers in their suitability assessment when distributing insurance investment products and include them in the product selection and justification, as well as in an ongoing review of existing insurance contracts in the distribution of insurance investment products ((EU) 2017/2359).

In Germany, therefore, in 2007, with the **professional access regulations,** the hitherto largely unregulated insurance intermediation was transformed into a business activity requiring a commercial trade permission and registration. In addition, **professional practice regulations,** in particular information, advice and documentation obligations to be fulfilled towards the customer, were newly anchored in law. With the implementation of the IDD requirements, further regulations were added in 2018, as mentioned above.

13.5.2 Professional Access Regulations for (Commercial) Intermediaries

The **professional access regulations** require a **registration obligation** for intermediaries, which is either carried out as part of a licensing procedure at the locally responsible Chamber of Commerce and Industry (IHK) or by an insurance company (in the case of tied, license-free insurance representatives) (§ 34d para. 10 GewO). Employed intermediaries are not affected by this. Since 2008, the types of intermediaries permitted under GewO have been registered in an intermediaries register according to § 11a GewO and their number is published.

The prerequisites for a commercial trade permission as an insurance intermediary are derived, by implication, from the reasons for refusal mentioned in § 34d para. 5 GewO:

- **Reliability:** There should be no facts against the applicant that give rise to justified doubts about the suitability to run a commercial enterprise. Explicitly mentioned are final convictions in the last five years before the application was made for a crime or for theft, embezzlement, extortion, fraud, breach of trust, money laundering, forgery of documents, receiving stolen goods, usury, or an insolvency offense. This is not an exhaustive list, so there may be other facts such as a continued, serious violation of the information, advice, and documentation obligations of an insurance intermediary.

- **Orderly financial circumstances:** Insurance intermediaries carry out a responsible activity. In the case of sustainable financial difficulties of the intermediary, it is not to be expected that he will advise his customers appropriately and not take advantage of them out of financial distress. Possibly, an intermediary is also entrusted with certain funds from the customer for the insurer. Liability claims of the customer may not be enforceable in the case of an insolvency-threatened intermediary company. The law mentions facts which, as a rule, do not suggest orderly financial circumstances: Opening of insolvency proceedings over the assets of the applicant or entry of the applicant in the debtor register according to § 882b of the Code of Civil Procedure.
- **Professional liability insurance:** The intermediary must conclude and maintain liability insurance for the financial losses resulting from his professional activity. The financial loss liability insurer is obliged to inform the responsible IHK if the financial loss liability insurance is terminated or changed in such a way that it no longer fulfills the provisions of the §§ 11–13 VersVermV. The financial loss liability insurance can provide for market-standard exclusions, as long as they do not endanger the purpose of the insurance, above all the exclusion of knowing breach of duty.
- **Proof of expertise:** This is to be provided by successfully passing an expertise examination before an IHK, the content and procedural requirements of which are specified in the §§ 2–4 VersVermV and are based on the training program "Insurance expert". Credits of other professional qualifications or of foreign proof of competence are regulated by the §§ 5–6 VersVermV. The expertise examination can be taken by an appropriate number of authorized representatives (management/board, power of attorney, power of action) who supervise the employees directly involved in the mediation (§ 34d para. 5 s. 4 GewO). This provision is aimed, for example, at banks and savings banks or other commercial entities who do not operate insurance mediation as their main business.

The prerequisites for the commercial trade permission must generally also be fulfilled by those exempted from the permission upon application and by the license-free tied insurance agents:

- **Exemption upon application:** If a **product accessory insurance intermediary** wants to be exempted from the commercial trade permission according to § 34d para. 6 GewO, he must prove in the application to the IHK that he is working on behalf of one or more insurance intermediaries with a commercial trade permission according to § 34d para. 1 s. 1 GewO or insurance companies, i.e., he must present a corresponding agreement (agent contract or other intermediation agreement). He must have professional liability insurance. This can be taken out by the principal and his liability can be explicitly insured there. The requirements of reliability and orderly financial circumstances also apply; however, these can be checked by the principal and a corresponding declaration can be made to the IHK. A expertise examination is not necessary, but the principal must ensure adequate qualification. It is considered appropriate that the intermediary has received training corresponding to the requirements of the expertise examination in the branches he is allowed to mediate according to his intermediation agreement. Thus, the qualification can, for example, be limited to the knowledge required for motor vehicle insurance in the case of a car dealership with which a intermediation agreement for motor vehicle insurance has been concluded.

- **License-free tied agents** according to § 34d para. 7 s. 1 GewO: Insurers may only cooperate with them according to § 48 para. 2 VAG if they have convinced themselves of their reliability and orderly financial circumstances and ensure that the agents have the appropriate qualification, which is to be assessed according to the above-mentioned standard. Professional liability insurance is not required because the insurer assumes unlimited liability for the intermediation activity. He declares this automatically by entering the agent in the intermediaries register. Insurers must respond to customer complaints about their intermediaries, in the case of repeated complaints that may be significant for the assessment of reliability, they must inform the locally responsible IHK as the supervisory body (§ 51 VAG).

According to § para.1 VAG insurers may only cooperate with those intermediaries working on a commercial basis and who have a permission according to § 34d para. 1 GewO or an exemption from the permission according to § 34d para. 6 GewO or who are not subject to the permission requirement according to § 34d para. 8 GewO. The insurer must convince himself of this in each individual case by looking into the intermediaries register. In addition, he must regularly check the so-called deletion lists of the IHKs to see whether a license or exemption from the permission has been withdrawn. If there are other indications of a lack of reliability or disordered financial circumstances, the insurer must also take action, inform the responsible IHK and possibly terminate the cooperation.

Insurers are accountable to BaFin for compliance with these rules. For this purpose, more detailed regulations were issued with the BaFin circular 9/2007 (VA). Among other things, insurers were obliged to participate in the AVAD procedure as before.

Excursus on AVAD

The information office on insurance and building society sales force and insurance brokers in Germany e. V. (AVAD) has existed since 1948 and serves to keep unsuitable persons away from insurance distribution. For this purpose, insurers report all persons who have become active as employees or as insurance agent for the insurer or who have received a commission promise as insurance brokers (activity report). After the cooperation has ended, a report must be prepared, from which the type, duration and reasons for termination of the cooperation and possibly incriminating information such as the existence of open, unpaid claims or offenses of the intermediary emerge. Thus, AVAD also serves as an early warning system, because through it facts become known that are significant for the assessment of reliability and orderly financial circumstances, which remain completely hidden from the IHK due to the lack of reporting obligations of the courts or at least only become known after a final conviction and thus possibly only years after an offense.

(AVAD 2023)

Furthermore, insurers are obliged to operate controlling within the framework of their risk management in order to identify abnormalities such as the misconduct of individual persons or faulty processes and to counteract them. In addition, insurers must ensure that tied agents are requalified if necessary and prove these measures on request (§ 48 para. 2a VAG).

Insurance intermediaries often mediate investment funds, sometimes other investment products and financing, or offer investment advice. Here too, appropriate commercial trade permissions for financial investment intermediaries (§ 34f GewO) and real estate loan intermediaries (§ 34i GewO) are required.

13.5.3 Professional Regulations in Insurance Distribution

The **professional regulations** concern civil law **information, advice and documentation obligations** of insurance intermediaries, non-compliance with which is sanctioned with a liability for damages. In addition to this, intermediaries—just like insurers—are subject to the duties of conduct as well as the special information, advice and ongoing reporting obligations for insurance investment products. The duties of the agent are sometimes less than the duties of the insurance broker, which are derived from his legal position. For the broker, compliance with the duties regulated mainly in the VVG may therefore not be sufficient. For example, as his fiduciary, the broker has a duty to influence the customer, i.e., he must strive to convince him of necessary insurance coverage, and for this purpose carry out more detailed investigations and risk assessments.

Insurance intermediaries are subject to a whole range of legal regulations and obligations in their professional everyday life. The following duties are specifically anchored (see for legal evaluation: Reiff 2018; Werber 2019):

- **Acting in the best possible interest of the customer** (§ 59 para. 1 VVG):
  The intermediary must always act honestly, fairly and professionally in the best possible interest of the policyholders in his distribution activity.
- **Regular further education** (§ 34d para. 9 GewO):
  There is also an obligation for regular further education of 15 hours per year for all intermediaries (agents, brokers, advisors) with the exception of product accessory intermediaries. As with the proof of expertise, it is sufficient if the further education is proven by an appropriate number of authorized employees who supervise the employees directly involved in the mediation. Contents, form, provider, documentation and review of the further education are specified in § 7 VersVermV.
- **Initial information** (§ 15 VersVermV):
  At the first business contact, the intermediary has to provide the customer with a number of details about himself in text form, clearly and understandably, including the type of intermediation according to GewO, possibly information on participations in or by insurance companies with more than 10%.
- **Basis for advice** (§ 60 VVG):
  Insurance brokers must adhere to an unrestricted basis for advice, unless they expressly limit this on a case-by-case basis before application. This means that they

must examine a sufficient number of insurance contracts and insurers to be able to recommend a contract suitable for their customer's needs from a professional point of view. An insurance broker therefore does not owe the recommendation of the cheapest or the best contract (best advice), which would be associated with considerable effort in practice due to the variety of market offers and customer wishes and needs, but the recommendation of a suitable contract (suitable advice)—unless he promises the customer something else. Insurance agents and brokers who limit their basis for advice in individual cases must inform the customer in text form before application on which selection of insurers their advice is based. Agents must also indicate for which insurers they are active, and whether they are exclusively active for these. Anyone who gives the impression to the customer of providing the services of a broker is also considered an insurance broker (§ 59 para. 3 sentence 2 VVG). Especially multi-tied agents thus run the risk of being liable as so-called "pseudo brokers" if they give the impression of brokerage activity in their appearance and do not make it clear that they are tied agents.

- **Occasion-related advice** (§ 61 para. 1 s. 1 VVG):
  The intermediary has to ask the customer about his wishes and needs—this is the objectifiable need such as e.g. provision gaps, insurable values, possible dangers etc. Although there is no general obligation to investigate, there must be a reason, which can be based on the complexity of the offered insurance contract or on the person and situation of the customer. However, this can be interpreted to mean that in most cases there is a reason for questioning, because the complexity is to be assessed not only objectively, but also subjectively according to the customer's prior knowledge and experience, and because for most insurances it is necessary to ask the customer for information in order to calculate the tariffs according to their needs.
- **Advice and justification of the advice** (§ 61 para. 1 s. 1 VVG):
  During the consultation, a reasonable relationship between effort and premium to be paid can be maintained. The idea behind this is that simple, less explanatory products are usually also cheaper. However, this does not protect the intermediary from further requirements if he still recognizes a need for advice, according to the legislative justification. In addition, every advice given on a particular insurance must be justified.
- **Documentation** (§ 61 para. 1 s. 2 VVG):
  The contents of the consultation, including advice and justification, are usually to be documented clearly and understandably in text form and transmitted to the customer before the contract is concluded.
- **Possibilities of waiver** (§§ 60 para. 3, 61 para. 2 VVG):
  The customer has the right to waive the notification of the basis of advice, the advice itself or the documentation. This must be done by separate written declaration. If the customer waives advice or documentation, the intermediary also has the obligation to inform the customer of possible disadvantages in enforcing claims for damages in this waiver declaration.

- **Liability for damages** (§ 63 VVG):
  The intermediary is liable for damages for violation of the aforementioned duties, unless he is not responsible for the breach of duty, i.e. it was not culpable. The main source of claims for damages is the duty to advise. The advice can lead to the customer suffering financial loss, either because an insurable risk was not insured, although there was a reason to do so, or because the risk was insured too expensively and the customer paid too much premium.
- **Additional information obligations for insurance-based investment products** (IBIP) (§§ 59 para. 1, 7b VVG):
  For IBIP, the policyholder must be provided with appropriate information about the distribution of IBIP and all costs and fees in good time before the contract is concluded. This includes, if advice is given, information about whether the policyholder is offered a regular suitability assessment of the recommended IBIPs according to § 7c, guidelines and warnings about risks associated with proposed investment strategies, at least annual information about advisory costs and costs of the IBIPs (total costs, reduction in yield) and how the policyholder can make payments (see possible tightening in the course of the EU retail investment strategy excursus on this in Sect. 3.4.2).
- **Additional advisory obligations for IBIPs** (§§ 59 para. 1, 7c para. 1–3 VVG):
  The advice must be based on a suitability assessment against the background of the customer's knowledge and experience, financial situation, and investment objectives (risk tolerance). In addition, an appropriateness test must be carried out and a warning issued if the customer does not provide the information he needs (e.g., about his experience or assets). It is possible to waive advice, but only if cumulatively the following conditions are met: The products are not considered complex financial instruments and do not have a structure that makes it difficult for the policyholder to understand the risks associated with the investment, or other non-complex insurance investments, the distribution activity is initiated by the policyholder, he is clearly informed that no appropriateness test of the IBIP is being carried out (warning), the intermediary fulfills his obligations to avoid conflicts of interest (see possible tightening in the course of the EU retail investment strategy excursus on this in Sect. 3.4.2).
- **Reporting obligations for IBIPs** (§§ 59 VVG, 7c para. 5 VVG):
  The regulations are quite diffuse and vague. They are ultimately almost literally taken from Art. 30 para. 5 of the IDD—they were not specified in the Delegated Regulation (EU) 2017/2359 on information and conduct obligations, and probably the German legislator did not know what to do with them either. The policyholder must be provided with appropriate reports on the services provided, which contain regular communications that take into account the nature and complexity of the respective insurance investment products and the type of service provided, and possibly the costs associated with them. If advice is given on a IBIP, the policyholder receives a statement on a durable medium before the contract is concluded, listing the advice provided and the

preferences, objectives, and other customer-specific characteristics taken into account. If the intermediary has informed the policyholder that he will carry out a regular assessment of suitability, the regular report must each time contain an updated statement as to the extent to which the insurance investment product corresponds to the preferences, objectives, and other customer-specific characteristics of the policyholder.

- **Payment security** (§§ 64, 69 para. 2 VVG, 20–24 VersVermV):
  Insurance agents are generally considered authorized to receive certain payments from the customer on behalf of the insurer. If they embezzle these or remit them too late, the payment is still considered made. Insurance brokers, on the other hand, must either be expressly authorized by the insurer to receive payments or secure payment before accepting it, e.g., through a fidelity insurance or certain guarantees. They must provide the customer with proof of payment security on request. Conversely, all insurance intermediaries may only receive payments from the insurer for the customer if they have been expressly authorized to do so in writing by the customer. Otherwise, the insurer risks that he has not made his payment with discharging effect.
- **Establishment of a complaint management system** (§ 17 para. 1 and 2 VersVermV): The intermediary must establish guidelines for complaint management, set up a complaint management function that investigates complaints and identifies and avoids conflicts of interest, register a complaint, allow the responsible IHK to inspect at any time and continuously evaluate the data for complaint processing, confirm the receipt of a complaint and inform the complainant about the complaint handling procedure, forward a complaint to the responsible office and inform the complainant about it, publish information about the complaint handling procedure in a suitable manner and thoroughly examine a complaint and respond to the complainant immediately in understandable language.
- **Conciliation** (§ 214 VVG):
  Insurance intermediaries have been included in the conciliation process, which was set up by the insurance industry via the insurance ombudsman. The purpose of this institution is to relieve the courts and to settle disputes as far as possible out of court first. If the policyholder calls the conciliation board, the intermediary working on a commercial basis is obliged to participate in the conciliation process (§ 17 para. 4 VersVermV).

Excursus on Obligations of the Insurance Company

According to § 6 para. 4 VVG, insurance companies are additionally obliged to consult and advise customers even during the contractual relationship, if a reason for this is apparent. This can be the case when the customer has queries, when damage and performance reports are made, or when legal changes have an impact on the insurance contract. There is no identical obligation for insurance intermediaries. However, insurance agents are usually also obliged to take care of their customers by means of an agency contract, so that they take over the occasion-related consulting and advisory duty in this case for the insurer. However, the insurer remains liable for damages to the customer for the proper fulfillment. The same applies to pre-contractual advice: For this, the insurer is obliged according to § 6 para. 1 VVG, identical with the agent, but the advice only has to be given once to the customer. However, this means that the insurer must monitor the fulfillment of the obligations and, if necessary, perform them himself.

This does not apply to insurance brokers. In their case, the insurer is not obliged to provide advice according to § 6 para. 6 VVG, neither before nor after the conclusion of the contract. The obligation for ongoing support arises from the explicitly or implicitly concluded brokerage contract. If there is uncertainty about this, the fact that the broker receives ongoing remuneration is sufficient to indicate that he remains obliged to provide advice.

The **monitoring of compliance with professional access and professional practice obligations** is carried out either by the trade licensing authorities, the Chambers of Commerce and Industry, or the insurance companies, and indirectly by the BaFin. In addition, the ombudsman of the insurance industry play a role as a complaint authority for consumers. It is noteworthy that the responsible authority (IHK) can publicize and display incontestable legal violations in the register (§ 34d para. 11 GewO) and that it must set up a (if necessary, anonymous) whistleblower procedure (§ 34d para. 12 GewO). With both, the legislator has given emphasis to the distribution regulations.

Insurance intermediaries must also observe the provisions of competition law. A specification can be found in the **competition guidelines of the insurance industry,** to which insurance agents are obliged by the agency contract. The following regulations are provided (GDV et al. 2006):

- Fair competition:
  Competition may only be conducted "with honest and decent means", defamation of competitors is not permissible, false statements about services must be omitted.
- Cooperation with intermediaries:
  Sales applicants may not be recruited with misleading information or poached from competitors by unfair methods. No agency contracts may be concluded with the following professional groups: insurance executives, insurance brokers, members of the legal and tax consulting professions. Applications must be complete and truthful.
- Truth and clarity in competition:
  Exaggerations and deceptions must be avoided in advertising. Anonymous advertising is prohibited, the company of the intermediary must be clearly and completely named in his advertising. Advertising with politicians in high public offices or publication of thank you and recommendation letters are undesirable.
- Prohibition on the passing on of commissions:
  Bribes and passing on of commissions are prohibited.
- Poaching:
  It is not permissible to intrude into foreign insurance portfolios by unfair means. In life and health insurance, poaching is also otherwise impermissible if the customer has not been informed about the associated disadvantages. The consequence is the reversal of the poaching, possibly after an internal industry consiliation process.

For the very advertising-intensive insurance distribution, the provisions of the **act against unfair competition** (UWG) in the area of telephone advertising are particularly important. Unauthorized advertising calls can be punished with fines of up to 50,000 €. Therefore, prior explicit consent of the person called is required. In addition, calling with number suppression is prohibited (§ 7 para. 2 sentence 1 UWG) (see also Sect. 14.2.1, excursus on telephone advertising).

Presumably also to counteract the increasing regulation of insurance distribution as a result of a widespread negative public opinion, critical media reporting, and increasing mistrust on the part of politicians, various insurance associations developed and adopted **self-imposed codes** about ten years ago: Thus, in 2012, insurers decided on the **GDV code of conduct for the distribution of insurance products,** i.e., they imposed standards on themselves that have been in effect since 2013. Participation is in principle voluntary, but has been made public on the GDV website; moreover, the code of conduct has been made binding (and thus credible) by being provided with a self-commitment to introduce compliance regulations and to externally review its implementation, and if a certificate is not proven, a deletion from the member list occurs. The industry has imposed a lot on itself with this. In any case, the implementation of the code of conduct and the review of its compliance are complex and fraught with risks. A non-issued certificate and a deletion could lead to negative headlines just as much as non-membership. The same applies to the continuation of cooperation with intermediaries who violate the code. On the other hand, it was hoped that by adhering to the imposed rules, customer orientation would be anchored, the industry image (finally) improved, and further interventions by politicians would be preempted (Schmitt 2013, pp. 666–669).

Due to the company-specific design possibilities of the implementation of the GDV code, it was hardly possible for independent intermediaries to deal with the numerous different regulations. Apart from that, neither the GDV nor insurance companies may issue binding behavioral guidelines for insurance brokers, because neither have legislative powers. For these reasons, the code allowed the intermediary associations to establish alternative compliance rules that had to be reconciled with the GDV code of conduct. The intermediary associations had long since prescribed their own behavioral standards; thus, the Association of Insurance Brokers had developed a **Code of Conduct**, the compliance of which by the intermediaries corresponds to the requirements of the GDV code of conduct, but which is much more practical for the intermediaries to handle. And for non-organized insurance intermediaries, a working group from various associations (BDVM, BVK and Votum) created the **"basic code for insurance intermediaries"** (Sandkühler 2014, p. 44).

In recent years, however, things have been quiet around the codes. And the regularly initiated further tightening of distribution law from Brussels suggest that the codes (at least in this respect) have not helped.

Interim Conclusion on the Legal Framework Conditions of Insurance Distribution

The legal framework conditions of insurance intermediation have changed significantly. Above all, they have produced very far-reaching and sometimes (too) detailed regulations that severely restrict the entrepreneurial freedom of independent intermediaries in private and smaller commercial customer business and burden it even more with artificially generated administrative effort. Due to the extent, the deregulation of product and pricing policy from 1994 seems increasingly (over-)compensated. The intermediaries have a number of (new) regulations to observe, the violation of which can lead firstly to the withdrawal of the commercial trade license and secondly to personal liability. The new intermediary law influences the rights and obligations between insurer, intermediary and/or customers and is therefore of great importance for the strategic choice of distribution channels as well as for the subsequent operational distribution management (i.e., acquisition, retention and control of sales partners).

13.6 (Regulatory) Approaches to Customer-oriented Sales Policy

Consumer protection organizations as institutional protagonists for the enforcement of consumer interests repeatedly accuse intermediaries of being exposed to conflicts of interest and therefore—almost systemically—violating consumer interests. The media reporting and also the legislation pick up on this argument (see Sect. 1.1.3). Approaches to a customer-oriented sales policy, which are intended to reduce or eliminate conflicts of interest, therefore include initial and follow-up qualifications, advisory duties, comprehensive information about status, dependencies, product partners, earnings and components of earnings, as well as numerous product informations to target group, performance, price and risks. The EU regulation of insurance distribution (Sect. 13.5) has therefore primarily addressed the professional requirements for insurance intermediaries, the information and conduct obligations towards customers, advice in the best possible interest of the customer, and the disclosure of remuneration to the customer, and has issued extensive provisions for member state law. In addition, the European Commission repeatedly scrutinizes the intermediary´s commission and its replacement by fees from the customer (first in the IMD draft, then in the IDD draft, now in the draft of the EU retail investment strategy (see excursus on the retail investment strategy Sect. 3.4.2); see also OECD 2020). The following will briefly discuss these legally anchored approaches to a customer-oriented sales policy and the prohibition of commissions, which is repeatedly discussed in this context, also from a marketing perspective (see also for an economic and legal assessment Reiff and Köhne 2017; Köhne and Brömmelmeyer 2018).

13.6.1 Professional Requirements for Insurance Intermediaries

The professional requirements for an insurance intermediary include the professional admission requirements and professional practice requirements listed in the previous chapter. With the implementation of the IDD, the obligation for continuous further education was added as another professional practice requirement in national law.

However, the **required expertise and ongoing training evidence** introduced with EU distribution law in German law still allow for exceptions: For example, the insurer must ensure that product accessory agents (annex distribution), if they have taken out professional liability insurance, only need to demonstrate a qualification appropriate for their activity instead of proof of expertise, which can then be limited to a product, for example (§ 34d para. 9 s. 1 in conjunction with § 34d para. 6 GewO). The further education obligation does not apply to product accessory intermediaries or to agents registered by the insurer if they only sell insurance that represents an additional service to the delivery of a good or the provision of a service (§ 34d para. 9 s. 2 and 3 GewO). In addition, all intermediaries must complete ongoing training, but the results are not checked for content; simply "sitting through" would be sufficient (§ 7 para. 1 VersVermV).

The **sustainable guarantee of a certain qualification** for insurance agents is **economically sensible.** Just like the proof of expertise at the initial qualification, the obligation for further education is necessary to ensure a minimum level of know-how and skills. As a barrier to market entry, both approaches generally have predominantly positive effects because they lead to **minimum standards** without inducing a shortage of supply or inhibiting cheaper standard advice (Karten 2002, p. 54 f.; Höckmayr 2012).

However, the resulting diversity of recognized training and further education activities in Europe and Germany still means a lack of clarity for consumers and thus **lack of transparency.** Although private customers usually only deal with intermediaries from their country (and the qualification standards recognized there) and are therefore not confused by any different qualifications. Therefore, the member state regulation was sensible because the member states can recognize qualifications that are technically suitable for their insurance market, its products, legal and tax conditions, and social security system. But even for the implementation in Germany, the diversity of recognized training and further education activities and especially the possible wide variation in the quality of the offers do not help the customer in the end.

However, the signals set incorrectly appear more problematic from the customer's point of view: The legal requirements allow the criteria of the training system to be based on mere scope (15 hours per year) and attendance (focus on behavior), but little on the content conveyed or even on successfully completed exams (focus on results). Thus, the signal to the customer includes the intermediary's diligence in having spent a certain number of hours in training courses, but no more. Since it is a rather low hurdle for weaker brokers, the signal value is low. Therefore, **neither the quality uncertainty nor**

the behavioral uncertainty for the customer is noticeably reduced. The former means that the customer can hardly assess the quality of the advice and the intermediary's professional suitability; the latter follows from the fact that the customer does not know whether the intermediary is acting in the customer's interest or, for example, recommending the insurance product with the highest commission instead of the most suitable one.

Improvements to the regulations would be desirable and feasible: Quality uncertainties would be reduced if there were a standardized, independently conducted **suitability test** at **regular intervals,** e.g. if the proof of expertise had to be confirmed every five years. Behavioral uncertainties can hardly be reduced by qualification certificates alone. Here, a **combination of qualification and sanctioning** might be conceivable, which could consist, for example, of receiving negative points for incorrect advice, having to retake the test, or temporarily losing the permission to sell insurance (as with a driver's license) (see also Köhne 2014, p. 251 f.).

13.6.2 General Information Requirements and Conduct of Business Rules

Against the backdrop of financial market transactions that harm consumers, the EU has created conduct rules in MiFID 2, which it has now incorporated into the IDD in order to harmonize the various financial market directives and thus also imposed on insurance distribution.

This includes that insurance intermediaries (and insurers) must always act honestly, fairly, and professionally in the best interest of their customers in their insurance mediation activities. In addition, all information related to the distribution activity, including advertising communications to policyholders, should be fair, clear, and not misleading, and advertising communications should always be clearly identifiable as such (§§ 1a, 59 para. 1 VVG).

From a moral-ethical standpoint, this **well-intentioned principle is undisputed,** and it is generally agreed upon. However, the **way it is formulated goes too far.** Accordingly, all actors, including companies and insurance agents, should always act in the best interest of their customers (for a legal assessment, see Reiff 2018, p. 198). As in any other industry, insurers and their commercial agents can only sell their products. They do so under the assumption that their products are beneficial and in the best interest of the customer, even if they are not the best products on the market. And in a market economy, no provider sends customers to the competition because they supposedly offer better products. If this were to happen, it would ultimately lead to monopolies in individual product categories. It is precisely the **competition and** not least the **marketing that contribute to the improvement of existing services.** However, customers must then take responsibility themselves and reward better providers through demand.

Apart from that, insurance agents act as representatives of interests and vicarious agents of their insurer in accordance with § 84 HGB. The principle is, however, superfluous with regard to brokers, because as fiduciaries of the client, they are already obliged to act in the interest of the customer under existing law.

The **extension to "advertising communications"** ultimately questions basic economic principles. At first glance, it is certainly positive and plausible that all information and marketing communications to (potential) customers must be fair, clear, and not misleading, and always clearly identifiable as such. A quite **possible broad interpretation** of this formulation in future case law would **significantly restrict entrepreneurial action and marketing,** if not make it impossible (see also the excursus on the retail investment strategy in Sect. 3.4.2). Is it compatible, for example, to want to assert oneself against the competition if it has the better product? Is it fair and not misleading to influence the customer's perception through brand positioning and differentiation as well as corresponding communication design in such a way that he desires the advertised product and is happy with it after its acquisition, even though the competitor's product is actually better (Köhne and Brömmelmeyer 2018, pp. 728–730)? Marketing contributes to profit generation as a business function, and it is more than just a factual, emotionless presentation of facts. Numerous examples show that customers want to be seduced—think of Apple, Coca-Cola, or successful fashion labels. And especially when it comes to retirement provision: **"Seducing" customers to take responsibility for their own retirement provision and to forego current consumption is usually in their interest.**

From this principle, another fundamental question arises: Is the **suitable advice** according to § 60 para. 1 VVG (see Sect. 13.5.3) in the customer's interest or not? Strictly speaking, the formulation **"in their best possible interest"** actually requires brokers to provide best advice, i.e., the mediation of the best or cheapest insurance on the market. That this is not legally the case and that suitable advice is compatible with the recommendation in the best interest of the customer was clarified many years ago (currently confirmed and with references to then at Werber 2019, p. 328). Economically, suitable advice is a pragmatic alternative for the customer because it allows him to choose from various good products without every broker necessarily having to deal with all products. There are numerous brokers with a comprehensive but limited product range who serve private customers who would otherwise most likely not be served at all (Köhne 2014, pp. 254 f.).

13.6.3 Competent and Comprehensive Advice for Private Customers

The **basis for consultation** is regulated by § 60 para. 1 VVG: The insurance broker is obliged to base his advice on a sufficient number of insurance contracts offered on the market and insurers, so that he can make a recommendation based on professional criteria as to which insurance contract is suitable to meet the needs of the policyholder. A market restriction is possible if he explicitly points out to the policyholder before the contract declaration is made that there is a limited selection of insurers and contracts. The **duty to advise** is regulated in § 61 para. 1 VVG. Accordingly, the insurance intermediary has to ask the policyholder about his wishes and needs on an occasion-related basis and, also taking into account a reasonable ratio between the effort of advice and the premiums to be paid by the policyholder, to advise and give reasons for each advice given for a specific insurance. He has to document this taking into account the complexity of the offered insurance contract.

For insurance investment products, additional regulations apply (§§ 59 para. 1, 7c para. 1-3 VVG): The advice must be based on a suitability test against the background of the customer's knowledge and experience, financial situation and investment objectives (risk tolerance). In addition, an appropriateness test must be carried out and a warning must be issued if the customer does not provide the information he needs (e.g. about his experience or assets). A waiver of advice is possible under certain, restrictive conditions.

The conduct of business rules also flank the advice in the best possible interest of the customer through the business organization (directly and additionally indirectly also through the insurers): According to § 14 para. 2 VersVerrmV, the intermediary may not remunerate or evaluate his employees in a way that conflicts with their duty to act in the best possible interest of the policyholders. Furthermore, he may not make any arrangements through remuneration, sales targets or in any other way that could create incentives to recommend a specific insurance product to a policyholder, although he could offer another insurance product that better meets the needs of the policyholder (see the possible tightening in the course of the EU retail investment strategy in the excursus on this in Sect. 3.4.2).

In accordance with the already mentioned rules of conduct consistently, intermediaries and insurance companies that give advice to customers on the basis of an objective market survey—i.e. are not bound or have pointed out restrictions—are obliged to base this advice on an objective examination of a sufficient number of insurance contracts offered on the market, so that he or it can give a personal recommendation in the best possible interest of the customer as to which insurance contract would be best suited to meet the customer's needs.

That customer-oriented advice in the course of insurance mediation should start with the customer's wishes and goals as well as the recording of his risk situation is factually undisputed (Traub 1995, p. 80 f.; Höckmayr 2012, pp. 57-59). However, in insurance practice, the process does not always proceed in this way, but often presents itself more as a pure product sale (Schareck 2005, p. 105 f.; Habschick and Evers 2008, p. 113). Since the advisory service is a credence good, it is helpful to legally anchor minimum requirements in this regard due to the associated behavioral uncertainties. Thus, it **succeeds** in largely avoiding **under-advice.** However, possible over-advice, which also bypasses the (immediate) advisory needs of the customer, is not counteracted. Thus, different advisory services can still be offered (Höckmayr 2012, pp. 118-121).

Excursus on comprehensive consultation process in insurance

The needs-based provision of insurance service, as mentioned, usually only occurs in personal contact and often through the intermediary. The required **expert guidance of a private risk management process** by the intermediary ideally goes through the following steps:

1. Determination of the customer's wishes and goals
2. Assessment of risk tolerance
3. Identification and analysis of the risks of the private household
4. Prioritization of risks (risk assessment)
5. Advice on risk management measures
6. Advice on insurance products
7. Recommendation of specific insurance products
8. Application for specific insurance coverages.

The first four steps are essentially components of a customer needs analysis; the following four steps justify the choice of measures as well as the choice of suitable insurance products and their specific design. These ideal-typical steps of holistic advice for private customers also correspond to the currently required legal requirements from intermediary law.

In the context of legally compliant insurance advice, the first standard for the financial industry initiated by the DEFINO Institute for Financial Standards and developed at the German Institute for Standardization (DIN) should be mentioned, the **DIN 77230 "basic financial analysis for private households".** It was jointly developed by market participants, consumer advocates and scientists and published at the beginning of 2019. The DIN 77230 describes the standardized financial analysis of private households. The aim here is to create the correct diagnosis for optimal insurance, provision and wealth planning of the household objectively and neutrally, i.e., free from possible interests of the advisors and companies. For this purpose, 42 financial topics were initially identified that could potentially be relevant for a private household, and these were then sorted in a fixed order of importance and provided with orientation values. As a result of the analysis, the customer and advisor have a transparent basis—this corresponds approximately to steps 1-4 of the above-mentioned ideal-typical risk management process—for further financial advice in the sense of searching for customer-specific solutions (DEFINO Institute for Financial Standards 2023). Thus, a financial analysis based on the DIN standard 77230 should more than meet the partial steps required by the legislator of querying wishes and needs as well as the (necessary in the course of the consultation) recording of the initial situation and in this respect also increase the legal certainty for intermediaries (and insurers).

Already active before and somewhat broader in content is the **Working Group on Consulting Processes.** This is a non-profit initiative of several intermediary associations and service companies for joint, equal and cross-association development of practical aids for the daily routine of intermediaries. More than ten years ago, the working group began to develop a **"map for consultation"** for private customers; there is now also one for commercial customers. It provides a matrix that lists consulting aspects of risk coverage and wealth accumulation for private customers, such as liability risk or savings target, on one axis and their influencing factors, such as age or health status, on the other. The map provides an overall view in terms of comprehensiveness and structuring, but should not be used directly as a basis for consultation. For this purpose, additional guidelines for typical consulting constellations such as car purchase, acquisition of a self-used property, marriage or relocation, as well as numerous sample documents for various steps of the consulting process are provided or the map is supplemented by these. The practical recommendations and materials serve systematic, efficient and legally secure insurance and financial advice from the first contact to documentation. The developed working aids are available free of charge on the website of the working group.

For further information on the phases, contents and instruments of holistic consulting, the following sources are referred to:

Working Group on Consulting Processes (Ed.): Website, at: www.beratungsprozesse.de

DEFINO Institute for Financial Standards (Ed.): Website, at: www.defino.de

Further literature on the topic:

- Jaeger and Weinmann 2012.
- Köhne and Lange 2020, pp. 206–228.
- Sandkühler 2011.

In combination with the required **documentation in the consultation protocol**, the effort and thus the costs increase; apart from the material costs, this mainly affects the **opportunity costs for the intermediary,** which result from the reduced time for further customer discussions (Nickel-Waninger 2010, p. 554). At the same time, however, the documentation also has a **number of advantages:** It can clarify the intermediary's consulting service to the customer, and he has something tangible and enduring in his hand (signal effect). This also reduces the quality and behavioral uncertainty, as the insurance customer can possibly better substantiate liability claims. Despite the mentioned effort, the intermediary also benefits because he has a piece of evidence for liability relief in the event of correct advice in the event of a customer's claim for damages.

From an economic point of view, as mentioned, it appears **consistent** that intermediaries who want to advise customers based on an objective market investigation, i.e., **brokers,** according to the **suitable-advice** principle implemented in Germany, base this advice on an objective investigation of a sufficient number of insurance contracts offered on the market in order to be able to give a personal recommendation in the interest of the customer as to which insurance contract best meets the customer's needs.

Furthermore, the **product information sheet** should be mentioned, which according to § 4 VVG-InfoV is mandatory for all insurance products except insurance investment products (Sect. 10.2.1): Since customers are generally overwhelmed with the legally formulated insurance conditions, an information sheet focused on the essential features, short and concise, helps to better understand the performance features of the insurance product. It tends to reduce the quality uncertainty regarding the product performance and gives the insurance customer something in hand during the consultation, so that the **information asymmetry** between him and the intermediary is **reduced.** However, the prerequisite is that the customer deals with it. The information sheet improves understanding of the specific, affected insurance product. A comparison between different products is only supported if uniform standards and formats are specified for the information (Köhne 2014, p. 258). At least this is not the case for the risk classes, return calculations, and cost statements for the IBIP and state-certified pension products.

13.6.4 Disclosure of Remuneration to the Client

The disclosure of remuneration is often discussed particularly emotionally and controversially. However, this can vary in extent: at one extreme, the intermediary discloses to the client in euros exactly what he earns from the conclusion of the contract, at the other extreme, only the type of remuneration due at the conclusion of the contract is described qualitatively. There are numerous other variants in between. It is also differentiated whether the disclosure is fundamentally mandatory (hard disclosure) or only has to be made at the request of the policyholder (soft disclosure).

According to German law, the intermediary must inform the policyholder at the first business contact whether he works on the basis of a fee, a commission, any other remuneration, or a combination of both (§ 15 para. 1, nos. 5–8 VersVermV). He must therefore **name all types of remuneration,** including those after the conclusion of the contract, i.e., also contingent commissions, bonuses or possible kick-backs (rebates from product providers). Insurers must also **show the calculated acquisition costs as a total amount** for life, disability, accident insurance with premium refund and health insurance products (§§ 2, 3 VVG-InfoV).

The European Commission and many consumer advocates wanted to obtain precise information in euros about the amount of remuneration, broken down into acquisition commissions, contingent commissions, bonuses and follow-up commissions. They have anchored this in Art. 29 para. 1 IDD for insurance-based investment products: The insurer or intermediary must disclose the reduction in yield due to costs, and at the customer's request even broken down by individual cost items (Reiff and Köhne 2017, p. 655).

The moderate **regulations** in German sales law seem to be useful as minimum information on the one hand, but on the other hand also seem to be of **little added value,** as this information is likely to be conveyed in insurance practice anyway and insurance customers are generally likely to know who pays their intermediary. The somewhat more extensive cost disclosures for insurance investment products are also likely to provide the customer with little insight: What conclusion should he draw from a total amount of calculated acquisition costs, i.e., an amount assigned to a contract that results from intermediation, advertising and other acquisition costs (e.g., costs of application recording)? The effects on the customer's decision are therefore unclear.

The disclosure of remuneration is also demanded by some in the **scientific community** (Aschenbrenner-von Dahlen and Nagel 2004, p. 90; Sonnenberg 2013, pp. 240–246; Schwintowski 2013, p. 224). It is postulated that customers can better assess the intermediary's interest in a product recommendation if they know the specific incentive associated with each recommended insurance product. However, the informational value of this information for the insurance customer is questionable (Focht et al. 2013, p. 346): If the quality of the product and the advice can hardly be assessed, the question arises as to what conclusions a customer should draw from varying high remunerations depending on the insurance products? It remains unclear whether the intermediary recommends the product with the highest remuneration because it best meets the customer's needs or simply because it promises him the highest payment. *Schiller* shows that the disclosure of commissions does not necessarily have to lead to an elimination or sufficient reduction of quality uncertainty, even with completely rational customers—who are generally rather rare in the population (Richter and Schiller 2009).

From the perspective of **consumer protection,** it is argued that the insurance customer thus becomes aware that advice costs something. However, what insight can he derive from this? Perhaps the aim is rather to increase the willingness to pay separately for intermediation services, i.e., to increase acceptance for fee-based advice (Köhne 2014, p. 261).

However, there are also costs associated with disclosure. Apart from process and material costs, it is a practically almost impossible task to disclose the components of remuneration in a differentiated manner in advance, because they are sometimes only calculated at the end of a financial year (contingent commissions, bonuses). In addition, the question arises whether only the intermediary's remuneration components or also those of his executives should be applied (Nickel-Waninger 2010, pp. 560–563).

13.6.5 Fee-based or Commission-based Intermediation?

From the described information asymmetry between intermediaries and insurance customers, there arise **behavioral leeways for the intermediary,** which he can exploit to his advantage (see excursus in Sect. 13.1). Therefore, in connection with the (sales-dependent) remuneration by the insurer, a **potential conflict of interest** arises for the intermediary, because he might be inclined to sell the customer more insurance coverage than he actually needs. Apart from the already described disclosure requirements, there are also occasional proposals to completely ban commissions, as in some European countries, and to only allow fees to be paid by the customer (especially by consumer advocates, currently also Sebastian et al. 2023). A somewhat less far-reaching solution (which was also proposed in the draft of the IMD2 Commission and currently again in the EU retail investment strategy (see excursus on this in Sect. 3.4.2)) is to do this only for independent intermediaries. Thus, the **question of the (consumer-related) effects of different remuneration systems** arises.

Excursus on a slightly different argumentation …

In the context of today's discussions and arguments, a statement from the 1950s by *Trinkhaus* is very interesting:

> "In addition to (...) the commission system also speaks for the fact that the insurance agent as an independent businessman is not subject to the instructions of the insurer like the directorate employee (...) [He] can therefore also better represent the interests of the policyholder (...) in the interest of all. He is therefore also more popular."
>
> Source: Trinkhaus 1955, p. 33.

In principle, there is broad consensus that commission-based mediation can lead to conflicts of interest on the part of the intermediary if he receives an incentive to recommend a less suitable product through a higher commission. In model theory, it can be shown that a commission-based remuneration system can lead to over-advice, but a fee-based one can also lead to under-advice (quality uncertainty). And with the fee-based remuneration system, there are also **conflicts of interest** between the intermediary (agent) and the customer (principal): The longer the consultation lasts, the better the intermediary earns (behavioral uncertainty). However, in both remuneration systems, the importance of reputation for the intermediary also comes into play: Because a long-term customer relationship is lucrative for the intermediary, be it through follow-up commissions or the potential for additional sales (cross- or up-selling); for fee-based advisors, it is added that each follow-up consultation or service (claims settlement) is to be billed separately. Consequently, the benefit of short-term over- or under-advice must be higher than the cost of losing the customer relationship. This danger seems to be fundamentally given for rather sales-oriented sales organizations, which also focus primarily on life or—in the case of MEG—on health insurances (Traub 1995, p. 155; Karten 2002, p. 51; Cummins and Doherty 2006, p. 385; Höckmayr 2012, pp. 87–89; see also Karau 2015).

Economic studies overwhelmingly conclude that **commission-based compensation systems** in insurance intermediation in the private customer sector are equivalent, sometimes even superior, to fee-based ones (with further literature references: Köhne 2014, p. 262; Ruß et al. 2023). This is justified by their **control effect, which ultimately also benefits the insurance customer.** Insurers want (and need) to retain the decision-making power over whether they underwrite a risk or not. Therefore, while insurance intermediaries bring supply and demand together, they do not take possession of the insurance products. Rather, the insurers decide on the acceptance of the risk during the underwriting process. In doing so, they need and receive risk-relevant information about the insurance customers from the insurance intermediary. However, they have to incentivize the intermediaries more (in the case of the broker, who is on the customer's side) or less (in the case of the agent, who is the vicarious agent of the insurer) to provide them with this information in sufficient quality. This justifies a commission as it ignites the required control effect. In contrast, no control is possible with a fee paid by the customer. Ultimately, the insurance customer also benefits from this, as improved underwriting can offer more needs-based coverage, some risks—albeit possibly only with exclusions, limitations or deductibles—can be insured at all, and pricing becomes more risk-appropriate. This goes hand in hand with the avoidance of adverse risk selection (Cummins and Doherty 2006, pp. 386–389; Schiller 2011, p. 126; Focht et al. 2013,

p. 345 f.). Although the studies with regard to the underwriting argument partly refer mainly to the industrial and corporate business, this argumentation generally applies in the private customer sector as well.

Previous studies suggest another **disadvantage of fee-based systems,** which tend to lead to an **undersupply of consumers with insurance protection and retirement provision products** (Gravelle 1993, p. 52). Because in the case of explicitly known fees, fewer insurance customers seek advice. With regard to Germany, this finding has current practical relevance, because due to the mentioned low willingness to pay, it can be expected that only a few insurance customers, especially those with high incomes and wealth, will request paid advice. As a consequence, large parts of the population make an uninformed or even no purchase decision anymore (Köhne 2014, p. 263; Schiller 2011, p. 126). The low willingness to pay of customers was recently confirmed in a representative study conducted on behalf of the Quirin Privatbank in Germany, which specializes in fee-based consulting (Puls 2023). According to this, only 33% of those surveyed are willing to pay a market-standard fee for advice, while 39% state that they would no longer seek advice after a ban on commissions. 28% do not know how they would behave. Even in countries like the UK and the Netherlands, which have long been considered reference models for a ban on commissions, it has long been shown that fees lead to a shortage of demand for financial advice in broad sections of the population, while the financially upscale clientele is hardly affected (Schafstädt 2015, pp. 304 f., 309; see also the cited sources in Köhne 2014, p. 263).

Here another important aspect becomes apparent, which needs to be taken into account especially in the private customer sector. The mentioned economic studies assume rational decisions in their models, but admit that these cannot be expected from private insurance customers. Therefore, it seems promising to use behavioral economic approaches that could explain why **private individuals often do not make rational decisions, especially in retirement provision** (see Sect. 4.2). Examples include insufficient coverage against existential risks due to incorrect cognitive assessment of the consequences, the desire for annual guarantees due to selective perception and relative evaluation of gains and losses to a reference point (reference point effect), i.e., changes near the reference point are perceived as more significant than equal changes at a greater distance, as well as a general preference for guarantees in life insurance caused by loss aversion (Richter et al. 2018). And because current consumption is more promising than that in old age, they do not demand insurance and retirement provision products to a sufficient extent on their own, and therefore there is a threat of an insurance and provision shortage (from a welfare economic, but also individual perspective).

Commission systems thus motivate intermediaries to persuade customers to secure and provide for their old age—as mentioned, with the risk of over-advising. On the other hand, fee-based systems, as mentioned, are associated with the risk of under-advising; they deter customers because they have to request insurance and pension advice on their own and also have to pay for it. In this respect, **commissions** are a **remuneration for**

the intermediary's performance of "forcing the customer to their luck" (Köhne 2014, p. 263 f.).

But even under rational, purely cost-based considerations, fees are superior to commissions only in certain constellations. Especially for less well-off customers, commissions are even the cheaper option, as a current model calculation impressively shows (see excursus on the quantitative comparison of commission-based and fee-based systems). Some consumer advocates argue exactly the opposite (only without quantitative evidence) and thus not in the interest of their clientele.

Excursus on costs of commission-based and fee-based advice compared

A quantitative analysis by the Institute for Actuarial Sciences from 2023 shows which form of advisory remuneration is more cost-effective for which types of consumers. The calculation is carried out using typical examples of different remuneration models. It clearly shows that **for consumers who regularly save rather small amounts, commission-based models are usually more cost-effective** than **fee-based models.**

For the calculation, the authors use, for example, the costs of commission advice from the largest German life insurer, derived as the difference between its gross tariff (which pays commissions) and its net tariff (which does not pay commissions), and on the other hand a **fee-based model with standard hourly rates** and typical time expenditure for a complete, legally compliant and high-quality pension advice and ongoing support. In this case, for example, the commission model is cheaper for a contract term of 20 (or 30) years if the monthly premium rate invested in the pension product is less than 186 € (or 129 €).

This order of magnitude does not change even with a **variation of the hourly rate** (higher or lower) and **ongoing support** (more frequent or not at all). It is therefore relevant for many consumers with rather limited financial means.

In a further examination of fee-based models **with flat fee rates,** it was initially shown that fee schedules of fee-based advisors are not easy to find and moreover the offered models—even within the fee schedule of a provider—allow both rather cheap and (sometimes very) high-priced models. This means that fee-based models are not necessarily more transparent for consumers than commission models. Then, with regard to these models, the statement is confirmed that the premium rate below which the commission model is cheaper is relevant for many consumers. It applies: Typical amounts of volume-dependent fees p.a. always lead to a **higher reduction in return than** the **costs of commission-financed advice**.

Overall, these quantitative results impressively underline that a **coexistence of commission-based and fee-based models is desirable.**

(Source: Ruß et al. 2023, pp. 25–35)

Last but not least, a **macroeconomic component** appears to be overlooked in the discussion, which is at least relevant with regard to Germany: The current remuneration system creates double benefits for insurance customers, especially for those who do not have a high income or wealth. Firstly, through an inherent **redistribution,** advice on existential, but low premium products such as liability insurance is co-financed by those on high premium products; likewise, the rather low-paid advice for customers with lower incomes and wealth is co-financed by the rather high-paid advice for well-off people. Secondly, it can also be advantageous that customers have the impression of receiving free advice; they are more likely to request this **seemingly free advice** than if they have to pay for it separately (and consciously). Surveys among the population repeatedly underline how low the willingness to pay is in the case of fee-based advice (Köhne 2014, p. 261; Ruß et al. 2023, p. 10).

13.6.6 Economic Evaluation of Regulatory Initiatives

As a result of the economic consideration of customer orientation mandated by regulatory initiatives, it should be noted that **some regulations appear quite in the interest of customers and justifiable from a cost perspective.** These include the necessary commercial trade permission with registration and minimum qualifications, which enhance the professional image of the insurance intermediary, the product information sheet, which should facilitate customer understanding, the sanction mechanisms in connection with the whistleblower procedure, and last but not least, the obligation to participate in consiliation process, all of which increase the relevance for intermediaries.

On the other hand, **many regulations involve more effort than benefit, some even only involve effort for intermediaries (and insurers).** No relevant benefit can be derived from the product approval process, the (purely German) status of the insurance advisor, and especially the associated prescribed, complex administrative processes around the pass-through requirement of any commissions and the separate monitoring of records and business organization, as well as the overly detailed regulations around the (at least) annual reports, return, risk and cost statements for insurance investment products. Furthermore, both the disclosure of remuneration and the demanded prohibition of commissions are more counterproductive than helpful from a consumer perspective. A coexistence of commission and fee-based systems, on the other hand, allows competition between both types of remuneration and leaves the choice to the insurance customer. However, for the reasons stated (low willingness to pay, unclear benefits, higher costs with a smaller budget), it is unlikely that customers will accept the fee-based system. What is certain, on the other hand, is that the route via the status of the insurance advisor is associated with additional costs, which ultimately the customer has to bear, because two systems have to be managed and supported in terms of process. Economically more sensible and consistent would then be the regulation that brokers with private customers may agree on any type of remuneration, but they must make it transparent and the customer must agree to it, or—as in Austrian law—a common regulation for brokers and advisors by merging them into the professional image of the "insurance broker and advisor in insurance matters" (Werber 2019, p. 329).

Interim Conclusion on the Marketing Tool of Sales Policy

The sales policy of an insurance company is a very critical success factor in a buyer's market, where insurance is sold and not bought. This is especially true for the private customer sector. Insurers are therefore dependent on finding the "way to the customer"; this has resulted in a great variety of sales channels over the last decades, and sales channel strategies range from sales channel specialization on the one hand to multi-channel management on the other. Insurance sales are becoming more digital, both in terms of supporting traditional sales channels and in terms of seeking new ways to reach the digital native, usually via InsurTechs. The latter have not yet established themselves and cannot compete with traditional intermediaries in terms of revenue generation. However, new developments such as the emergence of virtual worlds (Metaverse), the potential use of AI in everyday life (ChatGPT), and the processing of ever larger amounts of data (big data) make future predictions much more difficult than in the past. It is clearer, on the other hand, that insurance sales currently suffer from excessive regulation, which has been largely initiated at EU level and continues to be pushed. While it has brought improvements, it goes too far in many respects. From a cost-benefit perspective, it is hardly economically justifiable; moreover, there is a risk that it will provoke market failure (for example, in the case of an actual ban on commissions for brokers).

Further Reading Recommendations for Chap. 13

- Bosselmann 1994.
- Eckhardt 2007.
- Farny 1971.
- Heimes 2009.
- Höckmayr 2012.
- Köhne 2013b.
- Köhne and Lange 2020, Chap. 3, 5.
- Nickel-Waninger 2010.
- OECD 2020.
- Schareck 2005.
- Schmidt-Jochmann 2008.
- Straßler 2005.
- Vogler 2009.
- Zinnert 2008.
- Zinnert 2009.

References

Akerlof, G.A: (1970): The market for "lemons": quality uncertainty and the market mechanism, in: Q. J. Econ., Vol. 84, 1970, No. 3, pp. 488–500.

Aschenbrenner-von Dahlen, S./Nagel, S. (2004): Insurance Intermediation—Theoretical Analysis and Practical Issues in the European Market, in: ZVersWiss, Jg. 93, 2004, pp. 67–99.

AVAD (Ed.) (2023): Informationen zur Auskunftsstelle über den Versicherungs- und Bausparaußendienst und Versicherungsmakler in Deutschland e.V., in: http://www.avad.de, Accessed: 11.11.2023.

BaFin (Ed.) (2023c): Ausgewählte Kennzahlen der Schaden- und Unfallversicherungsunternehmen 2021, in der Rangfolge der verdienten Brutto-Beiträge, Tabelle 560, Bonn, 2023, in: www.bafin.de.

Beenken, M. (2010): Der Markt der Versicherungsvermittlung unter veränderten rechtlichen Rahmenbedingungen, unter besonderer Berücksichtigung von Sourcingstrategien des Versicherungsvermittlerbetriebs, Karlsruhe, 2010.

Birkner, G. (2017): Versicherung digital 2017, Wie Versicherte die neue Versicherungswelt sehen, Frankfurt am Main, 2017.

Bosselmann, E.H. (1994): Versicherungsmakler und deregulierte Versicherungsmärkte, Karlsruhe, 1994.

Bundesverband der Versicherungsberater (BVVB) (Ed.) (2024a): Was ist Versicherungsberatung?, in: https://www.bvvb.de/fuer-ratsuchende/was-ist-versicherungsberatung/, Accessed: 21.01.2024.

Bundesverband der Versicherungsberater (BVVB) (Ed.) (2024b): Kosten der Versicherungsberatung, in: https://www.bvvb.de/fuer-ratsuchende/kosten-der-beratung/, Accessed: 21.01.2024.

Bundesverband Deutscher Versicherungskaufleute (Ed.) (2020): BVK-Agenturvertrag, Muster eines Vertrages zwischen Einfirmenvertreter und Versicherer, Bonn, 2020.

Cash Online (Ed.) (2023): Allfinanzvertriebe 2023: in: https://www.cash-online.de/cash-hitlisten/finanzvertriebe/allfinanzvertriebe-2023/, Accessed: 24.01.2024.

Cummins, J.D./Doherty, N.A. (2006): The Economics of Insurance Intermediaries, in: JoRI, Vol. 73, 2006, No. 3, pp. 359–396.

Dahmen, P. (2004): Multi-Channel Strategies for Retail Financial Services, A Management-Framework for Designing and Implementing Multi-Channel Strategies, Wiesbaden, 2004.

Damm, P. (1993): Ertragsbarwertbezogene Vergütungspolitik von Versicherungsunternehmen zur Steuerung von Absatzorganen, Karlsruhe, 1993.

Deutsche Industrie- und Handelskammer (DIHK) (Ed.) (2024): Statistiken Vermittlerverzeichnisse, Eingetragene Versicherungsvermittler, Stand: 1. Januar 2024, in: https://www.dihk.de/de/themen-und-positionen/recht-in-der-wirtschaft/gewerberecht/statistiken-vermittlerverzeichnisse-3344, Accessed: 21.01.2024.

Eckert, C./Eckert, J./Zitzmann, A. (2021): The status quo of digital transformation in insurance sales: an empirical analysis of the german insurance industry, in: ZVersWiss, Jg. 110, 2021, Nr. 2–3, pp. 133–155.

Eckhardt, M. (2007): Insurance Intermediation, An Economic Analysis of the Information Services Market, Heidelberg, 2007.

Eckhardt, M./Räthke-Döppner, S. (2010): The quality of insurance intermediary services—empirical evidence for Germany, in: JoRI, Vol. 77, 2010, pp. 667–701.

Farny, D. (1971): Absatz und Absatzpolitik des Versicherungsunternehmens, Karlsruhe, 1971.

Farny, D. (2011): Versicherungsbetriebslehre, Karlsruhe, 5. ed., 2011.

Focht, U./Richter, A./Schiller, J. (2013): Intermediation and (Mis-)Matching in Insurance Markets—Who Should Pay the Insurance Broker?, in: JoRI, Vol. 80, 2013, No. 2, pp. 329–350.

GDV (Ed.) (2000): Neufassung der Hauptpunkte eines Vertrages für selbständige hauptberufliche Versicherungsvertreter gemäß §§ 84 Abs. 1, 92 HGB, Berlin/Bonn/Köln, 2000.

GDV (Ed.) (2023a): Statistiken zur deutschen Versicherungswirtschaft 2023, Berlin, 2023.

GDV/Verband der privaten Krankenversicherung e. V. (PKV)/Bundesverband der Assekuranzführungskräfte e. V. (VGA)/Bundesverband Deutscher Versicherungskaufleute e. V. (BVK) (Eds.) (2006): Wettbewerbsrichtlinien der Versicherungswirtschaft, o.O., 2006.

Gimpel, H./Lanzl, J./Manner-Romberg, T./Nüske, N. (2018): Digitaler Stress in Deutschland, Eine Befragung von Erwerbstätigen zu Belastung und Beanspruchung durch Arbeit mit digitalen Technologien, Working Paper Forschungsförderung Hans-Böckler-Stiftung Nr. 101, 2018.

Gravelle, H. (1993): Product price and advice quality: implications of the commission system in life assurance, in: GP, Vol. 18, 1993, pp. 31–53.

Habschick, M./Evers, J. (2008): Anforderungen an Finanzvermittler—mehr Qualität, bessere Entscheidungen: Studie im Auftrag des Bundesministeriums für Ernährung, Landwirtschaft und Verbraucherschutz, Hamburg, 2008.

Hambach, S./Hiendlmeier, S. (2021): Steuerung der Vertriebsprozesse, in: Junglas, A./Schradin, H./Wiegard, M.: Steuerung von Versicherungsunternehmen, Stuttgart, 3. ed., 2021, pp. 391–408.

HanseMerkur Reiseversicherung (Ed.) (2023): Darstellung der Partner auf der Unternehmenswebsite, in: www.hmrv.de/partner/referenzen, Accessed: 12.09.2023.

Hasenbein, M. (2020): Der Mensch im Fokus der digitalen Arbeitswelt. Wirtschaftspsychologische Perspektiven und Anwendungsfelder, Berlin, 2020.

Hauri, M. (2018): Wird der Berater "wegdigitalisiert"? Wie Online-Angebot und klassische Beratung miteinander harmonieren, in: ZfV, Jg. 69, 2018, Nr. 8, pp. 245–248.

Hax, H. (1991): Theorie der Unternehmung, Information, Anreize und Vertragsgestaltung, in: Ordelheide, D./Rudolph, B./Büsselmann, E. (Eds.), Betriebswirtschaftslehre und Ökonomische Theorie, Stuttgart, 1991, pp. 51–72.

Heimes, H. (2009): Verkaufsverhalten im Ausschließlichkeitsvertrieb der Versicherungsindustrie, Eine empirische Untersuchung des Einflusses auf den Vertriebserfolg, Lohmar, 2009.

Helten, E. (1998): Restrukturierung im Assekuranz-Vertrieb, Theoretische Bemerkungen zur Verlagerung von betrieblichen Teilfunktionen und empirische Ergebnisse aus Sicht der Vermittlerbetriebe, in: VW, Jg. 53, 1998, Nr. 2, pp. 90–94.

Hielscher, J.-R. (1993): Strategische Vertriebswegepolitik mittelgroßer Lebensversicherer, Wiesbaden, 1993.

Höckmayr, G. (2012): Wandel der Beratungsqualität auf dem Versicherungsvermittlungsmarkt, Eine ökonomische Analyse der Veränderungen aufgrund der Anforderungen der EU-Vermittlerrichtlinie, Karlsruhe, 2012.

Jaeger, K./Weinmann, H. (2012): Die Funktionsweise eines strukturierten, ganzheitlichen Beratungsprozesses, in: ZfV, Jg. 63, 2012, Nr. 13–14, pp. 427–431.

Kaas, K.-P. (1990): Marketing als Bewältigung von Informations- und Unsicherheitsproblemen im Markt, in: DBW, Jg. 50, 1990, Nr. 4, pp. 539–548.

Kallerhoff, H.-J. (2018): Digitalisierung im Bankenvertrieb: erfolgreich in exklusiven Bank-Partnerschaften, in: Beenken, M./Knörrer, D./Moormann, J./Schmidt, D. (Eds.), Digital Insurance. Strategien, Geschäftsmodelle, Daten, Frankfurt a. M., 2018, pp. 341–362.

Karau, T. (2015): Qualitätsmessung in der Versicherungsvermittlung: Eine empirische Untersuchung der Unterschiede zwischen Provisions- und Honorarvergütung in der Altervorsorge, Lohmar, 2015.

Karten, W. (2002): Ökonomische Aspekte einer EU-Richtlinie zur Versicherungsvermittlung, in: ZVersWiss, Jg. 91, 2002, pp. 43–60.

Kendl, E. (1997): Reengineering im Versicherungsmarketing, Funktionsverlagerung auf Vermittlerbetriebe, Wiesbaden, 1997.

Köhne, T. (1997): Die Wirkungsversicherung im Privatkundengeschäft—Implikationen für eine kundenorientierte Marktleistungsgestaltung, St. Gallen, 1997.

Köhne, T. (2006): Marketing im strategischen Unternehmensnetzwerk, Erklärungsmodell und praktische Anwendung in der Versicherungswirtschaft, Wiesbaden, 2006.

Köhne, T. (2013b): Performance von Versicherungsvermittlern—Konzeption und Messung aus Sicht des Versicherungsunternehmens, Berliner Schriften zur Versicherungswirtschaft, ed. by Institut für Versicherungswirtschaft an der Hochschule für Wirtschaft und Recht Berlin, Nr. 5, Berlin, 2013.

Köhne, T. (2014): Ökonomische Aspekte der neuen IMD2 vom 26.02.2014, in: ZVersWiss, Jg. 103, 2014, Nr. 3, pp. 243–268.

Köhne, T. (2022a): Digitalisierung in der Versicherungsvermittlung, in: ZfV, Jg. 73, 2022, Nr. 23, pp. 679–682.

Köhne, T. (2022b): Digitaler Stress bei Versicherungsvermittlern, in: ZfV, Jg. 73, 2022, Nr. 24, pp. 713–716.

Köhne, T./Brömmelmeyer, C. (2018): The New Insurance Distribution Regulation in the EU—A Critical Assessment from a Legal and Economic Perspective, in: The Geneva Papers on Risk and Insurance, Vol. 43, No. 4, 2018, 704–739.

Köhne, T./Lange, M. (2020): Marketing und Vertrieb von Versicherungs- und Finanzprodukten für Privatkunden, Fach- und Führungskompetenz für die Assekuranz, Karlsruhe, 4. ed., 2020.

Köhne, T./Wendland, A. (2022): Digitalisierung im Versicherungsvertrieb—eine empirische Untersuchung bei Versicherungsvermittlern, in: Berliner Schriften zur Versicherungswirtschaft, herausgegeben vom Institut für Versicherungswirtschaft an der Hochschule für Wirtschaft und Recht Berlin, Nr. 14, Berlin, 2022.

Kottmann, D.A. (2018): Bancassurance 2.0: Werden Banken die digitalen Versicherungsmakler der Zukunft?, in: Beenken, M./Knörrer, D./Moormann, J./Schmidt, D. (Eds.), Digital Insurance. Strategien, Geschäftsmodelle, Daten, Frankfurt a. M., 2018, pp. 45–64.

Krauß, H. (2009): Die Vergütung des Versicherungsmaklers im Rahmen internationaler Entwicklungen, Karlsruhe, 2009.

Kutz, S. (1997): Die Aufgabenverteilung zwischen Versicherungsunternehmen und Einfirmen-/Konzernvertretern, Lohmar, 1997.

Lach, H. (1995): Vertikales Marketing von Versicherungsunternehmen, Berlin, 1995.

Lange, W. (1995): Verteiltes Vertriebscontrolling in Versicherungsunternehmen, Karlsruhe, 1995.

Maier, J./Faßbender, K. (2020): Versicherungsnehmer und Firmenverbundener Vermittler, in: Mahnke, A./Rohlfs, T. (Eds.), Betriebliches Risikomanagement und Industrieversicherung, Erfolgreiche Unternehmenssteuerung durch ein effektives Risiko- und Versicherungsmanagement, Wiesbaden, 2020, pp. 277–296.

Nastjuk, I./Trang, S./Grummeck-Braamt, J.-V./Adam, M.T.P./Tarafdar, M (2023): Integrating and Synthesising Technostress Research: A Meta-Analysis on Technostress Creators, Outcomes, and IS Usage Contexts, in: European Journal of Information Systems, 2023, pp. 1–22. (https://doi.org/10.1080/0960085X.2022.2154712)

Nickel-Waninger, H. (2010): Implikationen der Vertriebswegeentwicklung in der Versicherungswirtschaft, in: ZVersWiss, Jg. 99, 2010, pp. 545–568.

Nicoletti, B. (2021): Insurance 4.0: Benefits and Challenges of Digital Transformation, Cham, 2021.

OECD (Ed.) (2020): Regulatory and Supervisory Framework for Insurance Intermediation, o. O., 2020.

Pahl, M./Domazet, M./Ressel, J. (2020): Bedeutung und Zukunft des Industrieversicherungsmaklers in Deutschland, in: Mahnke, A./Rohlfs, T. (Eds.), Betriebliches Risikomanagement und Industrieversicherung, Erfolgreiche Unternehmenssteuerung durch ein effektives Risiko- und Versicherungsmanagement, Wiesbaden, 2020, pp. 297–318.

Puls (Ed.) (2023): Das Beratungs-Bezahl-Paradoxon deutscher Bankkunden. Ergebnisse einer repräsentativen Studie zu den Themen Provisionen, Honorare und Bezahlung von Bankberatung von puls Marktforschung GmbH im Auftrag der Quirin Privatbank.

Puschmann, K.-H. (2003): Praxis des Versicherungsmarketing, Karlsruhe, 2. ed., 2003.
Rayburn, S.W./Badrinarayanan, V./Anderson, S.T./Gupta, A. (2021): Continuous techno-training and business-to-business salesperson success: How boosting techno-efficacy enhances sales effort and performance, in: Journal of Business Research, Vol. 133, 2021, pp. 66–78.
Reiff, P. (2018): Das Versicherungsvertriebsrecht nach Inkrafttreten des Gesetzes zur Umsetzung der Versicherungsvertriebsrichtlinie, in: VersR, Jg. 69, 2018, Nr. 4, pp. 193–203.
Reiff, P./Köhne, T. (2017): Der Regierungsentwurf zur Umsetzung der Richtlinie (EU) 2016/97 (IDD) in rechtlicher und ökonomischer Sicht, in: VersR, Jg. 68, 2017, Nr. 11, pp. 649–661.
Richter, A./Schiller, J. (2009): Entlohnung und Regulierung unabhängiger Versicherungsvermittler, in: Schäfer, K./Burghof, H.-P./Johanning, L./Wagner, H.F./Rodt, S. (Eds.), Risikomanagement und kapitalmarktorientierte Finanzierung, Festschrift zum 65. Geburtstag von Bernd Rudolph, Frankfurt a. M., 2009, pp. 319–336.
Richter, A./Ruß, J./Schelling, S. (2018): Moderne Verhaltensökonomie in der Versicherungswirtschaft, Denkanstöße für ein besseres Verständnis der Kunden, Wiesbaden, 2018.
Ruß, L./Kling, A./Seyboth, A. (2023): Provisionsverbot und Kleinanlegerstrategie, Plädoyer für eine Koexistenz von Provision und Honorar bei Altersvorsorgeprodukten, Ulm, 2023.
Sandkühler, H.-L. (2011): Arbeitskreis Beratungsprozesse entwickelt Branchenstandards für bessere Beratung, in: AssCompact, 2011, Nr. 2, pp. 88–89.
Sandkühler, H.-L. (2014): Kodex, Compliance und Reputation, Regelkonformität im Spannungsfeld zwischen Versicherern und Vermittlern, in: VW, Jg. 69, 2014, Nr. 11, pp. 44–45.
Schafstädt, C. (2015): Das Spannungsverhältnis zwischen Provisionsberatung und Honorarberatung im Versicherungsmarkt, Karlsruhe, 2015.
Schareck, C. (2005): Wertorientierung im Versicherungsvertrieb, Karlsruhe, 2005.
Schiller, J. (2011): Ökonomische Aspekte der Entlohnung und Regulierung unabhängiger Versicherungsvermittler, in: ZVersWiss, Jg. 100, 2011, pp. 113–130.
Schmidt-Gallas, D./Grunert, S./Lütticke, F. (2018): Der persönliche Vertrieb im Zeitalter der Digitalisierung—teurer Luxus oder echter Mehrwert, in: ZfV, Jg. 69, 2018, Nr.1, pp. 10–13.
Schmidt-Jochmann, C. (2008): Strategische Erfolgsfaktoren von Versicherungsvermittlern—Eine empirische Untersuchung mit PLS-Strukturgleichungsmodellen, Lohmar, 2008.
Schmitt, F.C. (2013): Vertrieb und Compliance Management—eine ungenutzte Chance, Konsequenzen aus dem GDV-Verhaltenskodex zum Vertrieb von Versicherungsprodukten, in: VW, Jg. 68, 2013, Nr. 20, S, 666–670.
Schögel, M. (1997): Mehrkanalsysteme in der Distribution, Dissertation St. Gallen, Scheßlitz 1997.
Schwintowski, H.-P. (2013): Neue Vergütungsformen für Versicherungsmakler? (II), Deutsches Recht und die Auswirkungen der IMD 2, in: ZfV, Jg. 64, 2013, pp. 221–225.
Sebastian, S./Noth, L./Grafe, A.: The Effect of Commission Bans on Household Wealth: Evidence from OECD Countries, Studie, Universität Regensburg, 2023.
Sirius Campus (Ed.) (2023b): Kundenmonitor e-Assekuranz 2023—Der Vertriebswege-Monitor, Köln, 2023.
Sonnenberg, M. (2013): Vertriebskostentransparenz bei Versicherungsprodukten, Eine juristisch-ökonomische Untersuchung unter Berücksichtigung rechtsvergleichender Aspekte, Karlsruhe, 2013.
Straßler, H.-J. (2005): Theoretische Analyse und empirische Überprüfung von Einflussgrößen auf den Erfolg des Ausschließlichkeitsvermittlers eines mittelständischen Versicherungsunternehmens, Univ.-Diss. München, o.O., 2005.
Tarafdar, M./Tu, Q./Ragu-Nathan, S./Ragu-Nathan, T.S. (2007): The Impact of Technostress on Role Stress and Productivity, in: Journal of Management Information Systems, Vol. 24, 2007, No. 1, pp. 301–328.

Tarafdar, M./Cooper, C.L./Stich, J.-F. (2019): The technostress trifecta—techno eustress, techno distress and design: Theoretical directions and an agenda for research, in: Information Systems Journal, Vol. 29, 2019, No. 1, pp. 6–42.

Teichler, M. (2018): Die Versicherungs-Vertriebsrichtlinie (IDD) erfolgreich umsetzen, Freiburg i. B., 2018.

Traub, W. (1995): Marktfunktionen und Dienstleistung des Versicherungsmaklers auf der Grundlage informationsökonomischer Ergebnisse, Karlsruhe, 1995.

Trinkhaus, H. (1955): Handbuch der Versicherungsvermittlung, Band I, Berlin, 1955.

Vetter, R./Möbius, C. (2019): Zukunftskonzept für die Ausschließlichkeitsorganisation, in ZfV, Jg. 70, 2019, Nr. 17, pp. 515–518.

Vogler, D. (2009): Personenbezogene Einflussfaktoren für den Vertriebserfolg im Versicherungsvertrieb, Eine empirische Analyse bei Ausschließlichkeitsvertretern, Lohmar, 2009.

Wagner, F. (Ed.) (2017): Gabler Versicherungslexikon, Wiesbaden, 2. Aufl., 2017.

Wagner, S. (2006): Provisionssatzdifferenzierung in finanziellen Anreizsystemen für Versicherungsvermittler, Karlsruhe, 2006.

Werber, M. (2019): Kritische Nachlese zur Umsetzung der Richtlinie (EU) 2016/97 über Versicherungsvertrieb, in: VersR, Jg. 70, 2019, Nr. 6, pp. 321–329.

Wiswesser, R. (2018): Die Zukunft der persönlichen Beratung im digitalen Zeitalter, in: Beenken, M./Knörrer, D./Moormann, J./Schmidt, D. (Eds.), Digital Insurance. Strategien, Geschäftsmodelle, Daten, Frankfurt a.M., 2018, pp. 109–130.

Zietsch, D. (1985): Grundlagen der Gestaltung außenorganisationsbezogener Vertriebssteuerungssysteme in Versicherungsunternehmen, Karlsruhe, 1985.

Zinnert, M. (2008): Recht und Praxis des Versicherungsmaklers, Karlsruhe, 2008.

Zinnert, M. (2009): Der Versicherungsvertreter, Karlsruhe, 2009.

14 Communication Policy as a Marketing Tool of the Insurance Company

14.1 Basics of Communication Policy

Within the framework of brand policy and in personal communication with the customer, there are significant overlaps between the product design and communication policy in service companies. Nevertheless, or precisely because of this, communication must be consciously managed as an independent marketing tool in its own right in order to fully unleash its potential. This is particularly true against the backdrop of the initial situation already described in private customer business: insurance products are low-interest products that do not attract attention, customers pay little attention to this topic and are already exposed to an information overload. Therefore, insurers are particularly challenged to find a noticeable and at the same time differentiating message that informs about the product, its features, its price-performance ratio and its advantages and reaches the recipients. In short: a professional communication policy is required.

▶ **Communication Policy** generally aims at the creation and transmission of information and meanings to control opinions, attitudes, expectations and behaviors according to company-specific objectives.

(adapted from: Bruhn 2019b, p. 3; Homburg 2020, p. 827)

Companies pursue marketing goals with their communication policy, which are intended to support the achievement of the company's economic objectives. These include improving awareness, the company and product image, positively changing the company and product-related attitudes of demanders, and not least triggering purchase intentions (Meffert et al. 2019, p. 633 f.).

Communication policy objectives can be systematized according to the **AIDA formula,** a classic impact stage model that structures the sub-processes of communication

T. Köhne, *Insurance Marketing*, https://doi.org/10.1007/978-3-658-47345-7_14

impact and goes back to *Lewis* (Bruhn 2019b, p. 163): According to this, the customer's attention (Attention) for a product must first be won. In the next step, interest (Interest) in the product can be aroused, followed by desire (Desire). This finally triggers a specific behavior (Action), e.g. the conclusion of an insurance contract.

As part of the objectives determination, it must also be determined which communication goals are to be achieved with which target groups. The target group can be potential buyers or current customers, decision-makers or influencers, individuals, specific groups or the general public. The selection of the target group is important because the addressed target group is relevant for what is communicated, how and through which channels it is communicated, when and where it is communicated, who should communicate it and what effect should be achieved (Kotler et al. 2022, p. 677; Meffert et al. 2019, p. 633; in detail at Bruhn 2019b, p. 179–213).

Communication brings about the exchange of information, the influencing of communication partners and social relationships. Important **tasks of the communication policy** therefore include information, trust and image building, profiling, motivation to conclude and customer retention. The information function in insurance follows directly from the product characteristics: insurance as an information product thrives on appropriate and customer-feeling information. This is also related to the trust-building function: insurance as a credence good requires trust-strengthening measures, communication can contribute to this due to its nature and content (Kühlmann et al. 2003, p. 192).

For **insurance** products as service products, their **specific characteristics** have to be considered in the communication, namely the provision of the provider's performance capability (potential orientation), the integration of the external factor, and the intangibility and non-storability (see Sect. 1.1.1). *Meffert et al.* have succinctly summarized the resulting implications for the communication policy of service companies. These are transferred here to insurance (Table 14.1).

Precisely because insurance still has a rather negative image across the industry, the **communicative establishment of a likable corporate brand** is as important as it is challenging. Familiarity and a positive image are not performance components in themselves. Therefore, the distinguishing performance characteristics need to be communicated, namely the reasons why a customer should conclude a specific insurance product from a specific provider. Ultimately, in terms of the motivation and binding function, it is about awakening the need for security and motivating customers to conclude, as well as confirming existing customers in their decision and thereby binding them.

The **basic structure of a communication process** includes a sender (communicator) who encodes (= encrypts) a message to be conveyed, then transports it via a carrier medium to a receiver who must decode (= decrypt) the message. For example, an insurer (sender) can communicate the target group-oriented coverage design of its product (communication message) via an advertisement in a trade journal (carrier medium) to potential buyers, namely brokers (receivers). The subject of communication is therefore who (sender) says what (message) how (encoding) via which channel (carrier medium) to whom (receiver) and with what effect (reaction). Communication processes are thus

Table 14.1 Specifics of the communication policy of insurance companies. (Further developed from Meffert et al. 2018, p. 310)

Specifics of services	Implications for communication policy
Performance capability of the insurer	• Documentation of specific service components (e.g., revenue, product ratings, quality seals, etc.) • Materialization of the potential capabilities (e.g., financial ratings, presentation of prominent insured risks or insurer´s global locations)
Integration of the external factor	• Reference to on-site risk inspection • Presentation of internal (e.g., face of a salesperson) and external factors (e.g., customer feedback, customer ratings) • Use of communication tools in the service creation process (e.g., offering travel insurance during a consultation on motor vehicle insurance) • Communication as the subject of the service (e.g., information and advice without or before the conclusion of insurance) • Individual communication to build close customer-employee relationships (especially in sales force) and to collect customer data (e.g., risk data, preferences, etc.) • Automated integration of the customer (e.g., when the customer enters data into an app)
Intangibility	• Materialization by presenting tangible elements (e.g., images of wealth in old age through ownership of luxury goods, before-and-after presentation of apartment damage due to burglary, flooding, etc., and the repaired apartment) • Visualization by highlighting tangible elements (e.g., employees in the call center or sales force) • Attracting attention through sales promotion materials (e.g., standees or flyers with famous personalities (testimonials)) • Presentation and materialization of competence (e.g., through lectures or seminars on everyday risks, retirement provision, etc. in clubs, universities, web forums, podcasts, etc.)
Non-storability	• Support of short-term demand control (e.g., in the case of a "sell-out" of life insurance products before a legally required new and less favorable tax (e.g., AltEinkG) or actuarial (e.g., Unisex judgment) treatment)

complex and prone to interference: disturbances or distortions of the message can occur during encryption, choice of carrier medium, and decryption. Communication is also two-sided because it triggers a reaction from the receiver to the decrypted message and is usually associated with an exchange of information, as is particularly the case in personal sales. One-sided communication, where the receiver's feedback is omitted, is strictly speaking "only" information (mass advertising) (Homburg 2020, p. 827 f.; Bruhn 2019b, pp. 30–32; Kotler et al. 2022, p. 675 f.).

The reaction of the receivers to a message depends significantly on the following factors (Kühlmann et al. 2003, p. 196):

- Credibility and sympathy of the sender
- Content of the message
- Medium: The suitability for attitude changes in the receiver decreases from personal conversation to pictorial communication, communication via auditory media (e.g., radio advertising) to written media (e.g., newspapers).
- Personality of the receiver.

Communication conditions change over time. From the perspective of the receivers, there is initially a continuously increasing amount of information. Customers suffer from a constant information overload. On average, between 3000 and 5000 advertising messages flood a city dweller every day (Kotler et al. 2017a, p. 697). *Kroeber-Riel* has empirically proven some time ago that receivers only pay attention to about two percent of the possible information offer, which means that a whopping 98% of the offered advertising messages go unnoticed (Kroeber-Riel 1992). And the flood of information continues to rise: On the one hand, competition and the differentiation efforts of providers cause corresponding information. On the other hand, the multitude of carrier media and their providers promote information diversity and information duplications, with an increasing tendency in the internet age. Since the number of transmitted information continues to increase significantly, the volume of unnoticed information will also continue to increase. Thus, communication policy remains committed to the **struggle for perception and emotional conditioning.** However, the reactions of the information receivers to this are as understandable as they are disappointing for the senders: information intake and processing are becoming increasingly superficial and fleeting, and interest in information on the customer side is declining even further (Bruhn 2019b, p. 26 f.; Meffert et al. 2019, p. 96; Kühlmann et al. 2003, pp. 202 f.).

14.2 Tools of Communication Policy

Externally oriented, i.e., towards the customer, communication (understood as a communication mix) includes the sub-tools advertising, sales promotion, personal selling, direct marketing, digital communication, event marketing, sponsoring, and public relations. In addition, communication takes place within the company and between it and its (sales) partners, among other things to support external communication (= internal communication).

In practice, people talk about communication tools above-the-line and below-the-line: **Above-the-line** tools include traditional advertising measures such as TV, radio, cinema, newspaper, and outdoor advertising; all other, new communication tools belong to the **below-the-line** tools (Meffert et al. 2019, p. 654).

14.2.1 Advertising

The advertising as a communication tool with the aim of influencing potential demanders is carried out without personal contact via media, which the advertiser designs and uses entirely at their own discretion. In the insurance industry, advertising is directed at sales partners or (potential) customers.

▶ **Advertising** is the systematic dissemination of information and messages against a performance-related fee with the aim of simultaneously generating attention among a large number of people being courted, informing them, and steering their attitudes and behaviors.

The overarching **task** of advertising is to prepare for purchase decisions. To this end, it provides information to potential and existing customers with the aim of triggering purchase interest. Thus, advertising is intended to win new customers, confirm existing customers in their purchase decision, and generally support the sales people in distribution (Bruhn 2022, p. 195).

Among the **characteristics** of advertising is that it is usually made for longer periods and a larger number of recipients. It takes place via various communication channels at a distance, i.e., impersonally. Due to the use of various media as advertising means, it is also referred to as media advertising. In contrast to personal selling, advertising is a public form of communication with a wide reach. Its expressiveness through print types, music, sounds, and images is memorable, but may possibly distract from the actual sender or product. Ultimately, advertising remains one-sided and thus information, which makes it impersonal and therefore also non-binding (Bruhn 2019b, p. 333; Kühlmann et al. 2003, pp. 210 f.).

A classic **type of advertising** is print advertising with texts and images. This includes newspapers, general interest magazines, trade magazines, supplements (= inserts), advertising papers, or customer magazines. Equally important is television and cinema advertising, which combines language, sound, and image. In contrast, radio advertising relies only on language and sound, but has a very high reach: On average, almost 80% of the population listen to the radio daily, with a German citizen spending four hours a day in front of the radio. Outdoor advertising (out-of-home media) includes poster advertising (posters, illuminated city light posters or electronic video boards, advertising columns, advertising towers), signage media (signs on bicycle racks, clocks, poles, etc.), vehicle advertising on cars, buses or trams, perimeter and jersey advertising, as well as so-called ambient media, which address the demander in his direct living environment, such as banners, floor graphics, mirror advertising, beverage coasters, etc. in publicly accessible facilities such as airports, (subway) stations, supermarkets, gastronomy or cultural institutions. Outdoor advertising can be used in a location-specific manner regionally and locally on the way to or at the point of sale, and especially modern out-of-home media follow the trend towards environment-related concepts (point of sales (PoS), station, airport) and the trend towards interaction (via email, SMS/MMS, internet address, Bluetooth, QR codes, image recognition apps, augmented reality apps) (Homburg 2020, p. 876; detailed in: Meffert et al. 2019, pp. 655–700).

Excursus on telephone advertising in the insurance industry

The annoying advertising calls (cold acquisition) for most consumers have prompted the national legislator to establish more restrictive regulations for telephone advertising with the law to combat unauthorized telephone advertising. This is generally to be welcomed, but it poses certain challenges for the insurance industry in maintaining relationships with their customers. The long-term service process requires—also in the course of the ongoing occasion review of changed risk situations—occasional telephone contact. This is possible if it primarily and predominantly involves the care of an existing customer. Since every contact can at least indirectly promote sales, it is necessary to check, based on the so-called "overweight theory", what the call primarily serves. If a consultation appointment is arranged or the customer is made aware of a new, better rate for him, this is in his interest and allowed. However, if the content of the conversation is a new product, this is advertising and prohibited without the customer's prior explicit permission (Lenz and Rabe 2010, p. 1541).

According to § 7 para. 1 sentence 1 of the Act Against Unfair Competition (**UWG**), any business action that unreasonably harasses a market participant is prohibited. Such unreasonable harassment is always to be assumed in the case of advertising with a **telephone call** to a consumer without their prior explicit consent (§ 7 para. 2 no. 2 UWG). Calls from an insurer or intermediary to existing customers can also be classified as unwanted advertising if changes, additions or expansions of existing contracts are discussed or a new contract is offered. In the case of the broker, measures by the insurance broker that serve the purpose of managing the customer's insurance contracts and supporting him in the event of a claim follow the broker contract with the customer and are therefore not advertising, but generally permissible as fulfillment of contractual secondary obligations.

According to case law, an explicit consent is understood to mean any declaration of intent that is made without coercion for the specific case and with knowledge of the facts. A declaration of consent within the framework of general terms and conditions (GTC) requires a separate declaration of consent that relates solely to consent to advertising. In the case of a declaration of consent via a website, an effective declaration only exists if the declarant has to actively click a box (opt-in), a pre-set tick is not sufficient. For private customers, telephone calls **without the prior consent of the person called are therefore generally not permissible**. Since October 1, 2021, consent to telephone advertising must also be documented in an appropriate form at the time of granting and kept for five years from the date of granting.

Advertising via other telemedia is generally not permissible according to § 7 para. 2 no. 3 UWG **unless the person concerned has previously consented to it**. An exception applies to email advertising if the entrepreneur has received the customer's email address in connection with the sale of his service, the entrepreneur uses the address for direct advertising for his own similar services, the customer has not objected to the use and the customer is clearly and explicitly pointed out at the time of collection of the address and with each use that he can object to the use at any time without incurring any costs other than the transmission costs according to the basic rates (§ 7 para. 3 no. 1–4 UWG). **Mail advertising** is **generally permissible**, as long as it does not prove to be an unreasonable nuisance (§ 7 para. 2 no. 1 UWG).

Even if it is generally not to be expected in existing and functioning business relationships that satisfied customers will make a fine distinction between contract administration and business expansion during calls, it is nevertheless advisable to obtain a voluntary, clear and understandable declaration of consent from all customers for all or possibly individual telemedia in the long term and to permanently store this in the customer file (Sandkühler 2022).

Increasingly important is **online advertising** via websites on the World Wide Web (WWW): This includes integrated ads (= banners, which are usually linked to the provider's website), new-window-ads (= advertising windows such as pop-ups and interstitials, which appear additionally or temporarily replacing in the window and contain advertising messages), layer-ads (= ads that lie a level above the content page and are independent of scrolling on it) as well as search engine advertising, where an advertising company purchases advertising spaces that appear in connection with certain terms, or the placement in the list. Online advertising offers individualization options, advertising success control and a direct introduction to the conclusion, but only reaches selected user layers. Similar to TV advertising, it is increasingly clicked away with increasing advertising penetration and amount of information (Homburg 2020, pp. 888–891; Meffert et al. 2019, pp. 702–718).

Mobile marketing stands for marketing activities via mobile devices such as mobile phones: In the push variant, the advertiser contacts the individuals of the target group via SMS or MMS, in the pull variant he makes them aware through hints in other media to participate in information or actions by reacting via mobile medium. Direct marketing can also be understood as a subform of advertising, as long as it is one-sided from the advertiser to the recipient: This includes advertising letters, advertising postcards, mailings, faxes or emails (Homburg 2020, pp. 816 f., 819).

As part of the **advertising strategy**, several sub-decisions have to be made (Fig. 14.1): These decisions concern

- Advertising objectives,
- Target groups, advertising object and target area,
- Determination of advertising budgets,
- Creation of the advertising message,
- Media planning and
- Control of advertising effectiveness.

In the course of **setting advertising objectives, sales effect objectives** and communicative effect objectives can be distinguished. The former include, for example, increasing sales, profits and market shares, opening up the market for new insurance branches (e.g. dog insurance), supporting new sales channels ("pre-sale") or direct sales, compensating for or reacting to seasonal or regional fluctuations, and building a company or product brand; they are thus sales-oriented. **Communicative effect objectives** include increasing awareness and recall value, improving the company image, increasing product knowledge and confirming the customer's purchase; they aim, in contrast to the sales-related ones, more at influencing the perception of (non-)customers (Kotler et al. 2007, p. 704).

The determination of advertising objectives is closely linked to the **target groups** of advertising. These can, but do not have to, coincide with market segments, because the advertising approach can consciously target larger circles such as influencers of the

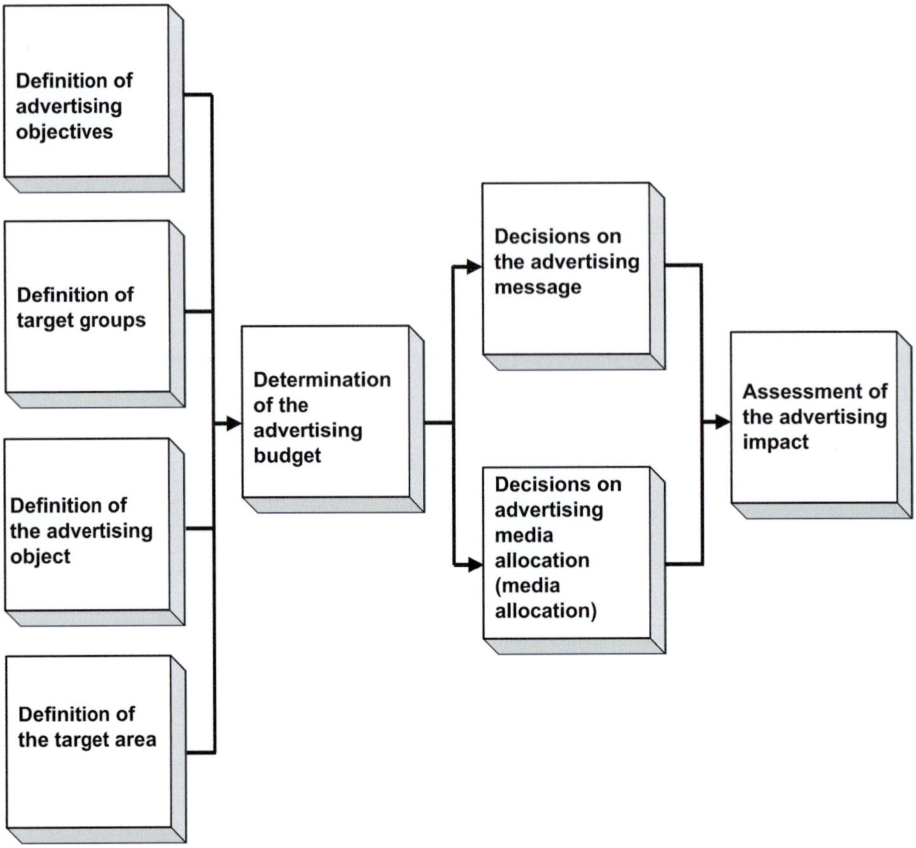

Fig. 14.1 Decisions on advertising strategy. (Based on Kotler et al. 2007, p. 702)

actual clientele. For a more precise definition and determination of the target groups, see Sect. 8.3.1.2. Derived from advertising objectives and target groups, the concrete **media objectives** are to be determined. They answer the question of what and to what extent is to be achieved through media planning. The two main media objectives are reach and advertising pressure. Reach expresses how many people in the target group should be contacted by the advertising, advertising pressure indicates how often this should happen (Meffert et al. 2019, pp. 792 f.).

Regarding the **object of advertising**, different levels of aggregation can be distinguished, which are also different distances from the actual sales act (point of sale) (Fig. 14.2). Industry-wide advertising (collective advertising) applies to the entire insurance industry, serves to promote the industry image compared to other industries, and is primarily placed by industry associations such as the GDV. Corporate resp. image advertising essentially serves to build and strengthen a corporate brand, i.e., the promotion of awareness and image. More specific is the actual product advertising, which can focus

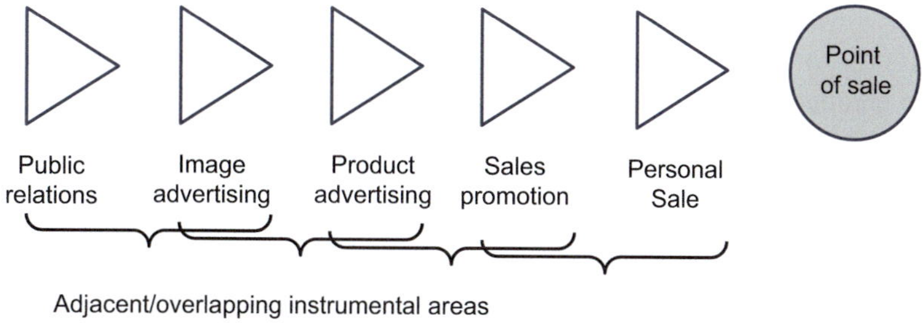

Fig. 14.2 Public relations, advertising, sales promotion, and personal sales and their proximity to the PoS. (Based on Puschmann 2003, p. 179)

on branches, target group solutions, or individual product brands. Sales promotion tools are already used in the sales act, and personal sales have the most direct effect at the point of sale.

Finally, the **target area** and the **period** of the advertising measures need to be determined (Meffert et al. 2019, pp. 805–809). This usually involves the regional extent, which can range from the neighborhood to the city, region, state, cross-country economic areas, to international, worldwide presence, which ultimately results from the insurer's business fields. The period of the advertising measures is related to the object of advertising: image advertising is essentially timeless, whereas advertising for motor vehicle insurance is time-bound and oriented towards the end-of-year switching business.

John Wanamaker, the department store king of Philadelphia, is said to have once said: "I know that half of my advertising is wasted, but unfortunately I don't know exactly which half it is." (quoted in: Kotler et al. 2017a, p. 711). In insurance companies, as in other companies, the approved **advertising budget** is fought for year after year, and the responsible board member is in need of explanation as to how he arrives at the amount of his advertising budget and what exactly it achieves. In this regard, there are **various approaches** (Kotler et al. 2017a, p. 711 f.; Homburg 2020, pp. 833–835):

An **orientation towards value or volume of sales** means that the largest departments or highest-selling products get the highest advertising budgets; in the case of an **orientation towards profit**, this applies accordingly to the areas with the highest profit. On the one hand, this is understandable and practical. On the other hand, it means investing in the future based on the past and ignoring market cycles, and—in the case of sales orientation—neglecting economic success. Pragmatic and therefore also practiced by one or the other insurer is an **orientation towards available financial resources**. However, there is a risk here of not advertising in times of economic downturn or crisis, thus not investing in the future and thereby exacerbating the situation.

The **orientation towards the budget of the previous period** is the result of an annual budget planning and the distribution battle for the available budget. This procedure is apparently simpler or time-saving, but not very economical. This "freezes" conditions and priorities. Moreover, this procedure does not encourage resource-saving handling, because not exhausting the budget would lead to cuts in the next year. Finally, this logic makes it difficult to invest in new areas and accompany growth spurts. The **orientation towards competition** is another, quite practiced procedure. This is due to the fact that the budget applicant often argues to the board that the budget size correlates with market presence, i.e., the competition would be more present there with a smaller budget. Economically, however, this is at best a reference point and should not be the sole benchmark. Ideally, the **orientation** of the advertising budget is towards the **advertising goals and tasks** of the insurer. But even this approach has its limits in terms of the amount of the available advertising budget. Therefore, a **mix of different procedures** is sensible, for example, an orientation of the advertising budget towards the advertising goals and tasks while at the same time capping the amount of the available budget. In this context, there will (must)—by the nature of the matter—always be negotiation processes between marketing and other departments.

In **Germany**, according to the Central Association of the German Advertising Industry (ZAW) and the Association of Private Media (VAUNET), total investments, which include fees, production, and media costs, amounted to approximately 36.2 billion € in 2022. Of this, around 25.7 billion € were attributable to the net advertising revenues of the media. Internet search (search engine placement) was the advertising medium with the highest net advertising revenues, at around 5.35 billion €. The display ads segment, including social networks, was in second place with around 5.2 billion €. Television advertising ranked third with more than 4.02 billion € (VAUNET 2023, p. 11). In 2020, around 6.8 million commercials were broadcast on German television; this number has slightly decreased compared to the previous year, but has almost tripled compared to 2002. In 2020, around 3.15 million minutes of TV advertising minutes were broadcast. Since 2009, the total number of advertising minutes has been continuously increasing and reached a record value. However, it should be noted that the number of channels evaluated has increased over the period (Central Association of the German Advertising Industry e. V. (2021a, b)).

An important decision in advertising strategy is the one about the **advertising message**. Insurers advertise a product that corresponds to an actual, rationally justifiable need: the protection of economic existence from the threat of unpredictable events and influences. The development of a specific advertising message must be aligned with this fact. An advertising message must also be desirable, distinct, and credible in order to ignite its effect. In the course of creating the specific advertising message, the following questions need to be clarified (Kotler and Bliemel 1999, pp. 940–945; similarly in Bruhn 2022, p. 199):

- What should be said? (Content of the message)
- Which motives should be chosen? (Appeal of the message)
- How can it be said in a coherent way? (Structure of the message)
- How can it be symbolically expressed? (Form of expression of the message)
- Who should say it? (Messenger of the message)

In relation to insurers, the content could, for example, address the benefits of risk prevention, support in the event of damage, or enabling activities through risk assumption. Appeals can aim to awaken needs or perceive risks, i.e., emotionally connect to the motive of security or desires for freedom. The **structure** of the message should follow the **KISS** rule (= keep it simple and short). A striking example of this is the former Allianz slogan "An Alliance for life". The form of expression of the message should symbolically express it. Nouns are useful in this regard due to their size, conciseness, and brevity, e.g., insurance, provision, assets. However, this combination is not distinct, as various financial services providers have used it and it is associated with many providers. Apart from words, information surrogates (= substitute information) such as symbols (e.g., rock in the surf of Württembergische, shield of HUK-Coburg) are suitable. The messengers of the message are usually professional, anonymous speakers and actors, sometimes also public figures, who are referred to as testimonials, e.g., Jürgen Klopp for DVAG, Dieter Bohlen, Til Schweiger and Barbara Schöneberger for VHV (Kotler et al. 2017a, pp. 707 f.; see Marketing Highlight in this chapter).

Marketing Highlight VHV:
Use of Testimonials using the Example of VHV Versicherungen
The VHV Allgemeine Versicherung, with around 2.5 billion € in gross earned premiums in 2022, is one of the (larger) medium-sized insurers in the German insurance market. It operates almost all branches of property & casualty insurance (except legal expenses insurance) and primarily relies on the distribution channel of independent intermediaries (brokers) (VHV Group 2023).

In the initial situation in 2007, the key question for VHV was: How can a medium-sized insurer with a small media budget and traditional broker distribution successfully make a mark in the market? After all, VHV's share of advertising in the financial services sector in 2007 was about one percent. The market shares in motor vehicle insurance, on the other hand, were four percent. VHV was an "unknown giant".

Brand positioning and communication strategy
Due to the heterogeneous target groups of brokers and end customers, as well as the limited media budget, VHV's brand appearance had to create a common communicative platform: In the sense of a dual strategy, it was necessary to generate more push among the intermediaries and more pull among the customers at the same time. In doing so, VHV positioned itself as an insurance expert, like the independent brokers, and formulated the performance promise "Insured by experts" (claim). The communication strategy followed a so-called fact-based strategy and decision-making process. Accordingly, VHV first sought reliable answers to the question of which factors have the strongest leverage effects for sales, together with the communication and media agency and through market research. Using a sales modeling approach (multivariate regression analysis), which takes into account a multitude of influencing factors that explain a new conclusion, it was determined, among other things, that brand awareness is directly significant for increasing new business. It thus became the pivot of the communicative and economic objectives, which followed the following hierarchy:

1. Increase in new business,
2. Expansion of brand awareness,
3. Expansion of advertising recall.

Testimonial with great leverage

In its advertising strategy, VHV therefore committed to an effective mechanism: Testimonial strengthens advertising recall strengthens brand awareness. Properly staged, a prominent testimonial can act as a communicative attention lever to increase brand awareness. In the selection of testimonials Dieter Bohlen (2009–2015), Til Schweiger (2015–2021) and currently Barbara Schöneberger, VHV aimed high. They all belong to the most famous Germans. The fact that they also polarize has been evaluated as an additional anchor for awareness and brand loyalty. To increase the impact of the testimonials for the brand, TV spots for the different VHV insurance offers—from accident to third-party private liability to motor vehicle insurance—were tailored to the respective person. The VHV testimonials are not the classic "hero" who proclaims a product unimaginatively. On the contrary, as a VHV testimonial, they play the role of a prominent injured party in quirky-humorous episodes. The selection of scenes followed a balance between story content (insurance product) and leverage (testimonial presence) (Figs. 14.3 and 14.4).

Vampire effect: Advertising for the testimonial or for the brand?

When using a testimonial, there is always the risk for the advertising brand that the testimonial overshadows the brand and thus works against the intended effect. This so-called classic vampire effect is addressed on two levels: On the one hand, the testimonials are an important part of the story, but the focus is not directed exclusively at them as in a presenter format. On the other hand, a clearer branding and a strongly standardized structure (Visual Design + Music + Sequence of Scenes) strengthen the brand transfer in the overall system of VHV's marketing communication.

Fig. 14.3 Print advertising towards brokers with testimonial and product information. (VHV Allgemeine Versicherung AG)

Fig. 14.4 TV commercial with Barbara Schöneberger. (VHV Allgemeine Versicherung AG)

Through a multitude of small optimizations, the celebrities are further developed into brand testimonials in the system of marketing communication. The basic strategy is never abandoned; the performance promise, the brand values, and the important structural elements of brand management form the long-term basis of the brand. And integrated market development ensures that the operational efficiency of marketing communication remains permanently high (Fig. 14.5).

Success Measurement
Since 2007, VHV's brand awareness has increased by more than 100%—with almost unchanged budget. The dynamics of brand awareness become visible from quarter 2/2009, with the start of the Dieter campaign (Fig. 14.6). The strong increase in VHV´s brand awareness until 2016 and the maintenance of brand values at the achieved level is even more impressive when considering the (below-average) and almost constant media budget over the years and the massive media inflation of recent years.

Due to the strong development in brand awareness and the continuously increased communicative leverage of the testimonials, VHV's products have been noticeably better perceived in the market. This has also had a demonstrably positive effect on brokers. For example, in the motor vehicle insurance market, the product preference for VHV in Q1/2023 was about 35.4% of the brokers surveyed—an increase of 5.3 percentage points since 2007. Thus, VHV has been able to further expand its already large lead over the competition; the second-placed insurer reached 12.6%.

Conclusion: Continuity of brand management is important
The example of VHV underlines that building brand awareness is an investment that must be considered in the long term. Especially in a highly competitive market environment, it is of central importance for a smaller, quality-oriented brand like VHV to rely on its own strengths and to communicate them consistently. The example also shows that success can be achieved with a rather small advertising budget if a holistic picture is obtained regarding brand and communication goals. The focus is then on the right variables, which not only influence image dimensions but are also

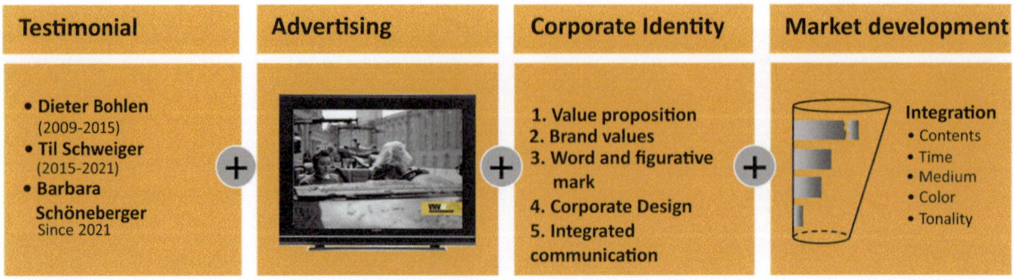

Fig. 14.5 System of VHV's marketing communication. (VHV Allgemeine Versicherung AG)

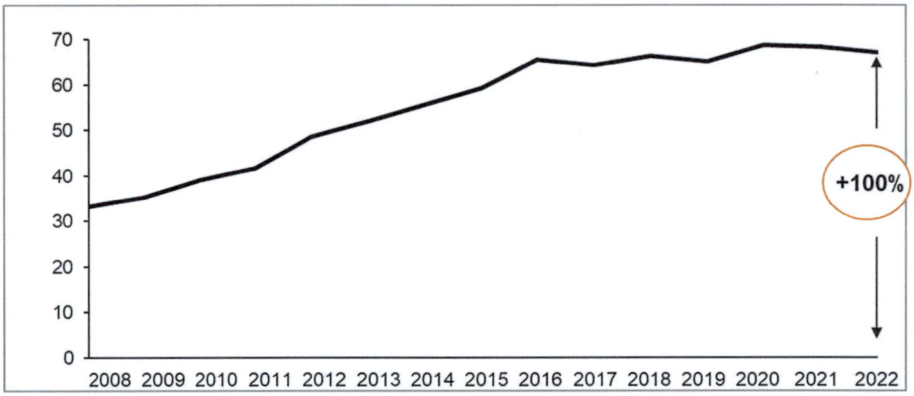

Fig. 14.6 Prompted brand awareness of VHV in the period 2008–2022 (in %). (VHV Allgemeine Versicherung AG)

clearly aimed at economic growth. The key lies in the intelligent use of the available data material and research methods. Thus, VHV's sales modeling not only defined the communicative target variable but also plays a central role in marketing planning. An elaborate approach that seems to pay off and also promotes close exchange between the company and the important service providers of communication and media agency as well as market research.

Sources:

- VHV Allgemeine Versicherung AG, Central Sales Development and Marketing Department.
- VHV Group (2023).

In **media planning,** it's about selecting suitable advertising media and determining the timing of advertising activities in the individual media. The individual advertising media have already been presented above in connection with the types of advertising. Media planning takes into account, as mentioned, the reach, frequency, and impression quality, i.e., an estimate of the strength of the attention generated by the individual media in determining the media to be used for an advertising strategy. Reach is important, for example, when introducing new products, frequency in the case of an immediate "advertising battle" with competitors (e.g., among direct insurers during the motor vehicle insurance switching season), with complex advertising messages and with products with high or cyclical purchase frequency (e.g., situational insurance, travel insurance).

In the course of **media type selection**, it's about the basic selection and weighting between the various media types such as electronic advertising media (TV, radio, cinema, teletext, video boards), print media (newspapers, consumer and trade magazines), outdoor advertising (posters, sign media, transport advertising, ambient media) and new digital advertising media (online advertising of all kinds). The subsequent detailed media selection serves the concrete selection and determination of individual, as target group-specific, cost-effective and yet effective advertising media in the selected media types. Decisive criteria are the cost per thousand contacts (= price to establish 1000 contacts with advertising recipients), for online advertising also the page views, page usage, session duration and the click-through rate as well as the target group accuracy, the intensity with which contact persons deal with the advertising medium (recall) and the editorial environment (image of the advertising medium, emotional world of the recipient). Finally, the **timing of media use** takes place: The macro planning takes into account seasonal and cyclical influences, the micro planning distributes the advertising expenditures within a short period of time (Kotler et al. 2017a, p. 735–742).

In the **insurance market**, the advertising volume over the period from July 2021 to June 2022 was around 850 million € across all sub-markets. Of this, a considerable 29% went into the product category health insurance (statutory and private health insurers, supplementary health, long-time care and supplementary long-time care). In comparison of the 15 analyzed sub-markets, the health/long-time care sector not only recorded the highest spendings, but also the highest absolute increase of over 20 million € compared to the previous year. The previous top product category motor vehicle insurance fell to rank two in the volume ranking after a decline to 20.7% of the advertising spendings. The third largest category was, as in previous years, image advertising (without direct product reference) with 13%. The concentration of expenditure in the insurance advertising market varies greatly depending on the sub-market: In the product categories motor vehicle and health insurance, there was a rather low concentration among a comparatively high number of strong advertising providers, which still resulted in about 50% of all advertising expenditures being accounted for by the three strongest spenders. Regarding the media type, TV and internet dominated as in previous years: 60% of the advertising expenditures were spent on television, almost 30% on internet advertising. The remaining categories (out-of-home, radio, newspaper, magazines) together accounted for less than ten percent. Also in the examined period, the traditionally most advertising-intensive months of October and November were the strongest (Matzner 2022).

The **evaluation of advertising measures** or the advertising effect can refer to economic and non-economic success: Economic success factors would be, for example, advertising revenue and advertising profit, achieved sales increase, market share increase or the increase in the number of customers. However, since these sizes cannot be directly derived from or related to advertising measures, they are—with the exception of certain advertising activities in the online area—difficult to measure due to unclear attributability. As a substitute, psychological advertising goals are often used, the achievement of which can be measured much better. These include awareness, sympathy, recognition, recall, building internal images or attitude effects (Kotler et al. 2011, p. 861; similarly Kotler et al. 2017a, p. 736–738).

14.2.2 Sales Promotion

The **high importance** of sales promotion in the insurance industry follows from the important role of the distribution of insurance products. Sales promotion occupies an intermediate position between sales and advertising, as it directly supports personal sales and—in the case of prior advertising—picks up advertising messages and external presentation again. It can be said that advertising pulls the customer to the product, while sales promotion pushes the product to the customer.

▶ **Sales Promotion** encompasses the analysis, planning, implementation, and monitor of temporary activities aimed at achieving a company's communication and sales objectives through additional incentives at downstream sales levels.

(Bruhn 2019b, p. 342)

Target groups are the **sales partners** (intermediary or sales force promotions through sales partner meetings, training, and competitions) as well as the **(potential) customers** (customer promotion through brochures, sweepstakes, coupon campaigns, product presentations). The sales partners (e.g., agencies) can also initiate sales promotion measures themselves (store design, websites, service actions, lectures).

The **objectives** of sales-promoting activities are to draw the customer's attention to the product, to offer incentives to the seller or customer, and to trigger an **activation to purchase**. They are intended to support the sale of a product directly—in contrast to advertising. They take place at the point of sale or refer to the incentive design of an entire sales organization.

In the insurance industry, important **sales promotion tools** include customer brochures (= product flyers), sales aids for intermediaries with the most important sales arguments (= sales folders), displays in agencies (= standees), window decorations, product-related documents (application, GIC; see in detail Sect. 10.2.1), promotional gifts, and finally—very important for the consulting and application recording process—IT-based expert systems are used. In the online area, customer-oriented apps are added, with the help of which the user can make calculations, obtain price information, and manage contracts.

Sales promotion takes place in three ways (Farny 2011, p. 738; Kühlmann et al. 2003, pp. 212–215):

1. **Promotion of the intermediary** (push strategy): These measures relate to the qualification and motivation of intermediaries. This starts with support in obtaining the (legally) required proof of expertise and the equally required further education. With regard to the product, it is about basic training and ongoing further education as well as ongoing information (e.g., at trade fairs), with regard to sales, it is about sales training, sales meetings (annual kick-off events), and competitions.
2. **Promotion of sales:** This includes merchandising offers that support the intermediary at the point of sale, such as displays, stickers, shop windows, and promotional gifts, as well as prepared mailings to existing customers (direct mailing) and pre-designed agency websites. In addition, all types of brochures (product flyers, image flyers, application forms, sales folders, etc.) directly promote sales. Finally, other actions such as an open house or lecture activities can promote sales.
3. **Promotion of the customer** (pull strategy): This involves activating the customer to conclude a contract. Corresponding measures are information (on new laws, provision possibilities, risks, etc.), customer magazines or newsletters, coupon campaigns, giveaways, or joint actions with other companies in annex distribution.

Evaluation: Not every insurer can afford advertising, but every insurer carries out sales promotion to a considerable extent. The otherwise intangible insurance product requires concretization by the intermediaries and the corresponding accompanying documents. Information, whether in flyers, information brochures, or on display walls, is important to convey company and product quality to the customer. In the private customer sector, insurance is usually sold and not bought, so promoting this sales process is of eminent importance. In addition, sales promotion activities support the conclusion of insurance contracts more directly compared to advertising and largely evade direct comparability with the competition.

14.2.3 Personal Selling

Given what has been said, it should be self-evident that personal selling, along with sales promotion, represents the **most important communication tool in insurance**. Its central **task** is to awaken and subsequently satisfy the existing, latent **need** in potential customers according to their circumstances.

In terms of communication, it is characterized—in contrast to advertising, which is one-sided and impersonal—by **two-way, personal communication** between the seller and the (potential) customer, whether face-to-face, over the phone, or via image and sound communication on a computer or smartphone. In complex sales situations, personal selling is significantly more effective than advertising and sales promotion. An agent can identify a customer's problems and state of mind, adapt the offer and communication to their specific requirements, and build a long-term and personal relationship with a customer (Kotler et al. 2022, p. 759). The **proximity to the customer** and the possibility of personal interaction, especially with insurance products, allow the complex, often incomprehensible and explanation-needing service value promise to be explained to the customer, answering questions and eliminating uncertainties. Thus, personal selling is a valuable tool for **reducing the** comparatively **large purchase uncertainty** that arises from the credence-based nature of insurance. The price for this is its not immediate controllability by the insurer (Kühlmann et al. 2003, p. 215).

In the service and insurance sector, the human being as a communication medium takes on a significant role anyway, as he is usually both the communicator and the service provider. The challenge, however, is to integrate personal selling with advertising statements, direct marketing actions, and especially sales promotion, and to achieve and control the required quality in this respect (Meffert et al. 2018, pp. 328 f.).

Evaluation: Personal selling is like no other communication tool in building trust, because it allows for a dialogue with the customer—in the case of the intermediary, face-to-face. This makes the otherwise abstract insurance service tangible and gives it a face. This can happen throughout the entire service process and does not have to be limited to the time of mediation. The advantages are offset by the comparatively high costs: An intermediary (or telephone service employee) can only conduct a limited number of conversations, and the quality of communication is more difficult to check the further the communicator operates from the company headquarters.

14.2.4 Direct Marketing

Direct marketing—not to be confused with direct sales—aims to **initiate** an **immediate dialogue through direct contact with the addressee** or to create the basis for it through indirect address. It traditionally uses correspondence, but increasingly also emails and telephone contact (see also the excursus on telephone advertising in Sect. 14.2.1). Direct marketing is rather standardized, designed for mass processing and directed towards the recipient. Its effectiveness and efficiency are promoted by database management (= the systematic recording, processing and analysis of various target group characteristics in so-called databases), as this creates the prerequisite for targeted scattering activities. However, database management requires more consistent customer-related data collection than before, systematic storage of this data in data warehouses, and evaluation using appropriate tools, which are then used for communication activities. Insurers have (theoretically) collected extensive customer data through the data recorded in the application, but often only partially incorporated this into their portfolio management systems, so that they are also only partially evaluable (Becker 2019, p. 633; Swift 2001, pp. 123–168).

In view of the risk of customer reactance to direct marketing activities, according to the idea of permission marketing, people who have expressed opposition to being contacted (e.g., by entry in negative lists such as the "Robinson List" and the list of the German Direct Marketing Association) should not be contacted (Homburg 2020, pp. 896–898). Apart from that, data protection law must be observed here—as with all data-based marketing actions.

▶ **Direct Marketing** includes all communicative activities that serve to initiate and maintain a direct, personalized interaction with current and potential customers; the interaction can also take place at different times.

(Meffert et al. 2019, p. 755)

Evaluation: The advantages of direct marketing activities lie in the targeted management, uniform quality over the entire information dispatch (= flight), the relatively low costs and the good controllability of success. However, they need to be very well coordinated with the entire communication mix. They should either directly support the work of the decentralized intermediators—in the sense of a sales promotion action—relieve them of certain tasks (e.g., information about new offers) or at least not impair or compete with them, for example by being directed only at customer bases that are not "processed" anyway. Otherwise, there is a risk that such activities will cause uneasiness in sales and be counterproductive.

14.2.5 Digital Communication

If one understands **digital communication** as all communication activities between companies and demanders as well as between demanders themselves, which are based on digital information and communication technologies, it is logical to subsume the communication tools **online communication, mobile communication and social media communication** under digital communication (see Meffert et al. 2019, Sect. 4.3). Today, companies have numerous communication possibilities in this area. However, the use of digital communication tools is associated with its own challenges, which result from the specific properties of digital communication processes. These include the immediate and direct feedback option of the message recipient and the resulting interaction possibilities. This results in a tendentially heterarchical communication structure, i.e., both the sender and receiver can change, as can the respective instruments within the media. In addition, some of the information is only provided by the companies and must be actively requested by demanders, while other information is directed directly at the demanders. Digital communication has a high temporal topicality and is globally available. Finally, it can offer various media formats at the same time (hypermediality) and, for example, provide information in the form of text, sound, image and/or film, so that the user can choose the presentation he prefers (Meffert et al. 2019, p. 701).

Even though the three more modern communication tools of online, mobile and social media communication are now presented separately, it is obvious that they are—not only technologically—very strongly connected and networked in their use.

The **online communication** utilizes the possibilities of all previously described communication tools and **combines online advertising, online sales promotion, and direct marketing using internet technology** (instead of conventional technology such as host computers, client/server systems, or Electronic Data Interchange (EDI)). Due to the technologically uniform standard, the processing via the Internet Protocol (IP), it promotes networking between partners and their communication.

▶ **Online Communication** includes all communication activities between companies and demanders, which influence the achievement of marketing and corporate goals and are processed via the Internet Protocol (IP).

(Meffert et al. 2019, p. 702)

Online communication therefore includes all communicative marketing activities that the internet supports online or even makes possible in the first place. From a company's perspective, these are traditionally **tools** such as the company and intermediary homepage, email marketing (newsletters), all tools of online advertising (see under advertising), search engine marketing and search engine optimization, as well as networking to platforms, discussion forums, and portals (Meffert et al. 2019, p. 730 f.; Homburg 2020, p. 888 f.).

For online communication, as for any communication with the customer, it should be designed to be recipient-friendly. In contrast to personal interaction, a website generally cannot respond individually to the user; he is left to his own devices in interpreting what he sees and reads. Especially then, it is important to pick him up at his typical behavioral patterns or heuristics and to consider these, if sensible, in communication, i.e., to refer to behavioral economic findings (Sect. 4.2 and guest contribution in Sect. 5.4). The Versicherungskammer Bayern has been doing this for several years to an increasing extent (see marketing highlight in this chapter).

Marketing Highlight Versicherungskammer:
Behavioral Economics in the Marketing Practice of Konzern Versicherungskammer

The Konzern Versicherungskammer is a multi-line insurer. It is the largest public insurer nationwide and the seventh largest primary insurer in Germany.

With a total of 11 insurers and three regional brands (Versicherungskammer Bayern, Feuersozietät Berlin Brandenburg, and SAARLAND Versicherungen), the group is the "insurer of the regions". In the health, long-term care, and travel insurance business, it operates nationwide. It also cooperates with some Allgemeine Ortskrankenkasse (AOK). In direct sales, the Konzern Versicherungskammer operates nationwide as a municipal and agricultural insurer and in online business with BavariaDirekt (Konzern Versicherungskammer2023).

Behavioral economic approaches were gradually established in the group's marketing over three years ago. The following exemplarily demonstrates how selected behavioral economic mechanisms are used in marketing practice today. Other approaches pursued in the group, for example in product development or behavioral pricing, are not discussed here.

Significance of Behavioral Economics in Marketing Practice

Neuromarketing has been applied in many industries, especially in retail, for many years. Behavioral economics is still a relatively young subfield in economics. It has gained a lot of attention in recent years, but so far it has not been able to find comparable resonance.

The reason for this is on the one hand the too low level of knowledge about the topic of behavioral economics, because many companies have not yet dealt intensively enough with this approach. On the other hand, the topic is simply not given enough importance, which is why no adequate training and further education of marketers is provided (Ackermann et al. 2020, p. 50 f.).

However, when one looks at market changes, it becomes clear that the use of behavioral economics for marketing is currently, and not just in the future, groundbreaking (see also Sect. 4.2 and guest contribution in Sect. 5.4). Because the world is changing: analog and digital are merging. This also changes people's needs, who long for high-touch in an increasingly anonymous high-tech world, for personalization. Whoever understands this development holds the key to success in their hands (Kotler et al. 2017b, p. 12). Behavioral economics deals precisely with this topic and can, when applied correctly, significantly influence the path to success.

Customer-Centric Marketing

The Versicherungskammer has been focusing on customer satisfaction for years. The basis for the orientation towards a consistent customer-centric view was the establishment of a group-wide customer satisfaction measurement system. The contact point-related and continuous measurement of customer satisfaction allows processes, working methods, and tools to be viewed from the customer's perspective and activities to be taken if dissatisfaction exists.

The company's internal customer barometer measures customer satisfaction at all relevant private customer contacts (e.g., claims settlement, consultation, or contract change) and brings the voice of the customer into the company with over 100,000 feedbacks annually. With the insights from the customer barometer, the customer experience is continuously improved and at the same time, a mindset for stronger customer centricity is created among the employees. The Versicherungskammer is breaking new ground and trying to make predictions about customer satisfaction using predictive data models—and this at a time when the customer has not yet formed a final judgment.

The insights about the customer, i.e., which aspects are important to him (fairness, appreciation, transparency, etc.) directly show the interface to behavioral economics. Behavioral economics can be effectively used in direct customer contact, among other things.

The Versicherungskammer therefore uses the approach of behavioral economics in addition to classical empirical market research. Because the better a company understands its customers and knows the purchase-deciding criteria, the more it knows which levers need to be set in motion to support customers in making informed and positive decisions for them.

Building Capabilities

To successfully establish behavioral economics in an organization or department, the systematic development of theoretical and practical skills is crucial. However, the topic of behavioral economics is too complex to train all employees as complete experts. Therefore, the marketing department of Versicherungskammer has chosen a very specific approach:

By forming expert core clusters that act as pioneers, the knowledge can be spread throughout the rest of the marketing department and all employees can be sensitized to the principles of behavioral economics. At the same time, it is not to be neglected that everyone at least knows the basics and has internalized the mindset.

Behavioral economics is now part of the internal further education concept of the marketing department, which serves to train employees in various formats and on various work-relevant topics. In a first step, all marketing employees were picked up in an online seminar on the basic knowledge of behavioral economics. In a second step, smaller (expert) groups were defined, which received more in-depth training or workshops on the behavioral economics approach. The circle of experts, for example, practiced the use of behavioral economics on very specific examples from marketing practice in a workshop with external specialists. The content included, among other things, the revision of a customer flyer according to behavioral economics aspects, which was then introduced and tested as a pilot.

In addition to this approach, the knowledge is also spread throughout the entire group through lectures. A suitable training program is currently even being developed in the marketing department for this purpose. In addition, bridges are being built to external partners. Because this not only strengthens networking in the field of behavioral economics but also promotes internal expertise through the exchange of best practices across company boundaries.

Application of Skills

After more than three years, the topic of behavioral economics has firmly established itself in the marketing department of the Versicherungskammer. It is now even considered a tool of the marketer. Because it is and remains an approach that has proven itself in its application. How exactly is exemplified by five examples from the marketing practice of the regional brand Versicherungskammer Bayern (VKB):

To successfully integrate behavioral economics on the websites, a separate study examined unused potentials in the customer journey, identified need dimensions, and uncovered barriers or decision bottlenecks when concluding various products online. The result is an optimized page concept for the product websites with a uniform structure and the use of firmly defined behavior patterns such as "Trust Bias", "Zeigarnik Effect", and "Social Proof".

Behavior Pattern are standardized behavior patterns that everyone carries within themselves and that underlie the majority of decisions made. There are now over 120 scientifically validated behavior patterns that "predict" our decision-making behavior (Spreer 2021, p. 27).

The **behavior pattern "Trust Bias"** (trust influences our judgment) (Spreer 2021, p. 116) describes the insight that trust is the basis for considering the purchase of a product at all.

This insight is particularly applicable in the context of insurance conclusion. Because it requires a high degree of trust to place the protection against losses or the security of one's own future in the hands of an insurer. In case of a loss, the customer wants to be able to rely on the insurance partner to handle this loss and to provide additional support. To create this basis of trust, trust-building elements are integrated into the website of the Versicherungskammer Bayern, among

Fig. 14.7 Trust-building facts about VKB. (Versicherungskammer, Corporate Marketing Department)

other things. At first glance, they are just a few numbers, but upon closer inspection, they convey that the Versicherungskammer Bayern is a competent, trustworthy partner (Fig. 14.7). And that's exactly what these numbers are supposed to trigger in customers: the emotion of trust.

The **"Zeigarnik Effect"** (we want to finish tasks we have started) (Spreer 2021, p. 281) describes that it is in human nature to want to finish things we have started. An unfinished process is perceived as unpleasant. One way to support customers in this is by visualizing a progress bar on the website (Fig. 14.8). Because a sales funnel, i.e., the purchasing process, often extends over several weeks. The reason is that many customers do not immediately conclude a purchase, but often hesitate and leave the website to inform themselves elsewhere or to reconsider the purchase. The art here is to cleverly pick up the potential customer at the last stage of leaving when they return to the website and to motivate them to conclude the contract with the right choice of words.

With the **behavior pattern "Social Proof"** (our judgment depends on the behavior of others) (Spreer 2021, p. 114), another support tool is used to facilitate a customer's decision-making process. Because if a customer does not know which decision to make when making a purchase, they orient themselves on the behavior of other people. For this reason, the Versicherungskammer Bayern has collected various regional customer statements and visualized them on the website through experience reports with quotes and pictures (Fig. 14.9).

In this way, two goals can be achieved at once: On the one hand, it helps uncertain customers in their decision-making process, and on the other hand, regional statements strengthen the brand positioning of the Versicherungskammer Bayern. Because this stands, among other things, for the value of regionalism, which is thus underlined.

Currently, the online marketing department of Versicherungskammer is also dealing with the optimization of online completion routes according to behavioral economics principles. A possible optimization potential is provided by the **pattern "Zero Risk Bias"** (the elimination of the last residual risk is very valuable to us) (Spreer 2021, p. 172), which is being tested with customers of Versicherungskammer Bayern using an A/B testing procedure. The pattern suggests that consumers tend to consider offers only when they perceive a low risk associated with them. If the customer is thus conveyed that there is no risk involved in taking out insurance, they are reinforced in their purchase decision.

This can be achieved, for example, by giving the customer the option to receive an offer first towards the end of the online completion route (Fig. 14.10). They can reconsider the conclusion of the insurance and decide for or against the purchase at a later point in time. This, in turn, reduces the perceived risk. The art here is to balance between an optimized conversion rate (the customer buys immediately) on the one hand and the zero risk bias on the other hand.

Ultimately, sVersicherungskammer Bayern was able to record a double-digit percentage increase in online completions last year through the use of behavioral economics on its websites.

Fig. 14.8 Visualization of the sales funnel. (Versicherungskammer, Corporate Marketing Department)

Fig. 14.9 Regional customer statements as a decision aid in insurance purchase. (Versicherungskammer, Corporate Marketing Department)

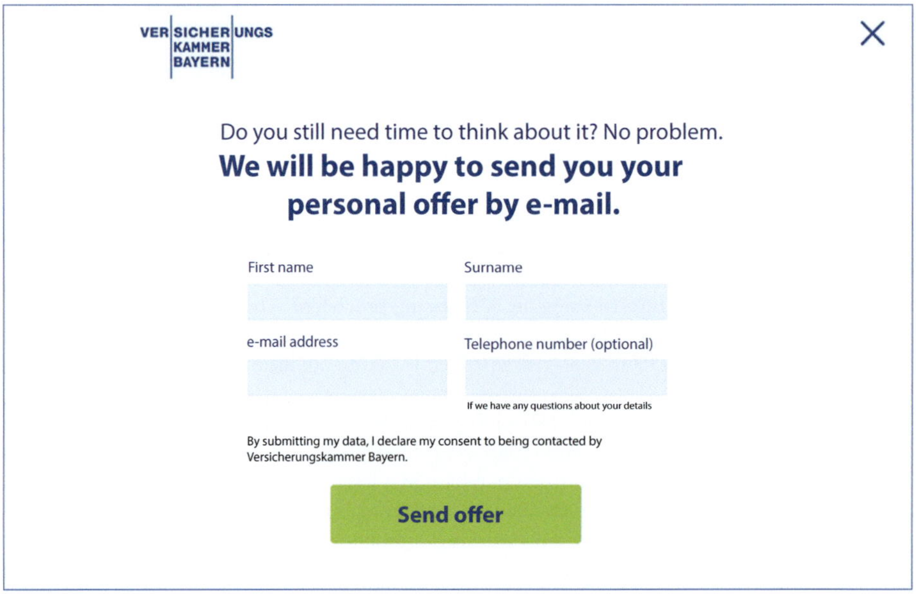

Fig. 14.10 Deferral option as a response to the zero risk bias. (Versicherungskammer, Corporate Marketing Department)

Of course, behavioral economics is not only used online, but also offline, such as in direct customer communication by letter.

The **pattern "Loss Aversion"** (losses hurt us more than gains please us) (Spreer 2021, p. 226) is addressed, for example, in a customer letter regarding a premium increase. In this sensitive issue, it is important to set the course correctly. Because such adjustments initially cause incomprehension and pain of loss in the customer. To counteract this, Versicherungskammer Bayern pursues a deactivation strategy in the corresponding letter through the formulation of good, understandable reasons for the price adjustment and the confirmation that the insurance coverage continues unchanged and there will be no restrictions in the event of a claim, such as:

- "Of course, we do everything to keep the premium adjustment as low as possible."
- "You don't have to worry about your insurance coverage at all."

The goal is to give customers a good feeling. After all, the aim is to be able to guarantee full insurance coverage in the future, even with rising claims costs.

The result: Customers feel demonstrably better taken care of, well informed. Conversations with customer advisors are subsequently more peaceful and solution-oriented, which supports customer loyalty and satisfaction.

The Responsibility of Marketing

Despite the many positive effects that the use of behavioral economics brings with it, it comes with a responsibility not to be underestimated. Because the degree between justifiable and dishonest influences is very narrow. The wrong handling of the approach can quickly lead to abuse. Not without reason do critics label the use of behavioral economics as ethically questionable.

Basically, it is the responsibility of the marketing department of the Versicherungskammer to ensure that the use of behavioral economics does not aim to manipulate or deceive customers. Rather, it must be about better understanding customers and helping them make informed decisions. The core concern must always be to support people in acting according to their own intentions or to their own advantage.

If this is taken into account, the use of nudges, i.e., small incentives, is unproblematic. However, it is important that behavioral economics is used carefully and responsibly. The benefit for the customer must always be at the center. To ensure this, a code of conduct can be formulated. The clearer the differentiation, the more clearly protection against abuse is guaranteed.

A code of conduct can be formulated as follows (excerpt):

1. Respect and integrity: Treat customers with respect and always act with integrity, without deceiving or manipulating.
2. Voluntary decisions: Ensure that customers make decisions voluntarily and informed, without pressure or misleading practices.
3. Customer needs in focus: Strive actively to understand the needs of the customers, promote their satisfaction, and improve the user experience.
4. Value customer feedback: Value the feedback of customers and use it for continuous improvement of the services offered.
5. Data protection: Respect the privacy of customers and act in accordance with applicable data protection policies.
6. Long-term customer relationships: Strive for long-term, trusting customer relationships through sincere cooperation.

Conclusion

The art, therefore, is to tailor behavioral economics precisely to customer needs and to use it in such a way that the user experience is concretely improved. For this, it is essential to understand the rational and emotional behavior of customers and to help them make informed, positive decisions for themselves. Because the benefit for the customer is always at the center. Increased customer satisfaction through personalized communication, offline and online, is the basis for long-term success.

Sources:

- Ackermann et al. (2020).
- Konzern Versicherungskammer (2023).
- Kotler et al. (2017b).
- Spreer (2021).

Evaluation: Compared to offline communication, online communication can be coordinated more easily and directly, integrated and varied more quickly due to the restriction to one medium, and its effect can be directly controlled and measured. Especially in the **insurance sector**—at least among customers who want to actively inform themselves—customer behavior plays a significant role, which is referred to as "Research online, Purchase offline" (RoPo) because customers inform themselves online about products and services and then buy them offline later (see also Sect. 6.1.4). Customers thus use the internet to inform themselves in advance, possibly even to make an independent selection. But the purchase itself often still takes place through the intermediary, i.e., personally, which is due, among other things, to the credence good properties of the insurance and the remaining purchase uncertainty after the preliminary information. Against this background, online marketing is indispensable for insurers. Since insurers generally already have well-developed internet presences, 'only' costs for the new development of online communication tools are incurred. However, it should be noted that despite a now very widespread internet use in the population, only a part of the potential customers can be reached via this medium, as large parts of the population are not interested in insurance issues (see Sect. 1.1.1), while the internet, on the other hand, requires the activity of the users.

In **mobile communication**, companies can send advertising messages directly to consumers via mobile devices, e.g., smartphones, tablets, or notebooks. Mobile devices can be used regardless of location. They can reach consumers directly in their personal environment and communication activities can be aligned accordingly (Kreutzer 2018, p. 356 f.). Through increasingly powerful mobile devices, consumers can directly access the internet, blurring the boundaries between online, social media, and mobile communication. The importance of mobile communication is steadily increasing and allows the use of special **mobile communication tools** (Meffert et al. 2019, pp. 744–751):

- In **SMS/MMS marketing** (short message service/multimedia messaging service), the focus is on sending text-based or multimedia short messages. The advantages are the high personalization of advertising messages, low costs, and the fact that recipients can hardly ignore the messages. However, this is offset by a decreasing frequency of use among smartphone users.
- **QR code marketing** uses and sends QR codes to refer to additional information carriers. For example, QR codes can establish a connection between traditional and digital communication tools when a QR code is integrated into an advertising poster

to provide additional information by linking to a website. Companies can thus offer additional information on traditional advertising media in a cost-effective and space-saving manner (e.g., for products that require explanation such as insurance) (Kreutzer 2018, p. 158).

- The sub-tool of **Bluetooth marketing** is based on the principles of QR codes. However, its advantage over these is that data transmission at Bluetooth locations does not take place via the mobile network, but directly via the Bluetooth interface, so that no transmission costs are incurred. In addition, passers-by who use the Bluetooth download can attract the attention of other passers-by. However, security gaps in the technology can occur if, for example, external attackers manage to introduce malicious programs via Bluetooth transmission.
- A newer sub-tool is **company-owned mobile applications (apps),** additional programs that provide the user with special functions beyond the basic system functions of the device, e.g., provide additional information or integrate additional service functions. Due to the enormous and still increasing number of offered apps, the challenge is that these are found by users at all. Better findability of company-owned apps can be achieved through so-called app store optimization, which is intended to facilitate the finding of an app in the store, similar to search engine optimization. On-page measures include the selection of the right search terms or informative description texts of the app. Off-page measures (e.g., star ratings of users, total number of downloads or download speed of the app) can only be indirectly influenced by the company. In addition, paid search ads can be integrated into app stores to be placed as high as possible in the search results of app stores (app store advertising).
- In the context of mobile apps, there is also the sub-tool of **mobile display advertising**. Here, ads are placed in apps from external providers.

Evaluation: Mobile communication is characterized primarily by its high reach and precise controllability. It particularly promotes the information of users and their purchase intention. Especially for simpler and situational **insurances**, it is predestined to give the recipient the decisive "push" at the right time, for example at the valley station of a ski area with the link to the conclusion of a ski break, ski theft, or temporary accident insurance. However, the range of applications for apps goes much further: Online brokers offer new users and existing customers apps with comprehensive comparison and optimization as well as administration functions and serve them via the app from a single source via the smartphone. Insurers can do the same, but will be more limited to their own product range and less set up across the market.

Finally, **social media communication** is aimed at influencing communication activities via social media not only between companies and demanders, but also between demanders themselves. Social services (social media) stand for all services and tools of Web 2.0 that enable the exchange of user-generated content on the internet: This includes opinions, experiences, and information. The use of social media has been becoming increasingly popular for years: In 2013, there were already 1.72 billion users worldwide, in 2023 there were already 4.76 billion users (we are social and Meltwater 2023). In Germany, 64 million people were already using social media in 2023. And in the coming years, the number of users is expected to continue to rise, worldwide to 5.85 billion users by 2027 and in Germany to almost 75 million users by 2028 (Statista 2022, 2023). The daily dwell time on social media was 1 h and 41 min in Germany in 2023. In that year, there were over two billion users each on Facebook (2.96), YouTube (2.51), WhatsApp, and Instagram (each 2.0) (we are social and Meltwater 2023). Therefore, it is not surprising that companies and insurers are increasingly moving on social media channels and the advertising revenue in social networks is gigantic. In 2022 alone, Meta (Facebook, Messenger, Instagram, WhatsApp, Workplace) realized worldwide advertising revenues of 113.6 billion US $ (Meta 2023, p. 2).

Cross-platform social media tools refer to communication activities whose area of responsibility is largely independent of the underlying social media platform. These include viral marketing and influencer marketing. Viral marketing stands for the intentional triggering of word of mouth, which leads to a rapid and exponentially growing spread of company-related content. Influencer marketing means the targeted use of opinion leaders in social media (influencers) to achieve communication goals. With the exception of review platforms, both instruments can be used in connection with all the platform types listed below. The most common **platform-specific social media tools** in technical-functional terms include weblogs, online communities, social networks, media sharing platforms, microblogging services, and review platforms, which are evaluated in more detail in Table 14.2 (in detail at: Meffert et al. 2019, pp. 721–743):

- **Weblogs**: Individual people express their opinion on their own websites, readers can react.
- **Online Communities**: Groups of people who share common interests exchange ideas.
- **Social Networks**: People network digitally, they release private information for a predefined group of recipients within the network.
- **Media Sharing Platforms**: Groups of people exchange photos and videos, or make them available for upload on platforms.
- **Microblogging Services**: They publish short (max. 140 characters) text messages (tweets), as a follower (interested party) you can follow these tweets.
- **Review Platforms**: Individuals can rate companies or their services and share experiences.

Social media is a special communication tool of the internet and could therefore also be considered in the context of online marketing. Although social media is based on internet technology, it operates differently from traditional online marketing in its concept. In social media, users are primarily networked with each other and generate the content or information exchange themselves. It is not at all - or only driven by the users -about

Table 14.2 Evaluation and examples of the most important social media tools. (Based on Meffert et al. 2019, pp. 724–726)

Social Media Tools	Advantages	Disadvantages	Examples
Weblogs	Increased reach in collaborations Provision of value-adding content	Identification of suitable external blogs Continuous updating necessary Loss of control, little influence on brand-related statements Low dynamics	Company-owned blogs (e.g., Gothaer2Know)
Online Communities	Direct exchange with demanders Strengthening of brand loyalty High interaction intensity	Little influence on brand-related statements Continuous updating and monitoring necessary Low dynamics	Company-owned communities (e.g., Helvetia Community)
Social Networks	Direct exchange with demanders Increased reach Provision of value-adding content Strong dynamics of content (viral effects)	Little influence on brand-related statements Continuous updating and monitoring necessary Advertising can be disruptive	Advertisements in the news feed of Facebook Company-owned accounts on Facebook (e.g., Allianz, DEVK, Gothaer, R+V, Zurich)
Media Sharing Platforms	Direct exchange with demanders High entertainment value Increased reach Strong dynamics of content (viral effects)	Little influence on brand-related statements Continuous updating and monitoring necessary Advertising can be disruptive	Advertisements in the news feed of Instagram Advertising videos on YouTube Company-owned: YouTube channel (e.g., Allianz, AXA, Generali) Instagram (e.g., Allianz, Generali, HUK-Coburg, LVM, R+V) TikTok (e.g., CosmosDirekt, Debeka) Pinterest (e.g., ERGO, HUK-Coburg)

(continued)

Table 14.2 (continued)

Social Media Tools	Advantages	Disadvantages	Examples
Microblogging Services	Direct exchange with demanders Informative content Fast dissemination of advertising content Strong dynamics of content (viral effects)	Little influence on brand-related statements Continuous updating and monitoring necessary Advertising can be disruptive Limitation of advertising content	Advertisements in the news feed of X (Twitter) Company-owned: X (Twitter) (e.g., Allianz, R+V)
Review Platforms	Direct exchange with demanders	Little influence on brand-related statements Low dynamics	TripAdvisor

the exchange with companies, rather about communication about companies. Therefore, social media marketing should be distinguished from online marketing.

▶ **Social Media Marketing** is marketing through the targeted use of social media with the possibility of publishing online user-generated content and exchanging information about them.

(Homburg 2020, p. 878, and the literature cited there)

In the course of marketing on social media, it is necessary to **differentiate how actively a company wants and can participate in the communication and opinion formation** about the company brand or selected products of the company. Brand and product communication can take place within the communities without the company's participation, but social media at least offers the company the opportunity for market and customer observation. If the company actively participates in the communication, e.g., as a participant or as a respondent to user questions or complaints, it should however observe some rules: Due to the speed of interaction in social media, interaction competence is required that enables consistent, relevant, and quick interactions. Success factors include the integration of social media activities into the overall brand communication, the authenticity of the brand, transparency regarding the communicating actors (brand and employees), and the attractive benefit of communication for the user. In contrast, PR announcements and undifferentiated advertising messages are counterproductive. Furthermore, the generation of word of mouth is of great value for brand management and generates a stronger demand response than traditional advertising, as empirical studies show (Trusov et al. 2009); however, this applies to both positive and negative reactions. An interesting tool in this regard are viral videos, which convey messages without being directly perceived as advertising, and spread rapidly in social networks (Meffert et al. 2019, p. 741 f.).

In the **insurance industry**, YouTube is highly popular, with a large proportion of insurers having an official account on this platform. Among 100 insurance companies surveyed in 2022, YouTube leads the popularity scale of the four analyzed social media platforms (in addition to Facebook, Instagram, X (Twitter)) with a usage rate of 91%. In recent years, Instagram has caught up; now two out of three insurers have an official channel there. In their posts, postings, and videos, the insurers refer to their products. Among the top 10 posts by likes on Facebook and Instagram, in addition to product-specific posts, there are also some sweepstakes, while the top posts by likes on X (Twitter) and YouTube refer to climate and nature. In the social media ranking of the evaluation of performances on the four platforms together, nine of the ten leading insurers have an account on all four analyzed platforms. Among these, Allianz, HUK-Coburg, and Zurich stand out; these three brands also place themselves among the ten best performers in all four individual platform rankings (research tools 2022).

Evaluation: In terms of achieving marketing goals, social media marketing can generate high awareness (although usually in smaller target groups), noticeably influence user attitudes, serve competitive differentiation (although usually in smaller target groups), and sometimes influence purchase and repurchase intentions more than traditional communication. Information can be disseminated quickly and up-to-date, but the reach and depth is lower compared to online marketing. However, the target group-specific reach is high, and the costs are lower compared to traditional media and also to online advertising. Feelings and emotions can be conveyed very well. The design possibilities (text, images, sound, and moving images) are diverse, and the tools can be used indefinitely. On the other hand, the process costs should not be underestimated: If the company's commitment in social media is to be sustainable, it must be networked throughout the company, and appropriate personnel resources must be built up for communication. The communication effect can indeed be influenced by the high degree of interaction. However, the specific contents of the communication made by the users with reference to the brand can hardly be influenced (Meffert et al. 2019, p. 742 f.).

Insurer-related, the use of social media marketing can thus serve brand management, customer retention, new customer acquisition, image influence, and the integration of customers into product design. However, the context in which insurance is related must be considered, because users generally do not want to be "commercially harassed" and only want to be confronted with insurance topics in certain situations. Since communication in social media channels is not or hardly controllable, it can 'backfire'. Especially the insurance industry is traditionally exposed to a dangerous spiral of consumer advocates, media and politics (see Sect. 1.1.3), which is supplemented and intensified in social networks by—rightly or wrongly—dissatisfied customers. Social media marketing can therefore be counterproductive. At the same time, a informative, authentic and quick reaction on the part of the insurers in this discussion offers opportunities for clarification, transparency creation and image improvement. In contrast to many other industries, the residual risk of this communication in the insurance industry appears to be comparatively high. Uncontested, on the other hand, is the benefit of social media marketing in the course of market research as a source of information about customers or their preferences or opinions, as well as in internal communication and sales support (information, exchange of experience, qualification).

14.2.6 Event Marketing

An event is an organized occurrence where something special is offered to the target groups. As company- or product-related events, events enable personal and direct contacts with the addressed in a casual, pleasant situation for them. Due to the **high experience orientation**, the feeling of participating in something special, and the on-site experience, a **high emotionalization** is achieved, and ideally a sense of community between the organizer and the target group (customers or intermediary retention) is created. For this to succeed, events must be target group-oriented, original, topical and creative, and ideally establish a connection to the provider. Then further goals such as the transmission of specific information, increasing awareness or building or enhancing an agency or product image can be achieved (Homburg 2020, p. 907).

▶ **Event Marketing** stands for the systematic planning and implementation of events, which trigger a strong activation process through experience-oriented and possibly product-related orientation via emotional and physical stimuli.

(Kühlmann et al. 2003, p. 222)

Essential **characteristics** of events are the direct, personal and intensive contact as well as the constant dialogue orientation, which creates sympathy, attention and trust. Another essential characteristic is the experience mediation, which ensures that the experience and the organizer are not forgotten (Meffert et al. 2019, p. 769).

Evaluation: For an event to achieve its goals and not just represent a costly event, it must be carefully planned and staged. The art lies in achieving a synthesis (= integration) of an exciting and memorable communication of the message, i.e., skillfully combining information and entertainment (= infotainment) and thus addressing the right target group. If this is successful, an increase in image, new customer acquisition and strengthening of customer loyalty are possible. However, due to the not to be underestimated costs, the selection of the target group is crucial for success: The event participants must be good customers with a corresponding premium volume or can become such, or as multipliers convey such customers (e.g., selected brokers). Otherwise, there is a risk that events—especially for a single intermediary agency—become a cost trap (Kühlmann et al. 2003, pp. 223–225).

14.2.7 Sponsorship

Another form of communication used by some insurers is the sponsorship of events, with the aim of promoting the company's image.

▶ **Sponsorship** includes activities associated with the provision of money, resources or services to promote individuals and/or organizations in the sports, cultural and social sectors in exchange for a specified return to the sponsor, which is intended to support the goals of corporate communication.

Sponsorship distinguishes itself from other communication tools through the combination of its **characteristics**:

- Principle of performance and quid pro quo
- Communicative objective
- Promotion of sports, cultural, social or other concerns
- Systematic planning and decision-making.

The classic forms of sponsorship are sports, culture, environment, social and (recently) TV program sponsorship. But also so-called product placement, where a sponsor visually and/or verbally places his product or product name in the editorial environment of media, is part of sponsorship. In this way, a sponsor can specifically showcase his branded product as a real prop in the plot of a movie or television film. Insurance products are less suitable in this respect. Accordingly, **insurers** mainly engage in **sports and cultural sponsorship** (see also marketing highlight on Allianz in this book in Sect. 8.2.2).

Excursus on clever sponsorship using the example of AXA and Liverpool FC

The costs for sponsors, especially in international professional sports with worldwide broadcasting such as club football, have risen enormously. This applies disproportionately to the main sponsors, who are depicted on the official season jerseys worn in the game. Here, AXA has made a clever move and made itself a "second class" sponsor partner, who is present on the training and warm-up jerseys of Liverpool FC among other opportunities. This is cheaper than being the main jersey partner, but it certainly also creates presence, especially in the pre- and post-reporting. Thus, the coach (Jürgen Klopp) was regularly seen with an AXA logo in interviews before or after the game, comparatively rarely with the jersey with the main sponsor 'standard chartered'.

Evaluation: Compared to traditional communication tools, sponsorship has the advantage of addressing customers and potential customers in non-commercial situations. And the importance of leisure activities and thus higher impact in the target group is increasing. Moreover, it may be cheaper to place the company name as a sponsor in public than it would be possible through advertising. The reporting on many sponsored activities in the media is intensive and the brand is therefore more present than in advertising. Sponsorship can also take place geographically flexibly, from international to local events. However, it is less suitable for longer messages, as the main focus is on the sponsored event and only the company or product name is noticed. On the other hand, it can contribute well to the awareness and possibly sympathy of the sponsor. However, sponsorship is not necessarily effective, especially at particularly audience-strong events, as empirical studies in the context of the Confed Cup and the Football World Championships have shown; at the 2006 World Cup in Germany, for example, only three of the sponsors were able to increase their awareness, the same phenomenon was seen four years later at the Football World Cup in South Africa (Meffert et al. 2019, p. 775 f.).

14.2.8 Public Relations

Public relations is one of the classic communication tools. Unlike advertising, its purpose is not directly to increase sales, but to maintain relationships with the public. This includes the population, the media, politics, analysts, owners, lenders, and other stakeholders (Abschn. 6.2.4).

▶ **Public Relations** (PR) involves the systematic building of relationships between the company and various public target groups with the aim of influencing them in line with the company's objectives and thus simultaneously achieving the objectives of corporate communication.

(Homburg 2020, p. 825, and the literature cited there)

Its typical **tools** are media work (press reports, press kits, interviews, podcasts), events (press conferences, speeches and lectures by company representatives, seminars, annual general meetings, business reports, factory tours), relationship management (meetings with opinion leaders and multipliers from media, industries, politics; participation in industry meetings; donations (lobbying)), communication with stakeholders (participation in communication in social networks) and crisis management. It basically addresses any target group with whose members the company maintains direct or indirect relationships via the sales, financial, procurement or labor markets (Homburg 2020, pp. 900–902).

For **insurers**, public relations means conscious communication with the social corporate environment. It becomes particularly relevant when insurers, certain insurance products or intermediaries are criticized, or—in the case of private health insurance and life insurance—entire insurance branch groups or—in the case of residual debt insurance—certain insurance branches are the subject of political discussion. Coordinated, uniform communication with the public is particularly important in such cases, and should therefore be organized in advance. It can essentially only be accomplished centrally.

Evaluation: Public relations is not a pure marketing tool, because it targets not only direct sales partners and end customers, but also other stakeholder groups and supports non-marketing goals. Nevertheless, it indirectly also has effects on buyers and (potential) customers, increases awareness and possibly improves the image. In addition to the classic communication tools, it should be used in a targeted manner; however, it cannot replace advertising, and especially sales promotion and personal selling.

14.2.9 Internal Communication

In contrast to the communication tools discussed so far, internal communication primarily focuses on the communication of messages and information within a company and is thus essentially **employee communication**. In doing so, it supports the external communication of its employees by informing, motivating, and guiding them. The tasks of employee communication include (Meffert et al. 2018, p. 427):

- Communication of all personnel policy measures, programs, and tools (e.g., outlining career opportunities, introducing further training offers),
- Supporting managers at all levels in their communication tasks,
- Informing employees and managers about change projects,
- Demonstrating the strategic connections within the company and the role of employees in achieving the company's and market-oriented objectives of the service provider.

The most significant **tools** of employee communication include impersonal, usually one-sided information tools such as reporting and information systems, internal job market, employee magazines, company brochures, notices and circulars, email and intranet, as well as computer-aided databases, agency systems, expert systems, or management information systems. Some companies even have their own business TV in this regard. In contrast, communication tools such as employee interviews, work meetings, sales force meetings, company meetings, staff forums, workshops, or online meetings are much more personal and two-sided. *Meffert et al.* categorize these tools according to the medium of address into personal (face-to-face) and media-based employee communication, and according to the continuity of use into continuous and sporadic employee communication. A four-field matrix of these two dimensions can be used to form four groups of employee communication tools (Table 14.3).

Evaluation: Internal communication is undoubtedly of central importance, whether factually in terms of necessary information and knowledge transfer, or emotionally for building and maintaining sufficient employee motivation and a corporate culture. From a marketing perspective, communication about the benefits of products and services begins with and among employees. Especially in a service company, it is important to implement the desired market positioning through correspondingly thinking and acting employees without and, above all, with customer contact. The most successful

Table 14.3 Tools of internal communication. (Based on Meffert et al. 2018, p. 429)

	Personal Address	Medial Address
Continuous	• Employee meeting • Quality groups • Project meetings	• Management newsletter • Employee magazine, company TV • Internal job magazine • Extranet
Sporadic	• Management meeting • Workshops • Company assembly • Employee coaching	• Employee communication • Notices, announcements on the intranet • Databases • Company-internal Facebook

companies with the most impressive market positions have managed to get their employees to identify with the vision and the marketing strategy based on it and to personify it (also in external customer contact).

14.2.10 Integrated Communication in the Communication Mix

The **increasing diversity of communication channels and advertising tools** challenge marketing, because consumers do not differentiate (or want to differentiate) between a company's messages and the channels through which they are disseminated. For consumers, all transmitted messages form a total message that they associate with the company or the company's brand. Contradictory messages are therefore counterproductive, as they cause confusion and undermine the credibility of the sender. The cause of uncoordinated communication channels is often the distribution of competencies for individual communication tools across different departments (e.g., advertising, sales promotion, brand management, product marketing, sales, PR, etc.). Insurance companies, in particular, are affected by this, because in many companies, traditional sales training is still conducted in the sales department, product marketing in branch departments, PR in a staff position of the CEO, and brand policy and advertising in the advertising department.

Against this background, **integrated communication is becoming increasingly important**. Its goal is to convey a clear, consistent, and irresistible message about the company, its range of products and services, and its brand positioning. To achieve this, all communication impressions triggered by various contact media about the same communication object (e.g., company brand) must complement and reinforce each other.

▶ **Integrated Communication** as a strategic and operational process is aimed at creating unity from the different sources of a company's internal and external communication, in order to convey a consistent appearance of the company or a reference object to the communication target groups.

(Bruhn 2019b, p. 78)

However, the coordination of all used communication tools requires that a company is aware of all contact points through which a current or potential customer can connect with it. The messages and positioning of the company and its service offerings must then be coordinated across all channels in order to create a strong brand identity: TV advertising and ads, flyers and agency signage have the same appearance and tone as online communication and the personal consultation and sales talks of the agents (Kotler et al. 2022, p. 674).

A systematic coordination of communication tools must be carried out **in terms of content, form, time, and geography** (Table 14.4).

In the context of integrated communication, internal communication plays a major role in supporting a uniform external appearance. In this regard, one also speaks of communication strategic guiding concepts such as corporate identity and corporate communication as one of its instruments: The **Corporate Identity** as the company's self-image is the strategically planned and operationally used self-presentation (corporate design), behavior (corporate behavior), and communication (corporate communication) of a company internally and externally. The **Corporate Communication** claims the coordination and control of all communication activities and the development of overarching communication programs aimed at synergy effects (Harbrücker 1992, pp. 208–219; Kühlmann et al. 2003, p. 227 f.).

Evaluation: Through integrated communication, an insurer can achieve higher consistency (= coherence) in market communication and an improved distribution effect. Coordination at one point increases the ability to address the right customers with the right advertising messages at the right time in the right place with the right medium, thereby effectively and efficiently using the communication budget.

14.2.11 Interim Conclusion on the Marketing Tool of Communication Policy

In the private customer´s business (and the following also applies to large parts of the commercial customer business), insurance products are low-interest products that do not attract attention. Customers pay little attention to this topic and are also exposed to an information overload. In addition, insurances are credence goods, resulting in a comparatively high purchase risk. Therefore, insurers are particularly challenged to create a noticeable and at the same time differentiating and trust-building message that informs about the provider and in the further course of communication the product, its features, its price-performance ratio and its advantages and that also reaches the recipients. This makes the communication policy and its diverse instruments an indispensable marketing tool in the insurance industry. This supports above all the psychographic marketing objectives and the establishment of a (strong) corporate brand (Sect. 7.2.3), all of them pioneers for achieving the economic objectives, and thus for the sale of insurances. Advertising can initially create awareness and sympathy. Since insurances are sold and

Table 14.4 Integrated communication. (Based on Bruhn 2019b, p. 81)

Forms		Subject	Goals	Tools	Time horizon
Content Integration	Functional	Thematic coordination through connecting lines	Consistency, autonomy, congruence	Uniform slogans, messages, images	Long-term
	Instrumental				
	Horizontal				
	Vertical				
Formal Integration		Formal design principles	Presence, conciseness, clarity	Signs, logos, corporate design manual	Medium to long-term
Temporal Integration		Coordination within and between planning periods	Consistency, continuity	Event planning	Short to medium-term
Geographical Integration		Coordination in different regions	Consistency, presence	see above	Medium to long-term

not bought, i.e., push marketing must be used, however, the communication tools of sales promotion and personal selling are of even more central importance for the successful sale of insurance products. The other communication tools, in turn, contribute to awareness, sympathy, trust building and/or preference for a provider and thus to the reduction of purchase risks and unleash their full effect in the sense of integrated communication. Nevertheless, personal selling in the insurance sector appears to be the most decisive communication tool.

Further Reading Recommendations for Chap. 14

- Bruhn (1998).
- Bruhn (2019b).
- Harbrücker (1992).
- Hujber (2005).
- Kling (2013).
- Schultz et al. (1993).

References

Ackermann, K. A./Heim, N./Collenberg, A./Lenggenhager, V./Müller, S./Furchheim, P. (2020): Swiss Behavioral Economics Studie, Winterthur, 2020.

Becker, J. (2019): Marketing-Konzeption: Grundlagen des ziel-strategischen und operativen Marketing-Managements, München, 11. Aufl., 2019.

Bruhn, M. (1998): Internes Marketing als Schnittstelle zwischen Marketing- und Personalmanagement, in: Bruhn, M./Meffert, H. (Eds.), Handbuch Dienstleistungsmanagement, Wiesbaden, 1998, S. 707–732.

Bruhn, M. (2019b): Kommunikationspolitik, Systematischer Einsatz der Kommunikation für Unternehmen, München, 9. Aufl., 2019.

Bruhn, M. (2022): Relationship Marketing. Das Management von Kundenbeziehungen, München, 6. Aufl., 2022.

Farny, D. (2011): Versicherungsbetriebslehre, Karlsruhe, 5. Aufl., 2011.

Harbrücker, U. (1992): Wertewandel und Corporate Identity, Perspektiven eines gesellschaftsorientierten Marketing von Versicherungsunternehmen, Wiesbaden, 1992.

Homburg, C. (2020): Marketingmanagement, Strategie – Instrumente – Umsetzung – Unternehmensführung, Wiesbaden, 7. Aufl., 2020.

Hujber, T. (2005): Werbung von Versicherungsunternehmen, Wiesbaden, 2005.

Kling, M. (2013): Irreführende und vergleichende Versicherungswerbung, in: ZVersWiss, Jg. 102, 2013, Nr. 4, S. 389–422.

Konzern Versicherungskammer (Ed.) (2023): Geschäftsbericht Konzern Versicherungskammer 2022, München, 2023.

Kotler, P./Bliemel, F. (1999): Marketing-Management, Analyse, Planung, Umsetzung und Steuerung, Stuttgart, 9. Aufl., 1999.

Kotler, P./Keller, K.L./Bliemel, F. (2007): Marketing-Management, Strategien für wertschaffendes Handeln, München, 12. Aufl., 2007.
Kotler, P./Armstrong, G./Wong, V./Saunders, J. (2011): Grundlagen des Marketing, München, 5. Aufl., 2011.
Kotler, P./Keller, K.L./Opresnik, M.O. (2017a): Marketing-Management, Konzepte – Instrumente – Unternehmensfallstudien, Halbergmoos, 15. Aufl., 2017.
Kotler, P./Kartajaya, H./Seitiawan, I. (2017b): Marketing 4.0, Chicago, 2017.
Kotler, P./Armstrong, G./Harris, L.C./He, H. (2022): Grundlagen des Marketing, Halbergmoos, 8. Aufl., 2022.
Kreutzer, R.T. (2018): Praxisorientiertes online-marketing. Konzepte–Instrumente–Checklisten, Wiesbaden, 3. Aufl., 2018.
Kroeber-Riel, W. (1992): Konsumentenverhalten, München, 5. Aufl., 1992.
Kühlmann, K./Wolf, H.-P./Wallenwein, C./Swoboda, U. (2003): Marketing und Vertrieb, Funktionsorientierte Qualifikationen, Karlsruhe, 2. Aufl., 2003.
Lenz, T./Rabe, D. (2010): Telefonwerbung – Eine Betrachtung aus der Praxis der Versicherungswirtschaft, in: VersR, Jg.61, 2010, Nr. 34, S. 1.541–1.546.
Matzner, U. (2022): 24 Versicherer mit achtstelligen Werbeausgaben, in: Versicherungswirtschaft-heute vom 14.08.2022.
Meffert, H./Bruhn, M./Hadwich, K. (2018): Dienstleistungsmarketing, Grundlagen – Konzepte – Methoden, Wiesbaden, 9. Aufl., 2018.
Meffert, H./Burmann, C./Kirchgeorg, M./Eisenbeiß, M. (2019): Marketing, Grundlagen marktorientierter Unternehmensführung, Konzepte – Instrumente – Praxisbeispiele, Wiesbaden, 13. Aufl., 2019.
Meta (Ed.) (2023): Meta Earnings Presentation Q3/2023, in: https://s21.q4cdn.com/399680738/files/doc_earnings/2023/q3/presentation/Earnings-Presentation-Q3-2023.pdf, Accessed: 24.01.2024.
Puschmann, K.-H. (2003): Praxis des Versicherungsmarketing, Karlsruhe, 2. Aufl., 2003.
Research tools (Ed.) (2022): Versicherer in Social Media: Agila platziert sich neben den Großen der Branche unter den Top 10-Performern, Pressemitteilung vom 21.12.2022, Esslingen am Neckar, 2022.
Sandkühler, H.-L. (2022): Unerlaubte Werbeanrufe und Co., in: AssCompact, 2022, Nr. 4, S. 74–75.
Schultz, D.E./Tannenbaum, S.I./Lauterborn, R.F. (1993): The new marketing paradigm. Integrated marketing communications, Lincolnwood/Illinois, 1993.
Spreer, P. (2021): PsyConversion, Wiesbaden, 2. Aufl., 2021.
Statista (Ed.) (2022): Number of social media users worldwide from 2017 to 2027 (in billions), 2022, in: https://www-statista-com.ezproxy.hwr-berlin.de/statistics/278414/number-of-worldwide-social-network-users/, Accessed: 26.01.2024.
Statista (Ed.) (2023): Number of social media users in Germany from 2019 to 2028 (in millions), 2023, in: https://www-statista-com.ezproxy.hwr-berlin.de/statistics/568943/predicted-number-of-social-network-users-in-germany/, Accessed: 26.01.2024.
Swift, R.S. (2001): Accelaterating Customer Relationships, Using CRM Technologies, New Jersey, 2001.
Trusov, M/Bucklin, R.E./Pauwels, K. (2009): Effects of word-of-mouth versus traditional marketing: Findings from an internet social networking site, in: JoM, Vol. 73, 2009, No. 5, S. 90–102.
VAUNET – Verband Privater Medien e. V. (Ed.) (2023): VAUNET-Werbemarktanalyse, Audio- & audiovisuelle Werbung in Deutschland 2022/2023, Berlin, 2023.
VHV Gruppe (Ed.) (2023): Geschäftsbericht 2022, Hannover, 2023.
We are Social/Meltwater (Ed.) (2023): Digital 2023, Global Overview Report, The essential guide to the world's connected behaviours, o. O., 2023.

Zentralverband der deutschen Werbewirtschaft e. V. (Ed.) (2021a): Ausgestrahlte TV-Werbeminuten in Deutschland in den Jahren 2002 bis 2020, Stand: 2021, in: Statista (Ed.), in: https://de-statista-com.ezproxy.hwr-berlin.de/statistik/daten/studie/4769/umfrage/tv-werbesekunden-in-deutschland-seit-2000/, Accessed: 26.01.2024.

Zentralverband der deutschen Werbewirtschaft e. V. (Ed.) (2021b): Anzahl der in Deutschland ausgestrahlten TV-Werbespots in den Jahren 2002 bis 2020 (in Millionen), Stand: 2021, in: Statista (Ed.), in: https://de-statista-com.ezproxy.hwr-berlin.de/statistik/daten/studie/4771/umfrage/anzahl-der-tv-werbespots-in-deutschland-seit-2000/, Accessed: 26.01.2024.

15 Integration of Marketing Tools in the Marketing Mix of the Insurance Company

Companies are exposed to the **risk of unintended instrumental effects** when designing their marketing mix. In this context, the marketing tools can ignite both their own effects resp. temporal combined effects—namely so-called delay, carry over, decay, and spill over effects (Steffenhagen 2004, p. 278 f.)—as well as factual combined effects, i.e., they can have opposing effects on each other (Becker 2019, pp. 787 f. and 799).

Even **insurers** encounter these instrumental effects (Bechmann and Köhne 1997, pp. 4–6):

Marketing tools often only take effect **delayed** ("time lag"), e.g., internal training to promote service mentality, advertising measures to improve brand image, and also when the tool is no longer used. Thus, tools have a **"carry over"** effect, for example, when a well-known, memorable advertising message "carries over", even though it has long been replaced by another (e.g., the slogan "An Alliance for life" for many years). Also, if one of the employees acts damaging to the image in customer contact, it usually has a long-lasting negative effect on the entire company. The same applies to the nightclub visit by insurance intermediaries a few years ago as part of a sales promotion competition: Intensive press reporting at the time fed the cliché of many citizens that insurance intermediaries earn too much and led to a lasting "memory" among current and potential customers. However, this should have 'faded' by now.

Marketing tools also show **signs of decay** when their effect unintentionally decreases: For example, the offer of assistance services initially contributed to differentiation, whereas in the age of professional assistance providers, such services become standard. And product renewals, especially product modifications, only attract customer attention for a short time—if at all—as competitors quickly catch up. However, the insurer has the opportunity to counteract this decay effect of product policy in cooperation with other service partners in ecosystems through genuine and individual problem solutions.

T. Köhne, *Insurance Marketing*, https://doi.org/10.1007/978-3-658-47345-7_15

Finally, **spill over effects** occur when a marketing tool has an effect beyond the targeted area by influencing parallel or competing product areas or upstream or downstream service areas: Parallel or competing product areas (branches) are influenced, for example, when an insurer mediates liability insurance both through sales force and direct sales, offering the same product in the form of two brands (possibly at different prices). On the other hand, the mutual dependence of internal staff and sales force, product and sales, as well as communication specialists and lawyers, leads to instrumental effects on upstream or downstream areas: For example, increases in acquisition commissions can induce thoughtless product sales and thus lead to a pile-up of complaints in the internal service, too complex products can lead to understanding problems with the employee in customer contact, and simplifications of conditions can lead to a pile-up of legal disputes, etc. Last but not least, service partners who operate upstream and downstream of the insurer (e.g., sales partners or partners in ecosystems) are negatively affected by all deficiencies in the marketing mix, provided that customers associate the deficiencies with the partner companies (negative image transfer). The same applies in the opposite direction, for example, when a partner repair shop appears on behalf of the insurer and repairs a damage poorly.

Apart from the mentioned instrumental effects, there is the **risk of an inconsistent marketing mix**: This means that the marketing tools are not coordinated with each other, i.e., they have opposing effects or do not aim in the same direction. The resulting counterproductive effect impairs the customer's perception and reduces the effectiveness of the marketing mix. For example, an insurance service communicated as particularly needs-based and flexible is only perceived as such to a limited extent if there is a standard coverage on the product side, only one possible distribution channel is available on the distribution side, or a needs- resp. risk-appropriate premium cannot be calculated on the price side. The fact that a single marketing tool can jeopardize an entire marketing strategy is demonstrated by the mentioned example of a sales organization belonging to an insurance group, which caused negative headlines by visiting a nightclub as part of an incentive trip and thus severely disrupted the parallel, costly image campaign of the insurance group. The problem of an inconsistent marketing mix is even more serious and consequential against the backdrop of the need for sustainable positioning in the market than the previously described instrumental effects.

Therefore, an **integrated marketing is indispensable** for the insurance company, which coordinates all marketing tools (= marketing mix) in the sense of a service benefit perceived by the customer from his point of view (Köhne 1997, p. 43).

This means (Köhne 2006, p. 365),

- firstly, to align the product design in the broad sense resp. the problem solution (product, product range, conditions, service and claims settlement) in a benefit-oriented way,
- secondly, to coordinate customer touchpoints across the entire service process and all contact functions across various distribution channels, and
- thirdly, to integrate the various communication tools (communication mix) in turn.

▶ **Integrated Marketing** stands for the holistic planning, coordination and control of the marketing mix, i.e., the product, price, service, claims settlement, sales and communication policy, from the customer's perspective.

This implies that integrated marketing **cannot succeed without the service partners**: As shown, the insurance service is not only provided at one point in time, but in a service process over the entire customer relationship (contract duration). Therefore, the various tools of the marketing mix need to be coordinated not only once, but adjusted again and again depending on the life situation and process phase. In addition, the insurance service is often carried out by several service partners in a decentralized manner (= outside the insurance company) during the service process; this is especially true in personal sales and in claims handling in the event of a claim. Therefore, the implementation of the integrated marketing mix requires a pronounced marketing mindset and **culture of customer orientation** from all partners—the central marketing (in the corporate headquarters) alone reaches its limits in this respect.

However, it is not enough for the headquarters to coordinate with decentralized service providers. Equally important is an exchange and a **coordination between the main departments responsible for service performance** at the corporate headquarters: Primarily, this refers to the collaboration between marketing, product development, and sales. In this context, traditional correlations between individual marketing tools must be considered:

- **Product and premium policy**:
  This involves the scope of coverage and additional services and the corresponding pricing, and ultimately, from the customer's perspective, the price-performance ratio of an insurance product. The latter is often difficult for customers to assess. However, the absolute premium amount often plays a role. Therefore, it makes sense to offer the customer differentiated levels of coverage and services at correspondingly premium rates. In the risk business area, coverage and premium design usually go hand in hand, as otherwise the insurer would violate the actuarial equivalence principle (= risk premium corresponds to the expected loss value) and the equal treatment requirement in certain branches. The pricing strategy plays an important role in terms of additional services. For example, in the case of a low-price strategy, cost-intensive service benefits are counterproductive.
- **Product and sales policy**:
  Standard products can basically be distributed via all sales channels; more individual, complex and thus advice-intensive products such as target group coverages or tax-optimized pension solutions including company pensions require selected sales channels that can provide appropriate advice. Conversely, special sales channels such as banks or other annex distribution channels require products tailored to their business and advisory processes and—to be able to mediate alongside other main products—tend to be standardized and simple insurance products. At the same time, the premium

amount must allow for certain commission volumes in personal selling; no intermediary can live from a mediated travel luggage insurance alone.

- **Product, sales, and communication policy**:
  On the one hand, communication through advertising messages and brand promises creates expectations among (potential) customers that the product and the sales channel must then fulfill during the service process. On the other hand, the products "communicate" through their presentation (e.g., in product brochures and flyers) and the sales channel through personal or impersonal media with the (potential) customers. In the case of professional marketing, the coordination between advertising messages and brand promises (as strategic communication guidelines) and, for example, advertising and sales promotion (as operational communication instruments) is not a problem, but the corresponding design of the insurance products (coverage and additional services) and the actual communicative behavior of the employees in customer contact certainly is. Helpful here is an anchoring of the brand promise, i.e., the positioning in the market, at the level of the top corporate objectives, so that the board members responsible for the marketing tools of product and sales policy are also integrated.

Equally necessary, because it is important for customer-oriented service provision at the moment of truth, is the consistent organizational **connection** between the product and sales department and—extremely rare in practice—**between the claims and marketing department**. The following task- and activity-related connections between claims and marketing aspects argue for this (Table 15.1):

- Service development (marketing department) and implementation (claims department) must be coordinated from the planning stage. In product design, the conditions for claims settlement services are set; legally in the insurance contract and sales-promoting in the product brochures.
- Customer-oriented claims settlement services require market research to explore the potential and customer-aware needs in the event of a claim (competence of the marketing department).
- Conversely, claims handlers in both internal and field service can provide important impulses for product development and marketing. This is already happening with regard to limiting claims costs and insurance fraud, but there is still potential for suggestions for service improvement (claims expertise and experiences from contacts with injured parties as competences of the claims department).
- Media for supporting customer contact can also be used for communication with injured parties (customer centers, external call centers, internet, sales force).
- The integration of the sales force into claims settlement to enable cross-selling requires a coordination of consulting, sales and support tasks and their implementation in the market.

Table 15.1 Fields of cooperation between the claims and marketing department. (Köhne 2003, p. 84)

Marketing department	Topic	Claims department
Service development within the framework of product design/ marketing	Design of claims settlement	Implementation or execution
Market research and functional thinking	Demand determination	Claims expertise and experiences from contacts with injured parties
Planning of customer contact via customer center, internet or sales force; possibly handling of standard cases	Contact media in the event of a claim	Handling of individual cases requiring expertise
Training of the claims inspector with a focus on customer orientation	Cross-selling to injured parties by claims inspectors or sales force	Technical support of the sales force
Design and promotion	Service guarantees	Design and fullfilment
Execution of performance controlling	Controlling of service provision	Implementation of findings

- A marketing task is the measurement of customer satisfaction with regard to claims handling and the control of service quality, the task of the claims department is the provision or initiation and possibly improvement of the claims settlement service.

A suitable tool for quality assurance and improvement of processes in cross-departmental service provision are **service guarantees** (Sect. 12.2). They serve to define clear service goals, continuous measurement of goal achievement, measurability of service deficits and the costs caused by them, as well as the optimization of internal processes for the benefit of the customer or injured party. The injured party receives compensation in case of service deficiencies and it is made clear to him that his objections are taken seriously and pursued. Service guarantees also support market profiling by drawing the customer's or injured party's attention to services that can distinguish the provider from the competition.

In the context of presenting individual marketing tools, it has often been shown that their respective design allows for many possibilities and thus already represents a complex undertaking at the tool level. In addition, however, the marketing tools must be coordinated with each other to ensure the highest possible effectiveness and efficiency in terms of goal, strategy, and task fulfillment in insurance marketing. This again shows that operational marketing must be guided by the overarching, strategic marketing.

Further Reading Recommendations for Chap. 15

- Bechmann and Köhne (1997).
- Becker (2019, pp. 647–664 and 765–814).
- Homburg (2020, pp. 1008–1019).

References

Bechmann, T./Köhne, T. (1997): Integriertes Marketing: Schlüsselfunktion im dynamischen Versicherungsmarkt, Sonderausgabe der IVW Management-Information, Band 1, St. Gallen, 1997.

Becker, J. (2019): Marketing-Konzeption: Grundlagen des ziel-strategischen und operativen Marketing-Managements, München, 11. Aufl., 2019.

Homburg, C. (2020): Marketingmanagement, Strategie—Instrumente—Umsetzung—Unternehmensführung, Wiesbaden, 7. Aufl., 2020.

Köhne, T. (1997): Die Wirkungsversicherung im Privatkundengeschäft—Implikationen für eine kundenorientierte Marktleistungsgestaltung, St. Gallen, 1997.

Köhne, T. (2003): Schadenmanagement als Marketinginstrument oder: Kundenorientierung im „Moment of truth", in: El Hage, B./Jara, M. (Eds.), Schadenmanagement, Grundlagen, Methoden und Instrumente, Praktische Erfahrungen, St. Gallen, 2003, S. 67–90.

Köhne, T. (2006): Marketing im strategischen Unternehmensnetzwerk, Erklärungsmodell und praktische Anwendung in der Versicherungswirtschaft, Wiesbaden, 2006.

Steffenhagen, H. (2004): Marketing, Stuttgart u. a., 5. Aufl., 2004.

Part VI

Marketing Management Process as Part of the Insurance Marketing Conception

16 Marketing Management: Planning, Implementation and Controlling of Marketing Activities

Marketing management, in the sense of the classical management concept, is to be understood as a process that includes planning and thus goal formulation (Sect. 16.1), strategic and operational implementation (Sect. 16.2), and controlling goal achievement (Sect. 16.3). This process impements the three other sub-areas of marketing conception—the identification of the marketing situation with the tasks of analysis and forecast (Part III: Chapter 6), strategic marketing with the tasks of goal, strategy, and task determination (Part IV: Chap. 7, 8 and 9) and the product and service design in the marketing mix (Part V: Chap. 10, 11, 12, 13, 14 and 15).

16.1 Marketing Planning

Marketing planning can be both strategic and operational. The **strategic marketing planning** directly follows the purpose, policy, and strategy of the insurance company and includes the fulfillment of the following tasks (Meffert et al. 2019, Chap. 4; Kotler et al. 2007, pp. 90–104; similarly in Kotler et al. 2017a, p. 45):

- Formulation of marketing objectives
- Planning of market participant-indepent and market participant-oriented strategies
- Definition of strategic business units (SBU) on the company side and business fields on the market side (portfolio evaluation)
- Definition of marketing tasks and their weighting depending on the strategic business fields
- Long-term marketing budgeting for the strategic business fields and SBU
- Definition of sub-goals and specifications for marketing tools such as internal transfer prices.

T. Köhne, *Insurance Marketing*, https://doi.org/10.1007/978-3-658-47345-7_16

Its planning horizon refers to **medium to long-term** planning (3 to 5 years); accordingly, strategic marketing planning is a **permanent basic planning** (Becker 2019, p. 832 f.). It is characterized by a diverse interplay between market-oriented corporate planning, market-oriented business field planning, and marketing mix planning (Fig. 16.1).

The **operational marketing planning** essentially concerns the concrete design of the marketing tools and is therefore a marketing mix planning. Its central goal is to find the optimal combination of marketing tools in terms of which tools are to be used by whom at what times, with what intensities and designs, and at what costs (budgets). Its planning horizon refers to **short-term** planning (usually 1 year, sometimes in quarters); accordingly, operational marketing planning is a **action planning**. This optimal coordination of individual marketing tools or activities presents a significant problem in theory and practice despite numerous developed procedures. This is due to the large number of combination possibilities of marketing tools, the dynamics in the development of new tools, interdependencies of marketing tools, spill over effects between business fields, uncertainty regarding the effect of measures, resource constraints due to time, financial and/or personnel restrictions, and coordination problems between different executives.

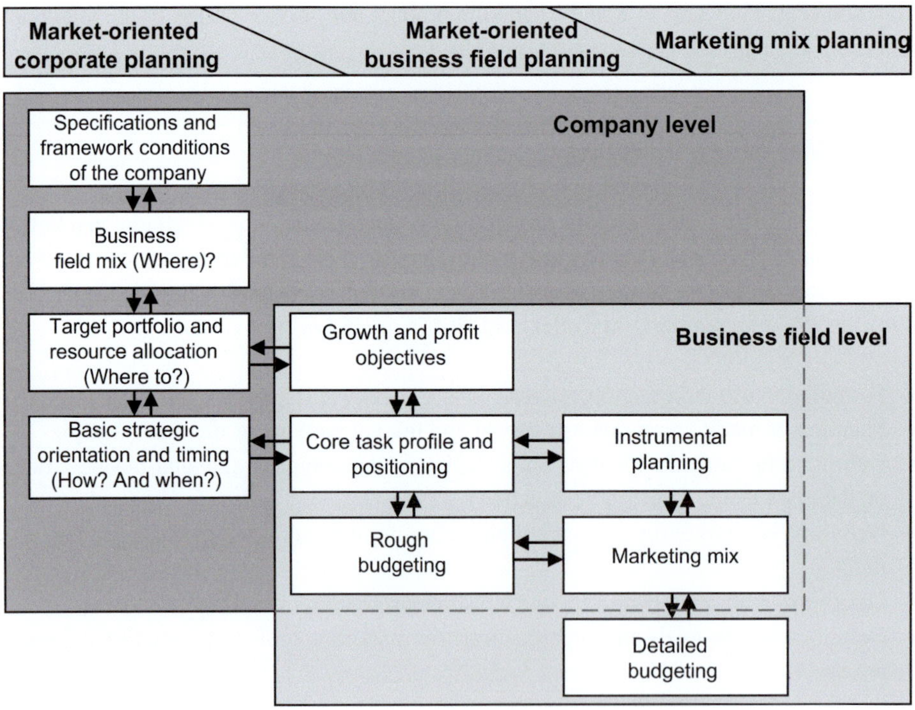

Fig. 16.1 Levels of marketing planning. (Based on Tomczak et al. 2014, p. 118)

Precisely for this reason, operational marketing planning is required as instrumental guiding planning to reduce complexity and concretize the **specifications for detailed planning**. The instrumental guiding planning is initially based on the marketing strategy for the business fields being processed and for the marketing task profiles determined from the defined business fields. This guiding planning translates into concrete guidelines for detailed planning through instrumental strategy models and marketing mix manifestations that meet these, as well as a rough budgeting. Nevertheless, the detailed planning of the use of tools remains influenced by the limits of determinability of all effects and interrelationships (Tomczak et al. 2014, pp. 119 f.).

16.2 Marketing Implementation

Marketing implementation refers to the transformation of marketing plans into actionable tasks and ensuring goal-oriented task fulfillment. Two essential subtasks of marketing implementation are the **enforcement of the marketing conception** and its implementation. As part of the enforcement, the marketing management has to create acceptance for the strategy among the affected employees, departments, and service partners, i.e., to promote knowledge (knowing), comprehension (understanding), equipping with corresponding competencies (being able to), and the will (wanting). As part of the **implementation of the marketing conception**, the marketing strategy and marketing tasks are first to be concretized in terms of content in order to be able to design the marketing tools. The implementation of the marketing strategy takes place based on the specifications defined in the marketing conception as well as situational adjustments and requires a coordinated interaction of all participants. In addition, marketing needs to be implemented organizationally, and structures, processes, and systems need to be networked throughout the company (Meffert et al. 2019, p. 881).

In the **organizational implementation** of marketing, the question needs to be clarified as to how the marketing function can be optimally integrated into the company. In this context, **various stages of maturity** of the marketing idea in the company can be identified (Kotler et al. 2007, pp. 1142–1146):

- Stage 1: Marketing as a **staff unit** of sales: Primitive form of marketing.
- Stage 2: Marketing as a **sub-department** in sales: Increasing professionalization of operational sales.
- Stage 3: Marketing as a **main department** alongside sales: Strategically oriented marketing activities are implemented independently.
- Stage 4: Marketing as a **management or board position**: The markets and marketing are given the appropriate importance in the company.
- Stage 5: Marketing as an **integrating function** in the company: This stage is largely identical to stage 4, but differs in its integrating effect in the company. In this stage, other executives and employees in the company outside the marketing department have

internalized that this is not to be seen as a separate and self-responsible (competitive) department, but that all departments work for the customer and marketing represents an integrating corporate task, in which ultimately everyone must participate.

- Stage 6: Marketing in the **project- and process-led organization**: Companies at this stage have aligned their organization to core processes, so that departmental and divisional thinking gives way to cross-departmental projects. Accordingly, a cross-disciplinary team is assembled in a customer-related project and process management, in which employees from marketing are involved. The marketing professionals are then in double subordination, namely to one or more team leaders and to the marketing department.

According to the requirements for the marketing organization, which result from market and competitive dynamics as well as customer requirements, various organizational forms for marketing are discussed in the literature. Basically, function- or task-oriented organizational structures can be distinguished from object-oriented ones (e.g., branches, regions, business fields). The **function-oriented alignment** bundles the specialist knowledge and thus in principle ensures a qualified task fulfillment. However, in dynamic, fragmented markets, it reaches its limits because it only partially considers object-related coordination aspects such as product, customer, or area orientation. For more complex, diversified market and offer conditions, more differentiated **(object-oriented) organizational concepts** are recommended, such as product, category, customer or customer group, regional, or project management. In practice, both basic approaches are often combined to benefit from the advantages of function and task orientation (specialization) as well as those of object orientation (greater market proximity and differentiation). As a result, so-called **matrix organizations** are created with two equal-ranking instances (Kotler et al. 2017a, pp. 834–839; Bruhn 2022, pp. 272 f.).

The **organization of insurance marketing** (see also Sect. 2.1.1) is often still in stages 2 or 3, depending on the company. As a **main department**, it generally operates functionally for the entire company; in international insurance groups, brand management is centrally controlled, but most communication tools and other marketing tools are decided on a country-specific basis. In this respect, there is essentially an object-oriented (country-specific) organization. It is not known that insurers also have a customer-specific - even if it is at the level of the large customer segments of industrial, commercial and private customers -, a branch-specific or a distribution channel-specific marketing department. However, this is partly due to the fact that insurers often equate marketing only with communication (Köhne 1999), which can be centralized most easily of all marketing tools. Product-related, there are product managers in more and more insurance companies, distribution channel-related different sales managers and in the industrial and corporate insurance sector key account managers (see also: Görgen 2007, pp. 224–229). **Occasionally**, but rather rarely, there is even a **executive board department** for market and customer management in the commercial and private customer segment. Stage 6 seems generally unsuitable in the insurance industry because services rarely need to be "produced" individually for customers, involving all or many departments. Even in the industrial insurance sector, individualization mainly takes place at the level of insurance coverage and pricing. **In the case of start-up companies or new product developments**, a **project organization** is quite sensible and common, but usually limited in time.

As part of the organizational implementation of marketing, the **cooperation with service partners** in the context of cooperative service provision - in other words, the configuration of value creation - must also be taken into account, as well as the control of the service providers, especially the sales partners, in line with the marketing strategy. Both must be institutionally anchored, either in the marketing department itself or in a separate unit, which should then continuously coordinate with the marketing department. However, a customer-oriented service provision always requires a pronounced marketing mindset and culture among all partners involved in value creation. Despite the marketing competence in the hands of the respective department, marketing thus remains a company-wide task. In the course of implementing the marketing strategy, attention must therefore be paid to the **creation of the framework conditions for a** strategy-appropriate corporate identity, which promotes the **marketing culture** (Köhne 2006, p. 234).

16.3 Marketing Controlling

Controlling is a central function of management. In the marketing context, it serves to **control the realization of marketing objectives, strategies and tasks**, but also the **effectiveness of individual marketing activities**. The review of goal achievement takes place company-wide, per business field and also department-related.

Within the framework of the marketing management process, marketing controlling has to answer the following questions according to Kotler et al. (2017a, p. 856):

1. What do we want to achieve (goal setting and starting point)?
2. How is the goal achievement process progressing (measurement of efficiency)?
3. Why is the process progressing as it is (assessment of efficiency)?
4. What needs to be done or improved (initiation of activities)?

In a broader sense, marketing controlling includes tasks of information, planning, coordination and control. In insurance companies, its importance stems not least from the fact that at the interface between companies or sales partners and the market, plan revisions often occur, which are accompanied by ongoing target-actual comparisons, deviation analyses and suggestions for adjustment actitivies. According to the marketing planning, strategic and operational marketing controlling can be distinguished.

The **strategic marketing controlling** aims at the systematic creation and preservation of future success potentials, is oriented towards the company and its environment and thus the establishment of new product-market relationships, and primarily performs the tasks of information supply, control, and coordination with the aim of result control (Tomczak et al. 2014, pp. 264–268):

- The **information function** is particularly important in the context of customer, competitor, and market analyses and not least during ongoing cooperation within the company in the exchange of information between top management, departments, and sales partners regarding sales, market share, sell-off, customer satisfaction, and quality indicators.
- The **control function** serves to uncover misdevelopments and deviations from marketing objectives, strategies, and tasks and thus aims at a current control of the marketing conception. It is therefore the core of marketing controlling.
- As part of its **coordination task**, strategic marketing controlling coordinates the various sub-plans formally and in terms of content, e.g., in new product planning with communication policy and sales planning of the various sales partners. Specifically, this task formally includes the initiation of planning processes, the permanent monitoring of planning progress, the ongoing scheduling of individual planning committees, and the coordination with operational plans, as well as content-wise the priority control.

Part of a strategic marketing controlling is a **marketing audit**, which serves to review the entire marketing system and analyzes its premises and conditions for planning, control, and monitoring. Compared to target-actual controls, the marketing audit is thus future-oriented (Meffert et al. 2019, p. 928; Kotler et al. 2017a, pp. 1213–1219).

The main task of **operational marketing controlling** is, on the other hand, the control of marketing activities, the analysis of deviation causes, and the initiation of adjustment activities. This approach is based on key data defined in advance in operational marketing planning, which are periodically checked and evaluated in target-actual comparisons. The instruments of operational marketing controlling, as well as the respective users and those responsible, can be modified in accordance with a company organization (Table 16.1).

In operational marketing controlling, there is a need for a marketing manager, (at least one) marketing controller, and a contact person on the part of the service and sales partners. With regard to partner-related expense and revenue control, it is questionable to what extent this can provide marketing-specific insights. However, the company-wide application of a **sales segment accounting**, which can reveal sources of profit and loss in a very differentiated form, seems sensible. Sales segments are conceptually distinguishable subareas of the company's market relationships and sales activities, e.g. customers, product branches or sales channels (as in the determination of business fields). With the aim of a causation-based cost and revenue allocation, costs and revenues are only allocated to those sales segments to which they can be directly and clearly assigned. In this way, costs and revenues can aggregate upwards across different sales segments. Service

Table 16.1 Areas of application of operational marketing controlling and their instruments. (Based on Kotler et al. 2007, p. 1183)

Type of control	Main responsibility	Purpose of control	Instruments
Annual plan control	Management	Check achievement of planned results	Sales volume comparison Market share comparison Expense comparison Financial figures comparison Customer Scorecard Partner Scorecard
Expense and revenue control	Marketing manager, Marketing controller	Determine company-wide profit-loss portfolio	Expense and revenue accounting for: • Products • Areas or SBU • Customer groups • Sales channels and partners Sales segment accounting
Efficiency control	Marketing manager, Marketing controller, Service partners	Efficiency control and efficiency improvement	Efficiency studies for: • Sales • Advertising • Sales promotion • Internal marketing processes Service Level Agreements

partners can only be directly classified as sales segments and thus controlled if they represent a product or a sales channel (Homburg 2020, pp. 1320–1322).

The **ongoing performance control** in the course of operational marketing controlling follows several steps:

1. Determination of control variables in accordance with marketing objectives
2. Determination of tolerance ranges
3. Recording of control variables
4. Analysis of the reasons for deviation
5. Development of corrective activities.

Typical key figures of ongoing performance control **in the insurance sector** include, for example, the premium volume per branch (market share and growth), contribution margins (costs or profit), the number of contracts per customer, customer satisfaction, complaint frequency (all customer loyalty), brand awareness and brand sympathy, cancellation rates (quality of advice and products) or the change in new business (customer acquisition and growth) (Kühlmann et al. 2003, p. 285).

In the sense of systematization, a strategic and an operational focus on marketing controlling can also be distinguished in insurance marketing. The **strategic marketing controlling** primarily aims to verify the achievement of economic (sales and profit, market share, contribution margins; all business field-specific) and psychographic marketing objectives (awareness, sympathy, preferences, purchase intention, customer satisfaction, customer loyalty). The aim is to keep an eye on the marketing conception and its success as a whole and, if necessary, to make adjustments to ensure future success. The **operational marketing controlling** is about the more detailed success measurement of the marketing tools used and their differentiated control or adjustment. Product controlling is determined on the one hand by realized sales, i.e. ongoing sales variables (new and existing business) are relevant here. On the other hand, product success is determined by costs, primarily risk costs, and is therefore not the subject of marketing controlling, but of actuarial activity and risk-oriented controlling. The communication policy and its tools can be well tested or measured; the corresponding success controls such as advertising success measurements or web tracking in online marketing are, however, not specific to insurance (Görgen 2007, p. 239).

Industry-specific features, on the other hand, are shown by the insurer's market partners, the intermediaries and the customers: The customers - in their dual role as demanders and cost causers via the risk object to be insured - have a strong influence as participants in the service provision and on the technical results (Sect. 1.1). The intermediaries are significant in activating and controlling demand (insurer's perspective), and due to their personal proximity and interaction, they have a great influence on customer satisfaction (Sect. 14.2.3). Therefore, the exploitation of customer potential and the control of sales channels are crucial for success.

The **customer-related controlling** can economically determine and reflect the customer value and psychographically the customer satisfaction, customer loyalty, customer retention, and complaint sensitivity with reference to the marketing objective categories (see also: Görgen 2007, pp. 256–287). The psychographic objectives have already been presented (Chaps. 7 and 9). The customer value as an economic measure of controlling is composed of the sum of all net present values of the contracts concluded by the customer himself and those mediated or recommended by him (Fig. 16.2). Each net present contract value results from the difference of all revenues, more precisely actually payments, and all expenses, more precisely actually disbursements, that have flowed over the term, all of which are discounted or compounded to the same point in time.

▶ **Customer equity (Customer Lifetime Value)** describes the value that a customer creates from the insurer's perspective over the course of his customer relationship through the discounted contribution margins of his own contracts as well as through the contribution margins of the contracts of other customers mediated through his reference.

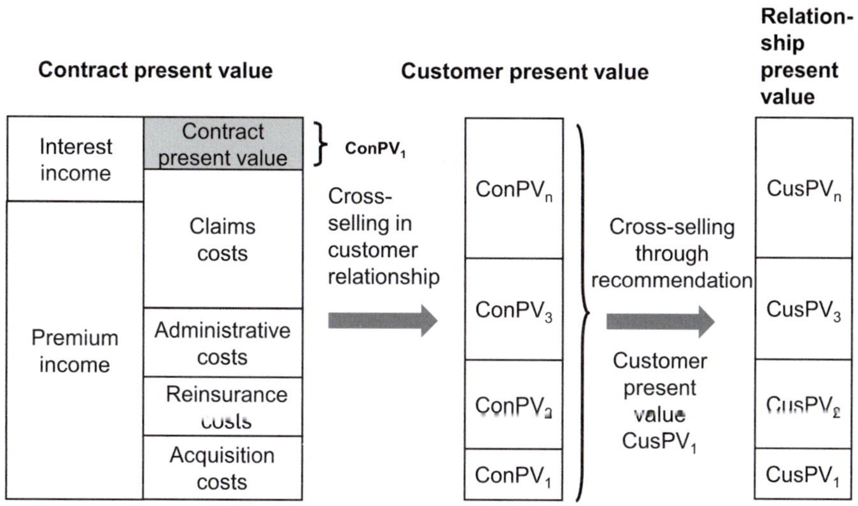

Fig. 16.2 Customer Lifetime Value of an insurance customer. (Based on Jara 2000, p. 68)

The method is theoretically consistent, but proves difficult to implement in practice because many future cash flows are associated with uncertain estimates and cannot be precisely predetermined in time. As a conceptual construct for understanding the value-relevant components of a customer relationship, the **customer lifetime value** is quite suitable: It illustrates on the inflow side the prepayment effect of the premiums and on the outflow side, which expense items in addition to expected loss and commission payments are to be attributed to a single customer contract. Furthermore, it shows that with each additional contract a customer relationship tends to become more profitable and a single negative contract present value does not necessarily result in a negative customer present value. The same applies to the relationship present value even at the level of all customer contracts, if the customer overcompensates his own negative customer present value by creating access to other, profitable customer relationships, e.g. as a managing director who enables access to his employee business. Therefore, it seems sensible in practice to at least calculate with auxiliary values and to better accommodate the fact that not only a single contract, but the entire customer relationship must be evaluated from an economic point of view.

Also the **intermediary-related controlling** can be oriented towards economic and psychographic target sizes. However, the operational implementation of the performance evaluation of insurance intermediaries ultimately depends on which corresponding key figures can actually be collected in practice. Economically, an intermediary-related contribution margin and thus, analogous to the customer lifetime value, a kind of salesperson lifetime value can be calculated (Schareck 2005, pp. 191–193). However, like the customer lifetime value, this is based on forecasts and assumptions. Therefore, pragmatically, alternative key figures can be used to evaluate the intermediary's performance, such as the number of new contracts, premium income of new contracts, number of customer contacts in relation to contract conclusions (closing rate) and number of conclusions in relation to the number of offers, based on existing customers e.g. premium income in the portfolio, number of cancellations in relation to the number of new customers (customer base turnover rate), customer-related cross-selling rate (bundling rate), customer equity or customer contribution margin. Psychographic measures of intermediary success are e.g. the average customer satisfaction with the individual intermediary (however, this is rarely consistently measured), the number of complaints to the insurer, ombudsman or BaFin as well as the willingness to recommend (e.g. based on the net promoter score) (see also Köhne 2013b).

Compiled in a different systematics, the following key figures are conceivable and helpful for sales controlling, for example (Homburg et al. 2016, p. 140; Görgen 2007, pp. 288 and 310–312; Hambach and Hiendlmeier 2021, p. 399):

1. **Economic Indicators**:
   - Premium income from existing and new business, related to distribution partners, sales regions, branches, products, customers, contacts, target groups
   - Potential premium income (ditto)
   - Contribution margin ex ante and ex post (ditto)
   - Shares of new and increased business in premium income
   - Granted discounts on tariff premiums (ditto)
   - Lost premium income and cancellation rates (ditto)
   - Reinvestment rate in life insurance
   - etc.
2. **Customer-related Indicators**:
   - Share of new customers, recoverd and lost customers in the total customer portfolio
   - Average customer retention period
   - Existing customer structure data
   - (Branch-specific) bundling rates
   - Customer satisfaction values (satisfaction with intermediary, willingness to conclude, willingness to recommend)
   - Complaint rate (share of customer complaints in the contract portfolio)
   - Payment rate (share of those customers among a intermediary's customers who converted their contract into a fully paid-up insurance)
   - etc.
3. **Sales-related Indicators**:
   - Customer visits per day/week/month/customer/conclusion
   - Appointment rate (ratio of appointments received to inquiries)
   - Closing rate (ratio of closings to appointments)
   - Offer success rate (ratio of closings to offers)
   - etc.

Although numerous controlling indicators for insurance sales are conceivable and current empirical findings also underline that the measurement of sales-related activities using so-called measurement-performance systems positively influences the financial success of companies (Homburg 2020, p. 1329), this measurement actually only takes place partially in the insurance industry. Rather, qualitative facts such as communicative competence, technical know-how or willingness to perform as well as corresponding indicators such as customer and employee satisfaction or appointment and contact rates—if at all—are usually only recorded at the aggregated level of the entire sales organization.

In contrast, almost all insurers record indicators for the final result of the sales process, e.g. the number of contracts concluded, the premium volume of the new business achieved, the cross-selling rate or the cancellation rate. And although value orientation, or at least profit orientation, is the top corporate objective for many companies, profit-related indicators such as the contribution margins generated by intermediaries or customer equity are hardly widespread. This is likely due primarily to the insufficient practicability due to the complexity and the sometimes necessary model assumptions in the allocation as well as the lack of acceptance among insurance intermediaries (Brozy and Mangold 2004, p. 476 f.; Friederichs-Schmidt 2006, p. 219; Görgen 2008, p. 1596; Hambach and Hiendlmeier 2021, p. 406 f.).

Further Reading Recommendations for Chap. 16

- Becker (2019, Part 4, p. 815–898).
- Friederichs-Schmidt (2006).
- Köhne (2013b).
- Kotler et al. (2007, p. 90–131 as well as Chap. 24 and 25).
- Tomczak et al. (2023).

References

Becker, J. (2019): Marketing-Konzeption: Grundlagen des ziel-strategischen und operativen Marketing-Managements, München, 11. Aufl., 2019.

Brozy, L./Mangold, C. (2004): Effizienter Vertrieb in der Assekuranz, in: ZfV, Jg. 55, 2004, Nr. 16, S. 476–479.

Bruhn, M. (2022): Relationship Marketing. Das Management von Kundenbeziehungen, München, 6. Aufl., 2022.

Friederichs-Schmidt, S. (2006): Kundenwert aus Sicht von Versicherungsunternehmen, Wiesbaden, 2006.

Görgen, F. (2007): Versicherungsmarketing, Strategien, Instrumente und Controlling, Stuttgart, 2. Aufl., 2007.

Görgen, F. (2008): Vertriebscontrolling: Mehr als Prämieneinnahmen, Cross-Selling und Stornos, in: VW, Jg. 63, 2008, Nr. 19, S. 1596–1599.
Hambach, S./Hiendlmeier, S. (2021): Steuerung der Vertriebsprozesse, in: Junglas, A./Schradin, H./Wiegard, M.: Steuerung von Versicherungsunternehmen, Stuttgart, 3. Aufl., 2021, S. 391–408.
Homburg, C. (2020): Marketingmanagement, Strategie – Instrumente – Umsetzung – Unternehmensführung, Wiesbaden, 7. Aufl., 2020.
Homburg, C./Schäfer, H./Schneider, J. (2016): Sales Excellence, Vertriebsmanagement mit System, Wiesbaden, 8. Aufl., 2016.
Jara, M. (2000): Zielorientierte Neugestaltung des Schadenmanagements in Versicherungsunternehmen, St. Gallen, 2000.
Köhne, T. (1999): Versicherungsmarketing: Vom „Mauerblümchendasein" zur strategischen Instanz, in: IVW HSG (Ed.): Risk Tomorrow, IVW-Jahresbericht 1998, St. Gallen, 1999, S. 35–38.
Köhne, T. (2006): Marketing im strategischen Unternehmensnetzwerk, Erklärungsmodell und praktische Anwendung in der Versicherungswirtschaft, Wiesbaden, 2006.
Köhne, T. (2013b): Performance von Versicherungsvermittlern – Konzeption und Messung aus Sicht des Versicherungsunternehmens, Berliner Schriften zur Versicherungswirtschaft, ed. by Institut für Versicherungswirtschaft an der Hochschule für Wirtschaft und Recht Berlin, Nr. 5, Berlin, 2013.
Kotler, P./Keller, K.L./Bliemel, F. (2007): Marketing-Management, Strategien für wertschaffendes Handeln, München, 12. Aufl., 2007.
Kotler, P./Keller, K.L./Opresnik, M.O. (2017a): Marketing-Management, Konzepte – Instrumente – Unternehmensfallstudien, Halbergmoos, 15. Aufl., 2017.
Kühlmann, K./Wolf, H.-P./Wallenwein, C./Swoboda, U. (2003): Marketing und Vertrieb, Funktionsorientierte Qualifikationen, Karlsruhe, 2. Aufl., 2003.
Meffert, H./Burmann, C./Kirchgeorg, M./Eisenbeiß, M. (2019): Marketing, Grundlagen marktorientierter Unternehmensführung, Konzepte – Instrumente – Praxisbeispiele, Wiesbaden, 13. Aufl., 2019.
Schareck, C. (2005): Wertorientierung im Versicherungsvertrieb, Karlsruhe, 2005.
Tomczak, T./Kuß, A./Reinecke, S. (2014): Marketingplanung, Einführung in die marktorientierte Unternehmens- und Geschäftsfeldplanung, Wiesbaden, 7. Aufl., 2014.
Tomczak, T./Reinecke, S./Gollnhofer, J. (2023): Marketingplanung, Einführung in die marktorientierte Unternehmens- und Geschäftsfeldplanung, Wiesbaden, 8. Aufl., 2023.

Bibliography

Aaker, D./Joachimsthaler, E. (2000): Brand Leadership, New York, 2000.

Abell, D.E. (1980): Defining the Business, The Starting Point of Strategic Planning, Englewood Cliffs N.J., 1980.

Accenture (Ed.) (2020): Ökosysteme in der Versicherungsindustrie, Potenziale und Umsetzungsstrategien, Whitepaper, 2020.

Ackermann, K. A./Heim, N./Collenberg, A./Lenggenhager, V./Müller, S./Furchheim, P. (2020): Swiss Behavioral Economics Studie, Winterthur, 2020.

Adams, P./Hunt, S. (2013): Encouraging Consumers to Claim Redress: Evidence from a Field Trial, in: Financial Conduct Authority (Ed.), Occasional Paper, Nr. 2, London, 2013.

Agnew, J.R./Anderson, L.R./Gerlach, J.R./Szykman, L.R. (2008): Who Chooses Annuities? An Experimental Investigation of the Role of Gender, Framing, and Defaults, in: American Economic Review: Papers & Proceedings, Vol. 98, 2008, No. 2, pp. 418–422.

Akerlof, G.A: (1970): The market for "lemons": quality uncertainty and the market mechanism, in: Q. J. Econ., Vol. 84, 1970, No. 3, pp. 488–500.

Allianz Konzern (Ed.) (2023): Allianz Konzern Geschäftsbericht 2022, München, 2023.

Allianz SE (Ed.) (2023a): Allianz SE Geschäftsbericht 2022, München, 2023.

Allianz SE (Ed.) (2023b): OneAllianz Creators Platform, München, 2023.

Allianz SE (Ed.) (2024): Unser Purpose lautet: We secure your future, in: https://www.allianz.com/de/ueber-uns/strategie-werte/strategie.html, Accessed: 02.01.2014.

Altemeyer-Bartscher, M./Hohenstein, J./Ketzler, R./Theis, A./Wiener, K. (2019): Kosten und Nutzen der Regulierung, in: Volkswirtschaftliche Themen und Analysen, Nr. 9, Ed. by GDV, Berlin, 2019.

Altenburger, R. (2003): Electronic Business im Erstversicherungsunternehmen unter besonderer Berücksichtigung des Marketing, Leipzig, 2003.

Altuntas, M./Gößmann, G. (2015): Stand zur Internationalisierung deutscher Versicherungsgruppen im Schaden- und Unfallgeschäft, in: VW, Jg. 70, 2015, Nr. 9, pp. 283–288.

Amerirad, B./Cattaneo, M./Kenett, R.S./Luciano, E. (2023): Adversarial Artificial Intelligence in Insurance: From an Example to Some Potential Remedies, in: Risks, Vol. 11, 2023, pp. 20–37. https://doi.org/10.3390/risks11010020

Anderson, J./Narus, J. (1999): Welchen Wert hat ihr Angebot für den Kunden?, in: Harvard Business Manager, Jg. 21, 1999, Nr. 4, pp. 97–107.

Ansari, A./Essegaier, S./Kohli, R. (2000): Internet Recommendation Systems, in: JoMR, Vol. 37, 2000, No. 3, pp. 363–375.

Ansoff, H.I. (1966): Management-Strategie, München, 1966.

T. Köhne, *Insurance Marketing,* https://doi.org/10.1007/978-3-658-47345-7

ARAG Holding SE (Ed.) (2015): Geschäftsbericht 2014, Konzernabschluss, Düsseldorf, 2015.

ARAG Holding SE (Ed.) (2023): Geschäftsbericht 2022, Konzernabschluss, Düsseldorf, 2023.

Arps, L. (1965): Auf sicheren Pfeilern—Deutsche Versicherungswirtschaft vor 1914, Göttingen, 1965.

Aschenbrenner-von Dahlen, S./Nagel, S. (2004): Insurance Intermediation—Theoretical Analysis and Practical Issues in the European Market, in: ZVersWiss, Jg. 93, 2004, pp. 67–99.

Aschoff, D./Heitmann, J. (2020): Klassische Risiken im Überblick, in: Mahnke, A./Rohlfs, T. (Eds.), Betriebliches Risikomanagement und Industrieversicherung, Erfolgreiche Unternehmenssteuerung durch ein effektives Risiko- und Versicherungsmanagement, Wiesbaden, 2020, pp. 89–114.

Assekurata Assekuranz Rating-Agentur GmbH (Ed.) (2022): Assekurata-Studie: Run-off in der Lebensversicherung 2022, Pressemitteilung vom 12.12.2022, Köln, 2022.

AVAD (Ed.) (2023): Informationen zur Auskunftsstelle über den Versicherungs- und Bausparaußendienst und Versicherungsmakler in Deutschland e.V., in: http://www.avad.de, Accessed: 11.11.2023.

AXA Versicherung AG (Ed.) (2023): Geschäftsbericht 2022, Köln, 2023.

Backhaus, K./Erichson, B./Gensler, S./Weiber, R./Weiber, T. (2021): Multivariate Analysemethoden, Eine anwendungsorientierte Einführung, Berlin, 16. Aufl., 2021.

Bätscher, R. (1989): Financial Services für den privaten Haushalt—Entwicklung, Funktionen und konzeptioneller Ansatz im Lichte des Service-Gedankens, Dissertation, St. Gallen, 1989.

BaFin (Ed.) (2010): '09 Jahresbericht der Bundesanstalt für Finanzdienstleistungsaufsicht, Bonn, 2010.

BaFin (Ed.) (2018): Big Data trifft auf künstliche Intelligenz. Herausforderungen und Implikationen für Aufsicht und Regulierung von Finanzdienstleistungen, Studie, o. O., 2018.

BaFin (Ed.) (2020): Merkblatt zum Umgang mit Nachhaltigkeitsrisiken, o. O. 2020.

BaFin (Ed.) (2021): Big Data und künstliche Intelligenz: Prinzipien für den Einsatz von Algorithmen in Entscheidungsprozessen, o. O., 2021.

BaFin (Ed.) (2022): Nachhaltigkeit: Daran kommt niemand mehr vorbei, in: BafinJournal vom 22.12.2022, Bonn, 2022.

BaFin (Ed.) (2023a): Ausgewählte Kennzahlen der Schaden- und Unfallversicherungsunternehmen 2021, in der selbst abgeschlossenen Kraftfahrzeug-Haftpflichtversicherung, in der Rangfolge der verdienten Brutto-Beiträge, Tabelle 5631, Bonn, 2023, in: www.bafin.de.

BaFin (Ed.) (2023b): Ausgewählte Kennzahlen der Schaden- und Unfallversicherungsunternehmen 2021, in der selbst abgeschlossenen sonstigen Kraftfahrtversicherung, in der Rangfolge der verdienten Brutto-Beiträge, Tabelle 5632, Bonn, 2023, in: www.bafin.de.

BaFin (Ed.) (2023c): Ausgewählte Kennzahlen der Schaden- und Unfallversicherungsunternehmen 2021, in der Rangfolge der verdienten Brutto-Beiträge, Tabelle 560, Bonn, 2023, in: www.bafin.de.

Balderjahn, I. (1995): Bedürfnis, Bedarf, Nutzen, in: Tietz, B./Köhler, R./Zentes, J. (Eds.), Handwörterbuch des Marketing , Band 2, pp. 179–190.

Barb, C./Klein, K./Kraft, M. (2018): Auswirkungen von Smart-Home-Technologien auf die verbundene Hausrat- und Wohngebäudeversicherung—Markt, Ausgestaltungsmerkmale und Preisbereitschaft, in: ZVersWiss, Jg. 107, 2018, pp. 495–516.

Barberis, N.C. (2013): Thirty Years of Prospect Theory in Economics: A Review and Assessment, in: Journal of Economic Perspectives, Vol. 27, 2013, No 1, pp. 173–196.

Barbier, E. (2023): Verschmelzende Geschäftswelt: Nach den ersten Ökosystem-Ausflügen der Branche macht sich Katerstimmung breit, in: Newsletter 'Versicherungswirtschaft-heute' vom 25.06.2023, 2023.

Barinka, A./Wippler, P. (2019): Personalisierte Links ersetzen Apps und Portale, in: Reich, M./ Zerres, C. (Eds.), Handbuch Versicherungsmarketing, Berlin, 2. Aufl., 2019, pp. 423–434.

Bechmann, T./Köhne, T. (1997): Integriertes Marketing: Schlüsselfunktion im dynamischen Versicherungsmarkt, Sonderausgabe der IVW Management-Information, Band 1, St. Gallen, 1997.

Becker, J. (2019): Marketing-Konzeption: Grundlagen des ziel-strategischen und operativen Marketing-Managements, München, 11. Aufl., 2019.

Beenken, M. (2010): Der Markt der Versicherungsvermittlung unter veränderten rechtlichen Rahmenbedingungen, unter besonderer Berücksichtigung von Sourcingstrategien des Versicherungsvermittlerbetriebs, Karlsruhe, 2010.

Benartzi, S./Thaler, R.H. (1995): Myopic loss aversion and the equity premium puzzle, in: The Quarterly Journal of Economics, Vol. 110, 1995, No. 1, pp. 75–92.

Bender-Scheel, M.S. (2012): Die Satisfaction-Profit Chain in der Logistikdienstleistungsbranche, Eine Längsschnittanalyse, Wiesbaden, 2012.

Berekoven, L./Eckert, W./Ellenrieder, P. (2009): Marktforschung, Methodische Grundlagen und praktische Anwendung, Wiesbaden, 12. Aufl., 2009.

Berenberg-Gossler, P./Bertelsmann, T./Hanisch, M. (2023): Branchenprognose Versicherungswirtschaft: Aussichten für 2023 und 2024 hellen sich auf, in: Insurance Perspectives, Nr. 3, Ed. by GDV, Berlin, 2023.

Berry, L.L. (1986): Big Ideas in Service Marketing, in: Venkatesan, M./Schamelensee, D.H./ Marshall, C.E. (Eds.), Creativity in Service Marketing, Chicago u. a., 1986, pp. 6–8.

Betschart, A./Mussak, P. (2021): Steuerung der Produktentwicklungsprozesse, in: Junglas, A./ Schradin, H./Wiegard, M.: Steuerung von Versicherungsunternehmen, Stuttgart, 3. Aufl., 2021, pp. 359–390.

Biedebach, M. (2023): Industrial-age Ecosystems and Digital Innovation—Implications for Structures, Roles and Value Capturing, Univ.-Diss., Kassel, 2023.

Birgikt, K./Stadler, M. (1986): Corporate Identity, Landsberg am Lech, 3. Aufl., 1986.

Birkner, G. (2017): Versicherung digital 2017, Wie Versicherte die neue Versicherungswelt sehen, Frankfurt am Main, 2017.

Bittl, A. (1998): Vertrauenserwerb durch innovative Problemlösungsangebote, in: ZfV, Jg. 49, 1998, Nr. 24, pp. 727–735.

Bittl, A./Vielreicher, P. (1994): Individuelle Wahrnehmung und Versiche rungsnachfrage, Konsequenzen für Produktgestaltung und Unterneh menskommunikation von Versicherungsunternehmen, in: ZVersWiss, Jg. 83, 1994, Nr. 1–2, pp. 193–217.

Blodgett, J./Wakefield, K./Barnes, J. (1995): The Effects of Customer Service on Consumer Complaining Behavior, in: Journal of Service Marketing, Vol. 9, 1995, No. 4, pp. 31–42.

Blum, R./Weller, S. (2013): Der Schlüssel ist der Mensch, Der Wertewandel durch neue Technologien zwingt die Versicherer zu radikalem Umdenken, in: VW, Jg. 68, 2013, Nr. 16, pp. 48–50.

Boemke, B./Ulrici, B. (2014): BGB Allgemeiner Teil, Heidelberg, 2. Aufl., 2014.

Bosselmann, E.H. (1994): Versicherungsmakler und deregulierte Versicherungsmärkte, Karlsruhe, 1994.

Braun, A. und Schreiber, F. (2017): The Current InsurTech Landscape: Business Models and Disruptive Potential, I.VW-HSG Schriftenreihe, Band 62, St. Gallen, 2017.

Breuer, W./Zimmermann, K. (2019): Werkstattmanagement–Schadensteuerung im Spannungsfeld zwischen Kunde und Versicherung, in: Reich, M./Zerres, C. (Eds.), Handbuch Versicherungsmarketing, Berlin, 2. Aufl., 2019, pp. 615–624.

Brown, J.R./Kling, J.R./Mullainathan, S./Wrobel, M.V. (2008): Why Don't People Insure Late-Life Consumption? A Framing Explanation of the Under-Annuitization Puzzle, in: American Economic Review, Vol. 98, 2008, No. 2, pp. 304–309.

Brozy, L./Mangold, C. (2004): Effizienter Vertrieb in der Assekuranz, in: ZfV, Jg. 55, 2004, Nr. 16, pp. 476–479.

Bruhn, M. (1998): Internes Marketing als Schnittstelle zwischen Marketing- und Personalmanagement, in: Bruhn, M./Meffert, H. (Eds.), Handbuch Dienstleistungsmanagement, Wiesbaden, 1998, pp. 707–732.

Bruhn, M. (2019a): Qualitätsmanagement für Dienstleistungen, Handbuch für ein erfolgreiches Qualitätsmanagement. Grundlagen, Konzepte, Methoden, Berlin, 11. Aufl., 2019.

Bruhn, M. (2019b): Kommunikationspolitik, Systematischer Einsatz der Kommunikation für Unternehmen, München, 9. Aufl., 2019.

Bruhn, M. (2022): Relationship Marketing. Das Management von Kundenbeziehungen, München, 6. Aufl., 2022.

Bruhn, M./Hennig, K. (1993): Selektion und Strukturierung von Qualitätsmerkmalen, Auf dem Weg zu einem umfassenden Qualitätsmanagement für Kreditinstitute, Teil 1, in: Jahrbuch der Absatz- und Verbrauchsforschung, Jg. 39, 1993, Nr. 3, pp. 214–238.

Bruhn, M./Homburg, C. (Eds.) (2017): Handbuch Kundenbindungsmanagement, Strategien und Instrumente für ein erfolgreiches CRM, Wiesbaden, 9. Aufl., 2013.

Bruhn, M./Meffert, H./Hadwich, K. (2019): Handbuch Dienstleistungsmarketing. Planung—Umsetzung—Kontrolle, Wiesbaden, 2. Aufl., 2019.

Brutyan, A./Guxha, D./Schmeiser, H. (2019): Versicherungen aus Kundensicht: Erkenntnisse aus der Wissenschaft, in: ZVersWiss, Jg. 108, S. 365–381. (https://doi.org/10.1007/s12297-019-00447-8)

Bundesministerium der Finanzen (Ed.) (2014): Eckpunkte des Lebensversicherungsreformgesetzes, Mitteilung vom 14. Juni 2014, Berlin, 2014.

Bundesministerium für Wirtschaft und Klimaschutz (Ed.) (2023): Gesundheitswirtschaft, Fakten & Zahlen, Daten 2022, Ergebnisse der Gesundheitswirtschaftlichen Gesamtrechnung, Berlin, 2023.

Bundesverband der Versicherungsberater (BVVB) (Ed.) (2024a): Was ist Versicherungsberatung?, in: https://www.bvvb.de/fuer-ratsuchende/was-ist-versicherungsberatung/, Accessed: 21.01.2024.

Bundesverband der Versicherungsberater (BVVB) (Ed.) (2024b): Kosten der Versicherungsberatung, in: https://www.bvvb.de/fuer-ratsuchende/kosten-der-beratung/, Accessed: 21.01.2024.

Bundesverband Deutscher Versicherungskaufleute (Ed.) (2020): BVK-Agenturvertrag, Muster eines Vertrages zwischen Einfirmenvertreter und Versicherer, Bonn, 2020.

Burkhardt, J./Steul-Fischer, M. (2014): Versicherungsunternehmen in Social Networks—Ein Überblick über aktuelle Forschungsfelder und eine experimentelle Studie zur Kundenansprache, in: ZVersWiss, Vol. 102, 2014, Nr. 5, S. 473–490.

Cash Online (Ed.) (2023): Allfinanzvertriebe 2023: in: https://www.cash-online.de/cash-hitlisten/finanzvertriebe/allfinanzvertriebe-2023/, Accessed: 24.01.2024.

Cassab, H./MacLachlan, D.L. (2009): A consumer-based view of multi-channel service, in: JOSM, Vol. 20, 2009, No. 1, pp. 52–75.

Chewning, E.G./Harrell, A.M. (1990): The Effect of Information Load on Decision Makers' Cue Utilization Levels and Decision Quality in a Financial Distress Decision Task, in: Accounting, Organizations and Society, Vol. 15, 1990, No. 6, pp. 527–542.

CosmosDirekt (Ed.) (2024): Unsere Mission, in: https://www.cosmosdirekt.de/unternehmen/ueber-uns/leitbild/, Accessed: 02.01.2014.

Crane, D.B./Froot, K.A./Mason, S.P./Perold, A.F./Merton, R.C./Bodie, Z./Sirri, E.R./Tufano, P. (1995): The Global Financial System, A Functional Perspective, Boston/Massachusetts, 1995.

Cummins, J.D./Doherty, N.A. (2006): The Economics of Insurance Intermediaries, in: JoRI, Vol. 73, 2006, No. 3, pp. 359–396.

Dahmen, P. (2004): Multi-Channel Strategies for Retail Financial Services, A Management-Framework for Designing and Implementing Multi-Channel Strategies, Wiesbaden, 2004.

Damm, P. (1993): Ertragsbarwertbezogene Vergütungspolitik von Versicherungsunternehmen zur Steuerung von Absatzorganen, Karlsruhe, 1993.

Debeka Gruppe (Ed.) (2024): Unternehmensleitbild, Über den Sinn und Zweck unseres Handelns, Stand: 12/2021, in: https://www.debeka.de/ueberuns/portrait.html, Accessed: 02.01.2024.

Delisle, E. (1971): Marketing in der Versicherungswirtschaft, Beiträge zu wirtschaftswissenschaftlichen Problemen der Versicherung, Band 5, Karlsruhe, 1971.

Delisle, E. (1981): Marketing in der Versicherungswirtschaft, Beiträge zu wirtschaftswissenschaftlichen Problemen der Versicherung, Band 5, Karlsruhe, 2. Aufl., 1981.

Dellaert, B.G.C./Johnson, E.J./Duncan, S./Baker, T. (2024): Choice Architecture for Healthier Insurance Decisions: Ordering and Partitioning Together Can Improve Consumer Choice, in: Journal of Marketing, Vol. 88, 2024, No. 1, pp. 15–30. (https://doi.org/10.1177/00222429221119086)

Der Bundesbeauftragte für den Datenschutz und die Informationsfreiheit (Ed.) (2022): Datenschutz-Grundverordnung—Bundesdatenschutzgesetz, Texte und Erläuterungen, BfDI-Info Nr. 1, Bonn, 2022.

Deutsche Bundesbank (Ed.) (2023): Finanzierungsrechnung Juni 2023, Frankfurt a.M., 2023.

Deutsche Industrie- und Handelskammer (DIHK) (Ed.) (2024): Statistiken Vermittlerverzeichnisse, Eingetragene Versicherungsvermittler, Stand: 1. Januar 2024, in: https://www.dihk.de/de/themen-und-positionen/recht-in-der-wirtschaft/gewerberecht/statistiken-vermittlerverzeichnisse-3344, Accessed: 21.01.2024.

Deutsche Rentenversicherung (Ed.) (2023): Die Digitale Rentenübersicht: Fragen und Antworten, o. O., 2023.

Dolan, P./Elliott, A./Metcalfe, R./Vlaev, I. (2012): Influencing Financial Behaviour: from Changing Minds to Changing Contexts, in: Journal of Behavioural Finance, Vol. 13, 2012, No. 2, pp. 126–142.

Doyle, P. (2000): Valuing Marketing's Contribution, in: European Management Journal, Vol. 18, 2000, No. 3, pp. 233–245.

Drucker, P. (1954): The Practice of Management, New York, 1954.

Duden (Ed.) (2023): Heuristik, in: https://www.duden.de/rechtschreibung/Heuristik, Accessed: 29.12.2023.

Duft, C. (1983): Insurance Marketing, Zürich, 1983.

Ebert, S./Koos, B./Schneider, J.C. (2012): On the optimal type and level of guarantees for prospect theory investors. Paris December 2012 Finance Meeting EUROFIDAIAFFI Paper.

Ebner, M.D. (2010): Preispolitik in der Kompositversicherung, Dissertation, Karlsruhe, 2010.

Eckert, C./Eckert, J./Zitzmann, A. (2021): The status quo of digital transformation in insurance sales: an empirical analysis of the german insurance industry, in: ZVersWiss, Jg. 110, 2021, Nr. 2–3, pp. 133–155.

Eckert, C./Neunsinger, C./Osterrieder, K. (2022): Managing customer satisfaction: digital applications for insurance companies, in: GP, Vol. 47, 2022, No. 3, pp. 569–602. (https://doi.org/10.1057/s41288-021-00257-z)

Eckhardt, M. (2007): Insurance Intermediation, An Economic Analysis of the Information Services Market, Heidelberg, 2007.

Eckhardt, M./Räthke-Döppner, S. (2010): The quality of insurance intermediary services—empirical evidence for Germany, in: JoRI, Vol. 77, 2010, pp. 667–701.

Eckhardt, P. (2023): Die neue EU-Kleinanlegerstrategie. Viel Schatten, wenig Licht, CEP-Studie, Ed. by Centrum für Europäische Politik, Freiburg, 2023.

Ehrler, B. (1999): Kernkompetenzorientiertes Management der Versicherung—Strategien in Risiko- und Finanzdienstleistungsnetzen, St. Gallen, 1999.

Eichner, D./Fritsch, C./Kothe, G.-L./Kühner, S./Remond, Y./Warnke, J. (2023): Risikowahrnehmung durch und nach Corona, in: Arnold, R./Berg, M./Goecke, O./Heep-Altiner, M./Müller-Peters, H. (Eds.), Risiko im Wandel, Herausforderung für die Versicherungswirtschaft, Wiesbaden, 2023, pp. 35–60.

Eickenberg, V. (2009): Marketing für Versicherungsvermittler, Karlsruhe, 2. Aufl., 2009.

Eickenberg, V. (2022): Erfolgsfaktor Vertrauen bei der Versicherungsvermittlung. Theorie und Praxis eines effektiven Marketings, Wiesbaden, 2022.

Eisen, Roland (2017): Versicherungsmarkt, in: Gabler Versicherungslexikon, Ed. by Fred Wagner, Wiesbaden, 2. Aufl., 2017, pp. 1010–1013.

Eling, M./Lehmann, M. (2018): The Impact of Digitalization on the Insurance Value Chain and the Insurability of Risks, in: GP, Vol. 43, No. 3, 2018, pp. 359–396.

Eling, M./Luhnen, M. (2010): Frontier Efficiency Methodologies to Measure Performance in the Insurance Industry, in: GP, Vol. 35, 2010, pp. 217–265.

Eppler, M.J./Mengis, J. (2004): The Concept of Information Overload: A Review of Literature from Organization Science, Accounting, Marketing, MIS, and Related Disciplines, in: The Information Society, Vol. 20, 2004, No. 5, pp. 325–344.

ERGO Versicherung AG (Ed.) (2023): Geschäftsbericht 2022, Düsseldorf, 2023.

Esch, F.-R. (2018): Strategie und Technik der Markenführung, München, 9. Aufl., 2018.

Esser, M. (2004): Assistance in der Versicherungswirtschaft. Ein marketingorientierter Ansatz zur Unternehmenswertsteigerung, Karlsruhe, 2004.

Eurich, A. (2001): Bestandskundenmarketing von Versicherungsunternehmen, Lohmar, 2001.

Europäische Kommission (Ed.) (2023): COM (2023) 279, Vorschlag für eine Richtlinie des Europäischen Parlaments und des Rates zur Änderung der Richtlinien (EU) 2009/65/EG, 2009/138/EG, 2011/61/EU, 2014/65/EU und (EU) 2016/97 im Hinblick auf die Unionsvorschriften zum Schutz von Kleinanlegern vom 24. Mai 2023, o.O., 2023.

European Insurance and Occupational Pensions Authority (EIOPA) (Ed.) (2017): Draft Implementing Technical Standards concerning a standardised presentation format for the Insurance Product Information Document of the Insurance Distribution Directive, EIOPA-17/056, o.O., 2017.

European Insurance and Occupational Pensions Authority (EIOPA) (Ed.) (2022): Guidance on the integration of sustainability preferences in the suitability assessment under the Insurance Distribution Directive (IDD), EIOPA-BoS-22-391, Frankfurt a. M., 2022.

European Insurance and Occupational Pensions Authority (EIOPA) (Ed.) (2023a): Risk Dashboard January 2023, EIOPA-BoS-23-26, Frankfurt a. M., 2023.

European Insurance and Occupational Pensions Authority (EIOPA) (Ed.) (2023b): Risk Dashboard November 2023, EIOPA-BoS-23-392, Frankfurt a. M., 2023.

Fädler, K. (1972): Eine Marketing-Konzeption für den Versicherungsbetrieb?, in: SVZ, Jg. 40, 1972, pp. 66–75.

Farny, D. (1961): Die Versicherungsmärkte, Berlin, 1961.

Farny, D. (1965): Produktions- und Kostentheorie der Versicherung, Karlsruhe, 1965.

Farny, D. (1971): Absatz und Absatzpolitik des Versicherungsunternehmens, Karlsruhe, 1971.

Farny, D. (1975): AVB unter dem Gesichtspunkt der “Produktbeschreibung”, in: ZVersWiss, Jg. 64, 1975, Nr. 2, pp. 169–184.

Farny, D. (1990): Versicherungsbetriebslehre: Wirtschaftliche Theorie des Versicherungsunternehmens und seiner Beziehungen zur Umwelt, in: ZVersWiss, Jg. 79, pp. 1–30.

Farny, D. (1992): Buchführung und Periodenrechnung im Versicherungsunternehmen, Wiesbaden, 4. Aufl., 1992.

Farny, D. (1995): Die Gestaltung von Versicherungsprodukten im Marketing von Versicherungsunternehmen, in: ZVersWiss, Jg. 84, 1995, pp. 79–102.

Farny, D. (2011): Versicherungsbetriebslehre, Karlsruhe, 5. Aufl., 2011.

Finn, A. (2001): Mystery Shopper Benchmarking of Durable Goods Chains and Stores, in: Journal of Service Research, Vol. 3, 2001, No. 4, pp. 310–320.

Fleck, J./Herrig, C. (2015): Das "neue" Beschwerdemanagement—ein Erfahrungsbericht aus der Praxis, in: ZfV, Jg. 66, 2015, Nr. 3, pp. 88–94.

Focht, U./Richter, A./Schiller, J. (2013): Intermediation and (Mis-)Matching in Insurance Markets—Who Should Pay the Insurance Broker?, in: JoRI, Vol. 80, 2013, No. 2, pp. 329–350.

Fopp, L. (2002): Schadenmanagement aktiv gestalten, Die Combined Ratio drastisch senken mit Value driven Claims Management, in: VW, Jg. 57, 2002, Nr. 2, pp. 80–81.

Forsa (Ed.) (2023): dbb Bürgerbefragung Öffentlicher Dienst 2023, Berlin, 2023.

Friederichs-Schmidt, S. (2006): Kundenwert aus Sicht von Versicherungsunternehmen, Wiesbaden, 2006.

Friedrich, T.A. (2013): Brüsseler Steine ins Rollen bringen, Bericht über die europäische Gesetzesmaschine, in: VW, Jg. 68, 2013, Nr. 14, pp. 10–13.

Fritzsche, A./Bohnert, A. (2022): Implications of bundled offerings for business development ad competitive strategy in digital insurance, in: GP, Vol. 47, 2022, pp. 817–834. (https://doi.org/10.1057/s41288-021-00244-4)

Fröhner, R. (1969): Lebensversicherung der Assekuranz, Versicherungswirtschaft auf dem Weg zum Marketing, in: die absatzwirtschaft, Jg. 12, 1969, Nr. 5, pp. 17–24.

Fuest, C./Thum, M. (2021): Hilft eine Versicherungspflicht für Elementarschäden?, in: Handelsblatt vom 28. Juli 2021, pp. 48.

Gaedeke, O. (2021): Vertriebseffizienz mit Behavioral Economics und Entscheidertypen steigern, Select Typen in b4p Mediaanalyse und -planung, Sirius Campus-White Paper vom 16.08.2021.

Gaedeke, O./Müller, C. (2023): Erfolgreiche Kundenberatung und -betreuung mit den Select Typen, Ansätze zur wirksamen Gestaltung von Entscheidungsprozessen bei allen Kundenkontakten. Ein Handbuch für Marketing, Produktentwicklung, Vertrieb und Service, Ed. by Sirius Campus, Köln, 2023.

Gal, J. (2019): Rechtliche Rahmenbedingungen eines Versicherungsmarketing, in: Reich, M./Zerres, C. (Eds.), Handbuch Versicherungsmarketing, Berlin, 2. Aufl., 2019, pp. 97–119.

GDV (Ed.) (2000): Neufassung der Hauptpunkte eines Vertrages für selbständige hauptberufliche Versicherungsvertreter gemäß §§ 84 Abs. 1, 92 HGB, Berlin/Bonn/Köln, 2000.

GDV (Ed.) (2008): Jahrbuch der deutschen Versicherungswirtschaft 2008, Berlin, 2008.

GDV (Ed.) (2021a): Anbieterlandschaft: Mehr Stabilität als Wandel, in: Makro und Märkte kompakt, Nr. 38, 2021.

GDV (Ed.) (2021b): Versicherer—für die Herausforderungen von morgen, in: Makro und Märkte kompakt, Nr. 39, 2021.

GDV (Ed.) (2021c): Versicherung gegen Naturgefahrenereignisse in Deutschland, Gesamtkonzept der deutschen Versicherer, Berlin, 2021.

GDV (Ed.) (2023a): Statistiken zur deutschen Versicherungswirtschaft 2023, Berlin, 2023.

GDV (Ed.) (2023b): Fokus Digitalisierung. Grünes Licht statt Rotstift: IT-Jobs in der digitalen Versicherungswirtschaft, Nr. 10, Berlin, 2023.

GDV (Ed.) (2023c): Klimawandelszenarien im ORSA, Ansätze zur Umsetzung der aufsichtlichen Anforderungen, Version 2.0, Berlin, 2023.

GDV (Ed.) (2023d): Nachhaltigkeitspositionierung. Der Beitrag der deutschen Versicherer zum Klimaschutz, Stand: 19.01.2023, Berlin, 2023.

GDV/Verband der privaten Krankenversicherung e. V. (PKV)/Bundesverband der Assekuranzführungskräfte e. V. (VGA)/Bundesverband Deutscher Versicherungskaufleute e. V. (BVK) (Eds.) (2006): Wettbewerbsrichtlinien der Versicherungswirtschaft, o.O., 2006.

Gericke, S.H. (2001): Customer Relationship Management in der Assekuranz unter besonderer Berücksichtigung neuer Verfahren und moderner Informationstechnologie—Ziele, Nutzen, Inhalt und Umsetzung, Karlsruhe, 2001.

Gimpel, H./Lanzl, J./Manner-Romberg, T./Nüske, N. (2018): Digitaler Stress in Deutschland, Eine Befragung von Erwerbstätigen zu Belastung und Beanspruchung durch Arbeit mit digitalen Technologien, Working Paper Forschungsförderung Hans-Böckler-Stiftung Nr. 101, 2018.

Glaser, C. (2021): Wettbewerbsfaktor Vertrieb bei Finanzdienstleistern. Ein ganzheitliches Konzept zur Sales Excellence, Wiesbaden, 3. Aufl., 2021.

Görgen, F. (2002): Versicherungsmarketing, Stuttgart, 2002.

Görgen, F. (2007): Versicherungsmarketing, Strategien, Instrumente und Controlling, Stuttgart, 2. Aufl., 2007.

Görgen, F. (2008): Vertriebscontrolling: Mehr als Prämieneinnahmen, Cross-Selling und Stornos, in: VW, Jg. 63, 2008, Nr. 19, pp. 1596–1599.

Gomez, P./Probst, G. (2007): Die Praxis des ganzheitlichen Problemlösens, Bern, 3. Aufl., 2007.

Gottlieb, D. (2012): Prospect theory, life insurance, and annuities. The Wharton School Research Paper, No. 44, University of Pennsylvania, 2012.

Graf, S. (2017): Life-cycle funds: Much ado about nothing?, in: The European Journal of Finance, Vol. 23, 2017, No. 11, pp. 974–998.

Graf, S./Ruß, J./Schelling, S. (2017): As you like it: Explaining the demand for lifecycle funds with multi cumulative prospect theory. Working paper IFA Ulm, 2017.

Gravelle, H. (1993): Product price and advice quality: implications of the commission system in life assurance, in: GP, Vol. 18, 1993, pp. 31–53.

Grischuk, P. (2021): Mystery Shopping, in: BaFin Journal, Dezember 2021, pp. 18–21.

Grösch, M. (2020): The impact of product variety on customers' default acceptance and company perception. Experimental studies for the insurance industry, in: ZVersWiss, Jg. 109, 2020, pp. 377–398. (https://doi.org/10.1007/s12297-020-00458-w)

Grösch, M./Steul-Fischer, M. (2018): Less is more: How the number of insurance options influences customers' default acceptance, in: ZVersWiss, Jg. 107, 2018, pp. 517–529. (https://doi.org/10.1007/s12297-018-0415-4)

Grothe, T./Lohse, U. (2003): Kundenbindungsmanagement für Versicherungsunternehmen, Göttingen, 2003.

Grüner, T./Hiebl, K. (2014): Bändigung gewaltiger Datenvolumina, Big Data ermöglicht Generierung von Wettbewerbsvorteilen im gesättigten Marktumfeld, in: VW, Jg. 69, 2014, Nr. 4, pp. 60–63.

Guttenbacher, S./Steinbrück, P./Waschkowitz, A.B. (2021): Steuerung der Schadenbearbeitungsprozesse, in: Junglas, A./Schradin, H./Wiegard, M.: Steuerung von Versicherungsunternehmen, Stuttgart, 3. Aufl., 2021, pp. 475–514.

Habschick, M./Evers, J. (2008): Anforderungen an Finanzvermittler—mehr Qualität, bessere Entscheidungen: Studie im Auftrag des Bundesministeriums für Ernährung, Landwirtschaft und Verbraucherschutz, Hamburg, 2008.

Haedrich, G./Tomczak, T./Kaetzke, P. (2003): Strategische Markenführung, Planung und Realisierung von Markenstrategien, Bern, 2003.

Haller, M. (1975): Sicherheit durch Versicherung? Gedanken zur zukünftigen Rolle der Versicherung, Bern, 1975.

Haller, M. (1982): Risiko- und Versicherungsprobleme des privaten Haushalts—aus Sicht der Privatversicherung, in: ZVersWiss, Jg. 71, 1982, Nr. 3/4, pp. 383–437.
Haller, M. (1986a): Funktionen-Marketing—zur Bewältigung der "Financial Services (R) Evolution"? in: Belz, C. (Ed.), Realisierung des Marketing, Festschrift zum 60. Geburtstag von Prof. Dr. H. Weinhold-Stünzi, St. Gallen 1986, pp. 1.097–1.124.
Haller, M. (1986b): Risiko-Management, in: Jacob, H. (Ed.), Schriften zur Unternehmensführung, Band 33, Wiesbaden, 1986, pp. 7–43.
Haller, M. (2006): Funktionen-Ansatz, in: Belz, C./Bieger, T. (Eds.), Customer Value, Kundenvorteile schaffen Unternehmensvorteile, Landsberg a. L., 2006, pp. 745–760.
Haller, M./Ackermann, W. (1995): Versicherungswirtschaft—kundenorientiert, Zürich, 1995.
Hambach, S./Hiendlmeier, S. (2021): Steuerung der Vertriebsprozesse, in: Junglas, A./Schradin, H./Wiegard, M.: Steuerung von Versicherungsunternehmen, Stuttgart, 3. Aufl., 2021, pp. 391–408.
Hamel, G./Prahalad, C.K. (1995): Die Zukunft gestalten—schon heute, in: HBM, 1995, Nr. 1, pp. 36–42.
HanseMerkur Reiseversicherung (Ed.) (2023): Darstellung der Partner auf der Unternehmenswebsite, in: www.hmrv.de/partner/referenzen, Accessed: 12.09.2023.
HanseMerkur (Ed.) (2024): Unsere Philosophie, in: https://www.hansemerkur.de/hansemerkur#-section_46324, Accessed: 24.01.2024.
Harbrücker, U. (1992): Wertewandel und Corporate Identity, Perspektiven eines gesellschaftsorientierten Marketing von Versicherungsunternehmen, Wiesbaden, 1992.
Hart, C./Heskett, J./Sasser, W. (1990): The Profitable Art of Service Recovery, in HBR, Vol. 68, 1990, No. 4, pp. 148–156.
Hartmann, C. (2006): Customer Value im Bereich der Automobilität—empirische Analyse und strategische Implikationen für die Kfz-Versicherer als automobile Dienstleistungsanbieter, St. Gallen, 2006.
Hasenbein, M. (2020): Der Mensch im Fokus der digitalen Arbeitswelt. Wirtschaftspsychologische Perspektiven und Anwendungsfelder, Berlin, 2020.
Hassler, M. (2017): Web Analytics: Metriken auswerten, Besucherverhalten verstehen, Website optimieren, Frechen, 4. Aufl., 2017.
Hauri, M. (2018): Wird der Berater "wegdigitalisiert"? Wie Online-Angebot und klassische Beratung miteinander harmonieren, in: ZfV, Jg. 69, 2018, Nr. 8, pp. 245–248.
Hax, H. (1991): Theorie der Unternehmung, Information, Anreize und Vertragsgestaltung, in: Ordelheide, D./Rudolph, B./Büsselmann, E. (Eds.), Betriebswirtschaftslehre und Ökonomische Theorie, Stuttgart, 1991, pp. 51–72.
Heideker, S./Steul-Fischer, M. (2016): Werbeanzeigen von Versicherungsunternehmen zur Aufklärung über Gesundheitsrisiken, in: ZVersWiss, Jg. 105, 2016; pp. 549–561. (https://doi.org/10.1007/s12297-016-0355-9)
Heimes, H. (2009): Verkaufsverhalten im Ausschließlichkeitsvertrieb der Versicherungsindustrie, Eine empirische Untersuchung des Einflusses auf den Vertriebserfolg, Lohmar, 2009.
Hein, A./Weking, J./Schreieck, M./Wiesche, M./Böhm, M./Krcmar, H. (2019): Value co-creation practices in business-to-business platform ecosystems, in: Electronic Markets, Vol. 29, 2019, No. 3, pp. 503–518. (https://doi.org/10.1007/s12525-019-00337-y)
Heinonen, K./Strandvik, T./Mickelsson, K.-J./Edvardsson, B./Sundström, E./Andersson, P. (2010): A customer-dominant logic of service, in: Journal of Service Marketing, Vol. 29, 2010, No. 6/7, pp. 531–548.
Helten, E. (1998): Restrukturierung im Assekuranz-Vertrieb, Theoretische Bemerkungen zur Verlagerung von betrieblichen Teilfunktionen und empirische Ergebnisse aus Sicht der Vermittlerbetriebe, in: VW, Jg. 53, 1998, Nr. 2, pp. 90–94.

Herrmann, A./Homburg, C./Klarmann, M. (Eds.) (2008): Handbuch Marktforschung—Methoden, Anwendungen, Praxisbeispiele, Wiesbaden, 3. Aufl., 2008.

Hermann, R. (2009): Überlebenswichtig oder überflüssig? Marketing für Firmensachversicherungen sichert langfristig das Marktpotenzial, in: VW, Jg. 64, 2009, Nr. 19, pp. 1.498–1.504.

Hertel, A./Sartorius, B. (1994): Innovatives Zielgruppenmarketing für Versicherungen ab Juli 1994, Karlsruhe, 1994.

Hielscher, J.-R. (1993): Strategische Vertriebswegepolitik mittelgroßer Lebensversicherer, Wiesbaden, 1993.

Höckmayr, G. (2012): Wandel der Beratungsqualität auf dem Versicherungsvermittlungsmarkt, Eine ökonomische Analyse der Veränderungen aufgrund der Anforderungen der EU-Vermittlerrichtlinie, Karlsruhe, 2012.

Hohenstein, J./Theis, A./Wiener, K. (2020): Versicherungsschutz der Deutschen: Potenziale nicht ausgeschöpft, in: Volkswirtschaftliche Themen und Analysen, Nr. 10, ed. by GDV, Berlin, 2020.

Holzheu, F. (1991): Skalen- und Verbundvorteile von Unternehmen mit besonderem Blick auf Versicherungsunternehmen, in: ZVersWiss, Jg. 80, 1991, pp. 531–559.

Homburg, C. (2020): Marketingmanagement, Strategie—Instrumente—Umsetzung—Unternehmensführung, Wiesbaden, 7. Aufl., 2020.

Homburg, C./Schäfer, H./Schneider, J. (2016): Sales Excellence, Vertriebsmanagement mit System, Wiesbaden, 8. Aufl., 2016.

Huber, C./Schlager, T. (2011): To Buy or not to Buy Insurance? The Antecedents in the Decision-Making Process and the Influence of Consumer Attitudes and Perceptions, Working Papers on Risk Management and Insurance, No. 90, St. Gallen, 2011.

Huber, C./Gatzert, N./Schmeiser, H. (2015): How Does Price Presentation Influence Consumer Choice? The Case of Life Insurance Products, in: JoRI, Vol. 82, 2015, No. 2, pp. 401–431.

Hüther, M. (2023): Volkswirtschaftliche Einordnung der Pandemieschäden, in: Arnold, R./Berg, M./Goecke, O./Heep-Altiner, M./Müller-Peters, H. (Eds.), Risiko im Wandel, Herausforderung für die Versicherungswirtschaft, Wiesbaden, 2023, pp. 63–74.

Hujber, T. (2005): Werbung von Versicherungsunternehmen, Wiesbaden, 2005.

HUK-Coburg Versicherungsgruppe (Ed.) (2023): Bericht über das Geschäftsjahr 2022, Coburg, 2023.

HUK-Coburg (Ed.) (2024): So sind wir, Unternehmensleitbild der HUK-COBURG Versicherungsgruppe, Stand: 10/2017, in: https://www.huk.de/ueber-uns/unternehmen/leitbild.html, Accessed: 02.01.2024.

Hu, W.Y./Scott, J.S. (2007): Behavioral obstacles in the annuity market, in: Financial Analysts Journal, Vol. 63, 2007, No. 6, pp. 71–82.

Interbrand (Ed.) (2024): Best global brands, in: www.interbrand.com/best-global-brands, Accessed: 03.01.2024.

Isaacson, W. (2011): Steve Jobs, Die autorisierte Biografie des Apple-Gründers, München, 2011.

Jaeger, K./Weinmann, H. (2012): Die Funktionsweise eines strukturierten, ganzheitlichen Beratungsprozesses, in: ZfV, Jg. 63, 2012, Nr. 13–14, pp. 427–431.

Jahnert, J.R./Schmeiser, H. (2022): The relationship between net promoter score and insurers' profitability: an empirical analysis at the customer level, in: GP, Vol. 47, 2022, pp. 944–972. (https://doi.org/10.1057/s41288-021-00237-3)

Jahnert, J.R./Schmeiser, H./Schreiber, F. (2022): Pricing strategies in the German term life Insurance market: An empirical analysis, in: Risk Management and Insurance Review, Vol. 25, 2022, pp. 19–34. (https://doi.org/10.1111/rmir.12202)

Jara, M. (2000): Zielorientierte Neugestaltung des Schadenmanagements in Versicherungsunternehmen, St. Gallen, 2000.

Jayswal, M.M./Brahmbhatt, A.C. (2013): Exploring the Impact of Post Purchase Services by Bancassurance on First Year Policy Lapsation Rate in Life Insurance Selling, in: IJBIT, Vol. 6, 2013, No. 2, pp. 94–101.

Jeßnitzer, A. (2008): Auf zur Champions League der Schadenbearbeitung (I), in: VW, Jg. 63, 2008, Nr. 19, pp. 1.615–1.619.

Joho, C. (1996): Ein Ansatz zum Kundenbindungs-Management für Versicherer, Bern, 1996.

Jost, T. (2022): Kundenbeziehungsmanagement in der Versicherungswirtschaft: Ein Perspektivwechsel vor dem Hintergrund der Digitalisierung und der Entwicklung von Ökosystemen, Karlsruhe, 2022.

Kaas, K.-P. (1990): Marketing als Bewältigung von Informations- und Unsicherheitsproblemen im Markt, in: DBW, Jg. 50, 1990, Nr. 4, pp. 539–548.

Kaas, K.-P. (1991): Marktinformationen: Screening und Signaling unter Partnern und Rivalen,, in: ZfB, Jg. 61, 1991, Nr. 3, pp. 357–370.

Kahneman, D. (2014): Schnelles Denken, langsames Denken, München, 7. Aufl., 2014.

Kahneman, D./Tversky, A. (1979): Prospect theory, An analysis of decision under risk, in: Econometrica, Vol. 47, 1979, No. 2, pp. 263–291.

Kahneman, D./Knetsch, J./Thaler, R. (1991): The Endowment Effect, Loss Aversion, and Status Quo Bias: Anomalies, in: Journal of Economic Perspectives, Vol. 5, 1991, No. 1, pp. 193–206.

Kallerhoff, H.-J. (2018): Digitalisierung im Bankenvertrieb: erfolgreich in exklusiven Bank-Partnerschaften, in: Beenken, M./Knörrer, D./Moormann, J./Schmidt, D. (Eds.), Digital Insurance. Strategien, Geschäftsmodelle, Daten, Frankfurt a.M., 2018, pp. 341–362.

Kaluza, B./Kürble, G. (1986): Die Erfahrungskurve als Instrument des strategischen Unternehmensführung in Krankenversicherungsunternehmen, in: ZVersWiss, Jg. 75, 1986, pp. 193–232.

Kapoor, R. (2018): Ecosystems: broadening the locus of value creation, in: Journal of Organization Design, Vol. 7, 2018, No. 1, pp. 1–16. (https://doi.org/10.1186/s41469-018-0035-4)

Karau, T. (2015): Qualitätsmessung in der Versicherungsvermittlung: Eine empirische Untersuchung der Unterschiede zwischen Provisions- und Honorarvergütung in der Altervorsorge, Lohmar, 2015.

Karten, W. (1995): Versicherungsproduktgestaltung—ökonomische Grundlagen, in: ZVersWiss, Jg. 84, 1995, Nr. 1, pp. 57–77.

Karten, W. (2002): Ökonomische Aspekte einer EU-Richtlinie zur Versicherungsvermittlung, in: ZVersWiss, Jg. 91, 2002, pp. 43–60.

Keith, R.J. (1960): The marketing revolution, in: JoM, Vol. 24, 1960, No. 1, pp. 35–38.

Keller, B./Klein, H.-W./Tuschl, S. (2019). Zukunft der Marktforschung: Entwicklungschancen in Zeiten von Social Media und Big Data, Wiesbaden, 2. Aufl., 2019.

Kendl, E. (1997): Reengineering im Versicherungsmarketing, Funktionsverlagerung auf Vermittlerbetriebe, Wiesbaden, 1997.

Keuper, F.W. (1986): Grundlagen einer Marketingkonzeption im Versicherungsunternehmen unter besonderer Berücksichtigung der betrieblichen Nachfragestruktur, Wien, 1986.

Kling, M. (2013): Irreführende und vergleichende Versicherungswerbung, in: ZVersWiss, Jg. 102, 2013, Nr. 4, pp. 389–422.

Klopfer, L.-M./Steul-Fischer, M. (2020): Weiterempfehlungsprogramme: Die Wirkung des Akquisitionskanals und der Prämienaufteilung auf den Erfolg von Weiterempfehlungen, in: ZVersWiss, Jg. 109, 2020, pp. 361–376. (https://doi.org/10.1007/s12297-020-00466-w)

Klopfer, L.-M./Steul-Fischer, M./Zitzmann, A. (2022): Customer Experience Management—Eine qualitative Studie zur Umsetzung in der Versicherungsbranche, in: ZVersWiss, Jg. 111, 2022, pp. 245–276. (https://doi.org/10.1007/s12297-022-00531-6)

Klotzki, U. (2018): New life insurance products and product complexity in Germany, in: ZVersWiss, Jg. 107, 2018, pp. 143.161. (https://doi.org/10.1007/s12297-018-0404-7)

Knoller, C. (2016): Multiple reference points and the demand for principal-protected life annuities: An experimental analysis, in: Journal of Risk and Insurance, Vol. 83, 2016, No. 1, pp. 217–255.

Koch, P. (1988): Versicherungszweige, System und übrige Sparten, in: Farny, D./Helten, E./Koch, P./Schmidt, R. (Eds.), Handwörterbuch der Versicherung (HdV), Karlsruhe, 1988, pp. 1.251.

Koch, J./Gebhardt, P./Riedmüller, F. (2016): Marktforschung, Grundlagen und praktische Anwendungen, Berlin, 7. Aufl., 2016.

Köhne, T. (1997): Die Wirkungsversicherung im Privatkundengeschäft—Implikationen für eine kundenorientierte Marktleistungsgestaltung, St. Gallen, 1997.

Köhne, T. (1998a): Chancen und Grenzen der Produktpolitik im deregulierten Versicherungsmarkt (Teil I), in: IVW Management-Information, St. Galler Trendmonitor für Risiko- und Finanzmärkte, 1998, Heft 4, pp. 2–15.

Köhne, T. (1998b): Chancen und Grenzen der Produktpolitik im deregulierten Versicherungsmarkt (Teil II), in: IVW Management-Information, St. Galler Trendmonitor für Risiko- und Finanzmärkte, 1998, Heft 5, pp. 2–10.

Köhne, T. (1998c): Zur Konzeption des Versicherungsproduktes—neue Anforderungen in einem deregulierten Markt, in: ZVersWiss, Jg. 87, 1998, Nr. 1/2, pp. 143–191.

Köhne, T. (1999): Versicherungsmarketing: Vom "Mauerblümchendasein" zur strategischen Instanz, in: IVW HSG (Ed.): Risk Tomorrow, IVW-Jahresbericht 1998, St. Gallen, 1999, pp. 35–38.

Köhne, T. (2003): Schadenmanagement als Marketinginstrument oder: Kundenorientierung im "Moment of truth", in: El Hage, B./Jara, M. (Eds.), Schadenmanagement, Grundlagen, Methoden und Instrumente, Praktische Erfahrungen, St. Gallen, 2003, pp. 67–90.

Köhne, T. (Ed.) (2004a): Strategische Kooperationen in der Versicherungsbranche: Kernkompetenzen, Wertschöpfungspartnerschaften und Unternehmensnetzwerke, Wiesbaden, 2004.

Köhne, T. (2004b): Strategische Kooperationen und Unternehmensnetzwerke in der Versicherungsbranche—Möglichkeiten, Herausforderungen und Erfolgsfaktoren, in: Köhne, T. (Ed.): Strategische Kooperationen in der Versicherungsbranche: Kernkompetenzen, Wertschöpfungspartnerschaften und Unternehmensnetzwerke, Wiesbaden, 2004, pp. 325–356.

Köhne, T. (2006): Marketing im strategischen Unternehmensnetzwerk, Erklärungsmodell und praktische Anwendung in der Versicherungswirtschaft, Wiesbaden, 2006.

Köhne, T. (2008): Produktinnovationen in der Versicherungswirtschaft—Theoretische Grundlagen zur Analyse aktueller Praxisentwicklungen, in: Köhne, T. (Ed.), Produktinnovationen in der deutschen Versicherungswirtschaft, Theoretische Analyse aktueller Praxisentwicklungen, Karlsruhe, 2008, pp. 1–39.

Köhne, T. (Ed.) (2008): Produktinnovationen in der deutschen Versicherungswirtschaft, Theoretische Analyse aktueller Praxisentwicklungen, Karlsruhe, 2008.

Köhne, T. (2013a): Preisdifferenzierung in der deutschen Kfz-Versicherung—unverändert enorme Preisunterschiede, in: ZfV, Jg. 64, 2013, Nr. 3, pp. 81–84.

Köhne, T. (2013b): Performance von Versicherungsvermittlern—Konzeption und Messung aus Sicht des Versicherungsunternehmens, Berliner Schriften zur Versicherungswirtschaft, Ed. by Institut für Versicherungswirtschaft an der Hochschule für Wirtschaft und Recht Berlin, Nr. 5, Berlin, 2013.

Köhne, T. (2014): Ökonomische Aspekte der neuen IMD2 vom 26.02.2014, in: ZVersWiss, Jg. 103, 2014, Nr. 3, pp. 243–268.

Köhne, T. (2016): Versicherungsmarketing. Marketing und Vertrieb im Versicherungsunternehmen in Theorie und Praxis, Karlsruhe, 2016.

Köhne, T. (2018): Zur Preissituation im deutschen Kfz-Versicherungsmarkt, Studie im Auftrag der Verti Versicherung AG, Berlin, 2018.

Köhne, T. (2022a): Digitalisierung in der Versicherungsvermittlung, in: ZfV, Jg. 73, 2022, Nr. 23, pp. 679–682.

Köhne, T. (2022b): Digitaler Stress bei Versicherungsvermittlern, in: ZfV, Jg. 73, 2022, Nr. 24, pp. 713–716.

Köhne, T./Brömmelmeyer, C. (2018): The New Insurance Distribution Regulation in the EU—A Critical Assessment from a Legal and Economic Perspective, in: The Geneva Papers on Risk and Insurance, Vol. 43, No. 4, 2018, 704–739.

Köhne, T./Kopp, F. (2007): Produktinnovationen und Produktmodifikationen in der Versicherungswirtschaft: Rolle und Bedeutung nach der Deregulierung, in: ZVersWiss, Jg. 96, 2007, Nr. 2, pp. 227–259.

Köhne, T./Lange, M. (2009): Marketing und Vertrieb von Versicherungs- und Finanzprodukten für Privatkunden, Fach- und Führungskompetenz für die Assekuranz, Karlsruhe, 2009.

Köhne, T./Lange, M. (2020): Marketing und Vertrieb von Versicherungs- und Finanzprodukten für Privatkunden, Fach- und Führungskompetenz für die Assekuranz, Karlsruhe, 4. Aufl., 2020.

Köhne, T./Matz, S. (2010): Die Effizienz deutscher Kompositversicherer—Eine Untersuchung mittels Data Envelopment Analysis, in: ZVersWiss, Jg. 99, 2010, pp. 277–317.

Köhne, T./Melashenko, I. (2019): Produktinnovationen und Produktmodifikationen in der Versicherungswirtschaft zwischen 2006 und 2017, in: ZVersWiss, Jg. 108, Nr. 3–4, 2019, pp. 275–305.

Köhne, T./Wendland, A. (2022): Digitalisierung im Versicherungsvertrieb—eine empirische Untersuchung bei Versicherungsvermittlern, in: Berliner Schriften zur Versicherungswirtschaft, herausgegeben vom Institut für Versicherungswirtschaft an der Hochschule für Wirtschaft und Recht Berlin, Nr. 14, Berlin, 2022.

Kollmann, T. (2019): E-Business, Grundlagen elektronischer Geschäftsprozesse in der Digitalen Wirtschaft, Wiesbaden, 7. Aufl., 2019.

Konzern Versicherungskammer (Ed.) (2023): Geschäftsbericht Konzern Versicherungskammer 2022, München, 2023.

Kopp, F. (2008): Produktneuerungen in der deutschen Versicherungswirtschaft nach der Deregulierung—Eine empirische Untersuchung des Zeitraums zwischen 1996 und 2005, in: Köhne, T. (Ed.), Produktinnovationen in der deutschen Versicherungswirtschaft, Karlsruhe, 2008, pp. 41–76.

Koppelmann, U. (1994): Marketingüberlegungen im Versicherungsbereich, in: Schwebler u. a. (Ed), Dieter Farny und die Versicherungswissenschaft, Karlsruhe, 1994, pp. 285–306.

Kotler, P./Bliemel, F. (1992): Marketing-Management, Analyse, Planung, Umsetzung und Kontrolle, Stuttgart, 7. Aufl., 1992.

Kotler, P./Bliemel, F. (1999): Marketing-Management, Analyse, Planung, Umsetzung und Steuerung, Stuttgart, 9. Aufl., 1999.

Kotler, P./Keller, K.L./Bliemel, F. (2007): Marketing-Management, Strategien für wertschaffendes Handeln, München, 12. Aufl., 2007.

Kotler, P./Armstrong, G./Wong, V./Saunders, J. (2011): Grundlagen des Marketing, München, 5. Aufl., 2011.

Kotler, P./Keller, K.L./Opresnik, M.O. (2017a): Marketing-Management, Konzepte—Instrumente—Unternehmensfallstudien, Halbergmoos, 15. Aufl., 2017.

Kotler, P./Kartajaya, H./Seitiawan, I. (2017b): Marketing 4.0, Chicago, 2017.

Kotler, P./Armstrong, G./Harris, L.C./He, H. (2022): Grundlagen des Marketing, Halbergmoos, 8. Aufl., 2022.

Kottmann, D.A. (2018): Bancassurance 2.0: Werden Banken die digitalen Versicherungsmakler der Zukunft?, in: Beenken, M./Knörrer, D./Moormann, J./Schmidt, D. (Eds.), Digital Insurance. Strategien, Geschäftsmodelle, Daten, Frankfurt a.M., 2018, pp. 45–64.

Krauß, H. (2009): Die Vergütung des Versicherungsmaklers im Rahmen internationaler Entwicklungen, Karlsruhe, 2009.

Krausz, S. (2002): Strategische Unternehmenspolitik von Erstversicherern unter Verbindung von Zielgruppen-Marketing und Kernkompetenz-Management, Karlsruhe, 2002.

Krauth, W. (1979): Absatzstrategien im Versicherungsunternehmen, in: ZVersWiss, Jg. 68, 1979, Nr. 3, pp. 497–548.

Kremer, M. (1994): Das Nachfrageverhalten von Versicherungs- und Bankkunden aus ganzheitlicher Sicht—Konsequenzen für den Finanzdienstleistungsgedanken, St. Gallen, 1994.

Kreutzer, R.T. (2018): Praxisorientiertes online-marketing. Konzepte–Instrumente–Checklisten, Wiesbaden, 3. Aufl., 2018.

Kroeber-Riel, W. (1992): Konsumentenverhalten, München, 5. Aufl., 1992.

Kroeber-Riel, W./Gröppel-Klein, A. (2019): Konsumentenverhalten, München, 11. Aufl., 2019.

Kromrey, H. (1988): Empirische Sozialforschung, Modelle und Methoden der Datenerhebung und Datenauswertung, Opladen, 8. Aufl., 1988.

Krüger-Barvels, R. (1971): Marketing im Versicherungsbetrieb, Freiburg i.B., 1971.

Kromschröder, B. (1993): Qualitätsmanagement in der Versicherungswirtschaft, Karlsruhe, 1993.

Kühl, H./Ramezani, S. (2008): Schadenregulierung durch den Außendienst: Königsweg oder Sackgasse?, in: VW, Jg. 63, 2008, Nr. 2, pp. 94–98.

Kühlmann, K./Käßer-Pawelka, G./Wengert, H./Kurtenbach, W. (2002): Marketing für Finanzdienstleistungen, Frankfurt a.M., 2002.

Kühlmann, K./Wolf, H.-P./Wallenwein, C./Swoboda, U. (2003): Marketing und Vertrieb, Funktionsorientierte Qualifikationen, Karlsruhe, 2. Aufl., 2003.

Kühn, R./Fassnacht, R. (2001): Marketing für Versicherungen, Herausforderungen und Entwicklungstendenzen, gezeigt am Beispiel des schweizerischen Versicherungsmarktes, in: Tscheulin, D.K./Helmig, B. (Eds.), Branchenspezifisches Marketing, Grundlagen—Besonderheiten—Gemeinsamkeiten, Wiesbaden, 2001, pp. 79–98.

Kurtenbach, W. (1981): Versicherungsmarketing, Frankfurt a.M., 1981.

Kurtenbach, W./Kühlmann, K./Käßer-Pawelka, G. (1995): Versicherungsmarketing, Eine praxisorientierte Einführung in das Marketing für Versicherungen und ergänzende Finanzdienstleistungen, Frankfurt a.M., 4. Aufl., 1995.

Kuß, A./Wildner, A./Kreis, H. (2018): Marktforschung: Datenerhebung und Datenanalyse, Wiesbaden, 6. Aufl., 2018.

Kutz, S. (1997): Die Aufgabenverteilung zwischen Versicherungsunternehmen und Einfirmen-/Konzernvertretern, Lohmar, 1997.

Kuzmany, K. (2004): Werbemitteldesign und Markenpolitik in Versicherungsunternehmen, in: ZVersWiss, Jg. 93, 2004, pp. 739–751.

Laakmann, M./Rahlf, C. (2019): Customer Journey am Beispiel des Schadenprozesses in der Versicherungswirtschaft, in: Reich, M./Zerres, C. (Eds.), Handbuch Versicherungsmarketing, Berlin, 2. Aufl., 2019, pp. 401–422.

Lach, H. (1995): Vertikales Marketing von Versicherungsunternehmen, Berlin, 1995.

Lach, H. (2023a): Die EU-Kleinanlegerstrategie—zum Wohle des Verbrauchers oder Zuviel des Guten? (I), in : ZfV, Jg. 74, 2023, Nr. 17, pp. 480–483.

Lach, H. (2023b): Die EU-Kleinanlegerstrategie—zum Wohle des Verbrauchers oder Zuviel des Guten? (II), in : ZfV, Jg. 74, 2023, Nr. 18, pp. 516–518.

Lange, M./Robold, M./Berthold, C. (2013): Schaden- und Leistungsmanagement, Sachversicherungen für private und gewerbliche Kunden, Fach- und Führungskompetenz für die Assekuranz, Karlsruhe, 2013.

Lange, W. (1995): Verteiltes Vertriebscontrolling in Versicherungsunternehmen, Karlsruhe, 1995.

Latzel, C. (2020): Verhaltenssteuerung, Recht und Privatautonomie, Berlin, 2020.

Lauterborn, B. (1990): New marketing litany—four P's passe; C-words take over, in: Advertising Age, 1990, October, pp. 26.

Lehmann, A. (1989): Dienstleistungsmanagement zwischen industriell-orientierter Produktion und zwischenmenschlicher Interaktion, St. Gallen, 1989.

Lehmann, A. (1993): Dienstleistungsmanagement, Strategien und Ansatzpunkte zur Schaffung von Servicequalität, Stuttgart, 1993.

Lehmann, A.P. (1998): Qualität und Produktivität im Dienstleistungsmanagement. Strategische Handlungsfelder im Versicherungs- und Finanzdienstleistungswettbewerb, Wiesbaden, 1998.

Leon, S./Nakayama, M. (2020): Exploring factors that influence positive WOM in the health insurance industry, in: Health Marketing Quarterly, Vol. 37, 2020, No. 2, pp. 176–192. (https://doi.org/10.1080/07359683.2020.1756124)

Lemke, C./Brenner, W. (2015): Einführung in die Wirtschaftsinformatik, Band 1: Verstehen des digitalen Zeitalters, Berlin, 2015.

Lemon, K.N./Verhoef, P.C. (2016): Understanding customer experience throughout the customer journey, in: Journal of Marketing, Vol. 80, 2016, No. 6, pp. 69–96.

Lenz, T./Rabe, D. (2010): Telefonwerbung—Eine Betrachtung aus der Praxis der Versicherungswirtschaft, in: VersR, Jg.61, 2010, Nr. 34, pp. 1.541–1.546.

Levitt, T. (1960): Marketing Myopia, in: Harvard Business Review, Vol. 38, No.4, 1960, pp. 45–56.

Lobscheid, H.G. (1970): Grundzüge eines Marketing bei Versicherungsunternehmen, in: DVZ, Jg. 24, 1970, Nr. 5, pp. 111–119.

Lohmann, C./Sowietzki, S./Gewand, P. (2020): Industrieversicherer im Marktumfeld der Industrieversicherung, in: Mahnke, A./Rohlfs, T. (Eds.), Betriebliches Risikomanagement und Industrieversicherung, Erfolgreiche Unternehmenssteuerung durch ein effektives Risiko- und Versicherungsmanagement, Wiesbaden, 2020, pp. 319–353.

Lohse, U./Will, A. (2019): Rahmenbedingungen und strategische Herausforderungen für die Versicherungsbranche, in: Reich, M./Zerres, C. (Eds.), Handbuch Versicherungsmarketing, Berlin, 2. Aufl., 2019, pp. 3–14.

Lukowsky, T./Tidelski, O. (2023): Datengetriebenes Marketing und Kommunikationsmanagement der Allianz; in: Krämer, A./Kalka, R./Merkle, W. (Eds.): Stammkundenbindung versus Neukundengewinnung, Marketing und Vertrieb im Spannungsfeld von "Hunting" und "Farming", Wiesbaden, 2023, pp. 357–369.

Lusch, R.F./Nambisan, S. (2015): Service innovation: A service-dominant logic perspective, in: MIS Quarterly, Vol. 39, 2015, No. 1, pp. 155–175.

Lusch, R.F./Vargo, S.L. (2006): Service-Dominant Logic: Reactions, Reflections and Refinements, in: Marketing Theory, Vol. 6, 2006, No. 3, pp. 281–288.

LVM (Ed.) (2024): Leitbild, in: https://www.lvm.de/die-lvm/unternehmen/wir-als-versicherer/ueber-uns/ueber-uns-leitbild, Accessed: 02.01.2024.

Mahmoodi, O. (2012): PKV, Bundestag ratifiziert Provisionsdeckelung, in: procontra online vom 02.04.2012.

Mahnke, L./Schmidt, J.-P. (2022): Klimawandel und Personenversicherung, in: Heep-Altiner, M./Rohlfs, T./Berg, M./Schmidt, J.-P. (Eds.), Klima- und Nachhaltigkeitsrisiken für die Versicherungswirtschaft, Wiesbaden, 2022, pp. 241–268.

Maier, J./Faßbender, K. (2020): Versicherungsnehmer und Firmenverbundener Vermittler, in: Mahnke, A./Rohlfs, T. (Eds.), Betriebliches Risikomanagement und Industrieversicherung,

Erfolgreiche Unternehmenssteuerung durch ein effektives Risiko- und Versicherungsmanagement, Wiesbaden, 2020, pp. 277–296.
Maslow, A.M. (1970): Motivation and Personality, New York, 2. Aufl., 1970.
Matzner, U. (2022): 24 Versicherer mit achtstelligen Werbeausgaben, in: Versicherungswirtschaft-heute vom 14.08.2022.
McCarthy, E.J. (1960): Basic Marketing: A Managerial Approach, Homewood, 1960.
McIntyre, D.P./Srinivasan, A. (2017): Networks, platforms, and strategy: Emerging views and next steps, in: Strategic Management Journal, Vol. 38, 2017, No. 1, S. 141–160.
Meffert, H. (1986): Grundlagen der Absatzpolitik, Wiesbaden, 1986.
Meffert, H./Bruhn, M. (1995): Dienstleistungsmarketing, Grundlagen—Konzepte—Methoden, Wiesbaden, 1. Aufl., 1995.
Meffert, H./Burmann, C./Kirchgeorg, M. (2015): Marketing, Grundlagen marktorientierter Unternehmensführung, Konzepte—Instrumente—Praxisbeispiele, Wiesbaden, 12. Aufl., 2015.
Meffert, H./Bruhn, M./Hadwich, K. (2018): Dienstleistungsmarketing, Grundlagen—Konzepte—Methoden, Wiesbaden, 9. Aufl., 2018.
Meffert, H./Burmann, C./Kirchgeorg, M./Eisenbeiß, M. (2019): Marketing, Grundlagen marktorientierter Unternehmensführung, Konzepte—Instrumente—Praxisbeispiele, Wiesbaden, 13. Aufl., 2019.
Meidan, A. (1984): Insurance Marketing, Leighton Buzzard, 1984.
Menhart, M.: Innovationsdynamik und Lebenszyklen in der Versicherungsindustrie, Aachen, 2003.
Mertens, M. (1992): Kundentypologien im Versicherungsgeschäft mit Privatkunden, Bergisch Gladbach, 1992.
Meta (Ed.) (2023): Meta Earnings Presentation Q3/2023, in: https://s21.q4cdn.com/399680738/files/doc_earnings/2023/q3/presentation/Earnings-Presentation-Q3-2023.pdf, Accessed: 24.01.2024.
Monopolkommission (Ed.) (2022): Wettbewerb 2022, XXIV. Hauptgutachten, Bonn, 2022.
Moore, J.F. (1996): The death of competition: Leadership and strategy in the age of business ecosystems, New York, 1996.
Mossin, J. (1968): Aspects of Rational Insurance Purchasing, in: Journal of Political Economy, Vol. 79, 1968, pp. 553–568.
Müller, H. (1994): Marktsegmentierung im Privatkundengeschäft von Versicherungsunternehmen, Karlsruhe, 1994.
Müller, R. (2012): Träume, Formeln, Traumata: Das Marketing der Versicherung heute, in: VW, Jg. 67, 2012, Nr. 23, pp. 1.720–1.722.
Müller, W. (1981): Das Produkt Versicherung, in: Jung, M./Ralph, L./Seifert, W. (Eds.), Geld und Versicherung, Festgabe für Wilhelm Seuß, Karlsruhe, 1981, pp. 155–171.
Müller, W. (1994): Informationsökonomische Grundlagen und empirische Überprüfung eines Beschreibungsmodells für Versicherungsprodukte, in: Schwebler, R. (Ed.), Dieter Farny und die Versicherungswissenschaft, Karlsruhe, 1994, pp. 363–379.
Müller-Reichart, M. (1993): Risiko-Management privater Haushalte, in: Brunner, W.L./Vollath, J. (Eds.), Handbuch Finanzdienstleistungen, Stuttgart, 1993, pp. 191–201.
Müller-Reichart, M. (2002): International orientierte Produktinnovationspolitik globalisierter Versicherungsunternehmen, Karlsruhe, 2002.
Müller-Reichart, M./Graumann, K.V. (2022): Nachhaltigkeit der Finanzdienstleistungswirtschaft auf der Grundlage der EU-Taxonomieverordnung, in: ZfV, Jg. 73, 2022, Nr. 13–14, pp. 419–423.
Müller-Reichart, M./Schäfer, M. (2014): Mit Assistance auf dem Weg zu einem service- und vertriebsoptimierten Finanzdienstleistungsangebot, in: ZfV, Jg. 65, 2014, Nr. 8, pp. 222–226.

Müller-Reichart, M./Haisch, D./Graumann, K.V. (2023): Versicherungs-Assistance als Voraussetzung einer "Customer Journey", in: ZfV, Jg. 74, 2023, Nr. 11, pp. 322–327.
Müller-Stewens, G./Lechner, C. (2016): Strategisches Management, Wie strategische Initiativen zum Wandel führen, Stuttgart, 5. Aufl., 2016.
Musiol, A./Steul-Fischer, M. (2017): The psychological effects on tariff choices for car insurance, in: ZVersWiss, Jg. 106, 2017, pp. 525–538. (https://doi.org/10.1007/s12297-017-0395-9)
Musiol, A./Steul-Fischer, M. (2019a): Price framing and consumers' purchase intention on pay-how-you-drive tariffs, in: ZVersWiss, Jg. 108, 2019, pp. 407–419. (https://doi.org/10.1007/s12297-019-00440-1)
Musiol, A./Steul-Fischer, M. (2019b): Der Einfluss der Produktart und des Weiterempfehlungskanals auf den Erfolg von Weiterempfehlungen bei Versicherungen, in: ZVersWiss, Jg. 108, 2019, pp. 389–406. (https://doi.org/10.1007/s12297-019-00438-9)
Nalebuff, B./Brandenburger, A. (1996): Coopetition—kooperativ konkurrieren. Mit der Spieltheorie zum Unternehmenserfolg, Frankfurt a. M., 1996.
Nastjuk , I./Trang, S./Grummeck-Braamt, J.-V./Adam, M.T.P./Tarafdar, M (2023): Integrating and Synthesising Technostress Research: A Meta-Analysis on Technostress Creators, Outcomes, and IS Usage Contexts, in: European Journal of Information Systems, 2023, pp. 1–22. (https://doi.org/10.1080/0960085X.2022.2154712)
Nickel-Waninger, H. (1987): Versicherungsmarketing, auf der Grundlage des Marketing von Informationsprodukten, Karlsruhe, 1987.
Nickel-Waninger, H. (2010): Implikationen der Vertriebswegeentwicklung in der Versicherungswirtschaft, in: ZVersWiss, Jg. 99, 2010, pp. 545–568.
Nicoletti, B. (2021): Insurance 4.0: Benefits and Challenges of Digital Transformation, Cham, 2021.
Nordemann, W. (1995): Innovationsschutz für Versicherungsprodukte, in: ZVersWiss, Jg. 84, 1995, Nr. 1, pp. 129–137.
Oberholzer, M. (2003): Strategische Implikationen des Ubiquitous Computing für das Nichtleben-Geschäft im Privatkundensegment der Assekuranz, Karlsruhe, 2003.
OECD (Ed.) (2020): Regulatory and Supervisory Framework for Insurance Intermediation, o. O., 2020.
Oletzky, T. (1998): Wertorientierte Steuerung von Versicherungsunternehmen, Karlsruhe, 1998.
Oletzky, T./Staud, N./Boltz, J. (2015): Die Versicherungswirtschaft auf dem Weg zu wirklicher Kundenorientierung, in: Zimmermann, G. (Ed.), Change Management in Versicherungsunternehmen. Die Zukunft der Assekuranz erfolgreich gestalten, Wiesbaden, 2015, pp. 257–272.
Oliver Wyman/policen direct (Ed.) (2021): Die Zukunft von InsurTech in DACH, Der InsurTech-Radar 2021, o. O., 2021.
Osberghaus, D. (2021): Staatliche Fluthilfe: Kurzfristig notwendig, aber keine nachhaltige Lösung, in: ifo Schnelldienst, Jg. 74, 2021, Nr. 11, pp. 3–6.
Oster, O. (2019): Customer Experience—die Königsdisziplin, in: Reich, M./Zerres, C. (Eds.), Handbuch Versicherungsmarketing, Berlin, 2. Aufl., 2019, pp. 171–191.
Osterwalder, A./Pigneur, Y. (2010): Business model generation, Hoboken (New Jersey), 2010.
o. V. (2010): Interview mit Dr. Torsten Oletzky, in: Handelsblatt vom 07.12.2010, pp. 33.
o. V. (2014a): Radikalreform der britischen Altersvorsorge, in: ZfV, Jg. 65, 2014, Nr. 8, pp. 205.
o. V. (2014b): Wo Schaden zum Erlebnis wird, Vermittler engagieren sich immer stärker bei der Schadenregulierung, um sich von Billig-Anbietern abzuheben, in: VW, Jg. 69, 2014, Nr. 3, pp. 54–57.
o. V. (2015): YouGov: Reise- und Mobilitäts-Assistance sind gefragt, in: Versicherungswirtschaft-heute.de, Tagesreport vom 03.07.2015.

o. V. (2023a): Die 50 größten Lebensversicherer nach gebuchten Bruttobeiträgen, in: ZfV, Jg. 74, 2023, Nr. 16, pp. 431.
o. V. (2023b): Die 50 größten Schadenversicherer nach gebuchtem Bruttobeitrag, in: ZfV, Jg. 74, 2023, Nr. 22, pp. 639.
o. V. (2023c): Ökosystem zum Anfassen, in: VW, Jg. 78, 2023, Nr. 5, pp. 42–44.
Pahl, M./Domazet, M./Ressel, J. (2020): Bedeutung und Zukunft des Industrieversicherungsmaklers in Deutschland, in: Mahnke, A./Rohlfs, T. (Eds.), Betriebliches Risikomanagement und Industrieversicherung, Erfolgreiche Unternehmenssteuerung durch ein effektives Risiko- und Versicherungsmanagement, Wiesbaden, 2020, pp. 297–318.
Papon, T. (2008): The Effect of Pre-commitment and Past-Experience on Insurance Choices: An Experimental Study, in: The Geneva Risk and Insurance Review, Vol. 33, 2008, No. 1, pp. 47–73.
Parasuraman, A./Zeithaml, V.A./Berry, L.L. (1985): A Conceptual Model of Service Quality and its Implications for Future Research, in: JoM, Vol. 49, 1985, No. 1, pp. 4–50.
Peill, E./van Eck, R. (1997): Kundenbindung durch Service-Garantien, in: VW, Jg. 52, 1997, Nr. 15, pp. 1.071–1.073.
Perrenoud, P.-C. (1979): Marketing in der Rückversicherung, Zürich, 1979.
Pesendorfer, B. (1982): Zur Theorie von Angst und Gefahr, Sicherheit und Versicherung, Einige theoretische Grundlagen zum besseren Verständnis der Haltungen von privaten Versicherungsnehmern, Arbeitspapier, St. Gallen, 1982.
Petrovs, V. (2016): Telematik-Produktmodelle für die deutsche KFZ-Versicherung, Köln, 2016.
Pooser, D.M./Browne, M.J. (2018): The effects of customer satisfaction on company profitability: Evidence from the property and casualty insurance industry, in: Risk Management and Insurance Review, Vol. 21, 2018, pp. 289–308.
Popp, H. (1997): Individualisierung und Versicherung, Konsequenzen für ein gesellschaftsorientiertes Versicherungsmarketing, Wiesbaden, 1997.
Porter, M.E. (1980): Competitive Strategy, New York, 1980.
Porter, M.E. (1985): Competitive Advantage, Creating and Sustaining Superior Performance, New York, 1985.
Porter, M.E. (2004): Competitive Strategy, New York, Neuaufl., 2004.
Prahalad, C.K./Hamel, G. (1990): The Core Competence of the Corporation, in: HBR, Vol. 68, 1990, No. 3, pp. 79–92.
psyconomics AG/avanturo GmbH (Ed.) (2002): Aktives Schadenmanagement aus Kundensicht, Eine Untersuchung der Akzeptanz alternativer Modelle der Schadenregulierung, Köln, 2002.
Puls (Ed.) (2023): Das Beratungs-Bezahl-Paradoxon deutscher Bankkunden. Ergebnisse einer repräsentativen Studie zu den Themen Provisionen, Honorare und Bezahlung von Bankberatung von puls Marktforschung GmbH im Auftrag der Quirin Privatbank.
Puschmann, K.-H. (1986): Praxis des Versicherungsmarketing, Karlsruhe, 1986.
Puschmann, K.-H. (2003): Praxis des Versicherungsmarketing, Karlsruhe, 2. Aufl., 2003.
Radtke, M. (2008): Grundlagen der Kalkulation von Versicherungsprodukten in der Schaden- und Unfallversicherung, Karlsruhe, 2008.
Rayburn, S.W./Badrinarayanan, V./Anderson, S.T./Gupta, A. (2021): Continuous techno-training and business-to-business salesperson success: How boosting techno-efficacy enhances sales effort and performance, in: Journal of Business Research, Vol. 133, 2021, pp. 66–78.
Reich, M./Braasch, T. (2019): Die Revolution der Prozessautomatisierung bei Versicherungsunternehmen: Robotic Process Automation (RPA), in: Reich, M./Zerres, C. (Eds.), Handbuch Versicherungsmarketing, Berlin, 2. Aufl., 2019, pp. 291–305.
Reichheld, F.F. (1997): Der Loyalitäts-Effekt, Die verborgene Kraft hinter Wachstum, Gewinnen und Unternehmenswert, Frankfurt a.M., 1997.

Reichheld, F.F. (2003): The one number you need to grow, in: Harvard Business Review, Vol. 81, 2003, No. 12, 46–54.
Reichheld, F./Markey, R. (2011): The ultimate question 2.0—how net promoter companies thrive in a customer driven world, Boston, 2011.
Reiff, P. (2018): Das Versicherungsvertriebsrecht nach Inkrafttreten des Gesetzes zur Umsetzung der Versicherungsvertriebsrichtlinie, in: VersR, Jg. 69, 2018, Nr. 4, pp. 193–203.
Reiff, P./Köhne, T. (2017): Der Regierungsentwurf zur Umsetzung der Richtlinie (EU) 2016/97 (IDD) in rechtlicher und ökonomischer Sicht, in: VersR, Jg. 68, 2017, Nr. 11, pp. 649–661.
Reinecke, S. (2004): Marketing Performance Management, Empirisches Fundament und Konzeption für ein integriertes Marketingkennzahlensystem, Wiesbaden, 2004.
Reitzler, R. (2001): Versicherungen für Senioren, Wiesbaden, 2001.
research tools (Ed.) (2022): Versicherer in Social Media: Agila platziert sich neben den Großen der Branche unter den Top 10-Performern, Pressemitteilung vom 21.12.2022, Esslingen am Neckar, 2022.
Reuter, F. (1994): Markenartikel in der Versicherungswirtschaft, in: Mehring, H.-P./Wolff, V. (Eds.): Festschrift für Dieter Farny zur Vollendung seines 60. Lebensjahres, Karlsruhe, 1994, pp. 55–61.
Richter, A. (1996): Neuausrichtung des Finanzdienstleistungsmarketings, Wiesbaden, 1996.
Richter, A./Schiller, J. (2009): Entlohnung und Regulierung unabhängiger Versicherungsvermittler, in: Schäfer, K./Burghof, H.-P./Johanning, L./Wagner, H.F./Rodt, S. (Eds.), Risikomanagement und kapitalmarktorientierte Finanzierung, Festschrift zum 65. Geburtstag von Bernd Rudolph, Frankfurt a.M., 2009, pp. 319–336.
Richter, A./Ruß, J./Schelling, S. (2018): Moderne Verhaltensökonomie in der Versicherungswirtschaft, Denkanstöße für ein besseres Verständnis der Kunden, Wiesbaden, 2018.
Richter, C. (2014): Digital versichert—Wie die Assekuranz ihre Geschäftsprozesse der Zukunft neu denkt, in: ZfV, Jg. 65, 2014, Nr. 2, pp. 48–51.
Riege, J. (1990): Das Versicherungsprodukt, in: ZVersWiss, Jg. 79, 1990, Nr. 3, pp. 403–470.
Ronsdorf, K./Rossmann, S./Schlinck, P. (2009): Vorsorgekonzepte im 3-Schichten-Modell, Karlsruhe, 2. Aufl., 2009.
Rothschild, M./Stiglitz, J.E. (1976): Equilibrium in Competitive Insurance Markets: The Economics of Markets with Imperfect Information, in: Quarterly Journal of Economics, Vol. 90, 1976, pp. 111–125.
Rützler, P. (1994): Jugendmarketing für Versicherungen, St. Gallen, 1994.
Ruß, J./Schelling, S. (2017): Multi cumulative prospect theory and the demand for cliquet-style guarantees, in: Journal of Risk and Insurance. https://doi.org/10.1111/jori.12195.
Ruß, L./Kling, A./Seyboth, A. (2023): Provisionsverbot und Kleinanlegerstrategie, Plädoyer für eine Koexistenz von Provision und Honorar bei Altersvorsorgeprodukten, Ulm, 2023.
R+V Versicherung (Ed.) (2024): Leitbild, in: https://www.ruv.de/ueber-uns/unternehmen/wofuer-wir-stehen, Accessed: 02.01.2024.
Sandkühler, H.-L. (2011): Arbeitskreis Beratungsprozesse entwickelt Branchenstandards für bessere Beratung, in: AssCompact, 2011, Nr. 2, pp. 88–89.
Sandkühler, H.-L. (2014): Kodex, Compliance und Reputation, Regelkonformität im Spannungsfeld zwischen Versicherern und Vermittlern, in: VW, Jg. 69, 2014, Nr. 11, pp. 44–45.
Sandkühler, H.-L. (2022): Unerlaubte Werbeanrufe und Co., in: AssCompact, 2022, Nr. 4, pp. 74–75.
Sarstedt, M./Mooi, E. (2019): A concise guide to market research: The process, data, and methods using IBM SPSS statistics, Berlin, 3. Aufl., 2019.

Schafstädt, C. (2015): Das Spannungsverhältnis zwischen Provisionsberatung und Honorarberatung im Versicherungsmarkt, Karlsruhe, 2015.

Schareck, C. (2005): Wertorientierung im Versicherungsvertrieb, Karlsruhe, 2005.

Schiller, J. (2011): Ökonomische Aspekte der Entlohnung und Regulierung unabhängiger Versicherungsvermittler, in: ZVersWiss, Jg. 100, 2011, pp. 113–130.

Schlesinger, H. (1994): Zur Theorie der Versicherungsnachfrage, in: ZVersWiss, Jg. 83, 1994, Nr. 1/2, pp. 113–136.

Schmidt, D. (1995): Versicherungsmarketing Heute—Anspruch und Wirklichkeit, in: SCG St. Gallen Consulting Group (Ed.), Handbuch Management Versicherungsvertrieb, Wiesbaden, 1995, pp. 5–18.

Schmidt, M. (1994): Marketing in der Rückversicherung, Karlsruhe, 1994.

Schmidt-Gallas, D./Grunert, S./Lütticke, F. (2018): Der persönliche Vertrieb im Zeitalter der Digitalisierung—teurer Luxus oder echter Mehrwert, in: ZfV, Jg. 69, 2018, Nr. 1, pp. 10–13.

Schmidt-Jochmann, C. (2008): Strategische Erfolgsfaktoren von Versicherungsvermittlern—Eine empirische Untersuchung mit PLS-Strukturgleichungsmodellen, Lohmar, 2008.

Schmidt-Kasparek, U. (2013): Regulierung und Vertrieb verzahnen, Gleich bei zwei Veranstaltungen stand das Schadenmanagement im Fokus, in: VW, Jg. 68, 2013, Nr. 24, pp. 62 f.

Schmitt, F.C. (2013): Vertrieb und Compliance Management—eine ungenutzte Chance, Konsequenzen aus dem GDV-Verhaltenskodex zum Vertrieb von Versicherungsprodukten, in: VW, Jg. 68, 2013, Nr. 20, pp. 666–670.

Schmitz, M. (2007): Einfluss der Vermittler auf Zufriedenheit und Loyalität von Versicherungskunden, Tönning u. a., 2007.

Schögel, M. (1997): Mehrkanalsysteme in der Distribution, Dissertation St. Gallen, Scheßlitz 1997.

Schoemaker, P. (1995): Scenario Planning: A Tool for Strategic Thinking, in: Sloan Management Review, Vol. 36, 1995, No. 2, pp. 25–40.

Schradin, H.R. (1994): Erfolgsorientiertes Versicherungsmanagement, Karlsruhe, 1994.

Schröder, H.-H. (2008): Technologie- und Innovationsmanagement, in: Corsten, H./Reiß, M. (Eds.), Betriebswirtschaftslehre, Band 2, München, 4. Aufl., 2008, pp. 307–438.

Schröppel, Lina (2017): Digitalisierung am deutschen Versicherungsmarkt—Einschätzung des moderierenden Effekts der Online-Aktivität auf den Zusammenhang von Convenience instrumentalisierenden Attributen und Kundengewinnung im Neugeschäft der Assekuranz, Univ.-Diss., Neubiberg, 2017.

Schütze, U. (1972): Probleme der Produktgestaltung in der Versicherungswirtschaft unter besonderer Berücksichtigung der Produktinnovation, Karlsruhe, 1972.

Schulenburg, J.-M. Graf von der/Lohse, U. (2014): Versicherungsökonomik, Karlsruhe, 2. Aufl., 2014.

Schultz, D.E./Tannenbaum, S.I./Lauterborn, R.F. (1993): The new marketing paradigm. Integrated marketing communications, Lincolnwood/Illinois, 1993.

Schumacher, U. (2019): Versicherung 2.0—Marketing und Kommunikation im Social Media-Zeitalter, in: Reich, M./Zerres, C. (Eds.), Handbuch Versicherungsmarketing, Berlin, 2. Aufl., 2019, pp. 457–470.

Schwake, E. (1987): Überlegungen zu einem risikoadäquaten Marketing als Steuerungskonzeption von Versicherungsunternehmen, Karlsruhe, 1987.

Schwarz, S. (2015): Kulturwandel bei AXA: "Kundenzentrierung" als Erfolgsfaktor bei der Strategieumsetzung, in: Zimmermann, G. (Ed.), Change Management in Versicherungsunternehmen. Die Zukunft der Assekuranz erfolgreich gestalten, Wiesbaden, 2015, pp. 153–163.

Schwintowski, H.-P. (2013): Neue Vergütungsformen für Versicherungsmakler? (II), Deutsches Recht und die Auswirkungen der IMD 2, in: ZfV, Jg. 64, 2013, pp. 221–225.

Sebastian, S./Noth, L./Grafe, A.: The Effect of Commission Bans on Household Wealth: Evidence from OECD Countries, Studie, Universität Regensburg, 2023.

Seemann, K./Theis, A. (2023): Finanzsystem trotz widriger Umstände resilient, Financial Stability Perspectives 2023 Q1, ed. by GDV, Berlin, 2023.

Shavell, S. (1979): On Moral Hazard and Insurance, in: Quarterly Journal of Economics, Vol. 93, 1979, pp. 541–562.

Siddiqui, M.H./Sharma, T.G. (2010): Analyzing customer satisfaction with service quality in life insurance services, in: Journal of Targeting, Measurement and Analysis for Marketing, Vol 18, 2010. No. 3/4, pp. 221–238.

Sihler, P. (2019): Kundenakzeptanz verhaltensabhängiger Preise, Hamburg, 2019.

Simon, H.A. (1986): Rationality in Psychology and Economics, in: The Journal of Business, Vol. 59, 1986, No. 4, Part 2: The Behavioral Foundations of Economic Theory, pp. 209–224.

Sirius Campus (Ed.) (2019a): Entscheidertypologie im Versicherungsmarkt, Köln, 2019.

Sirius Campus (Ed.) (2019b): Erfolgsfaktoren für Kundenberatungen zur Berufsunfähigkeitsversicherung, Köln, 2019.

Sirius Campus (Ed.) (2022a): Strategien für den digitalen Kundenservice in der Assekuranz, Köln, 2022.

Sirius Campus (Ed.) (2022b): Erfolgsfaktoren im Ausschließlichkeitsvertrieb. Benchmark-Untersuchung zur Zufriedenheit, Motivation und Bindung im Versicherungsaußendienst, Köln, 2022.

Sirius Campus (Ed.) (2022c): Kundenmonitor Assekuranz, Köln, 2022.

Sirius Campus (Ed.) (2023a): Versicherung der Zukunft—Was sind Erwartungen junger Menschen an die Versicherung von morgen?, Köln, 2023.

Sirius Campus (Ed.) (2023b): Kundenmonitor e-Assekuranz 2023—Der Vertriebswege-Monitor, Köln, 2023.

Smith, K.T./Smith, L.M. (2021): Analysis of Social Media Usage and Relationship to Profit Margin among Insurance Companies, in: Services Marketing Quarterly, VOL. 42, 2021, No. 1–2, pp. 108–123. (https://doi.org/10.1080/15332969.2021.1948488)

Sonnenberg, M. (2013): Vertriebskostentransparenz bei Versicherungsprodukten, Eine juristisch-ökonomische Untersuchung unter Berücksichtigung rechtsvergleichender Aspekte, Karlsruhe, 2013.

Spontent GmbH (Ed.) (2023): Review GermanBeachTour Saison, Düsseldorf, 2023.

Spreer, P. (2021): PsyConversion, Wiesbaden, 2. Aufl., 2021.

Statista (Ed.) (2022): Number of social media users worldwide from 2017 to 2027 (in billions), 2022, in: https://www-statista-com.ezproxy.hwr-berlin.de/statistics/278414/number-of-worldwide-social-network-users/, Accessed: 26.01.2024.

Statista (Ed.) (2023): Number of social media users in Germany from 2019 to 2028 (in millions), 2023, in: https://www-statista-com.ezproxy.hwr-berlin.de/statistics/568943/predicted-number-of-social-network-users-in-germany/, Accessed: 26.01.2024.

Statistisches Bundesamt (Ed.) (2021): Ausblick auf die Bevölkerungsentwicklung in Deutschland und den Bundesländern nach dem Corona-Jahr 2020, Erste mittelfristige Bevölkerungsvorausberechnung 2021 bis 2035, o.O., 2021.

Statistisches Bundesamt (Ed.) (2023a): Haushaltsgrößen, in: https://www.destatis.de/DE/Themen/Gesellschaft-Umwelt/Bevoelkerung/Haushalte-Familien/Tabellen/1-2-privathaushalte-bundeslaender.html, Accessed: 02.01.2024.

Statistisches Bundesamt (Ed.) (2023b): Volkswirtschaftliche Gesamtrechnungen, Hauptaggregate der Sektoren, Vierteljahresergebnisse ab 1999, Stand: November 2023, o.O., 2023.

Statistisches Bundesamt (Ed.) (2023c): Vorausberechnete Privathaushalte, in: https://www-genesis.destatis.de/genesis/online?sequenz=tabelleErgebnis&selectionname=12421-0100#abreadcrumb, Accessed: 02.01.2024

Statistisches Bundesamt (Ed.) (2023d): Hauptwohnsitzhaushalte: Deutschland, Jahre, Haushaltsgröße, Haushaltsnettoeinkommensklassen, Tab. 12211-0300, 2022, in: https://www-genesis.destatis.de/genesis//online?operation=table&code=12211-0300&bypass=true&levelindex=0&levelid=1704284458136#abreadcrumb, Accessed: 28.12.2023.

Statistisches Bundesamt (Ed.) (2023e): Zahl der Woche Nr. 43 vom 24. Oktober 2023, in: https://www.destatis.de/DE/Presse/Pressemitteilungen/Zahl-der-Woche/2023/PD23_43_p002.html, Accessed: 03.01.2024.

Staudt, Y./Wagner, J. (2022): Factors Driving Duration to Cross-Selling in Non-Life Insurance: New Empirical Evidence from Switzerland, in: Risks, Vol. 10, pp. 187–207. (https://doi.org/10.3390/risks10100187)

Stauss, B./Seidel, W.: Effective Complaint Management. The Business Case for Customer Satisfaction, Cham, 2. Aufl., 2019.

Steel, P. (2007): The Nature of Procrastination: A Meta-analytic and Theoretical Review of Quintessential Self-regulatory Failure, in: Psychological Bulletin, Vol. 133, 2007, No. 1, pp. 65–94.

Stefanidis, A. (2013): "Das Selbstverständnis der Journalisten hat sich geändert", Interview mit Prof. Dr. Hans Mathias Kepplinger, in: GDV (Ed.), Positionen zu Politik, Wirtschaft und Gesellschaft, Nr. 87, Berlin, 2013, pp. 12–15.

Steffenhagen, H. (2004): Marketing, Stuttgart u. a., 5. Aufl., 2004.

Stigler, G. (1961): The Economics of Information, in: Journal of Political Economy, Vol. 63, 1961, No. 3, pp. 213–225.

Stöckli, E./Dremel, C./Übernickel, F. (2018): Exploring characteristics and transformational capabilities of InsurTech innovations to understand insurance value creation in a digital world, in: Electronic Markets, Vol. 28, 2018, pp. 287–305.

Störmer, T. (2014): Essays on Risk Differentiation and Price Transparency in the Insurer's Pricing Process, Univ.-Diss. St. Gallen, Meiningen, 2014.

Straßler, H.-J. (2005): Theoretische Analyse und empirische Überprüfung von Einflussgrößen auf den Erfolg des Ausschließlichkeitsvermittlers eines mittelständischen Versicherungsunternehmens, Univ.-Diss. München, o.O., 2005.

Stremitzer, H./Ennsfeller, K.C. (1994): Gedanken zur kundenorientierten Qualität von Versicherungsdienstleistungen, in: Hesberg, D./Nell, M./Schott, W. (Eds.), Risiko, Versicherung, Markt, Festschrift für Walter Karten zur Vollendung des 60. Lebensjahres, Karlsruhe, 1994, pp. 381–399.

Surminski, A. (1987): Das Image in der Versicherung, in: ZfV, Jg. 38, 1987, Nr. 1, pp. 2–16.

Surminski, M. (2015a): Lebensversicherung im Fadenkreuz—Wie kann sich die Branche gegen den Medienbeschuss wehren?, in: ZfV, Jg. 66, 2015, Nr. 5, pp. 140.

Surminski, M. (2023a): Die PKV im Jahr 2022, in: ZfV, Jg. 74, 2023, Nr. 19, pp. 526–545.

Surminski, M. (2023b): Die großen Kompositversicherer wachsen schneller als der Markt, in: ZfV, Jg. 74, 2023, Nr. 22, pp. 538.

Swift, R.S. (2001): Accelaterating Customer Relationships, Using CRM Technologies, New Jersey, 2001.

SwissRe (Ed.) (2013): Lebensversicherung—Fokussierung auf den Konsumenten, in: Reihe sigma, Nr. 6, Zürich, 2013.

Sydnor, J. (2010): (Over)insuring modest risks, in: American Economic Journal: Applied Economics, Vol. 2, 2010, No. 4, pp. 177–199.

Sydow, J. (1992): Strategische Netzwerke, Evolution und Organisation, Wiesbaden, 1992.

Tarafdar, M./Tu, Q./Ragu-Nathan, S./Ragu-Nathan, T.S. (2007): The Impact of Technostress on Role Stress and Productivity, in: Journal of Management Information Systems, Vol. 24, 2007, No. 1, pp. 301–328.

Tarafdar, M./Cooper, C.L./Stich, J.-F. (2019): The technostress trifecta—techno eustress, techno distress and design: Theoretical directions and an agenda for research, in: Information Systems Journal, Vol. 29, 2019, No. 1, pp. 6–42.

Tchoumta, J.-M. (2002): Allfinanz aus der Sicht der Assekuranz: eine vergleichende Studie, Frankfurt a.M., 2002.

Teichler, M. (2018): Die Versicherungs-Vertriebsrichtlinie (IDD) erfolgreich umsetzen, Freiburg i. B., 2018.

Thaler, R.H. (1981): Some Empirical Evidence on Dynamic Inconsistency, in: Economic Letters, Vol. 8, 1981, No. 3, pp. 201–207.

Thaler, R.H./Benartzi, S. (2004): Save More Tomorrow: Using Behavioural Economics to Increase Employee Saving, in: Journal of Political Economy, Vol. 112, 2004, No. 1, pp. 164–187.

Theil, M. (1998): Prospect Theory's Approach to Insurance Decisions; Aspects and Challenges, in: Association Internationale pour l'Etude de l'Economie de l'Assurance (ed) Etudes et Dossiers, 1998, Nr. 220, pp. 55–72.

Theil, M. (2002): Versicherungsentscheidungen und Prospect Theory, Die Risikoeinschätzung der Versicherungsnehmer als Entscheidungsgrundlage, Wien, 2002.

Theil, M. (2003): The Value of Personal Contact in Marketing Insurance: Client Judgments of Representativeness and Mental Availability, in: Risk Management and Insurance Review, Vol. 6, 2003, No. 2, pp. 145–157.

Theis, A. (2015): Regulierung und Versicherungswirtschaft: Chancen und Herausforderungen aus ökonomischer Perspektive, in: Volkswirtschaftliche Themen und Analysen, Nr. 7, Ed. by GDV, Berlin, 2015.

Theis, A. (2023): InsurTech-Startups: Eine Zwischenbilanz, in: Economic Research, Insurance Flash, Ed. by GDV, Nr. 2, 2023.

Theis, A./Wiener, K. (2018): Anbieterlandschaft am Versicherungsmarkt: Ein Ausblick, in: Volkswirtschaftliche Themen und Analysen, Nr. 8, Ed. by GDV, Berlin, 2018.

The London Institute of Banking & Finance (Ed.) (2023): Insurance Banana Skins 2023, The CSFI survey of the risks facing insurers, London, 2023.

Thiefes, D. (2022): Influencer Branding in der Versicherungswirtschaft, Wiesbaden, 2022.

Tomczak, T./Reinecke, S. (1996): Der aufgabenorientierte Ansatz, Einen neue Perspektive für das Marketing-Management, Fachbericht für Marketing, Heft 5, St. Gallen, 1996.

Tomczak, T./Reinecke, S. (1999): Der aufgabenorientierte Ansatz als Basis eines marktorientierten Wertmanagements, in: Grünig, R./Pasquier, M. (Eds.), Strategisches Management und Marketing, Festschrift für Richard Kühn, Bern, 1999, pp. 293–327.

Tomczak, T./Kuß, A./Reinecke, S. (2014): Marketingplanung, Einführung in die marktorientierte Unternehmens- und Geschäftsfeldplanung, Wiesbaden, 7. Aufl., 2014.

Tomczak, T./Reinecke, S./Gollnhofer, J. (2023): Marketingplanung, Einführung in die marktorientierte Unternehmens- und Geschäftsfeldplanung, Wiesbaden, 8. Aufl., 2023.

Torrance, S./Robinson, B. (2022): EMBEDDED INSURANCE 2.0, A Multi-Trillion dollar opportunity for brands and insurers, Ed. by aperture/Embedded Finance & Super App Strategies, 2022.

Traub, W. (1995): Marktfunktionen und Dienstleistung des Versicherungsmaklers auf der Grundlage informationsökonomischer Ergebnisse, Karlsruhe, 1995.

Trautinger, M.-J. (2015): Der Moment der Wahrheit—Eine empirische Untersuchung zu Zufriedenheitsfaktoren im Versicherungsschadenfall, in: ZVersWiss, Jg. 104, 2015, pp. 289–309.

Trautinger, M.-J. (2018): Kundenzufriedenheit als Steuerungsinstrument in einem Versicherungsunternehmen—nur Schall und Rauch oder ökonomisch sinnvoll?, in: ZVersWiss, Jg. 107, 2018, pp. 3–39. (https://doi.org/10.1007/s12297-017-0394-x)

Trinkhaus, H. (1955): Handbuch der Versicherungsvermittlung, Band I, Berlin, 1955.

Trumpfheller, J. (2005): Kundenbindung in der Versicherungswirtschaft, Eine theoretische und empirische Analyse unter besonderer Berücksichtigung des Versicherungsvertriebs über Versicherungsintermediäre, Karlsruhe, 2005.

Trusov, M/Bucklin, R.E./Pauwels, K. (2009): Effects of word-of-mouth versus traditional marketing: Findings from an internet social networking site, in: JoM, Vol. 73, 2009, No. 5, pp. 90–102.

Tscheulin, D.K./Helmig, B. (2001): Gibt es ein branchenspezifisches Marketing? Zur Bedeutung einer branchenorientierten Sichtweise des Marketing in Wissenschaft, Lehre und Praxis, in: Tscheulin, D.K./Helmig, B. (Eds.), Branchenspezifisches Marketing, Grundlagen—Besonderheiten—Gemeinsamkeiten, Wiesbaden, 2001, pp. 19–33.

Tversky, A./Kahneman, D. (1974): Judgment under Uncertainty: Heuristics and Biases, in: Science, Vol. 185, 1974, No. 4157, pp. 1.124–1.131.

Tversky, A./Kahneman, D. (1981): The Framing of Decisions and the Psychology of Choice, in: Science, Vol. 211, 1981, No. 4481, pp. 453–458.

Tversky, A./Kahneman, D. (1982): Availability: A Heuristic for Judging Frequency and Probability, in: Kahneman, D./Slovic, P./Tversky, A. (Eds.), Judgment under Uncertainty: Heuristics and Biases, Cambridge, 1982, pp. 163–178.

Tversky, A./Kahneman, D. (1986): Rational Choice and the Framing of Decisions, in: Journal of Business, Vol. 59, 1986, No. 4, pp. 251–278.

Tversky, A./Kahneman, D. (1992): Advances in prospect theory: Cumulative representation of uncertainty, in: Journal of Risk and Uncertainty, Vol. 5, 1992, No. 4, pp. 297–323.

Umweltbundesamt (Ed.) (2023): Monitoringbericht 2023 zur Deutschen Anpassungsstrategie an den Klimawandel, Bericht der Interministeriellen Arbeitsgruppe Anpassungsstrategie der Bundesregierung, Dessau-Roßlau, 2023.

Unger, F./Steul-Fischer, M. (2023): Rewards for a Healthy Lifestyle:The Impact of Reward Type and Timing in Pay-As-You-Live Pricing, in: Marketing ZFP, Vol. 45, 2023, No. 1, pp. 66–84.

Vargo, S.L./Akaka, M.A. (2012): Value cocreation and service systems (re) formation: A service ecosystems view, in: Service Science, Vol. 4, 2012, No. 3, pp. 207–217.

VAUNET—Verband Privater Medien e.V. (Ed.) (2023): VAUNET-Werbemarktanalyse, Audio- & audiovisuelle Werbung in Deutschland 2022/2023, Berlin, 2023.

Venohr, B. (1996): Kundenbindungsmanagement als Unternehmensziel. Leitmotiv für Versicherungsunternehmen, in: VW, Jg. 51, 1996, Nr. 6, pp. 365–368.

Vester, F. (1999): Die Kunst vernetzt zu denken. Ideen und Werkzeuge für einen neuen Umgang mit Komplexität, Frankfurt a. M., 1999.

Vetter, R./Möbius, C. (2019): Zukunftskonzept für die Ausschließlichkeitsorganisation, in ZfV, Jg. 70, 2019, Nr. 17, pp. 515–518.

VGH (Ed.) (2024): Leitbild, in: https://www.vgh.de/content/_microsites/unternehmen/ueber-uns/portrait/leitbild/, Accessed: 02.01.2024.

VHV Gruppe (Ed.) (2023): Geschäftsbericht 2022, Hannover, 2023.

Vielreicher, P. (1995): Produktinnovationsmanagement in Versicherungsunternehmen, Wiesbaden, 1995.

Vogler, D. (2009): Personenbezogene Einflussfaktoren für den Vertriebserfolg im Versicherungsvertrieb, Eine empirische Analyse bei Ausschließlichkeitsvertretern, Lohmar, 2009.

Wähling, S./Trumpfheller, J./Schulenburg, J.-M. Graf von der (1993): Die Nachfragemotive nach Kapitallebensverischerungen und ihre Struktur, Eine empirische Analyse, in: VW, Jg. 48, 1993, Nr. 3, pp. 173–180.

Wagner, F. (2001a): Gestaltung von Versicherungsprodukten nach dem Bausteinprinzip, in: VW, Jg. 56, 2001, Nr. 11, pp. 818–822.
Wagner, F. (2001b): Gestaltung von Versicherungsprodukten nach dem Bausteinprinzip, in: VW, Jg. 56, 2001, Nr. 12, pp. 916–920.
Wagner, F. (Ed.) (2017): Gabler Versicherungslexikon, Wiesbaden, 2. Aufl., 2017.
Wagner, S. (2006): Provisionssatzdifferenzierung in finanziellen Anreizsystemen für Versicherungsvermittler, Karlsruhe, 2006.
We are Social/Meltwater (Ed.) (2023): Digital 2023, Global Overview Report, The essential guide to the world's connected behaviours, o. O., 2023.
Webster Jr., F.E. (2005): Back to the Future: Integrating Marketing as Tactics, Strategy, and Organizational Culture. In: JoM, Vol. 69, 2005, pp. 4–6.
Wedlich, F. (2019): Digitalisierung, Robotic Process Automation und Künstliche Intelligenz in der Versicherungsbranche, Potentiale und Möglichkeiten im Schadenmanagement, in: ZfV, Jg. 70, 2019, Nr. 14, pp. 436–440.
Weiber, R./Adler, J. (1995): Informationsökonomische Erkenntnisse für das Marketing bei Qualitätsunsicherheit der Konsumenten, in: ZfBF, Jg. 47, 1995, Nr. 1, pp. 43–65
Werber, M. (2019): Kritische Nachlese zur Umsetzung der Richtlinie (EU) 2016/97 über Versicherungsvertrieb, in: VersR, Jg. 70, 2019, Nr. 6, pp. 321–329.
Weinhold-Stünzi, H. (1988): Marketing in zwanzig Lektionen, St. Gallen, 1988.
Werth, O./Schwarzbach, C./Rodríguez Cardona, D./Breitner, M.H./Schulenburg, J.-M. Graf von der (2020): Influencing factors for the digital transformation in the financial services sector, in: ZVersWiss, Jg. 109, 2020, pp. 155–179.
Wiedmann, K.-P./Seegebarth, B./Reuter, M. (2009): Reputation als strategischer Erfolgsfaktor in der Assekuranz: Herausforderungen im Beschwerdemanagementprozess für ein zukunftsorientiertes Reputationsmanagement, in: Institut für Marketing & Management (Ed.), Schriftenreihe Marketing Management, Hannover, 2009.
Wiener, K. and Theis, A. (2017): InsurTech(s): Zwischen Konkurrenz und Partnerschaft, in: Makro und Markte kompakt, Ed. by GDV, Nr. 9, 2017.
Wiersich, M. (2013): Der Einfluss von Emotionen auf Versicherungsentscheidungen, Dissertation, Nürnberg, 2013.
Wiswesser, R. (2018): Die Zukunft der persönlichen Beratung im digitalen Zeitalter, in: Beenken, M./Knörrer, D./Moormann, J./Schmidt, D. (Eds.), Digital Insurance. Strategien, Geschäftsmodelle, Daten, Frankfurt a.M., 2018, pp. 109–130.
Woodruff, R. (1997): Customer value, The next source for competitive advantage, in: JoAMS, Vol. 25, 1997, No. 2, pp. 139–153.
YouGov (Ed.) (2014): Kundenmonitor e-Assekuranz, Der Vertriebswege-Monitor, Köln, 2014.
Zagel, T./Steul-Fischer, M. (2014): Wahrgenommene Preisfairness bei Preiserhöhungen in der Schadenversicherung, in: ZVersWiss, Jg. 103, 2014, Nr. 5, pp. 447–459.
Zeier Röschmann, A. (2018): Digital insurance brokers—old wine in new bottles? How digital brokers create value, in: ZVersWiss, Jg. 107, 2018, pp. 273–291. (https://doi.org/10.1007/s12297-018-0413-6)
Zeithaml, V.A./Berry, L.L./Parasuraman, A. (1988): Communication and Control Processes in the delivery of Service Quality, in: JoM, Vol. 52, 1988, No. 4, pp. 35–48.
Zentralverband der deutschen Werbewirtschaft e.V. (Ed.) (2021a): Ausgestrahlte TV-Werbeminuten in Deutschland in den Jahren 2002 bis 2020, Stand: 2021, in: Statista (Ed.), in: https://de-statista-com.ezproxy.hwr-berlin.de/statistik/daten/studie/4769/umfrage/tv-werbesekunden-in-deutschland-seit-2000/, Accessed: 26.01.2024.
Zentralverband der deutschen Werbewirtschaft e.V. (Ed.) (2021b): Anzahl der in Deutschland ausgestrahlten TV-Werbespots in den Jahren 2002 bis 2020 (in Millionen), Stand: 2021, in:

Statista (Ed.), in: https://de-statista-com.ezproxy.hwr-berlin.de/statistik/daten/studie/4771/umfrage/anzahl-der-tv-werbespots-in-deutschland-seit-2000/, Accessed: 26.01.2024.
Zietsch, D. (1985): Grundlagen der Gestaltung außenorganisationsbezogener Vertriebssteuerungssysteme in Versicherungsunternehmen, Karlsruhe, 1985.
Zinnert, M. (2008): Recht und Praxis des Versicherungsmaklers, Karlsruhe, 2008.
Zinnert, M. (2009): Der Versicherungsvertreter, Karlsruhe, 2009.
Zweifel, P./Eisen, R. (2012): Insurance Economics, Heidelberg, 2012.
Zweifel, P./Pedroni, G. (1988): Chance und Risiko. Messung, Bewertung, Akzeptanz, Basel, 1988.

MIX
Papier aus verantwortungsvollen Quellen
Paper from responsible sources
FSC® C105338

If you have any concerns about our products,
you can contact us on
ProductSafety@springernature.com

In case Publisher is established outside the EU,
the EU authorized representative is:
Springer Nature Customer Service Center GmbH
Europaplatz 3, 69115 Heidelberg, Germany

Printed by Libri Plureos GmbH
in Hamburg, Germany